D0848874

ACCOUNTING CLASSICS SERIES

Publication of this Classic was made possible
by a grant from Arthur Andersen & Co.

Suggestions of titles to be included
in the Series are solicited and should
be addressed to the Editor.

ACCOUNTING PUBLICATIONS OF SCHOLARS BOOK CO.

Robert R. Sterling, Editor

Sidney S. Alexander et al., *Five Monographs on Business Income*
Frank Sewell Bray, *The Accounting Mission*
Raymond J. Chambers, *Accounting, Evaluation and Economic Behavior*
Arthur Lowes Dickinson, *Accounting Practice and Procedure*
John Bart Geijsbeek, *Ancient Double-Entry Bookkeeping*
Henry Rand Hatfield, *Accounting: Its Principles and Problems*
Bishop Carleton Hunt (Editor), *George Oliver May: Twenty-Five Years of Accounting Responsibility, 1911–1936*
Kenneth MacNeal, *Truth in Accounting*
George O. May, *Financial Accounting: A Distillation of Experience*
Paul D. Montagna, *Certified Public Accounting: A Sociological View of a Profession in Change*
William A. Paton, *Accounting Theory*
W. Z. Ripley, *Main Street and Wall Street*
DR Scott, *The Cultural Significance of Accounts*
Charles E. Sprague, *The Philosophy of Accounts*
George Staubus, *A Theory of Accounting to Investors*
Robert R. Sterling (Editor), *Asset Valuation and Income Determination*
Robert R. Sterling (Editor), *Institutional Issues in Public Accounting*
Robert R. Sterling (Editor), *Research Methodology in Accounting*
Reed K. Storey, *The Search for Accounting Principles*
Study Group on Business Income, *Changing Concepts of Business Income*

ACCOUNTING
AND ANALYTICAL METHODS

Measurement and Projection of Income and
Wealth in the Micro- and Macro-Economy

ACCOUNTING
AND ANALYTICAL
METHODS

*Measurement and Projection of Income and
Wealth in the Micro- and Macro-Economy*

RICHARD MATTESSICH

SCHOLARS BOOK CO.
4431 MT. VERNON
HOUSTON, TEXAS 77006

Reprinted 1977 by

Scholars Book Co.
with special permission of
Richard Mattessich

Library of Congress Card Catalog Number: 64-22113
ISBN: 0-914348-21-3
Manufactured in the United States of America

TO THE FAMILY OF PFAUNDLER

*My Mother's family, the chronicle
of which gives evidence of eleven
generations of accountants*

PREFACE

THIS BOOK is written for academically trained accountants and students of business administration and economics, but it will also serve professional economists, management scientists, engineers, and mathematicians in relating accounting to their own areas. The purpose of this study is to present a *unified frame* of accounting, and to acquaint the reader with new significant developments in this discipline. Since many of the recent influences stem from the management sciences and their quantitative analytical approaches, the inclusion of the term "analytical methods" in the title of this book seems to be justified. However, it must be stressed at the very outset that here we are little concerned with mathematical techniques and algorisms. Neither are we occupied with highly specialized models and empirical hypotheses of temporary validity. This work pivots on the foundations of accounting; its foremost concern is to clarify accounting concepts, a *prerequisite* for the application of analytical methods in a more narrow sense. At the first International Conference on Accounting Education,[1] the author expressed his belief that *conceptual clarification* is the foremost task of accounting to be attained by employing tools borrowed from the modern analytical approaches. The present book is a manifestation of this creed. It utilizes a few basic ideas and concepts of modern logic, mathematics, and decision theory to improve accounting. The future needs of our discipline and the criticism of accounting advanced by management scientists are further considerations that will be examined carefully. Such an approach should help to bridge the deplorable gap between accounting and other management sciences; it should be more readily accepted by accountants and students not trained in mathematical techniques and formalized logic than an approach that insists on extensive mathematical training. The analytical prerequisites required for comprehending the text do not extend to complicated calculi, and can relatively easily be conveyed in footnotes and appendices.

---

[1] See Richard Mattessich, "Opportunities for Research in Accounting—Mathematical Applications," *Proceedings: International Conference on Accounting Education* (Urbana: University of Illinois, 1962), pp. 100–106.

The essence of accounting can best be illustrated and understood when reflected upon in a historical setting; thus we shall not neglect the evolutionary side of our discipline and its relation to other economic sciences. The major objective, however, lies in a new synthesis of micro- and macro-accounting, in the formation of a basis that is general enough to comprise the great variety of accounting systems in existence. The connection between business accounting, and similar micro-accounting systems on one side and social accounting systems on the other has been demonstrated before, but not so the *formulation of a unifying foundation*. Only by abstracting are we able to adapt reality to the limitations of our mind, only by sacrificing the specific can we *create* the general and extract the essence.

Such a preoccupation with generalization and conceptual clarification seems to be out of line with the present trend of enunciating highly specialized, and usually unrealistic, hypotheses. But during our activity in five different countries—for at least five years in each—we were confronted again and again with new local practices and different scientific views or customs. This made us painfully aware of the *temporary* and *localized validity* of many accounting doctrines, academic opinions, and technicalities. The intensifying international exchange and the acceleration of technological progress call for a more general outlook and for a more permanent foundation. This need is reinforced by the strong—and in many respects beneficial—trend toward specialization which inevitably leads to an *atomistic* view, to a myopic vision that does not encourage the formation of a comprehensive, coherent, and organic over-all picture. Thus further specialization ought to be accompanied by the search for a structure or a *hull* which enmeshes the whole and prevents the parts from breaking off.

The accountant's dilemma to cope with analytical methods is not merely a problem of memorizing some formulas or learning new mathematical tricks, it is *a problem of transition* from the dogmatic thinking of the jurisprudent to the behavioral-analytical thinking of the scientist. The change of accounting arising from the managerial-scientific revolution is too fundamental to allow it to be the concern of a few specialists. This shift will affect all accountants; and those unwilling to cope with it will be forced to surrender the most challenging tasks to the operations analyst, even worse, will have to admit ignorance regarding the competitor's activity in the accountant's very own backyard.

The reader anxious to obtain a bird's-eye view of the major problems and highlights of this book need not hesitate to begin, so to speak, at the end. He may first read the *Summary* in Chapter 10 (Section 10.3); it will satisfy his curiosity and, as we hope, whet his interest in the content of the individual chapters. Most of this content is not difficult to comprehend, but occasionally the reader may encounter a passage of rough going (this is true especially for our discussion of the basic assumptions in Sub-Section 2.41 and in Appendix A). With some persistence or reference to the appendices,[2] these difficult passages might ultimately prove to be the most rewarding ones.

In expressing the author's indebtedness, the following institutions of the University of California ought to be mentioned for their help and support at various phases of this project: the Department of Business Administration, the Department of Economics, the Institute of Business and Economic Research, the Center for Research in Management Science, the Western Management Science Institute, and the Western Data Processing Center. Further acknowledgement is due to the Ford Foundation who granted to me in 1961–62 a Faculty Fellowship for the study of mathematical methods.

Special recognition and thanks are due to two of my colleagues: to Professor Maurice Moonitz, for his suggestions and repeated encouragement—without which I might not have found the strength to finish this book—, and to Professor C. West Churchman, whose arguments and works—in spite of a standpoint drastically different from my own—have had a decisive impact upon my thinking.

I also express my gratitude to all publishers and authors who gave permission to quote from their publications. Further thanks go to Professor Yuji Ijiri of Stanford University for reading the manuscript and for valuable suggestions concerning the mathematical presentation, to my former assistant, Mr. Peter Dickerson, who permitted the inclusion of some pages of his master thesis in Section 5.4, and to my former students and assistants Mr. Thomas C. Schneider, manager (in operations research) of Arthur Young & Co. (C.P.A.'s), and Mr. Paul Zitlau, operations analyst of Du Pont de Nemours & Co., who collaborated on the companion volume and, in doing so, supplied valuable suggestions for improving Sub-Section 9.26 of the present book. For the painstaking work of pre-editing most of the manuscript I should like to express my gratitude to Mrs. Maude Riley,

---

[2]Most of the book can be read without the aid of these appendices, but acquaintance with them will be important for the modern accountant.

The first part of Appendix A contains a concise explanation of set-theoretical terms such as *set, ordered tuples, one-to-one correspondence, isomorphism*, etc., helpful in reading Sub-Section 2.41 and Sections 3.2 and 3.3. The second part of Appendix A is an attempt to refine the basic assumptions (of Chapter 2) through a set-theoretical formulation and to illustrate the deduction of theorems (with proofs) from the axioms.

Appendix B offers a brief survey of the essence of matrix algebra. It is not a general prerequisite, but required for the understanding of Sub-Sections 8.12, and 8.13.

Appendix C is a short introduction to linear programing, required for comprehending Sub-Sections 6.21 and 8.13.

former secretary of the Institute of Business and Economic Research. Yet, my greatest debt belongs to Hermi Mattessich, my wife. Not only did she bear with me through the trying year of 1963 when the contents of this book assumed their final shape, she also typed the complete manuscript, did the proofreading, helped compose the index, and untiringly smoothed the many difficulties encountered. Her dedication to this book was as essential to its completion as was the author's contribution.

BERKELEY, CALIFORNIA
December 1963   R.M.

PREAMBLE

"The diversity of our opinions does not arise from some being endowed with a larger share of reason than others, but solely from this, that we conduct our thoughts along different ways, and do not fix our attention on the same objects. For to be possessed by a vigorous mind is not enough; the prime requisite is rightly to apply it. The greatest minds, as they are capable of the highest excellences, are open likewise to the greatest aberrations; and those who travel very slowly may yet make far greater progress, provided they keep always to the straight road, than those who, while they run, forsake it."

RENÉ DESCARTES
(*Discourse on Method*, Part I, transl.)

TABLE OF CONTENTS

PART I. ON THE ESSENCE AND FOUNDATIONS OF ACCOUNTING

PART II. ON VALUATION AND HYPOTHESES FORMULATION

PART III. ON PROJECTION AND PLANNING FOR THE FUTURE

PREFACE TO THE
REPRINT EDITION

ALMOST TWENTY years have passed since I began to write *Accounting and Analytical Methods* (AAM). In the meantime, many things have changed in our discipline. Thus, it might appear that mainly for historical reasons this book is still considered to be worthwhile reading. This view is reinforced by several circumstances: first of all, many changes have occurred in my own thinking and several improvements were made in the German and Japanese versions of this book—improvements that here could not be taken into consideration due to the nature of this reprint series; second, this book is already being discussed in publications on accounting history; and third, "the golden age in the history of *a priori* research in accounting," as Professor Carl Nelson called the sixties,[1] has vanished long ago, though not without traces. Thus, it would seem preposterous to assert that *AAM still has something to contribute to the ongoing search for a more commonly accepted, truly modern theory of accounting.* Yet there are several reasons why I venture to make such an assertion.

History works in cycles: ideas come into fashion, go out of it and return again. The reaction to analytical research in accounting, since the late sixties, was quite natural and beneficial; it was the result of an inevitable dialectical process. But now the critique that was raised against "*a priori* research" is finding its own critics in turn. Professor M. C. Wells recently argued that "Far from being unproductive, the works (of *a priori* research) referred to were a necessary step in the revolution currently underway in accounting thought. Far from being of doubtful value, those works have helped to place us in a significantly different position from that of 1960."[2] Wells then attempts

---

[1] As regards AAM, the term "*a priori* research" may not be quite fitting because the basic assumptions here presented were derived inductively by empirical investigations of many micro- and macro-accounting systems. Yet due to its strong analytical overtone, AAM undoubtedly belongs to *a priori* research in accounting as well.

[2] M. C. Wells, "A Revolution in Accounting Thought?" *The Accounting Review*, Vol. 51, No. 3 (July 1976), p. 471.

quite successfully to demonstrate that in the sixties a new accounting paradigm (in the sense of the renowned theory of Thomas Kuhn) emerged which was designed to overcome the anomalies of traditional accounting theory (for example, the inability to cope in practice with specific and general price-level fluctuations). But Thomas Kuhn's paradigmatic theory has meanwhile been formalized and further developed by Sneed and Stegmüller,[3] who demonstrated that a theory no longer ought to be regarded as a static collection of propositions but as a dynamic mathematical or systemic structure. To do so, one requires a special kind of axiomatization, one in which the axioms become constituents of the definition of a set-theoretical predicate. But precisely this kind of axiomatization was chosen in AAM (whether by sheer luck or by sound intuition is left to others to judge). Here (p. 19) the axioms are neither propositions nor propositional forms but structural constituents of the definition of our discipline—exactly as required by Sneed and Stegmüller. The superiority of a structural over a propositional view of theory is manifold. Above all, it offers a more accurate picture of what a theory is about. It also permits the representation and explanation of *theory dynamics* as manifested in the improvements (core extensions in "normal science") as well as the fundamental revisions (substitution of a new structural core in "revolutionary science" in Kuhn's terminology). It also might prove beneficial in creating normative models or "intended applications" (Sneed's terminology) designed to match specific accounting systems with specific information purposes; this I regard as one of the major challenges ahead of us. At any rate, we are still a good distance away from a satisfactory theory of accounting. Thus, the search for theory must be attacked from many sides, among which the exploration of basic assumptions and specific hypotheses still has highest priority.

Regarding the most important improvements, I should like to mention first that the German version of AAM presents nineteen instead of eighteen basic assumptions.[4] The additional assumption, contained only implicitly in the English version, is stated here:

> There exists a specific information need and purpose (to be specified and) to be served by the pertinent accounting system. The specific hypotheses (for which the surrogate assumptions 10 to 18—or 11 to 19 in the German version—reserve a place) will then depend on the information need specified in the hypothesis chosen under this (new) assumption.

---

[3] T. S. Kuhn, *The Structure of Scientific Revolutions* (Chicago: Chicago University Press, 1962; 2nd enlarged edition, 1970). J. D. Sneed, *The Logical Structure of Mathematical Physics* (Dordrecht: D. Reidel & Co., 1971). W. Stegmüller, *The Structure and Dynamics of Theories* (New York: Berlin, Springer Verlag, 1976).

[4] Richard Mattessich, *Die wissenschaftlichen Grundlagen des Rechnungswesens* (Düsseldorf: Bertelsmann Universitätsverlag, 1970). See especially pp. 34–36, 68–69.

The significance of this teleological assumption is two-fold: on one side, it would force us to define for a specific system the information purpose as clearly as possible; on the other side, it would enable us to derive the specific hypotheses for many, if not all, of the remaining basic assumptions (ten to eighteen) instead of postulating them more or less arbitrarily. This I consider an important step toward a normative theory of accounting relating means to ends.

Furthermore, the second volume of the Japanese version of AAM contains some set-theoretical improvements (stimulated by Saito) as regards the relationship between equivalence classes and transactors.[5] Since it deals with a pedagogic rather than a substantial improvement, we refer the reader to an English translation where the pertinent details are presented.[6]

I also should like to point out that I have always regarded the various versions of my semi-axiomatic system of accountancy as nothing but preliminary formulations. The barriers which I encountered in the attempt to approach a truly normative theory of accounting were mainly of methodological nature. This incited me, from 1967 on, to concern myself intensely with epistemological questions. The result of this concern was several articles,[7] as well as a philosophic work which presently is in print.[8] I sincerely hope that these studies, as well as the present reprint, will contribute to the intellectual advancement of our discipline.

The reprint process on which this series is based does not permit any revisions or corrections. Thus, I should like to apologize for all the errata still contained in the text. Corrections to the more important ones are listed in Appendix D. I also hope the reader is not disturbed by the consistently supermodern spelling of "mnemonic" as "memnonic" in Chapter 9.

Finally, I should like to express my gratitude to Professor Robert R. Sterling, Editor of the Accounting Classics Series, for publishing AAM in this distinguished reprint series, and to Arthur Andersen & Co., for the grant that made the reprint possible. Special thanks go to all the colleagues and readers who have

[5] Richard Mattessich, *Kaikei To Bunsekiteki-Hoho Johan,* ed. S. Koshimura (Tokyo: Dobunkan Ltd.), Vol. I, 1972; Vol. II, 1974.

[6] *Idem.,* "On the Axiomatic Formulation of Accounting: Comment on Prof. S. Saito's Considerations," English translation in *The Mushashi University Journal* (Japan), Vol. 21, 1973, p. 77–94.

[7] *Idem.,* "Methodological Preconditions and Problems of a General Theory of Accounting," *The Accounting Review,* Vol. 47 (1972), pp. 469–487 (Accounting Literature Award 1972 of the American Institute of Certified Public Accountants).

[8] *Idem., Instrumental Reasoning and Systems Methodology* (Dordrecht: D. Reidel & Co., 1978).

urged us with unrelenting enthusiasm to republish the English version of AAM which has been out of print for about a decade.

Vienna, May 1977   Richard Mattessich

                                          University of British Columbia
                                          Vancouver, Canada

                                          Technische Universität Wien
                                          Vienna, Austria

PART 1

On the Essence and Foundations of Accounting

Chapter 1

INTRODUCTION

1.1 THE NEED FOR RELATING RECENT ACHIEVEMENTS OF MANAGERIAL SCIENCE AND ECONOMICS TO ACCOUNTING

MODERN ACCOUNTING is a mode of thought, a manifestation of our chrematistic thinking and evaluating, a tool designed to help master our economic struggle. It unfolded in its full breadth during the last hundred years and cannot be regarded as having exhausted its potential of technical as well as intellectual growth. Whether it is a trivial or a sophisticated means, whether it furthers the cognitive process of science, or whether it is a dogmatic body for pursuing the ritual of an industrial age are still controversial questions. The answers to them appear to be more a matter of opinion than well-established fact. Hence, these issues deserve further scrutiny— perhaps from a fresh point of view. On the other hand, the mere fact of an increasing application of accounting concepts and methods, the variety of micro- and especially macro-accounting systems that were born during the last decades, should be justification enough for examining accounting in a more general perspective and from a more analytical standpoint than it has been done in the past.

Since we live in a world subject to continuous change there is no reason why accountancy should be spared from the evolutionary and revolutionary forces of time. Indeed, recent technological, mathematical, and scientific developments are at work to exercise an impact on the practice and theory of accounting which has hardly begun to make itself felt but which cannot be ignored, neither by the practicing nor the academic accountant. The adjustment process which these forces bring about entail a rethinking that starts at the very basis of our discipline. In consideration of this we attempt in the following to sketch a frame of accounting that should fit present as well as future needs, that is not concerned with petty improvements which get obsolete before being implemented, but which is basic enough to provide a more permanent foundation. Such an effort is motivated by the belief that a change or danger perceived and acted upon in time will lead to an evolutionary instead of revolutionary solution.[1] To look at micro- and macro-accounting through the spectacles of modern scientific methods might be a well-advised beginning, an outset on a long road, the end of which lies beyond our horizon. To get the stone moving and see how far it will roll is all we can do at present.

The state of accountancy, that is to say, its practice, theory, and teaching, is by many experts looked upon discontentedly; it is heavily criticized by our colleagues from related disciplines and a glance into the current literature of economics and management science[2] suffices to convince the reader that some of this contempt goes beyond mere interdisciplinary jealousy or snobbery. There will be plenty of occasion in this book to elucidate these important issues in many ways, but it seems opportune to give at the very outset a short summary of the main criticism to which traditional accounting has been subjected:

1. *Accounting practice* does not supply an objective scale of value that may be used for selecting optimal decisions and for evaluating managerial performance.
2. *Accounting theory* has developed a body of knowledge which is of a dogmatic rather than scientific-hypothetical character and which serves with satisfaction only purposes of a legalistic nature. It has failed to integrate the micro- with the macro-aspects of the income-wealth measurement.
3. The *pedagogic* side of academic accounting overemphasizes technical aspects and does not endeavor to relate new scientific achievements to the established body of accounting knowledge. It leaves the student at a loss when it comes to expressing accounting theory in terms of modern logic, epistemology, and quantitative analysis. It hardly equips the student with a knowledge general enough for the flexible thinking required by the application of electronic data processing to advanced accounting problems.

Objections of this kind may appear harsh; they possess, however, many aspects which cannot be rejected as untrue, and a detailed

---

[1] The idea of "revolutionary forces" is by no means as farfetched as it might seem to many a reader. A conversation with the more radical among the industrial engineers and operations analysts will reveal their conviction that in the future accounting as an academic discipline will be replaced by something entirely new. We neither share this view nor the belief that such an event would be beneficial to industry; we rather think the reform should grow out of accountancy itself and be linked to the traditional flow of thought in this field.

[2] See e.g., Joel Dean [1951], West C. Churchman [1961], E. O. Edwards and P. W. Bell [1961].

examination of them will be necessary in order to form an "objective" view. It will be the task of future chapters to go into these details while presenting accountancy in a way that tries to overcome some of these shortcomings. This should be possible by incorporating contributions that related disciplines, primarily economics and management science, have made to what is regarded as accounting theory in a broad sense of the term. Such an extension of the viewpoint seems urgent in the face of the success and the academic recognition which symbolic logic, management science, and electronic data processing have gained during the past decade.

1.2 THE NEED FOR A NEW APPROACH IN TEACHING ACCOUNTING

The increasing volume of information brought about by research, discovery, and invention subjects academic teaching to the same ever-changing, dynamic forces that dominate the structure of knowledge itself. A discipline which does not hold pace with its neighbors, which falls behind in the marching ranks of learning, will soon be replaced. This process also incurs a constant shift of a particular information or knowledge within the ranks of academic wisdom: what was regarded as "difficult" and advanced knowledge in former centuries or even a few decades ago, what then was taught to the highest echelons of the university community, belongs in the twentieth century to "general education" and is being taught at high schools. The infinitesimal calculus, and more recently the principles of set theory, are merely two of the many examples that can be listed in support of a contention which holds for accounting not less than for any other discipline. Conservatism is a major, estimable, and necessary quality of accountants. It is of great benefit if applied in legalistic reporting but it must not dominate our attitude toward acquiring and conveying new knowledge. Furthermore it must be considered that university teaching of accounting nurtured by new achievements arising from the practice of bookkeeping belongs to the past. Obviously, every "applied" discipline is in the dilemma of (1) either teaching technical routines before it can begin to convey more subtle knowledge, or (2) requesting the skill in such techniques as a prerequisite. In the case of accounting the American universities and schools of business administration have chosen the first way while many of the European institutions of higher learning decided for the second. In central Europe bookkeeping and elementary accounting courses are a prerequisite for the study of business administration that can be taken at the high school-junior college level or as a *noncredit course* at the university. In America many schools of business administration found the establishment of accounting laboratory courses a solution—albeit not always a satisfactory one—to this problem. As long as accounting courses are penetrated by technicalities there is the danger of getting lost in a host of practical details at the expense of the fundamental issues that dominate the many facets of income and wealth measurement. The concentration on the commercial-legal point of view and the neglect of scientific aspects in the present-day teaching of accounting is a characteristic outcome of this narrow-minded attitude. The idea of "measurement" may serve as a welcome illustration; the *term* is abundantly used in the literature of our discipline; but did the authors make sure that their readers and students do really know what lies behind the *concept*, have the teachers and authors themselves bothered to dig into the comprehensive literature of modern measurement theory? Very few have done so and for a long time none has tried to relate it to his discipline because the myopic concern with everyday problems and particular technicalities did not permit to devote time to many problems of accounting that form its foundation. Basic scientific questions that underlie *accounting*, not only business accounting, have been neglected for a long time. We therefore propose to formulate accounting in a less technical-specific but a more general-scientific fashion. Though we will not fail to give a survey of present-day accounting practice and theory, our chief object of investigation is not a specific system, for a specific purpose, in a specific country, with a specific political environment, at a specific time. It rather is our ambition to analyze and teach the problems posed by accounting as a universal economic phenomenon. In doing so we hope to show the reader our discipline from a new vantage point and hope to equip him with a profound understanding of the scientific foundations on which it rests, and with a plan of its limitations as well as future possibilities. This approach also might be helpful in making accounting more palatable to those who, thus far, have shunned it because of too heavy a technical content. We believe that the ignorance of a multitude of social scientists as to the essence of accountancy must be overcome, not for the sake of accounting, but for the benefit of the practice and theory of the economic sciences in general.

Recent years brought forth an awakening in the academic circles of business administration. The heavy criticism of traditional teaching methods, as contained in the Gordon-Howell report, the Pierson report, and many pamphlets and articles[3] is directed primarily at the too-technical presentation of various subjects of business administration; thus a heavier stress on an analytical approach is urged. Obviously, the aim of modern quantitative analytical methods need not be purely "teleologic" in the sense of immediate practical application; their *pedagogic value* ranks foremost in our concern for a more profound and more efficient education of the student of the economic sciences. Hence, the emergence of sophisticated mathematical and statistical tools in management science and economics, the call for a more intensive quantitative-analytical thinking in business administration, and last but not least, the need of an industry—whose complexity seems to grow along a logarithmic scale—for tools that are able to master the intricacy of this web, are reason enough to plead for a revision of the teaching methods in accounting.

But such a call may easily be misinterpreted. Since it is prone to shift our interest to mathematical methods, there is the danger that again we lose ourselves in the multitude of *technical* details provided by the operations analysts for the solution of optimization and similar problems. What is more urgently needed for the synchronization of accounting and organization theory is a knowledge of the achievements of modern logic, the philosophy of science, measurement theory, management and behavioral science, systems simulation, etc. Some of these achievements are badly needed—not for glamorizing accounting, as a naïve mind might suspect—but for sharpening our own tools, for clarifying our concepts, for disentangling a dusty web of dogmas, for tearing us loose from some old-fashioned views which are so deeply ingrained in our thinking that we cannot get rid of them without sharp incisions. There is much to be said for this purifying aspect of the analytical methods; it not only clairfies our thinking but prevents us from applying available techniques purely schematically. The application of so-called "library routines" at our disposal[4] for electronic computers—which enable us to solve intricate mathematical problems without knowing

---

[3]See R. A. Gordon and J. E. Howell, *Higher Education for Business* (New York: Columbia Univ. Press, 1959); Frank Pierson *et al.*, *The Education of American Businessmen* (New York: McGraw-Hill, 1959); M. W. Lee *et al.*, *Views on Business Education* (Chapel Hill: Univ. of North Carolina, 1960); and L. S. Silk, *The Education of Businessmen* (New York: Committee for Economic Development, 1960).

[4]These *library routines* not only shorten the time of computation but, what is even more significant, they abbreviate considerably the time of mathematical training. The existence and further elaboration of such devices that enable the solution of a mathematical problem with a mere routine knowledge of its essence, are a further reason why accountants no longer can neglect to formulate their problems in terms of modern analytical thought.

all the technical-mathematical aspects involved—can be handled more expertly and with deeper insight if the user is familiar with analytical methods and trained to think according to their terms.

1.3   THE NEED FOR A GENERAL THEORY OF ACCOUNTING

The essence of the scientific approach is *abstraction*. Although this phenomenon may be dissected into several phases—the observation of particular cases, their description and measurement, the extraction of their common features, the formulation of the generalized case, and finally the application of the abstraction to new but related individual events—this process can be comprehended only if looked upon as an entity. It is one of the most profound elements of thought; in its rigorous form it enables what Ernst Mach called the "economy of science." It is in this principle of abstraction and its efficiency that the success of science lies, not in the discovery of ultimate truth.

With regard to our discipline, the question then arises whether we have taken full advantage of this powerful tool, whether we have already exhausted the potential of abstraction in accounting, or whether there still is some room for application. It must be left to later chapters to advance propositions for a further implementation of this principle within the realm of accounting, but we may here give evidence that generalization has not yet been carried to an extreme in this field.

The need for a general presentation of accounting is manifested in different ways; one of them is the appearance of a considerable number of accounting systems in actual practice: financial accounting, cost and managerial accounting, government and institutional accounting, national income and product accounting, flow of funds accounting, input-output accounting, the balance of payment accounting, and finally the construction of national balance sheets. These systems fulfill different functions and yet are based on the same basic principles as we will demonstrate later. Another argument for a rigorous general formulation of these principles grows out of the traditional language of accounting, which is too limited, which does not clearly reveal the mathematical structure, and which makes many believe it is the ultimate way of conveying the ideas of accounting. The third and main argument, however, can be interpreted as an extension of the first point made above: it is embedded in the apparent need for more functional accounting systems and evaluation approaches in contrast to the customary multipurpose systems. We regard the traditional financial and cost accounting systems as multipurpose devices because they constitute a compromise that shall enable the systems to serve several goals simultaneously, e.g., the measurement of taxability, of creditworthiness, of earning power, of resource control, of managerial efficiency,. etc. Experience has shown that such compromise solutions are not very satisfactory and may occasionally be harmful. They favor some purposes at the cost of others and their success depends not only on the accuracy required from the pertinent measure but also on the intricacy of the events subject to it. The multipurpose systems also bear major responsibility for the futile controversies concerned with the question whether this or that practice is the "correct" one. As long as a specific purpose is not spelled out explicitly, this question is meaningless. Therefore it is likely that in the future several interrelated "monopurpose"[5] accounting systems will replace one multipurpose establishment. This change may take place only slowly and gradually but under the impact of management science and with the aid of the enormous computing power of electronic data processing, this occurrence must be anticipated.[6] Its investigation and its problems will form one of the important new areas of theoretical accounting.

---

[5]We are using the term "monopurpose" for lack of a more adequate expression. The designation "limited-purpose" might fit better since frequently it will be impossible to restrict a certain system to a single function.

[6]This obviously is not an entirely new development. It began with the separation of cost accounting from financial accounting and many authors have argued for abandonment of the multipurpose approach: e.g., "Management problems take innumerable forms, and an accounting system that would fit them all is hard to conceive. The accounts should instead be made a source of basic data that can be fitted in different ways to different particular needs." (Joel Dean, *Managerial Economics*, copyright 1951. By permission of Prentice-Hall, Inc., publisher; pp. 27–28.)

In the realm of national income accounting it is Ingvar Ohlsson [1953, pp. 25, 26] who pleads for monopurpose-directed accounting systems: "It is rather self-evident that an NA-system (national accounting system) should be shaped to suit the purposes that the system is to serve. In this respect national accounting does not differ from other tools used in economic analysis and planning. This in itself is therefore not a problem for discussion. The fundamentally significant question regarding the role that the purpose plays in national accounting is rather the following: is the *same* NA-system applicable for all the various purposes for which it is currently used, or must alternative systems be drawn up to fit these different purposes?

"The reason why the purpose has explicitly played a rather subordinate role in national accounting may be either that—for more or less good reasons—it is assumed that an NA-system can serve all the different purposes of current interest or that every NA-system is designed only for one specific or a few compatible purposes. The first supposition may signify that in one NA-system all the transactions can be given that are required in order to compose the systems that are suitable in the various practical cases. National accounting would become a kind of presentation of all the 'building blocks' that are required in order to obtain various usable accounting systems. This thought is evident in a work of J. R. N. Stone and K. Hansen." [Footnote omitted.]

As soon as various monopurpose systems are being developed the need for a general basis of accounting becomes even more urgent. For if no uniform frame is available from which an accounting model for a particular purpose and a specific situation can systematically be developed, we run the risk of generating an array of "standard models" which soon would grow rigid and would thus defeat the original purpose of diversification for the sake of flexibility.

To some, our suggestions might seem contradictory: first we plead for a generalization of accounting and then for a diversification. This antinomy is only imaginary, and a closer examination reveals that our proposal is in accord with the "scientific process" to which *deduction* and *induction* are not contradictory but complementary methods.

1.4   THE NEED FOR AN ANALYTIC-BEHAVIORAL INTERPRETATION

Accounting has frequently been reproached that it wears the mantle of academic honors without justice, for it is predominantly descriptive and classificatory, has no analytic content, nor does it employ any empirical hypotheses. To defend accounting against such a superficial criticism is not difficult. The first objection can be encountered with examples out of biology and many social sciences where the descriptive and taxonomic approaches flourish. The second and third argument must be rejected as false, something that will be demonstrated in the Chapters 5, 6, and 7 of this book. The unjust accusation is partly chargeable to accountants themselves, for they make neither the mathematical-analytic nor the empirical-hypothetical structure of their discipline very explicit and—what is worse—they, in their metrologic activity, do not consistently match the tools with the purpose. This means that many empirical hypotheses employed in accounting are not sufficiently checked for their validity and revised accordingly.

A further reason for a stricter observance of the analytic-behavioral accounting approach is the burgeoning interest in the formalization of decision-making processes. As long as entrepreneurs or managers act without an analytical apparatus, like an optimization model, etc., but merely on the basis of accounting records—the underlying assumptions of which they are being assumed to know—one may argue that the thought processes of these entrepreneurs adjust, filter, and modify the accounting data such as to make them valid for a momentary decision. This is a common assumption which is just as commonly gainsaid. But it is indeed hard to bring evidence that our executives do not possess a mental power which could perform an intricate task like the one described. As soon as operations research or other analytical models are put in between the accounting apparatus and the entrepreneurial brain, the situation becomes different. Mathematical models, as employed in the management sciences, must be fed the correct values of precisely defined variables; these models cannot be expected to assume a comprehensive task of modification, consideration, and evaluation, and are expected to supply the decision maker with a more definite answer.

It seems to be time for accountants to reflect upon this point. How can they connect accounting identities with operations research models? How can they impose upon accounting models significant empirical hypotheses that may lead to useful projections? To solve the whole complex of problems connected with questions of this kind will occupy accountants and operations analysts for many years to come. Nevertheless we will try at least to clear the ground for these endeavors and suggest some ways which might lead to a satisfactory achievement of this goal. The classical example of a combination between an accounting frame and a full-fledged mathematical model is, of course, Leontief's input-output system.[7] It constitutes the foundation of modern interindustry analysis and will have to be discussed at some length later on. The few attempts that were made to apply the basic ideas of input-output analysis to the micro-economy do not give any indication of great promise on a large scale. It rather seems that the solution to our problem lies in a somewhat different direction. Whether it will be found in the application of simulation studies to various aspects of the micro- and macro-economy under application of accounting models, or in purely analytical models that permit the application of an algorism is still a matter of controversy. The issue, however, will receive due consideration.

In connection with models for optimizing entrepreneurial or also macro-economic goals, another question arises which concerns accountants intimately: Is there a way for determining the *optimal accounting model*? Can the idea of optimization be applied to the classificational and evaluative frame of accounting itself? Finding a

---

[7] See e.g., Wassili Leontief [1951].

solution to this problem ought to be one of the major tasks of accounting, one should presume, but little has consciously been done along these lines—even with regard to such spade work as formulating the problem. We consider this issue as closely related to the previously mentioned problem of constructing specialized accounting systems for individual purposes. Only if we can find criteria for determining when an accounting model is "satisfactory," will we be able to construct monopurpose accounting systems. To develop a device for finding models that are "optimal" with regard to a particular purpose would, obviously, be the ultimate goal.

1.5 THE NEED OF ACTUAL PRACTICE FOR IMPROVED ACCOUNTING MODELS

Accounting can be regarded as an applied, *normative* discipline. In budgeting the normative aspect of our discipline is clearly revealed, but even the measurement of past events is closely tied to future expectations (e.g., valuation by discounting future yields) and ultimately serves goals which obviously involve value judgments. Accounting is concerned with the theoretical and practical problems of measuring various aspects of the income or flow of wealth phenomenon and hence may be considered a *service discipline* which cannot be studied in isolation but which must be viewed in the setting of a threefold relationship: (1) in dependence with its *master discipline* "economics," (2) in relation with the other tributaries of economics and business administration, and (3) in connection with the needs of economic practice.

The last facet has dominated traditional accountancy and it will be worth inquiring here what these needs are and to which forces of change they are subject. Every system of measurement, serving not purely theoretical investigations but purposes of everyday life, constitutes a compromise of three conflicting aspects; accuracy, economy, and versatility.

With regard to the first, we must admit: not only is the degree of accuracy of many accounting measures very low, but frequently accountants are operating in a vacuum of reliability which does not provide any error measurement at all. This, from the scientific as well as practical point of view, is a serious defect to which in the past little attention has been paid and which will have to be discussed at some detail in this book. The conflict between a high degree of accuracy and low measurement costs, on the other hand, is pretty obvious, and the search for an optimal combination under consideration of purpose, versatility, etc., may be in close connection with the quest for an optimal accounting model as mentioned in the preceding section.

Economy, no doubt, plays in accounting a decisive role and in the past, accuracy had to be sacrificed to parsimony as soon as the marginal cost of improved precision was considered higher than the marginal benefit from a more accurate accounting system. This criterion will, of course, be valid in the future as well, but the marginal costs of higher accuracy might be reduced through the application of electronic data processing to accountancy; by these means one might even dream of mitigating the difficult evaluation of the marginal yield that improved measurements promise.

Versatility of application is another requirement expected from a scale of measurement. The adaptability of the yard, the meter, and other scales for measuring distances is reflected in the wide range of application; these scales pertain, theoretically at least, to the distances within the molecule or atom, just as well as to the gigantic dimension of cosmic space. This does not imply that the "yardstick," as a tool of the tailor, can be applied to all the phenomena between those extremes. Different tools, whose appearances do not resemble each other and whose ranges of error are hardly comparable among themselves, are necessary for these similar and yet so different tasks. This analogy applied to accounting is very crude and limp, but might give the reader an inkling of the kind of problem we are confronted with when speaking of the desirability of many monopurpose accounting systems in the face of the need for a simple but versatile accounting body.

The more obvious needs of actual practice for improved and more sophisticated accounting methods result out of the growing complexity of modern industrial and economic life. The chief economic problem of the second half of the twentieth century might well be characterized as a search for surveyability, for goal-clarification, for making more manageable the gigantic economic apparatus which threatens to subjugate man and to pervert his mind. In such an age, the making of "correct" decisions by industrial as well as political executives of various echelons becomes more and more difficult; even the refined economic instinct of the born financial wizard and industrial captain begins to fail. The longing for an apparatus that may relieve us, at least to some extent, from the heavy, ulcer-generating burden of decision making is hardly surprising. Thus many people *approach* accounting for help in this decision-making dilemma and some even *reproach* it that it has not provided such an aid long ago. This, too, is not astonishing, since a new unfilled quest is prone to overshadow the real merits which are then taken for granted. It does not need any assurance that many purposes which traditional accounting has fulfilled will continue to exist and will also in the future be served by accounting, but it may well be that facilities and methods for attaining these goals assume a peripheral position vis-à-vis the decision-making problem which aims toward the center of our discipline.

A further need of actual practice is the relaxation of "ideological" tensions between the industrial engineer, the economist, and the accountant—in as much as they are working and "contra"-operating in one and the same enterprise. Controversies between these groups occasionally bear fruit but more frequently are harmful and sometimes even fatal. The creation of data-processing departments in many enterprises has definitely had a mitigating and beneficial influence upon relations between these three groups. Under the catalytic effect of the mathematician the other three groups have found a common basis, and in the data-processing department of many firms a pleasant co-operation of experts from various fields can be observed. A conversation with these people usually reveals the need for an analytic presentation of accounting that is stripped of the technical-descriptive embroidery which adorns accounting literature. The mathematicians, industrial engineers, etc., who are charged to co-operate on an accounting-computer problem are willing to learn some accounting but are allegedly repelled by the technical and specialized presentation of this subject;[8] what is even more surprising, however, is to learn that those accountants who co-operate in the data-processing departments now fully agree to the objections of their colleagues from other fields.

1.6   CONCLUSION

As we have seen, the call for a novel approach to accounting comes from several directions and the need for a broadening of our discipline has many facets. It thus appears that accountants are confronted with the choice of one of the following two alternatives:

---

[8]In describing this situation we have not put up any straw men but reflect our personal experience with experts from industry.

(1) to acquire a profound knowledge of many aspects of jurisprudence (civil law, commercial law, corporation and partnership law, and tax law) and develop their discipline into a *purely* legalistic-dogmatic field of knowledge; or (2) to acquire proficiency in modern quantitative analytical methods and try to maintain the old status of their discipline, namely that of the most important quantitative tool of economic practice.

We do not believe that these will become alternatives for the profession as such, rather than for the individual accountant. The past has revealed clearly the importance of accounting as an instrument for the fulfillment of legalistic requirements. Our present system of financial accounting, however, constitutes a compromise that neglects some legal aspects almost as much as some managerial aspects. It is now easy to recognize that this anticipated diversification of accounting does not need to create a chasm in our discipline, but may well-nigh lead to a close co-operation between specialists. But even those specializing in the legalistic aspects of accounting will need a basic training in analytical methods, just as those specializing in the managerial aspects cannot get along without any education in law.

The following chapters are not concerned with legal details. Legalistic aspects are discussed only where they are indispensable for an understanding of the history of accounting, and for the construction of some monopurpose systems. As far as the quantitative analytic problems of accounting are concerned, we do not profess that this book contains all the solutions to them, we merely claim it to be a modest, first attempt of teaching accounting from a new, more analytic, and, hopefully, scientific point of view.

Chapter 2

BASIC ASSUMPTIONS
AND DEFINITIONS

One of the most important and difficult of the responsibilities of the economist is to resist the authority of the accepted.

GALBRAITH [1956, p. xi]

2.1 ATTEMPTS TO DEFINE ACCOUNTING

A FAVORED APPROACH in constructing a sound definition is to start from the commonly accepted view about the content of a subject (or object), refine and clarify certain aspects of this view, then draw boundaries as tightly as possible. Adhering to this procedure in our discipline would mean to exclude all macro-accounting systems.[1] In practice, and to a considerable extent in theory, the term "accounting" is employed to designate micro-accounting[2] only. Yet, many definitions of accounting, including the "most" official one offered by the Committee on Terminology of the American Institute of Certified Public Accountants, do not succumb to such a narrow view: "Accounting is the art of recording, classifying, and summarizing in a significant manner and in terms of money, transactions and events which are, in part at least, of a financial character and interpreting the results thereof." (AICPA [1961], Accounting Terminology Bulletin No. 1, p. 9).

---

[1] In our terminology *macro-accounting* comprises: (1) national income and product accounts (carried out in the United States by the Department of Commerce), (2) flow-of-funds accounts (Federal Reserve Board), (3) interindustry accounts or input-output tables (Department of Commerce, previously by the Department of Labor), (4) the international balance of payments (Department of Commerce), as well as (5) all *regional* accounts similar to those listed (1–4). The inclusion of *other* regional or national accounts to be constructed in future is not precluded.

[2] *Micro-accounting*, as here understood, includes (1) financial and funds accounting, (2) cost and managerial accounting, and (3) periodic budgeting, each of this for (*a*) business enterprises, (*b*) nonprofit organizations (eventually individual households), (*c*) government agencies, as well as (*d*) aggregates of several firms or other agencies belonging to one and the same administrative unit.

This definition by no means limits accounting to the "micro-economic" recording process, it obviously is broad enough to encompass macro-accounting systems of all kinds. Furthermore it does not exclude the recording of future transactions and events, leaving open the door for incorporating periodic budgeting and other projections of *future* micro- or macro-economic events. We emphasize this extension because in spite of the above *general* definition, accountants, business men, and many professors of accounting —as the teaching by the latter manifests—regard macro-accounting systems as odd and distant relatives of "accounting" which by mere accident acquired a name that deceives about the concept behind it.[3] Apart from the fact that the AICPA Committee's definition implicitly includes macro-accounting—whether deliberately or unintentionally is not known—there have been forces recognizing the *desirability* of integrating micro- and macro-accounting on a theoretical level.[4] Our own view is more radical, we do not merely express a desirability of, but we assert the *necessity* for such an integration. A theory of accounting that tends toward a scientific-analytic, instead of a dogmatic-legalistic foundation cannot renounce the potential of generalization and cross-fertilization which a unification brings about.

Criticisms of the above stated definition were directed mainly at (1) the vagueness that adheres to a phrase like "in a significant manner," (2) the partial overlapping of the term "transaction" with the expression "in terms of money," "events" and "of financial character," and of the term "interpreting" with "recording" (cf. Kohler [1952], p. 9). Yet, it is the wide leeway which the word "recording" affords that makes the Committee's definition acceptable (by including "valuation," "projection," etc., in the term "recording"). On the other hand, the shadow of this advantage creates a certain vagueness that is open to criticism. Individual authors have not been too successful in improving upon the above stated delinea-

---

[3]This assertion is best evidenced by a glance into the books, especially textbooks, on accounting. The number of accountants (in the whole world) who have seriously attempted to interrelate micro- and macro-accounting in their own books can be counted on one or two hands. See Allais [1954], Powelson [1955a], American Accounting Association [1957], Meyer [1962].

[4]In addition to the literature cited in the preceding footnote, there exists a series of *articles* and *book passages* in the accounting literature that manifest the *interest* of a greater number of accountants in a close relation between accounting and economics in general and micro- and macro-accounting in particular. See Boulding [1962], Devine [1952], Flanders [1959], Friend [1949], Kohler [1952], Littleton and Zimmerman [1962, pp. 200–22], Mattessich [1956, '57, '58b, '59b], Murphy [1957], Perry [1955], Powelson [1955b], Smith [1952], Smyth [1959], Solomons [1955, 61], Wheeler [1955].

tion of our discipline. Chambers, one of the more progressive theo-reticians, for example, offers the following interesting definition: "Accounting is a method of monetary calculation designed to pro-vide a continuous source of financial information as a guide to future action in markets." (Chambers [1961], p. 43.) Obviously, his terminology brings this formulation more in conformity with the modern vocabulary, but the qualification "continuous" is not strong enough to distinguish accounting from operations research and re-lated quantitative methods, while the phrase "as a guide to future action in markets" makes the definition so narrow as to exclude a great deal of accounting—unless this phrase is interpreted so broadly that it becomes all-embracing and hence meaningless. On the other hand, the expression "a method of" is no doubt a more fortunate choice than the Committee's locution "the art of." Aside from the fact that fruitless discussions on whether a discipline has to be addressed as an art or a science are outdated, it is to our mind *the method*[5] which lends the designation "accounting" to a recording and measurement process. The methodology constitutes the com-mon denominator, uniting such varied systems as financial account-ing, national income accounting, etc. Yet, the method itself is not at all described in Chambers' definition and is only hinted at in that of the Committee—by referring to "classifying.... transactions." To describe a dog as an animal which is able to draw a cart, guide a blind man, and stand on his hind-legs, would, from an organic-biological viewpoint, be unsatisfactory. Although in examining ac-counting we must not overlook its teleologic character, a purely functional definition of accounting (as is Chambers') that neglects essential, *generic* features proves inadequate for our purpose.

A definition is brought about by creating a class of objects with common properties; thereby these objects are made distinct from those lacking the characteristic attributes. In extremely simple and concrete situations it may be easy to specify these attributes, but in cases of even moderate complexity a perfect definition is difficult to attain. It should contain neither too few nor too many properties, only those of constitutive nature; it ought to be without ambiguity and it must avoid circular reasoning. Yet, the chief criterion of a good definition is its *power of demarcation*—that is the ability to sepa-rate clearly objects belonging to the defined category from other or

---

[5]"Method" is here understood in the sense of the most basic conceptual frame, but not with reference to detailed treatment.

similar objects that do not belong to it. But, many definitions pay mere lip-service to this discriminatory purpose, they are configurations of words fulfilling a psychological need, without being operationally fruitful.

Thus, we are groping for a definition which sets fairly sharp boundaries and which has substance enough to serve as a basis for the development of a coherent and general theory of accounting.[6] Such a definition will be at bay with the blurred notion about the essence of accounting that predominates. This notion overemphasizes the mere data-processing activity and projects accounting as "*the* information system" of the firm. This view is not only extremely vague but flagrantly invades the territory of neighboring disciplines. In the long run such a notion must lead to confusion and conflict, rather harming than promoting a synchronization between accounting and organization theory. Instead, it seems preferable to *regard the quantitative methods of the economic sciences as one superdiscipline* to which a name like "management science," "activity analysis," etc., might be assigned. *Within the boundaries of this discipline the application of a specific model-type forms the subdiscipline "accounting."* These reflections lead us to the following definition:

Accounting is a discipline[7] concerned with the quantitative description and projection of the income circulation and of wealth aggregates by means of a method based on the following set of basic assumptions (after these assumptions are thoroughly tested they might be regarded as necessary and sufficient conditions):

1. Monetary values	10. Economic transactions
2. Time intervals	11. Valuation
3. Structure	12. Realization
4. Duality	13. Classification
5. Aggregation	14. Data input
6. Economic objects	15. Duration
7. Inequity of monetary claims	16. Extension
8. Economic agents	17. Materiality
9. Entities	18. Allocation

(the individual assumptions are specified in Section 2.41).

---

[6] Otherwise we would prefer Wittgenstein's [1953, p. 32] approach of circumscribing a subject by means of "family resemblances."

[7] The distinction between the academic discipline and its practical application could further be articulated by a convention which Jourdain [1910] applies to mathematics: spelling the first letter of the theoretical body—in our case Accounting—in capital and that of the activity of "doing it" in lower case. A further possibility would be to address the former as accountancy, the latter as accounting. In order to adhere to customary usage, we will not apply such discriminatory means, but rather state explicitly when only the academic side is referred to and when the practical one alone.

In a way, the rest of our book is an elaboration of this definition. The eighteen basic assumptions[8] should lend sufficient power to this definition to make it qualify as a foundation for a general and systematic theory of accounting—a meta-theory of which this work represents no more than a mere outline.

As regards individual expressions of the above definition we restrict ourselves for the time being to the following remarks: the term "quantitative description" is in common usage, it is equivalent to *measurement* in its broadest sense, including classification. Since the following chapters devote much space to measurement, as understood in this way, the present indication should suffice. The term "projection" refers to the activity of planning by means of estimates about the future—the prognostic value of these estimates is deemed sufficient for planning and control purposes, but is low in comparison to rigorous scientific predictions. Since "all description methodologically entails prediction" (Churchman [1961], p. 85), and since the success of both, measurement and prediction, depends on the hypotheses used, the *epistemological* problem of "projection" will be discussed under the topic of "hypotheses formulation" (Chapter 7), while the technical problems of "projection" are illustrated in the Chapters 8 and 9.

Finally, the expression "of the income circulation and of wealth aggregates" refers to the whole group of interrelated activities that arise out of the need for subsistence and economic growth, from the acquisition of goods to their consumption, from the creation of claims to their redemption. The next section will elaborate upon this problem.

2.2 INCOME AND WEALTH

The concepts of income and wealth are applied to both micro- and macro-economies. This fact calls for a formulation of an income concept that, on one side, expresses its universal applicability and, on the other, leaves leeway to create subconcepts serving specific purposes. Most economic entities can be envisaged as possessing the two extremes of production and disposition (consumption).

---

[8]We call this set of assumptions, for lack of a more appropriate name, the *duality syndrome* since it pivots on the duality principle (or as some authors call it *duality-aspect principle*, cf. Anthony [1960], pp. 33, 71). See also our basic assumption 4.

Hence, *we define income as the flow of goods and services,*[9] *within a well-defined period, between the production side and the consumption side of an entity.* Usually this flow is evaluated in monetary terms; it has many side channels, it is interrupted (by capital formation or disinvestment, intermediate consumption, output to outsiders or input from them) and must be regarded as possessing tributaries and leakages, feedbacks and recursive channels, reservoirs and bottlenecks. Furthermore, due to fluctuations between specific price levels, this circulation of wealth must be envisaged as *a flow whose medium carries a substance the intensity of which varies with different channels.* Hence the question arises: at which passage of the flow shall income appropriately be measured? As the many attempts of formulating income concepts during the past have demonstrated, there is no unique "threshold"; and to assert one dogmatically—as Fisher did by choosing personal consumption as the dominating passage— introduces a rigidity that is in conflict with the requirements of theory and practice. This led us to suggest the above stated definition of a general income concept from which individual subconcepts may be derived according to needs (see Subsection 3.81). Such a solution permits great flexibility by shifting the threshold at which income is to be measured. A flexibility which resembles that attained by accepting a shift of the boundaries of the entity (e.g., from micro- to macro-economics) for which income is to be defined. The latter shift has never been objected to (not even by Fisher who accepts an income concept for the entire economy), why should there be any objection to the former?

Fisher, of course, was fully aware of the complexities involved

---

[9]Since we do not accept the "household threshold" as the dominating criterion for income measurement, the term "flow of services" may here not be interpreted in the Fisherian sense. For us the notion of a "flow of goods and services" refers to the transfer of economic objects (see basic assumption 10) from one entity, subentity, agent, etc., to another. Fisher's view that a commodity becomes a service only when consumed by a human being encounters terminological difficulties, since then labor entering a commodity can no longer be regarded a service.   The process of a (labor) service becoming thus a potential service (a commodity) would not be feasible under Fisher's conceptual apparatus; only the reverse process, the conversion of a potential service into a service, is possible.

In this connection the question arises whether the distinction between income and wealth does not become endangered.   Let us regard the borderline case in which income consists of *potential* services only (e.g., a firm which retained all its "income" of the current period). Since potential services are wealth aggregates, is then income not identical to wealth? Yet, it is not more identical to wealth then is the differential of a function identical with the original function; that means income always is an increment (or decrement) of wealth and not something apart from it.

and, within the domestic area, made the following concessions:

...we have a picture of three successive stages, or aspects, of a man's
income:
Enjoyment or psychic income, consisting of agreeable sensations and
experiences;
Real income *measured* by the cost of living;
Money income, consisting of the money received by a man for meeting
his costs of living;
The last—money income—is most commonly called income; and the
first—enjoyment income—is the most fundamental. But, for accounting
purposes, real income, as measured by the cost of living, is the most practical." (Fisher [1930], p. 11. Footnote omitted.)

Fisher's "money income includes all money *received* which is not
obviously, and in the nature of the case, to be devoted to reinvestment" (Fisher [1930], p. 10). At another place Fisher [1906, pp.
234, 333] is forced to extend the above stated stratification by introducing an auxiliary income concept. This he calls "earned income" which obviously includes investment in general. Thus in
defining income one is confronted with the double-edged blade of
either excluding most income concepts in current use (e.g., gross
income, operating income, taxable income, national income at market value, personal income, disposable income) or accepting a formulation so broad as to embrace all secondary income concepts.
The choice of the latter forces us to reject Fisher's "domestic
threshold" as the decisive criterion of income measurement. A
criterion that Fisher could not cease emphasizing in spite of the
obvious need for auxiliary concepts: "...a definition of income
which satisfies both theory and practice, in both economics and accountancy, *must* reckon as income in the most basic sense all those
uses, services, or living for which the cost of living is expended even
though such expenditure may exceed the money income" (Fisher
[1930], p. 11).

This "real" or "realized" income excludes the capital formation of the entity and is usually referred to when Fisher speaks of
"income" without qualifying adjective. Accountants may regard
this definition as extremely unrealistic or even naïve. A superficial
examination of Fisher's income concept may indeed deceive about
its profundity and about the subtlety with which it solves one of the
intricate problems of income measurement. By excluding capital
formation Fisher saves his income concept from the vagaries of capital (or asset) evaluation. Consumption can be evaluated without
heed to the uncertainties about the future, but not so capital for-

mation. It requires additional, and usually vague, assumptions about future trends or revenues, expenses, interest rates, use and duration of assets, etc. The question merely is whether those in need of a non-Fisherian income concept are not willing to pay the high price of uncertainty by accepting a less reliable but more adequate measure: In practice this is frequently the case and becomes most obvious in situations where long-term income concepts are involved. There, the ratio of "capital accumulation divided by income disposed" usually decreases with increasing length of the period. That means in the long-run the capital accumulation of the specific entity becomes less and less significant relative to the disposition of income (for consumption purposes or other purposes outside the entity).

In contrast to Fisher's definition of (real) income[10] is Hicks definition which definitely includes capital formation: "... it would seem that we ought to define a man's income as the maximum value which he can consume during a week, and still expect to be as well off at the end of the week as he was at the beginning" (Hicks [1946], p. 172).

In juxtaposing Fisher's and Hicks' income concepts we not only notice a difference in the exclusion or inclusion of investment activity, we also observe the two fundamentally different ways by which income is being measured. The first one (Fisher's) is based on *flow* variables, the second (Hicks') is based on *stock* variables. Thus we are led back to the duality exploited by accountants when measuring income, on one hand, in the balance sheet through the difference of stocks and, on the other, in the income statement through the accumulation of flows. The logico-mathematical principle behind this phenomenon is easily stated: *Any change can be quantified in two ways: (1) by measuring the sum total of all contributing increments and decrements (flows) or (2) by measuring the difference between the two totals (stocks) connected by this change.* This intuitively self-evident proposition—applied to the concepts of income and wealth which may be formally deduced from the associative law for the *difference operator* in connection with addition (see S. Goldberg [1958], p. 25)—yields the two basic forms from which every definition of in-

---

[10] Fisher's income of individual persons may, of course, be aggregated to a national income. With regard to the latter he gives the following definition:

"The income of society as a whole is the total money value of all the services received by the members of society from all sources. . . . Most events are interactions; so that in a comprehensive view most services are also disservices and cancel out, leaving as a final uncanceled fringe only the psychic experiences—enjoyable or distasteful—of the consumer." (Fisher [1932], p. 623.)

come must be chosen. Hicks chooses the first, Fisher the second.[11] But these forms are independent of the threshold at which the measurement occurs, thus constitute another dimension of choice compared with those of entity and threshold. Fisher sets his threshold at the last quantifiable stage, at the event of consumption; thus he is forced to exclude saving. Hicks prefers an earlier phase, the stage of production; thus he is bound to include capital formation. Between the extremes of production and consumption (or disposition) lies the vast area of distribution. Indeed, modern national income statisticians measure the total income flow of a country in all three phases, i.e., at each of these thresholds. Yet, each of these phases must be conceived as a broad stretch not likely to be homogeneous. The decision to measure income in a certain phase, is not sufficient but, in addition, calls for a specification as to the precise location of the threshold. This problem arises in the micro- as well as macroeconomy, and occasionally constitutes a source of confusion or misunderstanding. The solution to it, as indicated above, lies in a general formulation of income which permits the formation of a variety of specific income concepts, each well tailored to a limited purpose.

The concept of *wealth* is often regarded as a derivative of income; but here, too, a more accurate formulation based on Fisher and preceding economists is desirable. From the definitions of the latter (e.g., Marshall [1920], pp. 56–57) and even from Fisher's own definition[12] it seems rather that it is income which must be interpreted as a derivative of the wealth function,[13] not vice versa. Yet, Fisher

---

[11] The majority of income concepts are based on flow variables cf. e.g.:
"... his true or *net income* is found by deducting from his gross income 'the outgoings that belong to its production.'" (Marshall [1920], p. 72, footnote omitted.) or
"We can then define the *income* of the entrepreneur as being the excess of the value of his finished output sold during the period over his prime cost." (Keynes [1936], p. 53, footnote omitted.)
From a practical point of view Hicks' income concept encounters the difficulty of measuring "well-offness." To determine whether a person is as well off at the end of a time period as at its beginning—under renunciation of the incremental-decremental approach—is cumbersome and does by no means enhance reliability or accuracy of the estimates.

[12] "I define wealth as consisting of material objects owned by human beings (including, if you please, human beings themselves). The ownership may be divided and parcelled out among different individuals in the form of partnership rights, shares of stock, bonds, mortgages, and other forms of property rights. In whatever ways the ownership be distributed and symbolized in documents, the entire group of property rights are merely means to an end—income. Income is the alpha and omega of economics." (Fisher [1930], p. 13.)

[13] In mathematics, the ratio of the increment of the dependent variable (along the cumulative function) to the increment of the corresponding independent variable is called the "difference quotient"—or in case of infinitesimal increments, the "derivative." If wealth is interpreted as the dependent variable and time as the independent one, then income becomes the *difference quotient* (of wealth to time) or the *derivative* respectively.

resolves this confusion by distinguishing between wealth as capital goods and wealth as capital value:

> It would seem then that income must be derived from capital; and, in a sense, this is true. Income *is* derived from capital *goods*. But the *value* of the income is not derived from the *value* of the capital goods. On the contrary, the value of the capital is derived from the value of the income. Valuation is a human process in which foresight enters. Coming events cast their shadows before. Our valuations are always anticipations.
>
> These relations are shown in the following scheme in which the arrows represent the order of sequence—(1) from capital goods to their future services, that is, income; (2) from these services to their value; and (3) from their value back to capital value:

$$\text{Capital goods} \longrightarrow \text{Flow of services (income)}$$
$$\downarrow$$
$$\text{Capital value} \longleftarrow \text{Income value}$$

> Not until we know how much income an item of capital will probably bring us can we set any valuation on that capital at all. (Fisher [1930], pp. 14–15.)

But such measurement of capital (= asset) value is one-sided and based on a controversial implication. It presumes that future income—derived from a specific asset—can always be anticipated with a fair degree of reliability. Above all, it overlooks the basic principle of anticipation. This "principle of insufficient reason," well testable by observing human (and even animal) behavior asserts that *in the absence of better evidence about the future one assumes continuation of the present state of an object or the past trend of an event.* What about situations where future asset yields and interest rates seem to be more uncertain than the persistence of a trend? Here this principle *would suggest to extrapolate past and present values into the future* instead of introducing further perplexity by the roundabout way of estimating future yields and discount rates. Then the extrapolation of a past value-trend is at least as reliable as Fisher's approach, and is certainly more in conformity with the general attitude toward uncertainty. Of course, a reasonable method of extrapolation must be chosen. Since "historical costing" as applied in traditional accounting rarely fulfills this requirement, our argument must not be taken as a defense of the cost basis of valuation in its crude form. Further attention should be paid to the *purpose* of value measurement. While Fisher's approach is well suited for specific managerial investment decisions, the method of "value extrapolation" seems to be a better compromise for general communication between the accountant and a group of anonymous consumers of information. The data use of the latter is manifold and calls for comparatively simple conventions the results of which should depend as little as possible on subjective value judgements. Further discussion of these problems must be postponed to Chapters 5 and 6.

Finally it ought to be reminded that the phrase "of income circulation and of wealth aggregates" not only refers to the income and wealth of an entity but is applicable to subentities and subperiods as well. Furthermore this phrase implies derivative concepts such as production, consumption, surplus, saving, investment, etc.

2.3   THE DUALITY PRINCIPLE—ABSTRACT NOTION VERSUS ACTUAL RECORDING

Much misunderstanding has been created among laymen by confusing or identifying bookkeeping with accounting. Yet, more confusion arises because of the accountants' failure to make a precise distinction between the act of making a "double entry" and the idea of subjecting certain economic events to the abstract, mathematical notion of a transaction. The essence of the latter lies in a fundamentally *two-dimensional* property that permits double classification within one set of classes. Whether this dual classification is fully carried out, or only conceived mentally—or carried out merely on the highest level of aggregation, whether it is executed in T-accounts, or in a matrix, or in form of an ordered tuple or a vector, or by graphical means of a network—is irrelevant for the *duality principle*. The decisive factor is the existence of an economic event dominated by a process of giving and taking, input and output, transferring out and transferring in. It is this property which creates an isomorphism between an empirical phenomenon and our *basically* two dimensional mathematical construct.

Of course, the conception of this duality constitutes nothing but the core. A series of conditions especially with regard to aggregation and evaluation, must be fulfilled before one can speak of an accounting system. But in our view, it is this syndrome—a mathematico-logical structure consisting of a set of assumptions—which makes us decide whether we are dealing with an accounting system or not. Every other criterion for delineating our discipline is too vague and will quickly perish in a time when quantitative methods are introduced into the administration of enterprises, or of entire economies, by disciplines which are not more than distantly related to accounting. It would be vain toil to convince the experts of statistics, econometrics, operations research, activity analysis, information and communication theory, systems engineering, etc., that they are ultimately concerned with accounting. Yet, in spite of this difficulty, many accountants reject a generic definition without being able to clearly stake the boundaries of their discipline by other means. The predominant reason why many experts shun our apparently narrow and formalistic definition, lies in the ingrained notion that accounting is inseparable from profitability and efficiency measurement in the narrow sense. Although these are important tasks of some accounting systems (which shall be sufficiently cultivated in this book) they are no constituents of accounting in general like the circulatory and other characteristics stated in our definition.

Returning to the core of this section we may interpret the *duality principle* as the assertion that a transaction or flow has basically two dimensions: an aspect and a counter-aspect (to avoid the terms *input* and *output* which have too concrete a flavor, or the terms *debit* and *credit* which have too strong a flavor of the technical recording process). More precisely, the principle asserts that *there exist economic events*[14] *which are isomorphic to a two-dimensional classification of a value within one set of classes.* This basically dual property of a transaction thus generalizes and extends those empirical manifestations which are associated with the phenomenon of change. Wherever— in our attempt to depict phases of the economic environment—we explicitly adapt our model to this double aspect, we are confronted with an accounting system. The evolution of national income measurement offers an example *par excellence* that the duality aspect may, but need not be, exploited in creating and presenting statistical data. But it also shows that often, for reasons of systematization, perspicuity, and analysis, the utilization of an accounting frame works to great advantage. Thus accountancy, as a part of quantitative economics, is characterized by a special methodology and a set of assumptions which we might call "the duality syndrome."

---

[14] Theoretically it should be possible to develop accounting systems for noneconomic flow structures as well; e.g., for the transfer of liquids in a network of pipelines and reservoirs, or for the tracing of chemical substances during the metabolism of plants or animals (e.g., research with radioactive tracers in the photosynthesis), etc. These potential accounting systems do not deal with income and wealth aspects in the ordinary sense, thus cannot be addressed as *economic* accounting.

Cf. Anton [1953], p. 1 and [1962], p. 11: "The flow concept has universality of meaning as a continuous process whereby additions to a corpus or deductions from that corpus are made. It has its roots in organic theory where antecedents and subsequent events are currently important. One finds it prevalent in many closed systems." (Footnote omitted.)

In the present volume other than *economic* accounting systems are not dealt with.

The necessity for an accounting approach arose in several quarters, more or less independently. It made itself first felt in *financial accounting*, when in the three centuries before 1500 the "double entry" approach evolved out of "single entry" bookkeeping. For centuries this remained the only area utilizing the duality principle —apart from some traces in the *balance of trade* concept—until Quesnay presented his *tableau économique* (see Chapter 4). Later, in the beginning of the past century the duality principle emerged again in a different attire, namely in the international balance of payments.[15] During our century it was first *cost accounting* which grew out of systematizing the originally "loose" cost figures found in business enterprises. Then Ragnar Frisch (1937) and somewhat later (1941) Meade and Stone[16] proposed a system of *national income accounts*—ultimately based on the Keynesian savings-investment identity—which obviously used the duality principle without recording every *individual* event twice, restricting the double classification to highly aggregated figures. Thanks to the National Accounts Research Unit of the Organization for European Economic Cooperation, this approach has been adopted, in one form or another, on an international scale. Meanwhile in a pioneering study Copeland [1952] presented his analysis of money-flows in accounts form. This approach was thoroughly elaborated and somewhat modified in the *flow of funds accounts* published periodically since 1955 by the Federal Reserve Board.[17] The fact that the flow-of-funds statisticians followed a path similar to that of the national-income statisticians, may be taken for granted since a good deal of flow-of-funds accounting is based on data from the national income and product accounts—though the latter use a classification system that is more *functional* while the former developed fairly detailed *institutional* sectors. But it is all the more striking that Leontief's [1951] *input-output analysis* (nowadays known under the more appropriate name of *interindustry analysis*), which originated in a very different branch of economics (from Leon Walras' general equilibrium analysis), utilizes an accounting frame that could not have evolved more naturally and inevitably. Finally, it seems that also *periodic budgeting* is being more and more drawn into a systematic frame of

[15] For further details see Chapter 4.
[16] Cf. Studenski [1958], p. 209.
[17] See Federal Reserve Bulletins [Oct., 1955 and Aug., 1959], Board of Governors of the Federal Reserve System [1955], and National Bureau of Economic Research [1962].

accounts (see the system of T-accounts at the end of Chapter 9). *All these systems employ the duality principle in order to present their quantitative descriptions and explanations in a more cohesive, analytical, and meaningful way.*

It was already hinted at, and it shall be demonstrated later (e.g., in Section 4.2) in further detail, that the duality principle must not be confused with the double entry technique. The former provides the conceptual structure for a two-dimensional classification of certain economic events, but does not enforce individual entries on an item-by-item basis. Social accounting as well as some business accounting systems prove that the advantage of the duality principle can be taken hold of even when the double classification is carried out in the "last phase" only, avoiding the cumbersome, costly, and often impossible task of applying a technique which requires entry and counter-entry for each individual transaction. It is paramount that every flow is conceived as having *basically* two dimensions, but it is irrelevant whether these two aspects are recorded for each single event or not. The collection of highly aggregate data by "purely statistical means" may often be considered adequate. Furthermore it can easily be demonstrated through input-output tables (or accounting matrices, as we will call them later, see Section 4.6 and Chapter 5) that, even on the highest level of aggregation, *pair-wise* entries are no necessity; single entries *satisfying the twofold classification* are more elegant and better amenable to mathematical treatment, though, for technical reasons, not always practicable.

The major advantage of the duality principle, and probably the reason why it has found such diverse acclaim, lies in the over-all view which it affords and the integration of many details to a unified picture. If, for instance, business accounting were abandoned (as some operations analysts propose) and substituted by a new information system of the firm, sooner or later this new system is likely to utilize the duality principle and thus develop again into an "accounting" system, though in many respects a very different one. It may well be that a time will come when the classifications and hypotheses of our present accounting establishments are outdated, and thrown overboard. Yet, the duality principle and most of the basic assumptions (which we shall discuss in the next section) will firmly stand. Thus it might be of great importance (1) to acquaint oneself with the mathematical, logical structure of that part of accounting which is permanent and (2) to examine, test, and improve the empirical hypotheses that effect our classifications as well as our transactions in order to move toward improved accounting models.

2.4 THE BASIC ASSUMPTIONS OF ACCOUNTING

Let us examine the present situation in the area of basic assumptions of accounting (variously called accounting "postulates," "principles," "standards," etc.). The deviation in terminology and the general uncertainty in this area derives from an arbitrariness that, in search for the ultimate foundations of accountancy, seems unavoidable. Only if scientific criteria can be disclosed that give a natural mold to the basic assumptions of accounting, this arbitrariness could be kept within bounds.

Canning [1929, p. 9] pointed out that "the work of the accountant, and the writings on accounting, until very recently, proceeded by a sort of patchwork and tinkering. To be sure, the patching was often shrewdly planned and executed, but it was patchwork nevertheless in the sense that there was little going back to fundamentals for a fresh start." Much has changed since; many an ingenious idea and much intellectual effort has been invested in developing accounting, and a host of details were explored. Yet, in spite of serious attempts, the fundamentals of our discipline have not yet found a formulation that is general and rigorous enough to secure a firm foundation. The improvement of accounting theory during the last decades is not denied, but only an isolated viewpoint would disregard the greater theoretical progress that other related disciplines have experienced meanwhile. Economics and management science both have undergone an enviable process of purification and clarification through a rigorous application of modern logic and mathematics. It seems that, for the social sciences at least, this purifying aspect of symbolic logic (which nowadays is so strongly fused with mathematics that no sharp line can be drawn between the two) has even greater significance than the application of various algorisms for solving mathematical calculations.

In the following we shall use the duality principle—together with the fact that *economic* accounting systems all deal with income and wealth aspects—as a starting point in developing a set of accounting principles which are basic enough to hold for accounting systems in general. This set of basic assumptions reveals the mathematico-logical structure of the duality principle, its planets and their satellites; these elements are independent of the form in which records are kept. If we speak of "sets," "operations," etc., we refer to mathematical concepts that have little to do with the actual carrying out of the operations.

It must be emphasized that here we do not employ the term "basic assumption" synonymously to "axiom." In our interpretation a basic assumption may refer either to a "primitive" notion, or to an axiom proper, or to a conditional definition (the conditions of which are of axiomatic nature). This comparatively "informal" presentation may help accountants to comprehend such a system. This may be furthered by the absence of mathematical formulations at this stage. Merely the understanding of a few set-theoretical terms—such as "ordered tuple (pair, triple, etc.)," "Cartesian product," "one-to-one correspondence," "isomorphism," etc.— is here required. These and other basic terms are explained in the first part of Appendix A. A closely related, but more rigorous set-algebraic formulation of fundamental accounting concepts is contained in the second part of Appendix A. For the sake of a profounder insight into the essence of accounting, the reader is urged to master the entire Appendix A. The importance of this appendix does not rank behind the following presentation, to which it is in many ways complementary.

Most of our basic assumptions deal with empirical notions. Yet, as previously asserted, our concern is not with individual empirical hypotheses for specific situations, but with a *meta-theory* which provides a hull for different categories of empirical hypotheses. This is achieved by the basic assumptions 11 to 18 which might be addressed as *surrogate assumptions*. Each of these is a "place holder" for a set of empirical hypotheses adapted to a particular purpose. The precise formulation of the hypotheses is not possible without specifying the task of an individual accounting system. Although those individual hypotheses[18] lack general character, the assumptions that such sets of hypotheses must exist are as general and as basic as are the first ten assumptions. Hence we may regard these eighteen basic assumptions as necessary and (hopefully) sufficient conditions for an accounting model—though some leeway for future improvements as well as for the inclusion of more or less imperfect accounting systems of the past ought to be granted.

In order to distinguish the basic assumptions from propositions

---

[18] The major problems of formulating these hypotheses are discussed in Chapter 7.

of secondary importance, we have added to most of the basic assumptions related definitions, explanations, etc.; these appendages
are denoted by lower-case alphabetic letters. Finally the reader
must be reminded that a presentation of *the foundations* of a discipline serves a different purpose, and ought to be read in a different
way, than other parts of this book. To use an analogy: photo-
graphs of a building are looked at and studied in a different way
than is the architect's plan of the same building. Both aim at something different, and the study of a detailed abstraction requires additional toil and concentration. If the following set of basic assumptions, together with Appendix A, shall serve as a source of reference
in dealing with all kinds of accounting systems, the formulations
must be as general and as precise as possible. Such requirements
always check the pace of the reader, whether in studying a code of
law, the axioms of a mathematical system, or the basic assumptions
of accounting. We do not claim that these goals of generality and
precision have here been attained in full perfection, but we hope that
our's is a first step in this direction.

2.41 A Set of Eighteen Assumptions (with Definitions and Remarks)

1. Monetary Values. There exists *a set of additive values*, expressed in a monetary unit; this set is isomorphic to the system of
(positive and negative) integers plus the number zero.

> *a)* The monetary unit, here refers to the *smallest* currency unit of a
> country with monetary autonomy.[19]

2. Time Intervals. There exists *a set of elementary (or minimal),
additive time intervals* (e.g., days).[20]

---

[19] Instead of the integer system we could choose some other number system, e.g., the ring
system of *rational numbers*, or the field of *real numbers*, but all the accounting systems known
to us get along with the integers, provided the set of monetary values is based on the smallest
monetary unit of a particular country (e.g., the *cent* in the United States, the *penny* in the
United Kingdom, etc. Though precisely speaking *half pennies* are still in existence in Great
Britain).

[20] Customarily these time intervals are called, in accounting and economics, "time
points." But we ought to be aware that a point (in time or space) is a dimensionless concept. Thus, by adding points we could never attain a time period (which is one-dimen-
sional). In consequence it is convenient to assume (elementary) time intervals as a basic
concept. (This aspect obviously borders on one of the major problems of philosophy and
mathematics, the problem of continuity). *It has the advantage of emphasizing from the very outset the discreteness (or discontinuity) of the time function with which accountants operate.* The
part of mathematics dealing with discrete functions is called *difference analysis* in contrast to
differential analysis (concerned with nondiscrete functions). It would be commendable to
concentrate in the academic curriculum of business administration (and eventually economics) more on the calculus of difference equations than on the differential or infinitesimal
calculus.

a) The sum of a specific number of subsequent time intervals may be chosen as an *accounting period*.

b) A sum of subsequent time intervals (not larger than the accounting period), the beginning of which coincides with the beginning of the accounting period, is called a subperiod or shortly a *period*.

3. Structure. There exists a structured set of classes (a hierarchy of equivalence classes) reflecting significant categories of an entity (for the latter see basic assumption 9).

a) This structured set of classes (or a set isomorphic to it) is called *a chart of accounts*.

b) The unstructured[21] collection of all equivalence classes contained in the chart of accounts is called the *set of accounts*, its elements are the *accounts*.

c) Depending on the comprehensiveness of an equivalence class and the number of its subsets available, we distinguish between accounts of higher and lower order (the latter are more specific and less comprehensive). For an explanation of the term equivalence class see item XI of Appendix A.

d) In traditional accounting we do not emphasize enough the distinction between an account as an equivalence class that pertains to many entities, and an account as a subset of a specific entity. Obviously, there the term "account" is used in a double sense. Here the term *"account"* refers to *a subset of a specific entity* unless otherwise stated or substituted by the expression "equivalence class."

e) While it seems obvious that the "Cash" accounts of two enterprises belong to the same equivalence class, it may seem surprising that the account "Accounts Payable to X Co." of the Y Company can be regarded as representing the same equivalence class as the "Accounts Receivable from Y Co." of the X Company. A thorough examination proves the identity of the equivalence classes represented by these different account names (cf. Remarks to item 18 of Appendix A). However, the *control accounts* "Accounts Payable" of the Y Company and "Accounts Receivable" of the X Company do *not* represent identical equivalence classes unless all the accounts receivable of Y are owed by X (this statement is confirmed in practice by the need for subsidiary ledgers). A similar example of two differently named accounts representing identical equivalence classes is the following: "Investment in Shares of X Co." by Y Company and "Owners' Equity" of the X Company, provided all shares of X are owned by Y; otherwise only a portion of the owners' equity account represent the same equivalence class as the above stated investment account. Consolidation problems clearly reveal the advantage of such an interpretation.

4. Duality. For all *accounting transactions* it is true that a value is

---

[21] The difference between the "structured" set C_n and the "unstructured" set A_n is illustrated in item 16 of Appendix A.

assigned to a three-dimensional concept (ordered triple) consisting of *two* accounts and a time instance (date).

a) Set-theoretically speaking, accounting transactions are relations or even operations (herein designated by the symbol F, for flow) maping integers (or other numerals) into the subset of a Cartesian product. The characteristic feature is the twofold use of the set of accounts (duality principle).

b) Most mathematical operations assigning values to ordered tuples determine this value from the elements of these ordered tuples by means of an algorism. Occasionally however, no calculus is applicable and one speaks of "a listing" of the value to be assigned (e.g., assume the operation $M(5,3)$ means $3 \times 5 = 15$, here the number 15 is assigned to the ordered pair $(5,3)$ by means of multiplication for which there exist mathematical rules to determine the numeral 15 from the numerals 3 and 5. On the other hand, take the accounting transaction $F(5,3,10) = 100$ which may signify that on the 10th of the month, account No. 3 is to be debited and account No. 5 is to be credited with $100. In this case the numeral 100 cannot be derived by means of a mathematical rule applied to the numerals 10, 3, and 5; only a list of empirical observations—e.g., the general journal—will yield this information). Such a listing is needed for every transaction; that means here the value has to be assigned exogenously (see basic assumption 11).[22]

c) If there are *two* or more transactions assigning the same or different values to the *same* ordered triple (i.e., to the *same* accounts pair as well as the *same* data) an additional sequence-index can be employed to distinguish clearly these two or more transactions.

d) The so-called "combined entry," occasionally encountered in bookkeeping, is mathematically an "impure" concept (see Section 3.6). Therefore it is assumed that in principle every combined entry can be broken down into two or more individual transactions, if necessary even under hypothesis of an arbitrary allocation.

e) The operation F is called a *closing transaction* if one of the two accounts is an immediate sub-account of the other, and if the value assigned to this transaction is identical with the value assigned to the balance (see item 5b) of the subaccount (account of next lower order). The latter is then considered *to be closed.*

f) The operation F is called an *opening transaction* if one of the two accounts is an immediate subaccount of the other and if the balance of this subaccount (at this time instance) is zero. Not all accounts may be subject to opening transactions.

g) The two accounts of a transaction need not belong to the same en-

---

[22] A physical quantity (expressed in units, pounds or kilos, gallons or liters, etc.) or an ordered pair consisting of such a quantity and a monetary value could be assigned instead of the monetary value alone. In the first case we speak of a purely physical accounting, in the second of an accounting with physical data. In both cases one or more sets of (physical) quantities has to be postulated.

tity. They may belong to different entities in which case a super-entity comprising both entities may be envisaged.

5. Aggregation. Every *balance* assigns a (monetary) value— i.e., the arithmetic sum of all (positive and negative) values aggregated during a period in an account—to an ordered pair; the latter consists of the pertinent account and the above stated period which starts with the accounting period.[23]

a) The term "balance," as a substantive, connotes a value *combined with* an account and *a period*.[24] If and only if this balance refers to the *stock* (see item 6a) of an economic object at the end of a period, it becomes the beginning stock (beginning balance) of the immediately succeeding period. Thus, such a balance may also refer to a *time interval* (the beginning of the new period). If this balance is positive we speak of a *debit* balance, if it is negative we speak of a *credit* balance.

b) The verb "to balance" connotes an operation of addition and subtraction (to distinguish this operation from that referred to in assumption 4 we shall assign the symbol B to it; see also Appendix A, item 18).

c) The set of all balances is called the *trial balance*. Frequently, the set of an ordered pair of monetary values is attached to the trial balance. (The first element of this ordered pair represents the arithmetic sum of all balances with positive values, the second element represents the sum of all balances with negative values).

d) An *accounting statement* is a set consisting of three subsets: (*i*) the set of *some* balances (all of its subaccounts are supposed to be closed), (*ii*) the set of *other* balances (all of its subaccounts are also supposed to be closed) and (*iii*) an ordered triple of (monetary) values, the first element of which is the arithmetic sum of all values contained in the first subset (see *i*), the second element is the sum of all values contained in the second subset (see *ii*) and the third element is the value resulting out of subtracting the second value from the first. To the third element a name and the pertinent date may be assigned; it then may be called *the balance of this accounting statement*. If the value of the third element is zero, any one of the balances con-

---

[23]Superficially, it may seem that the ordered pair, to which *this* value is assigned, consists of an account and a time interval (i.e., a specific date) and not of an account and a *period* (i.e., a series of days or months). This is a common fallacy which only a precise formulation can reveal. Accountants, in determining the balance of an account, implicitly assume that the balance of an account results from the sum of all values (positive and negative) assigned to the account *from the beginning date of the accounting period* up to the date specified (not necessarily the end of the accounting period). This may reveal why in the sentence of the above stated text the last phrase: "which starts with the accounting period" is essential.

[24] It is vital to observe that according to our definition "the balance" is not an isolated value but *an ordered triple* consisting of (*i*) an account, (*ii*) a date (or more precisely, a period that lasts from the beginning of the accounting period to this date—see preceding footnote), and (*iii*) a monetary value.

tained in the first or second set may, in principle, be chosen as the balance of the accounting statement. An accounting statement may be regarded as a *structured* account.

6. Economic Objects. There exists *a set of economic objects*, whose values and physical properties are subject to change.

a) Economic objects may be either real or financial objects. The value (or quantity) of an economic object, referring to a time interval, is called *a stock variable* (or stock); the change in value (or quantity) of an economic object during a period is called *a flow variable*.

b) Commodities, including services, are *real objects*.

c) Claims (to property and to money) may, under certain circumstances, be regarded as *financial objects*.

d) *Property claims* (ownership rights in a partnership, shares in corporations, etc.) must here be strictly distinct from monetary claims (bonds, notes, open book debts), mainly because of assumption 7. The property claims of all owners of an entity toward this entity is called *the owners' equity*.

e) Assumption 6 leads to the inevitable question: how is it possible that an economic object maintains its identity if its physical properties (quantity, etc.) change. This *problem of change* constitutes one of the oldest puzzles of philosophy and was attacked by Zenon and some of the pre-Socratic philosophers. Especially Heraclitus is well known for seeing the phenomenon of perpetual flux in its full depth. In contrast to Heraclitus, Parmenides argued that change presupposes an object that changes, but at the same time it presupposes that this object retains its identity, thus concluding that change is illusionary. Bertrand Russell [1945, p. 49] calls this "the first example in philosophy of an argument from thought and language to the world at large" and Karl Popper [1962, p. 145] traces the potent distinction between reality and appearance to this controversy. But it rather seems to be a semantic problem and the plausible solution, as Russell points out, lies in the fact that in many cases the hidden change in the content of a term does not effect the truth or falsehood of the sentence in which this term is embedded.

7. Inequity of Monetary Claims. There exists a custom to enter *debts* with the understanding to *redeem them in legal tender at face value*[25]—whether meanwhile price-level changes vis-à-vis this legal tender have occurred or not.

a) If the exchange value (expressed in legal tender) of a representative "basket" of real objects (or property claims) at a time t^1 is higher or lower than at a later time t^2, we speak of a change (increase or decrease respectively) of the price-level defined by the chosen basket of real objects. Whether this basket is representative of the envisaged price structure is often difficult to determine and is usually regarded to be a value judgement.

---

[25] The possibility of paying interest eventually is a separate matter.

b) Assumption 7 refers to an implied entity (superentity) but will affect all its subentities (entities).

c) Assumption 7 virtually belongs into the group of "surrogate" assumptions. There, we would postulate merely a set of hypotheses (customs) for settling debts. If a specific hypothesis has been selected above, it was because of the general validity and the profound economic impact of this convention. ("General validity" does not exclude the exception of individual debt contracts (e.g., gold clause) but refers to the common debt behavior in the various countries with monetary autonomy). Since this custom might be abandoned in a more distant future, the above formulation has temporary validity. Then it might be preferable to formulate item 7 as a surrogate assumption.

d) The gold standard with its equilibrating mechanism does not render the above stated formulation invalid. It merely mitigates the inflationary-deflationary effects and thus lessens the economic impact of the custom postulated. Yet, even under the gold standard strong price-level fluctuations vis-à-vis the legal tender (gold) is possible and evidenced by historical events (e.g., influx of great quantities of gold into Europe from the American continent in the 16th century, causing virulent inflationary trends).

8. Economic Agents. There exists *a set of economic agents* who set specific goals to an accounting system, command resources, and make plans and decisions with regard to economic actions.

a) Economic agents (shortly: agents) are natural persons engaged in the economic activities (actions) of producing, owning, managing, storing, transferring, lending, borrowing, and consuming economic objects. An economic agent cannot be owned.

b) Agents may be classified (into different groups such as owners, managers, employees, customers, suppliers, etc.).

c) This assumption seems to be dispensable in some accounting systems because of assumption 9 which postulates the related concept of entity. Assumption 8, however, constitutes an important link to economics, management science, behavioral science, etc., and has found occasional reflection in some accounting theories (e.g., proprietorship theory,[26] commandership theory). In our set-theoretical formulation we regard agents and objects as *primitive* concepts out of which the concept of entity is formulated (see item 1 of Appendix A).

9. Entities. There exists a *set of entities* setting the frame for economic actions.

---

[26] The problem of entity versus proprietary theory is discussed by Gilman [1939], pp. 48–52 and by L. Goldberg [1957], pp. 26–30.

"According to the entity theory, profit is an increase in the amount the entity owes to the proprietor, disregarding capital advances and withdrawals. According to the proprietary theory, profit is the excess of proceeds over outlays during the business process" (Gilman [1939], p. 48).

a) An entity is a social institution which may *own* and *owe* economic objects and which can (but need not) *be owned* by one or more agents or other entities. An entity may be regarded as owning or owing if its agents or subentities own or owe respectively.

b) An entity consists either of agents or objects or both of them. Thus every agent can be regarded as an entity but not vice versa.

c) An entity whose transactions affect economic objects *within this entity* only, is called "closed" (or "self-contained"). Such closed entities are rare: e.g., the world economy, or a completely autarchic national economy, or that of a tribe of natives, or that of a monastery during the medieval ages.

d) Sometimes it is useful to distinguish between subentities, entities, superentities, etc. The world economy may be regarded as the superentity of highest degree (as long as no interstellar economic exchange takes place).

10. Economic Transactions. There exists *a set of empirical phenomena*, called *economic transactions*. Each of these transactions assigns, by means of empirical hypotheses, a value to an ordered pair of transactors (categories) and a time instance.

a) Economic transactions are relations arising out of the actions of producing, holding, transferring, lending, and consuming economic objects.

b) Economic transactions take place within an entity (subentity, superentity, etc.) and affect an aggregate of economic objects in some or all of the following three ways:

(*i*) The value (or quantity) of the aggregate changes.

(*ii*) The value (or quantity) of individual elements of the aggregate changes.

(*iii*) Services (including disservices) are rendered by the aggregate to its owners or to other economic agents.

c) We distinguish between *requited* and *unrequited* transactions.[27] Requited transactions occur in pairs, hereby one transaction is the legal or economic "consideration" of the other.

Furthermore we speak of "inter-entity transactions" *between two entities* and of "*intra*-entity transactions" *within one entity* (see Figure 2–1 of this chapter and Table A–2 of Appendix A).

d) Economic transactions are recorded through accounting transactions. Thus, a pair of requited transactions may be reflected by two interentity accounting transactions each of which has the following four characteristics:

(*i*) The value assigned to one transaction is equal to the value assigned to the other.

(*ii*) Both transactors of any one of the two transactions belong to a *different* entity (or subentity).

(*iii*) The negative transactor of one transaction and the positive

---

[27] The terms "requited" and "unrequited" flows are taken from Aukrust [1955].

transactor of the *other* transaction belong to the same entity (or subentity).

(*iv*) Both transactors of any one of the two transactions represent the same equivalence class.

e) An *operation* on two or more simultaneously occurring accounting transactions is permissible if the ultimate results of these transactions are not altered by this operation. Thus, for example, two inter-entity accounting transactions (with the characteristics of a pair of requited flows) can be converted into two *intra*-entity accounting transactions. It follows that *a pair of requited flows can be expressed by either of two pairs of accounting transactions:* (*α*) one inter-entity pair that corresponds (one-to-one) to the requited flows (transactors are represented by accounts) or (*β*) one *intra*-entity pair which is *not* isomorphic to the requited flows, but which yields the same ultimate result. For this pair the conditions (*ii*) to (*iv*) of item 10*d* do not hold though all requirements of basic assumption 4, necessary for being an accounting transaction, are fulfilled. Each of these two *intra*-entity transactions shows that:

(*i*) The value assigned to one transaction is equal to that assigned to the other.

(*ii*) Both aspects of one transaction belong to the same entity (or subentity).

(*iii*) Positive and negative transactors of any one transaction represent different equivalence classes.

Therefore it follows from items 10*e* and *d* that the positive transactor of one of these *intra*-entity transactions represents the same equivalence class as the negative transactor of the other *intra*-entity transaction.

f) It follows from items 10*d* (*iii*) and 10*e* (*iii*) that regardless of whether one or the other alternative is chosen (in expressing a requited flow by a pair of transactions), each transaction of a specific pair has *inverse direction* of the other.

Since assumption 10 brings about several important conclusions, an understanding of these relations is vital; it will be facilitated by Figure 2–1, which offers a less abstract formulation and a way to intuitive proof.

Assume there are two enterprises (entities) A and B within the superentity S. Each of the enterprises has two accounts: c (Cash) and m (Merchandise);[28]

Then the pair of *requited* economic flows is isomorphic to the pair of accounting transactions (t_1, t_2). The reader may check the conditions, listed under item 10*d*, for this pair of "inter-entity transactions." An alternative interpretation is possible by regarding the

---

[28] When an account is debited we call this account the positive transactor, when it is credited it is the negative transactor.

FIGURE 2-1

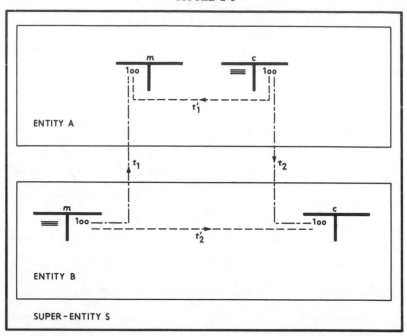

other pair of accounting transactions (t_1', t_2'). Again the reader may check the conditions, now listed under item 10e, for this pair of "*intra*-entity transactions." This seems fairly obvious as long as accounts like Cash and Merchandise are involved, but the situation becomes slightly more complex when the Cash is replaced in enterprise A by Accounts Payable and in enterprise B by Accounts Receivable. Here the two accounts "Payable" and "Receivable" represent identical equivalence classes (see item 3e), in spite of their different names.

The preceding example also demonstrates that *the discrimination between an economic transaction and an accounting transaction is important* since there need not be a one-to-one correspondence between them. An economic transaction may be reflected by different alternatives of accounting transactions depending on the structure of our entities. The following examples shall illustrate this:

(1) Let us assume the accounting system is designed merely from the viewpoint of superentity S *without* a need for subdivisions of S (e.g., in a financial accounting system of enterprise S where interdepartmental shipments from department B to A are not re-

corded). Then the requited economic transactions (shipment of merchandise and payment of cash) are not at all reflected by accounting transactions.

(2) Now we assume the system is designed from the viewpoint of superentity S *with* a need for a subdivision into entities A and B (e.g., if A and B are departments of an enterprise S). Then the same requited economic transactions will be reflected by a pair of accounting transactions (t_1, t_2). In this case the accounting transaction corresponds perfectly (or mathematically more precisely: "one-to-one") to the economic transactions (which therefore may also be called t_1 and t_2).

(3) Now we assume there are two accounting systems designed for the entities A and B, without regard to the superentity S (e.g., if A and B represent individual enterprises and S represents an economy, the accounting system of which is disregarded). Then the requited economic transactions are reflected in two separate accounting transactions which *do not correspond* (one-to-one) to the requited economic transaction. The accounting transaction t_1' for entity A neither corresponds to the economic transaction t_1 nor to t_2. And the accounting transaction t_2' for entity B corresponds neither to economic transactions t_1 nor to t_2 (here "accounting" transactions t_1 and t_2 do not exist[29]). We therefore conclude that accounting transactions may, but need not, correspond perfectly (i.e., one-to-one) to economic transactions or, in other words, that the set of accounting transactions is not necessarily isomorphic to the set of economic transactions. But the *structure* of an economic transaction still *fulfills the requirements* of an accounting transaction (cf. basic assumptions 4 and 10 and items 1 and 17 of Appendix A).

While the preceding assumptions (containing *a priori* as well as empirical notions) are of truly general nature, a series of secondary, empirical assumptions (in the following called "*hypotheses*") are required. These hypotheses will vary from instance to instance; the choice of one or the other will depend on the interrelation of (1) the purpose for which the resulting accounting data are d - signed, (2) the degree of accuracy or approximation desired or attainable, (3) the costs to operate the accounting system with a spe-

---

[29] Although these accounting transactions (t_1, t_2) are imaginable they here do *not* exist in the sense of "are being carried out." Once the individual debit and credit entries are made they can, according to the structure of the entity, be interpreted as accounting transactions (t_1, t_2) or (t_1', t_2'); but since these pairs are mutually exclusive and since the structure under example (3) requires transactions (t_1', t_2') the other pair is automatically eliminated.

cific set of hypotheses, and (4) the benefits derived or expected from the pertinent accounting system. Since the individual hypotheses cannot be stated generally, we *postulate* in the following—instead of the existence of sets and relations of "primitive" elements—*the existence of sets of hypotheses*, the details of which are open to specification. Then these stop-gap or *surrogate assumptions* acquire the same fundamental character which adheres to the basic assumptions listed previously.

The many alternate hypotheses available are abundantly discussed in books of conventional accounting and social accounting. A systematic survey and summary of the constraints within which accounting hypotheses have to be formulated is offered in Chapter 7 —though the main emphasis of that chapter is on epistemological problems of formulating accounting hypotheses in general. Furthermore, new assumptions and refined hypotheses brought about by modern analytical methods will receive separate attention—as for instance in Chapter 8, which contains hypotheses for planning purposes.

11. Valuation. There exists a set of hypotheses determining the value assigned to an accounting transaction.

   a) The discussion of individual valuation hypotheses and their sets does not belong to this Chapter (see Chapters 7 and 8), but the *fundamental distinction* between *original evaluation* of economic objects and *evaluation adjustments* should be mentioned in the following.

   b) *Original evaluations* of economic objects are based on a preference order among these objects at the time of transaction within the frame of reference of a specific entity and purpose.

   c) *Evaluation adjustments* are based on the recognition of value changes of economic objects since the time of original recording. Usually they are not connected with a new economic transaction but merely with a (fictitious) accounting transaction. In this connection one should further distinguish between the following two categories:

   (*i*) *Evaluation adjustments due to changes in prices or price level.* These are accounting transactions (usually at the end of an accounting period) giving recognition to a shift (since date of original entry[30]) in the preference between groups of economic objects or between "all" economic objects on one side and (a specific quantity of) money on the other.

   (*ii*) *Evaluation adjustments due to the expiration* (or nonexpiration) *of economic objects* (or portions of them). These accounting transactions (usually made at the end of an accounting period)

---

[30]"Original entry" may refer to the entry at the beginning of the current accounting period (in case evaluation adjustments were made in preceding periods).

give recognition to value changes of economic objects (since date of original entry) caused by usage, obsolescence, depletion, change in risk (to which an economic object or a group of them is subject) or the shifting of the expiration from one accounting period to another.

12. Realization. There exists a set of hypotheses, specifying which of the following three mutually exclusive effects are exercised by *a change* (in quantity, value, legal status, etc.) *of an entity's economic object(s).* Such a change either: (1) affects the value assigned to the current income of the entity; or (2) does not affect the owners' equity of this entity (within the specified period); or (3) affects the owners' equity without affecting the current income of the entity.

a) If such change contributes, positively or negatively, to the income of the entity, the economic object(s) affected are said to be *realized* as revenue or expense items respectively.

b) In discussing our general income definition (see Section 2.2) we have refused to fix the threshold at which a change in economic objects becomes an income particle. It is at this point that one has to provide hypotheses which establish this threshold for a particular situation.

c) Economic events that increase income are called "revenues," those that decrease it are called "expenses" (the terms "expenditures" and "receipts" refer to cash transactions only and must not be confused with the terms "revenues" and "expenses." But wherever a pure cash basis is applied these two pairs of expressions have identical content. Though this does not justify the abuse of the terms "receipts" and "expenditures" in national income accounting, it explains the usage). Expenses may be interpreted as intermediate consumption (from the viewpoint of the entity). "Value added" refers to an income concept that represents the value of the gross product of an entity minus the value of its intermediate consumption.

d) Alternative 3 of the basic assumption 12 refers to items like dividends declared by the entity, issue of new capital stocks, etc., as well as donations made to the entity and similar items which are to be excluded from income (e.g., appraisal surplus in micro-economic or capital gains in macro-economic entities).

e) At a first glance it may appear that in national income accounting, flow of funds accounting, etc., the concept of owners' equity is missing. If this were the case, the realization assumption would not be applicable to such systems. However in these macro-accounting systems the (owners') equity concept is represented by its "derivative," *the savings concept.* A change in net saving (as defined in these systems) is identical to a change in (owners') equity.

Thus assumption 12 also serves the function of *periodization.* By indicating the instant when a change in economic objects is (regarded to be) converted into an income particle, we are able to *allocate the aggregate income* (e.g., revenues, income, etc.) of a super-period to *individual periods* or subperiods.

13. Classification. There exists a set of hypotheses required to establish a chart of accounts.

a) We may make the *distinction* between "homogeneous" and "heterogeneous" accounts (though we admit that the criteria for separating one from the other is not yet satisfactorily formulated).

b) *Homogeneous accounts* primarily serve the aggregation of economic objects which have a dominating quality in common (i.e., whose degree of similarity is fairly concrete; e.g., Machinery, Liabilities, etc.)

c) *Heterogeneous accounts* serve the summarizing and juxtaposing of dissimilar economic objects (or aggregates) and the determination of a residual composed of heterogeneous elements (i.e., economic objects whose "similarity" is of a highly abstract nature, e.g., the profit and loss account).

d) Most *accounting statements* may be considered as heterogeneous accounts. Typical examples of heterogeneous accounts are some nominal accounts, as well as the Income Statement and the Balance Sheet. Its residual is the profit figure, a concept highly heterogeneous compared to the residuals in the cash account and many other real accounts. The distinction obviously is one of degree only.

e) Perfect class assignment should be informative, exhaustive, consistent and economical. In practice these requirements are rarely completely fulfilled. Therefore it would be desirable to determine the optimal combination of these requirements at various degrees of fulfillment—something that is difficult to carry out (for some remarks on the logic of "class assignment" see Churchman [1961], pp. 107–10).

14. Data Input. There exists a set of hypotheses required to determine the form of data input and the level of aggregation for which accounting transactions are to be formulated.

a) On a "low level of aggregation" it is usually possible to operate without a "residual due to statistical discrepancies"; on a "high level of aggregation" an imputed transaction called "statistical discrepancy" might have to be devised.

15. Duration. There exists a set of hypotheses about the expected life of the entity (or entities) under consideration, and the duration of individual accounting periods or subperiods.

a) The *duration (or life) of an entity* is the time of the existence of this entity expressed as the sum of a series of subsequent time intervals.

b) If this duration spans (or is expected to span) more than one accounting period, one may identify the life of the entity with a *superperiod* (which frequently is regarded as being of infinite length).

c) Customarily the accounting periods (or the subperiods) of a time series are of equal length. Yet, the latter is no precondition for an accounting system. Accounting periods may be identified with the duration of specific events (e.g., certain business ventures) of irregular length.

16. Extension. There exists a set of hypotheses specifying the empirical conditions under which two or more accounting systems can be consolidated and extended to a more comprehensive system.

a) An example of such an empirical proposition together with a theorem derived from it is offered in Appendix A, propositions 27 and 28.

17. Materiality. There exists a set of hypotheses (criteria) determining *if and when* an economic transaction or related event is *to be reflected by an accounting transaction.*

a) This assumption is not deemed to include the hypotheses that are taken care of by basic assumption 12 (realization).

18. Allocation. There exists a set of hypotheses determining the *allocation* of an entity's economic objects or flows of services *to subentities* and similar categories.

a) The subdividing of the main entity into *functional* areas (e.g., in financial accounting and national income accounting) is a dominant feature of accounting systems. A more recent development is the division into subentities of a more *institutional* type. This is reflected in cost accounting on the micro-level or in flow-of-funds accounting and interindustry analysis on the macro-level.

2.42 *Summary and Comparison of Moonitz' Postulates with the Basic Assumptions*

The set of eighteen assumptions discussed in the preceding section forms the criterion for accepting or rejecting a model as an accounting system. These assumptions pivot around the duality principle and are summarized under the term "duality syndrome." They are indispensable for the proper functioning of the micro- and macro-accounting systems presently known. Furthermore, the above presentation reveals that an accounting system is not a mere collection of "sterile" definitional equations. On the contrary, the majority of assumptions deal with empirical concepts—even if they themselves are not behavioral functions. But one of the important tasks of accounting theory is the formulation of various alternative sets of hypotheses required for specific purposes. Yet, before this task can be explored (see Chapters 7, 8, and 9) it was indispensable to acquire a clear notion about the foundations on which our discipline rests. If we have succeeded in providing an outline and first draft of these fundamental elements, credit must be given not only to the purifying influence of mathematical thinking but also to the pioneering works of Moonitz [1961] and Aukrust [1955].[31] The system of postulates developed by Moonitz crowns the search for the basic elements of financial accounting as reflected in the literature since the beginning of this century. These attempts to clarify and fortify our discipline are, in the long run, of much greater importance than many technical improvements. Yet we believe that the problem of formulating the basic assumptions cannot be solved as long as accounting is limited to micro-economic agencies. The recognition of conventions and empirical propositions serving solely the firm's statement presentation is insufficient as a basis for accounting. But the following juxtaposition of Moonitz' postulates to our basic assumptions suggests that the *essence* of many an assumption can be extracted from these postulates, though formulation and general applicability undergo incisive changes.

POSTULATES	BASIC ASSUMPTIONS
A–1 Quantification. Quantitative data are helpful in making rational economic decisions, i.e., in making choices among alternatives so that actions are correctly related to consequences.	Remark: *If the emphasis of A–1 is shifted from the helpfulness of quantitative data, our assumption 8 might come closest to A–1.* 8. *Economic Agents.* There exists *a set of economic agents* who set specific goals to an accounting system, command resources, and make plans and decisions with regard to economic actions.
A–2 Exchange.· Most of the goods and services that are produced are distributed through exchange, and are not directly consumed by the producers.	Remark: A–2 might be considered a special case of our assumption 10. *10. Economic Transactions.* There exists *a set of empirical* phenomena, called *economic transactions.* Each of these transactions assigns, by means of empirical hypotheses, a value to an ordered pair of transactors (categories) and a time instance.

---

[31] Aukrust lists twenty *"prinsipper"* or postulates. Two of these resemble two of our basic assumptions: postulate II (time) and postulate III (economic objects). But Aukrust postulates time in a continuous form, while we prefer the discrete one. Reason: (1) periods can be derived more easily from time intervals than from time points and (2) the time intervals are more in conformity with accounting practice. We also have adopted his notion of requited and unrequited flows. His remaining postulates are entirely different from ours because of the restriction of his system to National Income Accounts.

POSTULATES—*Cont.*

A-3 Entities. (including identification of the entity). Economic activity is carried on through specific units or entities. Any report on the activity must identify clearly the particular unit or entity involved.

A-4 Time Period (including specification of the time period). Economic activity is carried on during specifiable periods of time. Any report on that activity must identify clearly the period of time involved.

A-5 Unit of Measure (including identification of the monetary unit). Money is the common denominator in terms of which goods and services, including labor, natural resources, and capital are measured. Any report must clearly indicate which money (e.g., dollars, francs, pounds) is being used.

B-1 Financial Statements. (Related to A-1). The results of the accounting process are expressed in a set of fundamentally related financial statements which articulate with each other and rest upon the same underlying data.

B-2 Market Prices. (Related to A-2). Accounting data are based on prices generated by past, present, or future exchanges which have actually taken place or are expected to.

B-3 Entities. (Related to A-3). The results of the accounting process are expressed in terms of specific units or entities.

B-4 Tentativeness. (Related to A-4). The results of operations for rela-

BASIC ASSUMPTIONS—*Cont.*

9. Entities. There exists *a set of entities*, setting the frame for economic actions.

2. Time Intervals. There exists *a set of elementary (or minimal) additive time intervals* (e.g., days).

1. Monetary Values. There exists *a set of additive values*, expressed in a monetary unit; this set is isomorphic to the system of (positive and negative) integers plus the number zero.

5. Aggregation. Every *balance* assigns a (monetary) value—i.e., the arithmetic sum of all (positive and negative) values aggregated during a period in an account—to an ordered pair; the latter consists of the pertinent account and the above stated period, which starts with the accounting period.

Remark: *Once the principle of aggregation is stated, accounts and financial statements can be defined and derived from it, but need not be postulated.*

11. Valuation. There exists a set of hypotheses determining the value assigned to an accounting transaction.

3. Structure. There exists *a structured set of classes* (a hierarchy of equivalence classes) reflecting significant categories of an entity.

Remark: *The tentativeness of the measures resulting from these hypotheses can*

POSTULATES—*Cont.*

tively short periods of time are tentative whenever allocations between past, present, and future periods are required.

C-1 Continuity. (Including the correlative concept of limited life). In the absence of evidence to the contrary, the entity should be viewed as remaining in operation indefinitely. In the presence of evidence that the entity has a limited life, it should not be viewed as remaining in operation indefinitely.

C-2 Objectivity. Changes in assets and liabilities, and the related effects (if any) on revenues, expenses, retained earnings, and the like, should not be given formal recognition in the accounts earlier than the point of time at which they can be measured in objective terms.

C-3 Consistency. The procedures used in accounting for a given entity should be appropriate for the measurement of its position and its activities and should be followed consistently from period to period.

C-4 Stable Unit. Accounting reports should be based on a stable measuring unit.

C-5 Disclosure. Accounting reports

BASIC ASSUMPTIONS—*Cont.*

be deducted from various basic assumptions and the degree of approximation pertaining to the hypotheses of the above stated set. (Cf. also *12. Realization*).

15. *Duration.* There exists *a set of hypotheses* about the expected life of the entity (or entities) under consideration, and the duration of individual accounting periods or subperiods.

Remark: *In this contex the term "continuity" is imprecise. An enterprise which is being closed temporarily has no continuous operation but may have an assumed "infinite life." The latter assumption, although of fairly general acceptance, is better listed as a specific hypothesis.*

12. *Realization.* There exists a set of hypotheses, specifying which of the following three mutually exclusive effects are exercised by *a change* (in quality, value, legal status, etc.) *of an entity's economic object*(s): see (1), (2), and (3), p. 43.

17. *Materiality.* There exists a set of hypotheses (criteria) determining *if and when* an economic transaction or related event is *to be reflected by an accounting transaction.*

Remark: *In case of comparison between accounting measures for the same entity but different periods, or different entities and the same period, etc., it is possible to deduce the consistency requirement from basic assumptions.*

7. *Inequity of Monetary Claims.* There exists a custom to enter *debts* with the understanding *to redeem them in legal tender at face value*—whether meanwhile price-level changes vis-à-vis this legal tender have occurred or not.

13. *Classification.* There exists a set

POSTULATES—*Cont.*

BASIC ASSUMPTIONS—*Cont.*

should disclose that which is necessary to make them not misleading.

of hypotheses required to establish
a chart of accounts.

Remark: C–5 *is broader than assumption 13. But the latter is complemented
by our "introductory" statement valid for
all surrogate assumptions:* "These hypotheses will vary from instance to
instance; the choice of one or the
other will depend on the interrelation of (1) the purpose for which the
resulting accounting data are designed, (2) the degree of accuracy
or approximation desired or attainable. . . ." etc. (see pp. 41–42).

In the preceding section we asserted several basic assumptions
which are summarized in the following but which have no equivalent among Moonitz' postulates.

4. Duality. For all accounting transactions it is true that a value is
assigned to a three-dimensional concept (ordered triple) consisting of *two
accounts and a time instance (date),*[32]

6. Economic Objects. There exists a set of economic objects.[33]

14. Data Input. There exists a set of hypotheses required to determine
the form of data input and the level of aggregation for which accounting
transactions are to be formulated.

16. Extension. There exists a set of hypotheses specifying the empirical
conditions under which two or more accounting systems can be consolidated and extended to a more comprehensive system.

18. Allocation. There exists a set of hypotheses determing the allocation
of an entity's economic objects or flows of services to subentities and similar categories.

Before closing this chapter a further point shall be clarified. Besides Moonitz, there are other authors, especially Chambers [1961]
and Prince [1963], who recently endeavoured to formulate or list

---

[32]The fact that some theorists neglect this important basic assumption may surprise the
reader, but it can be explained by the common attitude to regard accounting as being independent of a specific type of model (e.g., the "duality model"). Some, like Moonitz,
imply this assumption, while others recognize it explicitly (e.g., the "dual aspect principle" by Anthony [1960], p. 33).

[33]Strangely enough this basic assumption is rarely encountered in the literature of
business accounting. A possible exception is Chambers [1961, p. 40] whose assumption
12 reads as follows: "*Means.* Wants are satisfied by the appropriation of means. Means
are scarce resources which are believed to be serviceable in satisfying wants. The utility
of a means subsists in the belief that it will be serviceable in satisfying a want."

Statisticians concerned with macro-accounting, on the other hand, are well aware of
the need for postulating economic objects (cf. Aukrust [1955], p. 83, Axiom III).

accounting postulates. Some of these postulates can be related to our set of basic assumptions, while others do not correspond[34] to any of our basic assumptions. It follows that either our set is incomplete or these "other postulates" cannot be regarded as foundation stones of accounting. To test our set for completeness in a rigorous sense is hardly possible at the present stage, but it is not difficult to illustrate why the "other postulates" cannot be regarded as basic assumptions. In Chambers' case some of his postulates indeed correspond to our basic assumptions, others are mere definitions and the rest are postulates that do not hold for accounting systems in general. The first argument and the last also apply to Prince's postulates.[35]

Our demonstration will be most significant by choosing the behavioral postulate of profit maximization which is in one form or the other contained in both sets of postulates. With Chambers [1961, p. 41] it assumes the following formulation:

20. Optimization. Because means are scarce (12) in relation to wants (2), deliberate actions are chosen according to their expected capacities for yielding the greatest aggregate satisfaction of a system of wants, e.g., the greatest gain for a given sacrifice (6, 9).

In Prince's study ([1963], p. 167 and 175) the basic hypothesis is "that the discipline of accounting theory should adopt the motivational postulate of maximization of long-term income" (I-A). Yet from a general viewpoint it can hardly be asserted that income maximization is essential for the existence and proper functioning of an accounting system. Neither the quantitative description of past income nor the projection of future income can depend on the ability or intention to maximize income. Quite obviously we are here, and in many other cases of behavioral propositions, con-

---

[34]The reader must also take into consideration that, occasionally, different authors may choose their postulates in such a manner that a postulate of one system does not correspond to any postulate of the other but to a *conclusion* based on the postulates of the other. In such cases there is no doubt that a *correspondence* between the two systems (or postulates of these systems) exists. Occasionally it is possible to interchange postulate and conclusion since criteria, determining which of the two propositions is more fundamental, are difficult to establish.

[35]Regrettably, Prince ([1963], pp. 50–51 and pp. 175–76), merely lists his postulates by names without giving them precise formulations. The following indicates those of Prince's postulates (pp. 175–76) of his "modified structure" (in Roman numerals with letters) that correspond to our basic assumptions (Arabic numbers):

II-A	9	II-G	12
II-B	15	II-J	17
II-C	4	II-K	3 & 13
II-E	14	III-A	2
II-F	1	III-B	6 ?

fronted with a confusion between hypotheses for specific situations and basic accounting assumptions of general validity.

This confusion is furthered by the impact of operations research models whose basic goal often is the maximization of some kind of profit concept. Since this confusion grossly distorts the essence of accounting, it cannot be emphasized strongly enough that—although the combination of optimization models with accounting seems desirable in many situations—the accounting model in general is independent of any kind of optimization or similar hypothesis.

Chapter 3

MODERN MEASUREMENT THEORY AND ACCOUNTING

3.1 EXPOSITION OF THE PROBLEM

OUR DEFINITION of accounting (see Subsection 2.1) states the purpose of this discipline as "the quantitative description and projection of income circulation and of wealth aggregates." The present chapter will *clarify the objective of accounting* by subjecting the phrase "quantitative description"—or in short, the terms "quantification" and "measurement"—to a thorough analysis. Mathematicians, philosophers, and social scientists, during the last few decades, have devoted much toil and mental effort to analyze the concepts connected with measurement and have extracted many subtleties. Social scientists in particular have tried to adapt the concepts of measurement to their own needs and have disclosed a series of new insights which for lack of a better name will here be called "modern measurement theory."[1] Accountants have neglected this body of knowledge for a considerable time and only recently, after some endeavors by the present author, they have begun to relate this knowledge to their own discipline.[2] Such an attempt is not a mere

---

[1] "It seems clear to us now that the process of measurement is the process of mapping empirical facts and relations into a formal model—a model borrowed from mathematics. But this conception took form only in very recent times. It is the product of long centuries of intellectual struggle, to which many of the foremost mathematicians contributed. It is a conception that was impossible, even unthinkable, until the nature of mathematics as a postulational system became clarified." (Stevens [1958], p. 383.)

But "modern measurement theory" must not be confused with *Measure Theory*, a new and highly abstract development of statistics and set theory. Prof. Ijiri [1964] has recently attempted to relate "measure theory" to accounting.

[2] Cf. Mattessich [1959a, 1962b], Homburger [1961], Devine [1962b, vol. 2, mimeogr.], pp. 144–159, Chambers [1963, mimeogr.], Bierman [1963], Firmin [1963], Anton [1964]. Here we are concerned only with papers relating some aspects of *modern measurement theory* to accounting.

filling of old wine into new skins, it is an inevitable step in the direction of systematizing accounting concepts and co-ordinating them into a broader frame of scientific definitions and conventions. The intensive concern of management scientists[3] with modern measurement theory and the sudden rise of interest among accountants in this area indicates the need for sharpening and purifying our tools of thought. The following quotation from an accountant may help to stir the interest of others in this area:

Accounting is the art of measuring and communicating financial information. This statement is not shocking or even surprising, yet the acknowledgement that accounting is concerned with measurement is the first necessary step towards a long awaited revolution in accounting. This revolution is not restricted to accounting; it has already taken place in other disciplines where measurement is crucial. For example, the classical concepts of measurement in physics and psychology have already undergone drastic changes. It is time for restrictive definitions of measurement in accounting to topple. (Bierman [1963], p. 501, footnotes omitted.)

Such restrictive definitions reveal the meaning of quantification; they make us aware of aspects that, though taken for granted, never entered our consciousness:

It is clear from even a cursory examination of current research practices that measurement and measures tend to be taken for granted . . . . As science moves into new areas, however, the carry-over of this unawareness of problems of measurement can lead to extremely ineffective research. In psychology, for example, only in recent years (largely as the result of Stevens' work) have researchers been giving measurement the attention it deserves. As a result there has been a noticeable tightening of procedures, bringing with it a scientific maturity that reduces the defensiveness which the psychologist must display before the physical scientists . . . .

Measurement, perhaps more than any other research activity, has been the principal stimulus of progress in both pure and applied science. (Ackoff [1962], pp. 215–16.)

The significance of commensuration in accountancy has been long recognized and is reflected in the frequent occurrence of the term "measurement" in accounting literature. Accountants and economists speak of measuring the magnitude of performance, the degree of liquidity, the sales quantity, the expenses, and the profit; they measure the quantitative and qualitative difference of assets, the size of the gross national product, the volume of the savings and investment activity, as well as the values of a multitude of other

---

[3]Churchman [1949, 1959], Lazarsfeld and Barton [1951], Coombs [1953], Coombs, Raiffa, and Thrall [1954], Adam [1959], Churchman and Ratoosh (eds.) [1959], Churchman [1961], pp. 93–136, 174–218, Ackoff [1962], pp. 177–217.

economic or business concepts. Is each of these activities *measurement* in the true and conventional sense of the word? Are perhaps different levels of measurement here involved? What is the "ultimate" meaning and purpose of the various kinds of measurement, scientifically speaking? Is there a difference between measuring and estimating, between classifying and measuring? Is measurement a primitive scientific occupation, or does it rank equal to hypothesis building and theory construction? What is the difference between quantitative and qualitative measurement? How valuable is measurement without indication of the measurement error? These and many more questions will have to be answered before accounting as a theory of measurement can be comprehended. Since traditional accounting literature does not reveal much about these problems, it is advisable to find some of the answers in the literature of other social or natural sciences, of mathematics, epistemology, and management science. Then, it should be possible to relate accounting to this wisdom, in order to answer the questions still open.

Accounting has many facets and is situated on the crossroad of several disciplines. It is this fact which makes it difficult to characterize its essence neatly and tightly. Does it belong to history because it records historical aspects of socio-economic aggregates? Is it a part of mathematics since it applies basic arithmetic? Can it be regarded as a legal discipline, because its application follows man-made laws and conventions? Or does anyone claim it to be a behavioral science with predictive powers? None of these questions can be answered with a straight *yes*, nor is a *no* quite fitting. Indeed, accounting does have historic, mathematical, legal, and even behavioristic aspects, but it cannot be put into the strait-jacket of one of these categories. The dilemma suggests that we choose a purely functional criterion to typify our discipline. Since the main functions of accounting are classification and evaluation, the thought of interpreting *accountancy* as *a theory of measurement* is not farfetched and sounds plausible. It will be the task of this chapter to clarify in what sense and to what degree this identification is justified.

3.2   FIRST ATTEMPTS TO PROBE INTO MEASUREMENT

The best known and earliest proponent of the advancement of science through intensive measurement activity is Galileo Galilei. He demonstrated in a series of experiments—which have become the foundation-stone of classical physics—that quantification is the best and most accurate way to acquire empirical knowledge. He confirmed this conviction with a proverb that has become a maxim for natural as well as social scientists: "Measure all that is measurable and attempt to make measurable that which is not yet so."

Meanwhile measurement has assumed many forms and has substantially contributed to the mental growth of our age. It is surprising, however, to learn that only comparatively lately have scholars begun to concern themselves with measurement as an *objective* of research, in contrast to measurement as a *tool* of research. The first serious epistemological attempts to gain insight into the foundations of measurement can be traced back not much beyond the turn of the century. Then it was Hermann von Helmholz [1895] and later Norman R. Campbell [1920, 1928, 1938] who laid the cornerstones of measurement theory. Some might wish to include here the names of Weierstrass, Cantor, Peano, and Zermelo, since the creation of modern number and set theory constitutes an important element in the understanding of measurement; but their contributions, as great and significant as they are, lie on the periphery of measurement theory. The early attempts were closely related to physics and in some respects their formulations are inadequate for application to the social sciences. To overcome these limitations a broadening and deepening of measurement theory has been undertaken by many social scientists during the last three or four decades. Though it is this development which bears importance for our topic, a concise survey of previous achievements is indispensable. Let us start with some simple common-sense reflections about measurement. In observing the more ordinary measurement activities, like that of determining length by way of a measuring rod, weight by means of a balance with counterweights, or the volume of a liquid by means of a vessel, we notice that the common feature is the confirmation of an *equivalence* by *comparison*, or what the mathematician calls the establishment of a *one-to-one correspondence* between two *sets*. The length of an object is compared with that of the rod, its weight with that of the stones, the volume of a liquid with the spatial capacity of the vessel. These media of comparisons are called scales and obviously may assume different appearances and different levels of abstraction, so different that it may take some time to recognize a particular device as a scale of measurement.

A savage, or a child, who *compares* a bundle of bananas with his right hand and observes that there are as many fruits in the bundle as there are fingers on his hand, must he not be considered as having measured the quantity of fruits (in units) even without knowing how to count and being aware of a number system? Such a process of "measuring," which can occasionally be studied on alert children in the age range of four to six who have not yet been "spoiled" by the sound and application of numbers, is enabled by the natural endowment of these human beings with fingers (digits !), that is, with a portable, though limited, *scale* for establishing a one-to-one correspondence between the *set* of bananas and the *set* of fingers. This gives rise to consider the system of integers for a moment. Its development is most likely due to the need for extending the scale we are carrying with us on our hands. If human mind is ingenious enough to create an *isomorphic relationship* (i.e., a one-to-one correspondence) between a collection of fingers and one of other objects, why should it not be capable of creating an "unlimited standard scale," or more expertly: a number system consisting of an *infinite set*, that can be stored and *transported in our brain*, and that may readily serve the purpose of counting—that is measuring the number of objects contained in another set by means of numerals. This illustration may enhance our awareness of the close relationship between number theory and metrology. Before leaving this topic we should be reminded that counting is essentially facilitated by still another ingenious trick, that of designating the whole set, serving for comparison, with the name of the *last* numeral. If we count five objects we do not refer to the fifth object alone but include the four preceding ones as well. Furthermore, the observant reader will have noticed our repeated use of the term "numeral" instead of the more conventional expression "number." This is not due to a predilection for variety in language but because of the important distinction between an object or its *property* on one side and its *name* on the other; a distinction that has become especially important in modern logic and that was emphasized by Campbell in connection with measurement theory. He confines the term "number" to a property which then is represented by a "numeral." If we speak of an asset which is valued at $500, this figure is a *number* since it expresses a property or quality of the asset (exactly speaking it is an attribute of the relation between an object and one or more human beings); if we say, however, that 500 designates the dollar value of an asset, we have used this figure in the sense of a *numeral* because in its *abstract use* it is not a property of anything but a mere label. This, as other semantic distinctions, is important for the understanding of our discipline and should be observed.

In classical measurement theory the ability to *combine* two or more elements of the object to be measured (additivity) is as important as the establishing of *equivalence* between object and scale (comparison). Out of these two major constituents Helmholz developed his axioms of measurement, a modern version of which is found in Menger [1959, pp. 97–101]. However, in a more recent study, which attracted international attention, Pfanzagl [1962] developed a refined set of axioms and demonstrated that *it is possible to construct (interval) scales of measurement even for objects with nonadditive properties*. This result is of special significance for the behavioral sciences where the additivity requirement is less frequently fulfilled (e.g., nonadditivity of utility, or of the intensity of tones) than in the physical sciences (though the latter also know instances of nonadditivity: temperature, density, etc.)

3.3 THE MEANING OF CLASSIFICATION

The natural consequence of a growing interest in quantification by social scientists led to their intensive occupation with the practical as well as theoretical aspects of measurement. Although, at present, economics seems to rank first among the social sciences in the application of quantitative analytical methods, the pioneering work in the theory of "measuring" social phenomena must be attributed to psychologists and sociologists (Coombs, Lazarsfeld, Stevens, Torgerson, and others). One explanation to this may be found in the pricing and information system of our modern industrialized economy which supplies ready-made, so to say, a great many economic data that otherwise would have to be created "artificially." This, however, can become a danger rather than a boon; since we are spoiled by the abundant supply of data from actual practice we do not think meticulously enough about their fundamental composition; while the psychologist and sociologist, who has to "create" his data for a specific research purpose, is forced to devote considerable time to thinking about the basis, the possibilities, and the usefulness of generating a new measure. Theoretical achievements in the measurement of utility as attained by J. von Neumann and O. Morgenstern [1944] or the metrologic activity within the boundaries of econometrics, will not be overlooked, but their impact upon general measurement theory is limited or at best indirect. Thus it is commendable to turn to S. S. Stevens [1946, 1951, 1959], a psychologist, who may well be looked upon as the dean of modern measurement theory. His system of categorizing measurement according to various scales is especially well suited to clarify the metrologic features of accountancy and shall be used as a basis for the exposition that follows. This perhaps one-sided picture shall then be complemented by further aspects of measurement theory as discussed by Churchman, Torgerson, Ackoff, and others; but before doing so we shall have occasion to relate measurement theory to our own discipline.

Stevens regards measurement from a broad point of view and accordingly accepts a definition which some scientists resist.[4] If one regards measurement, like Stevens, as *"the assignment of numerals to objects or events according to rules"*[5] it follows that the *most basic measurement* is *classification*, a fundamental discriminatory process, whereby the various categories can be identified and distinguished through numerals.[6] Such a broad definition seems not only justifiable but even desirable because it permits the preservation of a logical entity or continuity. By narrowing the definition of measurement in a way such as to exclude mere categorization, we resemble a botanist who denies that the root is part of the plant. Hence an array of categories or classes made distinct through the label of numerals is considered to be the natural basis of measurement and is called the *nominal scale*. Its mathematical properties correspond to those of

---

[4]The significance of Stevens' work lies partly in the merit of tracing measurement to classification and including the latter in his system. To understand this scheme we have to envisage a hierarchy of four scales: the *nominal, ordinal, interval,* and *ratio scale,* each serving as a mathematical model for measurement under conditions of increasing rigor. The achievement lies in the well-founded and systematic order of this hierarchy which defies any reproach of being arbitrary or artificial. It is attained by approaching the measurement problem from the mathematical viewpoint of *invariance,* that is, by classifying the scales of measurement in terms of the transformation group that leaves the scale-form invariant. Every scale, except the first, grows out of the preceding one by introducing an additional property or condition, thus restricting its application to a smaller but more specific area than that of the preceding scale. Thus, the scales correspond to well-established mathematical groups (see also footnote 7) and permit axiomatic formulation. This may be one reason why Stevens' system has been accepted with *relatively* little resistance and used by many as a basis for further development.

[5]This definition reveals the synonymy of the terms "quantification" and "measurement"; but Ackoff [1962, pp. 177–78] considers such a definition as incomplete and defines *measurement* as "the procedure by which we obtain symbols which can be used to represent the concept to be defined," thus measurement is regarded as an essential part of the process of defining.

[6]Stevens [1946, p. 678] admits, for the nominal scale, the substitution of numerals by other symbols. Also, H. Weyl [1927, p. 106] points out that "what is important in measurement is only the symbolic representation; the numerals are not the only usable symbols" (translated from German). This shall not be contradicted, but we must, in this connection, refer to our discussion of the *place value* system in Subsection 3.4. There we clearly recognize that the use of numerals combined with a place value system has a decisive advantage over the · use of other symbols—even at the nominal scale.

permutation groups.[7] To call a series of classes a scale of measurement might seem unaccustomed at first, but becomes obvious as soon as we look at scales of higher order. The next in hierarchy, the *ordinal* scale, consists of classes—characterized by numerals—which are subject to *order rank* in conformity with the numerals assigned. Hence here, the numbers not only serve the mere purpose of designation but have, as in the subsequent scales, a "normative" or preferential significance. While the nominal scale abstains from ranking the various classes, the ordinal scale enforces such an *order-ranking* and thus creates a hierarchy of classes or a "scale" in the true etymologic sense of the word. It is this order-ranking, not the classificatory activity, which some scholars consider the decisive criterion of measurement. As decisive as this criterion may appear at first sight, we are, with the ordinal scale still far away from measurement in a rigorous sense. The ordinal scale neither insists upon equality or regularity of class-size nor upon the existence of an "absolute" or "natural" zero class. It is, therefore, a matter of opinion which jump is regarded to be the critical one in determining what constitutes measurement and what not: the step from verbal description to numerical classification, that from the nominal scale, to the rank ordering of classes by means of the ordinal scale, or that from the latter to a scale which enforces regularity of class-interval and which Stevens calls *interval scale*, or even the step from the interval scale to *ratio scale* which requires a zero-point that is not arbitrarily chosen but given somehow beyond mere convention. Before we proceed with further considerations, an example from everyday life shall illuminate the previous statements.

Temperature, for instance, can be measured in different ways and on different scales. The crudest way of doing so is by mere classification into "cold," as soon as some medium (e.g., water) freezes, and "warm" if it does not. These two categories can be considered as constituting a nominal scale since there is hardly any order relationship involved; under some circumstances cold might be preferable to warm, under others it may be the reverse. This may

---

[7]The mathematical concept of a *group* offers a refined way of categorizing mathematical operations. Here we are dealing with a *permutation* group because the numerals assigned to the various classes of our nominal scale can freely be moved around (before the conventional agreement on a certain pattern) as there is no rank order involved. This arbitrary switching of the numerals corresponds to a *permutation*, hence it follows that by this kind of operation one nominal scale can be *transformed* into another while leaving the scale form itself unchanged. Since every mathematical operation belongs to a "group," the transformation group that leaves the *nominal* scale *invariant* is the permutation group. The transformation groups of all four scales can be seen from Table 4-2.

have been a way of caloric commensuration in ancient or prehistoric times and, as an illustration by Stevens suggests, the freezing point may still constitute the decisive classificational criterion with an Eskimo who is confronted with the task of measuring temperature. If one adds the boiling point as a second criteria, not only a third class—which we may designate with "hot"—is obtained, but a move to the ordinal scale is realized. For even a savage recognizes that "warm" lies between "cold" and "hot." Thus a very natural order relationship and, in consequence, an ordinal scale has arisen. The disadvantage of this new scale is, of course, the unequal sizes of our three categories. The first reaches from the absolute zero (−273 Centigrade) to the point of freezing, or in this case better called point of thawing (a range of 273 Centigrades); the second class reaches from the freezing to the boiling point (a range of 100 Centigrades) and the third class may be infinitely large, if not infinite, since no absolute ceiling-temperature has been established so far. Thus it is not surprising that the advent of empirical research during the Renaissance stimulated the development of precise methods of caloric measurement in subsequent centuries. Presently there are still four different scales of temperature in common usage: the Fahrenheit, Réaumur, Celsius, and Kelvin scale.[8] All four of them have class intervals of constant size but only the last has a natural zero point. Thus the Kelvin thermometer uses a ratio scale, while the other three thermometers, developed before the "discovery" of the unattainable but deduced thermic limit, have zero points that are arbitrarily set. This example is well fitted to demonstrate the whole gamut of Stevens' scales by means of a single task; it explicates the constitutional character which classification brings to bear upon measurement. What name we assign to the activity of applying the nominal scale, whether we call it "classification," "scaling,"[9] or "measurement," is a mere matter of labeling only if we recognize this activity as the ultimate basis of measurement in

---

[8]The *Fahrenheit* scale divides the temperature differential between freezing and boiling into 180 classes (degrees) and sets the freezing point (class) at 32°F. The *Reamur* scale sets the freezing point at zero (0°R) and graduates the distance between it and the boiling point into eighty degrees (80°R). The *Celsius* scale also sets the freezing point at zero (0°C) but divides the differential between it and the boiling point into one hundred centigrades or Celsius degrees. The *kelvin* scale uses the same temperature intervals as the Celsius scale but sets its zero point at −273°C, the lowest imaginable temperature at which, inferentially, all molecular movement would cease.

[9]C. H. Coombs [1953] for instance prefers to designate mere classification as "scaling" in contrast to "measurement" proper which he refers to the other scales. W. S. Torgerson [1958] would not even admit application of the term "scaling" to a mere classificational activity.

general and treat its complex of problems within measurement theory. Thus measurement can be regarded from at least two opposite points of view and the conflict between them seems to be fundamental rather than of mere terminological nature. While the traditional viewpoint stresses the "normative" aspect, the modern one penetrates to the root and therefore is forced to concentrate more on the taxonomic, or as we can call it now "taxonometric," characteristic. The recent approach recognizes that the information which measurement conveys is not by necessity purely quantitative but may consist of a numerical expression of qualitative features. This approach tries to bridge the chasm between quantitative and qualitative judgments as far as this is possible. Since even the most "precise" measurement is a mental process which assigns a class symbol to an empirical object or event (creation of a one-to-one correspondence between the object and one of the classes on the scale), the *undeniable fact* remains that *every measurement is classification.* The answer to the reverse question, whether every classification is measurement, depends, as we have seen, on the viewpoint. Do we consider a "simple order" imposed upon subsequent classes as indispensable to measurement and are we prepared, as a price for our insistence, to dichotomize what seems to be a logical entity? If so, do we not restrict measurement to too limited an area? Do we not impede progress, especially in the social sciences?

The preconception which has to be overcome in order to accept the modern standpoint would be slighter if people were more accustomed to the systematic and formal application of nominal scales. The fact that one aspect of accountancy is classification makes the accountant more susceptible to this new viewpoint. Those who use the nominal scale constantly develop a mental quality, let us call it a "sense of comparison" that enhances the information which nominal measurement conveys. This may become more obvious if we are reminded that for a child—unaccustomed to comparing linear measures—who is informed about his own height, the meaning of this information is much "smaller" than it is for a grown-up who can relate this datum to the height of other people, houses, mountains, to distances between cities, stars, etc. Is not the task of measurement to assign a numeral to an object in order to convey information which permits distinguishing one object from another and relating both to each other?

Let us illustrate in the following a fundamental point which is rarely formulated, in a clear and explicit manner. It offers a justification, hard to refute, for the superiority of numerals in identifying

classes of the nominal scale. Figure 3-1 depicts nineteen sets
(classes, boxes, or categories) to which numerals have been assigned. The main set is called 1, its four immediate subsets 1.0, 1.1,
1.2, and 1.3. The sub-subsets bear the numerals 1.00, 1.01, 1.10,
1.11, 1.12, 1.20, 1.30, and 1.31. Finally the sub-sub-subsets are
called 1.000, 1.001, 1.100, 1.310, 1.311, 1.312. This, mathematicians call a *place-value* system; it is well known to us from the common decimal classification, though there the class 1 would have ten

FIGURE 3-1
ILLUSTRATION OF ORDERING AND NUMBERING SUBSETS
ACCORDING TO A PLACE-VALUE SYSTEM

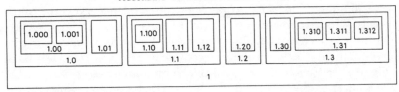

subsets (1.0 to 1.9) and each of these subsets would have ten sub-
subsets (1.00 to 1.09; 1.10–1.19, etc.) and so on, *ad infinitum.* Besides, we know that in such a case there exists an order ranking that
makes $1.0 < 1.100$, or $1.310 < 1.311 < 1.312$, etc.; furthermore we
know that there the difference between two classes of the same level
or phase are of equal "size," that means the interval between them
is the same (e.g.: $1.1 - 1.0 = 1.2 - 1.1 = 1.5 - 1.4 = 1.9 - 1.8$
or $1.001 - 1.002 = 1.007 - 1.008$, etc.); finally there exists a natural zero point in this scale.

In our example all the other conditions are lacking and we assume our set 1 as representing nothing but a nominal scale. Some
scholars argue that letters, names, or any other symbols are, for
classification and hence for the purpose of nominal measurement,
equally efficient and can replace the numerals. This view seems to
us incorrect and misleading. For, precisely speaking, numerals
identify the position of various sets to each other in *two* dimensions.
The first I would like to call the *horizontal dimension.* It indicates
that the set 1.1 is distinct or independent from the set 1.00. The
second, the *vertical dimension* indicates that the set 1.00 is a subset of
1.0, but contains two subsets called 1.000 and 1.001. While the
horizontal dimension of different sets or classes can be well expressed by any kind of symbolism, we know of no other *efficient* system to express simultaneously also the vertical dimension of classes,
subclasses, sub-subclasses, etc. Thus, numerals not only help to

discriminate among various classes, they also reveal the "internal structure" of a class with subclasses by means of a place-value system; they illustrate on which main or sublevel a certain set is placed. Such information is often valuable and plays a decisive role in many taxonomic systems.

In accounting and in classification systems like the one presented in Figure 3-1 we are actually dealing with *a subtle combination of nominal scales and ordinal scales.* To illustrate this we compare the four classes 1.0, 1.1, 1.2, 1.3; in spite of their deceptive labels we have assumed that these classes are subject to a nominal scale only, thus they cannot be connected by an order relation (i.e., the following formulation is *not* permissable: 1.0 < 1.1 < 1.2 < 1.3). But most of these classes contain subsets and sub-subsets which can be related by order relations like the following: 1.000 $\subset$ 1.00 $\subset$ 1.0 $\subset$ 1, or 1.001 $\subset$ 1.00, or 1.310 $\subset$ 1.31 $\subset$ 1.3 $\subset$ 1, etc. (the symbol < means "is smaller than," while the symbol $\subset$ means "is a subset of"). It follows that the *"horizontal dimension" uses mere nominal scales, while the "vertical dimension" enforces the use of ordinal scales.* The combination of both scale types yields a powerful classification system, the informational content of which is greatly enhanced. The *charts of accounts* are such systems that have been in use for more than three decades. With the rejection of Stevens' approach, the designation of measurement would be unduly denied to those systems. "Unduly," because these systems still extract significant information for comparison in research and practical decision making, information that often can efficiently be transmitted by numerals only.

3.4   THE NOMINAL SCALE IN ACCOUNTING

One of the systems that very frequently applies the nominal scale of measurement is accountancy. This, we hope, justifies the space devoted to the discussion of classification in general. Although, as we shall see later, accounting incorporates all four scales, its basis, the *chart of accounts* (or the "basic chart of accounts"), is a nominal scale. The aspect of classification has dominated this discipline and its antecedents for centuries, and it may well be asserted that accounting ranks historically first in "measuring" social events. Indeed, devices such as systematic ratings, ranking scales, quantitative indices, typologies, multidimensional classifications, etc., which we nowadays also encounter in other social sciences, were anticipated by accounting a long time ago. Besides, the activity of classification and aggregation gains increasing importance in other branches of business administration[10] and in all fields where huge masses of figures create an urgent need for orientation and data-reduction. The criterion for judging this categorizing as scientifically trivial or significant, will, in the long run at least, be the analytical and synthetical usefulness of this operation and not its purely "mathematical simplicity." It is a common trait of intellectual snobbery, on the one hand, to think that scientifically significant problems must always be associated with differentials and integrals, probability functions, difference equations, power series, or other "complicated" relations, while on the other hand, neither the complexity nor the importance of a "taxonometric" approach is perceived. In accounting, the activity of classification arises out of the need for a tight net of a large number of concepts. The fact that these concepts are related among themselves, frequently by definitional instead of behavioral functions, hardly alleviates the intricacy which is characteristic of every vast conceptual apparatus. As to the analytic-behavioral value of categorization, the Keynesian approach which pivots on classifying national income into the two categories of consumption and savings, which proved so revolutionary, and which ultimately gave rise to national income accounting, may be cited as an example. We have interpreted the basis of accounting as a nominal scale and are now faced with the task of investigating the peculiarities of this identification. The Anglo-American literature, even accounting literature—at least in the sector of micro-accounting—has been comparatively little concerned with the systematic articulation of classes and groups of accounts. This gives P. Scherpf [1955, p. 164], justification to write: "The American charts of accounts are a list of all the accounts available, with pertinent explanations, rather than a categorization according to a firmly determined idea" (translated). In continental European countries, on the other hand, the problem of highly articulated *"basic charts of accounts"*[11] has been studied for several decades and discussed very thoroughly. The reason for this concern lies partly in a different scientific orientation, but to a greater extent it is to be found in the support and stimulus imparted by governmental authorities. A generally accepted or imposed "basic chart of accounts" is not only

---

[10]As an example see Edward G. Koch: "Managerial Strategy through Classification and Coding," *California Management Review*, Vol. 1, No. 4 (1959), pp. 56–66.

[11]It seems that the only country of English language for which a *Kontenrahmen* has been designed is Australia, but even there the basic idea behind it could not attain a firm foothold. The term "basic chart of accounts" is the English translation of "Kontenrahmen" as used in Australia (see *Uniform Accounting*—the standard classification of accounts, edited by the Australian Institute of Management, Sidney, 1950).

of utmost importance to every planned or semiplanned economy, but it also facilitates auditing and control, improves cost accounting and price calculations as well as intra- and interindustrial comparison, and, last but not least, contributes toward more accurate data in national accounting and related statistics.[12]   As a consequence, most European countries have adopted such "basic charts" and under the impact of the Common Market are even considering the establishment of a uniform intra-European "basic chart of accounts."

These "basic charts" prescribe a well-devised and clearly defined system of classes, groups, and subgroups of accounts (nowadays called "synthetic accounts"[13]). Within this framework, every firm is at liberty to make further specifications and subdivisions so as to create its own "analytic accounts" and its chart of accounts according to individual needs.

This is mentioned here not to convince the experts of the Anglo-American hemisphere about the usefulness of such basic charts but rather because of its relevance to the problem of nominal measurement. First, the acceptance of uniform "basic charts of accounts" represents the establishing of national or even international standard scales; something which has great affinity to the general acceptance of "physical" units and scales of measurement during the last two centuries.[14]   Second, the request or desire to assign numerals

---

[12]In Austria, France, Holland, Switzerland, Yugoslavia, Czechoslovakia, Hungary, Poland, and Russia, the application of "basic charts of accounts" is either made compulsory or "recommended" by governmental or semigovernmental authorities, while it seems that in Australia, Denmark, Italy, Norway, Spain, and Sweden, the existing uniform basic charts are adopted on a more voluntary basis.

There exist tendencies toward a "Uniform European Basic Chart." The presently progressing economic integration of Europe seems to necessitate, sooner or later, such a means of organization.

[13]The designation of a group of accounts as a synthetic account and an individual account as an analytic account comes from a recent usage in Germany. This terminological distinction is important and corresponds to the distinction between set and subset.

[14]It is no accident that the adoption of the metric system was made in accordance with laws (first in France, 1795 and 1799) just as the general usage of the "basic chart of accounts" is based on legal decrees (first in Germany: Richtlinien für die Organisation der Buchführung—Pflichtkontenrahmen, 1937).

Another parallel between these two systems of measurement is the translation of one scale into another. The necessity to "translate" the Metric System into the older "British" system (of weights and measures) became acute soon after the adoption of the former. Recently, in a similar way, the conversion of one basic chart of accounts into another became urgent through the political and economic division of Germany. The "basic chart" of East Germany deviates nowadays considerably from that of West Germany. Since certain economic ties between the two parts still exist, it has been necessary to develop a "bridge of accounts" (Kontenbrücke) which serves to translate one "basic chart" into another— a formidable example of transforming one nominal scale of measurement into another.

Such conversions on an even larger scale will be necessary if a "basic chart" for the Common Market area should come into existence.

to the various categories is here fulfilled in an exemplary way. Most of the European "basic charts" adhere to a place-value system (which is occasionally also encountered in "charts of accounts" in America) in which the first digit of the account-number represents the main class to which the pertinent account belongs, the second digit represents the group (within this class), the third represents an eventual subgroup or the main analytic account itself. Further digits may represent subdivisions of various orders of the main analytic account. In this way it is possible to characterize very ex-

TABLE 3-1

The Basic Chart of Accounts as Developed by Eugen Schmalenbach

Class 0	Class 1	Class 2	Class 3	Class 4
Resting Accts.	Financial Accts.	Neutral Accts.	"Expense" Accts. Not Belonging to Other Classes	Store-Room and Wage Accts.
00 Land and buildings	10 Cash on hand	20–21 Accts. the balance of which is to be capitalized	30–31 Accts. without balance at years' end	40–43 Storeroom, including tools and reserve-parts
01 Machines implements, trucks, etc.	11 Cash in bank, overdrafts			
02 Patents, franchises, prepayments	12 Drafts	22–24 Neutral "expenses"	32 Accts. which are partly to be closed to assets	
03 Special investments	13 Foreign valuta		33–34 Accts. with debit balance	
04 Investments in subsidiaries	14 Marketable securities			44–45 Wages and pertinent fringe benefits
05 Long-term receivables	15 Short-term receivables (home currency)	25–27 Neutral revenues	35–36 Accts. with credit balance	
06 Deferred and accrued items	16 Short-term receivables (foreign currency)			
07 Reserves and corrective accts.	17 Doubtful accts. rec.		37 Accts. with changing balance	
08 Owner's equity	18 Payables	28–30 Reconciliation accts.	38 Auxiliary revenues without balances	48 Salaries and pertinent fringe benefits
09 Long-term liabilities	19 Dividend and interest, service, secret., acctg.		39 Auxiliary revenues with balance	49 Kitchens and cafeterias

pediently every synthetic and analytic account by a numeral and at the same time give expression to the position an account assumes within the whole structure. This not only has great resemblance to our "general decimal system" but makes it strikingly obvious that every place value system, whether it is used for measuring length or anything else, is a complex of classes with an infinite variety for creating subclasses, sub-subclasses and so on.

Eugen Schmalenbach developed his by now somewhat obsolete but still famous *Kontenrahmen* in 1927 on the principle of decentralized organization—a theoretical idea that is nowadays being revived by modern organization, information, and team theory—and

Class 5	*Class 6*	*Class 7*	*Class 8*	*Class 9*
Expense Accts. with Reserves	*Service Depts.*	*Producing Depts.*	*Work in Process and Finished Goods Inventories*	*Revenue and Profit Accts.*
	60 Depts. of general administration		80–84 Work in process accts.	90 General sales accts. without end-balance
	61 Building administration			91 General sales accts. with balances
	62 Power stations, water stations, etc.			92 Sales costs by regions
	63 Repair and tooling shops	*Time Costs* (approx. fixed costs):		93 Sales costs by products
	64 Conveyor depts.	Management Power Space		94 Rebates, discounts and returns, etc.
	65 Magazine administration	Maintenance	85 Finished goods and trading goods	
	66 Public relations dept.	*Quantity Costs* (approx. variable costs):		
57 Current reserves for risks, retrograd.	67 Control depts.	Material wages Depreciation Waste control Misc.	87 Merchandise in branches	97 "Expense"-summaries
	68 Welfare depts.			
	69 Miscellaneous depts.	Summary accts., profits	89 Merchandise on consignment	99 "Revenue" summaries, profit and loss, and balance sheet accts.

originally pursued the following aims:

1. Separation of profit-sources (*Erfolgsspaltung*).
2. Reliable and quick interim closings (*kurzfristige Erfolgsrechnung*).
3. Separation of fixed and variable costs (*Zeit- und Mengenkosten*).
4. Control of the various departments.
5. Intraindustrial comparisons.
6. Linking financial and cost accounting.
7. Determination of unit costs.

Since his *Kontenrahmen* became the prototype of most of the existing basic charts (excluding the "basic charts" of Russia) and since it represents *a classic example of an internationally applied nominal scale of measurement* we present in Table 3-1 this "basic chart" in English translation (see: E. Schmalenbach [1930], p. 13).

3.5 THE ORDINAL, INTERVAL, AND RATIO SCALES IN ACCOUNTING

The nominal scale although basic to the accounting process is neither the only nor the most important scale pertaining to our discipline. The evaluation process—the core of theoretical accountancy—utilizes the *ratio* scale; statement analysts primarily work with *ordinal* scales; and certain aspects of cost accounting can be considered as applying the *interval* scale. Before going into further details we recommend a study of Table 3–2 which juxtaposes the properties of the *nominal* to those of the other three scales and offers a concise survey of Stevens' system.

The understanding of the transformation permissible with various scales may be facilitated by geometrical representations (see Figures 3–2, 3–3, 3–4).

Suppose a bank, in judging the credit-worthiness of customers (from a certain industry), measures the liquidity—as revealed in the various balance sheets by the relation of current assets to short-term liabilities—by distinguishing the following six classes (scale x): excellent = 1, very good = 2, good = 3, sufficient = 4, deficient = 5, insufficient = 6. Table 3–3 indicates when the bank uses one or the other class.

Obviously this is not a mere *classification:* the second condition, that of *rank-order*, is here fulfilled and at first glance it even seems as though also the third condition, that of *equality* of class intervals, is attained. The latter, however, is not the case and only a very superficial judgment would make us believe that every class interval is of the size 0.5. Actually, class 1 reaches from infinity to 2.0; class

TABLE 3–2

A CLASSIFICATION OF SCALES OF MEASUREMENT*†

Scale	Basic Empirical Operations	Mathematical Group Structure	Typical Examples
Nominal......	Determination of equality	Permutation group $x' = f(x)$ where $f(x)$ means any one-to-one substitution	"Numbering" of football players Assignment of type or model numbers to classes
Ordinal	Determination of greater or less	Isotonic group $x' = f(x)$ where $f(x)$ means any increasing monotonic function	Hardness of minerals Street numbers Grades of leather, lumber, wool, etc. Intelligence test raw scores
Interval	Determination of the equality of intervals or of differences	Linear or affine group $x' = ax + b$ $a > 0$	Temperature (Fahrenheit or Celsius) Position Time (calendar) Energy (potential) Intelligence test "standard scores" (?)
Ratio.........	Determination of the equality of ratios	Similarity group $x' = cx$ $c > 0$	Numerosity Length, density, work, time intervals, etc. Temperature (Rankine or Kelvin) Loudness (sones) Brightness (brils)

*Measurement is the assignment of numerals to events or objects according to rule. The rules for four kinds of scales are tabulated above. The basic operations needed to create a given scale are all those listed in the second column, down to and including the operation listed opposite the scale. The third column gives the mathematical transformations that leave the scale form invariant. Any numeral x on a scale can be replaced by another numeral x', where x' is the function of x listed in column 3.

†Reprinted with the permission of J. Wiley & Sons, Stevens [1959] in Churchman and Ratoosh (eds.) [1959], p. 25. Attention should be drawn to the fact that for the isotonic group (ordinal scale) $f(x)$ can be an increasing or decreasing monotonic function, in contrast to the statement in the Table 3–2, but as evidenced by Figure 3–2.

Since the order relationship (<) dominates all scales except the nominal, the three conditions that must at least be satisfied by the nominal scale shall be listed below:

1. Transitivity: if $a < b$ and $b < c$ then $a < c$.
2. Closure: either $a < b$ or $b < a$.
3. Antisymmetry: if both $a < b$ and $b < a$ then $a = b$.

2 from 1.5 to *almost* 2.0; class 3 from above 1.0 to *almost* 1.5; class 4 comprises only a single event that of $a/b = 1$; class 5 reaches from 0.5 to *almost* 1.0; and class 6 from zero to *almost* 0.5. Hence the classes are by no means of equal size and we are confronted here with a typical *ordinal* scale. To demonstrate the possibility and condition of transforming this scale x into another ordinal scale x', we have renumbered the six classes from 2 to 7 instead of 1 to 6; that means the transformation (characterized by the isotonic group) is reflected by the function $x' = f(x) = x + 1$. Graph 1 depicts the two scales x and x', shows their relationship and illustrates the different sizes of the various scale intervals.

Modern measurement theory has frequently been related to sta-

TABLE 3-3
Illustration of an Interval Scale on the Example of
Balance Sheet Liquidity Measurement

Liquidity Coefficients	Description	Scale x	Scale x'
$a/b \geq 2.0$	Overliquidity (excellent)	1	2
$2.0 > a/b \geq 1.5$	Optimal liquidity (very good)	2	3
$1.5 > a/b > 1.0$	Under liquidity (good)	3	4
$a/b = 1.0$	Marginal-liquidity (sufficient)	4	5
$1 > a/b = 0.5$	Payment difficulties (deficient)	5	6
$a/b < 0.5$	Danger of bankruptcy (insufficient)	6	7

tistics and probability theory, chiefly because a single measure (of one and the same object or event) is not reliable enough and several measures are prone to deviate from each other according to the pattern of a frequency distribution. Therefore, it is important to indicate which kind of statistical procedures are permissible for various scales. Table 3-4 (adapted from Stevens) summarizes these statistical procedures with reference to the four scales of measurement.

TABLE 3-4
Examples of Statistical Measures Applicable to Measurements
Made on the Various Classes of Scales

CLASSES OF STATISTICS:	NOMINAL	ORDINAL	INTERVAL	RATIO
MEASURES OF LOCATION	MODE	MEDIAN	MEAN	GEOMETRIC MEAN; HARMONIC MEAN
DISPERSION	INFORMATION (H)	PERCENTILES	STANDARD AVERAGE DEVIATION	PERCENT VARIATION
ASSOCIATION OR CORRELATION	INFORMATION TRANSMITTED (T); CONTINGENCY CORRELATION	RANK-ORDER CORRELATION	PRODUCT-MOMENT CORRELATION; CORRELATION RATIO	---
SIGNIFICANCE TESTS	CHI SQUARE TEST	SIGN TEST; RUN TEST	CRITICAL RATIO TEST; t TEST; F TEST	---

It is the transformation group that—by way of the criterion of invariance under the transformation permitted by the pertinent scale—determines the applicability of a statistic. Thus obviously only simple and primitive statistical procedures are possible with regard to the nominal scale; to determine in such a case the median or mean, for example, would be meaningless since there exist neither rank-order, the prerequisite for any meaningful median, nor equality of intervals, a precondition for a relevant mean.

As Table 3–4 reveals, the ratio scale is most comprehensive in the sense that all statistics listed are applicable, while with every step down, in the hierarchy of our scales, additional restrictions—as regards applicable statistics—enter. This "cumulative" property of the table needs some qualifications:

The nominal scale involves only discrete categories or classes. When the categories are naturally discrete, e.g., *male* or *female*, the problem is straightforward. We can then count men and women and determine which, for example, is the modal class. But when categories are formed by partitioning a continuous variable, like stature, a certain arbitrariness enters in. If we group statures into class intervals 1 inch wide, we may, again, find the modal class for a given sample of people. However, if we change the boundaries of the class intervals, or if we make the intervals different in size, the modal value may change. If we make finer and finer measurements and reduce the size of the class intervals more and more, we may even find that no two statures are the same, i.e., there is no mode.

We see, then, that there is an essential difference between the concept of a mode as applied to naturally discrete classes and as applied to a continuous scale. In the discrete case, the mode remains invariant under all the scale transformations listed in Table 1 [our table 3–2], but, in the continuous case, the mode is not invariant under increasing monotonic transformations.[15]

In this connection it should be mentioned that in accounting most of the scales have *discrete* classes. This by definition holds for the nominal scales (charts of accounts) but it is also true for its ordinal (e.g., the measuring liquidity of an enterprise; see also Figure 3–2) as well as interval scales. Precisely speaking, this is even true for its ratio scales, since we usually do not record the $-values in smaller fractions or decimals than whole cents.

An example of the *interval* scale (see Figure 3–3) within the realm of accounting is found in standard costing. Here there exist several alternatives on which the standards may be based: the theoretical, the attainable, the average, or the normal performance.[16] In these

---

[15] S. S. Stevens [1959], in *Measurement* (New York: John Wiley & Sons, Inc.), p. 28. Stevens indicates his indebtedness to J. W. Tuckey, W. H. Kruskal, and L. J. Savage for calling his attention to this point.

[16] For an explanation of the various performance standards see Dickey [1960], p. 15.3.

FIGURE 3-2
ORDINAL SCALE ILLUSTRATED ON THE EXAMPLE
OF BALANCE SHEET LIQUIDITY MEASUREMENT

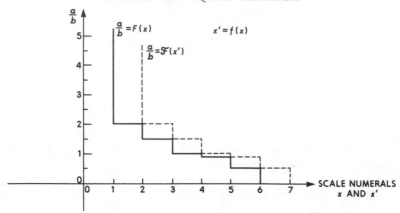

cases the standard variances are measured on scales with different
zero points. Since the choice of one of these performance levels as a
standard is more or less arbitrary—though the standard variances
themselves are expressed in dollars and cents, which means in constant intervals—we are confronted with an interval scale.

If we assume the scale x applicable to the theoretical performance
basis and the scale x' to the normal performance basis, we recognize
that the transformations under these $x' = ax + b$ conditions belongs
to the linear or *affine group*. However, the so-called *power group*
$(x' = kx^n)$, too, can, under certain circumstances dominate the

FIGURE 3-3
INTERVAL SCALE ILLUSTRATED ON THE EXAMPLE OF
MEASURING VARIANCES IN STANDARD COSTING

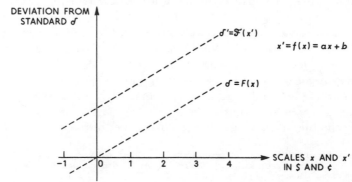

interval scales: in cases where the intervals are not assumed to be constant but are subject to change in accordance with a power parameter (n) such as to obtain a logarithmic scale. This, although a deviation from the ordinary interval scale, justifies its name since a *regularity*—though not an equality—of class-size is maintained.

The case of a ratio-scale in accounting is best illustrated by juxtaposing two or more monetary scales. Assume that an American parent company maintains assets and subsidiaries in Great Britain and Germany. It may in this case be necessary to measure these assets along three different ratio scales: the $-scale, the £-scale, and the *DM*-scale (see Figure 3–4).

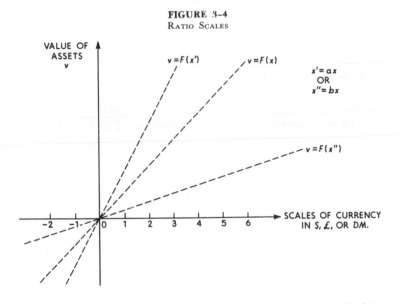

FIGURE 3–4
RATIO SCALES

If an asset is written off (that means reaches the zero value) it is zero in an absolute way: it is not only zero for the $-scale but also for the £ or *DM*-scale (similarity group). Hence all these scales must intersect at zero and the transformation ($x' = ax$ or $x'' = bx$) depends merely on the ratios or coefficients a or b respectively; these represent the reciprocal value of the exchange rates for the Dollar to the Pound Sterling or the *Deutsche Mark*.

Before closing this section, a word has to be said with reference to the *accuracy* of the various scales. In generating a measure one obviously tries to attain it through that scale which ranks highest in the hierarchy. Since the conditions of the ratio-scale are not always provided for, other rules for assigning numerals, less restrictive ones, will have to be accepted. This fact, however, is prone to deceive us in respect to the accuracy which the ratio scale makes possible:

Not ... all scales belonging to the same mathematical group are equally precise or accurate or useful or "fundamental." Measurement is never better than the empirical operations by which it is carried out, and operations range from bad to good. Any particular scale, sensory or physical, may be objected to on the grounds of bias, low precision, restricted generality, and other factors, but the objector should remember that these are relative and practical matters and that no scale used by mortals is perfectly free of their taint. (Stevens [1946], p. 680.)

3.6 A MULTIPLE SCALE OF ACCOUNTING

Thus far we have considered accounting in terms of Stevens' various measurement scales and have examined some aspects of our discipline that use various scales. The recording of accounto-economic transactions, however, is a multidimensional process and we cannot grasp its mathematical structure without integrating some of the elements discussed previously. It is in this section and the subsequent chapters that the reader will comprehend the necessity of having gone through elementary and elemental reflections upon measurement which seemed so familiar in content, but often strange in form; reflections that were necessary in order to make us fully aware of certain features and relations of measurement that may have been felt subconsciously only.

Multiple scales are frequently encountered in actual practice; the case of spatial measurement is the most familiar example. Here each of the three dimensions of space is determined by fundamental measurement along one and the same ratio-scale. The combination of these three measures of distance yields a new measure, the volume, which is determined along the same ratio-scale. There are, however, instances of multiple measurement, the dimensions of which are measured on scales that differ from each other; the accounting transaction is one of these cases and will now be analyzed in some detail. From our definition of transactions (see basic assumption 4, item *a*) three or four dimensions can be deduced. First, there are two objects involved that must be distinct from each other and therefore classifiable. Thus the "basis" of the transaction may be considered as consisting of two dimensions, measuring objects along one and the same nominal scale (the chart of accounts). The term "event" implies a *time* dimension which must not be neglected.

We suggest, for reasons that become obvious later, that for the time being this scale shall not be expressed in any of the customary time units such as hour, day, month, or year, but in terms of a purely chronologic-sequential order whereby the occurrence of the next event determines the scale. This is only a provisional device; this scale will later be changed to a discrete interval scale. Since we are, however, dealing with magnitudes of "properties" (values), we have to add another (this time a ratio) scale on which these magnitudes can be measured. This is the scale of dollar-values or of some other monetary unit, constituting the fourth dimension. Often this assignment of numerals is treated separately and not regarded as a dimension in the regular sense (see Subsection 3.84).

After this a tabular illustration (cf. R. Mattessich [1957], pp. 332–33) may be welcome and contribute to further clarification.

Let us assume a simple accounting system consisting of the following accounts: capital, cash, receivables, profit and loss, balance sheet.

We assume further, for the time being, six transactions (the unit in which the transactions are expressed can here be ignored):

	Dr.	Cr.		Dr.	Cr.
(1) Cash	500		(2) Receivables	400	
Capital		500	Cash		400
Owner's investment			Lending of money		
(3) Receivables	40		(4) Cash	250	
Profit and loss		40	Receivables		250
Charging interest			Repayment, first instalment		
(5) Profit and loss	10		(6) Cash	100	
Cash		10	Receivables		100
Expense payment			Repayment, second instalment		

These entries will be recorded in accounts whose formal appearance deviates somewhat from the traditional one. We open five accounts whose debit sides lie, in the form of columns, one beside the other, while their credit sides are arranged in the form of rows, one above (or beneath) the other. (The purpose of the last row and column does not seem evident but may be cleared up by comparing Table 3–5 with Tables 3–7 and 3–8). Making the above six entries in these "accounts," we obtain Table 3–5.

From Table 3–5 we recognize that the cash account has been debited with 500, 250, and 100, a total of 850; receivables have been debited with a total of 440 and profit and loss with 10. Hence all debits aggregate 1,300. The credits went to capital with 500; cash

TABLE 3-5

	Capital Dr.	Cash Dr.	Receivables Dr.	Profit and Loss Dr.	Balance Sheet Dr.
Capital Cr.		(1) 500			
Cash Cr.			(2) 400	(5) 10	
Receivables Cr.		(4) 250 (6) 100			
Profit and Loss Cr.			(3) 40		
Balance Sheet Cr.					

(in total) 410; receivables (in total) 350; and profit and loss 40; making a total of 1,300 for all credits. Thus our accounting equality has been observed although we have used only one entry for each transaction, in contrast to the traditional method by which every amount has to be entered twice. This table contains all four dimensions. The basic nominal scales utilize the two-dimensional surface of the paper, hereby the columns represent the debit sides and the rows the credit sides of the "accounts"; the time-sequence dimension can be recognized by the figures in parentheses, while the regular numbers represent points along the dollar-value dimension.

In this connection it should be pointed out that a matrix is but a rectangular array of figures. Matrix algebra, however, was developed to facilitate the solution of large systems of simultaneous linear equations and related mathematical operation. At present we do not use the accounting matrix for such purposes, yet may usefully apply one or the other matrix-algebraic notion. Every transaction can be interpreted as a separate matrix and Table 3-5 may be regarded as a matrix brought about by the addition of six transaction matrices. Matrix addition is simple, it requires matrices of identical format and the addition of corresponding elements. Figure 3-5 demonstrates this idea. If these six transaction matrices are envisaged one above the other the sequence or time dimension becomes even more obvious. Further details of this mode of representation are contained in Mattessich [1957]. Yet, all this is not designed to revolutionize bookkeeping techniques, rather to abstract the essence from the façade, to reveal the structural relations of accountancy in terms of a general and universally accepted language. It also emphasizes the multiple scale of accounting, which here consists of four dimensions, two of which are subject to the nominal scale, one to the interval scale and the fourth to the ratio scale. Although these four scales are tightly knit there is no fusion in the sense of a multi-

FIGURE 3-5

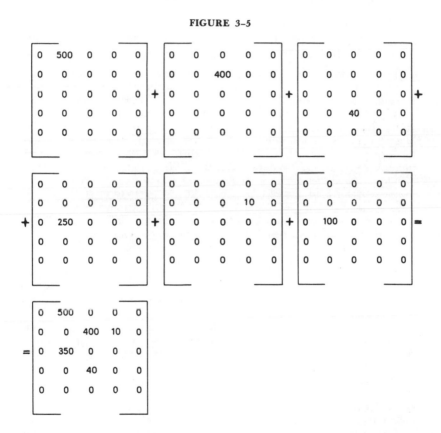

ple scale in the strict meaning of the word—as for instance in the example of volume measurement where the physical extension of each of the three dimensions are multiplied with each other and yield a single, newly compound measure. Thus it is questionable, or at least a matter of opinion, whether in accounting the term "multiple scale" is justified at all. It may be safer to speak of *a combination* of four dimensions along three distinct scales.

3.7 OTHER RECENT CONTRIBUTIONS

Scientific measurement is by no means attained by merely satis-fying the conditions stated in the preceding section, nor is the classi-fication of measurement into scale types the sole facet of modern measurement theory.

3.71 Kinds and Methods of Measurement

Torgerson presents a further classification, partly derived from Campbell, that is important for the comprehension and distinction of various metrologic activities.

The classification of scales into scale types was, in a sense, based on how *much* information about the property the numbers represented (which may depend on the nature of the property). It is also necessary to distinguish among what might be called the *kinds* of information the numbers repre-sent. This amounts to a consideration of the sorts of meaning attributed in a particular scale to those characteristics of order, distance, and origin that are represented. Here we distinguish three different ways in which these characteristics might obtain meaning. First of all, they might obtain meaning through *laws relating the property to other properties*. Density is an example of this kind of measurement. The law refers to the fact that the ratio of mass to volume for any amount of a given substance is a constant. Further, the ratio turns out to be different for different substances. Hence, the value of the ratio can be taken as the *density* of the substance. Campbell has called this kind of measurement, *derived measurement*, or measurement of *B magnitudes*.

A second way in which these characteristics might obtain meaning, after a fashion, is simply by arbitrary definition. We might call this *measurement by fiat*. Ordinarily, it depends on *presumed* relationships between observa-tions and the concept of interest. Included in this category are the indices and indicants so often used in the social and behavioral sciences. This sort of measurement is likely to occur whenever we have a prescientific or common-sense concept that on a priori grounds seems to be important but which we do not know how to measure directly. Hence, we measure some other variable or weighted average of other variables presumed to be re-lated to it. As examples, we might mention the measurement of *socio-economic status*, of *emotion* through use of GSR, or of *learning ability* through the number of trials or the number of errors it takes the subject to reach a particular criterion of learning. Whereas, with derived measurement, the characteristics possess constitutive meaning directly, and operational meaning only indirectly through the measurement of other variables, the indices and indicants possess operational meaning alone, at least initially.

A third kind of measurement depends upon laws relating various quan-tities of the construct to each other. Campbell calls this kind of measure-ment *fundamental* measurement or measurement of *A magnitudes*. Funda-mental measurement is a means by which numbers can be assigned according to natural laws to represent the property and yet which does not presuppose measurement of any other variables. *A construct measured fundamentally possesses both operational and constitutive meaning of and by itself.* The former, since definite rules are available for assigning numbers to represent particular quantities, and the latter, since the numbers reflect natural laws relating different quantities of the property. (Torgerson [1958], pp. 21–22.)

According to this categorization we have to distinguish between *fundamental measurement, derived measurement,* and *measurement by fiat.*[17] The last is the least desirable since it depends greatly on the intuition of the experimenter and offers frequently too large a number of definitional possibilities or alternatives.   We might measure the value of an asset by its purchase price (historic cost basis), by its discounted expected net revenues, by the potential of its liquidation yield, or many other variations and combinations.   There neither exists at present the possibility to infer accounting values through "natural laws" (i.e., by fundamental measurement) nor through a combination of two or more fundamental measures that result in derived measurement. Most of the economic and accounting measures belong in the category of measurement by fiat, which is reflected in a certain definitional arbitrariness of our discipline.   However, Torgerson emphasizes that the discovery of a stable relationship among variables measured upon a definitional basis can be as important as one among variables measured in other ways:

> Indeed, it really makes little difference whether the present scale of length, for example, had been obtained originally through arbitrary definition, through a relation with other, established variables, or through a fundamental process. The concept is a good one. It has entered into an immense number of simple relations with other variables. And this is, after all, the major criterion of the value of a concept. If the result is the same, the way in which a concept is originally introduced is of little importance. (Torgerson [1958], p. 24.)

This statement draws our attention to another important requirement for a useful measure: the latter must be able to enter into a great number of relations with other variables.   This quest will restrain us from carrying to an extreme the conversion of a multiple-purpose into a limited-purpose accounting measure since then the above stated imperative might not be fulfilled. Obviously the demand for more specialized measures is a double-edged blade and ultimately constitutes an optimization problem.

The major part of Torgerson's standard work on measurement is

---

[17]Of course any specific scale may be a mixture of various kinds of measurement. For example, the order may be determined fundamentally, but the "interval" may be determined by definition.

concerned with fundamental measurement, hence is of little relevance to accounting problems. This holds for the classifying of measurement methods—according to the differences in the allocation of the variability of the responses to the stimuli—into the "subject-centered approach," the "judgment approach," and the "response approach,"[18] as well as for the many statistical subtleties with which his book is endowed. However, with regard to the latter, a short reflection on the difference between deterministic and probabilistic measurement methods is made in the next subsection.

3.72 Probabilistic versus Deterministic Models of Measurement

The advantage of a probabilistic measurement model in contrast to a general or deterministic one, lies in the treatment of the *error problem*. The information of measurement is considerably enhanced if the degree of accuracy or error of the pertinent measurement is known. In many measurement activities of everyday life this problem of error measurement, though present, is pushed into the background and becomes rarely obtrusive. If we are engaged, for example, in measuring the various dimensions of a room by means of an ordinary yardstick we may be subconsciously aware that the accuracy which can be attained is limited within a range of several inches or so. This is best evidenced by the experiment of measuring the room many times, having many people do it as accurately as possible. The outcome will be a series of measures that are by no means identical. The differences between these results, if they are obtained in sufficient quantity, will form a probability distribution, which, with increasing number of measures, approaches a *normal curve*. From this a standard deviation or other error measure, that indicates the limits of reliability of the pertinent measurement activity, can be defined.

The accuracy or error-measure constitutes in the opinion of many scholars a most vital part of *every* measurement. Ackoff [1962, p. 205] rightly asserts that "a count, classification, rank, or interval or ratio measurement has little significance (if any) without some knowledge of its accuracy" and Churchman [1959, p. 92] even con-

---

[18]In the subject-centered approach the systematic variation in the reactions of the subjects to the stimuli is attributed to individual differences in the subjects (assignment of numerals to *subjects* only). In the judgment approach, the systematic variation in the reactions of the subjects to the stimuli is attributed to differences in the stimuli with respect to a designated attribute (assignment of numerals to *stimuli* only). Finally in the response approach the variability of reactions to stimuli is ascribed to both variation in the subjects and in the stimuli (assignment of numerals to both *subjects and stimuli*).

tends that "no procedure can claim the name of measurement unless it includes methods of estimating accuracy." These pleas should be borne in mind though at first glance, and in the face of the many deterministic measurement models applied in practice, it might seem exaggerated. For even a deterministic model calls for a theory of error or approximation, although an implicit rather than an intrinsic one. Whereas the probabilistic model of measurement lends itself to the setting up of statistical criteria on goodness of fit between model and data, the deterministic model must choose a more arbitrary, extraneous procedure of accepting or rejecting the pertinent method.

Probabilistic models and error measures in general have been neglected in accounting for a long time. Again Churchman [1961, p. 65] emphasizes that:

... two other aspects of costs that are definitely relevant to policy formation and are definitely lacking in accounting systems. Few (I'd be inclined to say "No") costs are known with certainty. The errors in cost figures (or return figures) are clearly important in decisions of management. They are important in deciding how much effort to put into the task of gathering cost information and transmitting it. The errors are also important in understanding the risks entailed in decisions. Yet company data-processing systems do not generate information about the errors of estimated costs, and in this respect, again, we lack a sound basis for verifying managerial decisions based on costs.[19]

It is also true that managers are often deceived by the absolute size of a cost variance and that it is important to know the extent to which the purely numerical size of the scale influences, in one way or the other, the behavior of the manager. There is, however, evidence that procedures of error measurement are available in modern accountancy by way of statistical control for standard costing. This approach exploits the experience gathered by industrial engineers in statistical quality control and applies it to the control of costs. Hereby a more objective method of calculating control limits is attained, and the pressing question which size of variance from standard is to be tolerated, should find an answer.[20]

It is difficult to surmise, at present, to what extent and in what fashion statistical methods will penetrate accounting. But the unfilled need of error measurement in many channels, the quest for

---

[19]West C. Churchman, *Prediction and Optimal Decision: Philosophical Issues of a Science of Values.* Copyright 1961. By permission of Prentice-Hall, Inc., publisher.

[20]See e.g., Bierman, Fouraker, and Jaedicke [1961a], pp. 108–24, [1961b], Gaynor [1954], and Noble [1954]; and Section 7.5 of this book.

relating decision theory to accounting models, and the ambition of incorporating a theory of learning into our discipline (cf. Churchman [1961], p. 336) mark this border area as a fertile soil for future experimentation (cf. Bierman [1962]).

3.73   A Functional Viewpoint of Measurement

While the preceding sections have shown a strong *operational* tendency in treating the problems of measurement, this one concludes such reflections by illuminating measurement from a more teleologic standpoint. The assertion that accounting is measurement, even if proven so operationally, cannot reveal its full meaning before the purpose of measurement in general has been clarified. What is the meaning of measurement? Why does this term imply a comparatively high academic prestige? Why has quantification become the—sometimes secret and occasionally unattainable—goal of every science?

We agree with Churchman [1959 and 1961], who is much concerned with the functional aspect of measurement, that it is the contrast between "precise" and "vague" information, the usefulness of this information in a "wide variety" of problems, and above all the value of this information for "purposive decisions" to which mensuration owes its high social and scientific status. Churchman attempts to formulate measurement itself as a decision-making endeavor that ultimately is to be evaluated by decision-making criteria. He must confess, however, that: "In this sense, of measurement taken as a decision-making activity designed to accomplish an objective, we have as yet no theory of measurement. We do not know why we do what we do. We do not even know why we measure at all. It is costly to obtain measurements. Is the effort worth the cost?"[21]

Let us start with the nominal scale of accounting, that is, with the subdivision of a single concept such as wealth into its concrete and abstract manifestations, and the further categorization of these two concepts into a multitude of subclasses of different levels. What is the force behind this pursuit? Obviously, the need for differentiation of our physical as well as mental surroundings arises out of the gain in knowledge which this differentiation brings about. Different parts of an object, event, or concept, frequently "behave" differently and any information about this behavior in relation to the specific part may prove useful, be it for the purpose of making a decision or

---

[21]Churchman, *op. cit.*, p. 102.

for the mere satisfaction of curiosity. If we know how "large" the assets of our enterprise are, this may be very useful, but with regard to the decision of whether to incur any immediate cash outlays, this information will not be sufficient and a certain subcategorization into liquid means and other assets will be inevitable if such a decision is to be reached. The knowledge that an asset or a liability, a revenue or an expense item amounts to, say, $3,000 can constitute significant information, provided this figure can be related to some other information and purpose. The simple fact that this item is worth $3,000 may cost something to deduce but perhaps is of no purposive significance. One may ask whether an activity that creates "worthless" information deserves to be regarded as measurement? Is it the purpose that sanctifies measurement?

Those who are of the opinion that purpose-directedness is an indispensable condition of measurement may refuse—in spite of operational acceptability—to designate the generation of many accounting and statistical-economic data as measurement on purely teleological grounds. The criterion of rejection, however, must be clarified. It is not so that many of these data are entirely without worth—there exists hardly any information (unless it is an incorrect or misleading one) for which no purpose can utlimately be found—but the goal is not *preconceived* and cannot be pinned down in advance with accuracy. This realization must constitute a heavy burden for every conscientious accountant and economic statistician, for it seems that in a majority of cases the collection of economic data is determined by the ease of accessibility and not by a clearly defined purpose to be served. The intent is often justified with reference to tradition or competition. There exist accounting, cost-accounting, and perhaps social accounting systems which owe their existence to an original aim which long has been abandoned, to the ambitions of small "empire builders," or to the urge to keep up with the Joneses (hereby it makes little difference whether the Joneses are identified with a department, a firm, a region, or a state). How difficult it is to escape these temptations only those who have tried to resist them in actual practice will fully appreciate.

To facilitate the attainment of the teleologic quest of measurement, a clear decision with regard to the following aspects ought to be made:

1. The *language* which communicates the results.
2. The *specification* as to *object* and *circumstances* to which the results shall pertain.
3. The *standards* for using the results.

4. The *evaluation* of the results with regard to *accuracy* and *control*.

For a discussion of the general significance of these aspects we refer the reader to Churchman's excellent presentations [1959; 1961, chap. 5]. In the following a few comments with specific reference to accounting shall be added.

The *language* of accounting is comprehensive enough to warrant the transmission of information to a great many potential users. It is a language that—though it may change in dialect—is well proven. Not only has the debit and credit apparatus endured for centuries but it has only recently found a new and fertile soil in the area of social accounting. The almost universal adoption of this language in national income statistics, in input-output analysis, and in flow of funds analysis has a profound meaning that is explored in the next chapter. As mentioned before, the chief problem is to find the golden middle between the quests for "simplicity" of language and "diversity" of its application.

The foremost concern of the *specification* problem in accounting measurement—also mentioned previously—is found in the reconciliation between cost for and return from information. It is precisely this economical aspect which sets the accountant and economic statistician a limit in yielding to the request of the theoretician and epistemologist for improved methods of measurement.

The creation of "basic charts of accounts" and of common evaluation procedures are the traditional routes by which *standardization* should have been attained. However, there exist three impediments. As we have noticed the first route, that of accepting basic charts, seems not to be acceptable in the Anglo-American hemisphere, whereas the second did not lead to the desired goal because of the compromise enforced by systems designed to satisfy concurrently legal, administrative, as well as managerial purposes. These goals apparently are too diverse to be combined in the *stem* of a single system. If a combination can be attained it will come through *branching out* into various areas from a *common basis*. The third obstacle lies in the difficulty of interpreting results that were not obtained under standard conditions. Churchman distinguishes three levels of standardization in this respect: (1) restricting to data that remain invariant enough with time and place such as to make adjustments superfluous; (2) rejecting data not collected under standard conditions; and (3) adjusting the nonstandard-data by means of "laws." In accounting, the third level is commonly chosen but the "laws" by which adjustments are made do not go much beyond "working hypotheses" of limited reliability.

The last consideration too, that of *accuracy* and *control*, has not yet found any definite formulation in accounting although—as pointed out—there exists, at least in standard costing, a theoretical basis for determining control limits.

3.8   FORMS OF PRESENTING ACCOUNTING MEASURES

A flow, accounting, or transaction system can be presented in various forms. The transition from one form to the other changes the appearance (though not the essence) of an accounting system radically and may lead to confusion. The most important of these variations are the network form, the double-entry form, the matrix form, the journal entry form, and the vector form. Though in this book we are not concerned with technicalities, we shall offer a short discussion of these forms and present at the end of this subsection a juxtaposition of these five versions (in schematic presentation) that will facilitate comparison.

3.81   The Network Form

This is a graphic version of presenting the flow, circulation, or duality phenomenon. It reveals at first glance the flow structure and the various accounting identities of the system. In the literature it is encountered in connection with macro- as well as micro-accounting systems. For the purpose of demonstrating national income accounting systems Allais [1954, pp. 44–47], makes use of such flow diagrams, so does Frisch [1942], Ohlsson [1953, p. 53], and others. Allais' and Lesourne's *Schematic Presentation of the Principal Equations* of a national income accounting system (see Figures 3–6 and 3–7), gives an illustration of the network form, and underlines our point (made in Subsection 2.2) of the need for measuring income, saving, etc., at various thresholds of the economic flow. The definitional equations can be read off either at specific points (nods) of outflows and inflows (e.g., from point 9 in Figure 3–6 we can formulate the following identity $R_N = B + I + S$; the inflows are equal to the outflows) or it can be derived from "cross sections" of the system (e.g., from cross section 15 in Figure 3–6 we can formulate the following identity $P_F = A_\Sigma + R_I + R_C$). Auxiliary or other equations not to be read off the graph may be added separately (e.g., in item 14 of Figure 3–6, $P_F = P - F$).

In micro-accounting Blocker and Weltmer [1954] make abundant use of a slightly modified version of a network presentation. A more abstract form of a complete business accounting system is given by

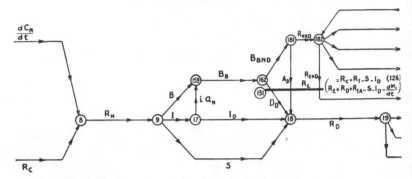

Key to Symbols to Figures 3–6 and 3–7 (translated from French):

A_D	= capital consumption allowance distributed	$\dfrac{dC_\Sigma}{dt}$	= total change in inventory
A_{IM}	= capital consumption allowance of fixed capital	$\dfrac{dC_{IM}}{dt}$	= total change in fixed assets
a_N	= sum of net assets		
A_Σ	= quantitative change of inventory	D_D	= dividends distributed
B	= net profits (of enterprises)	E	= total spontaneous saving
B_B	= "gross" profits $[B_B =$	E_B	= gross saving
	$(P_{IM} - A_{IM}) + (P_\Sigma + A_\Sigma) + R_\epsilon]$	E_N	= net saving
B_{BND}	= undistributed part of gross profits	E_S	= spontaneous saving by individuals
$\dfrac{dC_N}{dt}$	= change in national capital	E_T	= total saving
		F	= intermediate (consumption of) goods

*The diagram has been established by Mr. Lesourne, engineer to the Corps of Mines.
†The numbers placed inside the circles situated at the node of the network refer to the corresponding equations. The vertical bars correspond to the relations which have not been able to be represented by the nodes.

Source: *Les fondements comptables de la macro-economique* de M. Allais. (Paris: Presses Universitaires de France, 1954), tableau II—PP. 44–45.

Mattessich [1958a, p. 476] and is reproduced in Figure 3–8. Herein the capital letters A', C' and A, C symbolize the total asset and capital[22] values at the beginning and end of the accounting period respectively. The symbols a'_{100}, a'_{200}, ..., a'_{422} represent the beginning balances of various balance sheet subtotals, accounts, subaccounts, etc. while a_{100}, a_{200}, ..., a_{422} reflect the ending balances of the same subtotals, accounts, subaccounts, etc. The delta symbols Δa_{110}, Δa_{121}, ..., Δa_{410} stand for values of aggregate changes in the accounts numbered 110, 121, ..., 410. The remaining symbols, such as a_{500}, a_{510}, a_{520}, a_{521}, a_{600}, etc. indicate balances in nominal accounts (or subaccounts) before closing. The pertinent accounting identities

---

[22]Includes debt capital as well as owners' equity.

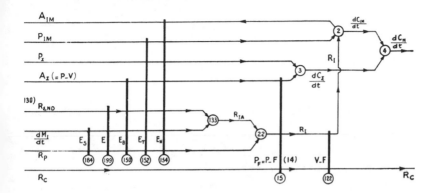

i = rate of pure interest	R_ϵ = entrepreneurial income
I = interest on total capital	$R_{\epsilon ND}$ = non-distributed entrepreneurial
I_D = interest distributed	income
$\dfrac{dM_I}{dt}$ = change in disposable monetary means (personal sector)	R_I = investment
	R_{IA} = self-investment of enterprises
	R_N = national income
P = gross product	R_{NND} = non-distributed part of national
P_F = final product	income
P_{IM} = value change of fixed assets	R_p = investment from personal sector
P_Σ = value change of inventory	S = salaries and wages
R_C = final consumption	V = total sales revenues of enterprises
R_D = disposable income	V_F = final sales

can be derived in similar fashion as described before (e.g., $a'_{100} = a'_{110} + a'_{120} + a_{130}$, or $a'_{311} + \Delta a_{311} = a_{311}$, $a_{600} + a_{500} = a_{422}$, or $A = C$).

In the last few decades a new branch of mathematics, known as *theory of graphs* (closely related to linear programing, see e.g., chap. 10 of Hadley [1962], pp. 331–78) has assumed increasing importance in various applied fields; primarily in electrical engineering, more recently in economics and management science. The central problem of the theory of graphs is the determination of maximal flows in networks. An accounting study by Charnes, Cooper, and Ijiri [1963] (for further details see our Section 8.4) gives evidence that this problem may become relevant to our discipline. Thus attention must be drawn to this new area which constitutes another door that opens the possibility of intertwining accounting identities with behavioral hypotheses.

3.82 The Double-Entry Form

This is the most common form in which accounting is manifested. There is hardly need to bring in examples from business,

FIGURE 3-7
SCHEMATIC REPRESENTATION OF PRINCIPAL AGGREGATE EQUATIONS
DIAGRAM 2 *†

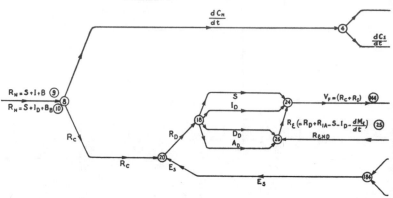

*The diagram has been established by Mr. Lesourne, engineer to the Corps of Mines.
†The numbers placed inside the circles situated at the node of the network refer to the corresponding equations. The vertical bars correspond to the relations which have not been able to be represented by the nodes.

Source: *Les fondements comptables de la macro-économique* de M. Allais. (Paris: Presses Universitaires de France, 1954), tableau III—pp. 46–47.

government accounting, etc. Illustrations of this form as applied to macro-accounting systems are given in Subsections 4.53 and 4.54.

3.83   The Matrix Form

The foremost use of this version is to be found in Leontief's [1951] interindustry analysis. There the *transaction matrix* combined with the idea of Walrasian production coefficients makes it possible to exploit its full matrix-algebraic potential (for further details see Subsection 8.11). But the basic idea of presenting accounting in matrix form can be encountered before the appearance of Leontief's work. The first evidence of the appearance of this idea, known to us, is Gomberg's [1927] "geometrical" presentation of bookkeeping methods (see Figure 3–9), but it also seems to have been known in American business accounting under the name of "spread sheet" (see Kohler [1952], pp. 387–89; see our Table 3–6).

Figure 3–9 gives a reproduction of Gomberg's accounting matrix. The rows and columns do not represent sides of individual accounts but whole areas or sectors—interestingly enough the latter are formed on the basis of statistical, legal, and economic results of accounting—similar to the spread sheet—but in contrast to Leontief's transaction matrix and recent conventions, the rows represent debit, and the columns credit sides. The separation of each square

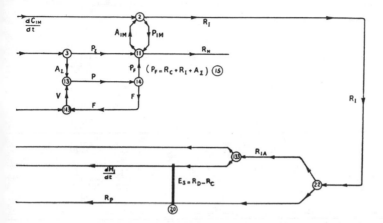

FIGURE 3-8
CHART OF ACCOUNTING IDENTITIES

Courtesy: Editor of the *Accounting Review*.

FIGURE 3-9
DIE VOLLSTÄNDIGE BUCHHALTUNG
KONTENMÄSSIGE VERRECHNUNG ALLER ERGEBNISGRUPPEN (KONTENVERKEHR)

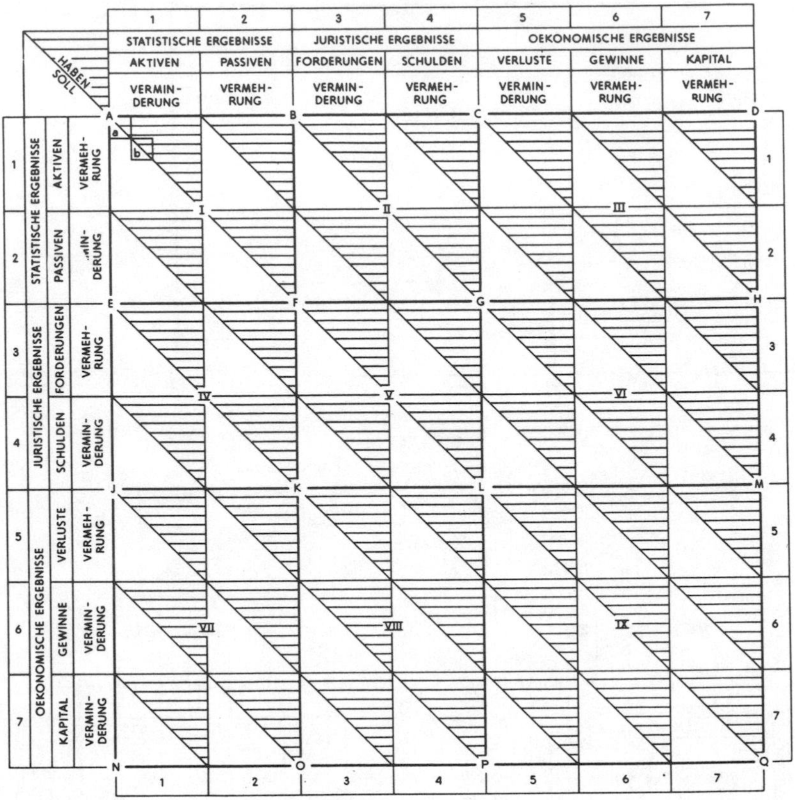

into a plain and a shaded area apparently attempts to convey the duality aspect of each figure entered.

Table 3-6 reproduces Kohler's *spread sheet* which is "a worksheet providing a two-way analysis or recapitulation of costs or other accounting data"; basically it corresponds to an accounting matrix. Its most obvious advantage is to achieve a *dual classification* (in the debit and credit account) by means of a *single entry*.

But for decades Gomberg's "geometrical" presentation and the American spread sheet were in oblivion, and it was interindustry analysis which gave new impact to formulate a more general version of an accounting matrix, one that is not restricted to the inputs and outputs of interindustry flows, but which is applicable to all situa-

TABLE 3-6

M COMPANY ACCOUNT ANALYSIS YEAR 19-1

(In Dollars; 00.00's Omitted)

Account		Cash	In-vest-ments	Re-ceiv-ables	In-ven-tory	Pay-ables	Capi-tal Stock	Sales	Pur-chases	Ex-penses	Totals
Debit ↓	Credit →										
Cash .... (a)			1.0	21.5			20.0			0.3	42.8
Investments .. (b)		5.1									5.1
Receivables... (c)								32.4			32.4
Inventory..... (d)									5.6		5.6
Payables ..... (e)		28.8									28.8
Capital stock											
Sales .... (f)				0.8							0.8
Purchases .... (g)						28.7					28.7
Expenses .... (h)				0.2		6.3					6.5
Totals.........		33.9	1.0	22.5	—	35.0	20.0	32.4	5.6	0.3	150.7

Key to transactions, reading across:

(a) Sale of investment	(b) Purchase of investments	(f) Return of sale
Collections of accounts	(c) Sales of merchandise	(g) Purchases of merchandise
Sale of capital stock	(d) Purchases unsold	(h) Bad debt written off
Refund of overcharge	(e) Payment of liabilities	Operating expense

Eric L. Kohler, *A Dictionary for Accountants*, copyright 1952, 1957, p. 389. By permission of Prentice-Hall, Inc., publisher.

tions that use a debit-credit pattern. The present author[23] suggested such an approach in 1957, utilizing it for axiomatizing the *a priori* aspects of accounting. As a consequence, accounting matrices became more popular and found reflection in the current literature (e.g., Richards [1960], p. 432; Kemeny, Schleifer, Snell, and Thomson [1962],[24] pp. 349, 354, 355; Ijiri [1960, 1963]; Charnes, Cooper, Ijiri [1963], pp. 26, 33). Two of these matrices are here reproduced to illustrate technical variations and to discuss the convention regulating which side (debit or credit) shall be represented by the matrix column and which by the row.

Both variations provide beginning and ending balance sheet accounts. To treat the balance sheet in account form and to use a "beginning balance sheet account" in which, by necessity, the assets are contained in the credit side and the capital items in the debit side, is necessary for a systematic opening and closing of the accounting cycle. To use such opening and closing accounts has been a long-established practice in Continental Europe but seems to be new in American accounting where these accounts could be dis-

---

[23] Mattessich [1957], then unaware of the two precursors mentioned above.

[24] This book has a special merit: after almost half a millenium (since Pacioli's treatise) it is again *a book on mathematics* which bothers to deal with accounting.

TABLE 3-7

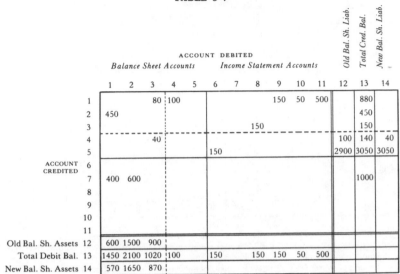

ACCOUNT CREDITED		1	2	3	4	5	6	7	8	9	10	11	12 (Old Bal. Sh. Liab.)	13 (Total Cred. Bal.)	14 (New Bal. Sh. Liab.)
	1			80	100					150	50	500		880	
	2	450												450	
	3								150					150	
	4			40									100	140	40
	5						150						2900	3050	3050
	6														
	7	400	600											1000	
	8														
	9														
	10														
	11														
Old Bal. Sh. Assets	12	600	1500	900											
Total Debit Bal.	13	1450	2100	1020	100		150		150	150	50	500			
New Bal. Sh. Assets	14	570	1650	870											

ACCOUNT DEBITED — Balance Sheet Accounts / Income Statement Accounts

John G. Kemeny, Arthur Schleifer, Jr., J. Laurie Snell, Gerald L. Thompson, *Finite Mathematics with Business Applica-tion*, copyright 1962. By permission of Prentice-Hall, Inc., publisher.

TABLE 3-8
SPREAD SHEET EXTENSION

Debits \ Credits	Beginning	Cash	Goods	Raw Materials	Net Worth	Sales	Ending Balance	Total
Beginning Balance					50.00			50.00
Cash	30.00					10.25		40.25
Goods	10.00	3.00						13.00
Raw Materials	10.00	2.75						12.75
Net Worth		4.50					49.00	53.50
Sales			3.00	3.75	3.50			10.25
Ending Balance		30.00	10.00	9.00				49.00
Total	50.00	40.25	13.00	12.75	53.50	10.25	49.00	228.75

Courtesy: *Journal of Accounting Research*

pensed with, as the counterentries to real balances are usually made on the same accounts of the succeeding period. The version of Kemeny et al. [1962] in addition provides a column to total all credit entries and a row to total all debit entries of each account. This is a merely pedagogic means and auxiliary device. By arranging the rows and columns of the balance sheet (opening and closing) ac-counts at the end (i.e., at the left-hand side and the bottom re-

spectively) the version of Kemeny et al. [1962] has the advantage
—over the version of Charnes et al. [1963]—of providing a form that
permits *matrix partition*[25] without further rearrangement of rows
and columns. This version indeed suggests such partitioning (see
various horizontal and vertical lines in Figure 3–7) for the purpose
of separating *real accounts* from *nominal accounts*,[26] etc.

As regards the use of columns and rows as debit and credit sides
respectively, this obviously is a mere convention. Hence the inverse
practice must also lead to correct results if consistently adhered to.
But thus far the practices are divided, Leontief [1951] and all economists, mathematicians, etc., using interindustry transaction matrices, as well as Kemeny et al. [1962] using business accounting
matrices, adhere to the convention of regarding the columns as
debit, and rows as credit sides. Gomberg [1927], Kohler [1952],
Richards [1960], and Charnes et al. [1963] use the other convention
of debiting in the rows and crediting in the columns. We shall
adhere to the former (Leontief) convention, not in order to balance the scale, but to follow an important precedent: Interindustry analysis and its convention is well entrenched all over the
world in economics, econometrics, and related fields of applied
mathematics, there is no hope for the accountants to convince these
experts to change their convention. In accounting, however, the exploitation of transaction matrices is novel and not yet customary.
If we accept the "other" convention we may erect, quite unneces-
sarily, a formidable barrier against the future integration of micro-
and macro-accounting. At this point of time we see into the future
only a few steps ahead of us, but it is not unlikely that two changes
will occur: a more intensive use of the matrix form and a closer co-
operation or co-ordination of micro- and macro-accounting. The
simultaneous use of both conventions will be all the more confusing
since the convention is also reflected in the sequence of the subscripts when using matrix algebraic symbolism. The mathematical

[25] A matrix is being partitioned by drawing horizontal or vertical lines, creating two or
more *submatrices*. These lines cannot be jagged lines. Thus in Charnes' et al. [1963] version 9 submatrices would have to be formed before the matrix containing ordinary transactions (excluding opening and closing)—that is the heavily framed central part of Figure
3–7—can be isolated. Occasionally such partitioning may be necessary but frequently the
operation accounting matrices may be restricted to the matrix algebraic operations of addition and subtraction (see Mattessich [1957], p. 332).

[26] A *real account* is a subaccount of the balance sheet (account) and a *nominal account* is a
subaccount of the profit and loss account. But Kemeny el al. [1962] addresses the real accounts as balance sheet accounts, a dangerous terminology which may lead to confusion with
the *balance sheet closing and opening accounts*.

convention states that the first subscript refers to the row and the second to the column. Hardly anyone would change this rule. But to it an accounting convention must be added. If we favor the Leontief convention, the first subscript refers to the account to be credited, the second subscript to the account to be debited (e.g., t_{23} may indicate a transaction that credits account No. 2 and debits account No. 3 with the value represented by the entire symbol). If we accept the "other" convention, we have here the reverse situation. The latter may indeed be closer to the taste of accountants who are used to listing the debit before the credit. But this weak argument can be countered with another, at least as strong, namely that the outflow (credit) must occur before the inflow (debit).

3.84   The Journal Entry Form and the Vector Form

The journal entry form is carefully described in Pacioli's [1494] treatise and may be older than the double-entry form. It usually consists of a data, the name of the account to be debited, with the corresponding value in a debit-column; and (if it is not a compound entry) below this, would be stated the name of the account to be credited with the corresponding value in a credit column. Further supplementary data, like reference marks, explanatory text, etc. are usually added. This form permits an easy way of listing chronologically a series of transactions but makes it difficult to survey transaction-aggregates from a functional point of view.

For us this form is of special interest since it comes close to the *vector presentation* of accounting transactions used in our formulation of the duality principle (assumption 4) and related assumptions (see 3b of 2.4). There the vector form was chosen because it is indispensable in a set-theoretical formulation of accounting. Its necessity cannot be fully understood without a study of Appendix A. Mathematically speaking a vector is an *ordered* array of elements. Thus a matrix consisting of a single column is called a column vector and a matrix consisting of a single row is called a row vector. In a Cartesian system of co-ordinates, the location of a point may be described by a vector—e.g., an ordered pair (2,4) in a two-dimensional space, see Figure 3–10a or, e.g., an ordered triple (2,4, 3) in a three-dimensional space, see Figure 3–10b.

If a monetary or other value is assigned to such a vector we may give expression to this relationship by inserting a symbol (e.g., a capital letter) in front of the vector and identify this expression with the value. So, for instance, the mathematical expression

$$F(2, 4, 3) = 78$$

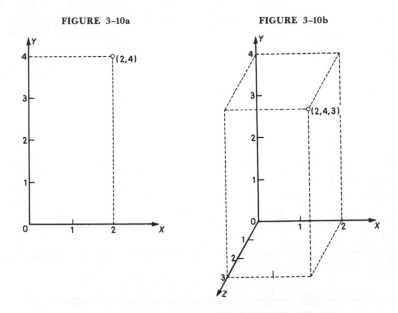

FIGURE 3-10a   FIGURE 3-10b

seems, indeed, to be a concise and efficient way of expressing the following journal entry:

	Dr.	Cr.
Jan. 3, Receivables (acct. no. 4)	$78	
Sales (acct. no. 2)		$78

Of course, it only works if certain conventions are agreed upon in advance: e.g., (1) that the first element in the vector always expresses the number of the credit account, the second the number of the debit account, and the third the day of the month—hence *ordered* triple—(2) that a chart of account is available in which accounts and account numbers can be readily identified; (3) that the month is agreed upon in advance (otherwise the last element of the vector will become more complex or a fourth element must be added; (4) that the left-hand side of the equation expresses the dollar amount assigned to the transaction (the latter *relation* being symbolized by the letter F for flow).

Since these conventions can be established in advance without difficulty, the vector form[27] has definite advantages, especially in

---

[27] Another version of this vector form is the following: (2,4,3,78); here the operator or relation sign is omitted (which may lead to confusion in dealing with different relations and vectors of different types); furthermore the value assigned ($78) is interpreted as belonging to a fifth *dimension*, thus being incorporated *in* the vector.

connection with the mathematical presentation of accounting axioms, theorems, proofs, etc. Another prospective area of application of this form is electronic data processing.

3.85 A Schematic Comparison

The following survey offers a schematic comparison of the five alternative forms discussed in the preceding subsections (cf. Adam [1959], p. 27). The repeated use of the same symbols will facilitate relating one form to another. The symbol t_{31} for instance stands for a transaction and the value assigned to it; the first figure of the subscript (e.g., 3) refers to the account to be credited, the second figure of the subscript (e.g., 1) refers to the account to be debited. (If account numbers with several digits were used, a comma between the first and the second figure would be required). We express the account numbers in bold figures, except where used as subscripts. The first three versions do not express the sequence or time dimension (something that could be added). The last two versions use the time dimension in form of a simple sequence index (1 to 9).

(a) *Network Form.*

FIGURE 3–11

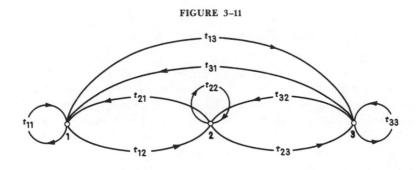

$$(t_{11} + t_{21} + t_{31}) + (t_{11} + t_{12} + t_{13}) + (t_{13} + t_{23} + t_{33}) =$$
$$= (t_{11} + t_{12} + t_{13}) + (t_{21} + t_{22} + t_{23}) + (t_{31} + t_{32} + t_{33}).$$

(b) *Double-Entry Form.*

1			**2**			**3**		
Dr.	Cash	Cr.	Dr.	Receiv.	Cr.	Dr.	Equity	Cr.
t_{11}		t_{11}	t_{12}		t_{21}	t_{13}		t_{31}
t_{21}		t_{12}	t_{22}		t_{22}	t_{23}		t_{32}
t_{31}		t_{13}	t_{32}		t_{23}	t_{33}		t_{33}

(c) *Matrix Form.*

		1 Cash Dr.	**2** Receiv. Dr.	**3** Equity Dr.
1 Cash	Cr.	t_{11}	t_{12}	t_{13}
2 Receiv.	Cr.	t_{21}	t_{22}	t_{23}
3 Equity	Cr.	t_{31}	t_{32}	t_{33}

(d) *Journal Entry Form.*

	Dr. Cr.		Dr. Cr.		Dr. Cr.

1. Cash............ t_{11}
   Cash .... t_{11}
		4. Receiv........... t_{12}
		   Cash .... t_{12}
				7. Equity .... t_{13}
				   Cash .... t_{13}	

2. Cash............ t_{21}
   Receiv. .... t_{21}
		5. Receiv........... t_{22}
		   Receiv. .... t_{22}
				8. Equity .... t_{23}
				   Receiv. .... t_{23}	

3. Cash............ t_{31}
   Equity........ t_{31}
		6. Receiv........... t_{32}
		   Equity........ t_{32}
				9. Equity .... t_{33}
				   Equity........ t_{33}	

(e) *Vector Form.*

$$F\,(1,1,1) = t_{11} \quad F\,(1,2,4) = t_{12} \quad F\,(1,3,7) = t_{13}$$
$$F\,(2,1,2) = t_{21} \quad F\,(2,2,5) = t_{22} \quad F\,(2,3,8) = t_{23}$$
$$F\,(3,1,3) = t_{31} \quad F\,(3,2,6) = t_{32} \quad F\,(3,3,9) = t_{33}$$

Chapter 4

EVOLUTION OF THE ACCOUNTING MODEL

THE PRESENT chapter is not designed to compete with the many books and papers written on the historical development of accounting. Here again we are concerned with the basic assumptions (formulated in Chapter 2) but from an historic point of view. Not all assumptions will receive equal attention; the point of gravity will shift toward those which reflect best the metamorphoses the accounting model underwent through the ages. These changes are clearly manifested in assumptions 9 (Entities), 13 (Classification), 14 (Data input), and to some extent 4 (Duality). The remaining assumptions will be discussed whenever they deserve special attention within the constraints of the space available. Yet, this chapter has two further purposes, (1) to present opinions on accounting pronounced at different times in diverse quarters and (2) to give evidence of the variety of situations in which the accounting model found application.

4.1 NOTES ON SOME PREACCOUNTING CONCEPTS

Bookkeeping has been traced back some four thousand years to the Babylonian empire of Hammurabi (2123 to 2081 B.C.) where clay tablets were used to record "financial" and other transactions in cuneiform writing. Though the idea of coinage seems to belong to a later period (seventh century B.C.), the ancient Babylonians had monetary conventions with "currency" units expressed in "universally" accepted commodities. But the general adoption of *money as a medium of valuation*, and the *conception of the account*, are phenomena born during the *Graeco-Roman* age. Even there the various items of an account were not always reduced to the common monetary denominator and the *bilateral* account form, so well known to us, seems to have been the exception rather than the rule:

> The first document is an extract from the building account of the Parthenon, covering the Attic (i.e., Athenian) year 434–433 B.C. . . . the accounts were then inscribed on a large marble stele, which was set up on the Acropolis of Athens. . . . Here we have a good example of the tendency referred to earlier, for a Greek account occasionally to express the value of a particular piece of property in units other than those of the system of currency in terms of which the account is being kept.
>
> The second document is a small part of a very long inscription on marble, found at Eleusis in Attica, containing the accounts for the year 329–328 B.C. . . .
>
> This document, in its complete lack of tabulation and the minute details it gives of most items of expenditure, is unfortunately more typical of fifth and fourth century public accounts than the briefer and much better arranged Parthenon account [pp. 23–25].
>
> . . . it is only in one surviving document, a unique papyrus roll of the Roman period from Karanis in the Fayum, . . . that we find an ancient account drawn up in "bilateral form"; and here we have the other variety of bilateral form—receipts and payments not on opposite "pages" (the successive columns of a papyrus roll do not naturally fall into pairs) but separately aligned vertically side by side within each column of writing. The peculiar form of this papyrus account is not to be taken as a fundamental advance in book-keeping method, because it can only have been adopted for convenience in perusing the account and identifying individual items within it. De Ste. Croix [1956], pp. 20–21, footnotes omitted.)

This *ratio* (=account) with its *tabulae acceptum* (debit side) and *tabulae expensum* (credit side) thus served comparatively early the aggregation of positive and negative quantities and the determination of a balance. In one instance even a cross-reference to another account was found. But, as De Ste. Croix indicates ". . . the presence of cross-references . . . does not imply that the account . . . was in any way integrated with others in a unified system of accounts." That means, there exists no evidence that the duality principle was conceived and exploited by the Romans, though the first traces of the double-entry approach—belonging to the thirteenth and fourteenth century—were found on what once was Roman soil. This fact tempts some authors with speculations about the ultimate origin of this simple but fundamental idea which found its first expression in double-entry bookkeeping.

In the light of the foregoing remarks it might be worth examining which of our basic assumptions hold for recording processes of ancient times. The remaining basic assumptions will be discussed later and may help to further illuminate the *essence* of modern accounting.

1. Monetary Values. The traces of *quasi* monetary systems in Babylon, Sumer, and Egypt and the evidence supplied by accounts of ancient Greek and Rome leaves no doubt that this is one of the oldest notions of economic recording. Nevertheless it had not the all-pervading power of reducing almost every kind of "value" to a monetary abstract. A power that only modern man is about to assign to this concept.

2. Time Intervals. This notion is so general and goes so far beyond the recording of economic events that it needs no further elaboration. The conception of time as an *additive* phenomenon may go back to prehistoric ages but has its first evidence in the idea of the *calendar* (which emerged before 4,000 B.C.).

Assumptions 3 and 4 seem not to belong to ancient recording processes and will be discussed later.

5. Aggregation. Even without the evidence provided by Graeco-Roman accounts, early mathematics and history of economic life would offer many clues that a systematic aggregation of positive and negative quantities and values (of economic significance) goes back to a period far beyond the Middle Ages. Yet, since many of the ancient accounts do not evidence a single currency as common denominator,[1] this postulate must be interpreted in a more limited sense than is applied nowadays.

6. Economic Objects. In ancient times financial objects (monetary and property claims) were no less known than real economic objects (goods and services), hence assumption 6 also precedes the duality principle.

7. Inequity of Monetary Claims. Price-level fluctuations were inherent in most economic systems of the past. Since debt contracts were rarely adjusted for changes in purchasing power this assumption is valid for preaccounting times, though of little significance for ancient bookkeeping practice. Nevertheless the reflection reveals that bookkeeping, commerce, and finance, even on a primitive level, are closely tied to this fundamental, although usually implied, convention.

8. Economic Agents. The oldest precondition for economic activity.

9. Entities. Though business corporations seem to be a crea-

---

[1]It seems that ending balances (in ancient accounts) were occasionally handled in a similar way as we nowadays handle inventory accounts operated on a Fifo or Lifo basis. There the ending balance consisted of several amounts expressed in different currencies (or commodities); here, the ending balance consists of several quantities priced at different values.

tion of the modern time, the existence of states and, perhaps even more so, of republics and independent cities in ancient times—as well as the evidence of financial transactions by these corporate entities—proves the antiquity of this notion.

10. Economic Transactions. Another assumption that belongs to the oldest and most basic elements of economic activity.

11. Valuation. Aristotle's distinction between value in use and value in exchange (cf. Schumpeter [1954], p. 60) and his concern with the problem of a just price are indication enough that different rules of valuation were conceived long before the Middle Ages.

The remaining basic assumptions (3 and 4 as well as 12 to 18) are so closely connected with accounting in the modern sense that it is difficult to associate their origin with ideas preceding double-entry bookkeeping.

4.2 THE ADVENT OF THE DUALITY APPROACH

The double-entry system of the *massari* (stewards) of the Genoese commune for the year 1340 supplies evidence that the duality principle definitely was a cultural possession of early Renaissance and was not, as erroneously believed, an invention of Fra Luca Bartolomeo Pacioli, a fact that does not deprive this Franciscan monk, and friend of Leonardo da Vinci,[2] of his eminent role in the history of our discipline. It was his merit to have first *published*[3] a systematic presentation of double-entry bookkeeping. The famous chapter on "Particularis de computis et scripturis" (of Pacioli's *Summa de arithmetica, geometrica, proportioni et proportionalita*, published at Venice in 1494) will remain the mark-stone of a cultural event that has been ranked with the achievements attained by Columbus, Copernicus, Galileo, Descartes, and Newton. This may sound outrageous in a time when most of us are conditioned by a positivistic indoctrination[4] which often distracts our attention from cultural forces be-

---

[2]Cf. Durant [1953], Vol. V, pp. 222, 225.

[3]In 1458 already Benedetto Cotruglio Raugeo *wrote* a book *Della mercatura et del mercante perfetto* which contained a presentation of double-entry bookkeeping. But this treatise remained unpublished until 1573. See Peragallo [1938], pp. 54–55.

[4]Cf. ". . . the positivistic attitude appears at present to be triumphant, at least here in the United States, in the so-called behavioral sciences. The sociologist and psychologist aspire to construct their sciences on the model of physics and therefore have a marked penchant for data that are 'objective,' quantitative, and physical. To be sure, this attitude is more often than not an unconscious and crude positivism, maintained by savants who have a marked distaste for philosophy but who, nevertheless, are likely to philosophize unconsciously all over the map." (Barrett and Aiken [1962], Vol. 3, p. 20.)

yond the natural sciences and pure mathematics. But the following quotations demonstrate that eminent men like Goethe, Sombart, Spengler, Cayley, Friedell, and others who were deeply concerned with the cultural influences and changes of Western society, attribute utmost importance to the advent of the duality approach.

4.21   Some Views on Double-Entry Bookkeeping

Goethe in his educational fiction of *Wilhelm Meister* calls the double-entry bookkeeping "one of the finest discoveries of the human intellect." Werner Sombart, the prodigious economist-sociologist, expresses his believe that:

. . . double-entry bookkeeping is borne of the same spirit as the system of Galileo and Newton . . . . With the same means as these, it orders the phenomenon into an elegant system, and it may be called the first cosmos built upon the basis of a mechanistic thought. Double-entry bookkeeping discloses to us the cosmos of the economic world by the same method as later the cosmos of the stellar universe was unveiled by the great investigation of natural philosophy. (Sombart [1902], p. 119 trans.)

Oswald Spengler—writing at a time when many regarded Pacioli the "inventor" of the double-entry approach—refers to the monetary and economic thinking of Western society and points out that: ". . . the decisive event, however, was the invention . . . of double-entry bookkeeping by Fra Luca Pacioli in 1494 . . . and indeed its author may without hesitation be ranked with his contemporaries Columbus and Copernicus." (Spengler [1928], Vol. II., p. 490.)

Arthur Cayley, one of the founders of modern matrix algebra, was much interested in the double-entry phenomenon and asserts that: "The Principles of Book-keeping by Double Entry constitute a theory which is mathematically by no means uninteresting: it is in fact like Euclid's theory of ratios an absolutely perfect one, and it is only its extreme simplicity which prevents it from being as interesting as it would otherwise be." (Cayley [1894], p. 5.)

But the last phrase of this statement does not hold any more. Today we recognize beside the double-entry (or duality) principle seventeen further basic assumptions and are in a position to connect some of them to theorems, with rigorous proofs; today we apply these principles to consolidation procedures and deal with several (macro-) accounting systems that were unknown to our ancestors in the nineteenth century; furthermore we are now confronted with a huge number of complex hypotheses.

Egon Friedell even attempts to explain double-entry out of the general dualism which in his opinion dominates modern man:

Through all the phenomena that the age produced there runs a break, a split, a great seam, the feeling of a world-ruling dualism—the *man of two souls* makes his entry into history. . . . It was in this same period, too, that dualistic technique took charge in a very different sphere from that of theology—namely, commercial arithmetic. Under the newly-invented system of double-entry bookkeeping, *partita doppia, loi digraphique*, the usage of entering every item on two opposite pages made every account a *coincidentia oppositorum*. (Friedell [1930], Vol. I., pp. 134–135.)

Spengler also hints at a parallel between two methodological inventions, the Cartesian co-ordinate system (through which geometry was made accessible to algebraic, analytical formulation) and the double-entry bookkeeping system.

4.22 Duality, a Methodological Achievement

Indeed it is this thought which must be pursued to make the significance of the duality principle plausible—especially to those who discredit methodological innovations and regard behavioral research and mathematical deductions as the only areas from which the social sciences may expect any progress. Descartes' revolutionary achievement in mathematics, however, does not merely lie in the deduction of new theorems; above all, it is to be found in a fundamental methodological reorganization. Like the Cartesian system of co-ordinates, the duality approach offered a new framework for *organizing and systematizing data*. It is the need of a method for describing and quantifying economic events in a *systematic way*, together with its unique fulfillment in accounting, that has elevated this dualism to so lofty a place. It was neither a purely mathematical achievement nor one of empirical research, but a triumph of methodology. One that *permits the co-ordinating of economic events* by a simple but powerful principle that can be extended to a wide range of needs. It is the duality approach with its paraphernalia that *converts the loose quantitative data* of an economic entity *into a well-structured set*. In this regard the accomplishment can be compared to another turning point of cultural evolution: the formulation of sentences out of incoherent sounds. The latter may well serve to transmit information—and probably were used by early man in the same way as apes, dogs, birds, and other creatures still make use of them—but the informational content can be immensely enhanced if these loose sounds are being *structured* by means of sentences. Similarly, *one may subject certain economic data to a dual classification, thereby imposing upon these data a preconceived structure that lends added meaning to the information transmitted.* This argument roots in

Wittgenstein's philosophy, which regards "language" as a pervading means of organizing cognitive experience, not merely as an instrument of thought and communication.

But in spite of the obvious advantages of the accounting language, in spite of the high praise it has received from many eminent people and serious scholars, in spite of its versatile application, it has lost much prestige during recent years. Today, accounting is criticized as being based on empty identities, as being concerned with trivial problems, as propagating unscientific methods, as hampering progress in business administration and economics. These accusations can only be understood in the light of a one-sided pseudo-positivistic thinking which presently influences most of the social sciences. Positivism, as a philosophy, has contributed substantially to scientific advancement and the accusations brought forth against our discipline cannot be brushed off with a few phrases. In the last chapter—after accounting has been thoroughly illuminated—an attempt shall be made to explain these charges against our discipline and to answer the questions thus brought about.

4.23   Notes on the Remaining Basic Assumptions

The most decisive assumption introduced by the advent of double-entry, no doubt, is our basic assumption 4 (Duality) which can be extracted from the Chapters XI and XII of Pacioli's "Particularis de computis et scripturis." Since the duality approach necessitates a structuring of the entity by means of a set of interrelated accounts, and since there is no historical evidence of such interrelated accounts before the development of double-entry bookkeeping, our assumption 5 (Structure: cf. Chapter XIII of "Particularis...") may be regarded as a natural consequence of the duality principle. Much less obvious in early double-entry bookkeeping are the remaining assumptions (12 to 18). Many of them were made implicitly, often without awareness of the variety of alternative hypotheses and their consequences; other postulates assumed more explicit forms. Among the latter our assumption 12 (Realization) plays an especially important role. As de Roover [1956, p. 144] states: 'Accrual accounting, therefore, is nothing new; it antedates 1400. So does depreciation, since the statement of Francesco Di Marco Datini & Co. in Barcelona, Jan. 31, 1399, indicates that £16.17 s. were written off on office equipment and charged to expenses." But the awareness of this postulate and the choice of an appropriate hypothesis within this assumption was not universal. In the case of Quesnay's *tableau économique* the fallacy of regarding the agricultural sector as the only productive one, ultimately rests in the realization assumption. The next section offers evidence that this fallacy was due to Quesnay's failure to break down properly the total consumption into final and intermediate consumption. His oversimplified hypothesis obviously was a misleading choice of historical consequence.

Assumptions 9 (Entities), 13 (Classification), and 14 (Data input) hardly constituted difficulties in early bookkeeping. But the search for optimal classification hypotheses became more precarious with increasing complexity of the entity structure. Thus far the solutions were frequently of dogmatic nature and usually evolved out of trial and error (e.g., *the basic charts of accounts*, as used in Continental Europe, see Chapter 3). The constant improvement of the classification and the data input by experience is furthermore revealed in the changes in national income accounting (compare the 1954 *Supplement to the Survey of Current Business* with that of 1958) and other macro-accounting systems (e.g., compare the discussion of flow of funds analysis in the 1955 issue, pp. 1085–1124, with that of the 1959 issue, pp. 828–1062 of the *Federal Reserve Bulletin*).

Assumption 15 (Duration) customarily uses nowadays (with few exceptions) the hypothesis of *infinite life* of the entity (broken down in annual fiscal periods). In early bookkeeping similar hypotheses may have occasionally been implied. Frequently, however, a periodic accounting cycle did not exist and measurement was based on individual business ventures the length of which could be fairly well estimated, and at the end of which most assets were converted into ready-cash. Assumption 16 (Extension) became acute comparatively recently because of two events: (1) The construction of consolidated financial statements for parent companies and (2) the development of macro-accounting. In both cases specific consolidation hypotheses must be made wherever the measurement is based on data for subentities. Similarly, assumption 18 (Allocation) becomes significant only where subentities and similar subdivisions are present. Above all, this is the case in cost accounting where the hypotheses belonging to this assumption are vital but often controversial. The latter is due to the lack of a reliable organization-theoretical basis from which such allocation hypotheses could be derived.

4.3   THE TABLEAU ÉCONOMIQUE

Quesnay's *tableau économique* constitutes a further methodological achievement of our discipline. It is more closely tied to accounting than usually recognized and has been under the cross-fire of scientific controversy for some two hundred years: being highly praised by economists ranging from Mirabeau, through Smith[5] and Marx to Schumpeter, and being criticized or rejected by economists of lesser stature.[6] Schumpeter [1953, pp. 232, 239] points out that "Quesnay... has to this day been receiving less than his due as a scientific economist...." because "the over-all description of a stationary economic process which Quesnay embodied in his *tableau* is not, as his pupils and practically all critics believed, the centerpiece of that structure but an addition to it that is separable from the rest.... What it [the *tableau*] depicts is the flow of expenditures and products between social classes...." This quantitative description of flows of economic objects makes the *tableau* one of the historic foundation stones of modern accounting.

4.31   Duality without Double-Entry

It is striking that on one hand Quesnay's system applied quite methodically the *duality principle* to a national economy (shift in entity!) without using double-entry bookkeeping.[7] On the other hand, it continued the tradition of national income statistics—so brilliantly introduced by Sir William Petty in his *Verbum Sapienti* 1665 (almost a century before Quesnay's *Analysis of the Arithmetical Formula of the Economic Table of the Distribution of the Annual Expenditure of an Agricultural Nation*, completed in 1758 and published in 1760)— without renouncing the power of co-ordinating otherwise unstruc-

---

[5]See also Adam Smith [1776], p. 637 and on p. 643 Smith's quotation of Mirabeau that "There have been... three great inventions which have principally given stability to political societies, independent of many other inventions which have enriched and adorned them. The first, is the invention of writing, which alone gives human nature the power of transmitting, without alterations, its laws, its contracts, its annals, and its discoveries.   The second, is the invention of money, which binds together all the relations between civilized societies. The third, is the Oeconomical Table, the result of the other two, which completes them both by perfecting their object; the great discovery of our age, but of which our posterity will reap the benefit." In the light of our evidence that Quesnay came extremely close to present-day national income and product accounting, Mirabeau's statement now appears less of an exaggeration than it did some decades or a century ago.

[6]E.g., Gray [1931], p. 106] who, referring to the *tableau*, asserts that "it may be doubted whether it will ever be anything but a vast mystification, a subject to be treated gingerly by commentators, rendered uneasy by the feeling that they do not quite understand what they are talking about."

[7]The earliest version of the *tableau* is depicted on p. 107:

tured information into an organic whole.[8]   We believe that this hybrid position—of being neither a double-entry system in the old-fashioned sense of bookkeeping, nor plain income statistics, but a combination that draws upon the advantages of both—which emerged first in the *tableau économique*, will be characteristic for future accounting systems in general.   Today this feature is typical for "social" accounting systems, but before long business account-ants too, will realize that the advantages of accounting do not de-pend on double-entry but on double-classification (which is attain-able by a single entry or other means); do not depend on the punctilious recording of individual events but on the recording of (sometimes highly) aggregated transactions.

Notably, the interest in Quesnay's work has recently been re-vived.   Due to Leontief's [1951, p. 9] recognition of the *tableau's* ancestry to interindustry analysis, and Phillips' [1955] attempt to present the *tableau* as a simple Leontief model, Quesnay's work

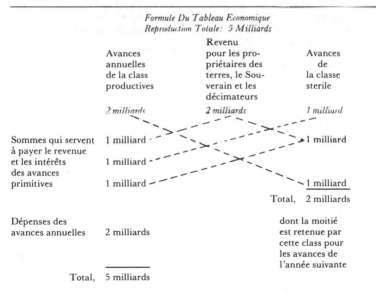

Quesnay "Analyse du Tableau Économique," collected by Oncken [1888], p. 316. Another version is found under the title "Problème Economique" in the *Journal de l'agri-culture, du commerce et de finance*, August, 1766, collected by Oncken [1888], p. 500.

[8]Before the appearance of the *tableau économique* there existed at least eight national income estimates (six for England and Wales and two for France).   The pioneers in national income measurement are Sir William Petty (1623–87) and Gregory King (1648–1712) on the English side, Pierre le Pesant de Boisguillebert (1646–1714) and marshal Sebastien de Vauban (1633–1707) on the French side.   Cf. Studenski [1958], pp. 26–62.

seems to experience a new vogue.[9] However, the *tableau* is at least as closely related to national income accounting as it is to input-output analysis, and we shall try to explain Quesnay's *tableau économique* by presenting it in accounts form, examining its essential features and its deviation from the present-day notion of national income and product accounting.

4.32   The Elements of the Tableau

Quesnay hypothesizes for the economy of France under Louis XV the following three social classes and economic sectors:

I. The farmers (*class productive*) which cultivate the land rented from the landowners. The Physiocratic school around Quesnay regarded this the truly "productive" sector of the economy since it alone is supposed to produce a "surplus" (*produit net* that goes as rent payment to class II). That means only agriculture is assumed to create—with a given amount of permanent land improvement (*avances foncières*) and fixed capital (*avances primitives*)—an output larger in value than all its inputs (*avance annuelles* consisting of labor, seed, other recurring expenses—except rent—interest, and depreciation). Our accounting presentation will reveal that the fallacy of this approach lies in the Physiocrats' specific hypothesis of the *realization principle* (see our basic assumption 4).

II. The landowners (*class des proprietaires*) comprising the feudal landlords, the state (*le souverain*) and the Church, who own the land with all its belongings and who have a claim on rent income.

III. The artisans (*class stérile*), comprising what corresponds in brought terms to the *bourgeoisie*, produce manufacturing goods (and services which are neglected) without creating any surplus, merely reproducing the value of all the inputs to this sector.

Quesnay is concerned in his *tableau économique* with two major problems:[10]

(1) To estimate the values of the transactions between the three sectors and to determine the participation of these sectors in the creation and consumption of the national product. (It can hardly be

---

[9]This is signified by the number of papers published about Quesnay: Vol. I (1886–1924) of the *Index of Economic Journals* (Homewood: Irwin [1961]) lists two articles about Quesnay by the same author; Vols. II (1925–39), III (1940–49), and IV (1950–54) list none; and Vol. V (1954–59) lists three articles by three different authors.

[10]Cf. with Bauer [1895, p. 9] who lists *three* fundamental problems which in our presentation are somewhat reformulated and consolidated into two.

denied that this is a typical task of national income and product accounting in the modern sense.)

(2) To determine that flow of goods (for consumption and investment purposes) between the three sectors which leads to a *maximal* national income. This is a typical optimization problem and discloses one relationship between the *tableau économique* and Leontief's *input-output table*. Obviously, Quesnay had to search for his "solution" by trial and error, that means without the analytical apparatus at the disposal of modern mathematical economics. But the mere vision of these problems and the courageous attempt to find— in spite of much adversity and personal sacrifices—a solution to the precarious situation of the French economy in the second half of the 18th century, are fundamental achievements of theoretical and applied economics alike. The *tableau* is not free from obscurities and conceptual difficulties. Its original version reveals that the idea of duality was materialized by descriptive means which have little to do with *comptabilité* and the *loi digraphique*.

4.33 The Tableau in Accounts Form

Quesnay (as a famous doctor and court physician of Madam Pompadour) does not seem to have been very familiar with the idiosyncrasies of the double-entry system. This may be regretted, as the *tableau* could have been presented much more lucidly by means of bookkeeping techniques. Further difficulties arise out of the time series that were incorporated into the *tableau*, breaking down a single accounting period according to the monetary redistribution: "Quesnay was apparently troubled by the problem of explaining where the money came from to get his process started. To solve this he used a sort of period analysis not completely unlike that used in the Robertsonian method for analyzing national income" (Phillips [1955], p. 142). Since this aspect of period analysis only distracts from the main problem we shall here abstain from pursuing the money circulation and repeated redistribution problem (in form of geometric progressions), but concentrate on global transactions between the sectors.

We may assume, at the beginning of a fiscal period, the following consolidated balance sheets[11] for Quesnay's three classes or sectors:

---

[11]These balance sheets contain only those values relevant immediately for the economic flows to be depicted; they do not contain the land and other *noncirculating* properties held by the various classes.

CONSOLIDATED BALANCE SHEET OF THE FARMERS
(At the Beginning *or* End of the Fiscal Period)

Dr		Cr
Cash 2,000	Liabilities.......... 2,000	
Food 3,000	Owners' Equity 5,000	
Raw Material 2,000		
7,000	7,000	

CONSOLIDATED BALANCE SHEET OF THE LANDOWNERS
(At the Beginning *or* End of the Fiscal Period)

Dr		Cr
Receivables 2,000	Owners' Equity 2,000	

CONSOLIDATED BALANCE SHEET OF THE ARTISANS
(At the Beginning *or* End of the Fiscal Period)

Dr		Cr
Mfg. Goods 2,000	Owners' Equity 2,000	

The *tableau économique* does not present these data in account and balance sheet form but such a presentation indicates the starting point of our circulatory system much better. Since Quesnay's economy is perfectly *stationary*, the above-stated balance sheet data hold for the beginning as well as the end of the fiscal period. The ensuing aggregate transactions are shortly explained in the following and for the sake of clarity are listed in (what accountants call) "journal entry form." (The first listing refers to the debit, the second to the credit aspect).

1. The farmers, owing rent to the landowners (see consolidated balance sheets) in the amount of 2,000 (all figures are in '000£) from the preceding fiscal period, redeem this debt by cash payment:

   Liabilities—farmers................................. 2,000
       Cash—farmers 2,000
   Cash—landowners.................................... 2,000
       Receivables—landowners 2,000

2. The landowners purchase (always against cash) food, etc., from the farmers in the amount of 1,000:

   Food—landowners................................. 1,000
       Cash—landowners 1,000
   Cash—farmers..................................... 1,000
       Food—landowners 1,000

3. The landowners purchase manufacturing goods, etc., from the artisans in the amount of 1,000:

   Mfg. Goods—landowners 1,000
       Cash—landowners 1,000
   Cash—artisans 1,000
       Mfg. Goods—artisans 1,000

4. The artisans purchase food from the farmers in the amount of 1,000:

```
Cash—farmers...................................  1,000
    Food—farmers..............................          1,000
Food—artisans .................................  1,000
    Cash—artisans.............................          1,000
```

5. The farmers purchase manufacturing goods from the artisans in the amount of 1,000:

```
Cash—artisans .................................  1,000
    Mfg. Goods—artisans.......................          1,000
Mfg. Goods—farmers ...........................  1,000
    Cash—farmers..............................       •   1,000
```

6. The artisans purchase raw material from the farmers in the amount of 1,000:

```
Cash—farmers...................................  1,000
    Raw Material—farmers .....................          1,000
Raw Materials—artisans.........................  1,000
    Cash—artisans.............................          1,000
```

The remaining (intrasectoral) transactions correspond to closing entries and serve the construction of an *income and product account*. These transactions are implied by Quesnay but were not so explicitly formulated as they are in our presentation.

7. Consumption of the food purchased by the landowners:

```
Income and Product—landowners ..................  1,000
    Food—landowners..........................          1,000
```

8. Consumption of manufacturing goods purchased by the landowners:

```
Income and Prod.—landowners.....................  1,000
    Mfg. Goods—landowners.....................          1,000
```

9. Consumption of self-produced food by the farmers:

```
Income and Prod.—farmers .......................  1,000
    Food—farmers..............................          1,000
```

10. Consumption of self-produced raw materials by the farmers:

```
Income and Prod.—farmers .......................  1,000
    Raw Mat.—farmers..........................          1,000
```

11. Consumption of manufacturing goods purchased by the farmers:

```
Income and Prod.—farmers .......................  1,000
    Mfg. Mat.—farmers.......................:...          1,000
```

12. Production of food (new harvest) by the farmers:

```
Food—farmers...................................  3,000
    Income and Prod.—farmers..................          3,000
```

13. Production of raw material (new harvest) by the farmers:

```
Raw Mat.—farmers...............................  2,000
    Income and Prod.—farmers..................          2,000
```

14. New rent (*produit net*) due—from farmers to landowners for the current fiscal period in the amount of 2,000:

```
Income and Prod.—farmers .......................  2,000
    Liabilities—farmers.......................          2,000
```

Receivables—landowners 2,000
    Income and Prod.—landowners 2,000

This is the only intersectoral transaction among our closing entries, thus it appears as a *requited* flow similar to the transactions 1 to 6 (Cf. comment (*c*) to basic assumption 10).

15. Consumption of food purchased by the artisans:

Income and Prod.—artisans 1,000
    Food—artisans 1,000

16. Consumption of raw material purchased by the artisans:

Income and Prod.—artisans 1,000
    Raw Mat.—artisans 1,000

17. Production of manufacturing goods by the artisans in the amount of 2,000:

Mfg. Goods—artisans 2,000
    Income and Prod.—artisans. 2,000

We now may record all these transactions, including the beginning balances, in a system of accounts. To attain a good survey we use for this purpose an accounting matrix; there the columns represent the debit sides and the rows the credit sides of the various accounts. We regard each sector (or social class) as a subentity for which a closed accounting system exists.

The agricultural sector (class of farmers) has the following accounts:

Cash	Manufacturing Goods
Liability	Income and Product
Food	Owners' Equity
Raw Material	

The capital sector (class of landholders) has the same accounts with the following exceptions:

1. Receivables instead of Liabilities
2. no Raw Material account

The manufacturing sector (class of artisans) has the same accounts as the agricultural sector with the exception of the Liability account which is not required.

The main figures in the accounting matrix (Table 4–1) represent the values assigned to the aggregate transactions (in '000£) while the numbers in parentheses indicate the transactions in conformity with the preceding explanations and "journalizations." Where there is no such number but an asterisk in front of a figure, the latter indicates a beginning balance. Readers not familiar with this kind of representation are referred to Section 3.6. The main purpose of the matrix presentation is surveillance and economy through double classification by means of a single entry. In cases of requited flows (transactions 1 to 6, and 14) obviously two entries will be encountered.

TABLE 4-1

The Tableau Economique Presented in Form of an Accounting Matrix
(Aggregate Transactions Only)
(in '000£)

		Cash	Receiv.	Liabil.	Food	Raw Mat.	Mfg. Goods	Income & Product	Owners' Equity
I Agriculture Sect.	Cash		(1) 2,000				(5) 1,000		
	Liabil.	* 2,000						(14) 2,000	
	Food	(2)1,000 (4)1,000						(9) 1,000	
	Raw Mat.							(10) 1,000	
	Mfg. Goods							(11) 1,000	
	Income & Product				(12) 3,000	(13) 2,000			
	Owners' Equity				* 3,000	* 2,000			
II Proprietory Sect.	Cash	*			(2) 1,000		(3) 1,000		
	Receiv.	(1) 2,000							
	Food							(7) 1,000	
	Mfg. Goods							(8) 1,000	
	Income & Product		(14) 2,000						
	Owners' Equity		* 2,000						
III Manufacturing Sect.	Cash				(4) 1,000	(6) 1,000			
	Food							(15) 1,000	
	Raw Mat.							(16) 1,000	
	Mfg. Goods	(3)1,000 (5)1,000							
	Income & Product						(17) 2,000		
	Owners' Equity						* 2,000		

By adding the debit side (column) and credit side (row) of each account, the reader may check that, indeed, the ending balances are identical with the beginning balances taken from the consolidated balance sheet. To relate this picture to our present-day national

income and product accounting we first extract from the accounting
matrix the income and product accounts:

INCOME AND PRODUCT ACCT.—AGRICULTURAL SECTOR
(For Fiscal Period)

Debit	Credit
(9) Consumption of food..........1,000	(12) Production of food...........3,000
(10) Consumption of raw mat. 1,000	(13) Production of raw mat........2,000
(11) Consumption of mfg. goods ...1,000	
(14) *Rent* (Surplus) 2,000	
5,000	5,000

INCOME AND EXPENDITURE ACCT.—PROPRIETORY SECTOR
(FOR FISCAL PERIOD)

Debit	Credit
(7) Cons. of food 1,000	(14) *Rent* (income)................2,000
(8) Cons. of mfg. goods 1,000	
2,000	2,000

INCOME AND EXPENDITURE ACCT.—MANUFACTURING SECTOR
(FOR FISCAL PERIOD)

Debit	Credit
(15) Cons. of food 1,000	(17) Production of mfg. goods......2,000
(16) Cons. of raw mat..............1,000	
2,000	2,000

These income and product (or expenditure) accounts reflect the
thesis that only the agricultural sector creates a surplus (*produit net*)
—which goes as rent to the landowners (Government and Proprietory Sector). Why, in this system, does agriculture alone appear
to be "productive," and why is Quesnay's *produit net* so much at
variance with the "net product" or Net National Product of social
accounting? From the following analysis we shall conclude that this
is due to *the failure to distinguish clearly between final and intermediate consumption.* Although the Physiocrats were aware of such a distinction,
they did not draw the necessary consequence of eliminating intermediate consumption (from their income and product calculation).
Had they followed more closely the conceptual scheme proposed by
earlier authors like Sir William Petty, much confusion could have
been avoided.[12]

---

[12]Some of the conceptual confusions (for example the notion that services are not "productive" and do not enhance the income of a nation) were taken over by Adam Smith and
led classical economics far astray. This in spite of Sir William Petty's clear formulation
of the national income concept as the sum of the "Annual Value of the Labour of the

4.34   Quesnay's Failure to Distinguish Properly between Final and Intermediate Consumption

Thus far our presentation used exclusively figures supplied by Quesnay. Yet, in order to link the *tableau économique* to modern national income accounting one additional set of assumptions is necessary. This is the breakdown of the total consumption, or as we shall call it total acquisition, into final and intermediate consumption (and, if desired, acquisition for capital formation). Quesnay did not assume net capital formation (beyond investment for replacement) but for the sake of comparison we shall, in the following, assume detailed data not only for final and intermediate consumption but also for investment purposes. (We hypothesize that the agricultural sector's investment is for replacement purposes only, while the investment of the other sectors serves economic expansion). The reader will notice from Table 4-2 that for each commodity and sector the total of final consumption plus intermediate consumption plus investment, corresponds to Quesnay's original data, contained on the debit sides of the first set of our income (and product or expenditure) accounts.

TABLE 4-2
ASSUMED BREAKDOWN OF QUESNAY'S "TOTAL ACQUISITION OF GOODS"
BY INDIVIDUAL SECTORS

	Final Consumption	Intermediate Consumption	Investment and Reinvestment*	Total Acquisition
Agricultural Sector:				
Food...............	1,000	-----	-----	1,000
Raw Material......	-----	1,000	-----	1,000
Mfg. Goods........	200	500	300*	1,000
Government and Proprietory Sector:				
Food...............	1,000	-----	-----	1,000
Mfg. Goods........	600	-----	400	1,000
Manufacturing Sector:				
Food...............	1,000	-----	-----	1,000
Raw Material......	-----	900	100	1,000

With the help of this additional information we may construct *revised* income accounts for the three sectors: hereby it proves advantageous to complement the sectors I and III with income and expenditure accounts (in addition to their income and product accounts). All this results in the following set of revised accounts:

People" and of the "Annual Proceeds of the Stock of Wealth of the Nation" which he equated to the "Annual Expenses of the People" and the surplus remaining after the expenses. Cf. Studenski [1958], p. 13.

REVISED INCOME AND PRODUCT ACCT.—AGRICULTURAL SECTOR
(For Fiscal Period)

Dr   Cr

Expenses, Expenditures, etc., for:	Revenues, Income, etc., from Sales of:
(a) Raw Material 1,000	Food to:
(b') Mfg. Goods 500	(e) Own sector 1,000
(b'') Mfg. Goods—rein-	(f) Propr. & Govm. Sect. 1,000
vestment. 300	(g) Mfg. Sect. 1,000
(c) Rent. 2,000	Raw Material to:
(d) Agri. Profit. 1,200	(a) Own sector 1,000
	(h) Mfg. Sector 1,000
5,000	5,000

APPROPRIATION ACCOUNT—AGRICULTURAL SECTOR
(For Fiscal Period)

Dr   Cr

Expenses, Expenditures, etc., for:	Revenues, Income, etc., from:
(e) Food 1,000	(d) Agri. Profit 1,200
(b''') Mfg. Goods—cons. 200	
1,200	1,200

APPROPRIATION ACCOUNT—PROPRIETORY SECTOR
(For Fiscal Period)

Dr   Cr

Expenses, Expenditures, etc., for:	Revenues, Income, etc., from:
(f) Food 1,000	(c) Rent 2,000
Mfg. Goods:	
(i') consumed. 600	
(i'') invested. 400	
2,000	2,000

REVISED INCOME AND PRODUCT ACCOUNT—MANUFACTURING SECTOR
(For Fiscal Period)

Dr   Cr

Expenses, Expenditures, etc., for:	Revenues, Income, etc., from:
(h') Raw Material 900	Mfg. Goods to:
(j) Mfg. Profit. 1,100	(b) Agri. Sector 1,000
	(i) Propr. & Govmt. Sect. . . . 1,000
2,000	2,000

APPROPRIATION ACCOUNT—MANUFACTURING SECTOR
(For Fiscal Period)

Dr   Cr

Expenses, Expenditures, etc., for:	Revenues, Income, etc., from:
(g) Food 1,000	(j) Mfg. Profit 1,100
(h'') Raw Mat.—invested. 100	
1,100	1,100

To facilitate the study of the double classification (or here even double-entry) we have assigned lower-case letters from (a) to (j) to each item. Occasionally there will be several debits or credits to one "transaction" but the debit-credit balance is maintained in each case. E.g., "transaction" (b); this transaction is interesting for another reason as well: it demonstrates that basically there is *no* difference between the purchase (of mfg. goods by the Agricultural Sector) for intermediate consumption on one side and reinvestment (i.e., for replacement) on the other.

4.35   The Tableau as a System of National Income Accounts

The last step is to construct a consolidated income and product account as well as a consolidated income and expenditure account for the entire economy. In doing so one more refinement may be added by revealing the activity of gross and net capital formation in a separate (consolidated) savings and investment account. Thus we obtain the last and ultimate set of accounts which, indeed, shows great affinity to present-day national income and product accounting.

INCOME AND PRODUCT ACCOUNT (CONSOLIDATED)
(For Fiscal Period)

Dr		Cr
Expenses, Expenditures, etc., for:	*Revenues, Income, etc., from Sales for:*	
(c) Rent....................2,000	Consumption:	
(d) Agri. Profit. 1,200	(e + b''') Agri. Sector 1,200	
(j) Mfg. Profit..............1,100	(f + i') Proprietory Sector ..1,600	
	(g) Mfg. Sector.........1,000	
	Investment in:	
	(i'') Mfg. Goods........ 700	
(b'') Capital Consumption	(h'') Raw Mat. 100	
Allowance (= rein-		
vestm. of Mfg. Goods) ... 300		
Gross Product 4,600	Gross Product 4,600	

APPROPRIATION ACCOUNT (CONSOLIDATED)
(For Fiscal Period)

Dr		Cr
Expenses, Expenditures, etc., for:	*Revenues, Income, etc., from:*	
(e + f + g) Food 3,000	(c) Agri. Profits 1,200	
(b''' + i') Mfg. Goods 800	(d) Rent 2,000	
(i'' + h'') Net Savings 500	(j) Mfg. Profits 1,100	
Personal Expenditures 4,300	Personal Income...........4,300	

SAVING AND INVESTMENT ACCOUNT (CONSOLIDATED)
(For Fiscal Period)

Dr			Cr	
Investment in:			*Savings from:*	
(i'') Mfg. Goods	700		(i'') Proprietor. Sect.	400
(h'') Raw Mat.	100		(h'') Mfg. Sect.	100
			Net Savings	500
			(b'') Agri. Sect.	300
Gross Investment:	800		Gross Savings:	800

4.36   Conclusion

Section 4.3 pursued three purposes: (1) To demonstrate that Quesnay's *tableau économique* for the first time used the duality principle in macro-economics and without recourse to a double-entry bookkeeping system.   (2) To prove that the *tableau's* conceptual structure is very close to the modern system of national income and product accounts, and that the former is separated from the latter merely by Quesnay's failure to break down properly the total consumption into final and intermediate consumption (and perhaps to introduce systematically net capital formation).[13]   (3) To illustrate the essence of the *tableau économique* by presenting it (with the original data supplied by Quesnay) in form of an accounting matrix as well as a double-entry accounting system, and to expand the latter by assuming additional data for the breakdown into final consumption, intermediate consumption, and investment (see Table 4–2).

4.4   THE INTERNATIONAL BALANCE OF PAYMENTS

Out of the basic needs to correlate systematically the international transactions of Great Britain, after the Napoleonic wars, a

---

[13]Net capital formation and its significance for economic growth of a nation was undoubtedly understood by Quesnay.   He writes: "Different states of prosperity and adversity of an agricultural nation offer a multitude of other cases than the one cited, each characterized by a different set of figures..."   Cf. Oncken [1888], p. 311.   In a later publication Quesnay presents such a different alternative, based on a "less effective use of its resources, i.e., providing more income to proprietors and less to the sterile class, larger investments by proprietors in agricultural improvements and, hence, a higher ratio of production to the annual advances of producers...." (Cf. Studenski [1958], p. 65.)

Yet, the incorporation of capital formation was incorrectly executed by Quesnay.   The reason for this failure might be better understood by considering the desolate state of the French economy in the second half of the 17th century.   There a net capital formation might have been doubtful indeed.

As regards distinguishing between final and intermediate production, Quesnay did not fail to see the issue, but his criterion (of productive versus unproductive labor) was an unfortunate choice for this crucial distinction.

parliamentary committee began in 1819 "to obtain a rough measure of the gold and silver movements of Great Britain. As the members of the committee phrased it, they wanted to determine the "balance of payments of the country" (Lewis [1927], p. 12). Thus originally this tool was designed to measure the net amount of specie passing to or from Great Britain during a year. It gave impact to the development of a system of "international accounts" during the nineteenth century in various countries (Great Britain, U.S.A., Russia, and Austria).[14] Structurally, the balance of payments is a very simple form of an accounting system. The duality principle is here manifested in several ways:

First, in the (theoretical) equality of the debit and credit side of a country's balance of payment with *any* other country (and hence with that of *all* foreign countries, i.e., *the international balance of payments* of the pertinent nation or economy).

Second, in the system of international accounts of the entire world (or a segment of it—cf. Meade [1951], p. 335). This reveals the need for double classification and hence the accounting character of such a system.

Third, in the close connection of the balance of payment with national income accounting. Most of the latter systems (that of the U.S.A., the U.N., the OEEC, etc.) contain a *foreign transactions account* (also called "rest of the world account"; see Subsection 4.53) which is a modified version of the country's international balance of payment. Apart from minor classificational deviations and some simplifications the main difference is characterized by the fact that the international transaction account is a *reflection* of the international balance of payments. In the latter the imports appear on the debit side, the exports on the credit side; while the international transaction account, which is an account of "the rest of the world," must obviously show imports (from the rest of the world) as credits, and exports as debits.

It cannot be the task of this section to discuss the international balance of payments in detail. The interested reader is referred to Meade's [1951] thorough treatment of this topic. For the sake of illustration a schematic presentation of an International Balance of Payment (based on the form used in the United States) follows.

The concepts used in the balance of payment are similar to those used in the foreign transactions account (of the national income ac-

---

[14]Cf. Lewis [1927], p. 11–15.

INTERNATIONAL BALANCE OF PAYMENTS

Expenditures for:	*Receipts from:*
Merchandise imports	Merchandise exports
	(other than govmt. financed)
Military services, etc.	
	Services, income, and military sales
Other services, income remit-	
tances, and pensions	Foreign capital flow (net):
	Changes in holdings of foreign
Unilateral transfers (net):	short-term assets and govmt.
Private remittances, etc.	securities
Govmt. (nonmilitary)	
	Changes in holdings of
Capital outflow (net):	other foreign assets
Direct investment	
Portfolio and short-term	Gold transfers
investment.	
	Errors and omissions
Total charges to Balance of Payments.	Total credits to Balance of Payments.

counts) but are *not* identical and are to be reconciled by accounting identities.

Finally a transaction matrix of several countries, as presented by Meade, shall further demonstrate the connection between national and international payments as well as the usefulness of an accounting approach in such an analysis (Table 4–3).

It assumes "a world" consisting of five countries and illustrates the relationship between national incomes, domestic expenditures, and the (visible plus invisible) imports and exports of the countries concerned. Meade uses this accounting matrix to analyze international equilibria and disequilibria, the impact-effect of changes in domestic expenditures upon national incomes and balances of payments (under the assumption of varying marginal propensities to import). He also considers multilateral price adjustments under varying elasticities of demand and varying exchange rates.

Such an approach not only manifests the duality principle but the other basic assumptions as well. These assumptions are rarely systematically presented, many of them are merely implied, but the following passage illustrates how assumptions 11 (*Valuation*) and 12 (*Realization*) and the hypotheses arising out of them are made explicit:

First, how should the imports and exports be valued? Here the most obvious example of the many possible causes of divergence is the question whether imports should be recorded as including the insurance and freight involved in shipping them from the country of export (c.i.f.) or whether

TABLE 4-3

NETWORK OF NATIONAL AND INTERNATIONAL PAYMENTS
FOR VISIBLE AND INVISIBLE TRADE*

$ m

Receiving Countries	Paying Countries					Total i.e., National Income	Total Excludg. Diagonals i.e., Exports	Balance of Trade i.e., Exports Minus Imports
	D_1	D_2	S_1	S_2	B			
	(a)	(b)	(c)	(d)	(e)	(f)	(g)	(h)
D_1 (1)	1,000	8	56	16	5	1,085	85	−70
D_2 (2)	65	500	5	23	12	605	105	−60
S_1 (3)	60	47	1,000	40	83	1,230	230	+95
S_2 (4)	5	82	53	500	5	645	145	+35
B (5)	25	28	21	31	700	805	105	0
Total i.e., domestic expenditure (6)	1,155	665	1,135	610	805	4,370		
Total excluding diagonals, i.e., imports (7)	155	165	135	110	105		670	

Courtesy: Oxford University Press.
*From Meade [1951], p. 335.

they should be recorded as including only the value of the goods when put on board the ship at the exporting country's port (f.o.b.). (Meade [1951], p. 20.)

A second and similar problem arises in determining the point of time at which commodity trade should be valued. Goods are exported from country A to country B. Should this appear in the exports of A and the imports of B when payment is made for the goods, when the liability for the transaction is incurred, or when the goods actually move from A to B, and in this last case should it be when the goods leave A or when they reach B? (Meade [1951], p. 22.)

4.5   CONTRIBUTIONS OF THE TWENTIETH CENTURY

4.51   Fisher's Income and Wealth Analysis by Means of the Accounting Model

Previous centuries laid the foundations, and created the pre-conditions for the application of accounting in various micro- and macro-economic areas. But during the twentieth century the duality approach found even more diverse application. This was greatly facilitated by Irving Fisher's theoretical spadework. From the viewpoint of theory, accounting and economics (before Fisher), were separate areas which nobody bothered to connect. Accounting was strictly for the business man and had little to do with economic theory until "Irving Fisher took a first step toward co-ordinating the economist's and the accountant's work," as Schumpeter [1954, p. 945] formulates it. Fisher's *Nature of Capital and Income* [1906] "forms a sort of philosophy of economic accounting" and supplies "a link long missing between the ideas and usages underlying practical business transactions and the theories of abstract economics," as Fisher [1906, p. vii] himself asserts. Though the above-stated work primarily refers to micro-economic aspects of income and wealth, it has equal impact on macro-economics and national income accounting. To this Ohlsson [1953, p. 48] offers the following evidence: "But although Fisher's work was not intended as a basis for practical statistical work of a national accounting type, he gives certain definitions and arguments which could very well have been taken from present-day works about national accounting.

"Fisher aims at giving clear-cut definitions for the concepts of capital and income, and one thing he uses for this is an accounting technique." Reference to some of Fisher's concepts was made in Section 2.2, and although these concepts could only be used as starting points, we fully recognize the importance of Fisher's ingenious stroke of using the balance sheet (or "capital account" as he calls it) and the income statement (or "income account") for the conceptualization of fundamental economic notions as well as for the analysis of many income and wealth aspects. Among accountants this particular contribution to our discipline seems to be underrated or underemphasized.[15] But Fisher's memory is definitely preserved in *The Economics of Accountancy* written under Fisher's inspiration by his disciple John Canning [1929], and in the area of capital budgeting which is closely related to the valuation problems of accounting.

4.52   Cost, Managerial, and Funds Accounting

Though the beginnings of cost accounting are not to be found in the twentieth century, the "general" acceptance of cost accounting practice and the creation of a specialized theoretical body belongs

---

[15]Most books in the history of accounting neither bother to mention Fisher's contribution nor do they list his name in the index. Ohlsson [1953, p. 51] has a similar complaint: "Fisher's system has, I believe, attracted too little notice in the theoretical discussions of national accounting."

to this century. Individual features of cost accounting can be traced to a time between 1400 and 1600. Thus already in the first stage of double entry bookkeeping it was realized that its principal ideas are applicable to a wide range of situations. On occasions these principles were extended to the costing of manufacturing processes. Records from various industries, such as weaving, mining, and printing, provide evidence that raw material and payroll accounts, manufacturing or work in process accounts, job-order and perpetual inventory accounts were known long before the industrial revolution got under way. But the conception of an idea is not to be confused with its application on a large scale. In many instances cost data were first collected on a purely "statistical" basis without any application of the duality principle. Later the aggregate value flows within the area of manufacturing—i.e., the prorating of the manufacturing costs to the various departments and the further prorating of these costs to the various products by means of factory overhead coefficients—were recorded on a work sheet utilizing double classification. This approach utilizes all features of accounting without, however, recording details on a double-entry basis. A further stage of development is the recording of cost data by means of double entries, bringing about a complete integration of financial and cost accounting in many enterprises.

With the advent of cost and managerial accounting, *discussions about alternative hypotheses* became more acute. It was realized that the problems of valuation, realization, classification, data input, extension, materiality, and allocation offer a variety of alternative solutions. But instead of a systematic analysis, matching a specific purpose with a specific alternative, discussions and controversies often arose about "*the* correct method." For major issues (e.g., direct costing versus absorption costing) a more functional approach was finally realized.

The development of the *flow of funds statement* as an additional instrument of information—besides the balance sheet and income statement—stems from a definite need felt by management and the accounting profession. The "traditional" financial statements are too vague with regard of information about the use and application of liquid funds within the area of long-term assets and claims. Thus by introducing additional hypotheses on classification, materiality, and allocation, the flow of funds statements—derived by means of double-entry principles and closely tied to financial accounting—provide the relevant data.

With the emergence of new theories in capital budgeting and investment (see Subsection 6.22) a certain conflict between cost accounting and investment theory seems to arise; or as Engels [1962, p. 163] asserts, there exists the danger that investment concepts overgrow or dominate those of cost accounting, just as previously cost accounting concepts dominated those of investment theory. In practice still, wrong decisions are caused by treating investment problems (expenditures for development and research, advertising, etc.) as those of costing. Here the difference between the investor who merely buys stocks and the investor who buys machinery in order to produce becomes acute. In the first case the investor has little choice left, unless he intends to sell the investment; in the second case further decisions must be made, and it ought to be *the task of cost accounting* to control and correct the decisions subsequent to the investment. Based on the necessity for further decisions Churchman [1961, p. 60] rejects the *rate of return* as an evaluation criterion for "entrepreneurial" investments.

A further stage, and one of special significance for the combination of accounting with mathematical methods, was the development of standard cost accounting, periodic budgeting, and related planning activity. Recently several important contributions appeared which illuminate standard costing (Danielson [1963]), periodic budgeting (Stedry [1960]), and the planning activity of the firm (Bonini [1963] and Cyert and March [1963]) from the viewpoint of management science. Further reference to these contributions will be made in the Chapters 8 and 9.

4.53 National Income Accounting

The utilization of the *tableau économique* as a practical tool of economic analysis was restricted to a brief time-span during the seventeenth century. The failure of this first national income accounting system was primarily due to insufficient conceptual clarification (as demonstrated in Subsection 4.34) and due to the close connection of the *tableau* with the quickly vanishing Physiocratic movement and its philosophy. However, national income estimates were continued, and Studenski [1958] gives evidence of no less than 50 estimates for Great Britain and France up to the close of the nineteenth century. To this must be added three lost Russian estimates (eighteenth century), as well as estimates of the United States (1843), Austria (1861), Germany (1863–99), Australasian Colonies (1886), and Norway (1893). The twentieth century brought a progressive continuation of this trend and reintroduced the *accounting* approach to national income statistics. The priority right, in this process of reincarnation of national income accounting, is a controversial issue. English, Scandinavian, and Dutch economists lay claim to this right.[16]   Indeed, during the thirties, theoretical work began independently in at least three countries. This led in the forties to the first publications on national income accounting in Holland (Van Cleeff [1941]), Norway (Frisch [1942]) and Great Britain (Stone [1947]). The United States presented its first official income estimates in account form in 1947 (*Survey of Current Business: 1947 Supplement*). The fact that a problem was attacked simultaneously, yet independently, by several different groups is not unique in the history of science. Usually it is interpreted as a sign expressing the significance and inevitability of such a development. This significance is reflected in Gainsburg's portentous remark (see U.S. Congress [1957], pp. 50–51):

The introduction and development of an integrated system of national accounts promises to rank in historic significance with some of the more heralded inventions of recent decades in the fields of physical sciences. This growing family of income and product statistics is without question

---

[16]Compare the following three statements: "The development of the idea of a double-entry national account of income and expenditure for the whole economy led to the subsidiary idea of constructing similar double-entry accounts of income and expenditure for each sector of the economy. Actually, these two ideas were conceived simultaneously by the same group of English economists—Meade, Stone, and Kaldor—under Keynes's guidance." (Studenski [1958], p. 154.)

"NA have been prepared in Norway for a fairly long time. Most of this work bears the stamp of Ragnar Frisch. The theoretical presentations in Norway have often been made graphically and have become known as the 'Økosirk-system.' It is, however, usually easy to translate this visual presentation to accounting terms, and in practice the Norwegian calculations have as a rule been presented in accounting form. The theoretical work in Norway began in the early thirties and has continued since that time. Unfortunately the results have frequently not been published in printed form but have been presented as mimeographed papers." (Ohlsson [1953], pp. 51, 52.)

"In 1941, the Netherlands Central Bureau of Statistics made an attempt to construct a system of national accounts for the year 1938. This study was stimulated by two articles by Mr. Ed. van Cleeff [1941] in the Dutch monthly *De Economist*.

Mr. van Cleeff, who also initiated the term 'national book-keeping,' used fictitious figures and his system of tables was different from that adopted later by the Central Bureau of Statistics. Owing to the war, the results could not be published, but they were circulated in mimeographed form and were later incorporated in the first postwar publications on the national accounts of the Netherlands. After the war, when contacts with the Anglo-American countries could be re-established, it was found that similar ideas had been developed in the United Kingdom and other countries. However, whereas in the Netherlands the work was concerned mainly with the statistical problems of estimating the various flows in the national accounts, the work in Great Britain was concerned mainly with the development of concepts and definitions." (Derksen's statement cited from Studenski [1958], p. 332. Footnotes omitted.)

one of the major contributions—if not the greatest—of the economic fraternity thus far in the 20th Century.

But the accounting approach was not embraced by all economists. Controversies sprang up, and clarified many conceptual technical and even fundamental issues. Among the arguments and counterarguments we find—in reply to a critical paper by S. Kuznets [1948]—a defense of the accounting approach by a group of well-known economists (Milton Gilbert, George Jaszi, Edward F. Denison, and Charles F. Schwartz [1948]). This statement has become a classic, and shall here be reprinted:

Advantages of the Accounting Approach

In view of the scepticism expressed by Professor Kuznets as to the usefulness of formulating and presenting national income statistics as a system of accounts, we should like to list what we consider to be the main advantages of this approach.

(1) The most important advantage has already been indicated, namely, that a system of economic accounting is a tremendous aid in revealing the structure of the economy and thereby contributes toward a better understanding of its functioning. We believe that the widespread use of such data as an interrelated system in econometric literature is abundant proof of this proposition.

(2) We have found in practice that the accounting approach provides a powerful tool for the solution of many intricate problems that arise in the consistent formulation of national income concepts. The treatment of financial intermediaries, nonprofit institutions, imputed income, and similar problem areas can be worked out consistently for both the national income and national product most readily by setting up the relevant transactions on the debit and credit sides of a system of accounts.

(3) From the reaction of many readers of our report and from our teaching experience, we are much impressed with the usefulness of the accounting approach as a pedagogical device for explaining the nature of national income statistics and the interrelationship of the various aggregates and their components. For instance, to demonstrate effectively that the following equation holds: gross national product − capital consumption allowances + subsidies − current surplus of government enterprises − indirect business tax and nontax liability − business transfer payments − statistical discrepancy = national income (Department of Commerce definitions), it is virtually necessary to establish a national economic accounting system containing separate accounts for the various sectors of the economy.

To give another example, in teaching national income we have found that students have difficulty in fully grasping Professor Kuznets' treatment of government from the explanation he gives in *National Income and Its Composition*. However, it becomes rather easy for most of them to understand when it is cast in the form of a set of accounts (conforming, of course, to Kuznets' definitions). It may be noted, in this connection, that Professor Kuznets' formulation of national income statistics in that volume is based upon a quite rigorous accounting framework, though for some reason he has never chosen to make it explicit.

The pedagogical utility of the accounting approach is not confined to strictly technical national income matters. For example, an explanation of why, and in what sense, savings equal investment is greatly facilitated if it is made with the help of a set of national economic accounts.

(4) We consider the accounting approach to be a great aid in defining the task of statistical collection. Once the particular accounting framework providing the most useful summary of the economic structure has been decided upon, a comprehensive list of requirements for economic statistics emerges rather automatically. As far as we know, a list of requirements obtained in this way provides the only assurance that the collection of primary statistical data will be organized so as to yield the information most relevant to economic analysis. It is our belief, moreover, that organizing the collection of value statistics so as to yield balanced debits and credits from every economic unit that is covered would greatly increase the accuracy of the data and one's knowledge of their precise content.

(5) Finally, the use of the accounting approach facilitates the estimation of the various national income aggregates and their components from the available statistical material. It does this by making clear that many items of information can be obtained from the records of either the buyer or the seller, and hence affords flexibility in adapting estimating methods to available information. In addition, it enables one to check every account for internal consistency by comparing the debit and credit totals as well as the relations among the various debit and credit entries. It also enables one to derive as residuals components of the national economic accounts which cannot be estimated directly from available data. This technique, of course, has been used by estimators who did not employ the accounting approach. Nevertheless, an interrelated system of national accounts had to be implicit in their work, for by no other means can meaningful residual estimates be obtained. We think it is useful to work out the system of accounts in detail so that the potentialities of this technique can be fully explored and understood. (Gilbert et al. [1948], pp. 181–82.)

Stone [1951, pp. 5–6] also emphasizes that "experience seems to show that from a teaching point of view there are great advantages in presenting national income and expenditure estimates and estimates of transactions generally in the form of a simple closed accounting system, because in this way the relationships of the parts to one another are immediately displayed." He then continues to summarize the advantages of the accounting approach (See Stone [1951], pp. 7–8. An earlier statement of similar nature is found in Stone [1947].)

The following five accounts shall enable the reader to survey the structure of present national income accounting. This illustration is a compromise between three similar systems[17] and is simplified enough to be suitable for pedagogic purposes.

I. Income and Product Account

Dr   Cr

Expenses, Expenditures, etc., for:

			Revenues, Income, etc., from Sales to:	
	1.10 Wages, etc.	(2.4)	1.40 Consumers	(2.1)
	1.11 Property income,		1.50 Government	(3.1)
Factor	etc.	(2.5)	1.60 Gross domest. investment	(5.1)
payments	1.12 Corpor. savings	(5.3)	1.70 *Net* exports—imports	(4.1–4.5)
	1.13 Corpor. taxes,			
	etc.	(3.5)		
Other	1.20 Bus. transfers	(2.6)		
values	1.21 Indir. taxes	(3.7)		
added	1.22 Surplus of gvmt.			
	enterprises	(3.4)		
	1.30 Depreciation,			
	etc.	(5.6)		

Gross national product	Gross national "expenditures"

II. Personal Appropriation Account

Dr   Cr

Expenses, Expenditures, etc., for:		*Revenues, Income, etc., from:*	
2.1 Consumers' purchases	(1.40)	2.4 Wages, etc.	(1.10)
2.2 Personal taxes, etc.	(3.6)	2.5 Property income, etc.	(1.11)
2.3 Transfers from r.o.w.	(4.7)	2.6 Business transfers	(1.20)
2.4 Personal saving	(5.4)	2.7 Transfers from govmt.	(3.2)
		2.8 Transfers from abroad	(4.3)

Person. expendts. plus saving	Personal income

III. Government Appropriation Account

Dr   Cr

Expenses, Expenditures, etc., for:		*Revenues, Income, etc., from:*	
3.1 Govmt. purchases	(1.50)	3.4 Surplus of govmt. enterprises	(1.22)
3.2 Govmt. transfers	(2.7)	3.5 Corporation taxes, etc.	(1.13)
3.3 Transfers to r.o.w.	(4.6)	3.6 Personal taxes	(2.2)
3.4 Govmt. saving	(5.5)	3.7 Indirect taxes	(1.21)
		3.8 Transfers from abroad	(4.2)

Govmt. "expendts" plus saving	Government revenues

---

[17]These systems are those of the United States (see U.S. Dept. of Commerce [1958]), of the United Nations (U.N., Studies in Methods No. 2 [1953]), and of the Organization for European Economic Co-operation (OEEC Publication [1952]). For further discussions of national income accounting systems for international comparisons see National Bureau of Economic Research [1958] and [1957] respectively.

IV. FOREIGN TRANSACTIONS ACCOUNT

Dr			Cr
Charges to rest of world:		*Credits to rest of world:*	
4.1 Exports to r.o.w.	(1.70)	4.5 Imports from r.o.w.	(1.70)
4.2 Transfers to govmt.	(3.8)	4.6 Transfers from govmt.	(3.3)
4.3 Transfers to pers. sector	(2.8)	4.7 Transfers to pers. sector	(2.3)
4.4 Net borrowing from r.o.w.	(5.6)	4.8 Net lending to r.o.w.	(5.2)
Total charges to r.o.w.		Total credits to r.o.w.	

V. SAVING AND INVESTMENT ACCOUNT

Dr.			Cr.
Investment:		*Saving:*	
5.1 Gross domestic investment	(1.60)	5.3 Corporate saving	(1.12)
5.2 Net lending to r.o.w.	(4.8)	5.4 Personal saving	(2.4)
		5.5 Govmt. saving	(3.4)
		5.6 Net borrowing from r.o.w.	(4.4)
		5.7 Depreciation, etc.	(1.30)
Gross addition to national wealth		Gross addition to national wealth	

In addition, the following accounting identities reveal important concepts such as national product, national income, personal income, and disposable income, etc.:

+ Personal consumption
+ Gross private domestic investment
+ Net foreign investment
+ Government expenditures

Gross national product
− Capital consumption allowance

Net national product (= national income at market prices)
+ Subsidies (less surplus of govmt. enterprises)
− Indirect business taxes, etc.
−Business transfer payments
− Statistical discrepancy

National income (at factor cost)
− Undistributed corporate profits
− Corporate profit taxes
− Corporate inventory valuation adjustments
− Contributions to social insurance
− Excess of wage accruals over disbursements
+ Net interest paid by government
+ Government transfer payments
+ Business transfer payments

Personal income
− Personal tax payments (etc.)

Disposable income

| Disposable income |
| – Personal savings |
| Personal consumption |

Explanation. The national income and product accounts[18] are based on a combination of functional and institutional classification —hereby the former predominates (in contrast to flow of funds accounting—see next subsection). The Income and Product Account bears resemblance to the profit and loss account or income statement of business accounting.[19] This account I reflects the production activity of the entire economy (not only of the business sector). The accounts II, III, and IV depict the appropriation (i.e., the income and acquisition) of the personal or household sector (which includes all nonprofit organizations), the government sector, and the rest-of-the-world sector. These three accounts are also related to the nominal accounts of business accounting, but a strict adherence to identifying the debit entries with expenses and the credit entries with revenues is not possible. Such concepts break down if applied to the whole economy. The account V is related to the balance sheet of business accounting, but instead of depicting the total assets and claims of the economy, it merely reflects their increments (an increment in assets is defined as investment and an increment in the corresponding claims, as saving). Thus, theoretically, the Saving and Investment Account can be derived by consolidating the changes of the balance sheets of all entities of the economy during a period. Apart from the fact that in practice the technique of data compilation is very intricate, it must be considered that the consolidation hypotheses—basic assumption 17 (Extension)—for national income accounting deviate occasionally from those applied in business accounting.

The foregoing presentation gives evidence of the presence of the first ten of our basic assumptions in national income accounting. Assumption 11 (Valuation) occasionally uses more refined hypotheses than traditional business accounting. The former includes price-level adjustments in respect to inventory valuation. Assumption 12 (Realization) together with assumption 17 (Materiality)

---

[18] In these five accounts we have identified every entry by a number on the left-hand side, the number on the right-hand side (in parentheses) indicates the corresponding counterentry.

[19] Powelson [1955, pp. 71, 253 ff.] demonstrates how, theoretically, income and product accounts can be derived from profit and loss accounts and how they are to be consolidated to a national Income and Product Account.

constitute crucial points in macro-accounting.[20]   The pertaining hypotheses determine which transactions are to be included (or to be recognized as income generating).   Thus they reveal not only major differences between micro- and macro-accounting (e.g., the emergence of capital gains and depletion allowances are legitimate transactions in business accounting, but *not* in national income accounting), they also distinguish various macro-accounting systems from each other (e.g., flow of funds accounting incorporates sales of second-hand goods, national income accounting does not do so.   The latter recognizes the imputed rent of owner-occupied houses as relevant transactions; the purpose of flow of funds accounting, on the other hand, would not permit such an hypothesis).

4.54   Flow of Funds Accounting

The need for analyzing the flow of payments or funds by a system of accounts seems to have been expressed first by Mitchell [1944], but it was Copeland [1952] who first presented a comprehensive study and analysis of money flows in form of a social accounting system.[21]   His disposition toward the accounting approach is expressed as follows:

Accounting patterns have a special advantage for economic analysis. The economic variables they link together in equations may fairly be characterized as independently measurable empirical magnitudes.   Yet because

---

[20]Of course, basic assumption 10 (Economic Transactions) also plays an important role in business accounting, but there, a long-established and rarely challenged (exception: Churchman [1959]) tradition exists that prescribes which transactions are to be included in the system.

[21]The following statement by Dorrance [1961, p. 100 n] indicates that here, too, the determination of priority becomes very complex as soon as historical details are examined:

"It should be emphasized that, except for the two pre-war tables referred to above, the development of financial accounts is a post-war development.   Columbia, Costa Rica, and New Zealand share the credit for publishing the first 'monetary analyses' in 1945.   The impetus for the development of this type of accounting was largely provided by R. Triffin's paper, 'Esbozo General de un Analisis de las Series Estadisticas Sobre Bases Uniformes y Comparables,' submitted to the first Meeting of Central Bank Technicians of the American Continent in Mexico City, 1946.   The United States 'Consolidated Condition Statement for Banks and the Monetary System' was first presented by Morris A. Copeland and Daniel H. Brill, 'Banking Assets and the Money Supply Since 1929,' *Federal Reserve Bulletin*, January, 1948.   Rudimentary monetary analyses for fifty-six countries appeared in the first issue of *International Financial Statistics* published in January, 1948, while complete monetary analyses were first presented in *International Financial Statistics* in January, 1955; they are now available for sixty-five countries.   The first attempt made by any official agency to extend financial analysis beyond monetary analysis is probably the study on 'Some Estimates on the National Wealth of the Netherlands in 1938,' Netherlands Central Bureau of Statistics, *Statistical and Econometric Studies*, 1947, No. 3.   It is believed that the first country to embark on annual publication of a general financial analysis was Finland; the first table appeared in the *Economic Survey* published in 1949."

they are based on double entries for individual transactions, the equalities they assert are firm and objective. When moneyflows measurements are approached from a social accounting viewpoint, they can be made to yield a good many such patterns, one for each transactor group into which the economy is divided and one for each type of transaction account the financial statements for various transactor groups employ. (Copeland [1952], pp. 32–33, footnote omitted.)

Copeland's system reflects the flow of money within several fairly homogeneous sectors of the U.S. economy. This system was modified, elaborated, and given official sanction by the Board of Governors of the Federal Reserve System, incorporating regular publications of *flow of funds* statistics in the *Federal Reserve Bulletin*.[22] In its present form the chief purpose of these accounts is to describe the saving and investment activity of eleven major economic sectors. The accounts corresponding to these sectors reflect details of saving and investment together with the corresponding sources and applications of liquid means.[23] To illustrate this we reprint the following Summary of Flow of Funds Accounts (from the Federal Reserve System [1963], p. 542 [cf. Table 4–4]). To make the entries more plausible we have extracted the Consumer (and Nonprofit) Sector

CONSUMER AND NONPROFIT SECTOR
OF FLOW OF FUNDS ACCOUNTS—FOURTH QUARTER, 1962
(Seasonally Adjusted, in Billions of Dollars)

Use of funds for:		Source of funds from:	
Consumer durables	49.6	Depreciation	48.7
Residence constr.	18.2	Net saving	34.4
Plant and equipmt.	3.7		
Inventory change	—		
Private Capital Expends.	71.6*	Gross Saving	83.1
Demand deposits, etc.	7.9		
Time deposits	26.7		
Life ins. & pension pls.	11.6	Credit market instr.	25.3
Security credit	1.0	Security credit	1.3
Partnerships, etc.	1.6		
Net acquis. of finan. assets	48.8	Net increase in liabilit.	26.6
Sector discrepancy	−10.7		
Total	109.7	Total	109.7

*Discrepancy of 0.1 because of rounding off.

[22]The theoretical foundations and revisions of these flow of funds accounts are given in Federal Reserve System [1955a, 1955b, 1959, 1962].

[23]These flow of funds accounts show some similarities with the flow of funds statements in business accounting, but there exist decisive differences between them, especially with regard to basic assumptions 9 (Entities), 13 (Classification), 14 (Data input), 17 (Materiality), 18 (Allocation), and it would be *misleading* to assert that the flow of funds statement on micro-level corresponds to the flow of funds accounts on the macro-level.

TABLE 4-4

1. SUMMARY OF FLOW OF FUNDS ACCOUNTS FOR FOURTH QUARTER, 1962—SEASONALLY ADJUSTED

(In billions of dollars)

Transaction category	Consumer and nonprofit U	Consumer S	Farm U	Farm S	Noncorp. U	Noncorp. S	Corporate U	Corporate S	U.S. Govt. U	U.S. Govt. S	State and local U	State and local S	Commercial banking U	Commercial banking S	Savings institutions U	Savings institutions S	Insurance U	Insurance S	Finance n.e.c. U	Finance n.e.c. S	Rest-of-world U	Rest-of-world S	All sectors U	All sectors S	Discrepancy U	Natl. saving and investment	
A Gross saving		83.1		4.1		9.0		42.6		-5.5		-6.1		1.5		1.0		1.7		-.7		-1.4		129.3	3.4	139.7	A
B Capital consumption		48.7		4.1		9.0		28.7						.3										90.9			B
C Net saving (A−B)		34.4						13.9		-5.5		-6.1		1.2		1.0		1.7		-.7		-1.4		38.4		124.9	C
D Gross investment (E+J)	93.8		4.1		9.0		31.0		-7.1		-6.3		3.7		.9		3.0		-1.6		.9		131.4			124.9	D
E Private capital expenditures (net of sales)	71.6		5.1		14.1		34.2																125.8			125.8	E
F Consumer durable goods	49.6																						49.6			49.6	F
G Nonfarm resident. constr.	18.2				2.8		2.8																23.8			23.8	G
H Plant and equipment	3.7		5.0		11.1		30.5																51.1			51.1	H
I Change in inventories			.3		.1		.9																1.3			1.3	I
J Net financial invest. (K−L)	22.2		-1.0		-5.1		-2.1		-7.1		-6.3		3.2		.9		2.6		-1.6		.9		5.6		-5.6	-.9	J
K Net acquis. of finan. assets	43.8		*		1.2		9.4		3.4		1.9		30.9		17.3		10.7		8.1		3.0		123.1			2.1	K
L Net increase in liab.		26.6		*		6.3		12.6		10.5		8.3		27.7		16.3		8.1		9.6		2.1		117.5	-5.6	3.0	L
M Gold and U.S. official fgn. exchange									-1.4	*			-1.5								.1		-1.4	-1.4		-1.5	M
N Treasury currency									.1																		N
O Dem. dep. and currency	7.9								.1		-1.1			12.8							.5		10.8	12.8		-.5	O
P Time and savings accounts	26.7													16.2		15.3							31.5	31.5		-1.4	P
Q At commercial banks	11.3													16.2									16.2	16.2			Q
R At savings institutions	15.3															15.3							15.3	15.3			R
S Life insurance reserves	3.0																	3.0					3.0	3.1			S
T Pension reserves	8.6									1.3								4.7					8.6	8.6			T
U Credit market instr.	*	25.3		2.6		1.1	-.1	16.0	4.5	9.1	1.8	5.5	29.9	.1	16.0	1.0	11.7		6.0	3.4	.9	4.1	71.0	70.8	-.2	3.2	U
V U.S. Govt. securities	-1.0						-.4			6.9	-.5		4.9		-.5		.7		2.6	.7	.5		4.6	4.8		-.5	V
W State and local securities	-1.0											4.6	3.3		-.5		2.2		1.5	1.8			4.7	4.6			W
X Corp. and foreign bonds	.2							3.5					.2		.5		2.1		.8		-.1	1.8				1.8	X
Y Corporate stock	-1.1							1.0											-.4	-.4						*	Y
Z 1- to 4-family mortgages	.4	15.4					1.2						2.7		12.1		1.4						17.6	17.6			Z
a Other mortgages	2.6	8.2		1.4		2.0		1.0				.2	1.3		2.9		1.3						8.8	8.8			a
b Consumer credit		8.2					1.7						2.7		.6								8.2	8.2			b
c Bank loans n.e.c.				1.1									3.3						1.8				9.4	9.4			c
d Other loans		.6					-.8	.5	4.2	2.2		.9	3.3		.1		-.6		.1	-.9	.5	2.6	9.4	7.3		-.2	d
e Security credit	1.0	1.3					2.2	-.3					4.5						1.6	5.8	-1		7.1	7.1		.1	e
f Trade credit	1.8			-.3	-.3		2.2	-3.2	.5	.7							-.8						1.8	-3.0	-4.8		f
g Proprietors' net invest. in noncorp. business	1.6			-1.3		2.9	1.4																1.6	1.6			g
h Misc. financial trans.	*		*		.1				-.3	-.7			-1.0	-1.1	.3		-1.3			.5			.6	-2.0	-2.6	-.7	h
i Sector discrepancies (A−D)	-10.7						11.6		.5		-.3		-2.2						.9		-2.3		-2.2		-2.2	5.8	i

NOTE.—Saving and investment concepts are described in notes to Table 2 and the Aug. 1959 BULL., pp. 831–43. Descriptions of sectors and of transaction categories are given in "Technical Notes," Aug. 1959 BULL., pp. 846–59. Seasonal adjustment procedures are described in Nov. 1962 BULL., p. 1399ff.

Courtesy: Board of Governors of the Federal Reserve System

and present it in a more conventional form. The debit side shows the application or use of funds (U), the credit side, the source of funds (S). On the debit side the first section reflects the private capital expenditures broken down into four main categories, the second section depicts "financial" investments of households and nonprofit institutions. But these institutions are not only lenders they are borrowers as well (see second section of credit side) and the balance between this lending and borrowing may be expressed in the following simple identity:

$$
\begin{aligned}
&\text{Net acquisition of financial assets} \dots\dots\dots\dots\dots 48.8 \\
-\;&\text{Net increase in liabilities} \dots\dots\dots\dots\dots\dots 26.6 \\
\hline
&\text{Net financial investment} \dots\dots\dots\dots\dots\dots 22.2
\end{aligned}
$$

This balance is contained in Table 4–4 but is not shown in our individual account. Yet it plays an important role in another accounting identity:

$$
\begin{aligned}
&\text{Private capital expenditures} \dots\dots\dots\dots\dots 71.6 \\
+\;&\text{Net financial investment} \dots\dots\dots\dots\dots\dots 26.6 \\
\hline
&\text{Gross investment} \dots\dots\dots\dots\dots\dots\dots 98.2
\end{aligned}
$$

Hence, in this situation gross investment for the consumer sector is larger than gross saving. Obviously the Keynesian *ex-post* savings-investment identity only holds for the entire economy, not for individual sectors. But, in flow of funds accounting another important factor, the "sector discrepancy" comes into play. Theoretically, the sum of private capital expenditures and net financial investment equals the amount of gross saving. Practically, this equality is difficult to establish, hence statistical discrepancies arise, which are especially sizable in the consumer sector of flow of funds accounting.[24] The data input and procurement not only constitutes a major problem in all accounting systems, it also forms a major link be-

---

[24]Statistical discrepancies are encountered in most macro-accounting systems. They are of minor nature in national income accounts and have been neglected in our presentation. In the U.S. income accounting system, items for statistical discrepancies are provided for at the debit side of the National Income and Product account and on the credit side of the Gross Savings and Investment Account. Since the second item constitutes the counterentry to the first, the double-entry equality is undisturbed. In the flow of funds accounts the sum of all sector discrepancies does not cancel out completely but usually assumes a much smaller magnitude than most of the individual sector discrepancies (cf. Table 4–4).

tween them. National income relies to a considerable extent on data from business, government, and other micro-accounting systems. Flow of funds accounting and interindustry analysis rely to some extent on national income accounting and on additional data from micro-accounting. This explains why some basic assumptions (e.g., Duration) and many hypotheses are merely implied in social accounting systems. The data problem gives impact to a further phenomenon: the search for an integration of national income and flow of funds accounting (cf. Sigel [1962]) and perhaps interindustry accounting. Thus it appears that macro-accounting pursues the reverse trend from that of micro-accounting: unification versus diversification. Yet, such a judgement needs many qualifications and can easily be misunderstood. The trend toward unification arises out of the fact that in the United States the three major systems of social accounting were developed by three different and separated agencies[25] (the Department of Commerce, the Federal Reserve System, and the Department of Labor). An integration of various social accounting systems is desirable and possible to a certain degree. It will avoid work duplication, reduce data-processing costs, etc., but the distinct purposes for which these systems are designed will not lose identity and cannot be merged.

4.55 Accounting for Interindustry Flows

The actions of every economic agent influence, directly or indirectly, the actions of every other agent. Thus each individual may be regarded as a transactor or entity—with his own account or accounting system—within a system that records these gradually attenuating economic interdependencies. Léon Walras [1874] utilized this idea in his general equilibrium approach which Schumpeter [1954, p. 242] called the "Magna Carta of economic theory." But Walras—realizing the unfeasibility of a practical macroeconomic approach with such a high degree of disaggregation— was satisfied with conceptualizing his system in general mathematical terms[26] without ambition of using this frame as a basis for a social accounting system. Yet, the seed was planted and today

---

[25] In other countries national income accounting and flow of funds accounting, and in some cases interindustry accounting, are handled by a single agency. For the development of flow of funds accounting in the United States as well as in other countries see Denizet [1961], Dorrance [1961], and National Bureau of Economic Research [1962].

[26] Stigler [1941, pp. 237–46] presents a concise summary of L. Walras' (static) equilibrium model.

Leontief's [1951] achievement in spite of much opposition, seems to be the natural and inevitable consequence of Walrasian economics. Leontief conceived the idea of converting this purely abstract model into a tool of economic measurement, analysis, and prediction. The first precondition was to accept a much higher, yet meaningful degree of aggregation. This was attained by replacing the individual economic agent through an entire industrial sector. Thus Leontief's input-output analysis starts from an accounting system that describes the commodity flows between the various industries of an economy. It connects these data with a set of economic hypotheses which lead to the projection of future commodity flows that again may be presented in accounting form.[27]   But this is an approach basic to periodic business budgeting and it shall be our task (in Chapters 8 and 9) to point out parallels and distinctions between these two methods.   Since Chapter 8 contains an introduction to the analytical aspects of interindustry accounting, and since the new input-output tables for the United States (based on the year 1958, and to be published by the Department of Commerce) are *imminent*, the present section is restricted to some general remarks on interindustry accounting.   The interindustry transaction matrix, in contrast to national income accounts, does not exclude intermediate (consumption of) goods and presents a concept that might be called *gross value of output* (the sum of the output values of all industries).   To clarify the relationship of this concept to the total money circulation on one side and to the gross national product (GNP) on the other, the following accounting identities may be helpful:

> Total monetary transactions
> − Debt payments (and related financial transactions)
> ± Imputed items
>
> ――
>
> Gross value of output
> − Intermediate consumption (excluding depreciation)
>
> ――
>
> Gross national product (GNP)
> ══

Although these are crude definitional equations which can be improved by many subtleties, they indicate that the difference between the total money flow (monetary transactions) of an economy within a period and the gross value of output lies in two global items.

---

[27]For an excellent introduction to interindustry analysis see Evans and Hoffenberg [1952] and Chenery and Clark [1959]; for further discussions on this topic see Leontief [1951, 1953] and National Bureau of Economic Research [1955].

First, in the payments made in creating and redeeming debts (debt payments and related financial transactions) and, second, in certain items that have to be "imputed." These include the purchases of second-hand goods (requiring financial transactions but constituting no output newly created during a period) which are to be *deducted;* they also include the addition of payments in kind (requiring no financial flows but constituting output newly created) which are to be *added* to the monetary transactions to attain the gross value of output. The difference between the latter and the GNP mainly consists in the intermediate (consumption of) goods. Precisely speaking, this intermediate consumption includes depreciation (capital consumption allowance), but due to the conventional difference between GNP and national income (at factor cost—see accounting identities of Subsection 4.53) the total depreciation must be excluded. This depreciation is then deducted from GNP to attain national income.

The reader will recognize that the global saving and investment concepts too can be derived from the transaction matrix and can be reconciled with the corresponding concepts of national income accounting and flow of funds accounting. The following remarks by Powelson [1955, pp. 444–45] are fitting to conclude this short discussion:

> This relationship between gross national product and the gross value of goods and services traded in the economy fills a long-existing gap in the practical application of economic doctrine. It is one of the basic tenets of economic theory that the intersection of supply and demand curves determines the price of a product. However, economists have long been accustomed to take these curves as "given." Demand has been related to consumer preferences, which were in turn based on sociological and psychological forces outside the realm of economics. The shape of supply curves, on the other hand, is determined by production functions, or the technological framework in which factors of production are combined, and the prices of those factors. Economic literature has traditionally disclaimed responsibility for evaluating the production function and has all too often accepted factor prices as being determined by forces beyond the control of the firm under study (except where that firm is a monopsonist, or sole buyer of a factor).
>
> By recognizing a relationship between consumer demand for final product and industrial demand for the factors that produce it, input-output accountants have come to accept demand curves as "given" only for autonomous sectors.... Thus, given the demand of autonomous sectors for the country's gross national product, plus engineering estimates of the physical requirements of production, it is possible to derive the demand positions of all the industrial sectors and to determine the gross (uncon-

solidated) expenditure of the community as a whole on goods and serv-ices.[28] (Footnote omitted.)

4.6　CONCLUSION

This chapter has tried to outline in rough strokes the development of the accounting model, from ancient pre-accounting concepts to the variegated accounting systems of the twentieth century. The ac-counting systems since the Renaissance contain most of our basic assumptions; frequently some of them are merely implied and occa-sionally one or the other assumption might seem dispensable (e.g., assumption 12 [Realization] in the case of balance of payment ac-counting). But from a broad point of view or by careful reflection one soon realizes that all of these basic assumptions are prevalent in each of the accounting systems discussed (e.g., in balance of pay-ment accounting the concept of [owners'] equity is not quite absent; its derivative is present in the form of the difference between U.S. capital outflow [net] and foreign capital outflow [net], as a conse-quence the realization principle is not absent either—cf. basic as-sumption 12 and explanations). In general we may conclude that there exist two prominent criteria for identifying an accounting system. The first criterion is the quantitative description of some aspects of the income-wealth phenomenon and the second is the duality aspect which is manifested in a process of giving and taking as inherent in many central events of economics. Producing and consuming, selling and purchasing, lending and borrowing, saving and investing; all these phenomena have a two-dimensional *basis* and enforce, in the course of their analysis, that model which is best suited to express the duality. This seems to be the accounting model, as Irving Fisher discovered more than half a century ago. We have seen that this duality principle is not equivalent to the double-entry technique, it is only most clearly evident in it.

Summarizing and classifying the various accounting systems and indicating their dependence on the basic assumptions, we may use the schema presented in Figure 4–1 (cf. Mattessich [1957], p. 331).

No space was devoted to government accounting in the preceding discussion. But, in this country government accounting is closely related to business accounting and a separate treatment did not seem to be warranted at this stage. Further omissions may be

---

[28]From *Economic Accounting*, by John P. Powelson. Copyright 1955. McGraw-Hill Book Company, Inc. Used by permission.

FIGURE 4-1

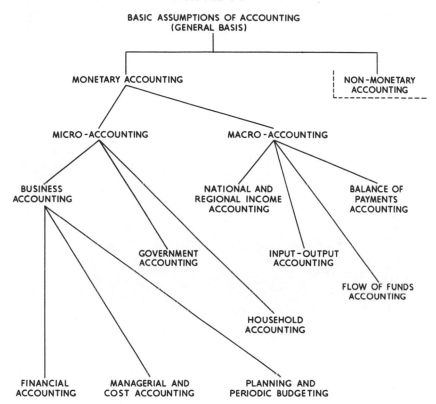

BASIC ASSUMPTIONS OF ACCOUNTING
(GENERAL BASIS)

MONETARY ACCOUNTING

NON-MONETARY
ACCOUNTING

MICRO-ACCOUNTING

MACRO-ACCOUNTING

BUSINESS
ACCOUNTING

NATIONAL AND
REGIONAL INCOME
ACCOUNTING

BALANCE OF
PAYMENTS
ACCOUNTING

GOVERNMENT
ACCOUNTING

INPUT-OUTPUT
ACCOUNTING

FLOW OF FUNDS
ACCOUNTING

HOUSEHOLD
ACCOUNTING

FINANCIAL
ACCOUNTING

MANAGERIAL AND
COST ACCOUNTING

PLANNING AND
PERIODIC BUDGETING

noted: the construction of national balance sheets (see Goldsmith
[1956], Goldsmith and Saunders [1959]) and related attempts (e.g.,
"The Balance Sheet of Agriculture,"[29] Federal Reserve System
[1961]). Although these have typical features of accounting systems,
they are still in a stage of transition. Finally, the emergence of the
"balance of trade," during mercantilism, was not mentioned. At
best it is a weak precurser of the "balance of payment" and although
the former contains a faint notion of duality, it was not well enough
structured to address it as a closed accounting system.

---

[29] Based on a report of the U.S. Department of Agriculture which presents the assets and
liabilities of agriculture (beginning 1961) "as though it were one large enterprise." This is
the 17th report in a series that began in 1940.

PART II

On Valuation and Hypotheses Formulation

Chapter 5

TOWARD A
GENERAL VIEW OF
VALUATION—ECONOMICS
AND ACCOUNTANCY

THERE ARE two areas in accounting where conceptual clarification seems to be most urgent. The first area comprises the basic assumptions and definitions, the second is the problem-complex of valuation. By devoting two chapters to a historical and critical examination of the valuation problem we also give preferential treatment to basic assumption 11 (Valuation). The hypotheses of most of our "surrogate" assumptions are not systematically presented in this book, but the major hypotheses of assumption 11, namely fundamental rules of valuation—together with valuation theories from which they evolve—will be contemplated more thoroughly. There is a further reason for including these two chapters: A systematic survey of valuation approaches—from different quarters of the economic sciences—will help to overcome the narrow attitude toward valuation so characteristic of traditional accounting.

5.1 FUNCTIONAL VERSUS SUBJECTIVE VALUE

We have interpreted an accounting system as a deterministic model of measurement that is dominated by two scales, the chart of accounts—a nominal scale enabling the two-dimensional classification of economic objects and events—and a ratio scale expressible in legal tender, serving the process of "valuation." Moreover, we have seen that the latter cannot be regarded as fundamental or derived measurement, but has to be considered as "measurement by fiat."

Hence *valuation*, the central theme of accounting, *is a procedure by which numerals are assigned to objects or events according to rules (to be discussed) in order to express preferences with regard to particular actions.* In accounting, the numerals assigned usually express *units of a standard "commodity."* In principle this standardization could be based on any commodity but, for obvious reasons, the monetary currency of a country is customarily chosen as such standard.

The chief concern of this and the next chapter is to explore rules of value measurement. But every set of valuation rules is embodied in a more or less explicitly formulated conception about value; no theory of *valuation* is imaginable without a theory of *value*, just as no theory of value exists without some notion about valuation. It is true that some theories of value concentrate on the coming about of value in general, stress the psychological, economic, epistemological, or ethical aspects of value, pushing the more technical problems of value measurement in the background. On the other hand we encounter valuation rules which seem to stand on their own, that is, appear to be independent of any theory of value. But each set of valuation rules must have a *raison d'être* and is embedded in a valuation model which roots in a particular conception of value. Thus we assume that every meaningful valuation procedure grows out of a value theory—even if the latter is implied, embryonic, or degenerate. Therefore, it will be necessary to outline the settings in which valuation theories have grown. It follows that we cannot be satisfied with a mere description of the current accounting conventions expressing and dominating the rules of value measurement in business. Most desirably one should examine all feasible value and valuation theories, illuminating their advantages and disadvantages, validities and invalidities, purposes and deceptions. This all too ambitious task may be reduced to reasonable proportions by analyzing and comparing the valuation procedures recommended by various schools or individuals within range of the economic sciences.[1] By doing so we shall have occasion to observe that a good deal of the discrepancies and controversies that exist between these camps derive from the different objectives these "schools" pursue in measuring value. As a consequence of this inquiry we shall have at the end of Chapter 6, a better notion about the ultimate elements of valuation, and shall examine the foundations of a more general

---

[1] Only the essential features and main results of the various theories, as well as their relationship and differences can here be outlined. For their detailed argumentation the reader must refer to the literature cited.

and functional theory, a theory which regards a particular purpose as only one among several peripheral alternatives, a theory which acknowledges no single autocratic valuation-purpose but a community of objectives, each of which has its own vote and area. Before attempting to disentangle the web of context that conceals many implicit relations and assumptions, let us briefly consider the purely metrologic aspects of valuation and the variations which the aforementioned elements display.

We noted in the beginning of Chapter 3 that every measurement process commands the establishment of a one-to-one correspondence between the object or event to be measured, and a scale. The value is then derived from the purchasing power of that quantity of legal tender which the *agent considers equivalent to the object* in question. We express no novelty if we brand this *subjectivity of comparison* as a major dilemma of economic science. However, economists, accountants, and ordinary mortals have become accustomed to living with this unalterable predicament, and begin to extract much consolation from the assertion of pragmatic and other philosophers that a good deal of scientific hypotheses are of subjective character and thus depend on value judgments.[2] To bestow upon this comparison between object and scale the nimbus of objectivity, and in order to attain an operationally acceptable form of measurement, one substitutes, wherever possible, for the value judgment of an individual, the value judgment of a social aggregate—in most cases a particular kind of aggregate, the market. To regard the value arising from this more or less "democratized" measurement process to be objective may be a matter of definition. Since market prices are (1) subject to monetary aberrations, (2) can be manipulated, and (3) are not always of world-wide validity, this kind of objectivity is not quite in conformity with the notion of objectivity employed in science. But a market although in many situations a comparatively small social aggregate, may, in the face of our dilemma, be considered as establishing a relatively objective "subjective value."

As to the scale itself, a strict distinction between object and scale ought to be made—a distinction seldom made explicit and, perhaps due to the subjective character of the valuation process, usually neglected. The best-known feature of such a scale is its *instability*. This characteristic is not restricted to the economic sciences; all scales

---

[2]See N. R. Hanson [1958], p. 157: "The observations and experiments are infused with concepts; they are loaded with the theories"; see also Churchman [1961], p. 87; and furthermore Minas [1961], p. 29.

(in the concrete sense) are subject to forces of change, but for "practical purposes," these changes can often be ignored. Yet, in accounting, it seems that we have reached a stage where the non-observance of changes in purchasing power constitutes a flagrant violation of economic thinking. *Hence value measurement is not only hampered by the undermining influence of subjectivity, but is handicapped also by the considerable and continuous changes of the standard scale.* We pointed out that often one measurement calls for another. This is here revealed in the need of measuring changes in purchasing power. A task so formidable that a detailed presentation of it would require a treatise of its own. Experience has shown that the concept of purchasing power is not only intricate but defies a *unique* solution. As a weighted average of the prices of a collection of commodities, this concept presupposes two major assumptions—one concerning the weight attributed to the individual commodity and the other referring to the selection of goods to be included in the collection. Both of these premises being of an extreme sensitivity are subject to debate, since scientific and political interests converge at this point. Those problems, however, are well known to accountants and economists and are abundantly discussed in the literature. Most valuation procedures in traditional accounting and economics utilize numerical ratio scales and yield a complete ranking of every element within its "universe," and thus are tied to what mathematicians call a linear or *complete ordering.* This is characterized by the following attributes: irreflexivity, asymmetry, transitivity, and connectedness.[3] Thus the value expressed by a numeral assigned to an object or event is supposed to indicate a rigorous preference for this object (over money, or goods, of any lower value) manifested by an individual or a social aggregate "in a well-defined context." The critical phrase in this sentence obviously is the part in quotation marks. What meaning do we attribute to this expression? It appears that in accounting and economics we often commit the sin of assuming that the context is well defined, even where circumstances under which we evaluate deviate considerably from those postulated or implied by theory. The important contributions of management science to this problem of "context" will be discussed in Subsection 6.23. But this does not exhaust the difficulties with which value measurement is beset. A simple illustration will

---

[3]These properties are explained in Appendix A, items XI and XII. Cf. Ackoff [1962], pp. 187–89.

illuminate another aspect of the imperfections of economic life that impede the development of a realistic theory of valuation: suppose we are offered the choice of a ripe peach or a bar of milk chocolate and would choose the former provided the purpose (decided upon in advance) is our personal consumption of the object in question. We might, however, very well choose the bar of chocolate if our intention is to give this object to the child which plays around the corner and whose liking of the sweet brown butter is well known to us.   This illustration of the purpose influencing our preference might be contested by the *homo oeconomicus* of the old school who would suggest we choose the object of higher market value under any circumstances; then, in case we do not need this object either for personal consumption or as a gift, sell it, buy the object desired (for whatever purpose) and pocket the difference.   Such an arbitrage, as desirable as it may seem, in the light of "profit maximation" will often prove unrealistic; that means the economic "imperfections" of life force us to recognize in theory as well as in practice the existence of different purposes and circumstances for one and the same object for which we have to attribute different values under otherwise *ceteris paribus* conditions.   In the above-stated case this means that the preference function of the child becomes (for a specific situation) our own.   Thus, in the face of the complexity or "imperfection" of economic life, the economist's assumption that every person is endowed with *one and only one* preference function may be unrealistic.   Another related reason for the quest of functional value measurement is rooted in the fact that frequently valuation arises out of administrative instead of economic needs.   In such cases (custodial control, cost allocation of joint products, etc.) purely dogmatic valuation procedures can be encountered and may sometimes be found satisfactory.

In spite of the fact that accountants have long-standing experience with most of these methods (though not necessarily with matching the appropriate method with the desired purpose), the belief lingers on that there must exist one approach that is *neutral* to all purposes, one way of assigning values that can satisfy all valuation needs.   This is not unlike the conviction of some economists that there exists only one true value, namely that which expresses the pertinent marginal utility.   To shed more light on these intricacies of value measurement is the purpose of the remaining sections of Chapter 5 and Chapter 6.   We shall examine and juxtapose the different hypotheses underlying the evaluation processes proposed by the three related disciplines: economics, accounting (together with other branches of business administration), and management science. As it seems too daring to formulate a "standard pattern" for each of these areas individual viewpoints are given some play.[4]

5.2   VALUE IN TRADITIONAL ECONOMICS

The history of the economic sciences (as well as of other social sciences and philosophy) illustrates the great variety of treatments to which the phenomenon of value and its measurement is amenable. The cause of this lies not only in the differing notions attributed to the term "value," it must be sought above all in the central position which this *class of concepts* assumes in economic thinking and which consequently has received such multiform attention. From the first steps of pre-classical economists, through Adam Smith's ambiguous and David Ricardo's one-sided presentation, to the early and profound psychological insight of Hermann Heinrich Gossen, the problem of value has constantly changed its attire. Even after some consolidation and clarification by the marginalists, this problem still proved inexhaustible and productive of a profusion of exciting ideas without, however, indicating any prospect for a definite solution.

5.21   A Sketch of Subjective Value Theory

The early marginalists based their theory of consumer behavior on the assumption that utility is measurable, in principle. Some of them, as for instance, Jevons and Menger, believed that sooner or later a practical way would be found to materialize this measure. In spite of the impressiveness of the present structure of this theory, two of Gossen's "laws"—unearthed after almost twenty years of obscurity—still form the foundation of subjective value theory. But even before Hermann Heinrich Gossen (1810-58), it was Augustin Cournot (1801-77) who made eminent contributions to the theory of exchange value. Though he neither inquired into the *causes* of value nor related utility to value, he derived the familiar theorem that "[instantaneous] gain will be maximized if the monopolist sets a price for which marginal revenue equals marginal cost" Cournot

---

[4]Especially on a subject such as "the problem of value" about which, as Enrico Barone [1920, pp. 26–27] says, libraries have been written, and whereby—as Karl Muhs [1928, p. 801] remarks even more cynically—"the number of constructed theories hardly remains behind the number of theorists" (transl.).

[1838, p. 57 transl.]. This may be regarded a "valuation rule" for profit maximizing monopolies.[5]

The first of Gossen's laws gives an explicit statement of the axiom of diminishing utility: "The amount of one and the same enjoyment diminishes continuously, until satiation, as we proceed with this enjoyment" Gossen [1854, pp. 4–5, transl.]. The fact that this at bottom is only a vaguely formulated empirical assumption that in some cases can be refuted, does not change its scientific-historical significance.[6] Gossen's second law expresses the way in which maximal enjoyment is to be achieved: "In order to obtain the maximum sum of enjoyment, an individual who has a choice between a number of enjoyments, but insufficient time to procure all completely, is obliged, however much the absolute amount of individual enjoyments may differ, to produce all partially, even before he has completed the greatest of them. The relation between them must be such *that, at the moment when they are discontinued, the amounts of all enjoyments are equal.*" Gossen [1854, p. 12, transl.]. This actually is a theorem based on the first law (which is an axiom) and on several implicit assumptions, the most important of which is the *principle of utility maximization*, nowadays recognized as a basic axiom. The second law then becomes plausible, considering that in case the consumer would spend his income in a different way, his total utility could be increased by rearranging his consumption pattern (consuming additional units of those goods that yield a marginal utility higher than the momentary average) such as finally to attain

---

[5]"He also showed how, on certain simplifying assumptions, this principle could be extended to markets with few sellers (our "oligopoly"), and to homogeneous markets with the number of sellers growing beyond any finite number (pure competition).   The usual statement now is that all profit-maximizing producers equate their marginal costs to their marginal revenue, but while for the purely competitive producer marginal revenue is the same as price, this is not true of producers operating in other market structures." From p. 107 of *Modern Economic Analysis*, by William Fellner.   Copyright 1960.   McGraw-Hill Book Co., Inc.   Used by permission.

[6]Gossen's [1854] mathematical formulation is more definite in as far as he assumes a linear marginal utility function.

To begin with Gossen's laws, and not with some later formulations has the advantage of demonstrating how propositions made at an early state of a discipline are later explained in part as explicit axioms, in part as theorems, and in part as implied axioms — a process of clarification that might be of some relevance to accountants who attempt to crystalize from loosely formulated principles a more exacting structure of basic assumptions and conclusions.

The reader interested in a mathematical formulation of subjective value theory (and the connection to econometrics) is referred to Klein's [1962] presentation that can be digested with a modest amount of knowledge in mathematics.   For the mathematically more sophisticated reader we recommend Samuelson [1947], Henderson and Quandt [1958], and the axiomatic, set-theoretical formulation by Debreu [1959].

"equilibrium." This leads to identifying the value of a commodity with its marginal utility (the first differential derivative). Indeed it is the satisfaction derived from the last increment of a commodity which settles our decision whether to purchase or not; or as Wicksteed [1914, p. 3] says: "... we are generally considering in our private budgets, and almost always in our general speculations, not the significance of a total supply of any commodity—coals, bread, or clothes, for instance—but the significance of the difference between, ... ten and eleven loaves of bread per week to our own family, or perhaps between ten days and a fortnight spent at the seaside."

This consumer theory was soon elaborated and extended into the market equilibrium theory which demonstrates that the interplay of the consumer—behaving as outlined above—leads, under idealized conditions, to a market price of a commodity that equals the anticipated marginal utility of the participants, because what A has to pay for it is determined by the difference it makes to the satisfaction of others. If B values the commodity more highly he will offer more for it, and obtain the good instead of A; but the greater the quantity of it B has, the less difference will an addition make to him; and the less quantity A has of it, the more A is willing to pay to get it, until finally equilibrium is established. Thus the (market) value of a commodity is actually determined by the marginal utility. The question remains, how is one to measure this utility? Around the turn of the last century Edgeworth, Fisher, and later Pareto noticed that this "mechanism" would work even without measuring the *cardinal* magnitude of utility, so long as the consumer can be expected to rank commodity combinations consistently according to his preference order. Thus cardinal utility was replaced by *ordinal utility;* and the *marginal rate of substitution* replaced marginal utility. Yet, the result of this transformation did not fulfill the expectations. The empirical determination of ordinal utility functions is possible, at best, in isolated laboratory experiments for a very limited number of goods.

But long before the general theoretical application of ordinal utility, with its *indifference* curves, the marginalists were confronted with the problem of deriving from their value theory of consumer goods a *value theory for means of production*. Menger, Böhm-Bawerk, J. B. Clark, and—if we define it comprehensively enough—Irving Fisher, were the major architects of this structure which towers over economics to this day as well as over many phases of business administration.

It was Karl Menger who took the decisive step—which seems so simple, but which Schumpeter calls "a genuine stroke of genius"— of asserting that *goods of higher order* (means of production) too, create utility, though indirectly by way of producing consumer goods: "The value of goods of higher order is always and without exception determined by the anticipated value of the goods of lower order in whose production they serve." (Menger [1871], p. 150, translated.)

Thus the realm of the marginal utility concept could be extended to the area of *production* as well as to that of distribution: "The greatest contribution of the theory of subjective value to theoretical economic analysis lies in the development of a sound theory of distribution. This means the view of distribution as the allocation of the total product among the resources which combine to produce it, through valuation by imputation." (Stigler [1941], pp. 151–52.)

The further fusion of this extended theory with the idea of market equilibrium follows by necessity:

The requisites or factors or agents of production are assigned use values: they acquire their *indices of economic significance* and hence their exchange values from the same marginal utility principle that provides the indices of economic significance and hence explains the exchange values of consumable goods. But those exchange values or relative prices of the factors constitute the costs of production for the producing firms. This means, on the one hand, that the marginal utility principle now covers the cost phenomenon and in consequence also the logic of the allocation of resources (structure of production), hence the "supply side" of the economic problem *so far as all this is determined by economic considerations*. (Schumpeter [1954], p. 913.)

5.22 Neoclassical Investment and Value Theory

The direct, modern extension of subjective value theory may be addressed as "neoclassical investment and value theory of the firm." Its most successful exponents are Friedrich and Vera Lutz [1951] and its central problem is the determination of the micro-economic investment level in terms of interest rate, prices (including wages), and technological conditions. As M. Gordon[7] [1962, p. 14] states:

On a very general level the structure of the neoclassical theory of a firm's investment and valuation is quite simple. It may be summarized as follows: the objective of the firm is assumed to be the maximization of

---

[7] Myron Gordon [1962] uses the neoclassical theory as starting point to develop his own theory of enterprise or share valuation (see also Subsection 6.22).

its present value; its present value is a function of its future income; and its future income is a function of its present investment. Hence, given these two functions, we may find the investment that maximizes the value of the firm, and given the behavior assumption, we may expect it to undertake this investment. Hence, the theory provides the investment and value of a firm to the extent it is able to establish information on the two functions stated above.

But the main merit of the Lutzian analysis lies in the introduction of many refinements: the distinctions between dependent and independent investment horizons, between these and fund horizons; between scale variability and technique variability; between different input and output, production and holding conditions, etc. The Lutzes first show that under several simplifying assumptions the following three decision imperatives are equivalent:

1. Invest up to the equilibrium point where marginal rate of return (on investment) equals (borrowing) rate of interest.
2. Maximize the internal rate of return.
3. Maximize the rate of return on owner's equity.

Yet, they demonstrate that under more realistic conditions the last two decision rules may not achieve maximization of the firm's present value. Their treatise and especially the chapter on "Cost Accounting" emphasizes "users" cost (opportunity costs) and marginal costs as valuation bases instead "initial" costs (historical costs) and average costs as frequently used in actual practice:

> ... The entrepreneur may not always have any very clear notion of the elasticity of demand for his product and may not attempt to estimate the demand *curve;* he may at best estimate one or two points on it. In such circumstances he cannot calculate a marginal revenue curve.
>
> As regards the cost side, it is probable that the entrepreneur in most cases looks at average cost and seldom at marginal cost. Moreover the average cost which he calculates may be the "full cost" including the "direct" operating cost plus an allowance for overhead or oncost and also a profit margin. In oncost he includes "indirect" (or discontinuously variable) operating costs (such as foremen's wages, lighting, etc.), and an allowance for the depreciation of equipment. The average cost thus includes several elements (discontinuously variable operating costs, durable goods costs, and the profit margin) which were absent from the cost curve which determined output and price in our theoretical solution. (F. & V. Lutz [1951], pp. 70–71, footnote omitted.)

Furthermore a multitude of models take into account a wide range of possible variations. Finally the consequences of withdrawing the major simplifying assumptions (certainty of knowledge about the future and free availability of money at a fixed interest rate) are considered in a less rigorous presentation. But M. Gordon [1962, p. 27] after several objections—which are, from our present point of view, of minor relevance—concludes that "at best the Lutz and Lutz theory of valuation under uncertainty is a rationale of entrepreneurial behavior that is far more complicated and no more informative than the simpler rationales that may be derived from the valuation rules stated at the start of this section" [i.e., under certainty, etc.].

5.23   Criticism from Within

The most critical axiom of economics is *the crass assumption that profit maximization is the correct and exclusive way of maximizing the utility function, hence is the ultimate and only entrepreneurial goal.* Apart from the question as to which profit concept shall be maximized, the above premise does not, in the short run, correspond to imperfect, that is real-world, competition. Maximizing dollar profit is not sensible unless conceived under constraints like maintaining goodwill, avoiding legal conflict, securing satisfactory working conditions, etc., while in the long run the profit maximization concept becomes so vague and all-embracing as to be meaningless.[8] A further difficulty is reflected by the insight that the maximization of a monetary value does not necessarily achieve a utility maximum. This cognition is by no means novel but recently has experienced repeated emphasis by management scientists.[9]

We have to admit, therefore, that this high elegance and comprehensiveness of subjective value theory has to be paid for by strongly restrictive assumptions. Besides, one ought to be aware that this value theory is not so much concerned with evaluating in-

---

[8]Cf. Dean [1951], p. 28: "But in recent years 'profit maximization' has been extensively qualified by theorists to refer to the long run; to refer to management's rather than to owner's income; to include nonfinancial income such as increased leisure for highstrung executives and more congenial relations between executive levels within the firm; and to make allowance for special considerations such as restraining competition, maintaining management control, holding off wage demands, and forestalling antitrust suits. The concept has become so general and hazy that it seems to encompass most of man's aims in life.

"This trend reflects a growing realization by theorists that many firms, and particularly the big ones, do not operate on the principle of profit maximizing in terms of marginal cost and revenues, but rather set standards and targets of reasonable profit." Joel Dean, *Managerial Economics,* copyright 1951. By permission of Prentice-Hall, Inc., publisher.

See also Scitovsky [1943], Lester [1946], R. A. Gordon [1948], Papandreou [1952], especially pp. 205–8, Lanzillotti [1958], Cyert and March [1963], pp. 9–10, 238–40, and Bonini [1963], p. 40. Cf. footnote 1 of Chapter 6.

[9]See, for instance, Miller and Starr [1960], pp. 55–65.

dividual assets as it is with setting up a framework that explains the coming about of value in general. Yet, the extension of this theory to capital formation (from Böhm-Bawerk [1889] to the Lutzes) and specifically to balance sheet asset valuation still lies within the bounds of economics. Irving Fisher [1906] recognized more clearly than others the chasm between valuations for consumption and valuations for production purposes, and tried to resolve this problem by moving as closely as possible to consumption. This he achieved, as stated in Chapter 2, by recognizing as realized income only that part of wealth-creation which has been made available for consumption during the economic process. It forced him to regard all goods as "capital": a loaf of bread, the luxury yacht of a millionaire, as well as a factory building or machine. The evaluation procedure he employed is based, first, on anticipating all the future (net) yields that an asset (or capital, in Fisher's terminology) is capable of generating and, second, is based on discounting these yields to the valuation date. This *"reverse" way of measuring value* (cf. Subsection 5.31) has profoundly influenced business economics, accounting theory, capital budgeting, and even national income accounting:[10] it is the most important link of economics to related disciplines because it forms the threshold on which the economists' value theory becomes a theory of valuation. Here again a body of measurement rules (for assigning numerals indicating preferences with regard to a specific purpose) is provided for. And so, academic accountants became interested in Fisher's formulation of capital and income theory and its application to financial statements; they investigated the differences between this "philosophy of economic accounting" and their own methods (Canning [1929]), attempting to some extent asset evaluation through discounting of expected net revenues, applying compound interest methods to depreciation and amortization procedures, and so forth.

But even though subjective value theory is the "official religion" of orthodox economists, there exists further dissent about the authority of this creed. One of the major opponents is Myrdal [1955] who already in the early thirties expressed criticism that comes now into high vogue in the light of management science. This author confirms that the marginal utility theory is logically independent of pure value theory, although in the literature they are often con-

---

[10]For the latter see Ohlsson [1953], p. 48.

fused, since "... it has always been the desire of marginal utility theorists to weave value arguments into their explanation of price formation in order to justify the claim that pure value theory is indispensable." (Myrdal [1955], p. 84.)

Subjective value theory, as we shall see, can be attacked from many positions, but Myrdal's confutation rests on the argument that this theory is valid only if hedonistic psychology is acceptable. Further criticism is summarized in the following quotations:

> Economic laws, i.e., propositions about the form of these [utility] functions, which apply to individuals are supposed to apply also to groups. Such assumptions are not even false, they are meaningless....
> The inconsistency between psychological premises and metaphysical deductions is quite understandable from our point of view. The subjective theory of value, like other theories with a normative intention, makes it appear possible to deduce, by logical process, rational political principles from its analysis of social phenomena. The argument of this book is that such a deduction must involve a fallacy somewhere; some link must be omitted in the chain of reasonings from positive analysis to normative conclusions. In this case, the fallacy is the assumption of interpersonal comparisons of feelings. Analysis is based on incomparability, conclusions on comparability. The theorist is often incapable of seeing the fallacy. It is latent in his approach to the whole problem for he sets out with the aim to arrive at certain conclusions which are precluded by his premise. (Myrdal [1955], p. 88.)

It is important to note that the above criticism refers not only to subjective value theory but partly also to management science's normative approach. On the other hand Myrdal anticipated the management scientists' assertion that an empirically well-founded value theory cannot do without psychological, that is, behavioral, studies (not to be confused with "behaviorism"). The following passages give evidence for this train of thought:

> The contention that the rational man is also the average man, that the so-called economic motives dominate actual conduct should, logically, lead the marginal utility theorists to a clear definition of the difference between "rational" and "irrational" impulses. But they have never been able to show what precisely this difference is. This is not surprising in view of the fact that they have never been in touch with empirical psychology. (Myrdal [1955], p. 93.)
> But modern psychology attempts to show that we ought to look behind the rationalizations of this introspective pseudoknowledge and that we ought to discover their causes. Rationalization is not an explanation but becomes itself a phenomenon which has to be explained. (Myrdal, [1955], p. 94.)

In view of its materialistic and rationalistic bias it is not surprising that the theory comes continually into conflict with modern psychology. All modern psychologists are agreed that the popular type of introspective rationalism to which hedonism tries to give a learned appearance is indefensible. (Myrdal [1955], p. 95.)

Of course, economics requires as its foundation a psychological explanation of the causes of supply, demand, and price. It is probable that the most important future advances will be made in this direction. But such psychological inquiries must be of a very different type from those of hedonism and subjective value theory (including the behaviourist interpretation). *Much can be learned from detailed statistical inquiries*, although *they must, in the first place, be interpreted empirically in terms of "stimulus" and "response," not "want" and "sacrifice."* We must overcome our old hedonistic prejudices. Social psychology and sociology may yield even more rewarding results. It will probably prove impossible to arrive at an elegant, logically coherent, psychological system, similar to that of subjective value theory. (Myrdal [1955], p. 100; italics ours.)

Myrdal stands by no means alone as a critic of subjective value theory among economists;[11] another important dissenter is Boulding [1950] and our analysis would be incomplete without citing his arguments. Boulding belongs to a group of eminent economists (like Irving Fisher, Joseph Schumpeter, Oskar Morgenstern, Ragnar Frisch, et al.) who believe in the pivotal position which accounting (the balance sheet approach) assumes within economics. Thus Boulding remarks:

The concept of the balance sheet, unfortunately, has not been employed to any extent in developing the static theory of the firm, so that as generally presented in the textbooks the firm is a strange bloodless creature without a balance sheet, without any visible capital structure, without debts, and engaged apparently in the simultaneous purchase of inputs and sale of outputs at constant rates. (Boulding [1950], p. 34.)

His view, in this respect, has hardly changed within the last decade or so. More recently Boulding [1960, p. 4] labels the "net revenue" concept of the Robinson-Chamberlin theory of imperfect competition[12] as "a curious quantity of which no accountant or businessman ever heard"; he argues that their firms are "creatures without past or future, balance sheet or net worth," and points out that "if it [the firm] is not maximizing profits it must be maximizing 'utility,' which is simply a more elaborate way of saying that it does

---

[11]Our choice of Myrdal and the specific quotations was strongly influenced by the fact that he, comparatively early, pointed into the direction of a behavioral (not "behavioristic") approach to the value problem, something that nowadays management science aims to bring about.

[12]Since we are here concerned with value theory—in the narrower sense of the word—there is no intention to discuss the complete theory of the firm.

what it thinks best." On the premise that marginal analysis provides
decision rules only under perfect knowledge, he finally concludes
that "a theory which assumes knowledge of what cannot be known
is clearly defective as a guide to actual behavior." But Boulding's
contribution is not limited to criticism, it is also highly constructive.
In his *Reconstruction of Economic Theory* he proposes a *theory of asset
preferences* which utilizes an accounting balance sheet ratio. This
"preferred asset ratio" is the *proportion of a specific asset to the total
assets* which an individual wishes to hold. It is a useful behavioral
parameter that expresses the structure of assets preferences and
may indicate changes in this structure.

Boulding then connects this accounting tool with the concept of
indifference curves or, more broadly speaking, with the theory of
preference, obtaining what he calls an "equipreference curve" (the
latter identical with the assets indifference curve *only* if satisfaction
is invariant with respect to price). Although this theory is not free
from the difficulties of the indifference curve approach, it simplifies
it to an extent that might facilitate its application in actual practice.

In the following section the reader will encounter further authors
that share the critical attitude toward subjective value theory; but
from the discussion so far it should be obvious that this theory—
in the narrow sense—is beset with embarrassing problems and is
not ideally suited to supply general rules for value measurement in
business life—except for specific cases where utility can be measured by behavioral laboratory experiments, or in connection with
probability combinations (Neumann-Morgenstern utility).[13]

---

[13]"The essence of the notion underlying the N-M utility (Neumann-Morgenstern
utility) is that its measurement (on an interval scale) can be derived from preferences
or lack of preferences among options involving two variables: commodities and probabilities. We first assume that, if a person shows no clear preference for either of a pair of
options, the two options have the same utility for him.... We get to an interval scale of
N-M utility by assuming that within equivalent options we can, so to speak, *trade probability
for utility* [our italics]. How this is done can be illustrated as follows:

"Suppose the subject in our experiment says he is indifferent between the prospect
of receiving $10 for certain and a fifty-fifty chance of gaining either $25 or $1. Since we are
concerned with an interval scale and can, therefore, assign two values arbitrarily, let us
say that the utility of $1 is 1 utile and the utility of $25 is 25 utiles. The utility of $10
is then assumed to be determined by an equating of the *expected* utilities of the two options.

$$1.0 \times U(\$10) = 0.5 \times U(\$25) + 0.5 \times U(\$1)$$
$$= 0.5 \times 25 \text{ utiles} + 0.5 \times 1 \text{ utile}$$
$$= 13 \text{ utiles.}$$

"In this example, then, the utility of $10 is 13 utiles. By starting from these known
utility values, and by devising additional options that combine other probabilities and
other sums of money, we could proceed to determine, on an interval scale, the utility of
other numbers of dollars." (Stevens [1959], p. 48.)

For objections to and further details on the measurement of utility see *idem.*, pp. 48–61.

5.3   VALUATION IN ACCOUNTING AND BUSINESS ADMINISTRATION

Accountants and many experts of business administration reject the subjective value theory of traditional economics as a *general* valuation basis for practical purposes. In so doing, they do not stand alone but have the support of individual members from the camps of economics, philosophy, management science, and psychology. The criticism of subjective value theory that follows will enlarge upon Myrdal's and Boulding's criticism by emphasizing the viewpoint of business administration and accounting in discussing the problem.[14] Then, the accountants' own approach will be taken to task.

5.31   Marginal Utility Unacceptable as a General Basis of Valuation

The marginalists' theory has met with great acclaim, partly because of its comprehensive elegance, but even more because of its implied promise for a *general* way of measuring economic values.

The early marginalists, as has been noted, believed in the possibility of a *direct* quantification of cardinal utility. In time this confidence, losing momentum, gave way to the hope of a *less direct* approach of quantification through operating with ordinal utilities. As this, too, proved disappointing, the modest path of an *indirect* measurement of marginal utility (= value) through the price paid for the pertinent commodity seemed to be the only solution. Thus the process was reversed: instead of being able to determine the price by way of value, the magnitude of the value had to be deduced from the price. Therefore, Wittmann [1956], in his detailed analysis of the value concept in business administration, asks what use a value has which cannot be determined except through recourse to the phenomenon it ought to explain. Pursuing the objection implied in this question, this author presents further arguments (Wittmann [1956], pp. 88–104) which shall be epitomized in the next paragraph.

There is Cassel's argument that all prices of pertinent goods would have to be available in order to permit a purchase decision. Another objection is that in reality many instances occur in which the consumer learns the price after the desire of purchase has been expressed, or even after the consumption has taken place. And

---

[14]There exist four "recent" noteworthy German books devoted exclusively to the problem of value in business administration and accounting: see Mellerowicz [1952a and 1952b], Wittmann [1956], and Engels [1962].

again, as Gisbert Kittig observes, prior decisions often influence, to a considerable extent, present expenditures. The consequence of this is that some purchases which presently have a low priority on the value scale may have to be satisfied first by force of some preceding purchase (e.g., the repair of a machine already in possession). This leads to Hans Mayer's argument that the subjective value theory isolates a single moment of the economic process without any consideration of a time co-ordinate. According to Wittmann, the most fundamental objection is to be found in the fact that the marginal theory assigns a value only if utility is accompanied by *rarity;* and he concludes that, when the direct measurability of marginal utility was abandoned, the law of determining the price through value became a self-evident truth which merely asserts that nobody pays for a commodity more than he wants to pay for it. Thus Wittmann concludes that:

> The impossibility of quantifying *the* value by direct means was emphasized already in examining its characteristics... The attempt to attain this quantification in an indirect way can be regarded as foundered. Thus the question after the applicability of the general value concept in business administration has to be denied—at least within accounting, the area under investigation.
> This result conforms with our outlines dealing with the essence of the magnitudes ("values") as actually used in enterprises. There it is demonstrated that none of these magnitudes constitutes a fact identical with the general value or which would contain it as an essential component. All "values" used in business administration can be proved to be monetary magnitudes, either in form of prices, debts or claims, hereby their disguise as "values" has neither been pertinent nor useful. (Wittmann [1956], p. 103, transl., footnote omitted.)

5.32   Rejecting or Maintaining the Value Concept?

The preceding quotation is less in contradiction with our view than it might appear at first sight. One must consider that what Wittmann calls "general value" is the marginalists' concept of subjective value; he refers to the psychological measurement of pleasure or utility when he speaks of "quantifying the value by direct means." To call quantifying the value by direct means an "impossibility," is somewhat rash in the face of the measurable Neumann-Morgenstern utility and recent behavioral studies;[15]

---

[15] Stevens [1959, pp. 46–59] discusses the following three approaches to measuring utility:
   (1) direct appraisals of subjective value,
   (2) deduction from choices made under circumstances involving risk (Neumann-Morgenstern utility),
   (3) deduction from choices that determine an indifference curve.
See also Davidson et al. [1955].

it thus would seem advisable to let Wittmann's qualifying remark "within accounting," quoted at the end of the second sentence, refer to the first as well. The major point at which out views seem to be at bay in the interpretation of values is in our definition (see Subsection 6.34), which does not conform to the view that values are a "disguise" of monetary magnitudes. *Just as a cupful of water is no disguise of its volume expressed in cubic inches or cubic millimeters, but is measured by it, so is the value of an asset, debt, equity, etc., no camouflage for a monetary label expressed in dollars, pound sterling, etc., but is made comparable by this standard (for a specific purpose) with other assets, debts, equities, etc.* Even the term, "value in general" still maintains significance in our conception (as a vector of specialized values, see 6.33), whereas it has lost any meaning for Wittmann. In consideration of the frequent use of this term in business administration it seems advisable *to set clear boundaries for this concept rather than deny its existence.* The term, "value" is so well entrenched in modern economic thought that we cannot consider doing without it.

Finally it must be noted that little of the criticism of marginalism is directed against Gossen's two laws insofar as they constitute the foundation for consumer economics. Of course, the convexity of the utility curve may be doubtful in exceptional cases, but we cannot deny that the individual possesses a mechanism of introspection which, *within limits*, enables him to rank various impressions of pleasure or pain (yet we are skeptical of the assertion that this mechanism works with equal "precision for far-off anticipations of pleasure and pain"). In general, we experience a decline in marginal satisfaction with increasing consumption of one and the same (or similar) good(s). We need not reject this axiom (so long as it is not extended to interpersonal comparison of pleasure and to the areas beyond consumption) nor the theorem deduced from it, that our tendency is to distribute income in a way that levels this marginal satisfaction for individual acts of consumption. But first, maximization of a man's total utility is still an ill-defined notion; second, the complex barriers and buffers between the areas of consumption, production, and investment are not yet sufficiently explored; and third, other imperfections of economic life (e.g., multiple preference functions) are usually neglected.

As regards marginalism in general, it shall not be denied that ideally and basically value (of an object) may be regarded a marginal concept (cf. the generalized marginalism of decision theory, Subsection 6.23) but first, there exist extreme cases in

which value of an object or event is an integral and not a differential concept (see Subsection 6.23), second, many total value
functions (from which the value of an object could be deduced by
differentiation) are step functions, hence undifferentiable, and
third the determination of these total value functions in actual practice often is prohibitively expensive if not impossible.

Thus traditional marginal value theory is helpful merely as an
analytical prop but becomes dangerous if taken as valid for practical situations where its preconditions are not fulfilled.   Such an
economic theory may still be of pedagogic use. We do not propose
to ostracize economic equilibrium theory from the university curriculum, but we emphasize that the usefulness of such a theory primarily is an exercise in logical deduction, or at best a study of
"isolated" economic phenomena. One must not invoke the impres-
sion that all practical value measurement can be reduced to marginalism and that this theory approximates reality closely enough
to be applicable to accounting purposes. Hence it seems opportune
to search for a theory of valuation that is in better accord with economic life, even at the price of relinquishing the impressive
theoretical machinery of traditional economics.

5.33   Adjusted Acquisition Cost as a Value Basis—Advantages and Criticism

The fundamental principle of traditional accounting for
evaluating assets is known under the term *cost basis*. In its crudest
form *the underlying hypothesis identifies the value of an asset item with the
cost (or price) paid for it at the date of acquisition.* The version encountered in actual practice[16] shows several refinements or, better
said, concessions. It takes into consideration an assumed decline in
value due to utilization, depletion, obsolescence, etc., through
periodically cumulative depreciation allowances on many fixed assets (such as furnitures and fixtures, machinery and equipment,
buildings, copyrights, patents, and the like). It puts a premium on
conservative evaluation by permitting adjustment only in cases of
value-*decline* since acquisition (inventory and marketable securi-

---

[16]For further details of the presently accepted conventions in valuing assets, etc., in the
United States, we refer to the *Accounting Research and Terminology Bulletins* (New York, 1961)
of the American Institute of Certified Public Accountants and the pertaining accounting
literature. Since many of these details are of local, conventional, and more or less temporary nature, they are on the periphery of our interest and do not lie within the range of this
book. For an outline of the above-named bulletins see Section 7.3.

ties: "cost or market value, whichever is lower"). It permits other occasional value adjustments (fixed assets) where there are significant value changes, and may allow consideration of anticipated losses in case of receivables. Finally, practice may exempt (from the principle of cost value) individual items such as precious metals, usually evaluated at the fixed market price; or it may stipulate surrogates where its application is not possible (e.g., the value of inventory manufactured by its own enterprise is calculated exclusive of administrative expenses incurred during the production process). These amendments, if applied rigorously, distort the cost basis so greatly that ultimately the rule consists of exceptions. Even where exceptions are moderate, the cost value is likely to become meaningless for most policy purposes, as time goes on. As vivid illustrations, one may cite the change in real estate prices during the last decades in this and many other countries, or the gigantic "growth" of some corporation stocks.

These changes by no means must be attributed to inflationary forces alone; obviously it is the dynamics of modern economic life which throw some commodities into vogue and toss others out of it. But how was it possible that the cost basis could survive academically and find popular support in actual practice under such unfavorable circumstances? The cost basis appears to be the most reliable method if the purpose of accounting is sought in the presentation of data which can be verified at a comparatively *high degree of objectivity*. It is true that the concept of objectivity itself is controversial but costs of acquisition can usually be well documented,[17] in a legalistic sense; they are somewhat less dependent on personal value judgments than many other economic or managerial criteria. There exist many academic accountants as well as practitioners of accounting who still uphold the opinion that the reader of the financial statements ought to make his own adjustments and computations (based on the specific purpose he pursues) rather than supplying him with data biased in an unwanted or unknown direction. This argument encounters several difficulties. One of them is the great bulk of additional information (impossible to include in financial statements) which would be required if reliable, detailed side-calculations are to be made for a specific ob-

---

[17] The focus of documentation is not—as it might appear at first sight—the fact that a purchase has been contracted at the pertinent price (acquisition cost), but the assumption that this price approximates "fair value" at date of acquisition. This subtle point has been repeatedly emphasized by W. A. Paton [1946, p. 193 and 1948, p. 288] and other authors, e.g., Sprouse and Moonitz [1962, p. 26].

jective—besides, the term "objective" as used above must be interpreted to mean *objective in the legalistic sense* and not in the
scientific sense. It would appear, then that the cost basis itself is
biased—namely, towards the purpose of valuation based on the
best legal evidence—and the argument that it helps the reader of
financial statements in his own side-calculations can just as well be
turned against the cost basis as against any other method.

The *cost basis* may, legalistically speaking, be more objective and
may circumvent some kind of "uncertainty," but in doing so *it
violates one of the most fundamental constituents of any value theory: the
fact that value of an object or event* is bound to time and circumstances.
Precisely speaking, a specific value is a momentary and highly un-
stable magnitude; it refers to a specific moment of time and may
change abruptly. *To assert continuity for valuation purposes is a very strong
assumption* and justifiable only in situations where there is no indication of the contrary and where no better information is available.
Accordingly, the resulting measure of profit and retained earnings
usually is a hodge-podge and of doubtful validity for most economic and business purposes; certainly it does not result in any
meaningful allocation of profit over time. As Boulding [1955, p. 852]
says: "Although this method [cost basis] has the virtue of avoiding
uncertainty, it also avoids the main problem which the accountant
has to solve. For the allocation of profit among various accounting
periods is the principal task of the accountant—otherwise accountancy would be mere arithmetic."

Or, as a recent report of an international firm of certified public
accountants states:

Present accounting practices are designed to account only in terms of
historical-cost dollars; these practices do not undertake to account in terms
of purchasing power or to recognize changes in the purchasing power of
the dollar. Therefore, property and other relatively long-term investments
and capital paid in by stockholders over the years are reported in balance sheets in terms of a mixture of dollars of various levels of purchasing
power; and in many instances these amounts in historical-cost dollars were
of much higher purchasing power than are the present-day dollars. The
monetary items (cash, receivables, liabilities, and other items, the amounts
of which do not change as a result of changes in price level) are reported in
terms of present-day dollars.

During a period of inflation, provisions for depreciation and amortization of property and other deferred costs that enter into the determination
of net income are expressed in terms of the higher-value dollars of the
earlier years in which the assets were acquired, while revenues and other
current costs are expressed in terms of lower-value current dollars. Costs
and net income are further misstated because of failure to account for (1)

the losses in purchasing power of cash and other monetary assets held during a period of inflation, and (2) the gains in purchasing power arising from the fact that liabilities can be repaid in current dollars which have a lower purchasing power than the dollars that gave rise to the liabilities. The net effect of these practices tends to result in overstatement of real net income (net income in an economic sense) and erosion of the purchasing power of the stockholders' investment in the company. Under conditions of deflation, the effects are the reverse. (A. Andersen & Co. [1962], p. 7.)

Finally one may wonder why exceptions were deemed necessary by the proponents of the cost basis. The obvious explanation is that objective, legal evidence can never be the only criterion for generating accounting information. Since other, competing criteria could not be suppressed, a hybrid evolved which few experts regard with satisfaction. To our mind the cost basis is acceptable only under realistic depreciation and price-level adjustments, in situations where other bases (market value, replacement value, appraisal value, etc.) are technically not feasible or not commendable for economic reasons. Since there is little hope of applying pure or limited-purpose accounting systems to any large extent during the next decade, a compromise will continue to be the solution. Yet, the following two questions remain to be answered: In spite of the practical handicap, is not accounting theory obliged to discern clearly the individual purposes of its measurements, and to determine systematically which measurement rules correspond to which ends? Secondly, can we not at present establish accounting systems that represent a more gratifying compromise in the light of changed economic and technological conditions? If the cost basis proved satisfactory in the twenties and thirties it will not do in the sixties and seventies. This problem of finding a new compromise has recently been attacked from several sides and hopefully approaches a more adequate solution. It found recent expression in two accounting research studies sponsored by the American Institute of Certified Public Accountants.[18] The first, preparing the ground and over-all frame, was analyzed in Chapter 3; the other, presenting the actual proposal, will be discussed in the following section.

---

[18] *The Basic Postulates of Accounting*, Accounting Research Study No. 1 (AICPA), by Maurice Moonitz [1961]; *A Tentative Set of Broad Accounting Principles for Business Enterprises*, Accounting Research Study No. 3 (AICPA), by Robert T. Sprouse and Maurice Moonitz [1962].

5.34   The New Compromise—Emphasizing the Market Value Basis

This section deals with an academic trend which—though not quite novel—has recently gathered strong impetus; it is abundantly reflected in contemporary accounting literature but two recent studies are paramount to it. One is by two (managerial) economists,[19] the other is by two accountants.[20] The latter exposition has a semi-official touch as it was sponsored by the main body of accounting practitioners of the United States without, however, representing the official position of the American Institute of Certified Public Accountants. Thus this trend, although offering no more than an improved compromise, has yet to be embodied in a system of actual conventions; yet it is the result of a thorough search for principles and constitutes the most satisfactory, presently feasible, solution for guiding accounting practice. The mere fact that this research study was carried out under the auspices of a powerful association of practitioners is indication enough that a need for a fundamental revision of valuation principles is being felt in actual practice. It also gives evidence of the responsibility and openmindedness of many public accountants toward theory and toward those needs that go beyond the mere auditing function; finally it gives hope that sooner or later these principles will officially be sanctioned and will materialize in business enterprises.   Many a theoretician and managerial philosopher might be disappointed over the "modesty" of such possible revisions, but those who are familiar with the numerous forces here at work, and the circumstances under which accounting practice has to operate, will be more understanding and would regard the acceptance of these tentative principles as a major practical achievement of our discipline.   The fact that accounting theory must go beyond these "compromising" propositions does not interfere with the above recommendation.   On the contrary, a clear distinction between the individual purposes and valuation procedures pertaining to each of them may indicate the area of validity of the Sprouse-Moonitz compromise.   Such theory is justifiable not only academically, but also practically, for in accounting the theory of today is likely to become the practice of tomorrow[21] and students have to be trained to think in terms general enough to include this tomorrow.

---

[19] See Edwards and Bell [1961].
[20] See Sprouse and Moonitz [1962].
[21] Provided the theory is not unrealistically distant from empirical phenomena.

The chief features of the recent trend are (1) the much stronger emphasis put upon market or replacement values, and, in connection with this, (2) the articulate distinction between gains derived from holding assets, on one side, and from operating profits on the other. The subordination of the cost basis in favor of the assigning of current values results from a shift in the objective of accounting, a shift away from the custodial aspect of documentable evidence toward the goal of facilitating managerial decisions as well as decisions *about* managers. One has become painfully aware that while traditional accounting has always stressed pure *custodial control* it neglects too much the *control of efficiency*. This becomes most obvious if we remind the reader that the income statement shows only how large or how small the profit (or loss) is, but fails to indicate what the profit could have been if certain investments or disinvestments (e.g., decrease of inventory), certain more realistic policies, or more efficient management had been chosen. Obviously, such an indicator can hardly be attained by switching from the cost to the current value basis. But a shift towards market values is a first step in the direction of an accounting for "decision-making" purposes; it leads to a closer connection between the "is" of the balance sheet or income statement and the "ought to be" of the budgeting system. It enables accounting to provide information for evaluating actions of the past to the benefit of the future.

There looms, however, the question of whether that proposed compromise goes far enough to attain a truly managerial accounting, or whether it were better to improve and purify traditional accounting in a legalistic direction (for the purpose of outside financial reporting), and to develop independently of it a new, internal information system based on scientific principles. As much as such a separation of the two might seem desirable to some people for a number of reasons, it may not be feasible. As shown in the previous section, an accounting system based on purely legal principles will always supply a meaningless profit figure. Not even shareholders, creditors, and governmental authorities rate legal objectivity so high that they would abandon all relevance to reality as it is (rather than as it was). Furthermore, existing accounting practice is too well entrenched to be changed radically, particularly as neither accountants nor management scientists are in a position to present a workable "scientific information system" that could readily substitute for the managerial or cost accounting systems now in use. The inertia, and the resistance encountered in considering the "comparatively modest" revision—from cost to market value—give an inkling of the resistance to be expected in case of more incisive changes. Therefore it is more likely that a slower evolutionary process will introduce (computerized) flow and budget models that will create gradually—and with increasing sophistication—substitutes for existing cost accounting tools.

Whether or not some kind of split between financial-legalistic accounting and managerial accounting will occur (perhaps in the form of a scientific information system) depends on several factors, some of which will be mentioned briefly: (1) The decision of the Accounting Principles Board of the AICPA as regards the acceptance in whole or in modified form of the Sprouse-Moonitz suggestions for a revision of accounting principles, certainly will have a decisive impact. The official acceptance of a watered-down version of this proposal could easily accelerate a break. (2) The attitude of the private (in contrast to the public) accountant as well as of management, might exert an even more important influence. If this group decides independently to use accounting systems and, above all, financial statements based *on a dual (or triple) evaluation basis*, showing in one column the *cost values*, in the others, the *current* (or other managerially relevant) *values* (as some firms already do) it might be possible to avoid the dangerous operation of separating our "Siamese twins." (3) Another strong factor could be the further development of operations research as an applied discipline—in distinction to operations research as a branch of mathematics and statistics. The dramatic theoretical structures that came forth from this field could deceive us into anticipating *general* applicability of OR techniques to problems of continuous flow. The inability so far manifested by this discipline to produce a workable, economically applicable, over-all framework of the firm suggests the possibility of a merger between OR and accounting, instead of absorption or even destruction of the latter by the former. (4) Finally, the vote of governmental authorities must not be overlooked in such considerations. Even though this problem may not be imminent, it is but a question of time until the government administration will be dissatisfied with the data presently supplied to it by business as raw material for its various social accounting systems. It would be "ostrich policy" to exclude the possibility of federal laws regulating evaluation principles of accounting for purposes other than income taxation.

After this marginal reflection, let us return to our main problem of examining the suggestions made by Edwards and Bell [1961], as well as Sprouse and Moonitz [1962].

5.4 SUMMARY AND TEST OF THE EDWARDS-BELL "MEASUREMENT OF BUSINESS INCOME"

For Edwards and Bell [1961], the ultimate asset disposition criterion is the difference between the subjective *ex ante* estimates of management, and the collective *ex post* judgment (current values) of the market. Asset composition (and the related production activity) must be planned in such a way that this difference—the "subjective goodwill" that ought to be converted as far as possible into market values during the planning period—becomes a maximum. To attain this,

> ... accounting data must provide separately, period by period, (1) an accurate measure of profit on operations and (2) an accurate measure of realizable gains which accrue as a result of holding assets which have risen in price. These are the key elements of information needed for evaluation by management of its own activities. To provide such information is the principal function of accounting. But, as we try to show at various points in our work, such data also provide the information necessary for the evaluation of management, that is, for measuring the performance of individual firms by outsiders. Still further, the data, when aggregated, yield the information needed for input-output and national income accounts which serve to measure the performance of the economy as a whole.
>
> Two further pieces of information, while less important for the evaluation process, are of vital significance if accounting is to serve its second principal function, that of providing data which form an equitable basis for taxation: (3) a record of holding gains which are actually realized on assets which have risen in price since time of purchase, either through direct sale of the asset (as realized capital gain) or through use of the asset in production which is sold (a realized cost saving); (4) a division of all gains into two parts, the portion that is real and the portion that is fictional, that is, money gains which simply keep pace with changes in the general price level.
>
> These are the data that are needed for reports on income and position if the purposes of accounting are to be fulfilled. Under present accounting practices, none of the necessary information is provided. (Edwards and Bell [1961], pp. 273–74.)

Edwards and Bell have developed a sizable conceptual apparatus of which the major tools are presented below in form of accounting identities. As pointed out, the chief difference between Edwards and Bell's proposal and the traditional accounting approach lies in the firm's evaluation of assets (minus liabilities) at *current values* in contrast to historic values. This results in a profit concept which these authors call *business profit* and which here is juxtaposed to the traditional *accounting profit*.

Current value of outputs −Current value of inputs	Sales (current values) −Expenses (historic costs)
Current operating profit +Realizable capital gains	Accounting operating profit +Realized capital gains
Business profit	Accounting profit

Hereby the concept of *realizable capital gains* (or *realizable cost savings*), excluded from accounting profit, must not be confused with the similarly sounding concept of *realized capital gains*.

Current cost of assets at end of period —Current cost of assets at beginning of period	Proceeds from irregular disposal of assets −Historic cost (minus deprec.) of irreg. disposed assets
Realizable cost savings	Realized capital gains

Business profit is recommended by Edwards and Bell as a useful, measurable, *long-run* profit concept which is undistorted by historic costing and which clearly separates operating from holding gains. In addition they suggest the use of a *short-run* profit concept called *realizable profit* which also is capable of objective measurement and which reflects profits arising from holding and using assets within the firm (rather than from asset disposition). It also constitutes an important link to the concept of *subjective profit* which depends to a high degree on the entrepreneur's value judgment about the future but the estimation of which is vital for managerial decisions. The subsequent identities shall illuminate these short-run profits and related concepts.

Market value of firm at end of period −Market value of firm at beginning of period	Subjective value of firm at end of period −Subjective value of firm at beginning of period
Realizable profit	Subjective profit
Subjective value of firm −Market value of total assets (minus Liabilities)	Subjective profit −Decline in subjective goodwill
Subjective goodwill	Realizable profit

Thus the three important, "objectively" measurable profit concepts are the *accounting profit*, the *business profit*, and the *realizable profit*. Since each of these can be expressed either in monetary or in real terms (price-level changes taken into account) we have to distinguish—apart from *subjective profit*—six different profit concepts.

Now we realize that these authors do not merely attempt to separate real from fictitious gains by making adjustments for price-level fluctuations; their major concern is with the value changes that occur between commodities over time—hence the strong emphasis on separating holding gains from operating profits. This separation alone, however, is not sufficient; for management purposes, it is also important to account for holding gains at the time they arise. Finally it is worth noting, even surprising, that these two *economists* favor current costs over opportunity costs for the purpose of practical valuation:

> This decision in favor of current costs over opportunity costs, which we feel is based upon sound theoretical considerations if a choice must be made, i.e., if both types of data cannot be kept, has the fortunate advantage of allowing us to develop a framework which upsets traditional accounting procedures hardly at all yet at the same time would provide the data which are needed, but are not now provided, for purposes of evaluation and taxation. (Edwards and Bell [1961], p. 275.)

Here we can neither present the detailed argumentation nor outline the techniques recommended in the above-cited work, but we shall present conclusions by Dickerson [1963],[22] who thoroughly tested the "Edwards and Bell proposal" in actual practice.

Conclusions by Peter J. Dickerson

Professors Edwards and Bell seem to assume that accountants currently measure the historic cost of all the assets and liabilities of the firm. I feel that this attributes to the accountant a degree of understanding of the terms cost, asset, and liability which he does not possess, and also imagines that if he did fully understand these words he would be able to overcome all of the problems of measurement. To suggest that the accountant does not understand the terms he uses is not necessarily an accusation of incompetence, for he is working with terms which are very difficult to define.

There are many areas in which the accountant recognizes the existence of a cost, asset, or liability, but fails to record it as part of the accounts because he feels that his attempts at measurement are so inadequate. The most obvious example of this is goodwill, which is traditionally recog-

---

[22]Mr. Peter J. Dickerson, a chartered accountant, has been the author's teaching and research assistant during the academic year 1962/63. He has given permission to use here the concluding chapter of his master thesis, "A Case Study in the Implementation of The Theory and Measurement of Business Income," written under the supervision of Prof. W. J. Vatter, Berkeley, Univ. of California [1963], 131 pp. with 34 tables.

nized in accounts only when purchased as such and not when created, at a cost, by the firm itself. It should be borne in mind that the theory requires the inclusion of what Professors Edwards and Bell refer to as objective goodwill among the assets. Even more frequently the accountant attempts to measure an item while recognizing well the inadequacy of his measurement. Countless examples of this may be found, and those that come to mind in this particular case are the use of a proportion of sale price to measure the costs of finished goods, the many problems which arise in the attempt to set depreciation rates, and the statement of the installment receivable at its face value.

The problems associated with the measurement of accounting income on a historic cost basis are therefore great; and while some of them could be overcome, others appear incapable of solution. I feel that Professors Edwards and Bell draw insufficient attention to these shortcomings, and that their techniques provide inadequate measures of current cost until considerable strides have been made in historic cost accounting. This criticism does not imply that we should reject their proposals, but that their proposals should be given only qualified acceptance. It does suggest, however, that it might be fruitful to try methods of measuring current cost which are independent of the historic cost figures and thereby avoid the problems mentioned above.

I have mentioned in the appropriate chapters two further points in which I feel that current cost measures are not provided by the techniques suggested by these authors. The first point was in connection with inventories where I consider that replacement cost ceases to be a relevant measure of the cost of an obsolete item and that in cases where such items are held, a more appropriate measure of cost would be the net realizable value. The second point was in connection with money claims where I consider the treatment accorded to fixed interest securities is incorrect, and would therefore prefer to see the interest expense, or income, based on the current cost of the claim rather than on the funds originally provided.

In many other areas the measures are, of course, no better than estimates of current cost and cannot be considered to have absolute accuracy. Such a situation arises particularly when index numbers are used, and when assumptions concerning the flow of various items into and out of the firm are introduced. Frequently this criticism also applies to historic cost figures; but here it is of even greater concern because we are using the already estimated historic cost, and adjusting it by additional estimated information to arrive at the current cost figures. For example, some differences of opinion exist as to how the historic cost of fixed assets should be determined; then to this historic cost figure are applied estimates of depreciation, and to the resulting figure the theory applies a three-figure index number, all of which means that even if the historic cost and the depreciation were correctly determined, and the index number was a true measure of cost movements, the resulting amount could still only be considered correct to three significant figures.

I shall now pass on to the discussion of the practicality of the suggested measures, and shall deal with the various items in the same order as is done in the text. I do not anticipate that firms will have much difficulty in obtaining market prices of raw material inventory, nor of the items entering into work in process and finished good inventory; my study did, however, indicate the difficulty of costing goods being produced by a firm and the type of estimate that has to be used to overcome this difficulty. I foresee more problems arising from an attempt to find the current market price of prepaid items, but as these usually form so small a proportion of a firm's assets (slightly over one per cent in this case) this is not likely to prove a significant defect in the theory.

It should be noted that the theory assumes the existence of perpetual inventory records and although the example with which I was dealing showed that this does not make it impossible to put the theory into effect, it does necessitate the introduction of additional assumptions concerning the flow of purchases over the time period. On the whole, however, my study does indicate that any problems which arise in connection with inventory are likely either to be minor or to arise out of the inadequacy of present historic cost accounting techniques.

When dealing with fixed assets, the first problem was the selection of the index numbers to be used. I feel that the indexes which I selected tended to be too general to produce a close resemblance to actual cost movements, but indexes of a more specific nature are hard to find and would have compelled a considerably expanded amount of tabulation. However, considering the type of depreciation estimate which is normally made and the possible degree of error which exists there, I do not think we are introducing an estimate that is likely to be more inaccurate than those which we ordinarily use. Perhaps a more important reason for approving the Edwards and Bell technique is that index numbers are likely to be sufficiently specific to say with confidence that the historic cost adjusted by a specific price index usually will be closer to current cost than is unadjusted historic cost.

The real problem with fixed assets is, however, the items classed as intangible assets, for here neither market prices, nor appraisals, nor index numbers were available and I had to report complete inability to find a measure of current cost in any way better than the historic cost which currently appears on the balance sheet. This seems to me to be an important limitation of the model, as although the percentage of total assets which most companies currently show as intangibles is small, this is largely a result of conservative policies on the part of the accountants. Frequently intangibles are written off at a rate much higher than that justified by their expiration, and it is not normal to capitalize much expenditure which yields future benefits to the firm and could be classified as an addition to goodwill. Therefore, if accountants modified their procedures so as to give a more accurate view of the historic cost of intangibles it seems probable that this class of asset would then become a significant proportion of the total assets.

I also found myself unable to implement Professors Edwards and Bell's proposals in connection with long-term money claims. They assume that all such claims have a market value, and this was not the case in the example with which I was dealing. The suggestions made could be implemented in cases where the security itself is regularly marketed, or where it is similar to some other security for which there is a regular market; but no consideration is given to the case wherein the claim is not marketed itself and where no claim of a similar nature has a regular market. As this second situation existed in the case which I was considering, it was not possible to arrive at a current cost of the assets in question and I was again forced to rely on the historic cost figures.

The long-term money claims in this particular example constituted only slightly less than 2 per cent of the total assets so that there is perhaps some question as to whether the amount is significant. I am certain however that a survey of accounts would show that there are many instances in which long-term money claims for which no market valuation is available form a significant proportion of total assets, for many firms have sizable investments in common stock which is not regularly marketed, while others have considerable long-term receivables. I therefore feel that this must be regarded as a significant failure of the model.

The method which Professors Edwards and Bell suggest for integrating their system into the bookkeeping of the firm appears to be quite adequate and is relatively easily understood, but, of course, it is not necessary to formally enter such data into the books in order to produce accounts in the form suggested. In producing the accounts I found that it was much easier to work directly from the tables used in making the calculations than from the journal entries; and frequently it was essential to refer to the tables because the required degree of detail was not carried in the journal entries. However there are advantages in being able to incorporate the adjustments into the bookkeeping if they are to form the basis for the accounts, and the fact that accounts in the revised form can be produced without making a single additional bookkeeping entry may encourage some people to use them as supplementary statements when they would not have done so had alterations in bookkeeping procedures been required. This flexibility is therefore most likely a desirable feature.

Any assessment of the practicality of a method of accounting must take into consideration the significance of the information which is provided and the cost of obtaining that information. I feel that I can say little on the subject of significance as the company with which I was working has been in existence for only seven years during which time the general price index rose 13 points, from 117 to 130. This is a relatively short life and a low rate of price change, and we would therefore not anticipate any sizable alteration in the accounts as a result of using current cost. The authors however do cite a number of studies which show that in many instances the changes disclosed by current cost are significant.

It is, however, of interest to note the changes which were brought about in this particular case. Looking first at the balance sheet we see that the current cost balance sheet for December 31, 1962, increases the stockholders' equity from $248,000 to $254,000 by the introduction of the unrealized surplus, a rise of a little over 2 per cent. More significant is the fact that the restatement in real terms shows that only $143,000 of the $154,000 of surplus constitutes a real gain, a reduction of approximately 7 per cent. Further, the unrealized surplus indicating the unrealized gain arising from holding assets while their cost rose is shown by the accounts in real terms to be negative, due to the fact that the prices of the items held did not rise as fast as the general level of prices, while without the general price level adjustment a gain is indicated. This seems to point at the desirability of any change in procedures incorporating the adjustments for the changing price level. The real accounting balance sheet for 1961, however, shows the dangers of making only an adjustment for general price-level changes for in this case it has resulted in an overstatement of stockholders' equity when compared with the current cost accounts.

On the income statement the operating profit is most likely the most important single figure and this is raised from $82,000 to $94,000 by the introduction of current costs, a rise of only slightly under 15 per cent, and once again the dangers of adjusting only for the change in the general level of prices are seen, as the real accounting statement shows a decrease in operating profit to $78,000 rather than the increase shown by the current cost statement. These figures lead me to conclude that even in the example with which I was dealing the differences caused by the introduction of current cost are significant and they could be expected to have a considerably greater effect in companies with a longer life during which changes in prices had been more spectacular.

The cost of producing the statements in the revised form was the 95 hours which I spent on the production of the figures which appear in the appendixes. This time was broken down approximately as follows:

Examining and analyzing the books of the firm . . . .   40 hours
Adjustment to inventories   15
Adjustment to fixed assets   20
Adjustments for changes in the general level of prices.   7
Preparation of the journal entries and revised statements   13
                                                                          ─────
                                                                          95 hours

The initial period of 40 hours arose because I started the project completely unfamiliar with the accounts of the firm, and as I had access to the books for only a limited time I had to copy a considerable amount of detailed information. If accounts in this form had been produced by the employees of the firm itself, this could have been completely eliminated. I also feel that little was gained by grouping the purchases of fixed assets monthly, and that the use of annual figures adjusted by the annual average index would have produced adequate results. This adjustment to the procedures would most likely have reduced the time needed by a further ten hours.

Accepting the above estimates we discover that the time likely to be required in this first year is approximately 45 hours. It is clear that a considerable amount of time must be spent in the first year devising the most advantageous form in which to set out the working papers and also in this year adjustments must be calculated to bring the initial balances to current costs. I would therefore suggest that in subsequent years the preparation of the data would take approximately one third of the time needed in the first year, that is about 15 hours.

The time required will obviously vary greatly between firms, and will increase as the size of the firm increases; but with the additional mechanical aids to computation that are available to the larger firm I feel that this increase is unlikely to be in direct proportion to the increase in the volume of assets. Each person must make his own decision as to whether the time involved in making the adjustments is justified by the usefulness of the resulting data. I do not propose to offer an opinion myself as it would be a mere value judgment which has no greater validity than that of any other observer of the facts which I have presented in this paper, and I do not consider it the function of a research paper to make such judgments but only to provide information on which they can be based.

To summarize my conclusions I have found that Professors Edwards and Bell have succeeded in devising a reasonably efficient method of restating inventories, tangible fixed assets, and regularly marketed money claims in terms of current costs by means of year end adjustments, but that they have not been successful in the areas of intangible fixed assets and money claims which are not regularly marketed. Further, even in the areas where they have been successful their success is limited by the shortcomings of present historic cost methods in arriving at the cost of an item. I have devised a set of working papers which I feel make the required adjustments with the minimum amount of work and which I hope will have some general applicability; and I have discovered the amount of time which is required to restate the accounts in the suggested form.

This examination by Dickerson reveals several difficulties that arise either out of shortcomings of the present accounting data or from inadequacies of the system proposed by Edwards and Bell [1961]. Yet, it also demonstrates that it is possible to amend—*on working papers*—the data of traditional accounting in an *inexpensive* way that provides financial statements in conformity with Edwards' and Bell's proposal. These *adjusted* statements no doubt supply a value scale that bears greater relevance to managerial decisions than traditional accounting statements. As to the difficulties, it must be reminded that most of them can be overcome with some effort in enterprises which intend to carry out such adjustments periodically.

5.5   ACCOUNTING AND VALUATION PRINCIPLES PROPOSED BY SPROUSE AND MOONITZ

It was mentioned before that the valuation aspects contained in the Sprouse and Moonitz [1962] study have great affinity with Edwards' and Bell's thoughts. But these (Sprouse-Moonitz') principles, developed by accountants, are formulated in such a way as to be better adaptable to actual practice. Though they explicitly refer to financial statements made availabe to third parties by management, these principles certainly would facilitate internal decision making based on accounting records. Such a more general validity is desirable for any measurement system, but must not be misunderstood. If Sprouse and Moonitz assert that "accounting draws its real strength from its neutrality as among the demands of competing special interests" (Sprouse and Moonitz [1962], p. 55), it must be added that this can never be anything else but a "neutrality" influenced by a certain viewpoint and biased more or less toward one or the other objectives, at best a "neutrality" that *weighs* (according to a specific *value judgment*) the bias by the importance of the functions which it favors or disfavors.

The Sprouse-Moonitz study develops eight main principles, some of which are in accord with traditional accounting. To give a concise survey we will characterize them with a few strokes, presenting in detail only those of importance to this chapter.

A. *Realization principle*[23] (emphasizing that profit is attributable to the whole process of business activity and not just to the moment of sale).

B. *Principle of profit separation* (related to Edwards and Bell's study requesting the classification of changes in resources according to price-level fluctuations, changes in replacement costs, sale or other transfers, and other causes).

C. *Balance sheet inclusion principle* (asserting the inclusion and existence of all assets independent of the means by which acquisition was financed).

D. *Asset valuation principle* (which shall be discussed in detail in the following pages).

E. *Principle of evaluating liabilities to be settled in cash* (recommending the discounting of future payments with the yield rate of interest seems to deviate from traditional practices, and was criticized by some practitioners).

F. *Principle of evaluating liabilities to be settled in goods other than cash* (recommending sales price as value basis).

G. *Owners' equity classification principle* (recommending the traditional classification into invested capital—according to sources—and retained earnings, with details about dividends declared and transfers to invested capital).

H. *Principle of classifying profit components* (requesting a minimum of presenting revenues, expenses, gains, and losses and giving definitions of these concepts).

These principles have been criticized from several viewpoints. One of the critics points out that the study does not show "why the conclusions represent a sound and coherent framework of accounting theory" and that "furthermore, there is very little attempt to

---

[23]In the original version these principles do not bear any names. For pedagogic reasons we have christened them in conventional fashion.

demonstrate how these principles flow from or are based on the postulates set forth in the previous study."[24] From the analytical viewpoint this argument has great weight and prompted us to discuss in Chapter 2 the possibility of a more coherent and more general structure of basic assumptions.

For the valuation problem, principle D is most important and is here reproduced in full detail:

The problem of measuring (pricing, valuing) an asset is the problem of measuring the future services, and involves at least three steps:

a. A determination if future services do in fact exist. For example, a building is capable of providing space for manufacturing activity.

b. An estimate of the quantity of services. For example, a building is estimated to be usable for twenty more years, or for half of its estimated total life.

c. The choice of a method or basis or formula for pricing (valuing) the quantity of services arrived at under b, above. In general, the choice of a pricing basis is made from the following three exchange prices:

(1) A past exchange price, e.g., acquisition cost or other initial basis. When this basis is used, profit or loss, if any, on the asset being priced will not be recognized until sale or other transfer out of the business entity.

(2) A current exchange price, e.g., replacement cost. When this basis is used, profit or loss on the asset being priced will be recognized in two stages. The first stage will recognize part of the gain or loss in the period or periods from time of acquisition to time of usage or other disposition; the second stage will recognize the remainder of the gain or loss at the time of sale or other transfer out of the entity, measured by the difference between sale (transfer) price and replacement cost. This method is still a cost method; an asset priced on this basis is being treated as a cost factor awaiting disposition.

(3) A future exchange price, e.g., anticipated selling price. When this

---

[24]"Comments of Leonard Spacek" in Sprouse and Moonitz [1962], p. 77; see comments by various critics pp. 60–83.

The chief causes of the objections are the following:

(1) Practical difficulties of establishing and working with these (more subjective) principles.

(2) Lack of conviction (and lack of an empirical test) that these principles lead to more meaningful and useful financial statements than the old principles.

(3) Looseness of the logic by which the postulates and principles are evolved and tied to each other.

(4) Pure dogmatism. Some of the objections (even a few contained in the printed comments to and with the Sprouse-Moonitz study) are pitiably dogmatic; in reading them one is inclined to compare the present state of accounting with that of astronomy in the sixteenth and seventeenth centuries when priests wrote treatises to refute the heliocentric theory and cardinals forced Galileo to abjure.

This comparison is not so far-fetched when considering the double nature, on one hand, of the knowledge of the heavenly bodies in the sixteenth century (theological *and* positive scientific), on the other, of contemporary accounting (legalistic *and* normative scientific).

basis is used, profit or loss, if any, has already been recognized in the accounts. Any asset priced on this basis is therefore being treated as though it were a receivable, in that sale or other transfer out of the business (including conversion into cash) will result in no gain or loss, except for any interest (discount) arising from the passage of time.

The proper pricing (valuation) of assets and the allocation of profit to accounting periods are dependent in large part upon estimates of the existence of future benefits, regardless of the bases used to price the assets. The need for estimates is unavoidable and cannot be eliminated by the adoption of any formula as to pricing.

1. All assets in the form of money or claims to money should be shown at their discounted present value or the equivalent. The interest rate to be employed in the discounting process is the market (effective) rate at the date the asset was acquired.

The discounting process is not necessary in the case of short-term receivables where the force of interest is small. The carrying-value of receivables should be reduced by allowances for uncollectible elements; estimated collection costs should be recorded in the accounts.

If the claims to money are uncertain as to time or amount of receipt, they should be recorded at their current market value. If the current market value is so uncertain as to be unreliable, these assets should be shown at cost.

2. Inventories which are readily salable at known prices with readily predictable costs of disposal should be recorded at net realizable value, and the related revenue taken up at the same time. Other inventory items should be recorded at their current (replacement) cost, and the related gain or loss separately reported. Accounting for inventories on either basis will result in recording revenues, gains, or losses before they are validated by sale but they are nevertheless components of the net profit (loss) of the period in which they occur.

Acquisition costs may be used whenever they approximate current (replacement) costs, as would probably be the case when the unit prices of inventory components are reasonably stable and turnover is rapid. In all cases the basis of measurement actually employed should be "subject to verification by another competent investigator."

3. All items of plant and equipment in service, or held in stand-by status, should be recorded at cost of acquisition or construction, with appropriate modification for the effect of the changing dollar either in the primary statements or in supplementary statements. In the external reports, plant and equipment should be restated in terms of current replacement costs whenever some significant event occurs, such as a reorganization of the business entity or its merger with another entity or when it becomes a subsidiary of a parent company. Even in the absence of a significant event, the accounts could be restated at periodic intervals, perhaps every five years. The development of satisfactory indexes of construction costs and of machinery and equipment prices would assist materially in making the calculation of replacement costs feasible, practical, and objective.

4. The investment (cost or other basis) in plant and equipment should be amortized over the estimated service life. The basis for adopting a particular method of amortization for a given asset should be its ability to produce an allocation reasonably consistent with the anticipated flow of benefits from the asset.

5. All "intangibles" such as patents, copyrights, research and development, and goodwill should be recorded at cost, with appropriate modification for the effect of the changing dollar either in the primary statements or in supplementary statements. Limited term items should be amortized as expenses over their estimated lives. Unlimited term items should continue to be carried as assets, without amortization.

If the amount of the investment (cost or other basis) in plant and equipment or in the "intangibles" has been increased or decreased as the result of appraisal or the use of index-numbers, depreciation or other amortization should be based on the changed amount. (Courtesy: American Institute of Certified Public Accountants, Sprouse and Moonitz [1962, pp. 55–58].)

This valuation principle clearly reveals, first, a trend toward current values (with a glance toward the future), and, second, a compromise that occasionally uses historical costs as a starting point. Already the proposal to discount (at least long-term) receivables is a move toward an evaluation procedure that is more realistic from the managerial point of view. Yet, this suggestion—similar to the proposed discounting of payables—has met with criticism from actual practice as being neither feasible nor desirable: "In view of normal fluctuations of earnings between years, I do not believe there is any 'interest rate' that can be identified as the rate which a given company is apt to earn, such rate to be applied on the assumption that this is how useful the delay in payment is to the company."[25] The evaluation of inventories at *net realizable values* (= anticipated sales revenues minus cost of completion and disposal) would be one of the most decisive changes vis-à-vis traditional accounting practice. So far this procedure is permissible only in the exceptional cases (e.g., where the sales revenues of the commodity are secured by an officially fixed price and the absence of substantial marketing costs—e.g., the trade in gold). It is also important to note the complexity of valuation rules introduced by practical difficulties which call for modification or even exceptions. Also important but less novel is the recommendation of price-level adjustments with regard to plant and equipment, or their eventual

---

[25]See "Comments of William W. Werntz" contained in Sprouse and Moonitz [1962], pp. 81–82.

evaluation at replacement costs. We thus encounter here, as in other situations of value measurement for practical purposes, a hierarchy of possibilities ranked according to feasibility or degree of materialization.

5.6 REPORTING GENERAL PRICE-LEVEL CHANGES

Closely connected with the Sprouse-Moonitz [1962] accounting principles is Accounting Research Study No. 6 by the research staff (under the directorship of Professor Moonitz) of the American Institute of Certified Public Accountants (AICPA [1963]). This work on the *Financial Reporting of Price-Level Changes* is a highly successful attempt to summarize the accounting problem of general price-level fluctuations and to suggest a feasible solution for *general* price-level adjustments. This semiofficial recommendation is in conformity with similar endeavors in other countries and constitutes a decisive step toward a more realistic presentation of financial statements. Since the Accounting Principles Board of the AICPA [1963, p. 1] has acknowledged that "the assumption in accounting that fluctuations in the value of the dollar may be ignored is unrealistic," it should be easier to remove a major barrier on the road to "reason" in our discipline.

This AICPA [1963] study has not been incorporated in the Sprouse-Moonitz [1962] accounting principles mainly in order to emphasize that price-level changes and their adjustments in financial statements constitute a problem *distinctly separate* from the problem of replacing the *historic* cost basis by the *current* cost basis:

... the essential difference between historical cost and current (replacement) cost is in the *timing* of the recognition of profit or loss, and this difference between the two kinds of cost is not affected by the presence of a changing dollar. What *is* changed is the validity of the measure of the *amount* of profit or loss as reported on either basis, historical cost or replacement cost. If an investment is made in assets in 1945 and recovered in 1962, the resultant amount of gain or loss is not measurable in any meaningful sense by a comparison of dollars received (recovered) with dollars paid out (invested). As in all types of accounting analysis, the problem at hand is not solved solely by a satisfactory determination of the *size* of a business event. Its solution requires a further determination as to the nature of the change, e.g., whether it represents a return of capital, a "return on capital," or a mere transfer or substitution of one item for another without effect on capital. (AICPA [1963], p. 8.)

To convince practitioners and private accountants to accept supplementary financial statements with data adjusted for *general* price-level changes is easier than to make them accept the current cost basis. Thus, the adoption of such supplementary statements in the annual reports of corporations by a sizable number of firms is the desired first step. The acceptance of the *current cost basis* is an independent matter that may follow later on. But even the solving of this second problem (current cost basis) can be made more attractive and more objective by applying price-level indices, though *specialized* ones for different commodity categories. The similarity of the means by which these two different problems can be settled has created much confusion among accountants. We cannot emphasize strongly enough that on one hand adjustments are made in order to eliminate the inflationary-deflationary trends by applying a *general* price-level index and on the other hand use is made of price-level indices *specialized* in order to separate gains and losses due to shifts in demand and supply between various groups of assets. The AICPA [1963] study is concerned with the first problem, the studies by Sprouse-Moonitz [1962] and Edwards and Bell [1961] are primarily concerned with the second. Obviously it is easier and apparently more "objective" to apply a *specialized* price or price-level index than to determine for each commodity the current cost.

The basic problem of general price-level changes[26] obviously lies in the different "behavior"—under inflationary-deflationary forces —of three major balance sheet items: *Debt claims* (i.e., monetary assets and liabilities) obviously do not change face value under our present legal-economic conventions, but a change of purchasing power does take place in *inverse* proportion to the change of the price-level index. The value of *nonmonetary assets* (excluding all debt claims) changes (on the average) in *direct* proportion to the change of the price-level index. But *owners' equity*, as a residual, changes in a *mixed* proportion, depending on the weight of the debt claims and nonmonetary assets contained in the balance sheet.

In order to illustrate this, we show below three balance sheets together with some algebraic formulations. We assume a price-level change $p = 10\%$ during the accounting period of 1947, hence

$$p = \frac{\text{Price level index (beg.) 1948}}{\text{Price level index (beg.) 1947}} - 1 = 0.1.$$

We furthermore assume that no business activity occured during 1947 and, apart from price-level changes, the balance sheet is un-

---

[26] See also Bierman [1959], pp. 464–70, Chambers [1961], pp. 21–22, A. Andersen & Co. [1962], pp. 13–14, and AICPA [1963], pp. 12–13.

affected (depreciations are neglected). Starting from the balance sheet at the beginning of 1947, we first postulate an Utopian society where legal regulations stabilize the purchasing power of old-debt claims (including previously issued money) during inflationary-deflationary trends. Accordingly, the second balance sheet presents the situation in Utopia at the beginning of 1948 in (beginning) 1948 dollars. Here *all* balance sheet items would increase by 10 per cent.

BALANCE SHEET
AT BEGINNING OF 1947
IN 1947 DOLLARS
(Valid for U.S.A. and for Utopia)

Monetary Assets, MA	2,000	Liabilities, LI	1,000
Nonmonetary Assets, NA	6,000	Owners' Equity, OE	7,000
Total Assets	8,000	Total Capital	8,000

BALANCE SHEET
AT BEGINNING OF 1948
IN 1948 DOLLARS
(In Utopia)

Monetary Assets, $MA(1+p)$	2,200	Liabilities, $LI(1+p)$	1,100
Nonmonetary Assets, $NA(1+p)$	6.600	Owners' Equity, $OE(1+p)$	7,700
Total Assets	8,800	Total Capital	8,800

BALANCE SHEET
AT BEGINNING OF 1948
IN 1948 DOLLARS
(In the U.S.A.)

Monetary Assets, MA	2,000	Liabilities, LI	1,000
Nonmonetary Assets, $NA(1+p)$	6,600	Owners' Equity, $OE(1+p) = 7,700$	
		$-(MA-LI)p = -100$	7.600
Total Assets	8,600	Total Capital	8,600

In our present-day economy the situation is different. As the third balance sheet indicates, the value of the debt claims remains unchanged, while the value of the nonmonetary assets changes in proportion to the price-level change $[NA(1+p)]$, and the owners' equity changes in mixed proportion $[OE(1+p) - p(MA - LI)]$ whereby the expression $(MA - LI)p = 100$ represents the net loss (or net gain) from holding and granting debt claims (including money). The AICPA [1963] recommends that this important net loss or net gain on "monetary" items should not be "buried" in the balance sheet, but be shown as a separate and ultimate item in the income calculation. To carry out these year-end adjustment calculations the Gross National Product Implicit Price Deflator is considered accurate enough and is recommended by the study. The difficulties arising from technological innovations and the resulting change in price index composition receive due acknowledgment in the AICPA [1963] study.

We may summarize the view of the accounting research staff of the AICPA with the following quotation:

In the preparation of these supplementary but completely adjusted financial statements, the necessary adjustments would usually be recorded at the end of the accounting period, and these statements would ordinarily be expressed in terms of the dollar at the end of the period. (The index for the last month or quarter would be used unless the price level was changing very rapidly). All nonmonetary items would be restated and brought up to date, the monetary items would appear unchanged, and the gain or loss in purchasing power of the monetary items would be recorded in the financial statements as a separate item.

In completely adjusted financial statements, all the amounts would be based on the same standard measuring unit and would therefore be comparable. As a result, the rate of return on the "adjusted" investment would be more accurate, the depreciation and related asset amounts would recognize price-level changes (but not necessarily current replacement costs), dividends could be interpreted in relation to more meaningful earnings, the proportion of earnings actually being taken by income taxes would be more apparent, the gains and losses from holding or maintaining monetary items would be disclosed, and so on. (AICPA [1963], p. 53–54.)

Chapter 6

TOWARD A GENERAL
VIEW OF VALUATION—
MANAGEMENT SCIENCE

THE PRECEDING discussion has shown that economics as well as accounting, in their traditional forms, supply one-sided and in many respects unsatisfactory valuation theories. Although branches of these two disciplines seem to move toward each other—and in the case of Edwards and Bell [1961], on the one hand, and Sprouse and Moonitz [1962] on the other, come very close together indeed—we ought to inquire into the contributions management scientists have made to value theory. The appropriate link to such an undertaking is Churchman's [1961] *Prediction and Optimal Decision* which has been called a "trail-blazing effort in a new dimension of management science" (Alderson [1962], p. 375), and which, (in its Chapter 3) subjects the measurements of accountants and business managers to a critical analysis. Yet, the present section is not intended to be a mere restatement of Churchman's critique; it attempts to evaluate these critical remarks from an accountant's point of view.

6.1 A MANAGEMENT SCIENTIST'S ATTITUDE TOWARD ACCOUNTING VALUATION

Scrutiny of the models of operations research, or any other *normative* discipline, reveals that these models are rooted in data and facts which actually turn out to be theories and value judgments instead of being ultimate scientific elements. Thus the need for a philosophic superstructure, for a "science" of values, has long been felt by those operation analysts who went beyond the mathematical-behavioral surface of OR-models. A circle of management scientists, grouped around the pragmatic philosopher E. A. Singer, who call themselves "Experimentalists," are at work to advance the philosophic basis of management science.   Churchman's [1961] book, which bears the subtitle *Philosophic Issues of a Science of Values*, is the most interesting, ambitious, and controversial thesis which arose from these endeavors. This book reflects a reciprocal giving and taking between a science and a philosophy, elevating this science to new heights.   There are numerous instances of philosophic constructs that were nurtured and inspired by other academic disciplines. Theology, mathematics, history, physics, biology, economics, etc., have served as a breeding ground for one philosophic system or another. Now, the science of the enterprise, of the decision-making process—and as such of business administration and accounting—serves as a catapult for a comprehensive philosophical inquiry. Churchman [1961, p. 67] admits this relationship to our discipline by affirming that "in a very general sense we are talking about managerial accounting in this book, if I understand the true intent of this term." The main significance of Churchman's [1961] book lies in the bold and honest attempt to expand the task of the management scientist from prescribing "technical" remedies to advising about normative and even ethical issues.

6.11   Summary of a Critique

Here we are not concerned with the problem of *imposing* ethical or related values on management, but shall focus attention on Churchman's attack of the accountants' approach to measuring values. Such criticism is introduced by the following remarks:

However, no business firm tries solely to maximize cash at a specific moment of time. Instead, firms are often said to maximize "profits" or "return on investment"; but there is no clear way of defining these concepts that will satisfy the requirements of value measurements. To substantiate this viewpoint, we shall argue that in most cases (1) the time over which profits are to be calculated is not adequately defined; (2) opportunity costs, such as alternative uses of capital and lost sales, are not usually included; (3) since a proper allocation of overhead presupposes a knowledge of the correct organization for the firm, the proper allocation is rarely made; (4) since costs act as motivators of human actions, cost accounting designed to measure values should depend on psychological considerations, but it rarely does. This does not mean that accounting figures are useless as far as managers are concerned. It does mean that accounting figures are not measures of the values or the goals of the industrial enterprise, and hence cannot be used directly as a means of verifying recommendation, that is, telling a manager what he ought to do.[1]

Before we evaluate these arguments in detail an important general observation may be opportune. Churchman looks at the accounting process from a "scientific," i.e., *maximizing*, point of view and inquires whether managers have command over a value scale upon which predictions (under full information and free choice) can be based. He then demonstrates in detail that accounting does not provide such a value scale and concludes as follows:

> It isn't that accounting systems are "slightly" defective here and there, and that the wise manager will ignore some figures and add or subtract from others. In view of the fact that asset utilization and non-utilization, and organizational policy are both highly critical in management decisions, and because the values of these policies are not measured by accounting information, it is safe to say that cost and profit information is seriously defective relative to a scientific understanding of policy information.[2]

6.12   Accounting Measures Do Not Serve Profit Maximization

But Churchman's approach to this problem seems to us artificial. If *maximization* of profit (or of a similar concept) is an unrealistic goal[3] that cannot even be clearly defined, why shall managers strive for it and why shall accounting provide tools for measuring it? Accountants have always refused to incorporate the idea of over-all profit maximization into their systems. Often enough they have criticized "pure" economists for distorting the issue of entrepreneurial behavior by accepting the oversimplified assumption of "profit maximization." Futhermore, accountants have never pretended that their data constitute measures and predictions in a rigorous scientific sense—not even operations analysts and econometricians can claim this for their own approaches.[4] Thus a careful

---

[1] West C. Churchman, *Prediction and Optimal Decision: Philosophical Issues of a Science of Value.* Copyright 1961. By permission of Prentice-Hall, Inc., publisher, pp. 50–51.

[2] *Ibid.*, p. 66.

[3] See footnote 8 of Chapter 5. The following motives other than profit maximization have been advanced: long-run survival (Rothschild [1947]), attaining targets of reasonable profits (Dean [1951], p. 28); making profits that are *satisfactory* from the standpoint of the entrepreneurial aspiration level (Simon [1952], and Margolis [1958], p. 188); maximizing sales, subject to a profit constraint (Baumol [1959], pp. 45–53); obtaining a satisfactory share of the market (Kaysen [1949]); and the combination of several objectives (Duesenberry [1958]). The hypothesis that funds generated internally influence investment activity of a firm, which has been recognized for some time (e.g., Tinbergen and Polak [1950]), also disproves the profit maximization objective.

In spite of the abundance of strong arguments against the assumption of profit maximization, scholars like Koplin [1963] accept it if applied to the firm, though rejecting it as meaningless in connection with the individual businessman.

[4] See Chapter 7.

analysis of Churchman's argument reveals that—although his logical deductions are impeccable—his premises contain the unwarranted implication that accounting evaluation ought to enable managers to maximize over-all profit or a related concept. Thus from his conclusion one can by no means infer that the accounting approach must be abandoned because it is "seriously defective"; it rather follows that the assumption of over-all profit maximization —so cherished by economists and many operations analysts—is untenable in connection with business practice. Neither can the criterion of "scientific prediction" be used for discarding accounting. *The usefulness or defectiveness of an accounting system can only be judged by the following two criteria:* (1) in the long run the costs of operating an accounting system must be lower than the benefits derived from it, and (2) this long-run differential or net benefit must be optimal relative to *available* competing systems.

The following example shall illustrate the crux of this problem. Assume the goal of an entrepreneur—in conformity with a *satisficing* procedure—is to increase (during the current period) profit by 10 per cent over last year's. In this situation accounting does provide a value scale for measuring the attainment or nonattainment of the entrepreneurial objective. But this argument would not satisfy Churchman, for he would not accept management's own goals; he rather proposes that management scientists tell the entrepreneur what his goal ought to be. But what is this goal supposed to be? Maximization of an indefinable profit concept? Churchman honestly searches for an answer to this question and in his Chapter 13 finally suggests the objective of *maximizing power* (see our Subsection 6.13). But this concept of power, as will be shown, does not solve our problem and, as Alderson [1962, p. 379] confirms, "is not yet fully integrated with his [Churchman's] root ideas for a science of ethics."

At this point we may well ask, what is the chief difficulty with the maximization principle? Is it that people want to maximize (profit, utility, etc.) and do not know how to go about? Or is it that life in general and human life in particular—including business life—does not lend itself to such a narrow pattern? Ultimately both difficulties may prove to have the same root, but we prefer to emphasize the latter cause.

Small segments of economic activity may be "idealized" and conceived under an optimization objective, but hardly so the entire sequence of a human life or the life cycle of an enterprise. In such cases the conceptual difficulties are so enormous that the assump-

tion of profit maximization becomes utterly unrealistic if not meaningless. Before one can systematically maximize a function, one
must possess the knowledge of how to go about it, and how to recognize its maximum state. Therefore the profit maximization assumption makes sense only in a well-defined and fairly transparent
context, it implies two essential prerequisites. This context must
be reflected in a scheme which (1) contains all relevant variables and
expresses all relations between them, including a realistic goal function and the economic as well as noneconomic constraints, and (2)
is amenable to a mechanism by which the absolute maximum (in
contrast to a *local* maximum) of the multi-dimensional goal function of the enterprise can be determined. Nineteenth-century economists could assume profit maximization with much better a
conscience then we can do. Today we can no longer believe that
the simple maximization model of the firm contains all the essentials
and offers a realistic view of entrepreneurial behavior.

6.13 Four Deficiencies of Accounting

The details of Churchman's arguments offer further points to
which objection can be raised from an accountant's point of view.
Some of these objections result from our rejection of the maximization principle. For instance, the problem of *defining the time over
which profits are to be calculated* becomes of secondary importance
as soon as the assumption of profit maximization is abandoned.
The maximization of a short-term profit might be in conflict with
the maximization of a long-term profit; but a profit goal (for a
longer period) based on a value judgment of management *can* be
broken down for subperiods by the same judgment procedure.

Furthermore Churchman objects that no time horizon (in the
sense of "the point of time beyond which one has virtually no information") is definitely given since "information is always created,
not taken."[5] But we believe that beyond such an "originally" established horizon, the costs of creating additional information about
the future are so enormously high, compared to the yield, that research into futurity is a very limited means of extending this
horizon.

---

[5]This argument is characteristic for Churchman, first, because it illustrates strikingly
how the variables are *interdependent* (this *mutatis-mutandis* thinking runs like a red thread
throughout Churchman's book and lends it an impressive comprehensiveness of design);
second, this argument emphasizes the interdependence or feed-back relationship *without
assigning weights* to the variables. As interesting as these feed-back relations are, there is
little evidence indicating the *magnitude* of their practical importance.

The neglect of *opportunity costs in accounting* is the second main point in Churchman's argumentation. Accountants have been criticized for many years on this score and have tried to take these complaints to heart. Churchman joins these critics by pointing out that:

Every business and industry faces the problem of the acquisition or nonacquisition of assets, and of their use or nonuse, once they have been acquired. In the case of this type of decision, only the acquisition and use are matters that are recorded in the usual P-and-L statement. If the manager fails to acquire an asset, no "cost" is directly recorded. Similarly, if he "holds" the asset without using it (for example, inventory, cash, and so on) there is no direct cost reported on the statement. These hidden costs are the well-known and well-neglected "opportunity" costs. As long as it is admitted that they are costs at all, it is clear that the "profit" line of the P-and-L is not necessarily a measure which the manager should try to optimize.

Of course, one may point out that opportunity costs do appear in P-and-L statements in an indirect way because inefficient holding of an asset, or failure to acquire an asset, generates lower profits in the long run. Indeed, this is exactly why these inefficiencies are taken to be "costs." But the question is: How do we know when a profit line is lower than it ought to be? The answer to this question is difficult to give simply because no business or industry keeps its records in such a manner that an answer to the question can be determined.[6]

But standard costing and especially budgeting are designed to tell management when a profit is lower than it ought to be. Thus the last sentence of the above quotation appears to be an incorrect assertion. But in fact it is not; at least not so long as this "ought to be" refers to an *optimal* profit[7] rather than to the managerial goal fixed in the budget. This shows that here again the argument stands and falls with the maximization assumption. Theoretically, cost accounting and budgeting provide structures that permit the incorporation of opportunity costs; if actual practice does not always take advantage of this, it is regrettable but gives no evidence for the inferiority of accounting. Yet, on some points cost accountants have to admit negligence. Opportunity costs such as interest on owners' equity and owners' salaries indeed ought to be imputed in the cost calculation. But even here the critique merely holds for the United States and not for Continental Europe where most basic charts of accounts enforce the imputation of such opportunity costs. Another deficiency, admittedly, is the impossibility of measuring marginal return for small increments of new investments. This deficiency

---

[6]Churchman, *op. cit.*, p. 57.
[7]Periodic budgeting does not command any optimization algorism (see Chapter 8).

may distort the shareholders' measure of the manager's abilities of investing (in machinery, factory buildings, etc.). It may lead to a measurement in terms of over-all return for a limited period. Again the seriousness of the argument should not be overrated, because managerial performance usually is judged on records that span periods of many years. Otherwise, a farsighted investment decision which causes a low profit in one year, but relatively higher profits at a later time, would result in dismissing the executive after the first year. Usually the wisdom of an investment decision of this nature can be made plausible in advance and will definitely be evidenced over the years.

The third point revolves around the *problem of overhead costing*. The arbitrary allocation of overheads in cost accounting is unceasingly complained of by economists and management scientist. Churchman illustrates through a waiting-line problem that the correct measurement of overhead costs depends on knowledge of the optimal organizational structure of the enterprise. Thus he comes to the conclusion that "organization theory and accounting for management decisions are inseparably tied together." This is a profound insight, the more so as he recognizes that accountants are approaching a solution to this problem through standard cost systems in which the organization of a firm ought to be reflected. And so long as organization theory does not provide reliable and practicable criteria for determining the optimal organizational structure, accountants will have to rely on their own less rigorous method of standard costing.

The last major point touches the *application of psychological considerations to cost accounting*. This indeed is an area neglected for too long a time by accountants. But one of them, Stedry [1960] made his reputation by examining the psychological effect of various budget levels (the timing and sequencing of budget information, and so forth) upon the performance of the individuals subject to the budget. This study was carried out by means of behavioral models and experiments; the results are still controversial and cannot as yet be recognized as generally valid. But Stedry is presently at work to further explore this important borderland of accounting and psychology.

6.14   A Transaction Theory

Churchman, in criticizing traditional accounting, does not fail to present (in Chapter 13, "Assets and Transactions") his own *trans-*

action or "net-profit" theory of optimal behavior. At some stretch of imagination one even may regard this theory as a translation of the financial statement approach into behavioral language. Although this proposal has interesting aspects, it is fragmentary and does not provide means for practical application as Churchman [1961, p. 336] himself admits. Churchman hopes that this transaction theory becomes "the basis of developing a theory of learning for the firm"; it pivots on the concept of *power*—power in the sense of an individual's potential choices.

First, a definition of transaction is offered "...when an action is construed as increasing or decreasing specific costs and returns, the action is to be called a *transaction*." Then, asset is defined in an unorthodox way as "...any aspect of an individual's environment which produces a potentiality of choice for a set of actions" whereby a distinction between *general* and *specific* assets is made according to the range of application ("variety of purposes") of such assets. The power of an individual (and we suppose also of a whole organization) is then simply identified with "the size of his assets," whereby this "theory of value ... asserts that the decision-maker tries to maximize his power." At first it looks as though this were in marked contrast with the economists' assumption of utility and profit maximization but ultimately these may become special forms of behavioral asset maximization. There also exists an element in this theory that resembles the idea of marginalism. Since "a *transaction* is the description of an action in terms of the differences," the phenomenon or idea of the *increment* has not vanished. The formal presentation of Churchman's first axiom follows below:

"Axiom I ('*Asset Maximization*'). Over a time span t_0 to t_1, the decision-maker, who is free to choose among a set of alternatives and knows the consequences of each, will select that alternative which maximizes the standardized size of his assets." (Churchman [1961], p. 328.)

There is, of course, the question whether this axiom is not just as tautological as the principle of utility maximization. But since asset or power is not defined "in the sense of ability to select the most effective action for a specific goal," emptiness or circular reasoning seems to be avoided. But even if the idea of maximizing a specific concept were realistic, for the accountant axiom 1 sounds too much like merely increasing the balance-sheet total. But Churchman points out that the idea of maximizing *behavioral* assets is general enough to include maximization of total assets, net worth or many another concept:

It may be that maximization of total 'balance-sheet assets' is equivalent to maximization of behavioral assets because the liabilities do not threaten a reduction in real assets in the next period.   If so, then the theory is equivalent to balance-sheet asset maximization.   Thus the theory is a possible basis for deciding which accounting measures (if any) the firm ought to maximize or minimize.   If a firm's objective is to maximize its potential for action, then risk considerations may be sufficient to determine what aspects of the balance sheet or operating statement are most important.[8]

This indicates that here the term "asset" is greatly at variance with traditional usage, and one wonders whether or not a less confusing name for the "substance" behind power should be chosen. This question becomes more acute if one considers that the withdrawal of an asset for the entrepreneur's personal consumption is in full accord with this asset maximization axiom—for such a consumption of an asset may not constitute a decrease but an increase in total assets, because the transaction enhances the health, the strength, the appearance, or the prestige of the individual.   Thus the increase in personal power may outweigh the general decrease. Apart from the risk that such an asset concept will become as all pervasive as the utility concept, it entails an old dilemma of economics: the separation of economic goods from personal qualities. This problem is frequently discussed in connection with national income measurement,[9] where its practical solutions by necessity have a strong dogmatic flavor.

Churchman's second axiom is even less realistic than his first, and expresses much wishful thinking: "Axiom 2 ('Closed System').   The optimal activity for the period t_0 to t_1 can be subdivided in such a way that it consists of asset maximization within each subdivision." (Churchman [1961], p. 328.)

A major reason why accountants reject the maximization of profits, or of asset holding, or of power, or of any other concept, is that they find it unrealistic to assume that in general one can subdivide economic activities according to maximization within subdivisions, whether these subdivisions are departments, branches, products, subperiods, or other partitions.   Nevertheless, axiom 2 is an important proposition if conceived as an imperative which we may try to approximate.

Churchman is not unaware of these difficulties and admits that "the transaction theory may not adequately account for reality"; he hopes, however, that "its acceptance in a certain form may be the

[8]Churchman, op. cit., 331.
[9]See e.g., Kuznets [1941], pp. 6–11 and Studenski [1958], pp. 188–91.

best method of learning from experience" if we act under the assumption that the system is closed (a system is closed when axiom 2 holds). Thus Churchman [1961, p. 335] inverts the original problem by pointing out that:

The most important problem of managerial accounting based on the transaction theory is to develop data that will reveal when a system is not properly closed. One way to go about solving this problem is to try to supply measures of statistical variations to costs, and hence, hopefully, to apply the resources contained in the literature of experimental design and statistical control. Those who have taken this step discover deep and mystifying complications; if current statistical theory is applicable to the control of segments of a firm, it is no simple matter to discover the application.[10]

After this admission it is understandable that accountants will reject criticisms by operation analysts so long as the latter are unable to propose solutions that are both better, and practically feasible. Many accountants welcome constructive criticism that helps to improve their models. But a wholesale rejection based on the maximization principle is not acceptable to them. So long as management scientists or economists are in no position to formulate a concept the maximization of which corresponds realistically to managerial behavior, accountants cannot be blamed for disregarding the idea of over-all maximization.

6.2   FURTHER CONTRIBUTIONS BY MANAGEMENT SCIENCE

Value theory is an area much favored by management scientists, and their contributions to it are as variegated as is the academic training of these experts. We shall start this discussion with an interesting aspect of valuation that arose out of linear programing. Next we shall shortly point to the contributions from the area of investment and finance. Our concern will then turn to the more esoteric contributions that decision theory has made by refining the value concept. Finally we shall concisely summarize both chapters on valuation and present our own conclusions.

6.21   Linear Programing, Valuation, and Accounting

The preceding criticism of the maximization assumption must not be misinterpreted. As emphasized, we do not object to *partial* or suboptimization, we merely object to profit-maximization—on

---

[10]Churchman, *op. cit.*

grounds of conceptualization—as the over-all goal of a person, of an enterprise, or of some other complex entity. Problems of limited scope for which an optimization algorism is available, or purely theoretical problems, may well be solved in this fashion. Optimization procedures are the backbone of operations research and as such have gained attention from theory as well as practice. In *linear programing*—one of the most successful areas of OR—a somewhat novel and interesting aspect of valuation has been disclosed.

Although the model type known as linear programing is applicable to a wide range of problems, one frequently encounters an economic standard-interpretation that takes the following form:

A series of n commodities shall be produced in such a way as to maximize profit within the capacity constraints to which the resources are subject in the short run. The problem is to determine the quantities at which the various commodities shall be produced under profit maximization. This can be formulated algebraically (see left-hand side) or in matrix algebraic form (see right-hand side) as follows:[11]

Key to Symbols.

a_{ij} . . . . Coefficient expressing quantity of resource i to produce one unit of commodity j. $(i = 1, \ldots, m; j = 1, \ldots, n)$.

A . . . . The $m \times n$ coefficient matrix of all a_{ij} coefficients.

b_i . . . . Capacity constraint of resource i $(i = 1, \ldots, m)$.

b . . . . Column vector of all m resource constraints.

c_j . . . . Profit margin (or contribution margin, or, frequently, net revenue) in \$ per unit of product j $(j = 1, \ldots, n)$.

c . . . . Row vector of all n profit margins.

O . . . . Zero column vector (consisting of n zero elements).

R . . . . Total profit (or contribution, or net revenues) in \$ (to be maximized).

x_j . . . . The (optimal) quantity of commodity j $(j = 1, \ldots, n)$ to be produced.

x . . . . Column vector of all quantities x_j $(j = 1, \ldots, n)$.

CAPACITY CONSTRAINTS

Algebraic Formulation   *Matrix Formulation*

$$a_{11}x_1 + a_{12}x_2 + \ldots + a_{1n}x_n \leq b_1$$
$$a_{21}x_1 + a_{22}x_2 + \ldots + a_{2n}x_n \leq b_2$$

$$\mathbf{Ax} \leq \mathbf{b}$$

$$\vdots \qquad\qquad\qquad\qquad \vdots$$

$$a_{m1}x_1 + a_{m2}x_2 + \ldots + a_{mn}x_n \leq b_m$$

----

[11] For further explanations of the matrix formulation and linear programing see Appendixes B and C.

NON-NEGATIVE QUANTITY CONSTRAINTS

$$x_1 \geq 0$$
$$x_2 \geq 0$$
$$\vdots$$

$$\mathbf{x} \geq \mathbf{O}$$

$$x_n \geq 0$$

OBJECTIVE FUNCTION

$$\text{maximize } R = c_i x_1 + c_2 x_2 + \ldots + c_n x_n \qquad \max R = \mathbf{cx}$$

Since the coefficients a_{ij} express the quantity of resource i needed to produce one unit of commodity j, it follows that each inequality of the *capacity constraints* expresses the following: the sum of all portions of resource i $(i = 1, \ldots, m)$ —as applied to the individual commodities $x_1, \ldots, x_n$—must be smaller or equal to the total capacity of resource i available. This limit is expressed in the variable b_i. If the left-hand side of the inequality is smaller than b_i, a portion of the capacity remains unutilized; if the left-hand side *equals* b_i, the total capacity of i is exploited in the production process.

The *non-negative production constraints*, as the term reveals, simply state that the production of x_j $(j = 1, \ldots, n)$ is either zero or larger than zero for it cannot be negative (i.e., product j cannot enter as a production factor).

The *objective function* expresses the need for maximizing the total profit or net revenues R. Since this profit consists of the product of profit margin (c_j) times product quantity (x_j) summed up for all commodities $(j = 1, \ldots, n)$, the right-hand side of this equation will pose no difficulties for accountants.

The solution, determining the commodity quantities to be produced, can be attained (under the introduction of slack variables) by means of one of several iterative algorisms that have been developed for linear programing. The algorism itself is a technical-mathematical process and shall not concern us here. Basically all this is nothing more than a simple problem of allocating (under conditions of constant marginal costs and purely competitive markets) a limited amount of resources in order to attain an optimal result. But resource allocation and valuation are two sides of a single coin, which means they are merely two different aspects of the same economic problem. From this we infer that a linear programing problem in which is known the amount of each commodity to be produced (under optimal resource allocation) may also be used to determine the optimal value or price structure of the resources. These *shadow prices* or *imputed prices* hold for the system expressed in the linear program, they need not be in conformity with the actual market price determined in a larger system. In other words we ask: which value has to be assigned to a unit of each resource in order to achieve optimal resource allocation within our framework. Obviously one product may be considered the standard commodity, the value of which is 1, and the values of the others can be expressed as ratios of this standard.

Indeed such a *dual* exists for every linear program and can be calculated *from the same data* required for the *primal* or original problem. If we call the determination of optimal product quantities the *primal* problem, the calculation of the optimal values to be assigned to the resources is the dual. If we prefer to regard the valuation problem as the primal, the allocation problem becomes the dual.

Such a dual assumes the following mathematical form: In addition to the previously used symbols we need the following:

w_i..............Value (= shadow price in \$ per unit) of resource i ($i = 1, \ldots, m$).

$\mathbf{w}$ ....Column vector of all m resource values.

$\mathbf{A'}$ ....$n \times m$ transpose of the coefficient matrix.

$\mathbf{b'}$..............Row vector of the resource constraints.

$\mathbf{c'}$ ....Column vector of the profit margins or net revenues per product unit.

K..............Total costs of all resources (to be minimized).

$\mathbf{O}$ ....Zero column vector (consisting of m zero elements).

CONTRIBUTION CONSTRAINTS

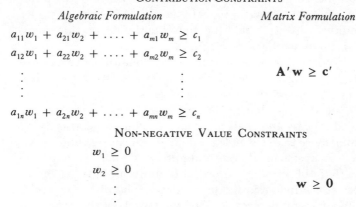

$$a_{11}w_1 + a_{21}w_2 + \ldots + a_{m1}w_m \geq c_1$$
$$a_{12}w_1 + a_{22}w_2 + \ldots + a_{m2}w_m \geq c_2$$

$$\mathbf{A'w \geq c'}$$

$$a_{1n}w_1 + a_{2n}w_2 + \ldots + a_{mn}w_m \geq c_n$$

NON-NEGATIVE VALUE CONSTRAINTS

$$w_1 \geq 0$$
$$w_2 \geq 0$$

$$\mathbf{w \geq 0}$$

$$w_m \geq 0$$

OBJECTIVE FUNCTION

minimize $K = b_1 w_1 + b_2 w_2 + \ldots + b_m w_m$ min. $K = \mathbf{b'w}$

The *profit or revenue constraints* express the fact that the values assigned to the resources used in producing one unit of commodity j must be equal to or larger than the profit (or the net revenues) per unit of this commodity j. This statement can only be understood in the light of optimal efficiency; for if the resource values were smaller than the net revenues of the pertinent product, then under perfectly competitive circumstances it would be worthwhile to expand the production of this commodity. This in turn indicates that previously the production program was not optimal. Actually, $w_i (i = 1, \ldots, m)$ measures exactly how much each additional resource contributes to the aggregated profit or net revenue at a specific point of the solution. Hence w_i is an opportunity cost in form of a marginal concept. The latter is clearly revealed in problems where a resource k, for instance, is not fully utilized; in such a situation the dual of the linear program assigns to the resource k the *zero value* $w_k = 0$. A further confirmation is found in the fact that the result for the maximal R of the primal problem is identical to the result of the minimal K of the dual, hence

$$\max R = c_1 x_1 + c_2 x_2 + \ldots + c_n x_n =$$
$$\min K = b_1 w_1 + b_2 w_2 + \ldots + b_m w_m$$

which merely expresses that under perfect competition total net revenues are identical to the total value of the resources employed.

The *non-negative value constraints* simply prevent the values, to be assigned to the resources, from becoming negative.

The *objective function* minimizes the total "opportunity cost" K at which the utilized resources must be evaluated.

Here, no doubt, we have *a new valuation model* that must be classified under the marginal valuation methods. Valuation by linear programing is a highly theoretical approach that supplies realistic results only under ideal circumstances. But there may exist potential areas of its application within the range of accounting as the following quotation indicates:

The dual variables have potential applications in cost accounting. Consider a large decentralized corporation which is broken down into a number of departments. Each department may make several products. In addition, there may exist a number of different activities for making a single product. These various departments jointly use manufacturing facilities and other services or resources which are in limited supply. Suppose that the chief executive officer has obtained an optimal solution to the linear programming problem for the entire corporation, and therefore knows which activities should be used and what their level should be.

Top management wishes to make sure that the department managers select the proper activities. However, this selection process should originate with the department managers and not come about as a result of directives from top management. Suppose that to each resource which is in short supply we assign the cost w_i, where w_i is the ith dual variable obtained from the optimal solution to the corporate problem referred to above. For each unit of resource i, a department manager must pay w_i (regardless of the actual cost of i). Then the cost of one unit of good i produced by activity j is $\Sigma a_{ij} w_i = z_j$. We now suppose that the department manager is paid c_j for each unit, c_j being the unit profit on j. If $z_j > c_j$, the department manager will find that his department is losing money when activity j is operated at a positive level. Consequently, the manager will be forced to avoid using activity j. He can find no activities for which $z_j < c_j$, and hence will automatically seek out activities for which $z_j = c_j$, i.e., activities that *should* be operated at a positive level. There remains the problem of getting the managers to operate these activities at the correct level. This cannot be done by means of the above costing procedure, and hence another approach must be used. For a unique, nondegenerate optimum, the activities for which $z_j = c_j$ form a basis. Thus only one thing can happen, i.e., the resources are not fully utilized. If the resources are utilized to the fullest extent possible, the activities must operate at the correct level. Thus it is only necessary to ensure that the available resources are used, and the production pattern will be optimal. When there are alternative optima, it is still true that the solution will be optimal if the resources are utilized to the fullest extent possible. In this case, however, the manager's optimal solution may not be basic. (Hadley [1962] p. 485.)[12]

Another important aspect of valuation by linear programing refers to planned economies. Theoretically the price mechanism in perfect competition leads automatically to an optimal resource allocation. Now it becomes possible, theoretically at least, to determine in a planned economy *that* price structure which optimizes resource allocation without any market mechanism. Economists generally agree that "this system of valuation is reminiscent of the operation of a competitive market in which resource users are forced by competition to offer to resource owners the full value to which their resources give rise, while competition among resource owners drives down resource prices to the minimum consistent with this limitation" (Dorfman et al. [1958], pp. 43–44). The same source (pp. 59–63) presents an illustration that demonstrates the

---

[12]George Hadley "Linear Programming" (Reading, Mass.: Addison-Wesley, 1962). In the above-cited passage and in other places in his book, Hadley uses the term "profit" for what accountants and economists call "net revenues."

use of shadow prices by planning authorities in order to guide production and foreign trade for the purpose of efficient resource allocation.   Since Kantorovich [1939][13] was the first to develop
the basic ideas of linear programing, "the Russians claim to have
solved the problem of value" (from an oral statement made by Prof.
R. W. Campbell).

6.22   Valuation in the New Theories of Investment and Finance

The transition from classical and neoclassical capital theory (see
Subsection 5.22) to the more practice-oriented theories of capital
budgeting took place during the fifties and sixties of our century.[14]
The most recent phase of this trend is the application of linear programing to the area of procuring and allocating capital;[15] this
promises a synthesis that supplies *simultaneous* answers to the question for an optimal investment and the question for an optimal way
of financing this investment.

These theories contain exciting ideas and hypotheses in great
abundance, their valuation approaches move along three main
roads: the first is value measurement by a *refined* procedure of discounting anticipated receipts and expenditures, the second is characterized by the use of linear programing, and the third determines
the trend of *share* values (and thus of the entire enterprise value)
by stochastic methods.[16]   The latter methods are encountered

---

[13]See also Kantorovich [1942, 1957], Koopmans [1960, 1962], and especially Charnes
and Cooper [1962], pp. 249–50.

[14]Apart from many important papers, the following books reflect this development:
Dean [1951], Solomon [1959], Bierman and Smidt [1960], M. Gordon [1962].

[15]Charnes, Cooper and Miller [1957], Massé [1959; transl. 1962], Albach [1960,
1962]; see also Kuh [1960] who does not use linear programing but who applies a maximization approach that tends toward a simultaneous solution of the investment and financing
problem.

[16]Furthermore one would have to mention the traditional and informal way of evaluating stocks about which M. Gordon [1962, p. 36] writes that "Observation of investment
analysts and reading the literature on security analysis, e.g., Graham and Dodd [1951],
reveal a highly pragmatic and subjective method for arriving at a share's value.   The
analyst looks at a corporation's record of earnings, dividends, book value, debt-equity
ratio, growth, instability of earnings, etc.   He then looks for any information not contained in the record of the above variables—information such as a change in unfilled orders
or prospects for new products—that make a change in earnings, dividends, and/or price
in the near future likely.   After considering all this information he arrives at a decision
whether the share is fairly priced, overpriced, or underpriced.

"The analyst may use bench-mark values for statistics such as the price-earnings
ratio in his analysis, but by and large his conclusion is reached through an unstructured
examination and interpretation of the data.   One should not be quick to criticize this
method of analysis.   In the absence of proven methods of scientific analysis, consideration
of all possible information, the use of judgment in conjunction with rules of thumb, and
the heavy emphasis on any information that indicates a change in dividends, earnings, etc.,
seem reasonable."

by authors such as Modigliani and Miller [1956], Durand [1959], M. Gordon [1959, 1962], etc. M. Gordon [1962] who bases the evaluation of a share on the dividend policy during the past, comes closest to the accounting approach in as far as he tries to base his model of stock price valuation on data available from accounting records, instead of using abstract concepts that evade measurement. M. Kennedy [1963, p. 115] in reference to M. Gordon's book asserts that:

> In economics super-profits are the oil which frees the mechanism of resource allocation and are generally of little interest; in business, super-profits are what the game is all about.
> And it is here that Gordon is probably at his strongest. For not only does he work out the policy implications of his empirical findings but he also tests the plausibility of his findings in terms of the reasonableness of these profit-maximizing policies. Here he saves himself from the inherent implausibilities of some of the earlier empirical work but he also shows us clearly how we must proceed if business accounts are really to be anything like as useful as they might be.
> If business decisions are to be influenced by accounting statements then clearly the values in these statements must be so designed that high values move conduct in one way, low values in another way. But a study such as this shows that optimal decisions depend entirely on the problem, on the nature of the world confronting us. Accounting values then, must be based not on self-evident great truths, not on legal rules or even on theory-less statistical measurements if they are fully to serve their purpose, but must take the sort of path followed in Gordon's investigation. (Footnote omitted.)

It may be added that Gordon's few objections to accounting mainly refer to traditional depreciation practices and seem to be fully justified.

In connection with this problem it must be pointed out that the discipline of "investment and finance" has assumed responsibility for evaluating the enterprise as a whole, a task that previously, especially in Continental Europe, was regarded to be the accountant's. However, the determination of a meaningful enterprise value is predominantly a problem of "finance" and thus far could not be attained by a pure accounting approach. In Subsection 6.34 (item 14b) we shall demonstrate that with some aid from the area of finance there exists a possibility to integrate the problem of changes in actual enterprise value with the current recording process of accounting. But usually accountants work with "monetary values" which are additive or, more precisely, they work with a homogeneous, linear value function (see MV-curve in Figure 6-1). The measurement of an enterprise value relevant to managerial or financial decisions requires nonlinear "utility" functions (of aggregate assets) as also demonstrated in Figure 6-1 (see *EV*-curve). The concept of goodwill may be used to bridge the gap between these two value functions. Thus the determination of the enterprise value function by econometric or other means is an indispensable supplement to a meaningful balance sheet presentation and must not be neglected by accountants however controversial the nature of these measurement approaches might be.

Before closing this subsection we present a general linear programing model for *evaluating* the optimal investment *and* financing activities *simultaneously*. Our presentation deviates in several respects from the models presented by Albach [1962]. The major difference lies in the formulation of the investment activity, which here is based on the *investment dollar* while Albach uses the asset (machine) unit as basis. Thus his approach emphasizes the indivisibility of the asset unit, while our model facilitates the discounting procedure, creates conformity between investment and financing parameters (which also utilize the dollar basis), and is easier to operate with in middle-sized and large-scale enterprises where groups of investments are considered rather than individual machines. As long as the indivisibility of the "asset unit" is not violated the approach here presented seems to be acceptable if not preferable. Similar to the presentation in Subsection 6.21 we present objective function and constraints in algebraic and matrix-algebraic formulation.

I. OBJECTIVE FUNCTION (TO BE MAXIMIZED)

Algebraic Formulation   *Matrix Formulation*

$$V = p_1 i_1 + \cdots + p_r i_r + q_1 f_1 + \cdots q_s f_s \qquad V = [\mathbf{p\,i} + \mathbf{q\,f}]$$

f_s.................Dollar volume of the sth financing alternative to be used.

$\mathbf{f}$.................Corresponding column vector of s financing alternatives ($\$$) to be used.

i_r.................Dollar volume of the rth investment object to be chosen;

$\mathbf{i}$.................Corresponding column vector of r investment objects ($\$$) to be chosen.

V.................Net present *value* (to be maximized) of r investment objects together with s financing requirements (i.e., "credits" which include capital raising through stock issues etc.).

p_r...................Present value *per investment dollar* of the rth investment object (= discounted net *receipts*—hence *positive*);

p.................Corresponding row vector of present values per dollar of each of the r investment objects.

q_s ....Present value *per "credit" dollar* of the sth financing alternative (= discounted net *outlays* including interest and redemption—hence *negative*);

q.................Corresponding row vector of present values per dollar of each of the s financing alternatives.

The problem posed is to find that combination of investment and financing alternatives $(i_1, \ldots, i_r, f_1, \ldots, f_s)$ which yields a maximal value V under the following four sets of constraints (II to V).

II. Liquidity Constraints

Algebraic Formulation   *Matrix Formulation*

$$l_{11}i_1 + \cdots + l_{1r}i_r + m_{11}f_1 + \cdots + m_{1s}f_s \leq -\lambda_1$$
$$l_{21}i_1 + \cdots + l_{2r}i_r + m_{21}f_1 + \cdots + m_{2s}f_s \leq -\lambda_2$$
$$\vdots$$
$$l_{t1}i_1 + \cdots + l_{tr}i_r + m_{t1}f_1 + \cdots + m_{ts}f_s \leq -\lambda_t$$

$$[\mathbf{L}\,i + \mathbf{M}\,\mathbf{f}] \leq -\lambda$$

$f_s, \mathbf{f}, i_r, \mathbf{i}$..........See explanations given after objective function;

l_{tr}.................Coefficient expressing funds required (−) or procured (+) in period t per asset dollar of investment object r.

L ....Corresponding (t times r) matrix of funds required or procured in t periods per asset dollar of each of the r investment objects.

λ_t.................Minimum amount ($) of liquid means at the beginning of period t.

λ.................Corresponding column vector of minimal liquid means for t periods (in most cases the liquid means will, of course, be larger than the mere difference between the receipts and expenditures caused by the investment and corresponding financing activities of the pertinent period).

m_{ts} ....Coefficient expressing funds procured (+) or required (−) in period t per "credit" dollar of financing alternative s.

M.................Corresponding (t times r) matrix of funds procured or required in t periods per "credit" dollar of each of the s financing alternatives.

The set of liquidity constraints can be made plausible by a series of cash flows of t periods as represented in Table 6–1.

If, for example, investment type 1 represents a machine bought

TABLE 6–1
CAPITAL BUDGET
(Receipts and Expenditures Due to Investments and
Its Financing Activities in Various Budget Periods)

Receipts (+) or Expenditures (−)		Budget Periods			
		1	2	. . . .	t
Caused by assets:					
Investment object	1	$l_{11}i_1$	$l_{21}i_1$	. . .	$l_{t1}i_1$
Investment object	2	$l_{12}i_2$	$l_{22}i_2$	. . .	$l_{t2}i_2$
⋮		⋮	⋮		⋮
Investment object	r	$l_{1r}i_r$	$l_{2r}i_r$	. . .	$l_{tr}i_r$
Liquid means available at beginning		λ_1	λ_2	. . .	λ_t
Caused by equities. *					
Financing alternative 1		$m_{11}f_1$	$m_{21}f_1$	. . .	$m_{t1}f_1$
Financing alternative 2		$m_{12}f_2$	$m_{22}f_2$	. . .	$m_{t2}f_2$
⋮		⋮	⋮		⋮
Financing alternative s		$m_{1s}f_s$	$m_{2s}f_s$	. . .	$m_{ts}f_s$
Sum		≥ 0	≥ 0	. . .	≥ 0

*Refers to debt equities as well as owners' equities.

(and fully paid for) at the *end* of the first period, then i_1 will represent the acquisition cost of this machine and $l_{11} = -1.00$ (i.e., a 100 per cent *outlay*—hence negative); furtheremore l_{21} (positive) represents the net cash in-flow, expressed in per cent of the original investment, during the second period and derived from investment type 1 (receipts in further periods are treated analogously). If, on the other hand, i_2 is an investment made (and fully paid for) at the *beginning* of, or during the first year, then l_{12} represents the percentagewise cash-inflow (positive)—due to investment type 2 in the first period —minus 1.00 (100 per cent outlay for acquisition cost). An assumption as regards the time of occurrence of the cash in-flows and out-flows—e.g., at beginning of each period—has to be made).

If financing type 1 represents a credit (fully) received at the end of period 1, then f_1 will be the amount of this credit and $m_{11} = +1.00$ (provided no interest or redemption is due during the first period); furthermore m_{21} represents the (negative) percentage (in terms of the credit's face value) to which interest and redemption amounts in the second period for financing type 1, etc. If, on the other hand, f_2 is a credit obtained at the beginning of, or during, the first year, then m_{12} represents the 100 per cent minus the percentage to be reserved for interest and redemption payment during the first period for investment 2 (hence $m_{12} < 1.00$).

III. FINANCING CONSTRAINTS

Algebraic Formulation   *Matrix Formulation*

$$f_1 \leq b_1$$
$$f_2 \leq b_2$$
$$\vdots \quad \vdots$$

$$\mathbf{f} \leq \mathbf{b}$$

$$f_s \leq b_s$$

b_s..................Credit (and capital procurement) limit for financing alternative s (in \$);

$\mathbf{b}$..................Corresponding column vector expressing capital procurement limits of s financing sources.

$f_s, \mathbf{f}$...............See explanations given after objective function.

IV. PRODUCTION CONSTRAINTS

Algebraic Formulation   *Matrix Formulation*

$$i_1 \leq k_1$$
$$i_2 \leq k_2$$
$$\vdots \quad \vdots$$

$$\mathbf{i} \leq \mathbf{k}$$

$$i_r \leq k_r$$

$i_r, \mathbf{i}$ ....See explanations given after objective function.

k_r..................Investment limit of asset type r (in \$);

$\mathbf{k}$..................Corresponding column vector of r investment limits.

V. SALES CONSTRAINTS

Algebraic Formulation   *Matrix Formulation*

$$c_{11}^1 i_1 + c_{12}^2 i_2 + \ldots + c_{1r}^1 i_r \leq s_1^1$$
$$\vdots \qquad\qquad\qquad \vdots$$
$$c_{t1}^1 i_1 + c_{t2}^1 i_2 + \ldots + c_{tr}^1 i_r \leq s_t^1$$

$$\mathbf{c}^1 \mathbf{i} \leq \mathbf{s}^1$$

$$c_{11}^2 i_1 + c_{12}^2 i_2 + \ldots + c_{1r}^2 i_r \leq s_1^2$$
$$\vdots \qquad\qquad\qquad \vdots$$
$$c_{t1}^2 i_1 + c_{t2}^2 i_2 + \ldots + c_{tr}^2 i_r \leq s_t^2$$

$$\mathbf{c}^2 \mathbf{i} \leq \mathbf{s}^2$$

$$\vdots$$

$$c_{11}^h i_1 + c_{12}^h i_2 + \ldots + c_{1r}^h i_r \leq s_1^h$$
$$\vdots \qquad\qquad\qquad \vdots$$
$$c_{t1}^h i_1 + c_{t2}^h i_2 + \ldots + c_{tr}^h i_r \leq s_t^h$$

$$\mathbf{c}^h \mathbf{i} \leq \mathbf{s}^h$$

c_{tr}^h ....Production contribution, in period t, per asset dollar of investment r toward producing commodity h;

$\mathbf{c}^i, \ldots, \mathbf{c}^h$ ....h corresponding (t times r) matrices of production contributions.

$i_t, \mathbf{i}$ ....See explanations given after objective function.

s_t^h ....Maximal sales volume in \$ (due to market satiation, etc.) of product h in period t;

$\mathbf{s}^1, \ldots, \mathbf{s}^h$ ....h corresponding column vectors of maximal sales volumes for t periods (hence each vector has t rows).

VI. Nonnegativity Constraints

Algebraic Formulation	*Matrix Formulation*

$$i_1 \geq 0, \quad f_1 \geq 0,$$
$$i_2 \geq 0, \quad f_2 \geq 0,$$

$$\mathbf{i} \geq 0, \mathbf{f} \geq 0$$

$$i_r \geq 0, \quad f_s \geq 0,$$

For symbols $i_r, f_s, \mathbf{i}, \mathbf{f}$ see explanation given after objective function.

Our presentation presumes that the dollar value of the investment objects considered equals the dollar value of the financing requirements

$$\sum_{d=1}^{r} i_d = \sum_{e=1}^{s} f_e .$$

For further details—especially as regards the choice of discount rates, the controversy with Dean's [1956] theory of capital budgeting, and the extension to a dynamic model, we refer to Albach's [1962] original work.

6.23 Value in Decision Theory

The preceding discussions, as sketchy as they are, reveal the existence of a great variety of approaches to value measurement, each of which serves a specific purpose. In consequence, our belief in the existence of a unique, or true, or neutral value of an object at a specific moment—independent of the objective and circumstances of measurement—is strongly shaken. A solution out of this dilemma might be found in a functional approach to valuation which recognizes different objective-oriented valuation models, but which emphasizes the common features of all of them. Before propositions toward such a functional theory of valuation are expressed, some contributions of modern decision theory[17] to the value problem ought to be shortly examined. Indeed this new area of statistics, not at least due to its interdisciplinary character, has illuminated many novel value aspects. It has contributed essentially toward formulating the interdependence between value and the *context* out of which value arises. In the following we shall draw upon the conclusions presented by Smith, Walters, Brooks, and Blackwell [1953], N. Smith [1952, 1954, 1956a and b], Schlaifer [1959, 1961], and Engels [1962].

N. Smith [1956a] who regards value from a very general point of view—he not only includes economic but also military and ethical aspects—asserts that a thing (i.e., "a particular way of classifying the universe") cannot be regarded apart from its environment. This is illustrated by the following quotation, which toward the end introduces a somewhat unaccustomed point of view:

> That the value of a dollar bill is not an absolute quantity but depends more on the circumstance in which it is exchanged can be illustrated very simply by noting the comparative effort a starving man would make to obtain a dollar bill compared to that which a rich man would make to get the same dollar bill. To the starving man the dollar bill represents something to eat, and therefore represents survival. It could in fact represent his whole chance to live, whereas to the rich man the dollar bill represents an increment toward the achievement of some further goal not necessarily of tantamount importance to his survival.
>
> Attention becomes directed not to the particular things or items in the system such as the man, the dollar bill, or ..., but to the system as a whole. It shall be seen that values are fundamentally to be associated with the state or condition of the entire system, and not necessarily with some linear combinations of the things comprising it. (N. Smith [1956], p. 112.)

Thus, *primarily, a value does not refer to an object but to the state of a system.* This is a somewhat novel aspect worth considering. On the

---

[17] The term "decision theory" designates a new approach to statistics. Game theory exercised a revolutionary, and in a way unexpected, influence upon statistics. This impact has been so strong that statistics nowadays is regarded to be the theory of decision making and no longer the science of numerical aggregates. "Years ago a statistician might have claimed that statistics deals with the processing of data. As a result of relatively recent formulations of statistical theory, today's statistician will be more likely to say that statistics is concerned with decision making in the face of uncertainty" (Chernoff and Moses [1959], p. 1). The foundation-stone to this development was laid by Abraham Wald [1950] through applying game-theoretical concepts (developed by Neumann and Morgenstern [1944]) to statistics. A further decisive step was made by L. J. Savage [1954] who incorporated subjective *a priori* probabilities and the idea of Bayesian strategy to this area. The fact that this modern version of statistics operates with such concepts as utility and opportunity cost matrix (regret matrix) indicates the close relation of this discipline to economics and business administration.

other hand, the fact that values are not necessarily additive—although frequently, especially in accounting, assumed to be so—is well known from economics and the personal experience of consumption. *The value of an object* or thing is then derived from the state values and becomes a *secondary* concept; it *is defined as "...the difference in state values of a system whose states differ by the thing under consideration."* This, at the bottom, is a highly generalized version of marginalism, since the value of an object is expressed in terms of the first, partial derivative of a function expressing the values of consecutive states ("state value function"). But while marginal economics rarely specifies sufficiently enough the entire context ("system state"), N. Smith makes provision for a finite number of elements or dimensions describing this context. Another difference, and at the same time the chief decision-theoretical feature of this new approach, is to be found in the use of stochastic variables (probabilities). Hence a system is defined as "a set of all states that are connected by nonzero transition probabilities" and "the value of the present state w is the average (or expected) value of a future state x, or in other words, is equal to the product of the probability of transition from state w at time s to state x at time t, with the value of the future state x at time t." (N. Smith [1956], p. 115.)

This finds expression in the following "value equation:"[18]

$$Q_{.}(w, s) = \sum_{x} P(w, s; x, t) Q(x, t) \qquad\qquad t > s$$

$Q(w, s)$........The value associated with the state w (consisting of a finite number of elements) at time s.

$Q(x, t)$ ....The value associated with a future state x at time t.

$P(w, s; x, t)$...The probability of transition from state w at time s to state x at time t.

The concept of *transition probability* has come into high vogue in connection with Markov Chains and transition matrices and is not entirely new in accounting. It has recently been applied by Cyert, Davidson, and Thompson [1962] to the problem of evaluating ac-

---

[18]This equation is subject to various implicit assumptions. Above all, a solution is possible only by assuming some boundary conditions about the end or equilibrium states which are called "trapped" states. The equation is derived from the Chapman-Kolmogorov equation (a special version of Bayes' [1763] theorem—see Kolmogorov [1931, 1933]) which can be interpreted in a forward looking way (a present state is given to predict the probability of a future state) or in a backward looking way where a future state (or its value) is given and the probability of the present state (or its value) is to be determined. Thus the latter form is already a version of the value equation and resembles somewhat valuation by discounting.

counts receivable and by Zannetos [1962] to the problem of group depreciation. It is worth noting that N. Smith uses the terms "transition" and "event" synonymously. Since changes are here interpreted stochastically, instead of deterministically, transition probabilities play a decisive role in value theory. But N. Smith throughout his discussion emphasizes the arbitrariness of these probability functions or constants:

Value determinations continually refer to future states, and those in turn to states further into the future, and so on, until either an endpoint is reached or until the state is so far into the future that prediction becomes impossible. At either of these points rational operation ceases and one must resort to an intuitive designation. These are essentially postulates of the value structure. Later in the discussion it will be suggested that there are more fundamental and more absolute principles that constrain the intuitive approach to the assignment of ultimate values; the application of these principles, however, does not lead to a unique set of values—that is, to a unique solution to the value equations. There is a natural repugnance felt by some readers that ultimate values are to be considered arbitrary and intuitive and they prefer to consider them otherwise. (N. Smith [1956], p. 116.)

Usually the transition paths from the present into the future—at least some of them—can be controlled or influenced by certain *decisions*. Thus for each of these decisions or actions there exists a value equation (as presented above). This is best illustrated in the situation where a commodity can be sold in different ways, but where only one way achieves the highest yield. Indeed, *often* we identify the *value* of this commodity with the *highest yield*. Smith proceeds along this path by considering first an optimization procedure which selects the value equation of the decision that assigns the largest numeral. But only simple situations are amenable to such a maximization approach. We know from game theory that under more complicated circumstances "arbitrary" decision criteria[19] must be introduced before a state can be evaluated. Recognizing this, N. Smith substitutes the maximization imperative by a more general operator that represents an objective function or *decision criterion* chosen according to the value judgment of the decision maker (and not necessarily identical with an optimization procedure).

---

[19] In game theory we encounter the following decision criteria, none of which can be regarded as a criterion of profit maximization: (1) A. Wald's criterion of pessimism (maximin criterion), (2) L. Hurwicz' criterion of optimism (maximax criterion), (3) L. J. Savage's criterion of minimum regret, and (4) Laplace's criterion of rationality (cf. Miller and Starr [1960], pp. 85–94).

This no doubt is an interesting approach to explain value, but one which imposes severe impediments for practical valuation purposes. A major difficulty lies in the requirement for an adequate description of the state of a value system. The more comprehensively a system is conceived, the more difficult it is to evaluate. Compare the value system of a man's total happiness with the value system of the monetary, short-run profit, pertaining to a storage system (inventory control model). It is relatively easy to determine how to accomplish the latter suboptimization, but to maximize the happiness in the first system is a hopeless undertaking. As Engles [1962, p. 46–47] points out: "though no actions are imaginable which are indifferent with regard to personal happiness, the imperative 'maximize your happiness' is so vague that it is difficult to derive from it concrete actions" (transl.).

Out of this dilemma arose two important and related ideas. First, the idea of *limiting or subdividing a value system:* that is reducing the context of such a system to a set with a smaller number of elements —or creating two and more subsystems—upon which a decision function (e.g., suboptimization) can be imposed without inherent difficulties. The state of such a subsystem can be evaluated with relative ease, provided each subsystem together with its decision function conforms to the over-all goal of the complete system or supersystem (cf. Churchman's Axiom 2, p. 192).

The second idea is the *resolution of conflicting value systems.* One may distinguish three conflict situations: "dominance," "schism," and "concrescence." (See N. Smith [1956], p. 135–41 and Engels [1962], pp. 47–50). Under *dominance*, one value system suppresses the other in the area of conflict. A *schism* leads to an "arbitrary" separation of the conflict area, in one part of which the first value system is dominant, in the other part the second. But the interesting situation is that of *concrescence*;[20] here a systematic solution exists, provided a third supervalue system can be found that conforms to, or "contains," both or all conflicting systems. The inventory control problem offers an illustration for such a case. Minimization of storage cost is in obvious conflict with minimization of losses caused by items out-of-stock. But there may exist a value system that embraces and reconciles both subsystems. This is the firm's total endeavor to generate income. After this supervalue system is con-

---

[20]Concrescence has played an important role in science where new observations enforce either changes of old postulates and additions of new ones or complete revisions of the axiomatic system. This resembles the evolution of a value system.

ceived, it should be possible to evaluate the state of this new system under the pertinent goal function (e.g., profit maximization). In such situations it is necessary to *assign weights* (Lagrange multipliers) to the set of elements of each subsystem.[21] An essential element of the decision-theoretical approach to value is the translation of monetary magnitudes into utility values. Only in particular situations can the "expected monetary value" be used as a guide to action:

> Expected monetary value should be used as the decision criterion in any real decision problem, however complex, if the person responsible for the decision would use it as his criterion in choosing between (1) an act which is certain to result in receipt or payment of a definite amount of cash and (2) an act which will result in either the *best* or the *worst* of all the possible consequences of the real decision problem.[22]

In all other cases Schlaifer [1961, p. 39] recommends that "any decision maker who wishes to choose among acts in a logically self-consistent manner must choose the act which has the greatest expected utility." Hence, if decision theory shall be used beyond the mere conceptualization of value, it becomes necessary to establish utility measures. The difficulty of such an undertaking has been pointed out with sufficient emphasis, but Figure 6-1 (Engels [1962, p. 180] uses a similar graph yet plots asset units instead of monetary values on the abscissa) illustrates how a utility approach would reflect entrepreneurial asset holding.

The abscissa of Figure 6-1 plots the *monetary value* of asset aggregates. The ordinate reflects *value* from a more general view point. The linear (45°) function MV (monetary value) serves as a comparison and merely projects the monetary value of the abscissa into the value scale of the ordinate. The function EV projects the enterprise (or utility) value on the ordinate and the corresponding monetary value on the abscissa. Thus, for example, an asset aggregate of $50,000 (monetary value) is estimated to have an enterprise value of $90,000. To overcome the difficulty of nonlinear asset functions in accounting, the concept of goodwill may be used in such a way as to

---

[21]The purpose of this presentation merely is to draw the reader's attention to these developments and to give a rough outline of recent insights—to be utilized in our own approach (see Subsection 6.34). A fair grasp of decision theories' contribution to the problem of valuation can only be attained by reading the literature cited and by getting acquainted with many new concepts that cannot be discussed within these few pages (e.g., "atrition system," "immortal value system," "trapped state," "variable field points," etc.).

[22]From *Introduction to Statistics for Business Decisions*, by Robert Schlaifer. Copyright 1961. McGraw-Hill Book Company, Inc. Used by permission, p. 29.

declare the difference of $40,000 (= 90,000 − 50,000, i.e., the difference between enterprise value and monetary value) as the *goodwill*. According to Figure 6-1 the identity of monetary value and enterprise value is "accidental" and holds only for two instances, namely at $30,000 and $100,000. Thus the determination of the enterprise value (Subsection 6.22) is an essential complement to the accountants evaluation approach. Engles [1962], who is concerned

FIGURE 6-1

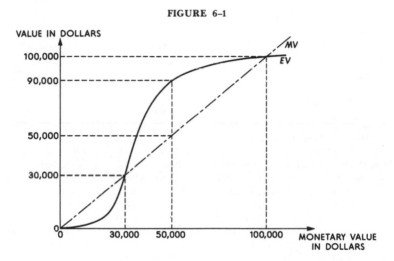

with the "valuation theory of business administration in the light of decision theory," recommends an approach that provides, what he calls, a "prognostic balance sheet" (*Prognosebilanz*). Basically, this theory—which operates with subjective or decision values (*Entscheidungswerte*) and current values aiming at the separation of holding gains (*Dispositionsgewinne*) from operating gains (*Umsatzgewinne*)—has strong affinity to the Edwards and Bell [1961] proposal, discussed in Subsection 6.37 (though Edwards and Bell's analysis is more thorough and offers tools for immediate practical application). But Engels [1962, p. 183], like Churchman[23] [1961, p. 336], emphasizes the importance of using accounting and the balance sheet for prognostic purposes in conformity with "learning

---

[23] Although Engels [1962] demonstrates extensive knowledge of the Anglo-American economic literature, it seems that the works by Edwards and Bell [1961] and Churchman [1961] appeared too shortly before his own publication to be taken into consideration (they are not even listed in his bibliography).

theory".[24] Indeed, a systematic learning-theoretical approach to accounting seems to be highly promising. But regrettably, neither Engels nor Churchman bother to exploit periodic budgeting—as it has been developed during recent decades—for this purpose. To our mind a practical effort towards the *projection* of accounting data into the future—utilizing the comparison between the "is" of the balance sheet and income statement, and the "ought to be" of the budget in a learning-theoretical fashion—cannot succeed without concern for improved budgeting techniques. Chapter 9 will elaborate on this point.

Yet, Engels, recognizing further aspects of the balance sheet, admits that

One can neither assume that business practice creates value data in vain nor that these data are altogether meaningless. The conclusion remains that objectives are being sought and goals are being achieved which cannot be pursued (or not so well) by means of decision values. Such a purpose is "communication."

If one classifies the values encountered in economics as decision values (*Entscheidungswerte*) and non-decision values (*Nicht-Entscheidungswerte*), one may soon find out that the latter occur only where information is transmitted from one person to another: The creditor receives information from the debtor, the revenue authority from the business man, the public from the corporation, the buyer or seller from the appraiser. These values too will ultimately serve the purpose of decision making: the acquisition of shares, the taxation, the granting of credits or price determination. But there is a great difference whether the evaluator and the decision agent are identical or not. If the evaluator himself makes the decision, he knows exactly the way by which he reached the value data and knows what he may conclude from them. But an outsider does not know it, he will gain no information or—even more dangerously—a false one. Therefore, under certain circumstances, it may be advantageous to convey a smaller amount of information securely than to transmit a value with large information content, but running the risk that the message is not correctly interpreted.

The precondition of every communication are conventions. There must exist an agreement about the meaning that adheres to the tokens. If I pronounce, for example, the word "*weiss*," then a German imagines a specific color; quite differently the Englishman, he associates with the

---

[24] *Learning theory* is based on the relation between *a priori* and *a posteriori* probabilities as stated in Bayes' theorem.

A priori probabilities are given or assumed (subjectively) *prior* to any information which the "experiment" may yield. *A posteriori* probabilities are the probabilities that result from the "experiment." For an easily comprehensible explanation of Bayes' theorem see Mosteller, Rourke, and Thomas [1961, pp. 143–52]. Bayes' theorem arises out of the concept of *conditional probability* and demonstrates how a newly acquired information (e.g., about market conditions) from the past may change our judgment about future events of the same sort.

same sound (vice) a tool or a blemish. The social conventions of the two peoples are different in respect of these sound articulations. (Engels [1962], p. 209, transl.)

The task of the theory of value conventions is a minimization of the information-loss that is inevitable. The "decision" is the ultimate purpose of subjective values as well as that of value conventions—even a value data generated by conventional rules is being transmitted with the objective to enable the making of a decision by the recipient. Thus it seems to be justified to use the term "value" for both categories, subjective values and value conventions in spite of the difference of their origin. The inherent relationship between both concepts weighs much stronger than the different methods for generating the value data. (Engels [1962], p.234, transl.)

6.3 SUMMARY, CONCLUSION, AND PROPOSALS

6.31 A Recapitulation

Value was conceived by classical economists as an intrinsic quality of a commodity. Intensive concern with consumer behavior led the marginalists to the more subtle conception of value as a relation between a commodity (object) and an economic agent (subject). They determined value, thereby, through the "satisfaction" which the last increment of this commodity (directly or indirectly) generates in the economic agent. Management scientists improved upon this view by emphasizing the context or the circumstances in which value is expressed. Thus we may regard value, primarily, as pertaining to the state of a value system. The value of an object, therefore, becomes a secondary concept which is derived from the discrepancy in value between two, chronologically different, states of a single value system.

Valuation, as the attempt to measure value, experienced an evolution that is closely tied to the individual steps of the metamorphosis undergone by the value concept. For classical and Marxian economics the labor invested in a commodity became its value measure. The marginal school in vain attempted to measure the "satisfaction" or the "utility," which the particle of a commodity causes, by direct means. Regress to value as expressed in the market was no more satisfactory a solution than was reformulating the (cardinal) utility to an ordinal utility concept. The newest version, the Neumann-Morgenstern utility—connecting utility with the concept of risk, thereby providing a more tangible measurement—could not supply a useful value measure beyond the laboratory.

In the face of this perennial dilemma the point of gravity of valua-

tion has been shifting from the direct, psychological aspect of measuring utility, to the *deduction* of value from a value judgment assumed to be given. Thus the "valuation calculus" has become the
dominant part of valuation. Different versions of such a calculus
(or rule for deducing value from some exogenous data) encountered
in business administration and economics have here been discussed. So, for instance, the "present value method" assumes as
given a series of future cash receipts and expenditures and infers
from these exogenous variables the value of an object (asset) at an
anterior date by means of discounting procedures. "Historical costing" on the other hand assumes the acquisition cost at a past date of
purchase as the correct value and deduces by means of a depreciation calculus and (hopefully) a price-level index, a posterior value
of this object. These and many other valuation rules are beset with
implicit assumptions, many of which hold up only under narrow
and specific circumstances. Decision theory introduced three important aspects to the valuation calculus. (1) The incorporation of
a priori probabilities, thereby refining the valuation process, (2) the
explicit formulation of *decision criteria* and objective functions for
valuation purposes, and (3) the overt specification of the *context*
within which the valuation is conceived. Thereby it was revealed
that the value to be assigned to a state or object may change if the
vector describing the state(s) of the value system is being extended
or contracted. This also brought into focus the necessity for subdividing and reconciling value systems. *Each* of these three aspects
enforces *a value judgment*. The assumption of *a priori* probabilities no
doubt is a normative process, so is the choice of a decision criterion
and the "arbitrary" limitation of the context or value system envisaged. Thus the question arises whether the reliability is not too
much infringed upon by the many subjective elements that enter the
picture. Is not a single normative decision about a value (as at today) as reliable as this long chain of deductions from a future value
that requires a multitude of subjective assumptions? But even if
the decision-theoretical approach is somewhat more accurate, from
a practical viewpoint the degree of reliability must be brought in
tune with the costs of measurement. It seems that in many situations the improvement of accuracy of the value measure by means of
stochastic models will be negligible compared to the much higher
expenses thereby caused. It will be necessary to confirm or refute
this supposition by empirical testing.

But many scholars reject the value concepts of decision theory for other reasons. Churchman [1961, p. 166] for example is disturbed by the fact that in case of two people disagreeing on the probability of future outcome "no one else, not even the scientists, can say which one is right when one adapts a Bayesian attitude and the other decides on the attitudinal basis of pessimism. . . . If this theory were adopted, there would be no ultimate basis for determining correct decisions." Obviously someone who believes that management scientists are in a position to determine *the* absolutely correct values or decisions—and therefore requests that the scientist must be permitted to impose these values and goals upon the decision maker—inevitable comes in conflict with Bayesian statistics. Churchman [1961, p. 168] cynically remarks that "Indeed, one cannot help being astonished at the naïve metaphysical presupposition underlying some of the thinking in current statistical theory, namely, that there is a Something-I-know-not-what, who in Her motherly way gives us mortals our data."

Whatever the objections are, from the viewpoint of conceptual clarification the contribution of modern decision theory to the problem of valuation is of far-reaching significance. The insight that valuation requires specification of the context as well as of the objective pursued, supplies evidence that the accountant's traditional multipurpose financial statements are indeed highly dogmatic tools. This situation can be remedied only if it is possible to endow the financial statements with a value scale that covers those ranges of purpose and context that are common to all business situations. Before a proposal for such improvement can be advanced, further discussion will be necessary. First let us examine and illustrate the interrelation of value measurement and its objective in the following simple situation.

6.32   An Illustration of the Interrelation between Valuation Objective and Valuation Model

We assume two commodities X and Y (e.g., a load of potatoes and a load of beets) and state their order of preference according to four different valuations: the first expresses the (acquisition) costs a month ago; the second expresses the market value as of today; the third, the present value (discounted, anticipated net revenues); and the fourth expresses the personal utility (measured on a utility index UI) in case the dealer is forced by circumstances to use one or the other commodity for consumption in his own household.

	Commodities	
Valuation Models	X	Y
I Cost value (past)	$100	$120
II Market value (current)	$110	$110
III Present value (anticipated)	$150	$130
IV Utility (current or anticipated)	UI 1	UI 2

The question we wish to answer is, which of these *four* valuation models is required for making the correct decision with regard to the following seven objectives?

a) Buying either commodity X or Y (in accord with profit maximization), if the decision maker has confidence in his future estimates (assuming he is not yet in possession of these commodities).

For this purpose market value and present value supply the models required to make the purchasing decision. In this case the acquisition of commodity X will be recommended.

b) Selling either X or Y, if the decision maker has confidence in future estimates (assuming he is in possession of these commodities).

Here again the market and present value models must be applied. Either commodity can be sold for $110, but to maximize a subjective profit it is advisable to sell commodity Y (in spite of a book loss of $10 which is irrelevant for this decision—hence the neglect of cost values).

c) Selling either X or Y, if the decision maker has no confidence in future estimations.

For this purpose a comparison of cost value with market value reveals an unrealized book profit of $10 for commodity X, but an unrealized book loss of $10 for commodity Y. To materialize a maximal accounting profit, commodity X ought to be sold presently.

d) Consuming either X or Y (in accord with utility maximization) by decision maker (or his family). We assume there is no possibility of consuming a part of X and a part of Y.

This objective requires the application of the utility model only. The decision obviously is to consume commodity Y, which according to the utility index yields twice as much utility to the dealer (and his family) than does commodity X.

e) Selling either X or Y, if decision maker wants to attain an accounting profit of at least $8 (aspiration level).

Again we are dealing with an accounting profit and require cost as well as market value models. Selling commodity Y would yield an accounting profit smaller than the aspiration level, while the sale of commodity X satisfies the objective. (Accounting profit is then $10 > $8).

f) Informing the decision maker—who owns X and Y but does not dispose of them—on a "conservative" or *minimal* estimate of his "wealth" (enabling him to make other financial dispositions).

Again, a comparison of cost value with market value is called for. Commodity X requires application of the cost value, while commodity Y is measured at market value ("cost or market value, which ever is lower").

g) Informing the decision maker—who owns X and Y but does not dispose of them—on a "legally objective" and documentable estimate of his "wealth" (enabling him to make other financial dispositions).

In this case only the cost value is required, provided that the acquisition cost is assumed to be the most reliable evidence from the viewpoint of legal objectivity. Preference rating goes here to Y but for different reasons than in situation (e).

This simple problem contains *six* different *objectives:* (1) maximization of economic profit (in *a* and *b*); (2) maximization of accounting profit (in *c*); (3) utility maximization (in *d*); (4) "satisficing" an accounting profit level (in *e*); (5) conservative profit reporting (in *f*); and (6) legalistically objective profit reporting (in *g*). It demonstrates that the objective determines the valuation model to be used and that different objectives may require different valuation models. We also notice that in the above illustration commodity X is rated higher than Y for the objectives (*a*), (*b*), and (*c*), while the reverse is the case for objectives (*d*), (*e*), (*f*), and (*g*). To conclude from this that the valuation models applied in the first three (or the last four) cases are equivalent among themselves or identical would be a superficial judgment. The exact difference in profit figures or other differentials is evidence of such a fallacy.

The preceding illustration calls for further examination of the concept "valuation model." Thus the next subsection presents the most basic model types, emphasizing the common characteristics of valuation models in general.

6.33   Basic Valuation Models

From the preceding discussion of the various approaches to valuation we conclude that most valuation models used in the economic sciences are characterized by *five* major elements:

1. The *object of comparison.* In order to express or measure a value, at least two objects (or events) are called for: the object to be evaluated and the scale, i.e., the object in terms of which the former (the *value object*) is to be evaluated. Since the object of comparison is usually an amount of cash there is the danger of overlooking the distinction between value object and value scale. However, as the following basic valuation models all use cash as a scale, this item can be neglected in the following comparison.

2. The *basic state* β, a set of exogenous variables (or functions), acceptable to the parties involved in generating and utilizing the measure to be derived. Frequently these given data are also values (*original* values) which must be distinguished from the value to be deduced (*opportunity* value).

3. The *valuation operation* ω, a set of mathematical operations relevant for deducing "the value" from the valuation basis β.

4. The *time structure* τ, a set of time points (or small intervals) ex-

pressing the temporal relation between the time points of the valuation basis on one side and the date for which the value is to be expressed (this date will be called "the time of value" or "the time of the preliminary state"). τ might be contained in ω and plays an important role when comparing different valuation models.

5. The (*opportunity*) value V, the end result or endogenous variable of the Valuation model. The information-worth of V will depend on the context within which it is used and on the degree of relevance of the model.

The subsequent illustrations enable a comparison of the main elements β, ω, τ, and V of well-known valuation models.

THE MARGINAL VALUATION MODEL

In many situations (though not in all) the value of an object can be equated with the utility which the last increment of this object is supposed to yield. Thus the insight of marginal economics re-emerges in a more generalized form in the value notion of decision theory.

Basic state β:	total utility function (occasionally also other related *total* functions like cost or revenue functions or indifference curves).
Valuation operation ω:	differentiation of the total (utility) function as at a specific instant (of consumption, production, etc.).
Time structure τ:	this set usually contains a single time point that is identical to the "time of value."
Value (to be measured) V:	equal to the first differential of the total function as at a specific instant.

FIGURE 6–2

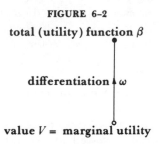

total (utility) function β

differentiation ↓ ω

value V = marginal utility

As previously discussed the difficulty of this valuation model lies in determining the total (utility) function or indifference curve, etc.

INVESTMENT VALUATION

The major exponent of this method of asset (and occasionally liability) valuation was Irving Fisher. It utilizes the actuarial calculation of discounting future revenues, and expenses connected with the asset item.

Basic state β:	anticipated receipts and expenditures (or expected net revenues, in case of identical time points). $\beta = \{\beta_1, \beta_2, \beta_3, \beta_4\}$.
Valuation operation ω:	discounting anticipated receipts (positive) and expenditures (negative) according to τ.
Time structure τ:	this set contains as many elements as time points of receipts and expenditures; it indicates the number of periods (or subperiods) each individual receipt or expenditure has to be discounted *backwards* to the time of value.
Value (to be measured) V:	equals the "present value."

FIGURE 6–3

DISCOUNTING PROCESS

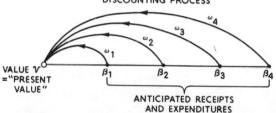

CURRENT VALUATION

It is based on an "informal" but reliable inquiry about the amount to be paid for an asset in the current market. Depending on whether the market is looked at from the sellers' or purchasers' side, one will speak of sales values, liquidation values, etc., *or* of replacement values, purchase values, market values, etc., respectively. Apart from these variations in the valuation basis, the further procedure is the same whether a liquidation value or a replacement value is referred to.

Basic state β:	the current quotation in the market.
Valuation operation ω:	the pertinent relation consists in a mere equating (=).
Time structure τ:	this set consist of a single time point, identical to the time of value.
Value (to be measured) V:	depending on the basis, it equals the sales value, liquidation value, replacement value, or purchase value, etc.

FIGURE 6–4

a market quotation β

equating ω
(=)

value V = **market value**

ADJUSTED COST VALUATION

The historical cost basis as traditionally used in accounting is justifiable from an economic viewpoint only if the original cost of acquisition is adjusted in two ways (1) with regard to value-changes due to utilization, etc., (2) with regard to value-changes due to price and price-level fluctuations.

Basic state β:	original cost of acquisition of asset.
Valuation operation ω:	applying a depreciation function and a function expressing other value changes.
Time structure τ:	this set contains a time point that (usually) is not identical with the time of value but is *prior* to it.
Value (to be measured) V:	equal to historical cost minus accumulated depreciation charges, plus or minus other value adjustments.

FIGURE 6–5

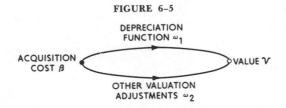

Many other valuation models could be listed (valuation by linear programing, valuation by means of regression models, etc.) but the purpose of this Subsection is not to explain valuation models, it is to *demonstrate the existence of the common elements* β, ω, τ *and* V, as well as *to illustrate the differences in the structure of these elements between various model types.* This and the preceding discussion may serve to prepare the reader for the following set of propositions which summarize the most important ideas on valuation. These propositions are presented in a fashion similar to our exposition of the basic assumptions (main items are listed with Arabic numbers, subitems, and explanations are listed with lower-case alphabetic letters). But the formulation of these valuation propositions is not rigorous enough to regard them as postulates in a formal sense. The last two items (13 and 14) of this set contain proposals that are especially relevant to future accounting.

6.34   Propositions and Definitions on Valuation

1. *Valuation* is a procedure assigning a preference order to either the state of a system or to an object (or event) by means of a valuation hypothesis.

  a) The numeral which usually expresses this preference order is called the *value*. Such a value may consist of one numeral or several of them.

  b) The valuation hypothesis is expressed by the *valuation model*, a set of rules and relations for assigning values (see Subsection 6.33).

  c) *The state of a system* is its condition at any moment in which the system is not undergoing any change. A state is expressed by a number of components (a vector) describing the relevant aspects of this state (context).

  d) A *value scale* is a standard of measurement (normally a ratio scale, occasionally merely an ordinal or interval scale) for evaluating an object, event, or state in terms of another object.

2. The *state of a value system* is described by a series of components considered to be relevant to a specific problem.

  a) The value system may be regarded as the *context* in which valuation occurs.

  b) The series of components may be presented in vector form (e.g., the anticipated receipts and expenditures in case of an investment problem).

  c) Two persons who do not agree on the relevance or irrelevance of the various components choose different systems and are likely to attain different values.

  d) Frequently the system has to be described very narrowly because of difficulties in procuring data for some of the relevant components. A narrow system is usually easier to evaluate than a broader one. Objectives can be defined more precisely for a narrow system.

  e) Therefore subdivisions of a system (too complex to describe or evaluate) are often necessary. Here it is assumed that the objectives defined on one or more subsystems are in conformity with the objective envisaged for the supersystem (e.g., suboptimization—cf. also with "closure" in Churchman's sense).

  f) If the objectives defined for two systems are in conflict, reconciliation may be attained provided there exists a common supersystem.

3. The *value of an ultimate state* of a system is assumed to be given or determined by psychological-experimental means.

  a) We ought to distinguish between psychological and economic value measurement. In psychology a person's preference order of an ultimate state is measured by observing that person's reactions or by questioning him.

    In the economic sciences we usually assume the value(s) which a person assigns to an ultimate state (or a set of ultimate states) as given, and then measure the preference order the person assigns to a preliminary state or, more frequently, to the object (or event) that causes the change(s) from the preliminary to the ultimate state(s).

  b) Hence the *ultimate state* of a value system is that state which can be evaluated "directly" or with greater accuracy than any other state of the same system.

c) Since the value of an ultimate state is a more or less spontaneous value judgment and since value judgments are conditioned by past events the ties between past and future may be considered strong enough to justify in some situations an *historical cost basis* adjusted for depreciations, price-level changes, etc.

d) The value of an ultimate state is closely related to the "conditional value" of modern decision theory.

Schlaifer [1959, 1961, p. 24] offers the following definition of the "*Conditional value* of an act given a particular event: the value which the person responsible for a choice among acts attaches to the consequence which that particular act will have if that particular event occurs."

4. In a *deterministic situation* there exists one ultimate state for a system. In a *probabilistic situation* there exist two or more ultimate states for one and the same system, and for a single preliminary state.

a) To the occurrence of each possible ultimate state a probability number (smaller than one) may be assigned in such a way that the sum total of these probabilities amounts to 1 precisely.

5. The *value of the preliminary state* of a system depends on the ultimate states and the probabilities with which one expects to attain each of the possible ultimate states.

a) The pertinent probability values are called *transition probabilities*.

b) The chronological occurrence of a preliminary state is prior to that of the ultimate state(s) of the same system. (The discounting method in which the "present value" is tied to a preliminary state that occurs before the cash receipts and expenditures, gives sufficient illustration).

6. The *transition probabilities* are based on personal value judgments, hence they are subjective *a priori* probabilities in the Bayesian sense.

7. The *value of an object* depends on the discrepancy between the values of the system states connected by this object.

a) Thus in a probabilistic situation a large number of alternative values can be assigned to an object. This number is equal to the number of possible ultimate states to be reached through the pertinent object (derived from propositions 3 and 6).

8. The *value* of an object at a preliminary state may be *derived* from the value of another preliminary state (or the value of the same object at this other state) provided the latter value has previously been determined.

a) We call the means of deriving the value of an object from another value the *valuation operation* (see Subsection 6.32). This other value may refer to the object at another preliminary state (or to the value of this other state) or to the value of an ultimate state.

b) This enables us for instance to accept a realistically adjusted historical cost valuation. The assumption here is that at the time of acquisition (i.e., at a preliminary state), the object at this state was determined as described in proposition 7. Then according to proposition 8 the value of this object at a later, but still at a preliminary, state can be derived by means of an appropriate valuation operation that takes all relevant factors into account.

c) The ultimate state or the first preliminary state (from which the value of the object at the second state is derived) will be called the *basic state*. This basic state may be *anterior* or *posterior* to the preliminary state (or its object) for which the value is to be derived.

9. An *action* (or decision) may influence the occurrence of one state or a limited number of specific ultimate states.

a) A corollary of proposition 9: different actions may influence the occurrence of different ultimate states.

b) If there exists one (or a group of) ultimate state(s) which is preferable to other possible ultimate states, and if the occurrence of the former can be influenced by an action, this action is called the *desired action*. The latter is expressed in the decision criterion or the objective function chosen.

c) The value assigned to the object under the desired action is usually regarded as "*the* value of the object" (though usually there exist other possible values of this object). Where clarity demands a strict distinction of this value from others it might be called the *opportunity value*.

d) It follows that the (opportunity) value of an object depends on the decision criterion (or the objective) that governs the valuation. This is an important conclusion that follows from propositions 8 and 9 and definitions 9*b* and 9*c*).

e) The statement of 9*d* indicates that multipurpose valuation provides satisfactory results only if every "value" contains a separate numeral for each major purpose (thus the need for multidimensional values— see item 13*a*).

10. The *decision criterion* and *objective* depend on a value judgment of the decision maker.

a) The decision criterion is not necessarily aimed at maximization of something; for technical and conceptual reasons maximization procedures are frequently infeasible. (For various decision criteria see footnote 14 of this chapter).

11. In valuation two extreme attitudes may be distinguished.

The numerals are assigned either (*i*) to convey "relatively" reliable information valid *for a well defined decision;* or (*ii*) to achieve *general information* at a low degree of reliability, but for a broad range of purposes.

a) A solution out of this dilemma could be attained by generating multidimensional values (see item 13*a*).

12. In using valuation models for decision making, the type and number of the model to be chosen will depend on the objective pursued.

a) The pursuit of a specific objective requires certain actions by the economic agent. These actions may be facilitated by using one or more valuation models.

b) A number of standard valuation models have been developed with regard to specific groups of objectives. In choosing a specific valuation model availability of data and cost of procuring these data are major considerations.

c) The most frequently used standard models are:

   (*i*) *Historical cost basis* (with several variations, each depending on the adjustment procedures incorporated).

   (*ii*) *Current value basis* (with variations depending on further circumstances, e.g., market value, replacement value, liquidation value).

   (*iii*) *Present value basis* (yield value).

   (*iv*) *Marginal value basis* (incremental value). Usually connected with utility functions (variations: cardinal, ordinal, and Neumann-Morgenstern utilities).

d) Theoretically each of these standard models could be conceived stochastically (as well as deterministically). However only the "present value basis" has a "basic state" posterior to the "preliminary state" (see 8*c*). Therefore this valuation model comes closest to the conception of value as expressed in proposition 4.

e) Before a specific valuation model is applied it ought to be carefully examined as to (*i*) whether it is applicable to the objective pursued, (*ii*) whether the basic data are procurable, and (*iii*) in which range of accuracy the results can be expected to fall.

f) For some purposes "related" models may be used instead of *the* "appropriate" model. In such cases a lower degree of reliability must be expected. The connection between "related models" and "degree of reliability" is an important area that is not yet sufficiently explored.

13. For a comprehensive evaluation of an object (or event) it may be desirable to assign to it a *vector of numerals* instead of a single numeral. Each element of this vector constitutes a value determined by a different valuation model.

a) Such a vector or ordered tuple of values will be called a value vector or a *multidimensional value*.

b) Such multidimensional values will be of special significance where the generator and the user of the data are not in direct contact with each other and where the data are used for various purposes.

c) Multidimensional values can frequently be measured only with *ordinal scales* and are subject to a *partial* ordering (the traditional value concept is subject to a *complete* order relation).[25] Under this new concept it may be inadequate to say the (multidimensional) value of object A is $500 and of object B is $300, but it may still be meaningful to say that the (multidimensional) value of A is greater than that of B. That means only the individual elements of the *value vector* are measurable upon ratio scales. To attain measurability of the multidimensional value on an ordinal scale our definition has to be complemented by a convention. One may regard the multidimensional value of A greater than that of B if at least one element of A is higher than the corresponding element of B and all other elements of A are at least as great as the corresponding elements of B. Similar conventions are occasionally encountered in mathematics. In some cases the (multidimensional) value of A will be *incomparable* with that of B (e.g., when some elements of A are greater but others are smaller than their correspondents in B). There, recourse to a comparison of individual elements is necessary or a more restricted multidimensional value (i.e., one with fewer dimensions) must be adopted.

We shall illustrate this new concept of multidimensional values with a simple example of three commodities A, B, and C and the following four *specific* value concepts: cost value, market value, present value, liquidation value.

		A	B	C
CV	Cost value	$3.00	$2.50	$4.00
MV	Market value	6.00	4.50	4.00
PV	Present value	7.00	5.00	6.00
LV	Liquidation value	5.00	4.00	5.00

If we designate the multidimensional values of A, B and C as $MV(A)$, $MV(B)$, and $MV(C)$ respectively we can write and compare three vectors:

$$MV\ (A) = (3.0,\ 6.0,\ 7.0,\ 5.0)$$
$$MV\ (B) = (2.5,\ 4.5,\ 5.0,\ 4.0)$$
$$MV\ (C) = (4.0,\ 5.0,\ 6.0,\ 5.0).$$

---

[25] For an explanation of various order relations see Ackoff [1962], p. 187–89.

Then, based on the above stated convention, we may conclude that $MV(A) > MV(B)$ and $MV(B) < MV(C)$ but $MV(A)$ is incomparable with $MV(C)$ because the first element of $MV(A)$ is smaller than the first element of $MV(C)$ but the second and third elements of $MV(A)$ are greater than the corresponding elements of $MV(C)$.

To propose such multidimensional values for the financial statement presentation is not so farfetched. Indeed a beginning has been made by the Accounting Research Study No. 6, AICPA [1963], which recommends to present the financial data in historical cost values as well as in price-level adjusted cost values (see Section 5.6). This is equivalent to the recommendation of a two-dimensional value vector. In future one may deem it advantageous—especially for internal reporting—to assign three or more-dimensional *value vectors consisting of an adjusted cost value, of a current value, of a present value*, etc. In addition to the information conveyed by each element of a value vector, *the relation and deviation of the various elements (of a specific vector) among each other will considerably enhance the informational content* of such a multidimensional value. A balance sheet endowed with such value components for each asset and equity item not only would be more informative than the traditional approach but would constitute a source of information satisfactory to the needs created by the every-increasing complexity of economic life.

A final and important proposition deals with the dilemma of nonlinearity and nonadditivity of many values relevant for decision making. A proposal for an accounting solution to this dilemma is offered in 14b.

14. The value of an entity over time may follow a nonlinear function.

a) Figure 6–1 (see also Figure 6–6) and the pertinent part of Subsection 6.23 has demonstrated this nonlinearity of the value function of an enterprise. There we distinguish between monetary value and enterprise value (also called "utility" or "decision" value) and assert that the determination of the enterprise value is an important complement to accounting, though thus far no procedure exists to reflect the change in enterprise value by accounting techniques.

b) An integration of the change in enterprise value and accounting procedures is feasible by fitting approximate linear functions to the nonlinear value function of the enterprise.

The presentation in Figure 6–6 illustrates such an integration and offers simple rules for practical application.

FIGURE 6-6

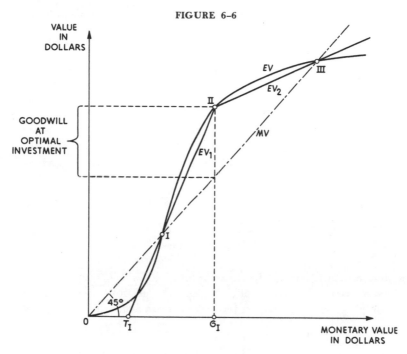

We assume the enterprise value function can roughly be estimated. This should prove to be no more difficult than estimating
total cost curves and constructing breakeven charts. Then one may
attempt to determine the points I, II, and III of the enterprise value
function EV. The points I and III are the intersections of EV with
MV (the monetary value function), while point II is characterized
by a marginal value (first derivative) of unity, that means it has a
45° tangent which in consequence is parallel to MV. The projection
of II on the abscissa may be regarded as the *point of optimal investment*
O_I. Finally the point T_I (we may call it the investment *threshold*) is
the intersection of EV_1 with the abscissa. The approximation of the
nonlinear curve EV partly by the linear curve EV_1 (passing through
points I and II) and partly by the linear curve EV_2 (passing through
points II and III) yields results which in the face of the *rough* estimation of EV might be regarded as acceptable.

After introducing some further concepts the bookkeeping rules
for integrating successive changes in enterprise value with current
accounting procedures can be stated.

   (*i*)   The slope of EV_1 is called value coefficient c_1.
   (*ii*) The slope of EV_2 is called value coefficient c_2.

(iii) The monetary value of fixed assets on hand (before acquisition of a new fixed asset) is designated by F.

(iv) The monetary value of a new acquisition or of fixed assets bears the symbol P.

(v) In addition to the well-known account "Goodwill" an account called "Goodwill Surplus" is needed. This account records the increase and decrease of owners' equity due to the idiosyncrasies of the enterprise value functions (EV_1 and EV_2).

Rules for recording goodwill (positive and negative) and the corresponding change in owners' equity (goodwill surplus) in case of purchases of additional capital equipment (here we *consider fixed assets only*):

Condition	Journal Entry	Dr.	Cr.
(a) If $F < T_I$ and if $(F + P) < T_I$ then			
	Dr. Goodwill Surplus..	P	
	Cr. Goodwill		P

Below (or at the left of) the investment threshold T_I every purchase of fixed assets is "written off," hereby the account Goodwill may be compared to an allowance for depreciation account.

(b) If $F > T_I$ and
    if $T_I < (F + P) < O_I$ then

Dr. Goodwill.......... $P(c_1 - 1)$
    Cr. Goodwill
        Surplus...... $P(c_1 - 1)$

Within the range between investment threshold T_I and investment threshold T_I and investment optimum O_I a *positive* goodwill has to be recorded. Since the approximate goodwill is the difference between EV_1 and MV, a goodwill ratio or coefficient (per \$1 purchase of fixed assets) can be expressed by ($c_1 - 1$), thus the total goodwill arising from this purchase is $P(c_1 - 1)$. We remind the reader that the slope of MV is unity and $c_1 > 1$.

(c) If $F > O_I$ then

Dr. Goodwill Surplus.. $P(1 - c_2)$
    Cr. Goodwill ..... $P(1 - c_2)$

Beyond (or at the right of) the investment optimum a *negative* goodwill has to be recorded (the slope of EV_2 is smaller than the slope of MV or in other words $c_2 < 1$). Since the fixed assets purchased within this range are recorded at full "monetary value" they must be written off in proportion to the difference between the slopes of the two curves MV and EV_2. Hence the negative goodwill of the additional purchase is $P(1 - c_2)$.

Purchases which pass over the investment threshold T_I or over the investment optimum O_I obviously ought to be broken down into a part below and a part above the pertinent point (T_I or O_I).

The above stated rules shall be illustrated in the following example of the X Corporation:

Assume

$$T_I = \$20,000 \qquad c_1 = 2.5$$
$$O_I = 50,000 \qquad c_2 = 0.3$$

Business events (all purchases of fixed assets are on a cash basis):

(1) Owners' original cash investment. $60,000
(2) Purchase of furniture 23,000
(3) Purchase of merchandise (on a credit basis). 12,000
(4) Purchase of machinery. 18,000
(5) Purchase of equipment. 11,000

CASH
(1)..........60,000 | (2a)..........23,000
                    | (4a)..........18,000
                    | (5a)..........11,000
                    | End. bal. 8,000
      60,000 | 60,000

PAYABLES
End. bal. ....12,000 | (3) 12,000

FURNITURE AND FIXTURES
(2a).........23,000 | End. bal. 23,000

MERCHANDISE INVENTORY
(3) ....12,000 | End. bal. 12,000

GOODWILL
(2c) 3,000 | (2b).........20,000
 × 1.5 = 4,500 | (5c) 2,000
(4b) 18,000 | × 0.7 – 1,400
 × 1.5 = 27,000 | End. bal. 23,600
(5b) 9,000 |
 × 1.5 = 13,500 |
      45,000 | 45,000

MACHINERY AND EQUIPMENT
(4a).........18,000 | End. bal. 29,000
(5a).........11,000 |
      29,000 | 29,000

GOODWILL SURPLUS
(2b).........20,000 | (2c) 4,500
(5c) .... 1,400 | (4b).........27,000
End. bal. ....23,600 | (5b).........13,500
      45,000 | 45,000

CAPITAL STOCK
End. bal. ....60,000 | (1) 60,000

BALANCE SHEET AT END OF PERIOD OF X Co.
Cash......... 8,000 | Payables.....12,000
Merch. ......12,000 |
F. & F. ......23,000 | Owners' Equity:
M. & E. .....29,000 | Stock Capit. 60,000
Goodwill ....23,600 | Goodwill
                    | Surpl. 23,600
      95,600 | 95,600

Most of the entries of this example are straight forward, the only exceptions are those in the goodwill and the corresponding goodwill surplus accounts. Entry (2b) provides a write-off allowance or negative goodwill for all fixed assets up to the investment threshold —the latter was assumed to be $20,000. That portion of the first purchase beyond the $20,000 (i.e., the remaining $3,000 of transaction 2) already participates in the creation of a (positive) goodwill. To this investment of a monetary value of $3,000 corresponds a "utility" value of $7,500 (= 3,000 × 2.5), hence the difference of $4,500 (7,500 − 3,000 or 3,000 × 1.5) represents the increase in goodwill (or decrease in negative goodwill). The value coefficient of 1.5 (= c_1 − 1) is therefore repeatedly encountered on the debit side of the goodwill account. A purchase, or a purchase portion, beyond the investment optimum reduces the goodwill (or creates a negative goodwill) as shown in entry (5c). Here the last $2,000 of transaction 5 fall into this range. To this monetary value of $2,000 a "decision" value of $600 (= 2,000 × 0.3) corresponds; the difference of $1,400 (2,000 − 1,600 or 2,000 × 0.7) represents the negative goodwill. Such an approach enables the continuous revision of the goodwill and facilitates the determination of an approximate enterprise value at any time. Our proposal also demonstrates that an accounting device exists for solving the dilemma of nonadditivity (or nonlinearity of "utility" or "decision" functions) of the value of the enterprise. Only recently Engels' [1962, p. 182] asserted that "the balance sheet is unfit to determine the total capital of an enterprise because there is no evaluation procedure which leads to the enterprise value by way of the partial values, not even if intangible parts of the firm are added (since their 'value' is gained merely by balancing, not by direct evaluation)" transl. The preceding discussion may convince the reader that Engels' assertion holds no longer, provided one accepts the rough estimation of enterprise value functions as an integral part of accounting and the balance sheet approach. This can be justified by reference to our basic assumption 11 (Valuation). One ought to be aware that the continuous "adjustments" made to Goodwill could have been recorded directly in the various fixed asset accounts. The reason why we abstained from such a procedure lies in our conviction that the balance sheet must show the "monetary" value of individual groups of assets as well as the total enterprise value. A balance sheet which contains no Goodwill but only records the "decision" values—instead of the monetary values —of the fixed assets, would be at least as deceptive as the traditional balance sheet, since the "decision" value of an individual asset varies—we have seen that this decision value depends on the investment stage at which such an asset was acquired.

One might however, argue that the accounting procedure suggested is cumbersome and confusing because of the need for constant alertness of the bookkeeper with respect to various thresholds and with respect to the question when a specific value coefficient has to be applied. This argument is weak since most of the investment decisions will be carried out within the range between the investment threshold and the investment optimum. In such cases it will be sufficient to multiply the monetary value of every additional fixed asset with the value coefficient $(c_1 - 1)$, debiting the resulting amount to Goodwill and crediting it to Goodwill Surplus.

However, it must be pointed out that several theoretical and practical issues pertaining to this problem need further thorough exploration. So for instance the problem of ordinary depreciation or the withdrawal of fixed assets from the enterprise. One may assume that such a decrease in fixed asset values follows the same paths as any increase, but Engels [1962, p. 181] indicates that the determination of an enterprise value function by way of value losses due to withdrawals of (fixed) assets supplies a curve that is differently shaped than the one presented and that the former yields higher enterprise values over most of the investment range. Another problem arises out of the question whether the full exclusion of cash and other current assets from the goodwill calculation by means of value coefficients is justified. Frequently a brand-name, a stock of customer, or other similar intangibles are important components of a goodwill concept that has to be fused or reconciled with the goodwill concept discussed here. A particular problem is the estimation of the enterprise value function and its integration with theoretical considerations of the optimal size of the enterprise.

Although the two major advances of accounting, "general price-level adjustments" and "current cost basis" are not yet generally accepted in business practice, it is by no means premature to reflect upon the problems next in rank. The stronger the demand becomes for a *managerial accounting* (in the sense of accounting for managerial decision making) the easier it will be to materialize in actual practice the ideas of *multidimensional values* and of *value additivity by means of value coefficients*.

Chapter 7

EMPIRICAL HYPOTHESES IN ACCOUNTING

7.1 PRAGMATIC VERSUS SCIENTIFIC HYPOTHESES

7.11 Induction and Statistical Hypotheses

OUR SCIENTIFIC and practical activities are crowded with more or less well-tested assumptions. While science tries to base its research on nonrefuted assumptions, the practical decision maker—under the pressure of circumstances—frequently cannot afford such a rigorous selection principle. Intuitions, beliefs, and guesses though lacking the formal credentials of high "reliability," (in the sense of Popper's [1959, p. 251 f.] "corroboration") perform such important tasks that human existence is hardly imaginable without them. Such "deficient" assumptions are just as abundant in business life as elsewhere; they even penetrate more formalized procedures like operations research, econometrics, and accounting. Thus it might be expedient to distinguish between two kinds of assumptions. On one side "general propositions about all things of a certain sort" (Braithwaite [1953], p. 2) to which a degree of validity is attributed that is high enough to class them as *scientific hypotheses*. On the other side, assumptions that are useful tools, facilitating decisions of everyday life, but whose degree of reliability (corroboration) is lower, so as to expect occasional or even frequent failure. The latter assumptions will here be addressed as *pragmatic hypotheses*, or *action hypotheses*. At the end of the next subsection (7.12) we offer a criterion for distinguishing action hypotheses from scientific hypotheses; but in a way such a distinction is arbitrary or is one of degree only—at least as long as Hume's rejection of the *induction principle* cannot be refuted on better and firmer grounds than has been the case thus far.[1] This arbitrariness is also confirmed by the more recent application of statistical hypotheses[2] in the physical sciences. Statistical hypotheses, in contrast to purely scientific ones, are not rejected by a single instance of refutation, their acceptance is subject to complex criteria that are connected with obvious value judgments and that have even been criticized as being based on circular reasoning. Braithwaite attests that statistical hypotheses were originally looked upon suspiciously:

> While statistical generalizations were current only in the social and biological sciences and in physical theories like the Kinetic Theory of Gases where non-statistical explanations were not excluded, it was reasonable for a philosopher of science to regard the statistical hypotheses as being acceptable *faute de mieux*, and only until they could be displaced by the non-statistical hypotheses . . . . But now that the most advanced of the sciences in the most sophisticated and far-reaching of its theories postulates an irreducibly statistical form of explanation, it will be unreasonable for a philosopher of science to ignore the special problems presented by statistical hypotheses. (Braithwaite [1953], p. 116.)

7.12   On the Metamorphosis of Statistics

While the science of past centuries was searching for *absolute* laws, modern science interprets most of its generalizations as tentative and relative. In consequence, statistical hypotheses became so well en-

---

[1]"Hume's scepticism rests entirely upon his rejection of the principle of induction. The principle of induction, as applied to causation, says that, if A has been found very often accompanied or followed by B, and no instance is known of A not being accompanied or followed by B, then it is probable that on the next occasion on which A is observed it will be accompanied or followed by B. If the principle is to be adequate, a sufficient number of instances must make the probability not far short of certainty. If this principle, or any other from which it can be deduced, is true, then the causal inferences which Hume rejects are valid, not indeed as giving certainty, but as giving a sufficient probability for practical purposes. If this principle is not true, every attempt to arrive at general scientific laws from particular observations is fallacious, and Hume's scepticism is inescapable for an empiricist. The principle itself cannot, of course, without circularity, be inferred from observed uniformities, since it is required to justify any such inference. It must therefore be, or be deduced from, an independent principle not based upon experience. To this extent, Hume has proved that pure empiricism is not a sufficient basis for science. But if this one principle is admitted, everything else can proceed in accordance with the theory that all our knowledge is based on experience. It must be granted that this is a serious departure from pure empiricism, and that those who are not empiricists may ask why, if one departure is allowed, others are to be forbidden. These, however, are questions not directly raised by Hume's arguments. What these arguments prove—and I do not think the proof can be controverted—is that induction is an independent logical principle, incapable of being inferred either from experience or from other logical principles, and that without this principle science is impossible." (Bertrand Russell [1945], pp. 673–674.)

[2]"Many of the generalizations which occur in science are not of the simple form of a *universal hypothesis* asserting that 100%, or that 0%, of the things which are A are also B, but are of the form of a *statistical hypothesis* asserting that a certain proportion between 100 and 0% of the things which are A are also B." (Braithwaite [1953], p. 115.)

trenched that statistics has officially been acknowledged as a major vehicle toward scientific cognition. The acceptance of statistical hypotheses was, under the impact of quantum theory and nuclear research, unavoidable. But once concessions were made, the further development away from the belief in the apprehension of an absolute, empirical truth, was just as inevitable. Indeed, as Schlaifer [1959, p. 607] remarks:

> In the first quarter of the twentieth century statisticians viewed their task as one of establishing the truth or falsity of statements or "hypotheses" rather than as one of showing how to choose among acts. The really great achievement of the theory which is now classical was to recognize that the establishment of ultimate truth is not an achievable goal for mere human endeavor and that the real problem of statistics is to aid in choice among acts under uncertainty, but the language of "hypotheses" remains as a historical residue.

Out of classical statistics grew modern *decision theory* in which the new task of facilitating choices in the face of uncertainty found its realization. It was game theory, which exercised, so to say unexpectedly, a revolutionary influence upon *statistics*, such that the latter is no longer defined as the art of processing aggregate data but is identified plainly as the theory of decision making.[3] The Bayesian[4] approach compels statisticians to make a strict distinction between rigorous *statistical hypotheses* (concerning *known* long-run frequency distributions) and *a priori* or *primary hypotheses* (concerning frequency distributions whose parameters or their biases are not exactly known but merely conjectured). These primary hypotheses (Schlaifer's [1959, p. 610] terminology) form a subset of that class which we have designated as pragmatic hypotheses; but the latter are by no means restricted to assumptions based on frequency distributions. *Most management decisions are built upon assumptions about objects and events that are not amenable to random sampling. The basis of these assumptions then consists of other, occasionally perhaps less convincing, evidence. The important thing, however, is to realize again that the distinction is merely a matter of degree and that it would hardly be justifiable to regard primary hypotheses as acceptable for formal decision-making purposes while labeling the*

---

[3] See footnote 17 of Chapter 6.

[4] Bayesian statistics is an extension of the concept of conditional probability to subjective evaluations of future events, whereby continuous experience is used to improve the subjective probabilities. Its "philosophy" involves some subtle reflections and hot controversies. In business administration it has recently come into vogue in connection with decision theory. See Bayes [1763], Savage [1954]; for an introduction see Schlaifer [1959, 1961], Raiffa and Schlaifer [1961], Chernoff and Moses [1959], Mosteller, Rourke, and Thomas [1961].

remaining pragmatic hypotheses as unacceptable. This discussion has particular bearing on accounting where systematic sampling procedures are relatively novel and where many aspects lie beyond the range of applying statistical tests. The critical question then asks for the tools with which, and the kind of evidence out of which, most of the pragmatic accounting hypotheses are molded. Before we attempt to answer this question a short, additional remark on the essence of pragmatic hypotheses is due. While statistical hypotheses might be regarded as the link between purely scientific hypotheses (if such exist) and pragmatic hypotheses, it must be borne in mind that the latter (in contrast to statistical hypotheses) do neither aim toward universal generality nor toward becoming scientific hypotheses. They merely express "more or less justified beliefs"—with regard to specific instances or purposes—on which decisions are to be based. Economic science, for a considerable time, has been utilizing such pragmatic assumptions, but unfortunately under the banner of statistical and universally valid hypotheses.[5] Accounting, on the other hand, is rarely concerned with the discovery of natural or behavioral "laws," but rather attempts to create an apparatus supplying information of different degrees of reliability for a variety of decision-making purposes. In this pursuit, choices between action hypotheses will be made in such a way that those hypotheses— how low their degree of reliability might be—will be considered acceptable which, in the face of uncertainty and economic constraints, are at least slightly more promising or more reasonable than their alternatives. Thus we propose *to exploit the process of invalidation as a criterion for distinguishing between pragmatic hypotheses* (or action hypotheses) *and scientific hypotheses:*

1. A scientific hypothesis is invalidated by instances (acceptable to the experts) which testify reliably to the *falsity* of this hypothesis.

2. A pragmatic hypothesis is invalidated (rejected) by demonstrating (or believing) that, *in the long run* or *on the average,* the actions based on it yield results that are *less satisfactory* than the results of actions based on another, available or procurable hypothesis.

Thus "invalidation" for a pragmatic hypothesis, means: "not acceptable because not good enough," while, for a scientific hypothesis it means: "not acceptable because not true."

Whether the result of an action is less satisfactory than that of another will depend in most cases on a comparison of *net* benefits or

---

[5] Although Papandreou [1958, 1959, 1963] attacks this problem from a different standpoint, his methodological investigations are highly relevant to the above mentioned aspect.

estimated net benefits. Hence the costs of determining and applying an hypothesis in relation to the *gross* benefits derived from these hypotheses plays a decisive role. The major difficulty obviously lies in measuring these benefits.

To illustrate the essence of a pragmatic hypothesis we recall the estimation of the total cost curve of an enterprise (e.g., for the purpose of constructing a break-even chart). A wide range of estimation procedures are available for finding such a cost function. The "low- and high-point method"—measuring two extreme points that relate cost and output volume, and connecting these points by a linear function—is a very crude but inexpensive method which occasionally is deemed satisfactory. The other extreme lies in the application of sophisticated econometric approaches, as carried out by Dean, Johnston, and others (see Johnston [1960], pp. 136–68). However, business practice rarely can afford the expenses involved in measuring cost curves by econometric means; indeed it seems that most examples listed by Johnston were financed as projects of scientific research and not out of the regular funds allocated to the pertinent accounting departments. Since the shape or formula of the total cost curve is a *pragmatic hypothesis*—as long as it serves decision-making purposes—its acceptance or rejection will depend upon the relation of the benefit of this hypothesis for the management of the firm to the costs of procuring this hypothesis and operating with it. Only in exceptional cases will incidental research funds be available for such a purpose. Thus in many instances the improvement in the decision-making process attained by more refined procedures of estimation will not warrant the employment of the most accurate tools available.

Furthermore it must be pointed out that even hypotheses developed with the aid of econometric niceties are merely action hypotheses and cannot claim the status or generality of scientific hypotheses. An examination of the hypotheses employed in interindustry analysis or in estimating consumption, investment, and other functions for the United States, reveals that these hypotheses are by far too crude to make their refutation difficult. For policy purposes, however, they may well be employed as the best hypotheses available—in spite of the fact that it is difficult to ascertain whether the funds spent on their construction yield equivalent or larger benefits.

We may summarize this short outline by stressing the belief that *the "empirical" task of the normative scientist* (the accountant, operations analyst, econometrician, etc.) *primarily lies in formulating and ranking competing action hypotheses rather than in a search for ("unrefuted") scien-*

tific hypotheses. At a first glance, this standpoint might resemble Friedman's [1953] view that the value of a theory does not depend on the realism of its assumptions (hypotheses) but on their power of prediction. Yet we emphatically dissociate our view from that held by Friedman (recent critics of his view are found by Nagel [1963], Samuelson [1963], and H. Simon [1963]). For a pure or *positive science* —and we wish to regard economics as such a science—the confutation of an hypothesis cannot be reversed by a "satisfactory" prediction performance of this hypothesis. For an applied or normative science, however, a *pragmatic* hypothesis may indeed be sanctioned by its (relative) power of prediction. But the absolute ability of such a theory to predict may be low. Thus, in connection with pragmatic hypotheses we prefer to speak of *projection* (into the future) instead of prediction wherever these hypotheses do not serve a mere explanatory purpose (for the distinction between "explanation" and "prediction" see Cyert and March [1963], pp. 299–301.)

7.13   The Persistency Assumption and the Trial and Error Principle

Even modest insight into human behavior reveals that many actions are founded upon crude and imprecise information, but also that this information need not be inadequate. Here, adequacy does not depend on accuracy alone but is closely tied to the sacrifice which procurement of the information has caused. Furthermore, many actions and reactions of living organisms in general, arise (in the absence of contrary evidence) from the supposition that a present trend will persist in the future. Most learning processes, for instance, are forced to place a high premium on the assumption of continuity and constancy. The usefulness and justification of learning processes of this kind is founded solely in the evidence that actions based on an assumed "uniformity of the universe" yield, *in the long run and in bulk*, better results than actions that disregard this assumption. It seems that *in the course of the evolutionary process* of life this experience has conditioned *the code of behavior of all creatures with a special kind of inertia or bias toward assuming the continuation of past trends.*[6] Such psychological insight is imperative also for the understanding of business management and accounting, at least for condoning the crudity of many of its premises. Since a "general policy" based on the extrapolation of past occurrences (in the absence of contradictory evidence) does not guarantee the success of *individual* actions, it is obvious that some of these actions will be failures —

---

[6] In the absence of any contradictory evidence.

then the assumptions, on which an *isolated* action was based, will, in the light of a failure, appear crude or absurd, while it may have been quite reasonable from the general viewpoint of past experience.

As Devine points out, accountants cannot legitimately be criticized for concerning themselves so heavily with history:

> Before turning to positive statements about accounting operations we turn to the old cliché that accountants always look the wrong way—that they always look at the past even though the utility of information arises from improved decisions that concern only the future. This criticism needs careful examination, for the charge is so obviously non-rational that some deceptively subtle points must be involved. We may start with a simple observation: so far as modern scientists know *no one*, not even the most adept fakirs and clairvoyants, *have ever learned anything from the future.* Obviously then one does not look to the future for knowledge, for understanding, for information or for guidance. One then asks from what sources do knowledge and information arise? What sources of information help form our mental attitudes and behavioral patterns? Only the most deterministic philosophers, the most devout believers in predestination or the most mystical mystics would argue that such sources are placed in one's experience in advance and are accessible to the mind before the events transpire. Perhaps some will maintain that individuals should look only to the present for guidance and for knowledge. An extreme interpretation of the usual epicurean dictum might seem to indicate such an approach, but it should be clear that if only the present has "meaning," then we can neglect both planning for the future and the heritage from the past. A closer look indicates that a sharp interpretation of "present" gets us involved in such mathematical devices as limits and that refuge in such methods soon leads us into an interval too short for any psychological span of recognition. If the interval is long enough for some sort of cognition, the present so defined must have enough of the past included in it to permit recognition and coordination with existing experience. Apparently scanning the present is not very helpful. (Devine [1962b], Vol. I, p. 13.)

Such statements need not bother the philosophic sceptic whose "contention is that any inference from past to future is illegitimate" (Ayer [1956], p. 37) because they do not assert a claim to knowledge, they mainly reflect observations about life in general and human behavior in particular, a behavior that is justified by long-run experience, but which does not pretend to constitute *rigorous* knowledge in the epistemological sense.[7]

---

[7] In this connection Ayer [1956, p. 34] remarks: "The main problem is to state and assess the grounds on which these claims to knowledge are made, to settle, as it were, the candidate's marks. It is a relatively unimportant question what titles we then bestow upon them. So long as we agree about the marking, it is of no great consequence where we draw the line between pass and failure, or between the different levels of distinction. If we choose to set a very high standard, we may find ourselves committed to saying that some of what ordinarily passes for knowledge ought rather to be described as probable opinion. And some critics will then take us to task for flouting ordinary usage. But the question is purely one of terminology. It is to be decided, if at all, on grounds of practical convenience."

Nevertheless the *continuity* or *persistency assumption* constitutes one of the pillars on which nonprobabilistic action hypotheses rest. Another one is found in the *trial and error principle* which justifies an hypothesis by the ultimate result arising from corrective interactions between a series of preliminary attempts (or experiments) and the observations of their outcome.[8] Those who disparage such a principle or its utilization in managerial decision methods ought to be reminded that *the trial and error approach has been the most successful approximation to optimizing and satisficing* since life began and, in many areas, will continue to fulfill this function. Yet, it must be conceded that the increasing complexity of industry, the growing predominance of mammoth concerns, and the anticipated, extensive automation of production, administration, and distribution, promotes sophisticated analytical methods at a degree unknown before.

7.14　Judgment Probability and Relative Frequency

The scientific recognition of the value of action hypotheses comes about hesitatingly only. As pointed out, Bayesian statistics with its subjective *a priori* hypotheses and its strategy of attributing (in the absence of contrary evidence) *equal* probability to each occurrence of various possible events, manifests the assumption of a homogeneous universe. This may be taken as evidence that management scientists have become aware of the need for solving, or at least exploring, the problem of pragmatic or action hypotheses. Closely connected with it is the question whether the concept of probability can and should be applied to action hypotheses or whether it ought to be restricted to the relative frequency of purely statistical phenomena. Braithwaite speaks of the term "probability" as being used in two different senses and illustrates this usage as follows:

For besides speaking of the hypothesis that the probability of a radium atom disintegrating within a period of 1700 years is 1/2, we also speak of Einstein's theory of gravitation being probable, or of its being more probable than Newton's theory, where it is a whole scientific theory that is asserted to be probable, or to be more probable than another, and not an

---

[8]The artillery practice of hitting a target by preceding trial shooting, the results (too far–too short) which are reported by an observation plane to the battery, is the classic example of this type of "optimization procedure," a procedure, the implicit application of which in business practice is so obvious and self-evident that many students of business administration are not aware of it. There exist many instances (e.g., waiting lines in self-service stores) where the trial and error approach, has lead to arrangements that come close to solutions offered by OR's analytic queuing models. Obviously there are countless cases in which systematic, analytical studies afford improvement, but frequently the costs of such studies, especially the determining of the necessary data, is so prohibitive that the net benefits of such studies are negative or too small to justify action.

event to which the theory itself assigns a probability" (Braithwaite [1953], p. 119).

To discern one from the other, probability in the second sense has variously been called "reasonableness" (Braithwaite), "confirmation" (Carnap), "judgment probability" (Churchman), "acceptability" (Kneale), and "credibility" (Russel). The chief argument for this distinction and particularly the rejection of the term "probability" (except by Churchman) for the *second* meaning, lies in the assertion that "relative frequency" (probability in the *first* sense) is measurable, while probability in the second sense is based on a value judgment and hence is deemed to be beyond measurability. But Churchman [1961, chap. 6] demonstrates in a very subtle analysis that the measurement of relative frequency by necessity also introduces value judgments: "the operation of verifying class membership is based on judgment; the operation of verifying the theory of sampling is based on judgment; the verification of a theory of the generation of events is based on judgment" (Churchman [1961], p. 168).

After a careful support of his arguments and a lengthy sequence of deductions, Churchman concludes that "good judgment" can be defined in terms of relative frequencies such that the latter concept may be used in expressing the degree of validity of a theory or a hypothesis:[9]

> It would certainly be naïve to suggest that we "count" the instances where the theory has held and the instances where it has failed—because our data are never of the form that clearly provides positive and negative instances. But we could count instances that are judged to confirm and instances that are not judged to do so. We could also count favorable expert opinions and unfavorable ones. Indeed, the whole idea of well-substantiated judgment seems to rest on such a counting procedure.
>
> Hence we conclude that either definition of probability is feasible. Reflection on the last chapter leads us to see that the issue is not one of logic but of decision-making. In effect, we want to know which is the better standard for probability measures: relative frequency or well-substantiated judgment? Relative-frequency standards have been much more carefully studied and developed; the judgment standard is often much easier to apply. Which is the better standard cannot be decided by an intuitive feeling about what probability 'really' means. But whichever standard is chosen it is essential that data collected under the other standard be adjustable; this means, simply, that relative frequencies must

---

[9]West C. Churchman, *Prediction and Optimal Decision: Philosophical Issues of a Science of Values.* Copyright 1961. By permission of Prentice-Hall, Inc., publisher, p. 169.

agree, by some acceptable method, with judgment probabilities and that judgment probabilities must agree with relative frequencies in those cases where both methods are applicable.

The reason for our concern with such definitional and epistemological problems, is easily explained. If accounting is to serve purposes that lie beyond purely legalistic considerations, its assumptions must be seen in the light of that body of knowledge which is presently being developed in management science for the purpose of formulating meaningful decision models. There, philosophers, logicians, and statisticians clear the ground for the practicing operations analyst as well as for the accountant. Yet, the latter can benefit from the endeavor of others only if he understands the problems involved, and tries to acquaint himself with the language in which scientists, logicians, and mathematicians communicate with each other.

Connected with the problem of hypothesis formulation, and the data resulting from subsequent deductions, is the problem of error measurement. This problem has been touched in Chapter 3 and is further illuminated in the following section.

7.2   THE DEGREE OF ACCURACY OF ACCOUNTING DATA

7.21   Two Predicaments of Accounting

The discussion of the previous section reveals two interrelated, major dilemmas of accounting. Both are manifested in the lack of reliable estimates and both are, at least partly, rooted in economic or budgetary constraints. The one is *the measurement* (or better said, the lack of measurement) *of the benefit of a specific accounting system* (or single hypothesis)—as compared to benefits from its alternatives. *The other is the error estimate* (or its absence respectively) *expressing the degree of accuracy of a particular accounting data.* Without these two measures the decision to choose between several hypotheses, or sets of hypotheses, or accounting systems, often becomes mere guess work. Our main consolation was found in the fact that this guessing is not quite arbitrary, but follows empirical principles which permit at least a rough orientation. From these statements one may infer two ways of mitigating the dilemma. If it were possible to find relatively inexpensive methods of measuring on one side the opportunity costs of choosing a specific hypothesis and on the other of measuring the "degrees of accuracy," the situation could be somewhat improved. The other possibility of achieving improvement would be to devise a more economic way of utilizing the *trial and error* procedure. The further exploitation of electronic data processing might well enable progress in both directions. The first, that of attaining measures on the opportunity cost and the accuracy of an hypothesis founded on indefinite data, might be attained through a recent development that is known under the term "sensitivity analysis."

7.22 "Sensitivity Analysis"—A Hopeful Concept

Sensitivity analysis is aimed at estimating the costs of making decisions with bad data and, correlatively, at estimating the value of procedures to improve the data. Cooper and Charnes and Dantzig developed techniques of sensitivity analysis as part of the apparatus for applying linear programming to management decisions. Sensitivity analysis and techniques for estimating the costs of inaccurate forecasts were developed for certain classes of dynamic programming models by Holt, Modigliani, Muth, and Simon in the United States and by Theil in the Netherlands. Out of this and similar work came a new understanding of forecast horizons: the degree of independence of current decisions from information about distant events. (Simon [1962], pp. 4–5.)

If sensitivity analysis can be designed to estimate the cost or risk of choices based on poor or meager information, it is precisely the technique accountants ought to be looking for. But to what extent accounting data are amenable to sensitivity analysis can be determined only by careful examination and sufficient testing. It may even be necessary to elaborate certain aspects of sensitivity analysis particularly for accounting and budgeting models. The latter, if expressed in mathematical form (see Section 9.5), offer some hope of utilizing this promising technique. This suggestion may be understood by conceiving a budget model which permits the exchange of certain hypotheses and sets of parameters against other hypotheses or other sets of parameters—all of which may help to depict "reality" more or less truthfully. But a sensitivity test may reveal those hypotheses or sets of parameters under which the model will respond most accurately in relation to a specific purpose. It is hoped that the present endeavors toward a unified, mathematical theory of sensitivity[10] will bear fruits that can also be enjoyed in the camp of accounting.

---

[10]See "The Mathematical Theory of Sensitivity," a paper by Kenneth Webb, presented at the 18th National Meeting of the Operations Research Society of America (for program-outlines see *Bulletin* [of the ORSA] Vol. 8, supplement 2 [1960], pp. B–120 to B–121).

The second possibility, that of utilizing the trial-and-error approach more economically, is offered through *system simulation*. In this way the trials, the errors, and the amendments are not incurred in actual practice but are simulated by means of a mathematical structure that is supposed to contain all essential variables and to reflect the chief relationships of the system under consideration. Since computers permit the imitation of a considerable number of alternatives over a long (fictitious) time-span within a few (actual) hours of computer running time, the costs of finding a satisfactory solution by trial and error could be dramatically reduced.

7.23   The Complexity of Accounting Measurement, an Innate Flaw

But, to return to our main problem of this section—the problem of error estimation in accounting—it must be borne in mind that often error measurement is not merely a budgetary problem, but is rooted more deeply. In some cases its difficulty seems to be inseparable from accounting to such an extent as to be unconquerable within this particular frame of reference. Oskar Morgenstern [1950 and 1963] has expressed profound thoughts on this problem of accounting analysis some of which are here reproduced in agreement with the Princeton University Press:

The Notion of Error in Accounting

From these [accounting] data of widely different quality there results a final *figure*, given down to two decimals, to which the ordinary concept of an "error of observation" could hardly be applied. Yet it is not an entirely meaningless figure. In particular, such figures cause people to act one way or the other. Furthermore, balances of most companies (probably incomparable in a rigorous sense) at a given time have most likely the same direction of bias, i.e., they are constructed by application of the same ideas and "theories" about depreciation, inventory evaluation, costs, etc. When prices move up or down, the same kind of optimism and pessimism prevails, although not to the same degree. But in such times views and practices differ among firms which are then apt to produce incomparable results on that account. In times of highly stable prices, however, balance sheets and operational statements give, for the same individual firm, some information which may even be consistent although it does not show what it purports to show. This is quite apart from the outright lying balances, which we do not consider, though they undoubtedly exist. It will, however, be noted that a "lie" is, in this context, not a simple and obvious concept. It is unmistakable when a false cash position is wilfully given or physical inventories are reported that do not exist. But when deliberately a more optimistic attitude is taken in interpreting the success of a year's operation—for example by small amortization—it will be hard to classify this statement as a "lie." Instead, it may be viewed as an error in judgment and as such to be proved or disproved by later events.

An individual balance sheet is therefore a cell looking somewhat like this:

FIGURE 7-1

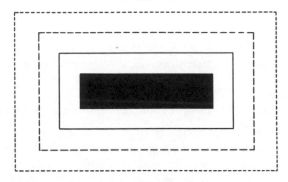

a single hard core or kernel of accurate figures to which the ordinary ideas or errors apply, surrounded by successive layers of figures, gradually farther and farther away in character from the core because of the manner in which they are conceived, although in outward monetary appearance indistinguishable in their presentation even down to the last decimals. An aggregation from several balance sheets is, therefore, the summation of such information; only the arithmetic *sums of the kernels* can have a claim to "accuracy" to which the customary notions of error can be applied.

The lack of definiteness of each cell is quite different from the "fuzziness" of natural and social data which is due to our inability to determine them more sharply. But even in physical theory (quantum mechanics) it was necessary to show that certain types of measurements, or rather combinations of measurements, are in *principle* impossible. Perhaps analogous notions have to be evolved for parts of economics, with correspondingly grave consequences.

It will be a serious task for statistics to develop a theory capable of dealing with such a situation: an ordered mixture or sequence of strict figures with guesses and estimates of increasing uncertainty. This sequence is not random but has its own rules, conventions and stability. The aggregation of such figures produces a certain amount of information, though not of the commonly accepted kind.

Summarizing, we see that the adoption of a correct statistical view on the nature of information produced by financial statements has profound *operational significance*. It must now be realized that combinations of financial statements yield far more limited information than is assumed by the nature and extent of the numerical operations carried out with these figures. For example, if the value of an asset depends on non-disturbance of the market by a sale of this asset, then the figures for all or many firms, showing such assets, are clearly *non-additive* (if the assets are estimated at all in close agreement with their market prices !). Yet additions are made and finally larger and larger aggregates are constructed.

Business gives itself the illusion of dealing with "accuracy" where there is none in an ordinary sense; nor does there exist a substitute notion. The economy as a whole is far less known in the financial field than one imagines if financial figures (other than those of type (a) above) are considered. This has deep significance in judging the possibilities and effects of policy, of prediction and is, of course, of paramount importance for economic theory. (Morgenstern [1950], pp. 30–32. Footnote omitted.)

From the second elaborate edition of the same book (which we highly recommend to the reader) we present the following excerpts:

To illuminate the true character of the various posts in a balance sheet, we proceed as follows:

It has already been stated that a balance sheet is the attempt to state the conditions of a firm at a given moment of time. The different component parts, shown in so many dollars have, however, different probabilities of being realized and in that sense "true." If we take "cash on hand," the probability of this cash being convertible into cash of the stated amount at the date of the balance sheet (or at least immediately thereafter) may be considered to be one. (In the terminology of probability theory a certain event has that probability, an impossible event that of probability zero, all others falling between these two limits). If we take as the next position "Government securities," shown for a certain number of certificates, to represent a certain amount of dollars, the probability of realizing this amount or more will be high, but less than one, since the market may not produce that much money when sold. Say, it will be .98. Going on to "accounts receivable," the probability may drop still further to, say, .85, or, depending on the state of business and the nature of the firm, even lower. When we come to "inventory," the probability of being capable of realizing at least the stated amount (always within a given time period, which is a further complication, to be neglected here) will fall even more, say to .75. Finally we come to "goodwill." If it is stated at a high, precise figure, its associated probability will perhaps be low. When it is given at one dollar, then that amount may have probability one.

So we see that for each item a "true" dollar value should be shown besides the given value. Such a dollar figure will have a probability distribution attached to it, the amount being obtained by adding (integrating) the various possible dollar values multiplied by their respective probabilities. This gives, in other words, the so-called "mathematical expectation." The probabilities can be determined in the customary way on the basis of experience as frequencies, though for some items they may have to be arrived at by more direct estimation. This point need not be discussed here further, since either procedure would yield numbers between zero and one.

Looking more closely at the above expected values, further refinements are necessary. An example will be helpful: if inventory is given as $1,000,000 and the probability of realizing it or more is .75, then the same physical inventory, set at a value of, say, $900,000, would have a probability of .85 to be realized. Surely all could be sold for, say, $500,000, hence it is worth this amount with a probability of one. Thus, the first stated probability is *marginal;* and for the particular item, in this case inventory, a probability distribution has to be determined and the mathematical expectation computed on that basis. For those cases, as cash, where the marginal probability is one up to the figure stated and zero above, the probability also is one for the total amount given. Dealing with the goodwill case, $1.00 has probability one of at least being realized, but since this is a deliberate understatement, probabilities for higher amounts and the corresponding mathematical expectations could also be computed.

A portion of the assets side of a balance sheet would thus have several columns for each item: The figures in column 3 would be comparable among each other and be subject to the ordinary arithmetic operations.

TABLE 7–1
PROBABILISTIC STRUCTURE OF ASSETS

Items	Stated $ (1)	Marginal Probability (2)	Mathematically Expected Value (3)	Standard Errors $ (4)
Cash	1,000,000	1.00	1,000,000	0
Securities	2,000,000	.95	2,075,000	50,000
Inventory	5,000,000	.80	5,400,000	600,000

As far as the liabilities are concerned, similar considerations apply. There the mathematical expectation will equal the stated amount in several categories, but it will differ sometimes significantly from the stated amount when capital, surplus and other reserves are considered. We shall not investigate whether a balance sheet of this probabilistic design necessarily must "balance" and what the nature of possibly needed balancing items would be.

The principle having been made clear, we dispense with further discussion at this juncture although considerable expansion of this approach is possible and necessary. This shall be done at another occasion.

The comparability of balance sheets of different firms is assured, as long as each indicates the probabilities it uses in order to arrive at the mathematical expectation. This holds under the restriction that the probabilities (i.e., the transactions) are not interrelated.

It is, of course, unlikely that balance sheets will be drawn up in the indicated manner; this is a matter for the future. But it is clear that present balance sheets already contain an element of expectation and speculation. Indeed, some accounting theorists emphasize this point, though without introducing also the probabilistic approach which is indispensable, since there cannot be an expectation without a probability attached to it. This would be meaningless.

At any rate, we note that a seemingly simple statement of the condition of a firm at a given date is in fact a very complicated matter and subject to the occurrence of many errors whose nature and amount are usually shrouded in mystery.

It follows that *profit and loss* statements cannot be easier to interpret. Indeed, they are beset with even more difficulties. In profit and loss statements some receipts and transfers of money such as interest received and monies transferred to surplus are again of highest accuracy, but what a "profit" or "loss" is, as already mentioned, depends on some theory which can never claim to be as convincing as a statement of the hard facts that certain sums of money were received and others were paid out.

Specifically, the notion of "cost" does not fall into the first category of immediate physical observations. It would lead too far to go into the wide variants of cost theory as understood either by economists or by accountants. But it is clear that in the absence of a convincing and complete theory there is no unique and objective way of accounting for costs when overhead, amortization, and joint costs have to be taken into consideration; of course, this is the case everywhere. These difficulties prevail even when prices are stable. "Cost" is merely one aspect of a valuation process of great complexity. Even if accountants should uniformly follow the same practices (i.e., hold the same "theories") or be compelled by law to apply certain procedures, these rules would never be sharp enough for a unique financial interpretation of the conditions and events of a business. Hence, wherever costs enter into financial accounts, non-objectively measured data are produced, having their own sources and forms of error. And where would "costs" not enter? (Morgenstern [1963], pp. 76–79. Footnotes omitted.)

7.24   Error Measurement in Accounting

By nature, measurement is a process of approximation;[11] hence to ask for the degree of approximation, or inversely for the measurement error, is not a farfetched thought. The question arises, at least implicitly, in almost every process of measurement. The essence of and necessity for error estimates has already been discussed in connection with probabilistic measurement models (see Subsection 3.72). There, we have pointed out that several measures (undertaken by the same individual or by several ones) of one and the same object may yield different results, the deviation of which (from their mean value) assumes a specific pattern. As the number of such measures increases, the distribution of the deviations will approach a *normal* frequency curve, a fact which seems to have been recognized first by Gauss in astronomy and which became of far-reaching importance for the statistical part of measurement theory. In this way the deviations, error limits, degrees of accuracy, or how one

---

[11]"If one imagines the possibility of formulating a scale in real numbers, it becomes obvious that the irrational part of this scale enforces relinquishment of perfect accuracy." (See Mattessich [1962a], p. 37.)

may call them, are amenable to precise statistical formulation. Thus in modern measurement theory one encounters concepts like standard deviation, confidence intervals, etc., and tries, through quantification of these concepts, to increase the information of the measurement act. Obviously, an evaluation process which assigns to an asset a value of $25,000 within an error range (e.g., twice the standard deviation) of $5,000 is of less information value than an act that determines the value within an error range of $1,000. But of what significance are accounting measures which *apparently* reveal no error limits at all? And how do the results of financial accounting, or cost accounting, or social accounting respond to an attempt of estimating their accuracy?

In judging the situation in accounting, again the difference between measurement for scientific purposes, and that for practical purposes must be stressed. The latter is more sensitive to measurement costs; here the threshold, where the incremental yield of a refinement in measurement is exceeded by its incremental costs, is reached much sooner than in case of measurement for research. Shall we convince the manager to improve his accounting measures for the sake of accuracy alone? It seems more reasonable of advising him to estimate cost and information value of an improvement in accounting technique before any reform is undertaken. To conjecture the value of information is often extremely difficult, yet is is imaginable that increasing competition will give those enterprises a premium that are in a position to determine more accurately the information value of an improved accounting system.

Next, we ought to inquire into the extent to which accountants and users of financial statements are ignorant about the accuracy of accounting data. Canning [1929] has repeatedly emphasized the importance of "degree of error" estimates in accounting valuation. Here, as in other deterministic measurement models, it would be delusive to believe that error estimates are not available because random samples are not being collected in sufficient quantities. It seems that in most situations the limits of accuracy are checked constantly by way of simple routines or rules of thumb. Just as it is not necessary to measure a room many times to determine the approximate degree of accuracy, probabilistic models are dispensable for many accounting purposes. This attitude must not be misunderstood; there are cases where such refined methods of measurement are possible and where they would benefit the enterprise—in future these cases may well increase. Occasionally the (usually

implicit) error estimates of accounting data are made explicit as
some national income estimates illustrate. Simon Kuznets [1941,
pp. 502–37 and Tabular Index] in his pioneering work on national
income of the United States appraised the probable error in his
estimates for each cell (component type of income paid out) as well
as for each industrial division. But what character do these reliability
estimates have? As Kuznets [1941, p. 501] admits: "To get a
quantitative measure the margins of error must be evaluated by
those who, being familiar with the estimates, dare to surmise how
far wrong they may be." That means we are not dealing here with
relative frequency concepts but with *judgment probabilities* (see Subsection 7.14). Similar reliability estimates were carried out by the
Organization for European Economic Co-operation in their national
income estimates of various countries and by the Central Statistical
Office of the United Kingdom [1956, p. 36] in their income estimates
for 1955 (U.K.). These reliability ratings employ *ordinal scales* only
(e.g., grade A less than 3 per cent *margin of error*, B from 3 to 10 per
cent, and C more than 10 per cent). The question arises whether it
would be commendable to grade data of micro-accounting in the
same way. To some extent this is done in accounting theory where
the students are being trained to distinguish one asset or liability
item from another, not only on grounds of the economic behavioral
characteristics of these items, but also with regard to the reliability
of the values assigned. Those familiar with financial statements,
more or less subconsciously, assign different error margins (or
ranges of different error margins) to the various balance-sheet
items.

Nevertheless we ought to ask whether there exist possibilities for
a systematic error estimation in accounting. Wherever statistical
samples of sufficient size can be employed there are good prospects
for such error determination. Since certain areas of auditing, accounting, and cost accounting[12] lend themselves to sampling techniques and to the application of control charts,[13] an expansion of
systematic error measurement in accounting can be expected.
Where samples are not available in sufficient quantities, regress to a
more conscious use of judgment probabilities may appear desirable.

[12]See Vance and Neter [1956], Trueblood and Cyert [1957], and especially Cyert and
Davidson [1962].

[13]See Gaynor [1954], Noble [1954], Bierman, Fouraker and Jaedicke [1961a], pp.
108–25, and Horngren [1962], pp. 746–65.

The difficulty of forming such judgments might be somewhat reduced by using *multidimensional values* (proposed in Subsection 6.34). A similar thought is encountered by Canning [1929, pp. 203–204]:

> If there are several good methods, [of valuation] each differing materially from the others with respect to one form of merit or another, there is no reason at all why more than one valuation should not be made and expressed. There is nothing whatever to hinder the valuing of an inventory both at cost, at market, at cost or market whichever is lower, at selling price, at selling price less allowances for selling and other expenses, and so on. Cases are plentiful in which more than one figure is enough better than any one to warrant the finding of more than one.... As between two good but materially different methods of valuation, the most sensible election is often to choose both. The parallel of this problem of choice is well known in general statistics. No longer do writers in statistics argue furiously about which of indefinitely many averages is "the best." If for any series the arithmetic, geometric, and harmonic means, the median, and the mode are given, more is told about the series than can be told by any one of these or by any set less than all of these.[14]

Canning does not refer specifically to the problem of error estimation, but by necessity the next step is to assume that an asset value expressed in three or more dimensions (adjusted cost value, current value, present value, etc.) reveals some *additional information about accuracy through the relationship and supposed interdependence of the individual value components* (similar to the comparison of mean, mode, and median of a probability distribution). The following assumption must be confirmed by further research, but it seems plausible to believe that a multidimensional value is more reliable if its value elements are relatively close to each other than one the elements of which deviate considerably from each other. Thus the value of asset A to which the value vector (100, 115, 109) is assigned ought to be more reliable than the value of asset B which carries the value vector (100, 185, 215). Experiments and empirical tests also may reveal clues about specific relations of certain *pairs* of value components.

A further problem of reliability measurement in accounting arises out of the merging of data with various degrees of error. Canning [1929, p. 200] already has drawn attention to this problem of accounting; it seems advisable to assign to an "aggregate" value that degree of reliability which corresponds to the lowest degree of reliability among the component values.

---

[14] John B. Canning, *The Economics of Accountancy* (N.Y.: Ronald Press Co., 1929).

7.3 A SURVEY OF PRESENT-DAY ACCOUNTING RULES IN THE UNITED STATES

7.31 Accounting Rules: Hypotheses or Constraints?

Traditional accounting theory rarely makes use of the term "hypothesis," whereas the term "rule" belongs to its standard vocabulary. Indeed, it requires some stretch of imagination to identify an accounting rule with a pragmatic hypothesis and it might be more realistic to speak of a constraint in this connection. In the past the chief concern of accounting was to give evidence according to rules. Many of these rules are recognized as "common law" and some of them even belong to "codified law"— at least in countries where the legal system is not dominated by the Anglo-Saxon tradition of jurisprudence. Managerial accounting, however, emphasizes the need for *efficiency control* (instead of mere custodial control) and —incited by the spirit of management science—tends to search for more effective organizational patterns of administration, production, and distribution. Thus it is not surprising that *this process of transition forces accounting to shift its emphasis from rules to hypotheses.* Modern accounting can no longer be satisfied to ascertain that certain legal or semilegal rules have been obeyed, its major task ought to be concerned with the question whether an optimal or satisfactory set of hypotheses was chosen for a specific objective within a well-defined context. For several reasons this statement sounds Utopian indeed. First, it must be considered that many accounting hypotheses are vaguely cast, though they require rigorous formulation. Second, it is often difficult to reconcile a specific hypothesis with a multipurpose or general-purpose information system. And third it is even more difficult to find out when a set of hypotheses is optimal or even satisfactory with respect to a specific objective and context. Much research effort will have to be invested as regards hypotheses formulation in accounting. But *all such effort will be in vain if accountants are not being trained to think in terms of empirical hypotheses instead of legalistic rules.* This statement may reveal the significance of the present chapter and justify the space devoted to this topic; furthermore the statement has immediate relevance to our set of basic assumptions which provide a frame for incorporating accounting *hypotheses.*

There is no intention that this book should disregard accounting rules presently accepted in this country. On the contrary a concise presentation of these rules (together with the established terminology) will be an important source of reference and will help to determine the boundaries within which the ultimate accounting hypotheses have to be formulated. The sources of these rules are the *Accounting Research Bulletins* Nos. 43 to 51, together with the *Accounting Terminology Bulletins* Nos. 1 to 4. These bulletins were issued in the time span between 1954 and 1959 by the American Institute of Certified Public Accountants. The full reproduction of such material is here not feasible, but in the following we present the gist and the highlights of these accounting research and terminology bulletins in form of an *outline* arranged by the United States General Accounting Office (Washington, D.C.: Office of Staff Management, 1962).[15] The study of this material reveals that occasionally an accounting rule can be employed as an ultimate hypothesis but in most cases additional specifications and assumptions will have to be made to formulate accounting hypotheses for a particular purpose. This additional information is frequently implied but ought to be made explicit. With progressive formalization and computerization of the accounting and budgeting processes, the precise formulation of all hypotheses employed in a specific accounting model will become inevitable.

---

[15] We hereby gratefully acknowledge the permission granted to reproduce this useful and well-arranged outline which contains the following introductory remark:

"The American Institute of Certified Public Accountants has published a Final Edition of the Accounting Research and Terminology Bulletins. Generally, the purpose of the bulletins is to clarify, and to standardize to the degree desirable, certain accounting principles and procedures.

"This memorandum presents a brief outline of their contents setting forth the definitions, conclusions and/or recommendations made by the Committee on Accounting Procedure, AICPA. This memorandum is not intended to replace the full discussion contained in the bulletins.

"The Accounting Research and Terminology Bulletins are of particular importance to accountants since they represent the considered opinion of the most widely recognized authoritative spokesman for the profession. For candidates preparing for the CPA examination, a thorough knowledge of their contents is mandatory.

"This summary was prepared for the Advanced Accounting and Auditing Study Program by General Accounting Office staff members. It is reproduced with permission of the American Institute of Certified Public Accountants and used in the General Accounting Office CPA Course given annually in Washington and the Regional Offices."

OUTLINE OF
ACCOUNTING RESEARCH BULLETINS

BULLETIN #43 (Restatement and Revisions of Accounting Research Bulletins)

General:

1. No opinion issued by the committee is intended to have a retroactive effect unless it contains a statement of such intention.

2. The committe contemplates that its opinions will have application only to items material and significant in the relative circumstances.

3. The committee recognizes that in extraordinary cases fair presentation and justice to all parties at interest may require exceptional treatment.

Chapter 1 - Prior Opinions

Section a. - Rules Adopted by Membership

1. Unrealized profit should not be credited to income either directly or indirectly. A sale in the ordinary course of business is the usual criterion for realization of profit.

2. Capital surplus should not be used to relieve the income account of current or future year's charges. Exception: Quasi-reorganization. However, in this instance, the facts should be clearly disclosed.

3. Earned surplus of a subsidiary company created prior to acquisition does not form a part of the consolidated earned surplus; nor can any dividend declared out of such surplus properly be credited to the income account of the parent.

4a. Treasury stock may be shown as an asset only if properly disclosed (perferably shown in equity section).

4b. Dividends on treasury stock should not be credited to income.

5. Notes and accounts receivable from officers, employees, and af-
filiated companies should be shown separately in the balance
sheet.

6. If a portion of stock issued for the acquisition of property is
donated to the corporation at about the time of issuance, par
value of the stock issued should not be recorded as cost of the
property. If such donated stock is subsequently sold, proceeds
should not be credited to surplus.

Section b. - Profits or Losses on Treasury Stock.

In a letter to members of the Institute issued in 1938, the following
question was discussed:

"Should the difference between the purchase and resale prices of
a corporation's own common stock be reflected in earned surplus
(directly or through income) or should such difference be reflected
in capital surplus?"

It was the opinion of the committee that such differences should be
reflected in capital surplus.

Chapter 2 - Form of Statements

Section a. - Comparative Financial Statements

1. The committee recommends extension of the use of comparative statements as enhancing the significance of reports and bringing out
more clearly the nature and trends of current changes affecting the
enterprise.

2. Changes in accounting policies or procedures which affect comparability should be disclosed.

3. It is the auditor's responsibility to satisfy himself that the
figures for the preceding year fairly present the position and
results for the enterprise.

Section b. - Combined Statement of Income and Earned Surplus

1. The committee expresses approval of the presentation of a combined
statement of income and surplus, where feasible, without recommending its general adoption.

2. The principal advantage of the combined statement is that it serves
the purpose of showing both earnings applicable to the current
period and modifications of earned surplus on a long-run basis.

- 2 -

3. The <u>principal disadvantage</u> of the combined statement is that income for the year will appear somewhere in the middle of the statement. If a combined statement is to be presented, care should be exercised to clearly indicate at what point income for the year appears.

Chapter 3 - Working Capital

Section a. - Current Assets and Current Liabilities

1. This section discusses the nature of current assets and current liabilities with a view to developing criteria as an aid to a more useful presentation in financial statements.

   a. The discussion takes cognizance of the recent tendency of creditors to rely more upon the ability of debtors to pay obligations out of the proceeds of current operations than upon their ability to pay in case of liquidation.

   b. The strict "one-year" interpretation of current assets and liabilities is ignored; the objective is to relate the criteria to the operating cycle of the business. (See Item 3 below.)

2. The term <u>current assets</u> is used to designate cash and other assets or resources commonly identified as those which are reasonably expected to be <u>realized</u> in cash or <u>sold</u> or <u>consumed</u> during the normal operating cycle of the business. This would generally include:

   a. Cash available for current operations or its equivalent.

   b. Inventories and operating and maintenance supplies.

   c. Accounts, notes, and acceptances receivable.

   d. Receivables from officers, employees, affiliates and others if collectible within a year.

   e. Installment or deferred accounts and notes receivable if they conform to normal trade practices and terms within the business.

   f. Temporary investments.

   g. Prepaid expenses which, if not paid in advance, would require the use of current assets during the operating cycle.

3. The <u>operating cycle</u> is deemed the average time intervening between the acquisition of materials or services entering the manufacturing process and the final cash realization. (However, when the operating cycle is one year or less, one year should be used as the basis for segregation of current assets.)

- 3 -

4. This concept of current assets contemplates the exclusion therefrom of:

   a. Restricted cash.

   b. Permanent or continuing investments.

   c. Receivables arising from unusual transactions and not expected to be collected within 12 months.

   d. Cash surrender value of life insurance.

   e. Unamortized costs of services received which are fairly chargeable to the operations of several years (deferred charges).

5. The basis of valuation of certain current assets, such as temporary investments and inventories, should be clearly disclosed in financial statements.

6. The term current liabilities is used to identify debts or obligations the liquidation or payment of which is reasonably expected to require the use of current assets or the creation of other current liabilities.

7. Current liabilities would include:

   a. Obligations for items which have entered into the operating cycle.

   b. Other liabilities requiring liquidation in a short period of time, usually 12 months.

   c. Income tax liability even though not payable within 12 months.

   d. Estimated or accrued amounts which are expected to cover expenditures within the year for known obligations. (Ex. Accrued bonus payments.)

   e. Current installments of long term periodic payments.

Section b. - Application of U. S. Government Securities Against Liabilities for Federal Taxes on Income.

1. The usual procedure of showing U. S. Treasury Tax notes as a current asset (temporary investment) is proper, and especially so if the notes are to be used for purposes other than payment of the tax liability.

2. If other government securities may, by their terms, be surrendered in the payment of taxes, it is permissible to deduct such securities from the tax liability in the liability section of the balance sheet as long as the full amount of each is shown.

- 4 -

Chapter 4 - Inventory Pricing

This chapter deals with the general principles applicable to the pricing of
inventories for mercantile and manufacturing enterprises. These principles
are not necessarily applicable to non-commercial businesses or to regulated
utilities.

1. The term "inventory" is used herein to designate the aggregate of those
    items of tangible personal property which (1) are held for sale in the
    ordinary course of business, (2) are in the process of production for
    such sale, or (3) are to be currently consumed in the production of
    goods or services to be available for sale.

2. A major objective of accounting for inventories is the proper deter-
    mination of income through the process of matching appropriate costs
    against revenues.

3. The primary basis of accounting for inventories is cost, which has been
    defined generally as the price paid or consideration given to acquire
    an asset. As applied to inventories, cost means in principle the sum
    of the applicable expenditures and charges directly or indirectly in-
    curred in bringing an article to its existing condition and location.

4. Cost for inventory purposes may be determined under any one of several
    assumptions as to the flow of cost factors (such as "first-in first-out,"
    "average," and "last-in first-out"); the major objective in selecting a
    method should be to choose the one which, under the circumstances, most
    clearly reflects periodic income.

5. A departure from the cost basis of pricing the inventory is required
    when the usefulness of the goods is no longer as great as its cost.
    Where there is evidence that the utility of goods, in their disposal
    in the ordinary course of business, will be less than cost, whether due
    to physical deterioration, obsolescence, change in price levels, or
    other causes, the difference should be recognized as a loss of the
    current period. This is generally accomplished by stating such goods
    at a lower level commonly designated as "market."

6. As used in the phrase "lower of cost or market," the term "market"
    means current replacement cost (by purchase or by reproduction, as the
    case may be) except that:

    a. Market should not exceed the net realizable value (i.e., estimated
        selling price in the ordinary course of business less reasonably
        predictable costs of completion and disposal); and

    b. Market should not be less than net realizable value reduced by an
        allowance for an approximately normal profit margin.

7. Depending on the character and composition of the inventory, the rule of
    "cost or market, whichever is lower" may properly be applied either
    directly to each item or to the total of the inventory (or, in some cases,
    to the total of the components of each major category). The method should
    be that which most clearly reflects periodic income.

8. The basis of stating inventories must be consistently applied and should be disclosed in the financial statements; whenever a significant change is made therein, there should be disclosure of the nature of the change and, if material, the effect on income.

9. Only in exceptional cases may inventories properly be stated above cost. For example, precious metals having a fixed monetary value with no substantial cost of marketing may be stated at such monetary value; any other exceptions must be justifiable by inability to determine appropriate approximate costs, immediate marketability at quoted market price, and the characteristic of unit interchangeability. Where goods are stated above cost this fact should be fully disclosed.

10. Accrued net losses on firm purchase commitments of goods for inventory, measured in the same way as are inventory losses, should be recognized in the accounts. The amounts thereof should, if material, be separately disclosed in the income statement. (Note: When firm purchase commitments are adequately protected by firm sales contracts, the utility of such commitments is not impaired and, therefore, there is no loss.)

Chapter 5 - Intangible Assets

This chapter deals with problems of accounting for intangible assets purchased, either individually or collectively with other assets, as opposed to intangibles developed within a company by research, etc.

1. The intangibles considered may be broadly classified as follows:

    Type (a). Those having a time of existence limited by law, regulation, agreement, or their nature (patents, copyrights, leases, etc., and good will if there is evidence of limited duration).

    Type (b). Those not having a limited time of existence as above, and for which there is no indication of limited life (generally includes good will, going value, trade names, secret processes, etc.).

2. Intangibles of all types should be stated at cost. If cash is not paid, cost may be measured by the fair value of (a) the consideration given, or (b) the property acquired.

3. The cost of type (a) intangibles should be systematically amortized over the period benefited.

4. The cost of type (b) intangibles may be carried continuously until:

    a. It becomes reasonably evident that their time of existence has become limited, in which event the cost should be amortized as in 3. above or, if such charges would result in distortion of the income statement a partial write down may be made to earned surplus, the balance to be amortized.

- 6 -

     b. It becomes reasonably evident that they have become worthless in which event the cost may be charged off to surplus or income, as deemed appropriate.

5. Excess paid by a parent over book value of equity acquired in a subsidiary should preferably be allocated as between tangible assets and intangible /types (a) and (b)/assets. The amounts allocated to intangibles should be treated as in 2, 3, and 4 above.

6. Lump-sum write-offs of intangibles should not be made to earned surplus immediately after acquisition, nor should intangibles be charged against capital surplus. If not amortized systematically, intangibles should be carried at cost until an event has taken place which indicates a loss or a limitation on the useful life of the intangibles.

Chapter 6 - Contingency Reserves

This chapter considers the accounting treatment of two types of reserves whose misuse may be the means of either arbitrarily reducing income or shifting income from one period to another:

    (a) General contingency reserves whose purposes are not specific;

    (b) Reserves designed to set aside a part of current profits to absorb losses feared or expected in connection with inventories on hand or future purchases of inventory.

1. The committee is of the opinion that reserves such as those created:

    (a) for general undetermined contingencies, or

    (b) for any indefinite possible future losses, such as, for example, losses on inventories not on hand or contracted for, or

    (c) for the purpose of reducing inventories other than to a basis which is in accordance with generally accepted accounting principles, or (See Chapter 4 above)

    (d) without regard to any specific loss reasonably related to the operations of the current period, or

    (e) in amounts not determined on the basis of any reasonable estimates of costs or losses

are of such a nature that charges or credits relating to such reserves should not enter into the determination of net income.

2. It is the opinion of the committee that if a reserve of the type described above is set up:

    (a) it should be created by a segregation or appropriation of earned surplus,

- 7 -

(b) no costs or losses should be charged to it and no part of it should be transferred to income or in any way used to affect the determination of net income for any year,

(c) it should be restored to earned surplus directly when such a reserve or any part thereof is no longer considered necessary, and

(d) it should preferably be classified in the balance sheet as a part of shareholders' equity.

Chapter 7 - Capital Accounts

Section a. - Quasi-Reorganization or Corporate Readjustment

A rule was adopted by the Institute in 1934 which read as follows:

"Capital surplus, however, created, should not be used to relieve the income account of the current or future years of charges which would otherwise be made thereagainst. This rule might be subject to the exception that where, upon reorganization, a reorganized company would be relieved of charges which would require to be made against income if the existing corporation were continued, it might be regarded as permissible to accomplish the same result without reorganization provided the facts were as fully revealed to and the action as formally approved by the shareholders as in reorganization."

This section does not deal with the general question of quasi-reorganization, but only with cases in which readjustment, as permitted in the rule, is availed of by a corporation.

1. Procedure in readjustment (quasi-reorganization).

a. Make a clear report to stockholders and obtain their formal consent.

b. The readjustment of values should be reasonably complete. (Include all company assets.)

c. The effective date of the readjustment should conform closely to date of stockholders consent, and should not be prior to close of the last fiscal year.

d. Charge write-offs against (1) earned surplus to the extent thereof, and (2) the balance against capital surplus. Consolidated earned surplus should not be carried through a readjustment in which some losses have been charged to capital surplus.

- 8 -

    e. Assets should be carried forward from readjustment at a fair
and not unduly conservative value, determined with due regard
for the accounting rules to be employed.

    f. Reserves may be set up to cover potential losses indeterminable
in amount but known to have occurred prior to date of readjustment. If such reserves are subsequently found to be excessive
or insufficient, balances should be carried to capital surplus.

2. Procedure after readjustment.

    a. After readjustment a company's accounting should be similar to
that appropriate for a new company.

    b. Carry no earned surplus forward under that title. Create a new
earned surplus account dated from the readjustment, and this
dating should be disclosed in financial statements until such
time as the effective date is no longer deemed to possess any
special significance. (See Bulletin No. 46.)

3. This statement deals only with readjustments wherein income or
earned surplus accounts of the current or future years are relieved
of charges which would otherwise be made thereagainst.

Section b. - Stock Dividends and Stock Split-Ups

This section deals with the issuance by a corporation of its own common
shares to its own common shareholders without consideration moving from
the shareholders to the corporation. A stock dividend involves an increase in the legal capital of the corporation, and is, therefore, distinguished from a stock split-up.

1. As to the recipient:

    a. An ordinary stock dividend is not income to the recipient.

    b. The cost of shares previouly held should be allocated equit-
ably to the total shares held after receipt of a stock dividend
or split-up.

2. As to the issuing corporation:

    a. Since the stock dividend implies a permanent capitalization of
earned surplus, it is necessary that the board of directors:

        (1) determine the aggregate amount to be capitalized.

        (2) observe legal requirements as to the per share amount to
be capitalized.

    b. The amount capitalized should be charged to earned surplus and
credited to capital stock, or to capital stock and capital surplus in an amount equal to the fair value of the additional
shares issued.

- 9 -

3. Where it is clearly the intent to effect a stock split-up, no
    transfer from earned surplus to capital surplus or capital stock
    is called for, other than to the extent occasioned by legal require-
    ments.

4. The committee believes that the corporation's representations to its
    shareholders as to the nature of the issuance is one of the principal
    considerations in determining whether it should be recorded as a
    stock dividend or a split-up.

Section c. - Business Combinations

This section has been superseded by Bulletin #48.

Chapter 8 - Income and Earned Surplus

The purpose of this chapter is to recommend criteria for use in identifying
material extraordinary charges and credits which may in some cases and
should in other cases be excluded from the determination of net income and
to recommend methods of presenting these charges and credits.

1. In the "all-inclusive" income statement, net income is defined accord-
    ing to a strict proprietary concept by which it is presumed to be deter-
    mined by the inclusion of all items affecting the net increase in
    proprietorship during the period except dividend distributions and
    capital transactions.

2. In the "current operating performance" type of income statement, the
    principal emphasis is placed upon the relationship of items to the oper-
    ations and to the year, excluding material extraordinary items which are
    not so related and which would impair the significance of net income
    if included.

3. It is the opinion of the committee that there should be a general pre-
    sumption that all items of profit and loss recognized during the period
    are to be used in determining the figure reported as net income. The
    only possible exception to this presumption relates to items which in
    the aggregate are material in relation to the company's net income and
    are clearly not identifiable with or do not result from the usual or
    typical business operations of the period.

4. Only extraordinary items such as the following may be excluded from the
    determination of net income for the year, and they should be excluded
    when their inclusion would impair the significance of net income:

    a. Material charges or credits (other than ordinary adjustments of a
        recurring nature) specifically related to operations of prior years,
        such as the elimination of unused reserves provided in prior years
        and adjustments of income taxes for prior years;

- 10 -

    b. Material charges or credits resulting from unusual sales of assets not acquired for resale and not of the type in which the company generally deals;

    c. Material losses of a type not usually insured against, such as those resulting from wars, riots, earthquakes, and similar calamities or catastrophes except where such losses are a recurrent hazard of the business;

    d. The write-off of a material amount of intangibles;

    e. The write-off of material amounts of unamortized bond discount or premium and bond issue expenses at the time of the retirement or refunding of the debt before maturity.

5. The following should be excluded from the determination of net income under all circumstances:

    a. Adjustments resulting from transactions in the company's own capital stock;

    b. Amounts transferred to and from accounts properly designated as surplus appropriations, such as charges and credits with respect to general purpose contingency reserves;

    c. Amounts deemed to represent excessive costs of fixed assets, and annual appropriations in contemplation of replacement of productive facilities at higher price levels; and

    d. Adjustments made pursuant to a quasi-reorganization.

6. The committee has given consideration to the methods of presentation of the extraordinary items excluded in the determination of net income under the criteria set forth in item 4 above. One method is to carry all such charges and credits directly to the surplus account with complete disclosure as to their nature and amount. The committee believes that this method more clearly portrays net income. A second method is to show them in the income statement after the amount designated as net income.

7. When a combined statement of income and earned surplus is utilized, the committee's preference is that the figure of net income be followed immediately by the surplus balance at the beginning of the period.

Chapter 9 - Depreciation

Section a. - Depreciation and High Costs

The committee recognizes the problem that, in reporting profits today, costs of material and labor are expressed in terms of a "cheaper" dollar than that represented in the cost of productive facilities purchased at a lower price level. But it feels that to recognize current prices in

- 11 -

providing depreciation, it is necessary to formally record appraised current value for all properties. It does not believe such a drastic step should be taken, at least until a stable price level is reached. The committee expresses a general disapproval of charging to current income amounts in excess of depreciation based on cost in order to provide for replacement at higher prices.

Section b. - Depreciation on Appreciation

When appreciation has been entered on the books income should be charged with depreciation computed on the written-up amounts. A company should not at the same time claim larger property valuations in its statement of assets and provide for the amortization of only smaller amounts in its statement of income. When a company has made representations as to an increased valuation of plant, depreciation accounting and periodic income determination thereafter should be based on such higher amounts.

Section c. - Emergency Facilities--Depreciation, Amortization and Income Taxes

In this section the committee considers the problem of accounting for certificates of necessity under which all or part of the cost of emergency facilities may be amortized over a period of 60 months for income tax purposes.

1. Depreciation considerations:

   a. The committee is of the opinion that from an accounting standpoint there is nothing inherent in the nature of emergency facilities which requires the depreciation of their cost for financial accounting purposes over either a shorter or a longer period than would be proper if no certificate of necessity had been issued.

   b. The committee believes that when the amount allowed as depreciation for income-tax purposes is materially different from the amount of the estimated depreciation, the latter should be used for financial accounting purposes.

2. Recognition of income tax effects:

   a. When the income taxes payable during the amortization period is significantly less than it would be on the basis of the income reflected in the financial statements, the committee believes that a charge should be made in the income statement to recognize the income tax to be paid in the future on the amount by which amortization for income tax purposes exceeds the depreciation that would be allowable if certificates of necessity had not been issued.

   b. In accounting for this deferment of income taxes, the committee believes it desirable to treat the charge as being for additional income taxes. The related credit in such cases would properly

- 12 -

be made to an account for deferred income taxes. Under this
method, during the life of the facility following the amortization period the annual charges for income taxes will be reduced
by charging to the account for deferred income taxes that part
of the income tax in excess of what would have been payable had
the amortization deduction not been claimed for income-tax
purposes in the amortization period. By this procedure the net
income will more nearly reflect the results of a proper matching of costs and revenues.

Chapter 10 - Taxes

Section a. - Real and Personal Property Taxes

This section deals with the proper allocation of property tax expense
between periodic income amounts and proper recognition of the tax
liability at balance sheet date.

1. Accounting for property taxes:

    a. Generally, the most acceptable basis of providing for property
        taxes is a monthly accrual on the taxpayer's books during the
        fiscal period of the taxing authority for which the taxes are
        levied. The books will then show, at any closing date, the
        appropriate accrual or prepayment.

    b. Treatment in financial statements:

        (1) Balance Sheet - An accrued liability for property taxes
            should be included as a current liability. When estimates
            are used, the liability should be described as estimated.

        (2) Income Statement - (a) charge to operating expenses; (b) show
            as a separate deduction from income; or (c) distribute among
            the several accounts to which they are deemed to apply, such
            as factory overhead, selling or general expenses, etc.

Section b. - Income Taxes

This section deals with a number of accounting problems involved in the
reporting of income taxes in financial statements.

1. These problems arise largely where:

    a. Material items affecting the computation of taxable income are
        not reflected in the income statement.

    b. Material items included in the income statement do not affect
        the computation of taxable income.

2. When necessary and practicable, income taxes should be allocated to
    income and other accounts, as are other expenses. In cases in which
    transactions included in the surplus statement, but not in the income

statement, increase the income tax payable by an amount that is substantial and is determinable without difficulty, an allocation of income tax between the two statements would ordinarily be made. It is appropriate to consider the tax effect as the difference between the tax payable with and without including the item in the amount of taxable income.

3. When an item resulting in a material increase in income taxes is credited to surplus, the credit to surplus should be reduced by the portion of the current provision for income taxes attributable to the special credit; such reduction being carried to the income statement either as a deduction from income taxes or as a separate credit clearly described.

4. When an item resulting in a material reduction in income taxes is charged to surplus, a deferred-charge or a reserve account, the charge should be reduced by the portion of the reduction in income taxes attributable to the item, a charge being made to the income statement either as an increase in income taxes, or as a portion of the item in question equal to the tax reduction. The charge to the income statement should be clearly disclosed.

5. Additional income taxes for prior years or refunds on taxes of prior years should be included in the current income statement, and if material, they may be charged or credited to surplus indicating the period to which they relate.

6. Refunds arising from the "carry-back" of losses should be included in the income statement of the year in which the loss arises. If the amount is material, it should be shown as a separate item after the determination of operating income exclusive of the refund; or the amount of taxes payable for such year may be shown in the income statement, with the amount of tax reduction attributable to the "carry-back" indicated in either a footnote or parenthetically in the body of the income statement.

7. Provisions for income taxes for the current or prior years should be shown as current liabilities in the balance sheet. Claims for refunds under "carry-back" provisions should be shown as current assets.

8. If, because of differences between accounting for income tax purposes and accounting for financial purposes, no income tax has been paid or provided as to certain significant amounts credited to surplus or to income, disclosure should be made. If a tax is likely to be paid thereon, provision should be made on the basis of an estimate of the amount of such tax. This rule applies, for instance, to profits on installment sales or long-term contracts which are deferred for tax purposes.

- 14 -

Chapter 11 - Government Contracts

Section a. - Cost-Plus-Fixed-Fee Contracts

This section deals with accounting problems arising under cost-plus-fixed-fee contracts.

1. Fees under CPFF contracts may be credited to income on the basis of a measurement of partial performance which will reflect reasonable assured realization; such as delivery of completed articles.

2. Where CPFF contracts involve the manufacture and delivery of products, reimbursable costs and fees are ordinarily included in revenue.

3. Unbilled costs and fees under CPFF contracts are ordinarily receivables rather than advances or inventory, but should be shown separate from billed accounts receivable.

4. Offsetting of Government advances against amounts due from the Government on CPFF contracts is permissible to the extent allowed in the agreement, but a more desirable procedure is to make the offset only if that is the treatment anticipated in the normal course of business transactions under the contract. The amounts offset should be clearly disclosed.

Section b. - Renegotiation

This section deals with certain aspects of the accounting for those government contracts and subcontracts which are subject to renegotiation.

1. The financial statements of contractors should fully disclose the possibility of renegotiation of contracts.

2. In keeping with the established accounting principle that provision should be made in financial statements for all liabilities, including reasonable estimates for liabilities not accurately determinable, provision should be made for probable renegotiation refunds wherever the amount of such refunds can be reasonably estimated.

3. In addition to any provision made in the accounts, disclosure by footnote or otherwise may be required as to the uncertainties, their significance, and the basis used in determining the amount of the provisions, such as the prior years' experience of the contractor.

4. Provisions made for renegotiation refunds should be included in the balance sheet among the current liabilities.

5. Provisions made for renegotiation refunds should be included as current liabilities in the balance sheet, and preferably as deductions from sales in the income statement.

- 15 -

6. The committee recommends that the difference between the renegotiation refund and the provision therefore be shown as a separate item
in the current income statement, unless such inclusion would result
in a distortion of the current net income, in which event the adjustment should be treated as an adjustment of earned surplus.

7. The committee believes that a major retroactive adjustment of the
provision made for a renegotiation refund can often best be disclosed by presenting a revised income statement for the prior year,
either in comparative form in conjunction with the current year's
financial statements or otherwise, it urges that this procedure be
followed.

Section c. - Terminated War and Defense Contracts

This section deals with problems in accounting for fixed price war
supply contracts terminated for the convenience of the Government.

1. Profits of the contractor accrue as of the date of termination.

2. Statements prepared subsequent to termination should include reasonably determinable termination claims. Material, but undeterminable,
claims should be footnoted.

3. The termination claim should be shown as a current asset separately
disclosed.

4. Advance payments received before termination may properly be shown
as a deduction from the claim receivable. Loans negotiated on the
security of the claim, should, however, be shown as current liabilities.

5. The contractor's cost and profit elements included in the claim should
be accounted for as a sale, separately disclosed. Costs and expenses
chargeable to the claim may then be given their usual classification.

Chapter 12 - Foreign Operations and Foreign Exchange

This section relates to the treatment of earnings from foreign operations,
of foreign assets, of losses and gains on foreign exchange, and to the consolidation of foreign subsidiaries. The recommendations made in this
chapter apply to United States companies which have branches or subsidiaries
operating in foreign countries.

1. Treatment of earnings:

Earnings of U. S. companies from foreign operations should be reported
in their own accounts only to the extent that funds have been received
in the U. S. or unrestricted funds are available for transmission.

2. Consolidation of foreign subsidiaries:

a. Foreign subsidiaries of U. S. companies may be excluded from consolidation of the parent and domestic subsidiaries, and summaries

- 16 -

of the foreign subsidiaries balance sheet and operating statements shown separately, <u>or</u>

b. Consolidation may include the foreign subsidiary, but in any event,

c. The financial position and operating results of the foreign subsidiary <u>must</u> be clearly distinguishable from those of the parent and its domestic subsidiaries, either by separate statements or otherwise.

3. Losses and gains on foreign exchange:

   a. Realized losses or gains on foreign exchange should be charged against or credited to operations.

   b. Provision for future declines in conversion value of foreign net current and working assets should be made and shown separately.

4. Translation of assets, liabilities, losses and gains:

   a. Current assets and current liabilities should be <u>translated</u> at the <u>rate</u> of exchange prevailing <u>on the date of the balance sheet</u>.

   b. Fixed assets, permanent investments, and long-term receivables should be translated at the <u>rates</u> prevailing <u>when</u> such assets were <u>acquired</u> or <u>constructed</u>.

   c. Long-term liabilities and capital stock should be translated at the <u>rates</u> prevailing <u>when</u> they were <u>originally incurred or issued</u>.

   d. The operating statements of foreign subsidiaries should be translated at the <u>average rate</u> of exchange applicable to each month.

<u>Chapter 13 - Compensation</u>

Section a. - Pension Plans - Annuity Costs Based on Past Service

This section deals with the accounting treatment of costs arising out of past service which are incurred under pension plans involving payments to outside agencies such as insurance companies and trustees.

1. The committee is of the opinion that:

   a. Costs of annuities based on past services should be allocated to current and future periods, except when immaterial, in which case they may be absorbed in the current year.

   b. Costs of annuities based on past services should not be charged to surplus.

2. The above opinions stem from the theory that costs of annuities based on past services are generally incurred in contemplation of present and future services.

- 17 -

Section b. - Compensation Involved in Stock Option and Stock Purchase Plans

This section deals primarily with stock options granted by corporations to their officers and employees. Generally, such options are a part of the corporation's cost of the services of officers and employees, and should be accounted for as such.

1. The date on which such stock options are deemed to accrue may be:

   a. The date of the option agreement.

   b. The date the option right becomes the property of the grantee.

   c. The date the grantee may first exercise the option.

   d. The date the grantee exercises the option.

2. The committee prefers the recording of the accrual for stock options on the date the right becomes the property of the grantee.

3. The value of the compensation should be measured by the difference between the option price and the fair value of the stock at the date of the recording.

4. Accrual of the compensation should be made by means of a charge against the income account.

5. Until the options are exercised or expire, the obligations of the corporation should be adequately disclosed in the financial statements.

Chapter 14 - Disclosure of Long-Term Leases in Financial Statements of Lessees

This chapter discusses proper accounting disclosure of "sell-and-lease-back" arrangements.

1. It is the opinion of the committee that when rentals or other obligations under such long-term leases are material:

   a. Disclosures should be made in the statements or in notes thereto of
      (1) the amount of the annual obligations and the period to run, and
      (2) any other important obligations or guarantee made under the lease.

   b. The information in a. above should be given in the year of origination and all subsequent years when the amount is material.

   c. Principal details of any important "sell-and-lease-back" arrangement should always be disclosed in the year of origination.

2. When the agreement is such that it is clearly evident that the leasee is, in substance, purchasing the property, by installment or otherwise, such property should be included in the assets of the leasee and the related liabilities and charges to income suitably accounted for.

- 18 -

Chapter 15 - Unamortized Discount, Issue Cost, and Redemption Premium on
           Bonds Refunded

This chapter discusses three methods of handling unamortized discount and
redemption premium on bonds refunded.

1. Direct write-off to income or retained earnings:

    a. It is acceptable accounting to write-off unamortized discount in full
        in the year of refunding.

    b. Where a write-off is made to retained earnings, it should be limited
        to the excess of the unamortized discount over the reduction of cur-
        rent taxes to which the refunding gave rise.

    c. The decision to charge the write-off to income or retained earnings
        should be governed by the materiality of the amount.

2. Amortization over the original life of the bonds refunded:

    a. This method conforms more closely to current accounting opinion and
        should be regarded as preferable.

    b. When this method is adopted, a portion of the unamortized discount
        equal to the reduction in current taxes resulting from the refunding
        should be deducted in the income statement and the remainder should
        be apportioned over the future periods.

    c. This method has the merit of reflecting the refinancing expense as
        a direct charge under the appropriate head in a series of income
        accounts related to term of the original bond issue.

3. Amortization over the life of the new issue:

    a. This method cannot be adequately supported by accounting theory and
        runs counter to generally accepted accounting principles.

    b. The committee concludes that this method is unacceptable.

    c. When this method is used, exception should be taken that the ac-
        counts do not conform to generally accepted accounting principle
        (except where this method is prescribed by regulatory bodies).

4. Other considerations:

    a. It is acceptable to accelerate the amortization of the discount on
        bonds refunded except where such charges would materially distort
        the income figure.

    b. The committee does not regard the charging of unamortized bond dis-
        count to capital surplus as an acceptable accounting treatment.

- 19 -

BULLETIN #44 - Declining-balance Depreciation

The declining-balance method of depreciation meets the requirements of being "systematic and rational."

1. In those cases where the expected productivity of the asset is relatively
    greater during the earlier years, or where maintenance charges tend to
    increase during the later years, this method may well provide the most
    satisfactory allocation of cost.

2. When a change to the declining-balance method is made for general ac-
    counting purposes, the change in method should be disclosed in the year
    in which the change is made.

3. The conclusions of this bulletin also apply to other methods, including
    the "sum-of-the-years-digits" method, which will produce substantially
    similar results.

BULLETIN #45 - Long-term Construction-type Contracts

This bulletin is directed to the accounting problems related to long-term
construction-type contracts. There are two generally accepted methods followed by contractors.

1. Percentage-of-completion method:

    a. The committee recommends that the recognized income be that percent-
        age of estimated total income, either:

        (1) that incurred costs to date bear to estimated total costs after
             giving effect to estimates of costs to complete based upon most
             recent information, or,

        (2) that may be indicated by such other measure of progress toward
             completion as may be appropriate having due regard to work
             performed.

    b. The principal advantages are:

        (1) periodic recognition of income as work on the contract progresses,
             and

        (2) a reflection of the status of the uncompleted contracts provided
             through the current estimates to complete.

    c. The principal disadvantage is:

        (1) it is necessarily dependent upon estimates of ultimate costs
             which are subject to the uncertainties frequently inherent in
             long-term contracts.

- 20 -

2. Completed-contract method:

    a. This method recognizes income only when the contract is completed. Costs of contracts in process and current billings are accumulated but there are no interim charges or credits to income other than provisions for losses.

    b. When this method is used, an excess of accumulated costs over related billings should be shown as a current asset and described as "costs of uncompleted contracts in excess of related billings." The excess of accumulated billings over related costs should be shown as current liability and described as "billings on uncompleted contracts in excess of related costs."

    c. The <u>principal advantage</u> is that it is based on results as finally determined, rather than on estimates for unperformed work.

    d. The <u>principal disadvantage</u> is that it does not reflect current performance when the period of any contract extends into more than one accounting period.

3. Selection of method:

    a. The committee believes that when estimates of costs to complete and extent of progress toward completion of long-term contracts are reasonably dependable, the percentage-of-completion method is preferable.

    b. When lack of dependable estimates or inherent hazards cause forecasts to be doubtful, the completed-contract method is preferable.

    c. The method followed should be disclosed.

BULLETIN #46 - Discontinuance of Dating Earned Surplus

The committee believes that the dating of earned surplus following a quasi-reorganization would rarely, if ever, be of significance after a period of ten years. It also believes that there may be exceptional circumstances in which the discontinuance of the dating of earned surplus could be justified at the conclusion of a period less than ten years.

BULLETIN #47 - Accounting for Costs of Pension Plans

This bulletin indicates guides which are acceptable for dealing with costs of pension plans in the accounts and reports of companies having such plans. The term pension plan is intended to mean a formal arrangement for employee retirement benefits.

1. The cost of pension plans to the employer usually is based in part on
    past services and in part on current and future services of the employees.
    The committee is of the opinion that past service costs should be charged
    to operations during the current and future periods benefited, and
    should not be charged to earned surplus at the inception of the plan.

2. Costs based on past services should be charged off over some reason-
    able period, provided the allocation is made on a systematic and
    rational basis and does not distort the operating results in any one
    year.. The committee prefers this method as the one most likely to
    effect a reasonable matching of costs and revenues.

3. The minimum period presently permitted for tax purposes is ten years
    if the initial past-service-cost is immediately paid in full, or twelve
    years if one-tenth of the initial past-service cost plus interest is
    paid each year.

BULLETIN #48 - Business Combinations

This bulletin differentiates between two types of combinations, the first of
which is designated as a purchase and the second as a pooling of interests,
and indicates the nature of the accounting treatment appropriate to each
type.

1. A purchase may be described as a business combination of two or more
    corporations in which an important part of the ownership interests in
    the acquired corporation is eliminated.

2. A pooling of interests may be described as a business combination of
    two or more corporations in which the holders of substantially all of
    the ownership interests in the constituent corporations become the
    owners of a single corporation which owns the assets and businesses of
    the constituent corporations. The continuance in existence of one or
    more of the constituent corporations in a subsidiary relationship to
    another does not prevent the combination from being a pooling of interests
    if no significant minority interest remains outstanding, and if there are
    important tax, legal, or economic reasons for maintaining the subsidiary
    relationship.

3. When a combination is deemed to be a purchase, the assets acquired should
    be recorded on the books of the acquiring corporation at cost, measured
    in money, or, in the event other consideration is given, at the fair
    value of such other consideration, or at the fair value of the property
    acquired, whichever is more clearly evident.

4. When a combination is deemed to be a pooling of interests, a new basis
    of accountability does not arise. The carrying amounts of the assets
    of the constituent corporations, if stated in conformity with generally
    accepted accounting principles and appropriately adjusted when deemed
    necessary to place them on a uniform accounting basis, should be carried
    forward.

- 22 -

5. Generally, one or more of the following circumstances give rise to a purchase:

    a. Stock received by several owners of one of the predecessor corporations is not substantially in proportion to their respective interests.

    b. Relative voting rights are materially altered through the issuance of senior equity or debt securities having limited or no voting rights

    c. A substantial change in ownership occurring shortly before or planned to occur shortly after the combination.

    d. If the management of one of the constituents is eliminated.

    e. Where one of the constituent corporations is clearly dominant (for example, where the stockholders of one of the constituent corporations obtain 90% to 95% or more of the voting interest in the combined enterprise).

6. No one of the above factors would necessarily be determinative and any one factor might have varying degrees of significance in different cases. However, their presence or absence would be cumulative in effect.

7. Where one or more of the constituent corporations continues in existence in a subsidiary relationship, and the requirements of a pooling of interests have been met, the combination of earned surpluses in the consolidated balance sheet is proper since a pooling of interests is not an acquisition as that term is used in paragraph 3 of chapter 1(a) of Bulletin #43.

- 23 -

BULLETIN #49 - Earnings Per Share

1. This bulletin deals with problems which arise in the computation and presentation of statistics concerning periodic net income (or loss) in terms of earnings per share.

2. The committee now reaffirms its earlier conclusions that:

(a) It is, in many cases, undesirable to give major prominence to a single figure of earnings per share;

(b) Any computation of earnings per share for a given period should be related to the amount designated in the income statement as net income for such period; and

(c) Where material extraordinary charges or credits have been excluded from the determination of net income, the per-share amount of such charges and credits should be reported separately and simultaneously.

3. In the computation and use of a single figure for earnings per share in this area of financial reporting, a clear explanation and disclosure of methods used are especially important.

4. The committee suggests the following general guides to be used in computing and presenting earnings per share:

(a) Where used without qualification, the term earnings per share should be used to designate the amount applicable to each share of common stock or other residual security outstanding.

(b) Earnings per share, and particularly comparative statistics covering a period of years, should generally be stated in terms of the common stock position as it existed in the years to which the statistics relate, unless it is clear that the growth or decline of earnings will be more fairly presented, e.g., in the case of a stock split, by dividing prior years' earnings by the current equivalent of the number of shares then outstnading.

(c) In all cases in which there have been significant changes in stock during the period to which the computations relate, an appropriate explanation of the method used should accompany the presentation of earnings per share.

- 24 -

Single-Year Computations

5. In computing earnings per share for a single year, small changes in the number of shares outstanding during the year may be disregarded; the number of shares outstanding at the end of the year may be used as the base. Where there has been a substantial increase or decrease in the number of shares outstanding it is proper to use a weighted average of the number of shares outstanding during the year as the base. When these shares have been issued at the end of the year they may be disregarded in the computation. Where the increase may be attributed to stock split or dividend or the decrease may be attributed to a reverse stock split, the computation should be based on the number of shares outstanding at the end of the year. In determining the number of shares outstanding, reacquired shares should be excluded.

6. If there has been a stock split or reverse split after the balance sheet date but before the financial report is issued, it is desirable to base the earnings per share computation on the new number of shares, since the reader's interest is presumed to be in the present stock position. When computations of earnings per share reflect changes in the number of shares after the balance sheet date, it is important to disclose this fact since it might be presumed that the earnings per share are based on the number of shares shown on the balance sheet. It is equally important to disclose significant changes in the number of shares after the balance sheet date when such changes are not reflected in the earnings per share computation.

7. Where there are shares outstanding senior to the common stock or other residual security, the claims of such securities or net income should be deducted from net income or added to net loss before the computation of per-share figures, since earnings per share is ordinarily used to identify the amount applicable to each share of common stock or other residual security outstanding. In arriving at net income applicable to common stock for purposes of the per-share computations, provision should be made for cumulative preferred dividends for the year, whether or not earned. In the event of a net loss, the amount of the loss should be increased by any cumulative preferred dividends for the year. Where the dividends are cumulative only if earned, no adjustment of this nature is required except to the extent of income available therefor. In all cases the effect that has been given to dividend rights of senior securities in arriving at the earnings per share of common stock should be disclosed.

8. The following are special considerations relating to convertible securities:

> (a) When debt capital, preferred stock, or other security has been converted into common stock during the year, earnings per share should ordinarily be based on a weighted average of the number of shares outstanding during the year. When the weighted average is used, adjustments for the year in respect of interest or other related factors are not made.

- 25 -

(b) When capitalizations consist essentially of two
classes of common stock, one which is convertible
into the other and is limited in its dividend rights
until conversion takes place as, e.g., when certain
levels of earnings are achieved, two earnings-per-
share figures, one assuming conversion, are ordinarily necessary for full disclosure.

Comparative Statistics

9. Presentations of earnings-per-share data for a period of several years
should be governed basically by criteria for single year presentations, but may
involve special considerations. Variations in the capital structure may have
substantial effects on earnings per share. The usefulness of comparative statistics depends in large measure on collateral historical information and disclosure of methods of computation used. The committee's recommendations which
follow are intended as guides to uniformity but not as substitutes for explanations and disclosures.

10. When computations of earnings per share for a period of years include periods in which there have been stock splits or reverse splits, the
earnings for periods prior to the dates of the splits should be divided by the
current equivalent of the number of shares outstanding in the respective prior
periods in order to arrive at earnings per share in terms of the present stock
position. Stock dividends should be treated similarly except that it is permissible not to extend such treatment to small recurrent stock dividends.
Where, during the period of years for which data are given, there have been
issuances or reacquisitions of stock for property or cash or issuances in
connection with conversions of debt capital, preferred stock, or other security,
the computations of earnings per share for the years prior to such changes are
not affected; it follows that earnings per share for these years should be based
on the number of shares outstanding in the various years. When both situations
have occurred, the effect of each should be reflected in accordance with the
foregoing recommendations.

11. When equity securities are being publicly offered:

(a) If there have been significant conversions of debt
capital, preferred stock, or other security during
the period of years for which data are given, it is
appropriate to present supplementary calculations
revising past figures to reflect subsequent conversions, on a pro forma basis.

(b) If the securities being offered or their proceeds,
are to be used to retire outstanding securities in
circumstances which assure such retirement, it
may be useful to present, in addition to otherwise
appropriate calculations, supplementary computations
to show pro forma earnings per share for at least

the most recent year as if such substitution of
securities had been made. When this is done,
the basis of the supplementary computation should
be clearly disclosed. Where, however, the securities
being offered, or their proceeds, are to be used, not
to retire existing securities but for other purposes,
earnings per share should be computed without adjustment for any increase in the number of shares anticipated
as a result of such offering.

12. Where there has been a pooling of interests during the period of
years for which data are given, in connection with which the number of shares
outstanding or the capital structure has been changed, the method used in
computing earnings per share for those years prior to the pooling of interests
should be based on the new capital structure. When there is to be a pooling
of interests in connection with which the number of shares outstanding or
capital structure will be changed, earnings per share for any period for which
income statements of the constituent companies are presented in combined
form should be computed on a basis consistent with the exchange ratio to be
used in the pooling of interest. In either case, earnings per share should be
computed in conformity with the foregoing paragraphs.

Earnings Coverage of Senior Securities

13. Where periodic net income is related to outstanding shares of
senior securities, i.e., preferred stock, under most circumstances, the
term earnings per share is not properly applicable because of the limited
dividend rights of these senior securities. Such information should not be
designated as earnings per share but might be shown as the number of times
or the extent to which the requirements of senior dividends have been earned.

Miscellaneous

14. In computing data relating to acquisitions, mergers, reorganizations,
convertible and participating securities, outstanding stock options, retirements
and combinations of these circumstances, a clear disclosure of the basis on
which the computations have been made is essential and these situations and
circumstances should all be dealt with in accordance with the recommendations
contained in this bulletin.

Dividends Per Share

15. In general, dividends per share constitute historical facts and
should be so reported. However, in certain cases, such as a stock split as
mentioned in paragraph 10, a presentation of dividends per share in terms of
the current equivalent of the number of shares outstanding at the time of the
dividend is necessary so that dividends per share and earnings per share will
be stated on the same basis. When dividends per share are stated on any
basis other than the historical, it is generally desirable that such statement
be supplemental to the historical record, and its basis and significance should
be fully explained.

- 27 -

BULLETIN #50 - Contingencies

1. A contingency is an existing condition, situation or set of circumstances, involving a considerable degree of uncertainty, which may, through a related future event, result in the acquisition or loss of an asset, or the incurrance or avoidance of a liability, usually with the concurrence of a gain or loss.

DISCUSSION

2. This bulletin deals with contingencies which are not predictable enough to record in the accounts, but which might materially affect financial position or results of operations. Examples of contingencies are: pending or threatened litigation, possible assessments of additional taxes, claims against others for patent infringement, price redetermination upward and claims for reimbursement under condemnation proceedings. Material contingencies of these types should be disclosed in the financial statements or in notes thereto.

3. Contingencies may exist where the outcome is reasonably foreseeable, such as anticipated losses from uncollectible receivables; these should be reflected in the accounts. However, contingencies which might result in gains usually are not reflected in the accounts since to do so might be to recognize revenue prior to its realization; but there should be adequate disclosure. (Probably footnote)

4. Contingencies that are inherent in business operations, such as the possibility of war, strike, business recession, need not be reflected in statements either by incorporation in the accounts or by other disclosure.

DISCLOSURE

5. Disclosure of contingencies referred to in paragraph 2 should be made in financial statements or in notes thereto. The disclosure should indicate the nature of the contingency, and should give an appraisal of the outlook. If a monetary estimate of the amount involved is not feasible, disclosure should be made in general terms, explaining that no amount is determinable. It may be appropriate to indicate a management opinion as to the amount which may be involved. Care should be exercised in the disclosure of contingencies in the case of gains or assets, to avoid misleading implications as to the likelihood of realization.

6. Certain other situations requiring disclosures have sometimes inappropriately been described as though they were contingencies, even though they do not possess the degree of uncertainty usually associated with a contingency. Examples are unused letters of credit, long term leases, assets pledged as security for loans, and commitments such as those for plant acquisition or an obligation to reduce debts, maintain working capital or restrict dividends. Even though these situations may develop into contengencies they should not be described (in the statements) as contingencies prior to such eventuality.

- 28 -

BULLETIN #51- Consolidated Financial Statements

Purpose of Consolidated Statements

1. The purpose of consolidated statements is to present the results of operations and the financial position of a parent company and its subsidiaries essentially as if the group were a single company.

Consolidation Policy

2. Ownership of a majority voting interest is the usual condition for a controlling financial interest; ownership by one company, directly or indirectly, of over fifty percent of the outstanding voting shares of another company is a condition pointing toward consolidation. A subsidiary should not be consolidated where control is likely to be temporary. A subsidiary should be consolidated even though it has a relatively large indebtedness to bondholders or others.

3. In deciding upon consolidation policy, the aim should be to make the financial presentation which is most meaningful to the reader in view of the circumstances. Even though the group of companies have diverse operations, their statements may be consolidated. Separate statements might be preferable for one or more subsidiaries if this would be more informative to stockholders and creditors of the parent company.

4. A difference in fiscal periods of a parent and a subsidiary does not of itself justify the exclusion of the subsidiary from consolidation. Where the difference is not more than three months, use statements for the subsidiary's fiscal period and disclose material intervening events; otherwise prepare special statements for the subsidiary to use for consolidation.

5. Consolidated statements should disclose the consolidation policy being followed through headings, information in the statements, or a footnote.

Consolidation Procedure Generally

6. In preparing consolidated statements, intercompany balances and transactions should be eliminated including receivable-payable and similar balances, security holdings, sales and purchases, and gross profits and losses on assets remaining within the group.

Elimination of Intercompany Investments

7. Where the cost to the parent of the investment in a purchased subsidiary, after provision for specific costs or losses incurred in the integration of the operations, exceeds the parent's equity in the subsidiary's net assets, the excess should be dealt with in the consolidated balance sheet according to its nature. (1) Any difference attributable to specific tangible or intangible assets, should be allocated to them with proper provisions for depreciation or amortization over their remaining life. (2) Any difference which cannot be applied, should be shown among the assets in the consolidated balance sheet with a descriptive caption. (The CPA Course Staff suggests the caption in the "Intangible assets" section of the balance sheet be " Excess of cost over book value in subsidiary".)

- 29 -

8. In general, parallel procedures should be followed in the reverse type of case - where the cost to the parent is less than its equity in the net assets of the purchased subsidiary. Attributable differences should be allocated to specific assets, with corresponding adjustments to depreciation or amortization. Any difference which cannot be applied may be shown in a credit account. (The CPA Course Staff suggests the use of the caption "Excess of book value over cost" in the "Stockholders Equity" section of the balance sheet.)

9. The earned surplus or deficit of a purchased subsidiary at the date of acquisition by the parent should not be included in consolidated earned surplus.

10. When one company purchases several blocks of stock of another company at various dates and eventually obtains control, the date of acquisition (for the purpose of consolidated statements) depends on the circumstances. If the purchases are made over a period of time, the subsidiary earned surplus at acquisition should generally be determined on a step-by-step basis; however, if small purchases are made over a period of time and then a purchase is made which results in control, the date of the last purchase may be considered the date of acquisition.

11. When a subsidiary is purchased during the year, there are alternative ways of dealing with results of operations in the consolidated income statement. One method is to include the subsidiary in the consolidation as though it had been acquired at the beginning of the year, and to deduct (at the bottom of the income statement) the preacquisition earnings applicable to each block of stock. Another method is to include only the subsidiary's revenue and expenses subsequent to the date of acquisition.

12. When the investment in a subsidiary is disposed of during the year, it may be preferable to omit the details of the operations of the subsidiary from the consolidated income statement, and to show the equity of the parent in the earnings of the subsidiary prior to disposal as a separate item in the statement.

13. Shares of the parent held by a subsidiary should not be treated as outstanding stock in the consolidated balance sheet.

Minority Interests

14. Eliminate 100% of intercompany profit or loss (paragraph 6) regardless of the existence of a minority interest. (NOTE: The last sentence of this paragraph pertains to a consolidation method not used in the GAO course.)

15. If losses applicable to the minority interest in a subsidiary exceed the minority interest in the equity capital of the subsidiary, such excess and any further losses applicable to the minority should be charged against the majority interest. However, if future earnings do materialize, the majority interest should be credited to the extent of such losses previously absorbed.

Income Taxes

16. When separate income tax returns are filed, income taxes usually are incurred when earnings of subsidiaries are transferred to the parent. If

- 30 -

undistributed earnings of a subsidiary are to be transferred to the parent in a taxable distribution, provision for related income taxes should be made on an estimated basis at the time the earnings are included in consolidated income. There is no need to provide for income tax where the income has been permanently invested by the subsidiaries.

17. If income taxes have been paid on intercompany profits on assets remaining within the group, such taxes should be deferred or the intercompany profits to be eliminated in consolidation should be appropriately reduced.

Stock Dividends of Subsidiaries

18. The capitalization by subsidiary companies of earned surplus arising since acquisition does not require a transfer to capital surplus on consolidation.

Unconsolidated Subsidiaries in Consolidated Statements

19. The preferable method of dealing with this matter is to adjust the investment through income currently to take up the share of the controlling company in the subsidiaries' net income or net loss. The other method is to carry the investment at cost and to take up income as dividends are received. When the latter method is followed, the consolidated statements should disclose the cost of the investment in unconsolidated subsidiaries, the equity of the consolidated group of companies in their net assets, the dividends received from them in the current period, and the equity of the consolidated group in their earnings for the period.

20. If the investment in the subsidiaries is carried at cost plus the equity in undistributed earnings and intercompany sales are made between the unconsolidated subsidiaries and the parent company, and elimination of unrealized intercompany gains and losses should be made to the same extent as if the subsidiaries were consolidated. If the investment is carried at cost, it is not necessary to eliminate the intercompany gain on sales to unconsolidated subsidiaries, if the gain on the sales does not exceed the unrecorded equity in undistributed earnings of the unconsolidated subsidiaries. If such gain is material, it should be disclosed. Intercompany gains or losses on sales by unconsolidated subsidiaries to companies in the consolidation should be eliminated to arrive at the amount of equity in the undistributed earnings of the unconsolidated subsidiaries.

21. When the unconsolidated subsidiaries are material in relation to the consolidated financial position, summarized information should be given in footnotes or separate statements.

Combined Statements

22. There are circumstances where combined financial statements (as distinguished from consolidated statements) of commonly controlled companies are likely to be more meaningful than their separate statements, for example, (1) where one individual owns a controlling interest in several corporations with related operations; (2) unconsolidated subsidiaries; and (3) companies under common management.

- 31 -

23. In preparing combined statements, intercompany transactions and profits or losses should be eliminated. Problems in the area of minority interests, foreign operations, different fiscal periods, e tc., should be handled in the same manner as in consolidated statements.

Parent-Company Statements

24. In some cases parent-company statements may be needed in addition to consolidated statements to show adequately the position of bondholders, other creditors, or preferred stockholders of the parent. Consolidating statements, using one column for the parent company and other columns for subsidiaries, are an effective means of presenting the pertinent information.

- 32 -

OUTLINE OF

ACCOUNTING TERMINOLOGY BULLETINS

The American Institute of Certified Public Accountants has published a final edition of Accounting Terminology Bulletins. Generally, the purpose of these bulletins is to promote uniformity in the use of terms in connection with business operations and financial statements.

This memorandum presents a brief outline of their contents setting forth the definitions, conclusions, and/or recommendations made by the Committee on Terminology, AICPA. This memorandum is not intended to replace the full discussion contained in the terminology bulletins.

These bulletins are of particular importance to accountants since they represent the considered opinion of the most widely recognized authoritative spokesman for the profession. For candidates preparing for the C.P.A. examination, a thorough knowledge of their contents is mandatory.

ACCOUNTING TERMINOLOGY BULLETINS

Bulletin #1

There follows a summary of the definitions and/or recommendations contained in this bulletin.

1. Accounting:

   The art of recording, classifying and summarizing in a significant manner and in terms of money, transactions and events which are, in part at least, of a financial character, and interpreting the results thereof.

2. Balance Sheet:

   A tabular statement or summary of balances (debit and credit) carried forward after an actual or constructive closing of the books of account kept by double-entry methods, according to the rules or principles of accounting. The items reflected on the two sides of the balance sheet are commonly called assets and liabilities, respectively.

   a. Asset (as a balance sheet heading):

      A thing represented by a debit balance (other than a deficit) that is or would be properly carried forward upon a closing of books of account kept by double-entry methods, according to the

- 33 -

rules or principles of accounting. The presumptive grounds
for carrying the balance forward are that it represents
either a property right or value acquired, or an expenditure
made which has created a property right, or which is properly
applicable to the future. Thus, plant, accounts receivable,
inventory and a deferred charge are all assets in balance-sheet
classification.

b. Liability (as a balance-sheet heading):

A thing represented by a credit balance that is or would be
properly carried forward upon a closing of books of account
kept by double-entry methods, according to the rules or
principles of accounting, provided such credit balance is not
in effect a negative balance applicable to an asset. Thus
the word is used broadly to comprise not only items which constitute liabilities in the popular sense of debts or obligations (including provision for those that are unascertained),
but also credit balances to be accounted for which do not
involve the debtor and creditor relation. For example, capital
stock, deferred credits to income and surplus are balance-sheet
liabilities in that they represent balances to be accounted
for by the company; though these are not liabilities in the
ordinary sense of debts owed to legal creditors.

3. Income Statement:

A statement which shows the principal elements, positive and
negative, in the derivation of income or loss, the claims against
income, and the resulting net income or loss of the accounting
unit.

4. Retained Income:

The balance of net profits, income and gains of a corporation from
the date of incorporation (or from the date when a deficit was
absorbed by a charge against the capital surplus created by a
reduction of the par or stated value of the capital stock or
otherwise) after deducting losses and after deducting distributions
to stockholders and transfers to capital-stock accounts when made
out of such surplus.

5. Value:

As used in accounts signifies the amount at which an item is
stated, in accordance with the accounting rules or principles
relating to that item. Generally, book or balance sheet values
(using the word "value" in this sense) represent cost to the
accounting unit or some modification thereof: but sometimes they
are determined in other ways, as for instance on the basis of
market values or cost of replacement, in which cases the basis
should be indicated in financial statements.

- 34 -

6. **Audit:**

   In general, an examination of an accounting document and of supporting evidence for the purpose of reaching an informed opinion concerning its propriety.

7. **Auditor's Report (or Certificate):**

   A document in which an independent accountant (or auditor) indicates briefly the nature and scope of the examination (audit) which he has made and expresses the opinion which he has formed in respect of the financial statements.

8. **Depreciation:**

   Depreciation accounting is a system of accounting which aims to distribute the cost or other basic value of tangible capital asset, less salvage (if any), over the estimated useful life of the unit (which may be a group of assets) in a systematic and rational manner. It is a process of allocation, not of valuation. Depreciation for the year is the portion of the total charge under such a system that is allocated to the year. Although the allocation may properly take into account occurences during the year, it is not intended to be a measurement of the effect of all such occurences.

9. **Use of the term "Reserve":**

   Four accounting uses of the term "reserve" are discussed and recommendations made as follows:

   a. Valuation reserves (reserves for depreciation, bad debts, etc.). Discontinue the use of the word reserve in this sense and substitute terms which indicate the measurement process, such as "less estimated uncollectibles," "less estimated losses in collection," "less amortization to date," "less accumulated depreciation," "less depreciation to date," etc.

   b. Liability reserves (reserves for damages, taxes, self-insurance, etc.). Discontinue the use of reserve in this sense and substitute such terms as "estimated liabilities," or "liabilities of estimated amount."

   c. The term reserve is often used in connection with appropriations of retained earnings. This use is correct and may be continued.

   d. The term reserve is often used to describe a variety of charges, including losses estimated as likely to be sustained because of uncollectible accounts, depreciation, etc. It is to be noted here that the term refers to the charge by means of which a reserve (in any of the three preceding senses) is created.

- 35 -

10. Use of the term "Surplus":

The Committee on Terminology discusses the ambiguity and poor
accounting usage of the term surplus, and presents the following
recommendations:

a. Use of the term "surplus" be discontinued.

b. Contributed portions of proprietary capital be shown as:

i. Capital contributed for, or assigned to, shares out-
    standing, to the extent of par or stated value.

ii. Capital contributed for, or assigned to, shares in excess
    of par or stated value, and capital received other than
    for shares, whether from shareholders or others.

c. Replace the term "earned surplus" with terms such as
    "retained income," "retained earnings," "accumulated earnings,"
    or "earnings retained for use in the business." Show deficits
    as a deduction from contributed capital, with appropriate
    description.

d. In connection with b.ii. and c. above, there should be
    clear indication of amounts appropriated or restricted as
    to withdrawal. Appropriations of retained income in the
    form of reserves should remain as part of stockholders
    equity.

e. Designate stockholders equities arising from appreciation
    increments as "excess of appraised or fair value of fixed
    assets over cost," or "appreciation of fixed assets."

Bulletin #2

    This bulletin considers the terms proceeds, revenue, income, profit,
and earnings.

1. Proceeds:

Proceeds is a very general term used to designate the total
amount realized or received in any transaction, whether it be a
sale, an issue of stock, the collection of receivables, or the
borrowing of money. Generally the term should be used only in
discussions of transactions.

2. Revenue:

Revenue results from the sale of goods and the rendering of
services and is measured by the charge made to customers, clients,
or tenants for goods and services furnished to them. It also

- 36 -

includes gains from the sale of assets (other than stock in
trade), interest and dividends earned on investments, and
other increases in the owner's equity except those arising from
capital contributions and capital adjustments. It does not include
items such as amounts received from loans, owners' investments, and
collection of receivables. The Committee on Terminology recommends
that the term "revenue" be more widely used in the preparation of
financial statements and for other accounting purposes.

3. Income and Profit:

Income and profit involve net or partially net concepts and refer
to amounts resulting from the deduction from revenues, or from
operating revenues, of cost of goods sold, other expenses, and
losses, or some of them. The terms are often used interchangeably
and are generally preceded by an appropriate qualifying adjective
or term such as "gross," "operating," "net.....before income taxes,"
and "net." The terms are also used in titles of statements showing results of operations, such as "income statement" or "statement
of profit and loss." The committee recommends that when the
terms are used in financial statements, they be preceded by the
appropriate qualifying adjective. When referring to the excess
of operating revenue over the cost of goods sold, the terms
"gross profit on sales" or "gross margin" are preferred. It is
also recommended that the terms "operating income," "net income"
and "income statement" be used.

4. Earnings:

The term earnings is not used uniformly but it is generally
employed as a synonym for "net income," particularly over a
period of years. The term is often combined with another word
in the expression "earning power", referring to the demonstrated
ability of an enterprise to earn net income. The committee makes
no recommendation at this time.

Bulletin #3

This bulletin considers the term book value.

Book value signifies the amount at which an item is stated in
accordance with the accounting principles related to them. The
committee recommends that the use of the term book value in referring
to amounts at which individual items are stated in books of account
or in financial statements, be avoided, and that instead, the basis
of amounts intended to apply to individual items be described specifically and precisely; for example, cost less depreciation, lower
of cost or current replacement cost, or lower of cost or selling price.

- 37 -

Bulletin #4

This bulletin considers the terms cost, expense, and loss.

1. Cost:

Cost is the amount, measured in money, of cash expended or other property transferred, capital stock issued, services performed, or a liability incurred, in consideration of goods or services received or to be received. Costs can be classified as unexpired or expired. The committee recommends that the term cost be used when appropriate in describing the basis of assets as displayed in the balance sheet, and properly should be used in income statements to describe such items as cost of goods sold, or costs of other properties or investments sold or abandoned.

2. Expenses:

Expense in its broadest sense includes all expired costs which are deductible from revenues. While the term expense is useful in its broad and generic sense in discussions of transactions and as a general caption in income statements, its use in financial statement is often appropriately limited to the narrower sense of the term, such as operating, selling or administrative expenses, interest, and taxes. In any event, items entering into the computation of cost of manufacturing, such as material, labor, and overhead, should be described as costs and not as expenses.

3. Loss:

Loss is (a) the excess of all expenses, in the broad sense of that word, over revenues for that period, or (b) the excess of all or the appropriate portion of the cost of assets over related proceeds, if any, when items are sold, abandoned, or either wholly or partially destroyed by casualty or otherwise written off. The committee recommends that the term loss be used in financial statements in reference to net or partially net results when appropriate in place of the term income or profit as described in Bulletin #2, item 3 above. In such cases the term should generally be used with appropriate qualifying adjectives. It should also be used in describing results of specific transactions, generally those that deal with disposition of assets.

7.32   Conclusion

The preceding illustrations indicate that an accounting rule rarely can be identified with an hypothesis. But in many cases such a rule provides the boundaries within which an hypothesis is permitted to be established. While the "basic assumptions" categorize the hypotheses into classes with fundamental characteristics, the accounting rules express imperatives and are strongly regulative. The *realization assumption*, for instance, calls for hypotheses that contain *detailed specifications* of the depreciations and other features of *accrual* accounting that are required for the allocation of revenues and expenses to the current period. The precise formulation of these pragmatic hypotheses will depend on the idiosyncrasies of the enterprise and other circumstances. Official pronouncements, as for example the *realization rules*, either illuminate a limited area only or indicate the general direction to be pursued. Usually they neither spell out all the details required for creating an individual hypothesis nor for establishing the complete set of hypotheses demanded by the pertinent basic assumption. Occasionally they may not even be accepted as constraints if such boundary conditions run counter to the specific objective pursued.

The low level of generalization on which most accounting hypotheses have to be formulated makes it difficult to evolve a comprehensive self-contained axiomatic system with a great number of generally applicable theorems. Thus we have to restrict ourselves to a few fundamental propositions (see Appendix A); something indicative for the "early scientific stage" of accounting. In the early stages the adepts of an academic discipline are concerned primarily with the formulation of the foundations (basic assumptions) and less with the whole gamut of conclusions that at this stage require additional specific or secondary assumptions. Nevertheless this "primitive" stage is indispensable for the evolution of every scientific discipline.

PART III

On Projection and
Planning for the Future

Chapter 8

PLANNING MODELS FOR THE MICRO- AND MACRO-ECONOMY

TRADITIONALLY, accounting has been directed toward the past; only relatively recently, with the spread of budgeting, standard costing, and input-output analysis, has an immediate orientation toward the future come about. This trend of planning and forecasting economic activity opens a vast territory of which only the fringes have been explored thus far; a territory into which pioneers of accounting, economics, and management science have begun to penetrate. There exist many tokens that accounting is in a position to make important contributions, on the micro- and macro-level, to the projection of future economic data. Thus during the next decades the center of gravity of accounting might shift from the descriptive-legalistic to the analytic-predictive side.

Chapter 8 and Chapter 9 both serve the illustration of planning models.[1] While Chapter 8 presents a survey of planning models developed by economists and management scientists, it is the task of Chapter 9 to demonstrate the way by which the accountant's traditional budget approach can be refined and brought in line with the new instruments of electronic data processing (EDP), activity analysis, and management science. The inclusion of the present chapter is justified by the relationship between accounting on one

---

[1] Most of the books introducing quantitative analytical methods to accountants and students of business administration (e.g., Bierman, Fouraker, and Jaedicke [1961a], Howell and Teichroew [1963], Kemeny, Schleifer, Snell, and Thompson [1962], Stern [1963] do *not* contain any treatment of the subjects discussed in this chapter. Thus there exists a need for presenting the essence of input-output analysis, macro-econometric models, etc., in a way that is comprehensible to accountants (with some moderate effort on their part).

side and Leontief-type models, Tinbergen-type models, and management control models on the other side. A knowledge of the essence of these constructs seems desirable for an understanding of planning models in general and budget models in particular. The modest mathematical prerequisites required for the understanding of the current chapter are given in Appendixes B and C.

8.1   ACCOUNTING FOR ANALYZING INTERINDUSTRY FLOWS

Input-output analysis, inspired by the general equilibrium approach of Léon Walras [1874] and originated by Wassily Leontief [1951], is concerned with analyzing the flows of commodities or services between the industrial sectors of an economy for the purpose of describing, analyzing, planning, and forecasting the industrial structure of a particular region. The many facets of interindustry analysis have been thoroughly explored in the literature;[2] especially the economic and mathematical problems have been treated intensively, while the accounting aspects have received comparatively little theoretical attention (see Powelson [1955, pp. 425–51] and the fundamental paper by Evans and Hoffenberg [1952]). The neglect of emphasis on the accounting facet in the literature—though not surprising in the face of the more glamorous analytical problems— leads to a misconception about the point of gravity of the input-output approach in actual practice. From the viewpoint of practical application in dozens of countries, the accounting features of interindustry analysis have been utilized to a far greater extent than the analytical-behavioral aspects. The majority of countries[3] for which interindustry studies were carried out, could afford no more than the recording of past transactions between the various industrial sectors; in many cases the pertinent coefficient matrices and inverse matrices which supply the parameters for predicting the "behavior" of the individual sectors were not available. Hence, for the time

---

[2] See the comprehensive bibliography by Riley and Allen [1955]. For an introduction into the mathematical aspects of input-output analysis see Allen [1956, pp. 343–65 and 483–92], Dorfman, Samuelson, and Solow [1958 pp. 204–64], Gale [1960, pp. 301–6], Hadley [1962, pp. 487–509]. As a general introduction we recommended in Subsection 4.55 the presentation by Chenery and Clark [1959].

For a *general* formulation of simple macro-economic transaction models see Stone [1951–52]. Regrettably this formulation does not include micro-economic models—something that would have accelerated the development of analytical budget models (see Section 9.1).

[3] A survey of nineteen countries using input-output tables, presented by Chenery and Clark [1959, pp. 184–85], indicates that only for eight of them inverse matrices were calculated. Meanwhile the picture may have changed to some extent.

being, the practical significance of *interindustry analysis* must be sought in its status as a social accounting system—indeed, in many ways, it ranks equal to national income accounting and flow of funds accounting.

8.11   The Transaction Matrix

The discussion of this chapter, though starting from the accounting aspect of input-output tables, pivots on a phenomenon that first was formally manifested in interindustry analysis, namely *the incorporation of behavioral-technological functions into an accounting system for predictive purposes.* Let us pose three questions which this chapter and the following (together with our companion volume) try to answer: In which way has interindustry analysis fused empirical hypotheses with a system of accounting identities? What are the prospects of adopting similar methods in other accounting systems? How do the structural parameters of input-output analysis compare with those used in budget simulation?

In Section 3.6 and Subsection 3.83 we acquainted the reader with the matrix presentation of accounting systems; and in Subsection 4.55 we referred to the U.S. input-output table (transaction matrix) for the Year 1958, forthcoming from the Office of Business Economics of the Department of Commerce. In this chapter we shall start with a highly aggregated transaction matrix (see Table 8-1) which subdivides the U.S. economy into eight industrial and four autonomous sectors.[4] This table was chosen in order to juxtapose a transaction matrix with concrete data to its abstract version, shown in Table 8-2. In these Tables 8-1 and 8-2 each row and its corresponding column represent the account of an individual sector. Hereby we adhere to the traditional convention of recording the credit entries in the rows and the debit entries in the columns (with the exception of the rows and columns containing totals and subtotals). In Table 8-1, for instance, the entry in row 4 and column 7 indicates that the industrial sector no. 4 supplied the industrial sector no. 7 with commodities in the value of 43 units—(i.e., $430 million). The industrial sectors (occasionally shortly called "industries") are here merely designated by numerals; in tables with a lower degree of aggregation they may be designated by names. The

---

[4]Although the data of Table 8-1 are not quite arbitrary (they are based on the U.S. input-output table for 1947), the degree of aggregation is so high and the additional assumptions (those separating the primary output into depreciation and labor supply) are so crude that these data should be treated as fictitious.

data contained in such a transaction matrix may be *determined historically* by a cumbersome process of data collection, *or* they may be *projected* in a way to be described in the following Subsection 8.13. In such a *projection*, the distinction between *industrial* and *autonomous* sectors becomes important, because only the figures of the industrial sectors can be projected, the figures of the autonomous sectors must be given exogenously ("open systems"). "Closed systems," where the variables of the nonindustrial sectors are also endogenous, are mainly of theoretical significance, but correspond closer to the Walrasian notion of the *interdependence* of *all* economic variables. The autonomous sectors are here designated by capital letters with the following meaning:

F ....Foreign sector   (rows contain import figures, and columns export figures of the various sectors).

G....Government sector   (rows show the amount of government services supplied to the remaining sectors, and columns show the purchases of the government from these sectors).

I .....Investment sector   (rows contain annual Allowances for Depreciation, and Inventory Depletion occured in the individual sectors, and columns show the sectors' contribution to the gross capital formation including inventory accumulation).

H....Household sector   (row data indicate the value of labor supply to the various sectors, and column data indicate the goods and services supplied by these sectors to the household sector—personal consumption).

The reader recognizes that these autonomous sectors show great affinity with the following accounts of the national income accounting system (cf. Subsection 4.53):

Foreign transaction account.
Government appropriation account.
Savings and investment account.
Personal appropriation account.

Indeed, at the construction of the forthcoming U.S. input-output tables much effort has gone into the task of reconciling the autonomous accounts with their corresponding counterparts of the national income and product accounts of this country.

We may now distinguish the following four quadrants (apart from the totals and subtotals): Quadrant I (compare Tables 8-1 with Tables 8-2) comprises only interdependent industry flows. Quadrant II contains the supplies (outputs) of the various industries to the four autonomous sectors. Quadrant III reveals the output of the autonomous sectors to the industrial sectors. Finally, quadrant IV contains transactions between autonomous sectors only. It should be noted that figures in the quadrants II and IV, taken together represent the total *final* demand (equal to the supply of final goods and services) of the economy the data of which, as has been pointed out, are usually given exogenously (so is the *supply* of the autonomous sectors). Therefore we also may address the sectors of quadrant I as the *intermediate* sectors (= industrial sectors) and the autonomous sectors (quadrants II, III, IV) as the *final* sectors.

TABLE 8-1
INTERINDUSTRY ACCOUNTING SYSTEM
(In $100,000)

Purchasing Sectors / Producing Sectors	Intermediate Use — Industry Sectors								Sub-Totals	Final Use — Autonomous Sectors				Total Gross Output (Supply)
	1	2	3	4	5	6	7	8		F	G	I	H	
1	0	6	27	32	4	3	98	4	174	34	15	−13	335	545
2	12	0	4	6	4	13	67	14	120	5	56	169	24	374
3	35	17	0	18	11	14	28	20	143	17	4	3	51	218
4	9	8	10	0	0	11	43	37	118	17	6	5	173	319
5	1	22	2	2	0	65	2	14	108	8	0	1	0	117
6	9	25	2	3	1	0	23	59	122	40	19	133	69	383
7	84	67	23	26	13	21	0	70	304	35	63	40	915	1,357
8	26	22	30	42	15	50	82	0	267	0	0	−8	0	259
Subtotals	176	167	98	129	48	177	343	218	1,356	156	163	330	1,567	3,572
F	28	3	9	13	6	2	5	1	67	0	13	0	13	93
G	32	15	17	22	8	23	139	22	278	8	0	3	313	602
I	30	19	9	15	5	18	87	2	185	1	30	0	2	218
H	279	170	85	140	50	163	783	16	1,686	7	271	2	0	1,966
Total input (Demand)	545	374	218	319	117	383	1,357	259	3,572	172	477	335	1,895	6,451*

F = Foreign sector.   I = Investment sector.
G = Government sector.   H = Household sector.

*The figure of the total gross output (or input) is incomparable with the figure contained in the transaction matrix of the U.S. 1947 supplied by the Bureau of Labor Statistics because in the above stated table the transactions *within* one sector have been eliminated (i.e., the elements of the main diagonal are zero).

8.12   Introducing Technological Functions

To explain the essence of interindustry analysis and its relation to accounting, the abstract version presented in Table 8-2 will be used. There, we notice that the elements of quadrant I are represented (in accordance with matrix algebraic conventions—see Appendix B) by a symbol (e.g., x) with two subscripts, the first re-

TABLE 8-2
INTERINDUSTRY ACCOUNTING SYSTEM
(Generalized Formulation)

Purchasing Sectors / Producing Sectors	Intermediate Use — Industry Sectors $1 \ldots 2 \ldots j \ldots n$					Subtotals	Final Use — Autonomous Sectors F	G	I	H	Total Gross Output (Supply)
1	x_{11}	$x_{12} \ldots$	$x_{1j} \ldots$	x_{1n}		W_1	E_1	Γ_1	I_1	C_1	X_1
2	x_{21}	$x_{22} \ldots$	$x_{2j} \ldots$	x_{2n}		W_2	E_2	Γ_2	I_2	C_2	X_2
.			. . . .			.		. . . .			.
i	x_{i1}	$x_{i2} \ldots$	$x_{ij} \ldots$	x_{in}		W_i	E_i	Γ_i	I_i	C_i	X_i
		Quadrant I				.		Quadrant II			.
.			. . . .			.		. . . .			.
n	x_{n1}	$x_{n2} \ldots$	$x_{nj} \ldots$	x_{ni}		W_n	E_n	Γ_n	I_n	C_n	X_n
Subtotals	U_1	$U_2 \ldots$	$U_j \ldots$	U_n		A	U_F	U_G	U_I	U_H	B
F	M_1	$M_2 \ldots$	$M_j \ldots$	M_n		W_F	M_E	M_G	M_I	M_H	X_F
G	G_1	$G_2 \ldots$	$G_j \ldots$	G_n		W_G	G_E	G_G	G_I	G_H	X_G
		Quadrant III						Quadrant IV			
I	D_1	$D_2 \ldots$	$D_j \ldots$	D_n		W_I	D_E	D_G	D_I	D_H	X_I
H	L_1	$L_2 \ldots$	$L_j \ldots$	L_n		W_H	L_E	L_G	L_I	L_H	X_H
Total Input (Demand)	Z_1	$Z_2 \ldots$	$Z_j \ldots$	Z_n		S	Z_F	Z_G	Z_I	Z_H	T

(Left column labels: "Industry Sectors (Intermediate)" for rows 1–n; "Autonomous Sectors" for rows F, G, I, H)

E_i = exports of sector i.
Γ_i = government purchases from sector i.
I_i = capital goods (incl. inventory incr.) bought from sector i.
C_i = consumption goods bought from sector i.

M_j = imports bought by sector j.
G_j = government services supplied to sector j.
D_j = depreciation, etc., in sector j.
L_j = labor input in sector j.

$$(i, j = 1, \ldots, H).$$

ferring to the row (output, credit, or supplying industry), the second referring to the column (input, debit, or consuming industry). Thus the general notation for interindustry supplies is

x_{ij} = the supply that flows from industry i to industry j (whereby i and j may refer to any of the n industries, i.e.: $i, j, = 1, \ldots, n$).

As regards the autonomous sectors we use a symbolism somewhat different and more suggestive. The pertaining symbols are explained at the bottom of Table 8-2. The subtotals and totals are fairly obvious and will be summarized below. Hereby one additional symbol has to be introduced, namely the *final* demand for products of industry i, represented by

$$\Upsilon_i = E_i + \Gamma_i + I_i + C_i \qquad (i = 1, \ldots, n)$$

and the total goods and services supplied by the autonomous sectors

$$V_j = M_j + G_j + D_j + L_j \qquad (j = 1, \ldots, n)$$

The equations listed below follow from Table 8–2:

$$W_i = \sum_{j=1}^{n} x_{ij} \qquad\qquad (i = 1, \ldots, n)$$

$$W_F = \sum_{j=1}^{n} M_j \qquad\qquad W_I = \sum_{j=1}^{n} D_j$$

$$W_G = \sum_{j=1}^{n} G_j \qquad\qquad W_H = \sum_{j=1}^{n} L_j$$

$$X_i = W_i + Y_i \qquad\qquad (i = 1, \ldots, H)$$

$$U_j = \sum_{i=1}^{n} x_{ij} \qquad\qquad (j = 1, \ldots, n)$$

$$U_F = \sum_{i=1}^{n} E_i \qquad\qquad U_I = \sum_{i=1}^{n} I_i$$

$$U_G = \sum_{i=1}^{n} \Gamma_i \qquad\qquad U_H = \sum_{i=1}^{n} C_i$$

$$Z_j = U_j + M_j + G_j + D_j + L_j = X_j \qquad (j = 1, \ldots, H)$$

$$A = \sum_{i=1}^{n} W_i = \sum_{j=1}^{n} U_j \qquad B = \sum_{i=1}^{n} X_i = \sum_{j=1}^{H} U_j$$

$$U_F = \sum_{i=1}^{n} E_i \qquad\qquad W_F = \sum_{j=1}^{n} M_j$$

$$U_G = \sum_{i=1}^{n} G_i \qquad\qquad W_G = \sum_{j=1}^{n} G_j$$

$$U_I = \sum_{i=1}^{n} I_i \qquad\qquad W_I = \sum_{j=1}^{n} D_j$$

$$U_H = \sum_{i=1}^{n} C_i \qquad\qquad W_H = \sum_{j=1}^{n} L_j$$

$$S = \sum_{j=1}^{n} Z_j = \sum_{i=1}^{H} W_i \qquad T = S + Z_F + Z_G + Z_I + Z_H$$

$$= B + X_F + X_G + X_I + X_H.$$

In actual practice the input-output tables are based on monetary values (i.e., all the preceding symbols would be expressed in monetary terms); but, as previously mentioned, in theory it is often advantageous to conceive the variables in quantitative terms.[5] In such cases only horizontal additions (row totals and row subtotals) are meaningful since no common denominator exists for vertical additions. Hence the column totals U_j, Z_j ($j = 1, \ldots, H$), A, B, S, and T of Table 8-2 would have to be omitted. The following equation systems are formulated for monetary input-output tables (but most of the equations will hold under quantitative terms as well). In expressing the Leontief system as a linear programing system, however, a change to a quantitative basis would be required (see remarks at the end of the current subsection).

We are now in a position to state the basic formulas of input-output analysis by way of a system of simultaneous equations. After this we shall reformulate this system by (1) introducing technological-behavioral functions with the aid of input coefficients a_{ij} ($i,j = 1, \ldots, n$) and (2) expressing our equations in terms of the *unknown* gross output of each industry. For pedagogic reasons we offer this and the subsequent equation systems in *three* equivalent forms; i.e.,

1. In traditional algebraic notation.
2. In sigma notation.
3. In matrix notation (the explanation of the matrix algebraic symbols in bold types is given at the end of the current subsection).

Algebraic Notation

$$x_{11} + x_{12} + \ldots + x_{1j} + \ldots + x_{1n} + Y_1 = X_1$$
$$x_{21} + x_{22} + \ldots + x_{2j} + \ldots + x_{2n} + Y_2 = X_2$$
$$\cdots\cdots\cdots\cdots\cdots\cdots\cdots\cdots\cdots\cdots\cdots\cdots\cdots$$
$$x_{i1} + x_{i2} + \ldots + x_{ij} + \ldots + x_{in} + Y_i = X_i$$
$$\cdots\cdots\cdots\cdots\cdots\cdots\cdots\cdots\cdots\cdots\cdots\cdots\cdots$$
$$x_{n1} + x_{n2} + \ldots + x_{nj} + \ldots + x_{nn} + Y_n = X_n$$

Sigma Notation   *Matrix Notation*

$$\sum_{j=1}^{n} x_{ij} + Y_i = X_i$$

$$[\mathbf{x} \vdots \mathbf{Y} \vdots \mathbf{X}]$$

$$(i = 1, \ldots, n)$$

super-matrix partitioned into one matrix and two vectors.

---

[5] Even where the input-output tables contain monetary terms it would be more accurate to show "quantitative" variables explicitly and to multiply them with the pertinent prices (see Allen [1956], p. 352). This approach has not been used in the following.

The above set of simultaneous equations follows from Table 8–2 (and the pertaining equations), it expresses the fact that the total output of each industry X_i $(i = 1, \ldots, n)$ is equal to the individual outputs of this industry to all other industries $(x_{ij}, j = 1, \ldots, n)$ plus the final demand Y_i for the product(s) of this (i^{th}) industry.

We now introduce the concept most characteristic for Leontief-type models, the *production coefficient* (or marginal input coefficient) a_{ij} which expresses the amount which the ith commodity contributes to the production of 1 \$ worth (or of one unit if *quantitative* instead of monetary terms are used) of commodity j, and which is defined as:

$$a_{ij} = \frac{x_{ij}}{X_j}.$$

If these production coefficients can be empirically determined (from past experience) then a projection of anticipated interindustry flows should be possible, provided the coefficients can be assumed constant, and provided some other conditions hold (to be discussed in Subsection 8.14). We therefore reformulate the last equation

$$x_{ij} = a_{ij}X_j,$$

then we substitute in the above stated system of simultaneous equations each x_{ij} $(i, j = 1, \ldots, n)$ by $a_{ij}X_j$ $(i, j = 1, \ldots, n)$—omitting in the algebraic formulation the jth column for simplicity's sake—so that the system assumes the following form:

Algebraic Notation

$$a_{11}X_1 + a_{12}X_2 + \ldots + a_{1n}X_n + Y_1 = X_1$$
$$a_{21}X_1 + a_{22}X_2 + \ldots + a_{2n}X_n + Y_2 = X_2$$
$$\cdots\cdots\cdots\cdots\cdots\cdots\cdots\cdots\cdots\cdots$$
$$a_{i1}X_1 + a_{i2}X_2 + \ldots + a_{in}X_n + Y_i = X_i$$
$$\cdots\cdots\cdots\cdots\cdots\cdots\cdots\cdots\cdots\cdots$$
$$a_{n1}X_1 + a_{n2}X_2 + \ldots + a_{nn}X_n + Y_n = X_n$$

Sigma Notation

$$\sum_{j=1}^{n} a_{ij}X_j + Y_i = X_i$$
$$(i = 1, \ldots, n)$$

Matrix Notation

$$[\mathbf{aX + Y}] = \mathbf{X};$$

If we bring all X_i $(i = 1, \ldots, n)$ to the left and the Y_i $(i = 1, \ldots, n)$ to the right we obtain:

Algebraic Notation

$$-(a_{11} - 1)X_1 - a_{12}X_2 - \ldots\ldots\ldots\ldots\ldots - a_{in}X_n = Y_1$$

$$-a_{21}X_1 - (a_{22} - 1)X_2 - \ldots\ldots\ldots\ldots - a_{2n}X_n = Y_2$$

$$\ldots\ldots\ldots\ldots\ldots\ldots\ldots\ldots\ldots\ldots\ldots\ldots\ldots\ldots\ldots$$

$$-a_{i1}X_1 - a_{i2}X_2 - \ldots - (a_{ij} - 1)X_j - \ldots - a_{in}X_n = Y_i$$

$$\ldots\ldots\ldots\ldots\ldots\ldots\ldots\ldots\ldots\ldots\ldots\ldots\ldots\ldots\ldots$$

$$-a_{n1}X_1 - a_{n2}X_2 - \ldots\ldots\ldots\ldots\ldots - (a_{nn} - 1)X_n = Y_n$$

Sigma Notation   *Matrix Notation*

$$\mathbf{X} - \mathbf{aX} = \mathbf{Y}$$

which is equivalent to

$$X_i - \sum_{i=1}^{n} a_{ij}X_j = Y_i$$

$$(\mathbf{I} - \mathbf{a})\mathbf{X} = \mathbf{Y};$$

$$(i = 1, \ldots, n)$$

since $X_1, X_2, \ldots, X_n$ are unknown and $Y_1, Y_2, \ldots, Y_n$ are exogenous variables (these final demands are assumed to be given) we have to present the equation system in such a way as to express *each* X_i as a function of *all* the $Y_j (j = 1, \ldots, n)$. The algebraic attempt to do this in a small system of simultaneous equations will prove to the reader that the new coefficients will be a more or less involved function of the coefficients $a_{11}, a_{12}, \ldots, a_{nn}$. Without going here into the calculation of these new coefficients (i.e., without discussing the determination of the inverse matrix) we shall designate them with $A_{11}, A_{12}, \ldots, A_{nn}$, then our system assumes the following appearance:

Algebraic Notation

$$A_{11}Y_1 + A_{12}Y_2 + \ldots + A_{1j}Y_j + \ldots + A_{1n}Y_n = X_1$$

$$A_{21}Y_1 + A_{22}Y_2 + \ldots + A_{2j}Y_j + \ldots + A_{2n}Y_n = X_2$$

$$\ldots\ldots\ldots\ldots\ldots\ldots\ldots\ldots\ldots\ldots\ldots\ldots\ldots\ldots\ldots\ldots\ldots$$

$$A_{i1}Y_1 + A_{i2}Y_2 + \ldots + A_{ij}Y_j + \ldots + A_{in}Y_n = X_i$$

$$\ldots\ldots\ldots\ldots\ldots\ldots\ldots\ldots\ldots\ldots\ldots\ldots\ldots\ldots\ldots\ldots\ldots$$

$$A_{n1}Y_1 + A_{n2}Y_2 + \ldots + A_{nj}Y_j + \ldots + A_{nn}Y_n = X_n$$

Sigma Notation   *Matrix Notation*

$$\mathbf{AY} = \mathbf{X}$$

which turns out to be the same as

$$\sum_{j=1}^{n} A_{ij}Y_j = X_i$$

$$(\mathbf{I} - \mathbf{a})^{-1}\mathbf{Y} = \mathbf{X}$$

$$(i = 1, \ldots, n)$$

The above equation system is the important result from which the desired gross output of each industry can be determined (when final demands are given). Then each x_{ij} can also be obtained by multiplying the X_j with the historically determined a_{ij}. The alternative formulations of the equation systems demonstrate that the Σ notation, and to a greater extent the matrix notation, enable "economy of expression." In regard to the matrix algebraic operations we refer the reader to Appendix B, but shall here identify the various matrix and vector symbols used above:

$$\mathbf{x} = \begin{bmatrix} x_{11} & x_{12} & \cdots & x_{1n} \\ x_{21} & x_{22} & \cdots & x_{2n} \\ \cdot & \cdot & & \cdot \\ \cdot & \cdot & & \cdot \\ x_{n1} & x_{n2} & \cdots & x_{nn} \end{bmatrix} ; \quad \mathbf{Y} = \begin{bmatrix} Y_1 \\ Y_2 \\ \cdot \\ \cdot \\ Y_n \end{bmatrix} ; \quad \mathbf{X} - \begin{bmatrix} X_1 \\ X_2 \\ \cdot \\ \cdot \\ X_n \end{bmatrix} ;$$

$$\mathbf{a} = \begin{bmatrix} a_{11} & a_{12} & \cdots & a_{1n} \\ a_{21} & a_{22} & \cdots & a_{2n} \\ \cdot & \cdot & & \cdot \\ \cdot & \cdot & & \cdot \\ a_{n1} & a_{n2} & \cdots & a_{nn} \end{bmatrix} ; \quad \mathbf{I} = \begin{bmatrix} 1 & 0 & \cdots\cdots & 0 \\ 0 & 1 & \ddots & 0 \\ \cdot & & \ddots & \cdot \\ 0 & 0 & \cdots\cdots & 1 \end{bmatrix}_{n \times n} ;$$

$$(\mathbf{I} - \mathbf{a}) = \begin{bmatrix} (1 - a_{11}) & -a_{12} & \cdots\cdots & -a_{1n} \\ -a_{21} & (1 - a_{22}) & \cdots\cdots & -a_{2n} \\ \cdot & \cdot & & \cdot \\ -a_{n1} & -a_{n2} & (1 - a_{nn}) \end{bmatrix} ;$$

$$\mathbf{A} = (\mathbf{I} - \mathbf{a})^{-1} = \begin{bmatrix} A_{11} & A_{12} & \cdots\cdots & A_{1n} \\ A_{21} & A_{22} & \cdots\cdots & A_{2n} \\ \cdot & \cdot & & \cdot \\ \cdot & \cdot & & \cdot \\ A_{n1} & A_{n2} & \cdots\cdots & A_{nn} \end{bmatrix}$$

Designations:

$\mathbf{x}$ .... Matrix of transactions (in \$ or in units) of intermediate sectors.
$\mathbf{Y}$ .... Vector of final demand.
$\mathbf{X}$ .... Vector of gross output.
$\mathbf{a}$ .... (Input) coefficient matrix.
$\mathbf{I}$ .... Identity matrix (n times n).
$(\mathbf{I} - \mathbf{a})$ .... Technology matrix.
$\mathbf{A}$ or $(\mathbf{I} - \mathbf{a})^{-1}$ Inverse matrix (of the technology matrix).

8.13 Interindustry Analysis as a Linear Program

Leontief's input-output analysis can be interpreted as a linear programing model and its dual. Such a reformulation is primarily

of theoretical interest, but since the dual of a standard linear programing model has already been encountered (see Subsection 6.21)
a few hints ought to be given as to its application in a Leontief-
economy. We limit ourselves to the statement of the primal and
dual in matrix algebraic notation, pointing merely at the meaning of
the variables.

The Input-Output System as a Linear Program

Primal:	Dual:
(1) $(I - a)X \geq Y$	(4) $(I - a)'V \leq L'$
(2) $X \geq 0$	(5) $V \geq 0$
(3) $\min L = L'X$	(6) $\max P = Y'V$

Explanation:

(1) The total output (supply) of each industry $(I - a)X$ (expressed in product units) must be at least as great as the *given* final demand Y (also expressed in product units) of each product.

(2) The total output of each industry X (in units) must be nonnegative (i.e., either positive or zero).

(3) The *objective* is to *minimize* the total labor input $L'X$ (expressed in labor hours).

(4) The total worth of all inputs for each sector $(I - a)'V$ (expressed in labor hours per unit) must not exceed the labor constraint L' (in labor hours per unit).

(5) The "value" (in labor hours) assigned to each input must be nonnegative.

(6) The *objective* is to *maximize* the national product $Y'V$ (measured in labor hours).

In case there exists a feasible solution to this problem the total labor
input min L is equal to the national product (in labor hours) max P
hence

$$L'X = Y'V$$

Since the variables are stated in *quantitative* terms (product units,
labor hours or combinations of both) the values are also expressed in
labor hours per unit. A conversion of the "values," contained in the
value vector V, into monetary terms (relative prices) requires a given
wage rate and depends on the assumption that the value added in
each sector is entirely due to labor.

Thus the following *additional* matrices and vectors are required:

The transpose of the
technology matrix: $(\mathbf{I} - \mathbf{a})' = \begin{bmatrix} (1 - a_{11}) & -a_{21} \cdots \cdots \cdots -a_{n1} \\ -a_{12} & (1 - a_{22}) \cdots & -a_{n2} \\ \vdots & \vdots & \vdots \\ -a_{1n} & -a_{2n} \cdots \cdots (1 - a_{nn}) \end{bmatrix}$

The column vector
of labor coefficients: $\mathbf{L} = \begin{bmatrix} l_1 \\ l_2 \\ \vdots \\ l_n \end{bmatrix}$;   its transpose $\mathbf{L}' = [l_1 \quad l_2 \cdots l_n]$

The transpose of the column
vector of final demand. $\mathbf{Y}' = [Y_1 \quad Y_2 \cdots Y_n]$

The column vector of values
(in labor hours): $\mathbf{V} = \begin{bmatrix} V_1 \\ V_2 \\ \vdots \\ V_n \end{bmatrix}$

The foregoing discussion on Leontief models indicates that it ought to be possible to project the gross output of each industrial sector as well as the interindustry flows, provided a reliable inverse matrix $\mathbf{A}$ is available (in addition to the availability of: a predetermined final demand for the product of each sector, a historically determined coefficient matrix, etc.). The linear programing version even indicates that it is theoretically possible to project future employment, the national product, and the price structure. The practical utilization of input-output analysis, though not in conformity with a linear program, follows ways similar to those outlined previously. This is evidenced by the following quotations:

To begin, the desired pattern of end-product deliveries must be stipulated.... A typical starting point would be the preparation of an estimate of the gross national product implied by the conditions assumed for the period under consideration, and a subsequent distribution of this total on the basis of data for the commodity flow side of the Commerce Department estimates of gross national product.   (Evans and Hoffenberg [1952], p. 125.)

The essential point is that a cross-sectional analysis, such as was made for 1947, is properly considered as a benchmark for the establishment of structural relationships. The structural interconnections revealed by it should not be considered as immutable or unchanging, but rather as the starting point appropriate to the period to which an analysis of input

structures is to refer.... Actually, the value of the approach is primarily
that it permits meaningful analysis of difficult problems which other
methods, regardless of labor, have failed to solve. (Evans and Hoffenberg
[1952], pp. 126–27.)

Interindustry analysis has been applied in a variety of ways. Although it seems to be best suited for purposes of planning and forecasting in socialized and underdeveloped economies, it has proved
useful in many private-enterprise economies. Input-output studies
facilitate the analysis of bottlenecks (created for instance by fluctuations in government orders to the weapons industry), structural
unemployment, inflationary-deflationary effects, interactions between wages and prices, etc. Transaction matrices have also profitably been employed in marketing and investment studies for specific
industries.

8.14 Basic Assumptions and Extensions

We have noticed that the matrix **a** of production coefficients
$a_{ij} = x_{ij}/X_j$ forms the basis of interindustry *analysis*. These coefficients, *assumed to be fixed over time*, are the structural parameters of
our technological-behavioral functions. They can be given an interpretation more familiar to accountants by juxtaposing the cost curve
of a firm (Figure 8–1a) to the production function of a Leontief-
economy (see Figure 8–1b).

Apart from the fact that a_{ij} represents the slope of the cost or the
production function (depending whether we use a monetary or
quantitative basis), we recognize the *linearity assumption* and the
much stronger (and in the short run more unrealistic) *homogeneity
assumption* implying the absence of fixed costs.

FIGURE 8–1a   **FIGURE 8–1b**

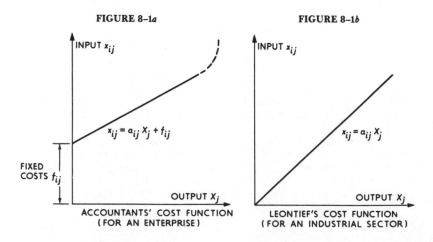

ACCOUNTANTS' COST FUNCTION
(FOR AN ENTERPRISE)

LEONTIEF'S COST FUNCTION
(FOR AN INDUSTRIAL SECTOR)

A fourth assumption which we may call the *assumption of limitational production*, or nonsubstitution, is illustrated in Figure 8–2*b*. It implies production conditions that permit no factor substitution (as it is possible under traditional assumptions—see Figure 8–2*a*), a consequence that leads to a degeneration of the iso-quants (equiproduct curves) which then become mere vertical and horizontal limits.

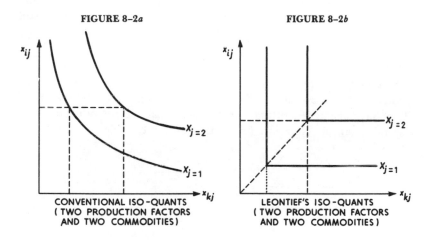

FIGURE 8–2*a*   FIGURE 8–2*b*

CONVENTIONAL ISO-QUANTS
(TWO PRODUCTION FACTORS
AND TWO COMMODITIES)

LEONTIEF'S ISO-QUANTS
(TWO PRODUCTION FACTORS
AND TWO COMMODITIES)

A fifth *assumption*, requires *that each productive sector possesses a single production function*. Among still other assumptions frequently encountered are the following:

a) There are no joint products.
b) A specific product is identified with a specific sector.
c) The production conditions are stationary with regard to the effect of capital formation.

Assumption (*c*) is abandoned in dynamic input-output systems where the acceleration principle is used to connect capital stocks with output, so that investments of one period become a function of the demands and production of subsequent periods. Since dynamic models are less suited for planning purposes than for studying structural interdependences, a few words of explanation may here suffice. Dynamic input-output models require—in addition to the input coefficient matrix (and technology matrix) representing the flow structure—*capital (and inventory) coefficient matrices* which reflect the capital structure of the economy. The capital coefficients indicate a specific stock of capital as a ratio (or percentage) of the total output of a product (or sector).

If we designate by k_{ij} the capital stock in units of the ith product held by the jth industry

and by X_j the output of the jth industry in *units* of product j,

then the *capital coefficient* is defined as

$$c_{ij} = \frac{k_{ij}}{X_j}.$$

Since capital stocks as well as outputs vary over time we may form the first derivative (as to time) of the equation $k_{ij} = c_{ij}X_j$ and obtain

$$\frac{dk_{ij}}{dt} = c_{ij}\frac{dX_j}{dt}.$$

This equation expresses the change in capital as resulting from the product of the *accelerator* dX_j/dt times our capital coefficient c_{ij}. Time-lags are here omitted but obviously can be introduced. The extended output equation (cf. Subsection 8.12) then assumes the following form:

$$\sum_{j=1}^{n} x_{ij} + \sum_{j=1}^{n} \frac{dk_{ij}}{dt} + Y_i = X_i \quad (i = 1, \ldots, n).$$

$$\vdots \qquad\qquad \vdots \qquad\qquad \vdots \qquad \vdots$$

| to inter- mediate industries | to capital formation | to con- sumption (or final demand ex- cluding in- vestments) | total output of i |

If the input and capital coefficients are inserted and if the *discrete* variables of period analysis are preferred (superscript t indicating current period and t' subsequent periods) we obtain:

$$\sum_{j=1}^{n} a_{ij}X_j^t + \sum_{j=1}^{n} c_{ij}\Delta X_j^{t'} + Y_i^t = X_i^t \quad (i = 1, \ldots, n)$$

The dynamic system is a good example of the attempts to convert exogenous variables to endogenous ones, thus helping to close the open system as far as possible.

8.2   ACCOUNTING DATA AND OTHER MODELS FOR MACRO-ECONOMIC PROJECTIONS

While the Leontief-type models constitute a genuine fusion of an accounting system with a set of technological-behavioral functions, purely macro-econometric models (i.e., *Tinbergen-type models*[6]) and macro-economic simulation models predominantly use the existing accounting data (usually from national income and product accounts) as raw material for determining structural parameters. Yet, there is a group-effort under way[7] to construct a comprehensive econometric model of the United States which imposes an accounting (input-output) matrix upon a Tinbergen-type model. Klein [1961, p. 36] the co-ordinator of this project, confirms that "one of the most interesting ideas growing out of the conference [at Dartmouth, 1961] was a method for combining input-output analysis with the usual type of econometric model. This has not previously been done. In the end, we should have a much more satisfactory explanation of prices, and this has been a weak point in other models." Thus the use of accounting data, the possible combination of an accounting matrix with a macro-econometric model, and the projection of accounting variables by Tinbergen-type models may justify a brief survey of attempts that have recently been made in this area.

8.21   Tinbergen-Type Models

In Subsection 7.12 we referred to the difficulty of financing micro-econometric studies (e.g., for determining enterprise cost curves) out of the administrative budget of a firm. We indicated that in many situations the additional benefits derived from such refined studies may not match the comparatively high expenses caused by them. Thus cheaper methods with a lower degree of reliability have to be accepted. As regards macro-econometric studies, due to the large-scale benefits derived from them, the prospects of employing highly refined estimation methods for policy purposes are much brighter. Indeed, a series of bold econometric models—predicting the behavior or time path of such *accounting variables* as national income, investment, consumption, corporate savings, depreciation, production, business liquidity preference, etc.—were undertaken during the past two decades.[8] Although, these models have gained in sophistication since their introduction, they do not yet enable prediction of business-cycle fluctuations. Since these studies were carried out, on a limited

---

[6]The designations "Leontief-type model" and "Tinbergen-type model" are borrowed from Christ [1957].

[7]Sponsored by the Social Science Research Council.

[8]By Tinbergen [1939], Clark [1949], Klein [1950], Christ [1951], Barger and Klein [1954], Klein and Goldberger [1955], Valvanis [1955], etc.

scale, by single persons or small teams, it is hoped that a large-scale group-effort leads to results that are satisfactory also from a practical point of view.   As already mentioned, a promising group scheme has been launched under the auspices of the Social Science Research Council.   Hereby two co-ordinators and a group of 16 principal investigators (each specializing in a major segment of the economy) are presently co-operating on an econometric model of the United States economy.   This model deviates markedly from traditional econometric models.

It is *based on an accounting frame of some 30 sectors*[9] (one for each major manufacturing industry, one for agriculture, mining, communication, transportation, public utilities, trade, finance, government, etc.) which are to be related to the sectors of final demand as revealed in the national income accounts.   From this model the following advantages are expected:

... a fuller picture of the inventory process between materials, goods in process, and finished goods; an explanation of orders and their influence in inventories; a more accurate distribution of the lag between housing starts and completions; a more useful explanation of the lag structures of business investment and the influence of capacity on capital formation; an improved explanation of the relationship between investment expectations and actual investment; a more complete explanation of foreign trade and an extension to the balance of payments; an endogenous explanation of part of government expenditures and a sharper assessment of the impact of government on the economy.   (Klein [1961], p. 36.)

As to the essence of Tinbergen-type models in general, the following four sets of functions of which these models are composed, should be noted:

1. A set of *accounting identities* (definitions from national income accounting).
2. A set of *institutional equations*, reflecting the conditions of social institutions such as the taxation system, or adjustment processes (e.g., of the monetary system), etc.
3. A set of technical or *technological equations* expressing the constraints imposed upon the economy by production limitations, import necessities, or similar conditions.
4. A set of *behavior equations*[10] describing the collective behavior of specific groups such as consumers, investors, wage and salary recipients, entrepreneurs, etc.

---

[9] These sectors differ from the more disaggregated sectors of the Leontief models which are designed for the intersectoral commodity flow, a purpose more limited than the model here discussed.

[10] The term "behavioral equation" is frequently used in a broader sense, including institutional and technological equations as well.

All equations belonging to the model are referred to as *structural equations*, while only part of them (excluding the definitions) are *stochastic equations*. The latter contain probabilistic variables that express the random error of the function (the model reproduced at the end of this subsection does not explicitly show these stochastic variables but the illustration in Figure 8-3 does—see the time path of u_2).

Accounting variables enter definitional as well as stochastic equations, and form the basis for parameter estimation; thus the structure of the accounting system and the quality of the accounting data is important to the success or failure of the prediction. Since econometricians rarely have influence on the collection and the procuring of accounting data, econometric studies constitute an additional responsibility for national income accountants.

Klein's [1953, p. 2] emphasis that econometrics is "a way of studying history," and his view that the task of the econometrician is "to piece together the fundamental aspects of economic behavior by looking at the interrelationships of the quantitative magnitudes generated historically" with the ultimate objective "to extrapolate past behavior" reveal the close affinity between this discipline and accounting. We close these remarks on Tinbergen-type models with the summary of a complete model of the United States economy (from Klein and Goldberger [1955],[11] pp. 89–114) consisting of twenty linear equations.[12] We also present a detailed illustration of the investment function, i.e., of one of the twenty equations.

Explanation of Symbols

$Y + T + D$ .. Gross national product, 1939 dollars.
C .... Consumer expenditures, 1939 dollars.
I .... Gross private domestic capital formation, 1939 dollars.
G .... Government expenditures for goods and services, 1939 dollars.
p .... Price index of gross national product, 1939: 100.
F_E .... Exports of goods and services, 1939 dollars.

---

[11] Hereby the "limited information method" was used for parameter estimation. Most of the data are expressed in billions of 1939 dollars, millions of persons, or indexes based on the year 1939.

[12] These equations contain *parameters* (assumed to be constant, over a specific time), unknown or *endogenous variables*, and *predetermined variables*. However, the latter is somewhat more comprehensive than the term "exogenous variables." Tinbergen-type models frequently operate with period analysis and hence with time lags whereby the predetermined variables consist of lagged *endogenous variables* (i.e., endogenous variables of preceding periods) as well as of *exogenous variables*.

F_I .... Imports of goods and services, 1939 dollars.

W_1 .... Private employee compensation, deflated.

W_2 .... Government employee compensation, deflated.

P .... Nonwage nonfarm income, deflated.

A_1 .... Farm income, deflated.

A_2 .... Government payments to farmers, deflated.

$A_1 + A_2 = A$. Total farm income, deflated.

D .... Capital consumption charges, 1939 dollars.

P_C .... Corporate profits, deflated.

S_P .... Corporate savings, deflated.

T .... Indirect taxes less subsidies, deflated.

T_W .... Personal and payroll taxes less transfers associated with wage and salary income, deflated.

T_P .... Personal and corporate taxes less transfers associated with nonwage nonfarm income, deflated.

T_C .... Corporate income taxes, deflated.

T_A .... Taxes less transfers associated with farm income, deflated.

B .... End-of-year corporate surplus, deflated, from arbitrary origin.

K .... End-of-year stock of private capital, 1939 dollars, from arbitrary origin.

F_A .... Index of agricultural exports, 1939: 100.

p_A .... Index of agricultural prices, 1939: 100.

p_I .... Index of prices of imports, 1939: 100.

N_P .... Number of persons in the United States.

N .... Number of persons in the labor force.

N_W .... Number of wage- and salary-earners.

N_G .... Number of government employees.

N_F .... Number of farm operators.

N_E .... Number of nonfarm entrepreneurs.

h .... Index of hours worked per year, 1939: 1.00.

w .... Index of hourly wages, 1939: 122.1.

i_L .... Average yield on corporate bonds.

i_S .... Average yield on short term commercial paper.

R .... Excess reserves of banks as a percentage of total reserves.

L_1 .... End-of-year liquid assets held by persons, deflated.

L_2 .... End-of-year liquid assets held by businesses, deflated.

t .... Time trend, years, from arbitrary origin.

(1) *Consumption Equation:*

$$C_t = -22.26 + 0.55(W_1 + W_2 - T_W)_t + 0.41(P - T_P - S_P)_t +$$
$$+ 0.34(A_1 + A_2 - T_A)_t + 0.26C_{t-1} + 0.072(L_1)_{t-1} + 0.26(N_P)_t$$

(2) *Investment Equation:*

$$I_t = -16.71 + 0.78(P - T_P + A_1 + A_2 - T_A + D)_{t-1} -$$
$$- 0.073K_{t-1} + 0.14(L_2)_{t-1}$$

(3) *Corporate Savings Equation:*

$$(S_P)_t = -3.53 + 0.72(P_C - T_C)_t +$$
$$+ 0.076(P_C - T_C - S_P)_{t-1} - 0.028 B_{t-1}$$

(4) *Relation of Corporate Profits to Nonwage Nonfarm Income:*

$$(P_C)_t = -7.60 + 0.68 P_t$$

(5) *Depreciation Equation:*

$$D_t = 7.25 + 0.10 \frac{K_t + K_{t-1}}{2} + 0.044(Y + T + D - W_2)_t$$

(6) *Labor Demand Equation:*

$$(W_1)_t = -1.40 + 0.24(Y + T + D - W_2)_t +$$
$$+0.24(Y + T + D - W_2)_{t-1} + 0.29t$$

(7) *Production Function:*

$$(Y + T + D - W_2)_t = -26.08 + 2.17[h(N_W - N_G) + N_E + N_F]_t +$$
$$+ 0.16 \frac{K_t + K_{t-1}}{2} + 2.05t$$

(8) *Wage Adjustment Equation:*

$$w_t - w_{t-1} = 4.11 - 0.74(N - N_W - N_E - N_F)_t +$$
$$+ 0.52(p_{t-1} - p_{t-2}) + 0.54t$$

(9) *Import Demand Equation:*

$$(F_I)_t = 0.32 +$$
$$+ 0.0060(W_1 + W_2 - T_W + P - T_P + A_1 + A_2 - T_A)_t \frac{p_t}{(p_I)_t} +$$
$$+ 0.81(F_I)_{t-1}$$

(10) *Farm Income Equation:*

$$(A_1)_t \frac{p_t}{(p_A)_t} = -0.36 + 0.054(W_1 + W_2 - T_W + P - T_P - S_P)_t \frac{p_t}{(p_A)_t} -$$
$$-0.007(W_1 W_2 - T_W + P - T_P - S_P)_{t-1} \frac{p_{t-1}}{(p_A)_{t-1}} + 0.012(F_A)_t$$

(11) *Relation of Nonagricultural Prices to Agricultural Prices:*

$$(p_A)_t = -131.17 + 2.32 p_t$$

(12) *Household Liquidity Preference Equation:*

$$(L_1)_t = 0.14(W_1 + W_2 - T_W + P - T_P - S_P + A_1 + A_2 - T_A)_t +$$
$$+ 76.03(i_L - 2.0)_t$$

(13) *Business Liquidity Preference Equation:*

$$(L_2)_t = -0.34 + 0.26 (W_1)_t - 1.02 (i_S)_t - 0.26 (p_t - p_{t-1}) +$$
$$+ 0.61 (L_2)_{t-1}$$

(14) *Relation between Short- and Long-Term Interest Rates:*

$$i_L = 2.58 + 0.44 (i_S)_{t-3} + 0.26 (i_S)_{t-5}$$

(15) *Money Market Adjustment Equation:*

$$100 \frac{(i_S)_t - (i_S)_{t-1}}{(i_S)_{t-1}} = 11.17 - 0.67 R_t$$

(16) *Definition of Gross National Product:*

$$C_t + I_t + G_t + (F_E)_t - (F_I)_t = Y_t + T_t + D_t$$

(17) *Definition of National Income:*

$$(W_1)_t + (W_2)_t + P_t + (A_1)_t + (A_2)_t = Y_t$$

(18) *Net Investment Identity:*

$$h_t \frac{w_t}{p_t} (N_W)_t = (W_1)_t + (W_2)t$$

(19) *Wage Rate and Labor Identity:*

$$K_t - K_{t-1} = I_t - D_t$$

(20) *Definition of Corporate Savings:*

$$B_t - B_{t-1} = (S_P)_t$$

Investment Equation

$$I_t = -16.71 + 0.78 (P - T_p + A - T_A + D)_{t-1} -$$
$$\underset{(4.74)}{} \quad \underset{(0.18)}{}$$
$$-0.073 K_{t-1} + 0.14 (L_2)_{t-1}$$
$$\underset{(0.067)}{} \quad \underset{(0.11)}{}$$
$$\delta^2 / S^2 = 2.08$$

In Figure 8–3 the dashed curve designated with I depicts the *actual* (historically measured) investment during the periods 1929–41 and 1946–52, the full curve designated with $\hat{I}$ represents the *projected* investment, estimated by means of the econometric investment equation 2 over the same periods. The other curves (beneath) reflect the behavior of the individual components of the investment equation, namely the profit component $0.78 (P - T_p + A - T_A + D)_{t-1}$ the capital component $-0.073 K_{t-1}$, the liquidity component $0.14 (L_2)_{t-1}$ and the stochastic random variable u_2 (indicating the deviation of $\hat{I}$ from I which is not shown in our

FIGURE 8-3

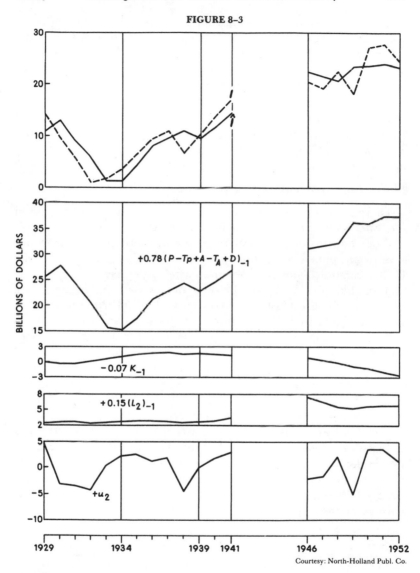

presentation of equation 10). Thus the investment $\hat{I}$ (*or precisely $\hat{I}_t$*) is expressed as a function of the entrepreneurial profits of the preceding period, the capital stocks in the preceding period, the liquid means held by business at the end of the preceding period, and the random variable. The figures of the equation (in front of each component) are the parameters that were estimated econometrically by sampling the pertinent variables for a period of 25 years (less 3 war years) and by applying the limited information method). The figures in brackets, underneath the parameters of the investment equation are a measure of reliability of the pertinent parameter (standard error of the sample). Finally there is—also beneath the investment equation—the ratio δ^2/S^2 which reveals (to the statistician) the presence or absence of autocorrelation.[13] Graphical presentations similar to that depicted in Figure 8-3 are available (by Klein and Goldberger [1955], pp. 89–114) for each of the stochastic equations.

8.22 Simulation and the Macro-Economy

There exists no sharp border between the input-output method and the econometric approach, nor exists one between these methods and system simulation. Indeed, simulation approaches have been applied with some success to Tinbergen-type models. The simulation study by Adelman and Adelman [1959] of the Klein-Goldberger model produced a time series containing cycles resembling the prosperity-recession pattern of the American economy. A comparison of the results of these simulation studies with historical-descriptive records, gives evidence of a high degree of conformity with the economic fluctuations manifested in actual practice. Yet, here we are not concerned with the border area of econometrics and system simulation, rather are we interested in the essence of this new approach, and in the macro-economic simulation studies that have thus far been completed—wholly or partly.

Social scientists have cause to envy physicists, chemists, and biologists for their vast opportunity of experimentation. Everyday life, no doubt, supplies social scientists with *surrogate* experimental material, the cognitive value of which shall by no means be underrated (cf. Schumpeter [1954], p. 16). But the most important features of the experiment, *control of certain variables* and *arbitrary*

---

[13]The term "autocorrelation" refers to the (usually undesirable) correlation of a time series with itself, when lagged by one or more time units. It constitutes a grave problem of most time series analyses; tests of significance help interpreting the reliability of parameter estimates (at least where the sample size is sufficiently large). According to the normal probability distribution and a 5% significance level, the values of δ^2/S^2 should lie within a range of 1.4 to 2.7 to warrant nonautocorrelation of an hypothesis. In the above presentation $\delta^2/S^2 = 2.08$, hence the investment function does not seem to be plagued with autocorrelation. The Klein-Goldberger [1955] model indicates for *every equation* a measure of autocorrelation, and for *every parameter* the standard error. Since the preceding system of equations merely serves an illustrative purpose we have omitted these statistical measures (except in case of the investment equation pertaining to Figure 8-3).

repetition, are frequently precluded in the economic sciences. Besides, experimentation with the whole economy or an individual firm is practically not feasible.

The advent of electronic data-processing systems and *system simulation*, however, seem to have opened the door to experimental ventures and adventures for the economic sciences. Such experiments, of course, are of a different nature than those of the traditional physicist, who deals with the "medium of reality" itself—not merely with a simplified structure reflected in a mathematical system. Simulation experiments do, however, permit the mental reproduction of a large number of alternative situations and help determining *satisfactory*, if not optimal, solutions. As Malcolm [1957, p. v] says:

System simulation has the most useful property of permitting the researcher and management to experiment with and test policy, procedures and organization changes in much the same way as the aeronautical engineer tests his design ideas in the laboratory or in the "wind tunnel." Thus we might think of System Simulation as a sort of "management Wind Tunnel" which is used to pretest many suggested changes and eliminate much needless "experimentation" with the "real" people, machines and facilities.

In contrast to the "wind tunnel," the simulation models of economists and management scientists are analytical[14] or analog models which frequently incorporate probability concepts. Where the latter holds—particular in cases which hinge upon a statistical distribution whose structure is not exactly known—a special simulation approach has been developed under the name of *Monte Carlo method*.[15] The term "simulation method," however, has a more

---

[14] Occasionally the term "analytical" is limited to models obeying an algorism (permitting solution by deductive means). Frequently, however, this term is defined widely enough to include system simulation.

[15] The Monte Carlo method is a technique of simulating stochastic (= probabilistic) events by means of *random digit tables;* it is used where either explicit probabilistic calculations are too complex and awkward to be executed or where the outcome cannot be observed in actual practice. In principle such a simulation can be carried out by purely mechanical devices such as drawing red and white balls from an urn, roulette wheels, dice, etc., but they supply the results slowly and clumsily in comparison to random digit tables. The latter are generalized results of independent trials, they are presented in tables each number of which has the same probability of occurrence. Thus for instance an event with a chance of 1/25 (or 0.04) is simulated by assigning any 4 out of 100 possibilities, e.g., the first 4 numbers may be accepted as representing "success," or the numbers from 28 through 31, etc. After this designation an arbitrary number is chosen from the table and judged as success or failure through comparison with the random digits labeled as "success" whereby it is advisable at the next "draw" to move to another part of the table, also to use different rules of selection at the next experimental series. For more detailed explanations see Miller and Starr [1960], pp. 273–80.

comprehensive meaning since not every simulation model relies on a "simulated probability distribution." Problems which cannot be forced into the straitjacket of an optimization model, or optimization problems of a forbiddingly complex mathematical structure, can be solved *approximately* by simulation—that is, by determining and scanning an array of alternative combinations and selecting the most favorable one. This of course is a fairly crude approach since "the result of a simulation is always the answer to a specific numerical problem without any insight into why that is the answer or how the answer would be influenced by a change in any of the data" (Dorfman [1960], p. 604). But it enables the "observation" of dynamic interactions between components of the system that otherwise must be analyzed in isolation (*mutatis mutandis* vs. *ceteris paribus*). This has been illustrated by Gillespie [1961] who, using the Holland-Tencer-Gillespie [1960] model for a study of exchange rate devaluation, found that it is not the elasticities of demand (traditionally believed to be the decisive factor), but "the induced effects on the pattern of investment allocation and the resistance of the system to inflation of prices" that form the important determinants. Holland [1962] referring to this study remarks that:

These results... make it clear that some of the most innocent-appearing *ceteris paribus* assumptions can be treacherous, and that exchange-rate policy had better not be decided purely on the basis of comparative statics. Farsighted theoreticians and policy-makers have already described the processes involved here and how they pertain to the effectiveness of a devaluation... But until the development of simulation, the means of exploring the problem fully have been lacking, and little has been done about it on the theoretical level beyond discussion.

As compared with maximization techniques, simulation permits a clearer separation of the technical investigation from the defining of policy objectives. No formal welfare function or over-all performance index is needed in the analysis itself. Thus it is not necessary to formulate value judgments in a vacuum before observing the effects of alternative policies. Since the effects show up as changes in such incommensurable criteria as the time profiles of income, employment, and prices and the stability of the foreign exchange rate, any such formulation is extremely dubious. A better approach is to choose among alternative outcomes in terms of all of their dimensions. With simulation this can be the final step and can be done, if desired, by decision-makers other than the experimenter. (Holland, [1962], p. 428.)

The above statement has more or less general validity, although Dr. Holland is concerned with the simulation of an underdeveloped economy (India), an area of especially favorable prospects for applying macro-economic simulation techniques.

The idea of simulating economic events is by no means new; as early as 1892 has Irving Fisher constructed a *hydrostatic* model to represent "in terms of mechanical interaction, that beautiful and intricate equilibrium which manifests itself in the 'exchanges' of a great city."[16]   And we take it that a more refined version of a hydraulic model has been used for many years in the London School of Economics to simulate features of a macro-economy. Although these mechanical models have no doubt some affinity with modern system simulation (they are the immediate ancestors of *analog* computers), the simulation technique came into its own through the versatility of general *digital* electronic computers. While previously the models, being limited to a few equations, were too crude, present-day electronic data processing—which permits the manipulation of systems consisting of hundreds of equations and variables—makes it a worthwhile task to refine macro- as well as micro-economic models.

In the following we shall mention only a few of the better known macro-economic simulation studies to indicate the variety of purposes pursued.   One of the earliest pioneering works of this kind was Cohen's [1960] simulation of the interconnection of three industries.   Since the shoe, leather, hide sequence forms a tight vertical hierarchy and since a solid empirical as well as theoretical foundation for research in these industries was available through Mrs. Mack's [1956] fundamental work, it is easily explained why just this sequence was chosen for simulating the aggregate market behavior of a group of retailers, manufacturers, and suppliers of raw material.   Thus the time paths of the endogenous variables (retail price, sales, shoe receipts, manufacturer's selling price, production, leather receipts, etc.) and those of the main exogenous variables (consumers' price index, disposable personal income and stocks of raw material) were traced by the computer through a nonlinear system of simultaneous difference equation with boundary conditions.   One submodel finds the values of the endogenous variables, the other explains the determination of these variables at future periods.   The results of this simulation for the years 1930 through 1940 show a "very close correspondence between the time paths generated by our process model and the actual values" (Cohen [1960], p. viii).

---

[16]Cited from Irving Norton Fisher's book, *My Father Irving Fisher* (New York, 1956), p. 48, which even presents a photograph of this hydrostatic model (see pictures between pp. 176 and 177).

Another simulation study on a multistage market with a significant vertical sequence is the work carried out by Balderston and Hoggatt [1962] on the lumber market of the West Coast (U.S.). Its main objective is to "explain relationships between flows (of information, commodities, and money payments) and the structural configuration of the market," thus pursuing empirical results of market behavior as well as "theoretical insight into the operation of decentralized decision systems." Although sectoral studies like Cohen's, or Balderston and Hoggatt's, are of macro-economic concern, they also illuminate important connections between individual firms and the social aggregate in which these are embedded. Thus costs, revenues, accounting parameters, and financial statements of the participating firms enter into those models.

A very different type of macro-economic simulation is reflected in the work carried out by the Social Systems Research Institute of the University of Wisconsin under the direction of Professor Orcutt (see Orcutt [1960], pp. 903–5 and especially Orcutt et al. [1961]). This is a demographic model of the U.S. household sector.

The basic components of the model are individuals and combinations of individuals such as married couples and families. The family units form, grow, diminish, and dissolve as married couples have children and get divorced and individuals age, marry, and die. These outputs of the basic components in a given month depend on the status variables that characterize each component as of the beginning of the month and on the inputs into each component during the month. The operating characteristics, which serve to relate outputs of components to input and status variables, are stochastic in nature; i.e., it is the probabilities of occurrence of certain outputs rather than the outputs themselves which are regarded as functions of input and status variables. For example, the probability that a woman will give birth to a child during a given month was estimated, on the basis of available data, to depend on a nonlinear, multivariate function of her marital status, age, number of previous births, interval since previous birth or since marriage, month, and year. The model is recursive in that the probabilities determined for the possible outputs of each component in any period depend only on previously determined input and status variables. (Orcutt [1960] p. 903.)

Such a study must rely on comprehensive statistical samples and must proceed in periodic steps (e.g., one month). Thus at the end of each period the members of each sample family are being reviewed, their status is being changed, or not changed, according to the result of a random "drawing" made from a probability distribution (by means of random numbers generated in the computer). In this way it should be possible to "predict" the population structure of an economy or a specific region at a specific point of time; a task that might become the cornerstone of a comprehensive simulation study of the entire economy. Indeed, a general model consisting of eleven sectors (similar to those of the *flow of funds accounting*) is envisaged as the ultimate goal.

8.3 MICRO-ECONOMIC SIMULATION: CONTROL MODELS OF MANAGEMENT SCIENCE

The macro-economic models considered in Subsection 8.22 all started in one way or the other, from the micro-level. Either individual firms and their economic behavior, or household units and their changes, were taken into consideration to attain macro-economic forecasts. This reveals the close ties between these two levels, and suggests that the traditional separation of micro- from macro-economics (or micro-accounting from macro-accounting) may not always be desirable.

8.31 Forrester's Industrial Dynamics

This example in our survey of simulation studies confirms the trend toward *general* applicability. Forrester [1961] explicitly states that his methodology may be applied to individuals, firms, whole industries, or entire economies. His major concern is the simulation of an economic system with specific emphasis on facilitating "management" policies through *improving the organizational structure* of this approach. The ultimate goal is not so much prediction or short-run planning but "enterprise construction," which means long-range planning of the organization's structure. In consequence, the focus of investigation is directed toward testing responses and fluctuations of the internal components of the system (firm, industry; or economy) caused by external events. This enforces an integration of separate functional areas such as marketing, investment, research, personnel, production, accounting, etc., and leads to the exploitation of the fact "that any economic or corporate activity consists of flows of money, orders, materials, personnel, and capital equipment." It is the co-ordination of these flows to an *information network* which (due to its feedbacks, delays, and amplifications) impresses upon the system its own *dynamics* and individuality. This can best be described by means of a concrete example. Forrester begins with a comparatively simple (73 equations) network of the orders and shipments between factory, factory warehouse, distributor, retailer, and customer, matching the production rate to the rate of retail sales. After assuming the basic policies governing these flows, as well as the delays inherent in the system, he tests the response of the *individual components* of this production-distribution system (e.g., manufacturing orders to factory, factory production output, inventory levels at each stage, retail sales, etc.), thereby demonstrating that a sudden 10 per cent increase in retail sales may, after considerable delays, lead to a 51 per cent increase in manufacturing orders to factory, a 45 per cent increase in factory production output, and may even a year after the original event still affect the flow of various orders. The conclusion is that internal conditions such as conventional manufacturing and sales policies may well create disturbances that are erroneously contributed to outside circumstances. Although the small original increase in retail sales gave the first impetus, a more adequately designed system may have avoided the strongly amplified fluctuations mentioned above. At this point it may be opportune to listen to the praise and critique expressed by a reviewer of *Industrial Dynamics:*

...Forrester could very well be credited with providing the missing link between the grand conceptions of classical Continental economists and the imaginative inventions of modern electronic wizards... Forrester listens to the heart beat, checks the respiration rate, and measures the reflexes of a firm as well as any fully outfitted medic does his ailing patient. Unlike many of the venerable ancients, Forrester does not restrict his view of the world to strictly linear systems. Instead, he employs for his model a set of stochastic non-linear difference equations subject to side constraints and containing virtually no simultaneity... No other management science model now operating efficiently on a computer has the same degree of combined flexibility and magnitude. The attractiveness of this feature is self-evident. But of equal importance is the accompanying uneasiness as to whether any such large complex system could really be a sufficiently accurate representation to yield reliable analyses. My concern is...that the methodology of industrial dynamics seems to suggest that a particular model is to be repeatedly tinkered with until it operates in a fashion consistent with some preconceived notion. In other words, the very extensive and sequential nature of the modeling approach appears to vitiate a means for obtaining independent tests of validity....

Perhaps the most serious imperfection in the book is the absence of any fundamental analysis of the problems caused by the introduction of stochastic elements...when probabilistic variables are added to a model, more than simple refinements in diagnostic techniques are required....

Does industrial dynamics represent a truly scientific approach? Or does it represent the judgmental approach of a particular scientist? Are there principles for applying industrial dynamics as a diagnostic tool which are not tied to the personality traits of a particular practitioner?

What is the likelihood of two industrial dynamists coming to the same recommendations when faced with the same strategic problem? (Wagner [1963], pp. 184–86.)

These critical remarks may well apply to simulation models in general. Another characteristic of Industrial Dynamics, but typical for many systems of this kind, is the subdivision of the entire network or feedback system into "building blocks" (see also Orcutt [1960], p. 901). By breaking down the complete system into smaller, exchangeable units, greater economy and convenience may be attained, especially in connection with changes, modifications, and improvements of the system. But apart from the computer programing which more or less enforces the writing of subroutines, this development—as some other features of system-simulation—was anticipated by the accountant's periodic budgeting approach.

Like the other simulation models, those presented by Forrester depend to a considerable extent on accounting variables and combine these with behavioral equations, policy, and decision functions, as well as with data generated outside of the accounting department. Finally it should be mentioned that industrial dynamics as described above relies on DYNAMO, a special-purpose compiler for producing the running code for computer simulation of information feedback systems. The ultimate result or output of this kind of simulation are time paths of various functions and groups of equations (in form of figure tables or diagrams) which indicate the fluctuations of the individual components (flows of orders, sales, cash inventories, etc.).

Since our special interest refers to the simulation of business and manufacturing enterprises we present the following quotation from Markowitz, Hauser and Karr [1963, p. 1]:

In the simulation of manufacturing systems, for example, the computer is told the physical structure of the manufacturing facility—the number of machines of each kind, the number of men of each kind on each shift, which men can work on which machines, and so on. It is also told the rules the system operates under, such as the dispatching rules for determining which order to work on first, and overtime rules for determining when men will work extra hours. Finally the computer is told the work load to be processed through the plant, including both the orders waiting at the start of simulation and the orders received during the course of simulated time. With this information the computer runs the orders through the plant, routing them from one machine to the other according to specified routing information, and making them wait their turn for men and machines already occupied. During the course of simulated time the computer keeps track of how well the simulated system performs, according to such measures as machine utilization, labor utilization, and the time required for orders to be completed.[17]

To facilitate the coding (programing) of simulation models Markowitz, Hauser, and Karr [1963] of the Rand Corporation have developed a simulation programing language (SIMSCRIPT) that seems to be more generally applicable than Forrester's DYNAMO or the SIMPAC (simulation language and computer program) developed by the System Development Corporation for similar purposes.

8.32   The MARK I of the Systems Development Corporation

Another model, which is characteristic of these types of simulation studies, is the MARK I, a fictitious manufacturing firm (a producer of durable industrial hard goods—standard models and custom-made designs, annual sales ca. $30 million, 1600 employees) for which a comprehensive and highly disaggregated simulation study has been constructed by the System Development Corporation (see Kagdis and Lackner [1962], Heyne [1960a, 1960b] and other publications of the SDC).

The prime purpose of these attempts to simulate a firm is to substitute for the pragmatic part of management an intricate system of decision rules. In other words, to construct an enterprise that runs more or less automatically. Since the pragmatic management functions are at bottom control decisions, one speaks of *management control models* defined by an aggregate of business control decision areas which determine the structure of the enterprise. Thus a careful identification of the individual decision processes is an indispensable precondition of every management control model. The above-mentioned prime purpose must not be misinterpreted, it does not so much serve the elimination of personnel, but the experimentation that leads to ultimate *criteria for designing improved control systems*[18] applicable in actual business practice—an aspect that was already noted in discussing Forrester's industrial

---

[17] Harry M. Markowitz, Bernard Hauser, and Herbert W. Karr, *SIMSCRIPT—A Simulation Programming Language*. Copyright 1963 by the Rand Corporation. By permission of Prentice-Hall, Inc., publisher.

[18] Further purposes of simulating the firm, that are to be attacked in MARK I, are hypothesis formulation and testing, as well as goal searching and goal attainment.

dynamics.   The special feature of MARK I is the interpretation of an enterprise as *a network of waiting lines and service centers.*[19]

A strict separation is made between internal activities and environmental influences, depending on whether a specific situation is within the area of managerial control or beyond it.   Especially in relation to the latter, ample use can be made of stochastic variables and the Monte Carlo method (see footnote 15 of the current chapter) as in the case of generating sales by means of a probabilistic submodel.   Similar to budgeting, the simulation of MARK I starts from the sales activity for which a series of "transfer-functions" (for prices, lateness of deliveries, advertising, salesmen, etc.) is available; these have the dual effect of influencing on one side business activity directly and on the other the perceptive organs of management, called "sensing" devices.   As mentioned, much emphasis is put on details so that the relations between sales volume on one side and product prices, qualities, delays in delivery (broken down according to causes), advertising volume, number of salesmen, level of sales support, on the other side, are taken into consideration—again, the basic outputs are in form of time series.

---

[19]Waiting line or queuing models serve to find optimal (or at least satisfactory) solutions to problems which cause *idle time* either to the units to be served or to the facilities providing the service.   It is the generalization of a problem which modern economic life offers in great variety (e.g., waiting at the cash register of the supermarket, waiting for being served by a salesman in the department store, airborne planes waiting for landing possibilities, even waiting of the vehicles at a cross-road in front of a traffic light).   The basic equations of the simple case of a waiting line are given by Sasieni, Yaspan and Friedman [1959, p. 129] as

$$P_1 = \frac{\lambda}{\mu} P_0$$

$$P_n = \frac{\lambda + (n-1)\mu}{n\mu} P_{n-1} - \frac{\lambda}{n\mu} P_{n-2} \qquad n = 2, 3, \ldots, k$$

$$P_n = \frac{\lambda + k\mu}{k\mu} P_{n-1} - \frac{\lambda}{k\mu} P_{n-2} \qquad n \geq k+1$$

Hereby signifies:

μ . . . . mean service rate

λ . . . . . . mean arrival rate

n . . . . number of units (people) in queue plus number of units being serviced

P_n . . . . probability that there are n units (people) in the system at a specific time

P_0 . . . . probability that there are 0 units in the system (determined from

$$\sum_{n=0}^{\infty} P_n = 1)$$

k . . . . number of "servicing stations."

It cannot be our task to go into details of this model, but its treatment of accounting aspects shall shortly be mentioned. The eight (somewhat unorthodox) subbudgets (Personnel, General Office, Sales, Engineering, Manufacturing Administration, Warehousing, Purchasing, Factory Labor) of the system consist of nearly fifty accounts which are credited through an explicit control decision rule with budget allocations, and are debited with "actual" expense items. The variance between total debits and credits of the individual accounts seems to influence the operations of the enterprise only insofar as *the budget allocations for the subsequent period are identical with the actual expenditures of the current period.* A crude set of accounting identities is available from which a profit and loss statement as well as a balance sheet can be produced. Furthermore a statement of source and application of funds, as well as a cash forecast is generated (see Kagdis and Lackner [1962], p. 20).

The entire arrangement forms a web of interacting events of which three "systems" may be distinguished, the "activity system," with its activity generating equations, the "control system" (an aggregate of servo-mechanisms) with its explicit decision rules, and the "environmental system" with its transfer functions. This intricate interdependency is furthermore "immensely complicated by the stochastic nature of signal transmission from servo to servo." In connection with this somewhat frightening complexity it must be mentioned that models of this kind take many years to be built and require a research staff of dozens, sometimes hundreds of experts and well-trained personnel. Accordingly the costs for such experimentation can run into millions of dollars.[20] Summarizing we offer the following conclusion:

In the development and completion of the Management Control Systems Project, the System Development Corporation has shown that it is possible to simulate realistically a business firm with a reasonable amount of computer time. During the course of the investigation, some basic tools were developed which make large-scale simulations easier to organize and build.

Some areas of investigation were postulated by the project and are presented here as suggestions for future research. Research with the current model can be conducted (1) to better learn how aggregated a model can be and still remain useful; (2) to study the effect of communications systems on business performance; (3) to study the effect of dif-

---

[20]The Rand Corporation has completed several laboratory experiments of similar kinds (inventory policies, inventory control, inventory data-processing systems) for the Air Force, "each problem has required the expenditure of well over a million dollars ... the duration of each experiment has been about two years" (Geisler [1962], p. 240).

ferent resource allocation policies on efficiency of production; (4) to study business operations under stressful conditions; (5) to study the effect of organization on business performance; (6) to study the effect of environmental phenomena, such as vendor performance, state of the economy, changes in the labor market, on the business; and (7) to study the performance of a business under different market conditions.

If the current version of the model is modified, other areas may be investigated. These areas would enable the investigator to compare alternate corporate planning techniques, such as budgeting; study the effect of behavior and learning theory on overall business performance; compare the use of the newer analytical techniques, such as dynamic and linear programming, game theory, etc., under identical controlled conditions; and compare several simulation techniques to determine which renders the most useful model for the effort expended. Unquestionably numerous other areas of investigation are possible with the business simulation vehicle and simulation techniques created by the Management Control Systems Project. It is hoped that this work will provide a basis for greater interest and research in the control of large organizations. (Kagdis and Lackner [1962], p. 24.)

8.33 *Further Management Simulation Models*

A series of micro-economic simulation models were developed on a less gigantic scale than the MARK I; further intensive activity in this area is expected. Without ambition to be exhaustive or to go into details, we briefly draw the reader's attention to some of these models.

The Task Manufacturing Corporation by Sprowls and Asimow (UCLA). This is a simulation model of a fictitious enterprise (400 employees, five hardwear-type products, annual sales of $3 million to $4 million with five submodels: employees, machines, vendors, customers, and financial institutions). Only the submodel of consumer behavior is discussed in Sprowls and Asimow [1960], but the remaining parts seem to be completed by now. "Each of these subsystems is sufficiently general, self-contained and complete that it can be dealt with as an entity." The models consist of two parts: the forecasting system which supplies an operating plan, and a production system which generates the data of the actual simulation experiment. The Task Mfg. Co. does not, in contrast to the MARK I, make automatic changes for subsequent periods. The forecast and the actual operation is linked by a human being outside the system; policy decisions, however, are included in the model.

Bonini's Simulation Model. Bonini's Simulation Model [1963] has a strongly psychological slant. Beyond the accounting and economic factors, it operates with behavioral concepts such as "aspiration levels," "psychological pressure," "reaction," etc. The major objective of this model is the study of the impact which informational and organizational factors exercise upon managerial decisions. "We have had limited knowledge of such variables as: the effects of tardy information, the effects of different distributions of information within the firm, the effects of differing degrees of centralization or decentralization, etc. A comprehensive model, such as the one proposed, is necessary to answer such questions" (Bonini [1962], p. 33). The hypotheses selected are based on changes of which three groups can be distinguished: changes in (1) the external environment (stable versus fluctuating costs and sales, different growth patterns); (2) the decision system (loose versus tight standard costs, sensitivity to "pressure," and transmission of "pressure" to subordinates); (3) the information system (LIFO versus average costing, managerial knowledge, emphasis upon different kinds of information objectives). Among the results of such investigations is of particular interest for accountants the effect of LIFO versus average inventory costing (see Bonini [1963], pp. 104–9).

The major effect of the use of LIFO versus the average cost method of inventory valuation was a significant increase in sales, pressure, and profits within the firm. And since the model did not include taxes, this increase in profits was not attributable to tax benefits.

How was this result achieved? LIFO, when used for internal reporting purposes, increased the variability of profits from period to period [footnote omitted]. The average cost method, on the other hand, tended to smooth out costs (by averaging) and hence produced more stable profits from period to period. The fluctuating profits under LIFO tended to keep the firm "on its toes " and quick to take advantage of cost saving and profit making opportunities. The firm with the more constant profit picture was more sluggish.

The importance of this result is not that it proves LIFO as the best policy, but that some surprising unintended results came from what appeared to be a simple accounting procedure. The result was achieved because the information affected others in the firm than those intended—those external to the firm. Tax savings and external reporting should not be the only considerations in deciding a policy of inventory valuation. (Bonini [1962], p. 35.)[21]

A Price-Output Simulation Model. Cyert and March [1963, pp. 128–236] present an interesting combination of micro- and macromodels for determining prices, outputs, and sales strategies for a

---

group of oligopolists. First, a specific model for one department of a large retail department store is developed (special decision processes are: original sales pricing, mark-up, mark-down, sales estimates, advance orders, and reorders). Out of this grows a general model for an individual firm as well as the model for simulating the interactions of the individual firms within the oligopolistic market. The various decision processes—for which detailed *flow charts* are available—conform to the behavioral theory of the firm as developed by these authors. Thus again psychological concepts, especially multiple-aspiration-level goals, memories, and feedbacks by learning processes, are heavily emphasized. A sensitivity analysis of price, inventory, market share, and profit indicates on one side the parameters that exercise a general impact, and on the other those parameters of predominantly local influence. However, the description of this model is designated by the authors as "a report on the first stage of a research"; thus a definite conclusion is hardly possible at this stage.

In closing this section it should be pointed out that, apart from the simulation of entire firms (and aggregates of firms), a series of simulation studies of more limited areas were carried out (e.g., for job shop scheduling by Rowe [1958], for manufacturing systems by Dickie and Throndsen [1960], for investment portfolio selection by Clarkson [1962]).

There cannot be any doubt that these endeavors[22] will ultimately benefit business practice and will in the long run decisively influence the science of business administration and management, but there is a need—and perhaps a more urgent one—for an entirely different way of simulating the firm. One that is not directed toward "enterprise construction," but one that merely aims at improving the existing system of operating budgets. One that does not substitute more or less rigid decision rules for middle management, but one that facilitates and improves the activity of management by means that are set moderately enough to be immediately realizable. Realizable in a large number of enterprises, even those of middle and small size, where neither vast financial means nor electronic computers are at the disposal of the individual firm. The novelty of computer simulation as applied to the enterprises may easily deceive us that a budget simulation model is nothing but a

---

[22] See also Hoggatt and Balderston [1963], and Feldman and Feigenbaum [1963].

paltry or diluted version of the management control models of the type just described. However, the goals, the range of expenses, the technical features, the expertness required, the range of application, and the effect on accounting, are entirely different ones in these two approaches. The individual differences between them shall be demonstrated in Section 9.2, yet before this can be done some other accounting models shall be described.

Chapter 9

BUDGET MODELS
OF THE FIRM

FROM PREVIOUS experience and the preceding chapter we conclude that the search for an over-all model of the firm shows two extremes and a great variety of possibilities in between. On the one side we find the unsophisticated but relatively inexpensive and easily adaptable balance sheet model of traditional accounting and budgeting. On the other side we find the immensely complex and exorbitantly expensive management control model, dealing with minute details of the flows and causal relationships of the enterprise. Within these extremes there are compromise solutions, variations, and mutations which will be explored in this chapter. Our treatment is not definitive but suggestive and designed to illustrate new methodologies. It is meant to stimulate the reader, to incite him to ventures into this newly exposed territory, and, above all, to introduce him to a conceptual apparatus and a way of thinking that may well become indispensable to the future managerial accountant.

The first part of this chapter (Section 9.1) deals concisely with the foundations of "analytical" budget models.[1] Although we have some reservations as to the practical usefulness of such *analytical* budget models, the discussion offers an opportunity to prepare the reader for the budget *simulation* model which, to our mind, has better prospects of practical realization. This budget simulation model will be discussed thoroughly in the second part (Section 9.2) of this chapter. While analytical models are comparatively simple and therefore enable the application of an algorism for determining *optimal* solutions, simulation models lack such an algorism. They

---

[1]The term "analytical" is here used in the true and narrow sense of the word, excluding simulation.

merely serve the comparison of a number of alternatives, a procedure that leads to "satisfactory" rather than to optimal solutions. But this procedure takes care of many details and complexities without which a meaningful budget system is hardly imaginable.

9.1 AN "ANALYTICAL" BUDGET MODEL

A major difference between the ordinary business accounting
model and the budget model is to be found not only in the "time-
direction" but also *in the degree of aggregation*. A historical accounting system records every "relevant" event in a separate entry, while
a budget system—similar to macro-accounting systems—records
an aggregate of many similar (future) events as a single, global
transaction. A consequence of this high degree of aggregation is the
eventual relinquishment of many subaccounts in the budget model,
without, however, renouncing the basic accounting frame of the
budget system. Thus the expression *accounting for the future* seems to
be well justified. In this section we present a simple and somewhat
unorthodox version of a budget model for a manufacturing enterprise. We illustrate the anticipated aggregate flows in two ways:
by means of T-accounts (Figure 9-1) and by means of an accounting
matrix (Table 9-1). All global transactions are characterized by
the symbol t with subscripts for further distinction. In conformity
with previously discussed conventions (see Subsection 3.83), the
first subscript refers to the account to be credited, the second subscript to the account to be debited. To facilitate a quick identification of the various entries, the *subscripts* now appear *in form of capital
letters* (a practice adopted from Charnes, Cooper, and Ijiri [1963],
p. 28 ff.), but no longer in form of numerals which are less suggestive. To distinguish in the matrix the opening and closing transactions (or the Beginning Balance Sheet Account B and the Ending
Balance Sheet Account E) from the other aggregate transactions
(or from the other accounts respectively) we separate the debit and
credit sides of the balance sheet accounts from the remaining accounts by bold lines. In the T-accounts the beginning and ending
balances are characterized by the "subscripts" without the symbol t.

In periodic budgeting we assume that the anticipated aggregate
flows are either given as exogenous data, or can be derived from
such data by means of budgeting hypotheses and accounting identities. Thus the aggregate sales transaction t_{SR} (assuming *all* sales
are booked through the accounts receivable account) can be ex-

FIGURE 9-1

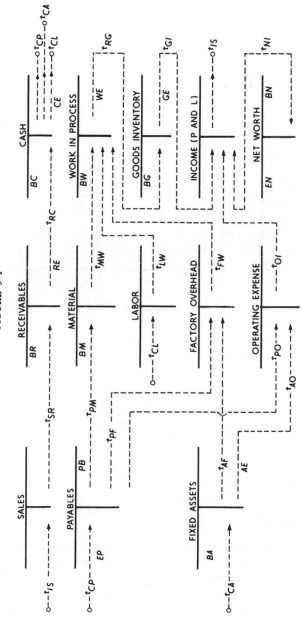

TABLE 9-1
SCHEMATIC AND MATRIX-PRESENTATION OF AGGREGATE TRANSACTIONS

		S	R	C	P	A	M	L	F	W	G	O	I	N	B	E
SALES	S		t_{SR}													
RECEIVABLES	R			t_{RC}												t_{RE}
CASH	C				t_{CP}	t_{CA}		t_{CL}								t_{CE}
PAYABLES	P						t_{PM}	t_{PL}	t_{PF}			t_{PO}			t_{PB}	
FIXED ASSETS	A								t_{AF}			t_{AO}				t_{AE}
MATERIAL	M									t_{MW}						t_{ME}
LABOR	L									t_{LW}						
FACT. OVERHEAD	F									t_{FW}						
WORK IN PROC.	W										t_{WG}					t_{WE}
GOODS INVT.	G												t_{GI}			t_{GE}
OPERATING EXPS.	O												t_{OI}			
INCOME	I	t_{IS}														
NET WORTH	N												t_{NI}		t_{NB}	
BEG. BALANCE	B		t_{BR}	t_{BC}		t_{BA}	t_{BM}			t_{BW}	t_{BG}					
END. BALANCE	E				t_{EP}									t_{EN}		

pressed as a function of the sales quantity (for product $i = 1, \ldots, n$) q_i and the sales price p_i:

$$(1) \quad t_{SR} = \sum_{i=1}^{n} q_i p_i.$$

Similarly, the transactions t_{MW}, and t_{LW} may be expressible as functions of the production volume[2]

$$(2) \quad t_{MW} = \sum_{i=1}^{n} c_{Mi} q_i,$$

$$(3) \quad t_{LW} = \sum_{i=1}^{n} c_{Li} q_i.$$

Herein c_{Mi} and c_{Li} designate the direct material and direct labor cost respectively (in $ per unit of product i). Before proceeding with the formulation of our system of simultaneous equations we list further

---

[2] If sales and production volumes differ, another variable e.g., q_i' might be introduced to designate the *production* volume of product i.

data *here assumed to be exogenous. Beginning* balances of:

Accounts receivable . . . . t_{BR}
Cash . . . . t_{BC}
Fixed assets . . . . t_{BA}
Material inventory . . . . t_{BM}
Work-in-process inventory . . . . t_{BW}
Finished goods inventory . . . . t_{BG}
Accounts payable . . . . t_{PB}
Owners' equity (or net worth) . . . . t_{NB}

Among the *ending* inventories the following are here assumed to be given:

Material inventory . . . . t_{ME}
Work-in-process inventory . . . . t_{WE}
Finished goods inventory . . . . t_{GE}

Another item to be given is the cash outlay for

Purchases of new equipment, etc. . . . . t_{CA}

Finally we simplify our illustration by assuming factory overhead and operating expenses as fixed and exogenously given:

Factory overheads . . . . t_{FW}
Operating expenses . . . . t_{OI}

Limiting ourselves to these transactions as externally determined, we may express the remaining 17 global transactions as functions of the above-stated 17 transaction variables. Thereby parameters are designated by the symbol a with subscripts corresponding to the subscripts of the attached transaction variable (parameters assumed to be unity are not made explicit). The linearity assumption accepted in this presentation is, of course, not a necessary condition for analytical budget models in general.

$$
\begin{aligned}
(4)\quad & t_{RC} = t_{BR} + a_{SR}t_{SR} \\
(5)\quad & t_{CP} = t_{PB} + a_{PM}t_{PM} + a_{PF}t_{PF} + a_{PO}t_{PO} \\
(6)\quad & t_{CL} = t_{LW} \\
(7)\quad & t_{PF} = a'_{FW}t_{FW} \\
(8)\quad & t_{AF} = a''_{FW}t_{FW} \\
(9)\quad & t_{PO} = a'_{OI}t_{OI} \\
(10)\quad & t_{AO} = a''_{OI}t_{OI} \\
(11)\quad & t_{PM} = t_{ME} + t_{MW} - t_{BM} \\
(12)\quad & t_{WG} = t_{BW} - t_{WE} + t_{MW} + t_{LW} + t_{FW} \\
(13)\quad & t_{GI} = t_{BG} - t_{GE} + t_{WG} \\
(14)\quad & t_{IS} = t_{SR} \\
(15)\quad & t_{NI} = t_{IS} - t_{GI} - t_{OI} \\
(16)\quad & t_{RE} = t_{BR} + t_{RS} - t_{RC} \\
(17)\quad & t_{CE} = t_{Bc} + t_{RC} - t_{CP} - t_{CL} - t_{AC} \\
(18)\quad & t_{AE} = t_{BA} - t_{AF} - t_{AO} + t_{AC} \\
(19)\quad & t_{EP} = t_{PB} + t_{PM} + t_{PF} + t_{PO} - t_{CP} \\
(20)\quad & t_{EN} = t_{BN} + t_{NI}
\end{aligned}
$$

The empirical character of these functions is especially obvious in equations 4, 5, 7, 8, 9, and 10, which are based on structural parameters $(a_{RS}, a_{PM}, \ldots, a_{OI}'')$ determined through past experience. Hence these equations may justly be addressed as *budgeting hypotheses*.

For instance, in equation 4:

$$t_{RC} = t_{BR} + a_{SR}t_{SR}$$

expresses the aggregate cash collection during the planning period as a function of the accounts receivable outstanding in the beginning of the period (assumed to be completely collectible during this period) plus a percentage (a_{SR}) of the sales transactions during the whole planning period. This obviously is a very crude hypothesis. No doubt, in actual practice a more refined relationship between the pertinent variables will evolve. In this book, however, individual hypotheses merely serve to illustrate the methodology.

In periodic budgeting we try to project and plan the flows between the major financial categories (accounts) of the enterprise. Indeed, given the exogenous data, and given the set of empirically determined parameters, we are in a position to project the remaining aggregate transactions. This approach, though less sophisticated, is basically not much different from that applied on the macro-level by interindustry analysis. Indeed this approach may lend itself to refinements by means of linear programing and thus to the determination of an optimal solution. If a budget system is to be converted into a linear programing model, the set of equations 1 to 10 may be used in formulating at least some of the constraints of the linear program. Capacity constraints, nonnegativity production constraints, etc., would have to be added; furthermore an appropriate objective function might be chosen and, theoretically at least, an analytical budget model in form of a linear program could be stated. Let us first consider the production constraint for the various manufacturing processes of the pertinent enterprise and then formulate the possible constraints of such an analytical budget model. After this has been done, we shall shortly consider one or the other objective function eventually to be chosen.

We assume the following simple production conditions at full capacity of department j:

$$K_j = \sum_{i=1}^{n} b_{ji}q_i$$

Hereby represent:

K_j................Maximal production of process (or department)
$$j = 1, \ldots, k.$$
q_i................The quantity (in units) produced of product i.
b_{ji}................The contribution of process j to product i.

Since production at full capacity may not be possible in every department, we have to formulate an inequality or introduce a so-called *slack variable* γ_j (indicating idle capacity):

$$K_j \geq \sum_{i=1}^{n} b_{ji} q_i \qquad \text{or} \qquad K_j = \sum_{i=1}^{n} b_{ji} q_i + \gamma_j$$

Assuming we produce four commodities ($i = 1, \ldots, 4$) manufactured in three processes ($j = 1, \ldots, 3$), then the following thirty *budget constraints*[3] are *available for a linear program* (cf. the preceding equations 1 to 20):

$$
\begin{aligned}
&(1) & p_1 q_1 &+ p_2 q_2 &+ p_3 q_3 &+ p_4 q_4 &- t_{SR} && = 0 \\
&(2) & c_{M1} q_1 &+ c_{M2} q_2 &+ c_{M3} q_3 &+ c_{M4} q_4 &- t_{MW} && = 0 \\
&(3) & c_{L1} q_1 &+ c_{M2} q_2 &+ c_{M3} q_3 &+ c_{L4} q_4 &- t_{LW} && = 0 \\
&(4) & t_{RC} &- a_{SR} t_{SR} &- t_{BR} && && = 0 \\
&(5) & t_{CP} &- t_{PB} &- a_{PM} t_{PM} &- a'_{PF} t_{PF} &- a_{PO} t_{PO} && = 0 \\
&(6) & t_{CL} &- t_{LW} && && && = 0 \\
&(7) & t_{PF} &- a'_{FW} t_{FW} && && && = 0 \\
&(8) & t_{AF} &- a''_{FW} t_{FW} && && && = 0 \\
&(9) & t_{PO} &- a'_{OI} t_{OI} && && && = 0 \\
&(10) & t_{AO} &- a''_{OI} t_{OI} && && && = 0 \\
&(11) & t_{PM} &- t_{ME} &- t_{MW} &+ t_{BM} && && = 0 \\
&(12) & t_{WG} &- t_{BW} &+ t_{WE} &- t_{MW} &- t_{LW} &- t_{FW} & = 0 \\
&(13) & t_{GI} &- t_{BC} &+ t_{GE} &- t_{WG} && && = 0 \\
&(14) & t_{IS} &- t_{SR} && && && = 0 \\
&(15) & t_{MI} &- t_{IS} &+ t_{GI} &+ t_{OI} && && = 0 \\
&(16) & t_{RE} &- t_{BR} &- t_{RS} &+ t_{RC} && && = 0 \\
&(17) & t_{CE} &- t_{BC} &- t_{RC} &+ t_{CP} &+ t_{CL} &+ t_{AC} & = 0 \\
&(18) & t_{AE} &- t_{BA} &+ t_{AF} &+ t_{AO} &- t_{AC} && = 0 \\
&(19) & t_{EP} &- t_{PB} &- t_{PM} &- t_{PF} &- t_{PO} &+ t_{CP} & = 0 \\
&(20) & t_{EN} &- t_{BN} &- t_{MI} && && && = 0 \\
&(21) & b_{11} q_1 &+ b_{12} q_2 &+ b_{13} q_3 &+ b_{14} q_4 &+ \gamma_1 && = K_1 \\
&(22) & b_{21} q_1 &+ b_{22} q_2 &+ b_{23} q_3 &+ b_{24} q_4 &+ \gamma_2 && = K_2 \\
&(23) & b_{31} q_1 &+ b_{32} q_2 &+ b_{33} q_3 &+ b_{34} q_4 &+ \gamma_3 && = K_3 \\
&(24) & && && && q_1 && \geq 0 \\
&(25) & && && && q_2 && \geq 0 \\
&(26) & && && && q_3 && \geq 0 \\
&(27) & && && && q_4 && \geq 0 \\
&(28) & && && && \gamma_1 && \geq 0 \\
\end{aligned}
$$

---

[3]The fact that most of these constraints are equations instead of inequalities is no impediment.

$$(29) \qquad\qquad\qquad\qquad\qquad \gamma_2 \quad \geq 0$$
$$(30) \qquad\qquad\qquad\qquad\qquad \gamma_3 \quad \geq 0$$

The inequalities 24 to 27 are required to indicate that none of the four commodities to be produced may be purchased from outside (no *negative* output). The inequalities 28 to 30 imply that the production facilities of a department (or process) may be underutilized but cannot be overutilized (idle capacity must be nonnegative). The pure identities (equations 6 and 11 to 20) *might* prove dispensable in the formulation of the linear program. On the other hand, it is possible to restrict the area of feasible solutions by inserting further constraints. Such additional boundaries may grow out of a desired structure of the ending balance sheet or of the income statement (e.g., a desirable range of liquidity, or a certain leverage, or a minimum rate of return). By means of such *statement ratio constraints* not only specific production and flow conditions are secured, even certain minimal balance sheet and income ratios can be attained.

The objective function to be maximized may assume various forms: a pure net profit function, a gross profit function, or, in particularly odd cases, even a cash or liquid-funds function. A further question arises as to the iterative algorism to be used for solving such a linear program. Charnes, Cooper, and Ijiri [1963, p. 36] suggested exploiting the advantages of the *incidence* (or net-work) *models* of linear programing.[4] This proposal may well be acceptable for their own model of *goal programing*[5] which is limited to transactions effected on a cash basis, and which does not articulate the features of a full-fledged budget system. For our model, which is in a position to reflect an entire "purchase-production-sales-collection cycle" of a manufacturing enterprise, the net-work method could, at best, fulfill an auxiliary function.[6] In our opinion, it should be

---

[4]For details on the *net-work model* see Charnes and Cooper [1961], Vol. 2, p. 628. See also Ford and Fulkerson [1962].

[5]"Goal programing" or "programing to goals" is a technique incorporating a constraint within the objective function (such a constraint is called a "goal"). For further details see Charnes and Cooper [1961], vol. 1, pp. 215–221.

[6]Many of our transaction variables have coefficients *different* from ±1; thus an important precondition for the application of the net-work model suggested by Charnes, Cooper, and Ijiri [1963] is *not* fulfilled.

The preceding outlines of an analytical budget model were developed independently and without acquaintance of the paper by Ijiri, Levy, and Lyon [1963]. Dittoed copies of our model were distributed in 1962 at the *International Conference of Accounting Education*. Yet, a special merit of Ijiri et al. [1963], which is not conceived in our model, is the utilization of the *dual* of the linear budget program for evaluating managerial aspects beyond the "optimal balance sheet." After this section was closed, a further development of

possible to apply one of the standard iterative algorisms (e.g., the simplex method) to the linear budget program, provided the number of accounts, of products, of departments, etc., is fairly small, and provided the budget hypotheses can realistically be expressed in *linear* functions.

However, there is a further possibility of extending and using a model of this type. This is reflected in the intriguing proposition—made by Charnes, Cooper, and Ijiri [1963] for cases where the data do not permit any solution to satisfying all constraints simultaneously—to incorporate into the linear program *pre-emptive priorities*, i.e., a set of *choices* with different "weights that could reflect the relative preferences (degree of priority) which a management might want to accord to the various account balances that it would like to see maintained" (Charnes, Cooper, and Ijiri [1963], pp. 30–33).[7] The future will reveal to what extent linear and nonlinear programming can be applied to periodic budgeting in actual practice. But the limitations of "mathematical programing" are strong enough to encourage the exploration of other techniques applicable to budgeting. A combination of linear programing with, or a shift to, simulation models seems to be more promising.

Before closing this subsection on *analytical* budget models, reference shall be made to Stedry's [1960] work which contains two independent attempts at applying methods of management science to budgeting. The first of these attempts stresses the behavioral and especially motivational aspects of budgeting. It examines the interrelations between the budgeted (expenditure) level, the department head's aspiration level,[8] and the level actually expected. Stedry

the basic ideas outlined herein was brought to our attention. N. Churchill [1964] presents several applications of linear algebra to the area of accounting (reciprocal cost allocations, cost allocations with inventories, financial statements and residual balances, and product costing). Previous attempts to apply matrix algebra to micro-economic allocation processes are found by Pichler [1953], Wenke [1956, 1959], Rosenblatt [1957], and Richards [1960], as well as Williams and Griffin [1964a and b].

[7]This is illustrated in a case where expenses exceed revenues. Since their model cannot handle any receivable and payable transactions, the above situation results in a cash shortage (beyond a specified lower bound). Management may now prefer to deplete inventories even beyond the desirable minimum, instead of accepting a shortage in cash reserves. In addition, management may have particular preferences as to the sequence in which various inventories shall be depleted. This exercise of optimal choice may be attained through goal programing by minimizing a function expressing the inventory "deficiencies" together with the weights expressing their various pre-emptive priorities.

[8]*Aspiration level* is defined "as the level of future performance in a familiar task which an individual, knowing his level of past performance in that task, explicitly undertakes to reach" (see Frank [1935], p. 119).

sympathizes with the notion that, from a motivational viewpoint, there exists an *optimal budget level*. Thus motivational rather than technological or accounting forces would determine the *standards* to be chosen. The following hypotheses, based on a series of empirical tests with student subjects, are postulated for the *behavior of a department head* for whom a budget is set:

(*i*)   If there is a *discrepancy* between the *expected actual level of expenditure* and the *aspired level of expenditure*, he will attempt to reduce this discrepancy by moving his aspiration level toward the actual level at a rate which depends on the size of the discrepancy.

(*ii*) In addition to the effect caused by the discrepancy, the *aspired level of expenditure* will be lowered in response to a lowering of the *budgeted level of expenditure*.

(*iiia*) The department head will be *encouraged* if the discrepancy (actual expected cost minus aspired cost) does not exceed some positive value known as the *discouragement point*.

(*iiib*) The department head will be *discouraged* if the discrepancy exceeds the *discouragement point* but does not exceed a larger value known as the *failure point*.

(*iiic*) If the value of the discrepancy exceeds the *failure point*, the system will cease to exist, or a new one will come into being; "the department head will resign."

(*iva*) If the department head is *encouraged*, he will attempt to reduce a positive discrepancy by reducing the *expected actual level of expenditure*; he will react to a negative discrepancy by allowing expected cost to rise. The rate of reduction or increase depends upon the size of the discrepancy.

(*ivb*) If the department head is *slightly discouraged*, he will reduce the discrepancy by reducing expected cost at a lower rate relative to a given discrepancy than he would if encouraged. If he is *moderately discouraged*, he will allow expected cost to increase, but at a sufficiently small rate that the discrepancy will not be increased. If he is *extremely discouraged*, he will allow expected cost to increase at a rate which increases the discrepancy. (Stedry [1960], pp. 24–25 [footnote omitted].)[9]

Based on these hypotheses a mathematical model is developed and various conditions—depending on the reactions of the "system" i.e., the individuals involved—are examined.

Stedry's approach has the merit of an original contribution to the area of accounting, but it has many controversial implications and has been criticized for several reasons. From an experimental point of view it must be objected that the psychological tests were carried out on students in the classroom and not on department heads in a

---

[9]Andrew C. Stedry, *Budget Control and Cost Behavior*, copyright 1960. By permission of Prentice-Hall, Inc., publisher.

business environment. Horngren [1962, p. 242] even asserts that Stedry's recommendation "smacks of manipulation of humans without their knowledge. It has unfavorable long-run overtones that may outweigh short-run benefits." To these considerations a host of practical and financial difficulties—such as measurement of the aspiration levels, discouragement points, restriction to an individual department, etc.—must be added. Here, as in many sophisticated mathematical models of management science, the cost of practical application would, at present, outweigh the benefits derived.

Stedry's second model again is concerned with an *individual department only*. It is directed towards (profit) planning and ultimately assumes the form of a linear program (limited substitution) the main features of which are outlined below:

x'_{ijk} . . . . Number of units of the kth factor of the jth subgroup used in production of the ith product.

a_{ijk} . . . . Number of product equivalents of the ith item produced per unit of x'_{ijk}.

y_i . . . . Amount of the ith item produced.

n_j . . . . Number of factors in the jth subgroup.

c_i . . . . Contribution per unit of the ith item to profit and overhead.

c'_{ijk} . . . . Cost of one unit of x'_{ijk}.

q_i . . . . There are p factor subgroups of which the ith item requires inputs from q_i of the subgroups.

L_i . . . . Lower limits to inventory.

U_i . . . . Upper limits to inventory ($L_i \leq y_i \leq U_i$).

$$x_{ijk} = x'_{ijk} a_{ijk}.$$

$$b_{ijk} = \frac{1}{a_{ijk}}.$$

$$c_{ijk} = \frac{c'_{ijk}}{a_{ijk}}.$$

Objective function to be maximized:

$$\sum_{i=1}^{m} \left(c_i y_i - \sum_{i \in q_i} \sum_{k=1}^{n_j} c_{ijk} x_{ijk} \right),$$

Under the following constraints:

$$\sum_{k=1}^{n_j} x_{ijk} - y_i = 0 \qquad\qquad i = 1, \ldots, m; \; i \in q_i$$

$$\sum_{i=1}^{m} b_{ijk} x_{ijk} \leq b_{jk} \qquad\qquad k = 1, \ldots, n_j; \; j \in q_i$$

$$y_i \leq U_i \qquad\qquad i = 1, \ldots, m$$

$$-y_i \leq -L_i$$

This may crudely be interpreted as a model maximizing the "profit"[10] of a single department under the constraints set by its production conditions (which are somewhat complicated by operating with "factor subgroups," by the limited substitution possibilities between these groups, etc.). Stedry also makes suggestions and gives illustrations on the computational scheme to be employed (the subdual method for dyadic problems, developed by Charnes, Cooper [1961], vol. 2, pp. 549–82).

Apart from the idiosyncrasies, difficulties, and limitations of Stedry's specific formulation, it has to be recognized that the idea of developing departmental, analytical budget models is theoretically sound and may sooner or later find practical application within the frame of an *over-all budget*. But if periodic budgeting is to be formalized, it seems that the formalization of the over-all budget (i.e., formalization on the co-ordinative level) can be carried out in practice with less difficulty than the construction of linear programing budgets for individual departments. The latter rather constitutes a refinement after the over-all budget model is established.

9.2   A BUDGET MODEL FOR SIMULATING THE FIRM

9.21   Introductory Remarks

In this section we shall indicate how the accountant's approach to budgeting can be refined and brought in tune with the new tools of electronic data processing (EDP) and management science. This shall be carried out by use of a comprehensive budget model which uses traditional methodology as a launching basis, incorporating some modest features of management science such as feedback mechanisms, explicit boundary conditions, and system simulation. We believe that such a step-by-step transition from traditional budgeting techniques to more sophisticated simulation models will prove practicable and more fruitful than a radical change to entirely unproved methods that can appeal from the theoretical viewpoint only. Our computer model, constructed as generally as possible under the circumstances, serves *four* main purposes:

---

[10]This *profit* is "the difference between the contribution of the outputs and the costs of the necessary inputs" (Stedry [1960], p. 119).

(1) To present *the complete operating budget* of a fictitious enterprise *in form of a mathematical model together with a computer program usable for various educational purposes*.

(2) To provide a *prototype of an operating budget that may serve in actual practice as a basis for constructing budget models and programs* satisfying the individual needs of particular firms.

(3) To demonstrate the *connection between operations research models and traditional budgeting*, and to overcome the shortcomings of the latter by conceptual clarification (making explicit budgeting hypotheses, separating endogenous from exogenous variables and parameters, introducing explicit boundary conditions, etc.).

(4) To introduce accountants—unfamiliar with the programing of electronic computers—to the fundamental symbolism used in computer languages.

This section together with the companion volume[11] offer opportunity to use the memno-technical features of FORTRAN (and similar computer source languages) to facilitate the perusal of the algebraic model by accountants.[12]

Periodic budgeting, as practiced in industry and taught in the accounting curriculum, combines estimates by individual departments in a process of co-ordinative aggregation. The purpose is to supply management with a financial plan for future operations. The chief purpose of this planning activity serves the future control of the enterprise; but occasionally budgeting is charged with the more ambitious task of "finding the most profitable course" (Heckert and Wilson [1955], p. 14). If by this is meant selecting a combination of managerial policies *optimizing* the profit of the enterprise, then the quoted task seems to overstate the potential of traditional budget activity. Such an interpretation would make us believe that we are dealing with a branch of accounting that is in a position to determine *optimal solutions*. Undoubtedly this is not the case since budgeting traditionally neither applies an algorism for optimizing the long-term profit function, nor provides any means for determining and comparing *all* the alternatives resulting from

---

[11]While the budget model is here presented and discussed in detail, the corresponding computer program together with comments, a historical survey, explanations, flow charts, and an illustrative output consisting of nine subbudgets) is supplied in the companion volume, *Simulation of the Firm through a Budget Computer Program* by Richard Mattessich (Homewood, Ill.: Richard D. Irwin, Inc., 1964).

[12]Thus, beyond the knowledge of algebra and a familiarity with the Σ notation, no mathematical or technical prerequisites are required to comprehend this budget simulation model—though some patience and endeavor on the part of the reader is expected.

the numerous factor and policy combinations feasible in an enterprise. If it means, however, finding a policy that yields a prospective profit considered to be *satisfactory*, the quoted task is acceptable (provided the term "satisfactory" is interpreted in the Simonean meaning of the best available solution within a limited range of alternatives and in conformity with a specified aspiration level). With the application of mathematical-scientific approaches to management problems and the progressive use of automatic data processing, the question arises: in what way can periodic budgeting be improved? As we have seen, traditional budgeting already offers a primitive procedure of *satisficing* a goal function. It suffers, however, from the shortcoming of including too small a number of possible alternatives from which to choose when determining the "most satisfactory" solution. Furthermore, we recognize the difficulty of adjusting the operating budget (in its traditional form) to suddenly changing conditions; it is at best "flexible" only with regard to a changing sales or production volume. Our proposal therefore rests on the simple assumption that a model which permits the calculation of a larger number of alternatives, based on more numerous "flexible" variables and eventually changing parameters, would yield a better approximation to the ideal but unknown optimal solution. This can be materialized by means of electronic computers and system simulation. Such a task requires the translation of a traditional budgeting system into algebraic terms and the elaboration of a computer program, an approach that ought to be strictly distinguished from the "computerization" of an ordinary accounting system. The latter pivots around a *continuing* process of recording; it utilizes primarily the computer's capacity of classifying, adding, subtracting, storing, and reporting a huge number of figures through sustained data generation; therefore it requires the permanent or at least frequent availability of a computer. Consequently this computerized bookkeeping will be feasible only where electronic data-processing systems (EDP) are owned or rented on a more or less permanent basis, and where the work load is large enough to warrant the considerable expense of maintaining an electronic computer. In contrast to this is budget simulation which requires only occasional use of the computer, and which utilizes its ability to master more complex operations. It follows that budget computer simulation is by no means restricted to large-scale enterprises, but is feasible for middle- and small-sized firms. In the latter cases the computation may be performed outside the enterprise at consulting firms, statistical service stations, or other computer centers. The major tasks, that is to say, the building of the budget model, the determination of the parameters, the choice of the exogenous variables, and the writing of the computer program, can be carried out independently of the EDP system (provided the kind of computer to be used is known). Once the program is available, a change or revision of the budget requires merely the substitution of new exogenous variables for old ones or requires, less frequently, a modification of parameters. At this stage a concise survey of the various phases in manipulating budget simulation is recommended.

9.22   Constructing the Model

The existing budget system will have to be examined and translated into mathematical terms, step by step, each subbudget for itself, as shown in the subsequent model. Although our model has been kept as general as possible, and thus might serve as a prototype for budget simulation models in actual practice, it must be borne in mind that ultimately the model is an illustration by means of a fictitious firm. Obviously the idiosyncrasies of each individual firm and budgeting system have to be reflected through appropriate choice of variables, parameters, and model structure. At this point one might consider the desirability of additional changes that improve the previously available budget system.

This activity of model building is the most interesting and most precarious phase in such an undertaking. The problem of weighing the degree of sophistication and reliability against operating costs and adaptability of the model will often have to be solved on the basis of a personal value judgement. The fact that computerization permits the incorporation of cybernetic control features into the budget model, provides important means of refinement, and might enable a successive transition from an old-fashioned budgeting system to a management control model proper. Indeed, the two major interconnected differences between traditional budgeting and management control models are (1) the *utilization of formal adaptive controls* by management scientists versus the informal trial and error procedures by accountants, and (2) the *explicit formulation of side-constraints* by the former versus the *implicit* assumption of such constraints by the latter.

To illustrate the preceding remark on the utilization of adaptive controls, we may think of a situation in which the monthly production activity is not fully synchronized with the sales activity, but follows—within the limit set by the total annual production volume—an independent course based on other criteria: e.g., (1) the leveling-out of production and employment fluctuations, (2) the benefit of *seasonal* purchases of raw material, (3) the overcoming of storage bottlenecks, etc. At times, this may lead to a precariously low level of finished-goods inventory. In the past a trial-and-error procedure has frequently been employed to attain production levels that are *generally* satisfactory and that secure minimal inventories. If this procedure is adopted in connection with budget simulation the following sequence occurs: certain parameters (prorating the annual production volume to the individual months) are originally assumed, the endogenous variables (e.g., finished-goods inventories) are computed, if these are not within the constraints, new inventories—based on a modified set of parameters, chosen by the budget director—are being calculated, and so on. Even if the computer running time of such a budget or subbudget is very brief, this is an awkward procedure and it might be advantageous to incorporate a feedback mechanism into the system that changes automatically the parameters according to a preconceived formula which ultimately yields "satisfactory" results. Such a feedback control can assume different degrees of sophistication and may range from a simple adjustment mechanism, as used in the model presented in this book, to a complete inventory control model with learning processes and other refinements excogitated by OR specialists. Similar problems arise with regard to raw material inventory, the holding of short-term marketable securities, the incurring of bank debts, etc. Our budget program contains several such, relatively simple and deterministic, adaptive control processes. These can later be refined and elaborated into regular OR models (eventually with probabilistic features) for which the budget system then constitutes the basic framework tying the individual parts together and forming a model for simulating the financial aspects of a firm.

9.23 Utilizing the Memno-Technic Advantage of the Source Language

The complete model now has to be translated into machine language, conveniently by way of an automatic coding system (source language).[13] This may become of far-reaching consequence

---

[13]Originally a computer program *had* to be written in *machine coding*, i.e., in the language (usually binary or octal number codes) that is "understood" by the pertinent electronic computer. This created many difficulties; above all the machine-language or

for accounting because the various source languages—developed by manufacturers of electronic computers and other institutions interested in the rapid emanation of computer work—contain features that unexpectedly may prove very useful for model building in accounting. Most of the source languages permit a combination of several letters as a symbol for one variable, or a set of related variables. These letters (etc.) can be arranged in a memnonical way, which means in a manner that will induce a relatively quick identification of the symbol with the name and concept behind it. Such a device accountants have been utilizing for a long time by symbolizing, for instance, the cost of goods sold with the letters CGS, the owners' equity with OE, the work in process with $W.i.P.$, etc. In contrast to this is the symbolism of high-school algebra which characterizes the variables by "impersonal" and less suggestive symbols. This is a technical or pedagogical impediment the severity of which must not be underrated in cases where these variables become numerous. Furthermore, there is the danger of running out of letters (of the Roman alphabet) which enforces regression to the Greek, Hebrew, and other alphabets. The memno-technical symbolism of source languages (which permits the combining of several letters in *many variations*) does not entirely remove these difficulties but reduces them considerably. Thus the question arises whether accountants might not profitably adopt the practice of writing their mathematical models directly in a symbolism that comes close to that of the source languages. This has not been customary in ordinary computer application where the mathematical model is presented in traditional symbolism while its computer program is written in the symbolism of source language. Accounting, however, is especially well suited to such an innovation—as our model, written in this peculiar symbolism—will demonstrate. A further advantage of this approach is the full *utilization of several dimensions* of a specific variable—which only recently has found occasional adaptation in accounting literature—by use of subscripts (or superscripts) and the sigma notation. This we shall illustrate shortly.

If the sales quantities of three commodities during six months is

---

object language is difficult and inconvenient to program. Therefore intermediate language systems (usually program-oriented) were devised for writing the *source program* which a compiler automatically converts into the object language. Since these *source languages* resemble ordinary English or the ordinary language of mathematics, the task of computer programing is greatly facilitated. Each of these languages has its idiosyncrasies (its rules of grammar, its punctuation, etc.) which have to be acquired and obeyed precisely.

to be symbolized, then three alternative formulations are possible:

(1) Old-fashioned algebra, which might use the following symbols:

Product Item	Month					
	1	*2*	*3*	*4*	*5*	*6*
1	A	B	C	D	E	F
2	a	b	c	d	e	f
3	α	β	γ	δ	ϵ	ζ

That means, the *sales value* of product 1 sold in March bears the label *C*; that of product 2 sold in January, the label *a*; and that of product 3 sold in May, the label ϵ, etc. We recognize that, apart from the confusing variety of letters, there exists no concise general symbolism for an arbitrary sales value that is to be specified later.

(2) Matrix algebraic notation, which simplifies the symbolism in the following way by using only one letter (e.g., the symbol *s*) combined with different subscripts. As we have noticed in previous chapters, the first subscript refers to the row (e.g., the month), the second to the column (e.g., the product).

Product Item	Month					
	1	*2*	*3*	*4*	*5*	*6*
1	s_{11}	s_{12}	s_{13}	s_{14}	s_{15}	s_{16}
2	s_{21}	s_{22}	s_{23}	s_{24}	s_{25}	s_{26}
3	s_{31}	s_{32}	s_{33}	s_{34}	s_{35}	s_{36}

Thus the sales value of product 1 sold during March is designated by s_{13}, that of product 2 sold during January by s_{21}, and that of product 3 sold during May by s_{35}, etc. The general symbol for any sales value to be specified later may then be written:

$$s_{ij} \qquad \begin{aligned} i &= 1,\ldots,3 \\ j &= 1,\ldots,6 \end{aligned}$$

(3) The memnonic symbolism of source languages (especially the FORTRAN language[14]) here used, which might employ the

---

[14] FORTRAN, the official abbreviation for *Mathematical Formula Translating System* (IBM) is, so far, the most popular automatic coding system and source language in use (for an excellent introduction to FORTRAN see Organick [1963]). It is modeled after ordinary algebra, but may be applied to commercial as well as mathematical programs. With regard to *some* "commercial" applications the limitations of FORTRAN are strong enough for them to prefer other source languages such as COBOL (Common Business Oriented Language).

following symbols:

Product			*Month*			
Item	1	2	3	4	5	6
1	SV(1, 1)	SV(1, 2)	SV(1, 3)	SV(1, 4)	SV(1, 5)	SV(1, 6)
2	SV(2, 1)	SV(2, 2)	SV(2, 3)	SV(2, 4)	SV(2, 5)	SV(2, 6)
3	SV(3, 1)	SV(3, 2)	SV(3, 3)	SV(3, 4)	SV(3, 5)	SV(3, 6)

Thus the sales value (or volume in \$) of product 1 in March is designated by $SV(1, 3)$, that of product 2 in January by $SV(2, 1)$, and that of product 3 in May by $SV(3, 5)$. The general symbol for any quantity to be specified later may now be expressed by:

$$SV(I, M\emptyset) \qquad \begin{aligned} I &= 1, \ldots, 3 \\ M\emptyset &= 1, \ldots, 6 \end{aligned}$$

or

$$SV(I, M\emptyset) \qquad \begin{aligned} I &= 1, 3 \\ M\emptyset &= 1, 6 \end{aligned}$$

The latter form of indicating the range of the *index variables* (those replacing the subscripts) is the only one permissible for FORTRAN-programing purposes, while the former is a compromise chosen by us for accounting models. It should here be added that only the letters I, J, K, L, M, N (fixed point mode,[15] or symbol combinations, of up to six alpha-numeric characters, *beginning* with one of the letters I to N can be used as index variables).

In the case of $SV(I, M\emptyset)$ we are speaking of a two-dimensional variable, the first dimension referring to the product item ($I = 1, \ldots, 3$), the second referring to the month ($M\emptyset = 1, \ldots, 6$)[16]. It

---

[15] Two *modes* of variables and constants are to be distinguished under FORTRAN (and other languages), the *fixed point* mode (restricted to integers) and the *floating point* mode (characterized by data with decimal points). One of the chief functions of fixed point values is their use as *indexes* (fulfilling the task of subscripts). Thus the reader will notice that in our model *no* symbol referring to an exogenous or endogenous variable, or to a parameter, *begins* with one of the letters I to N which are reserved for fixed point values. On the other hand, no index or "subscript" can begin with letters other than I, J, K, L, M, or N. The letters subsequent to the *first* letter can be chosen freely, but in FORTRAN the total number of letters representing a symbol, *or* its subscript-index, cannot exceed six alphabetical or numerical (alpha-numeric) characters.

[16] In computer work it is important to distinguish explicitly the letter "O" ($= \emptyset$) from the numeral "zero," the letter "*I*" or "l" from the numeral "one," etc. In everyday usage, especially in connection with typewriters, we may apply the same symbols for "O" and "zero," for "I" or "l" and "one." In "programing," such a double usage would be fatal, since the compiler cannot discriminate when a specific symbol refers to a letter or a numeral if identical symbols are used. Thus it is commendable to employ strictly distinct characters like $\emptyset$ and 0, or *I* and 1, etc., when expressing the symbols and formulas for programing purposes.

is obvious that this is a very economical way of handling a huge number of related variables.

The sum of the sales values of a specified number of product items and months (e.g., I = 1, ..., 2 and M$\emptyset$ = 1, ..., 4) can now be expressed in our model in the following way:

$$\sum_{I=1}^{2} \sum_{M\emptyset=1}^{4} SV(I, M\emptyset).$$

The total sales value (of all three products for all six months) would then be written as

$$\sum_{I=1}^{3} \sum_{M\emptyset=1}^{6} SV(I, M\emptyset).$$

This way of writing, again, is a compromise reserved for our accounting models; it is not permissible in the computer program itself. FORTRAN cannot utilize or read the sigma notation and cannot obey the command of the Σ operator. The procedure of summing up has to be programed as follows:

```
TSV(I, MØ) = 0.0
TSV(I, MØ) = TSV(I, MØ) + SV(I, MØ)
DØ 1    I  = 1, 3
DØ 1   MØ  = 1, 6
. . . . . . . . . . . . . .
. . . . . . . . . . . . . .
1 CØNTINUE
```

In this book we are concerned not with the computer program[17] but only with the mathematical model, hence we will go no further into the technical details of computer work, we merely mention that in the above program statements the symbol TSV(I, M$\emptyset$) is *ultimately* equivalent to what in the present example corresponds to

$$\sum_{I=1}^{3} \sum_{M\emptyset=1}^{6} SV(I, M\emptyset),$$

although at the start it assumes the figure 0.0 (similar to an adding machine which has to be *cleared* at the beginning); then step by step it adds with each cycle another value of the various SV(I, M$\emptyset$) I = 1, ..., 3 and M$\emptyset$ = 1, ..., 6. It begins with the value of SV(1, 1) to which the value of SV(2, 1) is added, then the value

---

[17]However, the companion volume *Simulation of the Firm through a Budget Computer Program* does present complete programs in FORTRAN IV for the IBSYS Monitor System applicable at several IBM computers, together with comments, flow charts, and the output tables with input and output data of budget systems.

of SV(3, 1); after this the value of SV(1, 2) is added, then the value of SV(2, 2), and so on until the last value of SV(3, 6) has been added, whereupon the total sum

$$\text{TSV}(I, M\phi) = \sum_{I=1}^{3} \sum_{M\phi=1}^{6} SV(I, M\phi)$$

has been accumulated, stored, and is eventually printed out. The individual values of the $SV(I, M\phi)$ $I = 1, \ldots, 3$ and $M\phi = 1, \ldots, 6$ were either previously calculated and stored in the computer memory, or formulas to compute these values have to be set up in the program (between the last $D\phi$-statement and the 1 $C\phi$NTINUE statement).

9.24 Assigning Values

As a next step, values must be assigned to the parameters and exogenous variables. The values of the former will be based on past experience and will often require extensive empirical studies or experimentation. The simple example of seasonal sales fluctuations might be used as an illustration. We assign the symbol $SQ(I, M\phi)$ to the sales quantity (in units) of product item I $(I = 1, \ldots, 10)$ during the month $M\phi (M\phi = 1, \ldots, 13)$. The figure *thirteen* as referring to the index variable $M\phi$ must be especially explained; it has a *threefold significance* in our model. Applied to a *flow variable* it refers to the complete budget period, not to a single month; thus

$$SQ(I, 13) = \sum_{M\phi=1}^{12} SQ(I, M\phi).$$

Applied to a *stock variable*, it refers to the stock at the *end* of the twelfth month, e.g.:

BI(I, 13) symbolizes the inventory of product I at the *end* of the budget period (in our case, the end of December), while the symbol

BI(I, 12) refers to the inventory of product I at the *beginning* of the twelfth month.

Finally it may refer to an *annual average* as in the example of PUC(I, 13) where the unit cost of product I is averaged over the entire budget period.

Assuming, now, the value of SQ(I, 13) is available for each product $(I = 1, \ldots, 10)$, it is possible to forecast the monthly sales quantities through multiplication of SQ(I, 13) with parameters that reflect the seasonal sales fluctuations, e.g.,

$$SQ(I, M\emptyset) = SQ(I, 13) * SK(M\emptyset) \quad M\emptyset = 1, \ldots ,12$$

The *asterisk* * in FORTRAN designates the operation of multiplication and shall also be adopted for our model. $SK(M\emptyset)$ is the
sales coefficient, an index or parameter that expresses a specific
monthly sales quantity as a percentage $(0 \leq SK(MO) \leq 1)$ of the
annual sales quantity for the pertinent product. The decision,
which kinds of parameters shall be employed, will depend on
questions like the following: Shall different coefficients for different
products be used or do all products conform to the same pattern
of seasonal fluctuations? The latter is assumed in our model, otherwise this coefficient would require *two* dimensions and would have
to be expressed as $SK(I, M\emptyset)$. Thus important decisions with
regard to the structure of the budget model and the determination
of the structural parameters have to be made at this stage. In our
model we have tried to adhere, as far as possible, to traditionally
accepted hypotheses; occasionally deviations were necessary, either
in order to embody adaptive controls or for the sake of convenience.
Yet, the significance of our model must not be sought in the choice
of the hypotheses—a criterion which is ordinarily applied in the
evaluation of economic models—but in creating a framework that
uses traditional budgeting and permits the successive incorporation
of analytical features (constraints, feedback controls, satisficing or
even optimizing procedures); *the significance lies in presenting a model
of the firm that has a highly general notation* and yet *is operationally feasible*,
even for small and middle-sized enterprises. Although many of our
hypotheses will be acceptable in actual practice, we ask the reader
to regard them as illustrations rather than as recommendations.
The controller of a particular enterprise, who considers the utilization of such a budget model, will have to do thorough soul-searching
as well as researching before a specific set of hypotheses is being
adopted (for details see Chap. 4 of our companion volume).

With regard to the exogenous variables the question arises where
to draw the boundaries of the model, i.e., where to separate the
analytical procedures from data to be assumed or determined outside the model. A simple model can be expanded by incorporating
into the model proper the process of determining those variables,
which originally were of exogenous nature. Thus the exogenous
variables become endogenous and a new set of exogenous variables
emerges. This expansion process can be continued and the model

will ultimately reflect a greater number of casual relationships, but will concomitantly grow more rigid, less manageable, and much more expensive to operate. The above consideration may well be illustrated by the sales budget. There, the question arises whether the future sales are to be determined by a highly sophisticated OR model or by an elementary procedure that starts from previous sales quantities and adjusts them through simple parameters based on business-cycle forecasts. Our model leans toward the latter approach; but this is of secondary importance, decisive is the framework which also would permit the use of more refined features.

At the time of compiling and selecting the exogenous data it must be decided which alternatives shall be computed. The basic difference between individual variations may lie in (1) the product-mix, (2) the factor combination or cost structure (e.g., more capital intensive versus more labor intensive production methods—as far as such choices are open within *short-term* planning), (3) the quality and price structure of inputs as well as outputs (e.g., production of qualitatively better products under decreasing sales quantity but increasing profit margin and price), (4) the liquidity position and financing methods, (5) the promotion and sales methods, etc. In actual practice it may be advantageous on one hand to distinguish between *basic alternatives* and *combinations* of basic alternatives, and on the other to devise a procedure that eliminates less favorable or unfeasible alternatives, reducing the amount of data to be compared to a manageable size ("data reduction"—one of the acute aspects of computer work). Simulating the firm under a considerable number of alternatives will facilitate the determination of that alternative which satisfies a specific aspiration level; most likely this will be an alternative which is more satisfactory than that one determined through a traditional, noncomputerized budget. Furthermore, a detailed plan is in this way provided for each alternative through which insight may be gained on some imponderables that cannot be fit into the ordinary scheme of satisficing or optimizing procedures but which influence choice (e.g., stable employment versus high fluctuations in employment within the enterprise). The resulting alternatives will primarily depend on the set of exogenous variables to be chosen, occasionally these alternatives may differ because of changing parameters, especially where more permanent changes of the enterprise are considered. In this connection it should be pointed out that the distinction between exogenous variables and parameters is not always obvious and, under circumstances, may become vague.

9.25 Program, Computation, and Output

Following this preparatory work, the computer program, based on the mathematical model, can be written. Obviously, the formulation of a model in a symbolism germane to the program's source language greatly facilitates the task of programing. Which source language shall be chosen will depend on the type of computer and many other circumstances. Our program (presented in the companion volume—see footnote 11 of this chapter) is written in FORTRAN IV for the IBM 360, 7040, 7044, 7090, 7094. The reason for this choice lies in the fact that FORTRAN, among "popular" computer languages, is most suitable for our purpose.

The computer output shall be arranged in such a way that the individual budgets will be printed with all details including the pertinent exogenous variables and parameters. (In this book no output-illustrations will be offered since the companion volume contains the complete output of the budget program giving nearly fifty tables of the various subbudgets and the projected financial statements). In actual practice the selection of the most satisfactory alternative may be carried out by visual inspection and comparison. In case of too large a number of alternatives (especially where a limited number of key figures—as for example: net profit, sales volume, asset and capital structure, liquidity ratio, etc.—are insufficient for selecting the most satisfactory alternative) it should be possible to complement the main program with a program of satisficing criteria such that the computer selects automatically the "most satisfactory" choice or a limited number of "best" alternatives from which executives can make their own selection. But even where the calculation of several alternatives (for the purpose of satisficing "factor combinations") is not the major task, a budget-computer model will become an invaluable tool in all situations where budgets have to be revised. The *revision of a budget* under conventional conditions is the nightmare of the controller or budget director; such revisions take many weeks or months, and sometimes the modified data arrive at a time when a *new* revision is due. With a computerized budget model the input variables are easily changed, and within minutes the revised version of the budget is printed out by the computer. This yields an additional benefit—it affords a much more frequent recomputation of the budget. Under traditional conditions the difficulty of revising the budget has limited such an undertaking to situations of drastic changes where a revision was inevitable. In future a continuous or, better said, intermittent procedure might be devised which generates from time to time budget data adjusted to the most recent environmental conditions. This leads to consideration of further possibilities, especially to the reconciliation of historical data, supplied from financial accounting, with the corresponding figures originally planned. The determination of variances of different kinds and their impact on future planning could be incorporated into the budget program and could ultimately be converted into a "learning process" of the enterprise.

9.26   A Verbal Outline of the Model

The purpose of this chapter is to introduce accountants to a formalized budget model. Thus we try to indicate the direction to be chosen in actual practice when constructing budget computer models. This task can be achieved only by relinquishing most of the refinements desirable in a sophisticated computer budget. In order to make this model palatable to accountants, in order not to confuse those uninitiated in computer work and control models, we shall concentrate on the essence and not on individual hypotheses. Since we cannot do without the latter, we have chosen fairly simple hypotheses that can easily be exchanged against more subtle ones. To acquaint the reader with these simple hypotheses we first offer a concise survey of the model in *verbal* form. But the originality of this model lies in *the methodology and the generality of its conception*, thus the essence of this chapter cannot be extracted from these brief outlines.[18] Furthermore it has to be borne in mind that the subsequent verbal formulation is much less precise and less exhaustive than the algebraic one, benefiting from the use of index variables.

I.   *General Description of Model*

10 products	3 types of raw material
12 months' budgets	12 separate overhead accounts
4 producing departments	5 separate operating expenses
2 service departments	

The model uses the process cost method of accounting. The parameters are "variables" in the program, and may be altered without rewriting the program.

Note: (G)...given data (= exogenous variable or parameter). Figures in parentheses indicate source of (endogenous) data.

---

[18]These outlines (Subsection 9.26) are adapted from Prof. Jay M. Smith (now at the University of Minnesota), who used a similar presentation in Summer, 1963, at Stanford University in order to explain our model to his colleagues and students. We are gratefully indebted to him for his interest in our work and his endeavor to propagate its idea.

Another verbal presentation (together with an algebraic one) of our model is contained in Chap. 3 of the companion volume.

II. *Quantity Computations in the Model*
  1. *Sales quantity by product*
     = [Sales of previous period(s) by product (G)] times [Sales index (G)]
  2. *Sales quantity by product by month*
     = [Sales quantity by product (1)] times [Sales coefficient for seasonal variation (G)]
  3. *Production quantity by products*
     = [Ending inventory by product (G)] + [Sales quantity by product (1)] − [Beginning inventory by product (G)]
  4. *Production quantity by product by month*
     = [Production quantity by product (3)] times [Production coefficient (G)] Not related to sales
  4a. *Adaptive mechanism*
     If the inventory at the end of a specific month of partially completed and finished goods (measured in equivalent units) falls below a minimum, production quantity is adjusted upward to meet the minimum. Since total annual production quantity is fixed (1 & 3), production in subsequent month(s) is reduced equivalently.
  5. *Material requirements by type of material, by product, by month*
     = [Production quantity by product (4a)] times [Amount of material required for one unit of product (G)]
  6. *Material purchase quantity by type of material, by product, by month*
     = [Material requirement by product (5)] times [Purchase coefficient (G)] Unrelated to timing of material requirements
     If raw material inventory threatens to fall below the minimum level required, an adaptive mechanism increases current purchase coefficient, reducing purchasing in subsequent month(s).
  7. *Labor hours by type of labor (department) by month*
     = [Standard labor hours per unit (G)] times [Production quantity by product by month (4a)]

III. *Monetary Extensions and Definitions in the Model*
  8. *Sales dollar value by product*
     = [Sales price by product (G)] times [Sales quantity by product (1)]
  9. *Sales dollar value by product by month*
     = [Sales dollar value by product (8)] times [Sales coefficient for seasonal variation (G)]
  10. *Cost of material used by material, by product, by month*
     = [Material requirements by type of material by product by month (5)] times [Unit cost of material (G)]
  11. *Direct labor cost by department by product by month*
     = [Standard labor hours by department by product (7)] times [Standard labor cost (G)]

12. *Fixed portion of overhead by department by cost item*
    = [Fixed overhead by cost item (G)] times [Percentage distribution by department (G)]

13. *Variable portion of overhead by department by cost item*
    = [Variable overhead rate by department and cost item (G)] times [Direct labor cost by department (11)]

14. *Allocation of service departments to producing as well as service departments*
    = [Total overhead before allocation (12 & 13) of service department costs] times [Percentage allocation to each department (G)] Includes a recursive allocation mechanism

15. *Annual overhead rate by department*
    = [Total overhead of production departments including allocation of service (12, 13, 14)] divided by [Total direct labor cost by department (11)]

16. *Factory overhead cost by product by department by month*
    = [Annual overhead rate by department (15)] times [Direct labor hours by product by department by month (11)]

17. *Unit production costs by product by month*
    = {[Production cost (10), (11), (16) by product by month] + [Product unit cost at beginning by product by month] times [Beginning inventory in equivalent units by product by month]} divided by {[Adjusted production quantity by product by month] + [Beginning inventory by product by month]} (Rough average costing).

18. *Value of finished and partly finished goods ending inventory*
    = [Inventory quantity (in equivalent units) by product (G)] times [Unit production costs (17)]

19. *Variable operating expenses by type of expense by month*
    = [Sales dollar value by product by month (9)] times [Expense expressed as a percentage of sales (G)]

20. *Fixed operating expenses by cost item (G)*

IV. *Cash Flow and Cash Balance Information*
    21. *Accounts receivable collection*
        = [Percentage of sales collected in first month after sale (G)] times [Sales of last month (9)] +
        + [Percentage of sales collected in second month after sale (G)] times [Sales of two months ago (9)]

    22. *Cash sales*
        = [Percentage of sales which are cash (G)] times [Total monthly sales (9)]

    23. *Payment of factory overheads*
        = [Percentage to be paid during first month (G)] times [Specific overhead item (G) and (13)]   Same for two more months. Payments spread between three months.

    24. *Cash balance at beginning of month*
        Adaptive mechanism—Maximum and minimum amount are es-

tablished for cash balances. If cash exceeds the maximum, marketable securities are purchased. If cash is less than minimum, securities are sold to bring balance back to minimum. If portfolio is exhausted, cash may be below "desirable" minimum or even become negative (indicates need for short-term loan).

25. *Payroll expenditures*
   = {[Direct Labor Cost (11) + Indirect labor expenditures in Factory Overheads] times [Payment coefficient (G)]} + {[Indirect Labor expenditures in operating expenses (19)] times [Payment coefficient (G)]}

26. *Vouchers payable expenditures*
   = [Purchases of material last month] + [Portions of factory overhead costs not included in (25)] + [Portion of operating expenses not included in (25)]

27. Capital expenditures, Stock changes, etc. (G)

28. *Payment of dividends* = [Percentage (G)] times [Profit after Taxes]

9.27   The Budget Model Proper

To facilitate understanding of the budget model presented herein, we list individual variables for each of the subbudgets together with short comments and eventual definitional or other illuminating equations, *and present at the end of each subbudget the hypotheses and main equations pertaining to it* (important definitional equations are occasionally repeated at the end of the subbudgets). In order to indicate which of the variables are endogenous, i.e., generated in the computer, and which are exogenous or treated as parameters, we have adopted the following convention: *exogenous variables* are listed *in a box*, *parameters* are *underlined*, and *endogenous variables* are *listed plainly*. In conformity with source language practice, the "dimensions" of variables and parameters are indicated in parentheses (instead of using subscripts) whereby the following index variables are used to characterize dimensions like product item, cost item, department, and month:

I   for *product item* $(I = 1, \ldots, N)$.
J   for *direct material cost item* $(J = 1, \ldots, JJ)$.
K   for *department* $(K = 1, \ldots, KK)$; occasionally symbols such as K1, K2, K3, KP, and KS are used for auxiliary purposes. Since our model operates with only one direct labor type per department, K can here be interpreted as the index of the *direct labor cost item* when it refers to producing departments.[19]

---

[19] In contrast to *producing departments* which participate *directly* in the production process, are the service departments (e.g., steam plant, generation of electrical energy, building administration, etc.) which only supply auxiliary services to various departments; consequently no direct labor costs arise in these departments.

L   for *factory overhead cost item*   (L = 1, ... , LL).

M   for *operating expense item*   (M = 1, ... , MM).

M$\emptyset$ for *month* if   M$\emptyset$ = 1, ... , 12.

If M$\emptyset$ belongs to a *stock variable* it refers to the *beginning* of the month indicated by the figure assigned to M$\emptyset$ (except where the variable explicitly refers to the *ending balance*, e.g., EI(M$\emptyset$)— see 2–3); if it belongs to a *flow variable*, it refers to the whole month indicated by M$\emptyset$. Consequently the case of M$\emptyset$ = 13 has two or, exactly speaking, three different meanings, depending on the context—that means whether encountered in connection with a stock variable, a flow variable, or an average. In the first case it refers to the end of the entire budget period (end of December, in our model); in the second case it refers to the entire budget period (the total of the twelve months, January to December). A third meaning is assumed in the case of an average (e.g., PUC(I, 13) ... annual average of product I unit costs).

Furthermore it becomes necessary to introduce the following symbols:

LM   for *last month* (with respect to M$\emptyset$ as indicating the current month),

MBL for *month before the last one* (with respect to M$\emptyset$), and

NM   for *next month* (with respect to M$\emptyset$), hence

LM   = M$\emptyset$ − 1, MBL = M$\emptyset$ − 2, and NM = M$\emptyset$ + 1.

In one instance an additional auxiliary index variable MS (explained in 7–9; references of this kind refer to the variables, parameters, or hypotheses listed below and must not be confused with references to sections, figures, or tables which have similar appearance) had to be used. When the Σ notation is used in connection with stock variables a further symbol MI (month indicated) becomes necessary (see 9–2).

For the sake of cross reference and easier identification of a specific variable with the subbudget to which it originally belongs, we assigned a double number (e.g., 1–4, expressing the fourth variable in the first subbudget) to each variable or parameter. At the end of this chapter all variables are listed alphabetically together with their numbers of identification.

(1) Sales Budget:

(1–1) | PSQ(I) | *previous sales quantity,*
in product units;
"previous" refers to that past period on which the sales forecast is based (e.g., preceding business year).

(1–2)   SI(I)   *sales index* for each product (I = 1, ... , N);
expected sales (for entire budget period) as

a percentage (in decimals $1.00 = 100\%$) from "previous" sales quantities in product units.

(1–3)   <u>SK(MØ)</u>   *sales coefficient,*

expressing the sales quantity (in product units) of month MØ (MØ $= 1, \ldots, 12$) as a percentage of the sales quantity for the entire budget period (MØ $= 13$). Hence $SK(13) = 1.00$. (Under some circumstances a model would be required that provides a separate coefficient SK(I, MØ) for each product.)

(1–4) $\boxed{\text{SP(I)}}$ *sales price,*

in dollars (actually $000' with respect to our model; the same holds for all subsequent variables expressible in dollars) per product unit (product prices are assumed to be constant during the budget period; not so, material prices).

(1–5)   SQ(I, MØ)   *sales quantity,*

in product units per product item;

$$SQ(I, 13) = \sum_{M\emptyset=1}^{12} SQ(I, M\emptyset).$$

(1–6)   SV(I, MØ)   *sales volume,*

in dollars per product;

$$SV(I, 13) = \sum_{M\emptyset=1}^{12} SV(I, M\emptyset)$$

$$SV(I, M\emptyset) = SQ(I, M\emptyset) * SP(I).$$

(1–7)   TSQ(MØ)   *total sales quantity,*

$$TSQ(M\emptyset) = \sum_{I=1}^{N} SQ(I, M\emptyset),$$
$$M\emptyset = 1, \ldots, 13.$$

Obviously this variable and the next are meaningful only where all products have common unit denominators.

(1–8)   TPSQ   *total previous sales quantity,*

in product units;

$$TPSQ = \sum_{I=1}^{N} PSQ(I).$$

In many situations the quantities of different product items may not be additive; then TPSQ becomes meaningless.

(1–9)   TSV (MØ)   *total sales volume,*
in product units;

$$TSV(MØ) = \sum_{I=1}^{N} SV(I, MØ),$$
$$MØ = 1, \ldots, 13;$$
$$TSV(13) = \sum_{Mo=1}^{12} TSV(MØ).$$

Basic hypotheses and equations of the sales budget:
(1–i) $SQ(I, 13) = PSQ(I) * SI(I), \quad I = 1, \ldots, N.$
(1–ii) $SQ(I, MØ) = SQ(I,13) * SK(MØ), I = 1, \ldots, N, MØ = 1, \ldots, 12.$
(1–iii) $SV(I, MØ) = SQ(I, MØ) * SP(I), I = 1, \ldots, N, MØ = 1, \ldots, 13.$

(2) Production Budget:
(2–1)   APQ(I, MØ)   *Adjusted Production Quantity,*
in (equivalent whole) product units;
$APQ(I, MØ) = PQ(I, 13) * PKN(I, MØ),$
$PKN(I, MØ) \ldots$ see (2–6);
compare $APQ(I, MØ), \quad I = 1, \ldots, N,$
$MØ = 1, \ldots, 13,$ with $PQ(I, MØ),$ see
(2–7) and (2–ii). It is important to realize
that $APQ(I, MØ) = PQ(I, MØ)$ if the
original *inventory* calculation yields $BI(I, MØ) \geq PMI(I)$, and if no adjustments for
earlier production has to be made;[20]
$$I = 1, \ldots, N,$$
$$MØ = 1, \ldots, 13.$$
If the original calculation indicates some
inventories below the minimum, automatic
adjustments are made such that the original set of production coefficients PK(I,
MØ)—see (2–5)—is replaced by a *new*
set of production coefficients PKN(I, MØ)
—see (2–6)—which, though it is a set of
parameters, is not an input but is generated by the computer. It is always true
that
$$APQ(I, 13) = PQ(I, 13).$$

(2–2)   BI(I, MØ)   *beginning inventory* of finished and partly
finished goods in (equivalent whole) prod-
uct units. No distinction is made here between partly finished goods and finished
products; $MØ = 1, \ldots, 13.$

---

[20] The minimum inventory level of product $I = 1, \ldots, N$ is represented by the symbol PMI(I) and listed as a parameter (see 2–13).

| BI(I, 1) | expresses the inventory of product I $(I = 1, \ldots, N)$ at the beginning of the *first* month (January). |

| BI(I, 13) | expresses beginning inventory of period subsequent to budget period. |

(2–3)   EI(I, MØ)   *ending inventory* of finished and partly finished goods
in equivalent whole units at the *end* of month MØ.

$$EI(I, M\emptyset) = BI(I, NM), \quad NM = M\emptyset + 1$$
$$M\emptyset = 1, \ldots, 12$$
$$NM = 2, \ldots, 13.$$

(2–4)   PC(I, MØ)   *production cost* (cost to manufacture); in dollars per product quantity;

$$PC(I, 13) = PUC(I, 13) * APQ(I, 13)$$

$$= \sum_{M\emptyset=1}^{12} PC(I, M\emptyset), PUC(I, M\emptyset) \ldots \text{see } (2\text{–}8)$$

$$PC(I, M\emptyset) = \sum_{K=1}^{KP} DLC(I, K, MO) +$$

$$+ \sum_{J=1}^{JJ} RMR(I, J, M\emptyset) * UCM(J, M\emptyset) +$$

$$+ \sum_{K=1}^{KP} TF\emptyset A(K, M\emptyset) * DLC(I, K,$$

$$M\emptyset)/TDLC(K, M\emptyset).$$

(2–5)   PK(I, MØ)   *production coefficient;* expressing the production quantity of each month as a percentage (in decimals: $PK(I, 13) = 1.00$, $I = 1, \ldots, N$) of the total production of the budgeting period as *originally* assumed. This coefficient might lead to inventories below a prescribed minimum; if the latter is the case, a *new* series of production coefficients PKN(I, MØ)—see (2–6)—observing these minimum inventories, is automatically computed. If, however, the minimum inventory has originally been respected by PK(I, MØ), then the value of this parameter becomes automatically the value of PKN(I, MØ) which is the production coefficient used from this stage on.

(2–6)   PKN(I, MØ)   *new production coefficient;*
$$PKN(I, M\emptyset) = PK(I, M\emptyset), \quad I = 1, \ldots, N;$$
$$M\emptyset = 1, \ldots, 13, \text{ unless } PK(I, M\emptyset) \text{ yields}$$

inventory figures below the minimum PMI(I) (see comments to 2–1 and 2–5). The rule for computing PKN(I, MØ), I = 1, ..., N and MØ = 1, ..., 12 (PKN (I, 13) = PK(I, 13) = 1.00) can be described as follows:

The computer tests whether the planned production (i.e., the original production coefficients) provides an ending inventory above the desired minimum. If the ending inventory is not above the minimum, the production will be adjusted upwards (by means of a new production coefficient) until the inventory is at the minimum level. The amount of adjustment is noted and then compensated for by a reduction of production of the subsequent month(s) if so permissible.

If the ending inventory is above the minimum, a check is made to see whether production adjustments are to be made because of production changes in preceding months; if yes, then production is reduced by an amount that compensates for an eventual production increase incurred in preceding months until the minimum inventory level might be reached. The adjustment again is noted for future reference. The result is an adjusted production plan based on "adjusted production coefficients" which secure minimum inventories (in equivalent whole units) for all product items and months.

(2–7)   PQ(I, MØ)   *production quantity;*
in (equivalent whole) product units

$$PQ(I, 13) = \sum_{MO=1}^{12} PQ(I, MØ)$$

(2–8)   PUC(I, MØ)   *product unit cost;*
          $\boxed{PUCØ(I)}$ in dollars per (equivalent whole) product unit (average during month or year)
PUC(I, MØ) = [PC(I, MØ) + PUC(I, LM) * BI(I, MØ)]/[(APQ(I, MØ) + + BI(I, MØ)], for MØ = 2, ..., 12;
PUC(I, 1) = [PC(I, 1) + PUCØ(I) * * BI(I, 1)]/[APQ(I, 1) + BI(I, 1)];

$$PUC(I, 13) = \left[\sum_{M\emptyset=1}^{12} PC(I, M\emptyset) + \right.$$

$$\left. + PUC\emptyset(I) * BI(I, 1) \right] / [APQ(I, 13)$$

$$+ BI(I, 1)].$$

The unit cost (per equivalent whole unit) of the finished and partly finished goods for product I $(I = 1, \ldots, N)$ at the *beginning* of the budget period (in our model: January 1) must be given. It would be appropriate to assign the symbol PUC(I, 0) to this unit cost, but FORTRAN does not permit a zero as value of an index symbol. For this reason and others (e.g., efficiency in storage space) we have chosen the symbol PUC$\emptyset$(I) to designate the unit cost of product I at the beginning of the budget period (beginning of January); see also (2–iii). The calculation of PUC(I, M$\emptyset$) is carried out in the *second part* of the production subroutine which can be computed only after the figures of the factory overhead cost budget are available.

(2-9) TBI(M$\emptyset$)
total beginning inventory (finished and partly finished goods); in (equivalent whole) product units;

$$TBI(M\emptyset) = \sum_{I=1}^{N} BI(I, M\emptyset),$$
$$M\emptyset = 1, \ldots, 13.$$

For the *evaluation* of this inventory see (9–40: TFI(M$\emptyset$)).

(2-10) TEI(M$\emptyset$)
total ending inventory; in (equivalent whole) product units at the *end* of month M$\emptyset$;

$$TEI(M\emptyset) = \sum_{I=1}^{N} EI(I, M\emptyset),$$
$$M\emptyset = 1, \ldots, 12.$$

(2-11) TPC(M$\emptyset$)
total product cost (cost to manufacture); in dollars;
$$TPC(M\emptyset) = TPV(M\emptyset) + VMI(M\emptyset) - VMI(NM) + TLC(M\emptyset) + F\emptyset(M\emptyset),$$
$$M\emptyset = 1, \ldots, 12;$$
$$TPC(13) = TPV(13) + VMI(1) - VMI(13) + TLC(13) + F\emptyset(13),$$
see (3–11), (3–13), (4–5), and (5–7);

$$TPC(M\emptyset) = \sum_{I=1}^{N} PC(I, M\emptyset),$$
$$M\emptyset = 1, \ldots, 13.$$

(2–12)　TPQ(M$\emptyset$)　　　*total product quantity;*
in (equivalent whole) product units;

$$TPQ(M\emptyset) = \sum_{I=1}^{N} PQ(I, M\emptyset),$$
$$M\emptyset = 1, \ldots, 13.$$

In our model only TPQ(13) is being calculated.

(2–13)　<u>PMI(I)</u>　　　*product (finished and partly finished goods) minimum inventory level;*
in equivalent whole units.

Basic hypotheses and equations of the production budget:

(2–i)　　$PQ(I, M\emptyset) = PQ(I, 13) * PK(I, M\emptyset)$
$I = 1, \ldots, N; M\emptyset = 1, \ldots, 12.$

(2–ii)　　$APQ(I, M\emptyset) = PQ(I, 13) * PKN(I, M\emptyset).$
$I = 1, \ldots, N; M\emptyset = 1, \ldots, 12.$

(2–iii)　　$PUC(I, 13) = [PC(I, 13) + PUC\emptyset(I) * BI(I, 1)]/[APQ(I, 13) + BI(I, 1)]$
$PUC(I, M\emptyset) = [PC(I, LM) + PUC(I, LM) * BI(I, M\emptyset)]/[APQ(I, M\emptyset) + BI(I, M\emptyset)],$
$I = 1, \ldots, N; M\emptyset = 2, \ldots, 12.$
Obviously this leads to a comparatively crude average costing procedure which could be refined by a hypothesis that takes account of the individual cost components of the beginning inventory, etc.

(2–iv)　　$PQ(I, 13) = BI(I, 13) + SQ(I, 13) - BI(I, 1)$

(3) Materials Budget:

(3–1)　　CMR(J, M$\emptyset$)　　　*cost of material requirement;* in dollars;

$$CMR(J, M\emptyset) = \sum_{I=1}^{N} RMR(I, J, M\emptyset) * UCM(J, M\emptyset).$$

(3–2)　　<u>PMC(J, M$\emptyset$)</u>　　　*purchases: monthly coefficient;*
expressing the *originally* planned, monthly purchases (in material units) of raw material item J (J = 1, \ldots, JJ) as a percentage (in decimals) of the total purchase per item J during the budget period (M$\emptyset$ = 1, \ldots, 13; PMC (J, 13) = 1.00). The *ultimately* planned percentual purchases are reflected in PMCN(J, M$\emptyset$) \ldots see (3–15).

(3-3)   <u>PMK(I, J)</u>   *purchases; material coefficient;*
expressing units of raw material $J(J = 1, \ldots, JJ)$ per unit of product I $(I = 1, \ldots, N)$.

(3-4)   PRM(J, M$\emptyset$)   *purchases of raw material;*
in material units;

$$PRM(J, 13) = \sum_{M\emptyset=1}^{12} PRM(J, M\emptyset),$$
$$M\emptyset = 1, \ldots, 13.$$

(3-5)   RMI(J, M$\emptyset$)

     RMI(J, 1)

raw material inventory at beginning of month; in material units; $M\emptyset = 1, \ldots, 13$ RMI(J, 13) ... material inventory at beginning of period subsequent to budget period. Analogous to the finished and partly finished goods inventory, there exists a feedback control with regard to raw material inventory. The purchasing of raw material is here assumed to follow a seasonal pattern, depending on prices, etc., while the raw material consumption depends on the production activity in the individual months. If one or the other original purchase coefficient PMC(J, M$\emptyset$) fails to secure the raw material minimum inventory RMMI(I)—see (3-16)—then the program generates new purchase coefficients PMCN(J, M$\emptyset$) in the same way as explained in item (2-6).

(3-6)   RMR(I, J, M$\emptyset$)   *raw material requirement;*
in units of item $J(J = 1, \ldots, JJ)$ in department 1 for product $I(I = 1, \ldots, N)$ (where the raw-material input occurs not only in the first but in various departments, a fourth dimension would have to be added; this creates difficulties under FORTRAN—unless the breakdown into product items is relinquished—but is feasible under some other computer languages). Another possibility of circumventing this difficulty is to set up a variable that specifies the material requirement with regard to the following three dimensions (J, K, M$\emptyset$), omitting a breakdown into product items.

(3–7)   TCM(MØ)   *total cost of material* (consumed in production); in dollars; see also (8–ii).

$$TCM(MØ) = \sum_{J=1}^{JJ} CMR(J, MØ),$$
$$MØ = 1, \ldots, 13;$$

$$TCM(13) \quad = \sum_{MØ=1}^{12} TCM(MØ).$$

(3–8)   TMI(MØ)   *total material inventory* (beginning inventory); in material units;

$$TMI(MØ = \sum_{J=1}^{JJ} RMI(J, MØ);$$
$$MØ = 1, \ldots, 13.$$

For the *evaluation* of this inventory see (3–13).

(3–9)   TMR(J, MØ)   *total material requirement;*
                              in material units;

$$TMR(J, MØ) = \sum_{I=1}^{N} RMR(I, J, MØ),$$
$$MØ = 1, \ldots, 13;$$

$$TMR(J, 13) \quad = \sum_{MØ=1}^{12} TMR(J, MØ).$$

(3–10) TPM(MØ)   *total purchases of materials;*
                              in material units;

$$TPM(MØ) = \sum_{J=1}^{JJ} APRM(J, MØ),$$
$$MØ = 1, \ldots, 13;$$

$$TPM(13) \quad = \sum_{MØ=1}^{12} TPM(MØ)$$

$$= \sum_{J=!}^{JJ} TMR(J, 13).$$

For   APRM(J,   MØ)...see   (3–14).

Meaningful only where material items have a common (nonmonetary) denominator.

(3–11) TPV(M∅)   *total purchases of material—value;*
in dollars per month

$$TPV(M\emptyset) = \sum_{J=1}^{JJ} APRM(J,M\emptyset) *$$
$$* UCM(J, M\emptyset), \qquad M\emptyset = 1,\ldots,12;$$

$$TPV(13) = \sum_{M\emptyset=1}^{12} TPV(M\emptyset).$$

(3–12) UCM(J, M∅)   *unit cost of material;*

UCM∅(J)   in dollars per unit of material item J (J = 1,…,JJ) per month [M∅ = 1,…,12— in contrast to the sales prices of the products which are assumed constant over the budget period, the material costs in our model are assumed to vary from month to month—the unit cost of the material beginning inventory (January 1) is designated by UCM∅(J) compare (2–8)].

(3–13) VMI(M∅)   *Value of (direct) material inventory;*
in dollars;
VMI(NM) = VMI(M∅) + TPV(M∅) −
− TCM(M∅),   M∅ = 1,…,12;

$$VMI(I) = \sum_{J=1}^{JJ} RMI(J,1) * UCM\emptyset(J),$$
$$NM = M\emptyset + 1.$$

(3–14) APRM(J, M∅)   *adjusted purchases of raw material;*
in material units;

$$APRM(J,13) = \sum_{M\emptyset=1}^{12} APRM(J,M\emptyset)$$
$$= PRM(J,13);$$
APRM(J, M∅) = PMCN(J, M∅)*
* APRM(J, 13),   M∅ = 1,…,13.

(3–15) PMCN(J, M∅)   *purchases, monthly coefficient—new;*
PMCN(J, M∅) = PMC(J, M∅),
M∅ = 1,…,12;
unless PMC(J, M∅) yields raw material inventory figures below the minimum RMMI(J). The rule for computing PMCN(J, M∅) can be extracted from the commentary to item (2–6) by substituting the word "purchase" for the term "production." Note that
PMCN(J, 13) = PMC(J, 13) = 1.00.

(3–16)   RMMI(J)   *raw material minimum inventory level;*
                                    in material units.

Basic hypotheses and equations of the material budget:
(3–i) $RMR(I, J, M\emptyset) = APQ(I, M\emptyset) * PMK(I, J);$
                      $M\emptyset = 1, \ldots, 13$ (for 3–i to 3–iii);
(3–ii) $PRM(J, M\emptyset) = TMR(J, 13) * PMC(J, M\emptyset)$
              $APRM(J, M\emptyset) = TMR(J, 13) * PMCN(J, M\emptyset);$
(3–iii) $RMI(J, M\emptyset) = RMI(J, LM) + PRM(J, LM) -$
                          $- TMR(J, LM), LM = M\emptyset - 1,$
(3–iv) $VMI(M\emptyset) = VMI(M\emptyset) + TPV(M\emptyset) - TCM(M\emptyset),$
                          $M\emptyset = 2, \ldots, 13.$

(4) Labor Budget:
(4–1)   DLC(I, K, M$\emptyset$)   *direct labor cost;*
                                    in dollars per product item I (I = 1,
                                    ..., N), department K (K = 1, ..., KK)
                                    and month M$\emptyset$,   M$\emptyset$ = 1, ..., 13;
                                    DLC(I, K, M$\emptyset$) = SLC(K) * SLH(I, K,
                                    M$\emptyset$), see (4–ii);

$$DLC(I, K, 13) = \sum_{M\emptyset=1}^{12} DLC(I, K, M\emptyset).$$

(4–2)   SLC(K)   *standard labor cost;*
                                    in dollars *per hour* of direct labor type per
                                    department.
                                    Our model assumes only one type of direct
                                    labor per department, hence the index K
                                    (K = 1, ..., KK) identifies the department
                                    as well as the type of labor—at least in-
                                    asmuch as producing departments are
                                    concerned. Where this assumption does
                                    not hold, a further, separate, dimension
                                    for direct labor types has to be added.

(4–3)   SLH(I, K, M$\emptyset$)   *standard labor hours,*
         SLH(I, K, 13)   hours per product I (I = 1, ..., N), de-
                                    partment K (K = 1, ..., KK) and month
                                    M$\emptyset$ (M$\emptyset$ = 1, ..., 13); see (4–i).
                                    Although K = 1, ..., KK and KK is the
                                    number of all departments (service de-
                                    partments included) *the value* of SLH(I,
                                    K, 13) for those K's which refer to service
                                    departments (in our model the last two
                                    K's) *will be zero.*

$$\sum_{M\emptyset=1}^{12} SLH(I, K, M\emptyset) = SLH(I, K, 13).$$

(4–4)   TDLC(K, MØ)   *total departmental labor cost* (direct labor only), in dollars;

$$TDLC(K, MØ) = \sum_{I=1}^{N} DLC(I, K, MØ);$$
$$K = 1, \dots, KK,$$

$$TDLC(K, 13) = \sum_{MØ=1}^{12} TDLC(K, MØ),$$
$$MØ = 1, \dots, 13.$$

(4–5)   TLC(MØ)   *total labor cost* (direct labor only); in dollars per month;

$$TLC(MØ) = \sum_{K=1}^{KK} TDLC(K, MØ),$$
$$MØ = 1, \dots, 13$$

$$TLC(13) = \sum_{MØ=1}^{12} TLC(MØ).$$

(4–6)   TLCP(I)   *total labor cost per product* (direct labor only); in dollars per product item per year;

$$TLCP(I) = \sum_{K=1}^{KK} DLC(I, K, 13);$$

Basic hypotheses and equations of the labor budget:
(4–i) $SLH(I, K, MØ) = SLH(I, K, 13) * PKN(I, MØ),$
$$I = 1, \dots, N,$$
$$K = 1, \dots, KK,$$
$$MØ = 1, \dots, 12,$$
$$PKN(I, MØ) \dots \text{see } (2–6);$$
(4–ii) $DLC(I,K,MØ) = SLC(K) * SLH(I,K,MØ),$
$$I = 1, \dots, N,$$
$$K = 1, \dots, KK,$$
$$MØ = 1, \dots, 13.$$

(5) Factory Overhead Cost Budget:
Although our fictitious enterprise basically is oriented toward process costing, some features of job-costing have been incorporated to make this model *more* suitable as a "prototype" from which projected process costing as well as job order systems can be evolved. Thus this subbudget is concerned primarily with the distribution of the factory overhead costs to the individual departments, and with the proration of the service departments, costs to the producing departments; this may later facilitate connecting the budget with a *standard cost system*.

In allocating the costs of service departments to producing departments and other service departments we take into consideration the possible interdependence of the service departments among themselves. In contrast to the oversimplified approach of traditional cost accounting we allocate service departmental costs among service departments recursively until, in the worst case, less than 0.1 per cent (of the costs to be distributed) is unallocated; this residual is distributed uniformly to the service departments involved.

In the following the symbol KP represents the number of producing departments, and thus refers to the *last* producing department; KI may refer to any of the service departments; KK is the number of *all* departments and occasionally the designation of the *last* service department.

(5-1)   DFF(K, L)   *departmental fixed factory overheads* for entire budget period;
in dollars per department K (K = 1, ..., KK) and per factory overhead cost item L (L = 1, ..., LL).

(5-2)   DF$\emptyset$(K)   *departmental fixed* factory *overheads* for all cost items and entire budget period; in dollars;

$$DF\emptyset(K) = \sum_{L=1}^{LL} DFF(K, L),$$

$$K = 1, \ldots, KK.$$

(5-3)   DVF(K, L, M$\emptyset$)   *departmental variable factory overheads;*
in dollars per department, cost item and month. (In our model we assume four producing and two service departments; we also assume that no variable factory overhead costs accumulate in the service departments.)

$$DVF(K, L, 13) = \sum_{M\emptyset=1}^{12} DVF(K, L, M\emptyset),$$

$$DVF(K, L, M\emptyset) = VFR(K, L) * TDLC$$
$$(K, M\emptyset), \quad \text{see (4-4), see (5-23).}$$

(5-4)   DV$\emptyset$(K, M$\emptyset$)   *departmental variable overheads* for all factory cost items;
in dollars per department and month;

$$DV\emptyset(K, M\emptyset) = \sum_{L=1}^{LL} DVF(K, L, M\emptyset),$$

$$K = 1, \ldots, KK,$$
$$M\emptyset = 1, \ldots, 12;$$

$$DV\emptyset(K, 13) = \sum_{M\emptyset=1}^{12} DV\emptyset(K, M\emptyset).$$

(5–5)   FF∅(M∅)   *fixed factory overheads* for all departments and cost items, in dollars per month;

$$FF∅(13) \quad = \sum_{K=1}^{KK} \sum_{L=1}^{LL} DFF(K, L),$$

$$FF∅(M∅) = \sum_{K=1}^{KK} \sum_{L=1}^{LL} DFF(K, L)/12.$$

(5–6) $\boxed{FFR(K, L)}$ *fixed factory* overhead *rate;* expressing the percentual distribution of the fixed factory overheads (per cost item) to the individual departments.

(5–7)   F∅(M∅)   *factory overheads,* in dollars per month;

$$F∅(M∅) = \sum_{L=1}^{LL} F∅C(L, M∅),$$

$$F∅(13) \quad = \sum_{M∅=1}^{12} F∅(M∅).$$

(5–8)   F∅̇B(K, L, M∅)   *factory overheads* before proration of service departments (restricted to producing departments), in dollars per department, cost item, and month;

$$F∅B(K, L, 13) = \sum_{M∅=1}^{12} F∅B(K, L, M∅).$$

(5–9)   F∅C(L, M∅)   *factory overhead cost* for all departments, in dollars per cost item and month;

$$F∅C(L, M∅) = \sum_{K=1}^{KP} F∅B(K, L, M∅) +$$

$$+ \sum_{K=KP+1}^{KK} F∅S(K, L, M∅),$$

producing departments: $K = 1, \ldots, KP$; service departments: $K = KP + 1, \ldots, KK$;

(5–10) $\underline{F∅K(K, KI, M∅)}$ *factory overhead coefficient* for prorating service department totals to producing departments;
K department to be charged with pro-rated amount, $(K = 1, \ldots, KK)$;
KI service department to be credited with prorated amount,
$$(KI = KP + 1, \ldots, KK).$$

(5–11) $F\emptyset P(K, M\emptyset)$

factory overheads prorated from service departments;
K refers to department receiving prorated amount, $(K = 1, \ldots, KK)$.

First, we take the service department costs $TF\emptyset S(KI, M\emptyset)$ and allocate them by means of the coefficients $F\emptyset K$ (K, KI, $M\emptyset$) to the variables $F\emptyset P(K, M\emptyset)$. But since service departments may serve each other, provision must be made for further proration of the residuals. These remaining, unallocated costs are found in $F\emptyset P(KI, M\emptyset)$, $KI = KP + 1, \ldots, KK$. Taking one service department at a time, we allocate as described; this being done $F\emptyset P(KI, M\emptyset)$ is set to zero for each service department. Then we test whether one per cent or more (of the total costs accumulated in the pertinent service department) is remaining. If yes, the second step is repeated. If not, the residual is distributed uniformly to the departments involved.

(5–12) $F\emptyset S(K, L, M\emptyset)$

factory overheads of service departments (before proration);
in dollars per department, cost item, and month;

$$F\emptyset S(K, L, 13) = \sum_{M\emptyset=1}^{12} F\emptyset S(K, L, M\emptyset).$$

(5–13) $\boxed{FPF(L)}$

fixed part of factory overheads;
in dollars per cost item and entire budget period.

(5–14) $TF\emptyset(M\emptyset)$

total factory overheads;
in dollars;

$$TF\emptyset(M\emptyset) = \sum_{K=1}^{KK} TF\emptyset A(K, M\emptyset).$$

(5–15) $TF\emptyset B(K, M\emptyset)$

total factory overheads before proration,
in dollars per department;

$$TF\emptyset B(K, M\emptyset) = \sum_{L=1}^{LL} F\emptyset B(K, L, M\emptyset).$$

(5–16) TFF

total fixed factory overheads for all cost items and entire budget period, in dollars;

$$TFF = \sum_{L=1}^{LL} FPF(L).$$

(5–17)   TFØA(K, MØ)   *total factory overheads after proration* of service departments, in dollars per (producing) department and month;

$$TFØA(K, MØ) = TFØB(K, MØ) +$$

$$+ \sum_{K=1}^{KP} FØP(K, MØ);$$

$$TFØA(K, 13) = \sum_{MØ=1}^{12} TFØA(K, MØ).$$

(5–18)   TFØS(K, MØ)   *total factory overheads of service* departments, in dollars per (service) department and month;
       or
      TFØS(KI, MØ)

$$TFØS(K, MØ) = \sum_{L=1}^{LL} FØS(K, L, MØ),$$

$$TFØS(K, 13) = \sum_{MØ=1}^{12} TFØS(K, MØ).$$

(5–19)   TTV   *total of total variable* factory overheads (for all cost items, departments and entire budget period), in dollars;

$$TTV = \sum_{L=1}^{LL} TVF(L).$$

(5–20)   TVF(L)   *total variable factory overheads* per cost item, in dollars;

$$TVF(L) = \sum_{K=1}^{KK} DVF(K, L, 13).$$

(5–21)   TVR(K)   *total variable factory overhead rate* per department, in dollars;

$$TVR(K) = \sum_{L=1}^{LL} VFR(K, L).$$

(5–22)   VFØ(MØ)   *variable factory overheads*, in dollars per month;

$$VFØ(MØ) = \sum_{K=1}^{KK} DVØ(K, MØ),$$

$$MØ = 1, \ldots, 12;$$

$$VF\emptyset(13) \quad = \sum_{M\emptyset=1}^{12} VF\emptyset(M\emptyset).$$

(5–23) $\boxed{VFR(K, \ L)}$ *variable factory overhead rate* per department and cost item, in dollars per labor dollar;

Basic hypotheses and equations of the factory overhead budget:

(5–i) $DFF(K, L) = FPF(L) * FFR(K, L).$

(5–ii) $DVF(K, L, M\emptyset) = VFR(K, L) * TDLC(K, M\emptyset)$

$$TDLC(K, M\emptyset)\ldots \text{see } (4\text{-}4).$$

(5–iii) $$F\emptyset C(L, M\emptyset) = \sum_{K=1}^{KK} [DVF(K, L, M\emptyset) + DFF(K, L)/12]$$

$$= \sum_{K=1}^{KP} F\emptyset B(K, L, M\emptyset) + \sum_{K=KP+1}^{KK} F\emptyset S(K, L, M\emptyset);$$

$$\left.\begin{array}{l} F\emptyset B(K, L, M\emptyset) \\ \text{or} \\ F\emptyset S(K, L, M\emptyset) \end{array}\right\} = [DFF(K, L)/12] + DVF(K, L, M\emptyset).$$

(5–iv) $$TF\emptyset A(K, M\emptyset) = TF\emptyset B(K, M\emptyset) + \sum_{K=1}^{KP} F\emptyset P(K, M\emptyset).$$

Obviously it would be feasible to base the variable factory overhead rate (and hereby the main hypothesis) on labor hours, machine hours, etc., instead of choosing labor costs as a basis.

(6) Operating Expense Budget:

(6–1) $\boxed{F\emptyset E(M)}$ *fixed operating expenses;* in dollars per operating cost item M
$$(M = 1, \ldots, MM).$$

(6–2) $\emptyset E(M, M\emptyset)$ *operating expenses* (total); in dollars per operating cost item;
$$\emptyset E(M, M\emptyset) = V\emptyset E(M, M\emptyset) + + [F\emptyset E(M)/12].$$

(6–3) $\underline{\emptyset EK(I, M)}$ *operating expense coefficient* expressing a particular operating expense in per cent of the sales value of a specific product item.

(6–4) $TF\emptyset E$ *total fixed operating expenses,* in dollars per entire budget period;

$$TF\emptyset E = \sum_{M=1}^{MM} F\emptyset E(M).$$

(6–5) $T\emptyset E(M\emptyset)$ *total operating expenses,*
in dollars per month;

$$T\emptyset E(M\emptyset) = \sum_{M=1}^{MM} \emptyset E(M, M\emptyset),$$
$$M\emptyset = 1, \ldots, 12,$$

$$T\emptyset E(13) \quad = \sum_{M\emptyset=1}^{12} T\emptyset E(M\emptyset).$$

(6–6) $TV\emptyset E(M\emptyset)$ *total variable operating expenses* per month,
in dollars;

$$TV\emptyset E(M\emptyset) = \sum_{M=1}^{MM} V\emptyset E(M, M\emptyset),$$
$$M\emptyset = 1, \ldots, 12,$$

$$TV\emptyset E(13) \quad = \sum_{M\emptyset=1}^{12} TV\emptyset E(M\emptyset).$$

(6–7) $TP\emptyset E(M)$ *total period operating expenses,*
in dollars per operating cost item;

$$TP\emptyset E(M) = \sum_{M\emptyset=1}^{12} \emptyset E(M, M\emptyset),$$
$$M = 1, \ldots, MM$$

(6–8) $V\emptyset E(M, M\emptyset)$ *variable operating expenses,*
in dollars per cost item and month;

Basic hypotheses and equations of the operating expense budget:

(6–i) $$V\emptyset E(M, M\emptyset) = \sum_{I=1}^{N} SV(I, M\emptyset) \overline{*} \emptyset EK(I, M), SV(I, M\emptyset)$$
$$\ldots \text{ see } (1\text{–}6).$$

(6–ii) $$T\emptyset E(13) = TF\emptyset E + \sum_{I=1}^{N} \sum_{M=1}^{MM} \emptyset EK(I, M) * SV(I, 13).$$

(7) Cash Budget:
(7–1)   <u>AC1</u>   *accounts receivable collection coefficient—for
sales of last month,* collectible during current
month,
in per cent of receivables outstanding for
less than or equal to one month.

(7-2)   <u>AC2</u>   *accounts receivable collection coefficient—for*
                                   sales past one month;
                                   in per cent of receivables outstanding for
                                   more than one month, collectible during
                                   current month.

(7-3)   ARC(Mϕ)   *accounts receivable collection;*
                                   in dollars per month;

$$ARC(M\phi) = AC1*TSVD + AC2*TSVN,$$
$$M\phi = 1$$
$$ARC(M\phi) = AC1*TSV(LM) + AC2*$$
$$*TSVD, M\phi = 2;$$
$$ARC(M\phi) = AC1*TSV(LM) +$$
$$+ AC2*TSV(MBL);$$

$$TSVD\ldots\text{see } (7\text{--}22)$$
$$TSVN\ldots\text{see } (7\text{--}23)$$
$$TSV(M\phi)\ldots\text{see } (1\text{--}9)$$
$$LM = M\phi - 1$$
$$MBL = M\phi - 2$$
$$M\phi = 3,\ldots,12$$

$$ARC(13) = \sum_{M\phi=1}^{12} ARC(M\phi)$$

Such a formula assumes that accounts
older than one to two months are not so-
licitable; it also requires a breakdown of
the accounts receivables at the beginning
of the year with respect to their "age"
(a more refined "aging process" is
obviously feasible and would require a
slightly more complicated formula).

(7-4)   CHB(Mϕ)   *cash on hand and in bank at the beginning of*
         | CHB(1) | *month;* in dollars;

$$CHB(NM) = CHB(M\phi) + TCR(M\phi) - TC\phi(M\phi),$$
$$M\phi = 1,\ldots 12,$$
$$NM = M\phi + 1;$$
$$CHB(13) = CHB(1) + TCR(13) -$$
$$- TC\phi(13)$$
$$= CHB(12) + TCR(12) -$$
$$- TC\phi(12);$$
$$TC\phi(M\phi)\ldots\text{see } (7\text{--}17),$$
$$TCR(M\phi)\ldots\text{see } (7\text{--}18).$$

The boundary conditions of this variable
are as follows:
CHB(NM) $\leq$ CASMAX ... see   (7-20),
and CHB(NM) $\geq$ CASMIN ... see (7-21).
An adaptive control system allocates any

eventual excess amount to, or replenishes any shortage from, short-term securities. That means the excess amount or shortage $SSM(M\phi)$—which may become negative —(see also 7–16 and 9–34) changes $SS(NM)$, $M\phi = 1,\ldots 12$ as long as the latter is nonnegative. Thus, the *cash maximum* (CASMAX) is an *absolute* boundary condition while the cash minimum (CASMIN) is relative with regard to the portfolio state of "short-term securities." If this portfolio is exhausted, $CHB(M\phi)$ may drop below the *relative Minimum* and even become negative (bank credit). The latter indicates the need for serious concern on the part of the managers of the financial plan.

(7–5) $CRI(M\phi)$ *cash receipts of interest on short-term securities,* in dollars per month;

$$CRI(6) \quad = \sum_{M\phi=1}^{6} SSI(M\phi),$$
$$SSI(M\phi)\ldots \text{see } (8\text{–}12)$$

$$CRI(12) \quad = \sum_{M\phi=7}^{12} SSI(M\phi),$$

$$CRI(M\phi) = 0 \text{ for } M\phi = 1,\ldots, 5,$$
$$7,\ldots, 11.$$

$$CRI(13) \quad = \sum_{M\phi=1}^{12} CRI(M\phi)$$
$$= CRI(6) + CRI(12).$$

Our model assumes a semiannual receipt of interest (during June and December).

(7–6) $CS(M\phi)$ *cash sales,* in dollars;
$$CS(M\phi) = CSC * TSV(M\phi),$$
$$M\phi = 1,\ldots, 13,$$

$$CS(13) = \sum_{M\phi=1}^{12} CS(M\phi),$$

see also (7–7) and (7–vii),
$$TSV(M\phi)\ldots \text{see } (1\text{–}9).$$

(7–7)   <u>CSC</u>   *cash sales coefficient;* expressing cash sales as a percentage of total sales.

(7–8)   FØF(I, K, MØ)   *factory overheads of finished (and partly finished) goods (inventory);* in dollars per product unit, department, and month;
$$\text{FØF}(I, K, \text{MØ}) = \text{PFK}(K) *$$
$$* \text{DLC}(I, \dot{K}, \text{MØ}),$$
$$K = 1, \dots, KK,$$
$$\text{MØ} = 1, \dots, 13,$$
$$\text{PFK}(K) \dots \text{see } (7\text{–}13),$$
$$\text{DLC}(I, K, \text{MØ}) \dots \text{see } (4\text{–}1).$$

(7–9)   <u>FPC(L, MS)</u>   *factory overhead payments coefficient;*
expressing that percentage of a specific overhead item (L = 1, ..., LL) to be paid during the first month (MS = 1), the second month (MS = 2) or the third month (MS = 3) of occurrence of this expense item. For cost items for which the delay between occurrence and payment is longer (e.g., depreciations), this coefficient becomes zero.   cf. (7–12)

(7–10)   ØCØ(MØ)   *other cash outlays,*
in dollars per month;
$$\text{ØCØ}(\text{MØ}) = \text{RCØ}(\text{MØ}) + \text{SSM}(\text{MØ})$$
if SSM ≥ 0,
$$\text{otherwise} \quad \text{ØCØ}(\text{MØ}) = \text{RCØ}(\text{MØ}),$$
$$\text{MØ} = 1, \dots, 13,$$
$$\text{RCØ}(\text{MØ}) \dots \text{see } (7\text{–}14),$$
$$\text{SSM}(\text{MØ}) \dots \text{see } (7\text{–}16),$$
$$\text{ØCØ}(13) = \sum_{\text{MØ}=1}^{12} \text{ØCØ}.$$

(7–11)   ØCR(MØ)   *other cash receipts,*
in dollars per month;
$$\text{ØCR}(\text{MØ}) = \text{CRI}(\text{MØ}) + \text{RCR}(\text{MØ}) -$$
$$- \text{SSM}(\text{MØ}), \quad \text{if} \quad \text{SS}(\text{NM}) \geq 0 \quad \text{and}$$
SSM < 0,
$$\text{otherwise} \; \text{ØCR}(\text{MØ}) = \text{CRI}(\text{MØ}) +$$
$$+ \text{RCR}(\text{MØ}), \qquad \text{MØ} = 1, \dots, 13,$$
$$\text{CRI}(\text{MØ}) \dots \text{see } (7\text{–}5),$$
$$\text{RCR}(\text{MØ}) \dots \text{see } (7\text{–}15),$$
$$\text{ØCR}(13) = \sum_{\text{MØ}=1}^{12} \text{ØCR}.$$

(7–12)   PE(MØ)   *payroll expenditures,*
in dollars per month;
$$\text{PE}(\text{MØ}) = \sum_{K=1}^{KK} \text{TDLC}(K, \text{MØ}) +$$

$$+ \sum_{L=1}^{L1} FPC(L, 1) * F\emptyset C(L, M\emptyset) +$$

$$+ \sum_{M=1}^{M1} V\emptyset E(M, M\emptyset) +$$

$$+ [F\emptyset E(M)/12],$$
$$M\emptyset = 1, \ldots, 12;$$

(for variables contained in this equation see 4–4, 7–9, 5–9, 7–11, 6–8, and 6–1).

$$PE(13) = \sum_{M\emptyset=1}^{12} PE(M\dot{\emptyset}).$$

Payroll expenditures consist of payment for direct labor plus the first three (L1 = 3) factory overhead cost items and the first two (M1 = 2) operating expense items which all are, in our model, assumed to be indirect labor costs. All labor costs are assumed to be paid in the month of their occurrence.

(7–13)   PFK(K)   *product factory overhead coefficient*;
expressing the standard rate of factory overheads per department as a percentage of the corresponding direct labor cost;
$$PFK(K) = TF\emptyset A(K, 13)/TDLC(K, 13),$$
$$K = 1, \ldots, KK,$$
$$TF\emptyset A(K, 13) \ldots \text{see } (5\text{–}7),$$
$$TDLC(K, 13) \ldots \text{see } (4\text{–}4).$$

(7–14)   RC∅(M∅)   *remaining cash outlays*,
in dollars per month;
not to be confused with "other cash outlays" (see 7–10) with which it may be equal but need not be—the possible difference lying in "short-term securities manipulation" (see 7–16).
$$RC\emptyset(M\emptyset) = SSX(M\emptyset) + PEX(M\emptyset) +$$
$$+ PIX(M\emptyset) + EMX(M\emptyset) +$$
$$+ HLX(M\emptyset) + BFX(M\emptyset) +$$
$$+ \emptyset LI(M\emptyset) + RFE(M\emptyset) +$$
$$+ SLI(M\emptyset),$$
$$M\emptyset = 1, \ldots, 13.$$
For the components of RC∅(M∅) see (9–34), (9–22), (9–26), (9–17), (9–19), (9–13), (8–6), (8–9), and (8–13); most of these variables *may* assume negative values, in such cases the pertinent item

should actually be envisaged as belonging to $RCR(M\emptyset)$ instead of $RC\emptyset(MO)$.

$$RC\emptyset(13) = \sum_{M\emptyset=1}^{12} RC\emptyset(M\emptyset).$$

(7–15) $RCR(M\emptyset)$ *remaining cash receipts,*
in dollars per month;
not to be confused with "other cash receipts" (see 7–11), the difference is in "cash receipts of interest" (see 7–5), and possibly in "short-term securities manipulation" (see 7–16).

$$RCR(M\emptyset) = SLX(M\emptyset) + TLLX(M\emptyset) +$$
$$+ PISX(M\emptyset) + RFR(M\emptyset) +$$
$$+ SCX(M\emptyset),$$
$$M\emptyset = 1,\dots,13.$$

For the components of $RCR(M\emptyset)$ see (9–33), (9–42), (9–25), and (8–10); the first three of these variables *may* assume negative values and should, in such a case, be envisaged as belonging to $RCR(M\emptyset)$ instead of $RC\emptyset(M\emptyset)$.

$$RCR(13) = \sum_{M\emptyset=1}^{12} RCR(M\emptyset).$$

(7–16) $SSM(M\emptyset)$ *short-term securities manipulation,*
in dollars per month;
this is one of the variables in the feedback mechanism regulating the cash within its lower and upper bounds. This variable *can assume negative value;* if $SSM(M\emptyset) \geq 0$ it is a component of $\emptyset C\emptyset(M\emptyset)$—see (7–10); if $SSM(M\emptyset) < 0$ it is a component of $\emptyset CR(M\emptyset)$—see (7–11).

(7–17) $TC\emptyset(MO)$ *total cash outlays,*
in dollars per month;
$$TC\emptyset(M\emptyset) = PE(M\emptyset) + VPE(M\emptyset) +$$
$$+ \emptyset C\emptyset(M\emptyset), \qquad M\emptyset = 1,\dots,13,$$
$$PE(M\emptyset)\dots\text{see } (7\text{–}12),$$
$$VPE(M\emptyset)\dots\text{see } (7\text{–}19),$$
$$\emptyset C\emptyset(M\emptyset)\dots\text{see } (7\text{–}10),$$

$$TC\emptyset(13) = \sum_{M\emptyset=1}^{12} TC\emptyset(M\emptyset).$$

(7–18) $TCR(M\emptyset)$ *total cash receipts,*
in dollars per month;

$$TCR(M\phi) = CS(M\phi) + ARC(M\phi) +$$
$$+ \phi CR(M\phi), \qquad M\phi = 1, \dots 13,$$
$$CS(M\phi) \quad \dots \text{see } (7\text{--}6),$$
$$ARC(M\phi) \dots \text{see } (7\text{--}3),$$
$$\phi RC(M\phi) \dots \text{see } (7\text{--}11),$$

$$TCR(13) = \sum_{M\phi=1}^{12} TC\phi(M\phi).$$

(7–19)   VPE(Mϕ)   *vouchers payable expenditures*
[excluding $\phi C\phi(M\phi)$ and PE(Mϕ)] in dollars per month;

$$VPE(M\phi) = \sum_{J=1}^{JJ} PRMD(J) * UCM\phi(J) +$$

$$+ \sum_{L=L2}^{L3} FPC(L, 1) *$$
$$* F\phi C(L, M\phi) +$$

$$+ \sum_{L=L2}^{L3} FPC(L, 2) * F\phi CD(L) +$$

$$+ \sum_{L=L2}^{L3} FPC(L, 3) * F\phi CN(L) +$$

$$+ \sum_{M=M3}^{M4} \phi E(M, M\phi),$$
$$\text{for } M\phi = 1;$$

$$VPE(M\phi) = \sum_{J=1}^{JJ} APRM(J, LM) *$$
$$* UCM(J, LM) +$$

$$+ \sum_{L=L2}^{L3} FPC(L, 1) * F\phi C(L, M\phi) +$$

$$+ \sum_{L=L2}^{L3} FPC(L, 2) * F\phi C(L, LM) +$$

$$+ \sum_{L=L2}^{L3} FPC(L, 3) * F\phi CD(L) +$$

$$+ \sum_{M=M3}^{M4} \phi E(M, M\phi),$$
$$\text{for } M\phi = 2;$$
$$APRM(M\phi) \dots \text{see } (3\text{--}14)$$

$$F\phi C(L, M\phi) \ldots \text{see} \quad (5\text{--}9)$$
$$F\phi CD(L) \qquad \ldots \text{see} \quad (7\text{--}24)$$
$$F\phi CN(L) \qquad \ldots \text{see} \quad (7\text{--}25)$$
$$FPC(L, M) \quad \ldots \text{see} \quad (7\text{--}9)$$
$$\phi E(M, M\phi) \ldots \text{see} \quad (6\text{--}2)$$
$$PRMD(J) \qquad \ldots \text{see} \quad (3\text{--}4),$$
$$UCM(J, M\phi) \ldots \text{see} \quad (3\text{--}12),$$
$$UCM\phi(J) \qquad \ldots \text{see} \quad (3\text{--}12);$$

$$VPE(M\phi) = \sum_{J=1}^{JJ} APRM(J, LM) *$$
$$* UCM(J, LM) +$$

$$+ \sum_{L=L2}^{L3} FPC(L, 1) * F\phi C(L, M\phi) +$$

$$+ \sum_{L=L2}^{L3} FPC(L, 2) * F\phi C(L, LM) +$$

$$+ \sum_{L=L2}^{L3} FPC(L, 3) *$$
$$* F\phi C(L, MBL) +$$

$$+ \sum_{M=M3}^{M4} \phi E(M, M\phi),$$

$$M\phi = 3, \ldots, 12,$$
$$LM = M\phi - 1,$$
$$MBL = M\phi - 2;$$

$$VPE(13) = \sum_{M\phi=1}^{12} VPE(M\phi).$$

$VPE(M\phi)$ comprehends (1) the payments for the purchases of direct material incurred in the *previous* month, (2) the portions of some factory overhead costs of previous months (see 7–9)—in our model these are the factory overhead cost items four to nine (hence L2 = 4 and L3 = 9; the factory overhead cost items one to three are assumed to be indirect labor costs and the factory overhead cost items ten to twelve are assumed to be depreciation costs), and (3) the operating expense item three, assumed to be paid in the month of occurrence (hence M3 = M4 = 3; operating expense items one and two are assumed to be indirect labor costs and operating expense items four and five are assumed to be depreciation costs).[21]

(7–20) $\underline{\text{CASMAX}}$ *cash maximum level allowed;*
in dollars (or 1,000 of dollars, etc.); it is an "absolute" upper-bound; see commentary to item (7–4).

(7–21) $\underline{\text{CASMIN}}$ *cash minimum level desired;*
in dollars (or 1,000 of dollars, etc.); it is a "relative" lower-bound; see commentary to item (7–4)

(7–22)   TSVD   *total sales value of (past) December;*
in dollars, etc.

(7–23)   TSVN   *total sales value of (past) November;*
in dollars, etc.

(7–24) $\text{F}\phi\text{CD(L)}$ *factory overhead costs of (past) December;*
in dollars per factory overhead cost item,
$$L = 4, \ldots, 9.$$

(7–25) $\text{F}\phi\text{CN(L)}$ *factory overhead cost of (past) November;*
in dollars per factory overhead cost item,
$$L = 4, \ldots, 9.$$

Basic hypotheses and equations of the cash budget:

(7–i) $\text{ARC}(\text{M}\phi) = [\text{AC1} * \text{TSV(LM)}] + [\text{AC2} * \text{TSV(MBL)}]$

(7–ii) $\text{CHB}(\text{M}\phi) = \text{CHB(LM)} + \text{TCR(LM)} - \text{TC}\phi\text{(LM)}.$

(7–iii) $\text{CRI}(\text{M}\phi) = 0, \text{ for M}\phi = 1, \ldots, 5, 7, \ldots, 11.$

(7–iv) $\text{CRI}(6) = \sum_{\text{M}\phi=1}^{6} \text{SSI}(\text{M}\phi) \text{ and CRI}(12) = \sum_{\text{M}\phi=7}^{12} \text{SSI}(\text{M}\phi).$

(7–v) $\text{PFK(K)} = \text{TF}\phi\text{A(K, 13)}/\text{TDLC(K, 13)}.$

(7–vi) $\text{CHB}(\text{M}\phi) \leq \text{CASMAX; excess} =$
$\text{SSM(LM)} > 0, \text{ CHB}(\text{M}\phi) > \text{CASMIN};$
[as long as permissible by SS(LM)];
shortage = SSM(LM) < 0.

(7–vii) $\text{CS}(\text{M}\phi) = \text{CSC} * \text{TSV}(\text{M}\phi),$
$$\text{M}\phi = 1, \ldots, 13.$$

(7–viii) $\text{F}\phi\text{F(I, K, M}\phi) = \text{PFK(K)} * \text{DLC(I, K, M}\phi),$
$$I = 1, \ldots, N,$$
$$K = 1, \ldots, KK,$$
$$\text{M}\phi = 1, \ldots, 13.$$

---

[21]This somewhat unconventional definition of vouchers *payable* and their expenditures (excluding payrolls, fixed asset purchases, etc.) might be justified by the assumption that payroll expenditures as well as other cash outlays are immediately paid when incurred.

$$(7\text{-ix}) \quad PE(M\phi) = \sum_{K=1}^{KK} TDLC(K, M\phi) + \left\{ \sum_{L=1}^{L1} [FPC(L, 1) * \right.$$

$$* F\phi C(L, M\phi)] + \sum_{M=1}^{M1} \{V\phi E(M, \dot{M}\phi) + [F\phi E(M)/12]\},$$

$$M\phi = 1, \dots, 13.$$

$$(7\text{-x}) \quad VPE(M\phi) = \sum_{J=1}^{JJ} APRM(J, LM) * UCM(J, LM) +$$

$$+ \sum_{L=L2}^{L3} FPC(L, 1) * F\phi C(L, M\phi) +$$

$$+ \sum_{L=L2}^{L3} FPC(L, 2) * F\phi C(L, LM) + \sum_{L=L2}^{L3} FPC(L, 3) * F\phi C(L, MBL) +$$

$$+ \sum_{M=M3}^{M4} \{V\phi E(M, M\phi) + [F\phi E(M)/12]\}, \quad M\phi = 3, \dots, 12;$$

see also other formulas of item (7–19).

(8) Projected Income Statement:

(8–1)   CGS(Mϕ)   *cost of goods sold;*
in dollars per month;
CGS(Mϕ) = TPC(Mϕ) + TFI(Mϕ) –
– TFI(NM),
Mϕ = 1, ..., 12,
NM = Mϕ + 1,
CGS(13) = TPC(13) + TFI(1)– TFI(12)

$$= \sum_{M\phi=1}^{12} CGS(M\phi),$$

TPC(Mϕ)... see (2–11)
TFI(Mϕ)... see (9–40)

(8–2)   CT(Mϕ)   *corporation taxes* (federal income taxes); in
dollars per month;
CT(Mϕ) = CT(13)/12, Mϕ = 1, ..., 12
for CT(13) see (8–i).

(8–3)   FME(Mϕ)   *financial and miscellaneous expenses (net);*
in dollars per month;
FME(Mϕ) = ϕLI(Mϕ) + RFE(Mϕ) –
– SSI(Mϕ) – RFR(Mϕ) + SLI(Mϕ) +
+ AEX(Mϕ) + PER(Mϕ),
Mϕ = 1, ... 13,

$$\varnothing\text{LI(M}\varnothing) \dots \text{see } (8\text{--}6),$$
$$\text{RFE(M}\varnothing) \dots \text{see } (8\text{--}9),$$
$$\text{SSI(M}\varnothing) \dots \text{see } (8\text{--}12),$$
$$\text{RFR(M}\varnothing) \dots \text{see } (8\text{--}10),$$
$$\text{SLI(M}\varnothing) \dots \text{see } (8\text{--}13);$$

$$\text{FME}(13) = \sum_{\text{M}\varnothing=1}^{12} \text{FME(M}\varnothing),$$

$$\text{AEX(M}\varnothing) \dots \text{see } (9\text{--}6);$$
$$\text{PER(M}\varnothing) \dots \text{see } (9\text{--}21);$$

(8–4)   GP(M$\varnothing$)   *gross profit*,
in dollars per month;
$$\text{GP(M}\varnothing) = \text{TSV(M}\varnothing) - \text{CGS(M}\varnothing),$$
$$\text{M}\varnothing = 1, \dots, 13;$$

$$\text{GP}(13) = \sum_{\text{M}\varnothing=1}^{12} \text{GP(M}\varnothing).$$

(8–5) $\boxed{\varnothing\text{IR(M}\varnothing)}$ *ordinary long-term liabilities' interest rate,*
(monthly or annual average).

(8–6) $\varnothing\text{LI(M}\varnothing)$ *ordinary long-term liabilities' interest (expense),*
in dollars per month;
$$\varnothing\text{LI(M}\varnothing) = \varnothing\text{IR(M}\varnothing) * [\text{TLL(M}\varnothing) +$$
$$+ \text{TLL(NM)}]/2, \qquad \text{M}\varnothing = 1, \dots, 12,$$
$$\text{NM} = \text{M}\varnothing + 1,$$
$$\text{TLL(M}\varnothing) \dots \text{see } (9\text{--}40);$$

$$\varnothing\text{LI}(13) = \sum_{\text{M}\varnothing=1}^{12} \varnothing\text{LI(M}\varnothing)$$

(8–7)   PAT(M$\varnothing$)   *profit after (federal income) taxes;*
in dollars per month;
$$\text{PAT(M}\varnothing) = \text{PBT(M}\varnothing) - \text{CT(M}\varnothing),$$
$$\text{M}\varnothing = 1, \dots, 13,$$
$$\text{CT(M}\varnothing) \dots \text{see } (8\text{--}2),$$

$$\text{PAT}(13) = \sum_{\text{M}\varnothing=1}^{12} \text{PAT(M}\varnothing);$$

(8–8)   PBT(M$\varnothing$)   *profit before taxes;*
in dollars per month;
$$\text{PBT(M}\varnothing) = \text{GP(M}\varnothing) - \text{T}\varnothing\text{E(M}\varnothing) -$$
$$- \text{FME(M}\varnothing), \qquad \text{M}\varnothing = 1, \dots, 13;$$
$$\text{GP(M}\varnothing) \dots \text{see } (8\text{--}4),$$
$$\text{T}\varnothing\text{E(M}\varnothing) \dots \text{see } (6\text{--}5),$$
$$\text{FME(M}\varnothing) \dots \text{see } (8\text{--}3);$$

$$\text{PBT}(13) = \sum_{\text{M}\varnothing=1}^{12} \text{PBT(M}\varnothing).$$

(8-9) $\boxed{\text{RFE}(\text{M}\phi)}$ *remaining financial (and other) expenses;*
in dollars per month; $\text{M}\phi = 1,\ldots,13,$

$$\text{RFE}(13) = \sum_{\text{M}\phi=1}^{12} \text{RFE}(\text{M}\phi), \qquad \text{cf. (8-3)}.$$

(8-10) $\boxed{\text{RFR}(\text{M}\phi)}$ *remaining financial (and other) revenues;*
in dollars per month; $\text{M}\phi = 1,\ldots,13,$

$$\text{RFR}(13) = \sum_{\text{M}\phi=1}^{12} \text{RFR}(\text{M}\phi), \qquad \text{cf. (8-3)}.$$

(8-11) $\boxed{\text{SIR}(\text{M}\phi)}$ *short-term securities' interest rate;*
(monthly or annual average)

(8-12) $\text{SSI}(\text{M}\phi)$ *short-term security interest income;*
in dollars per month;
$\text{SSI}(\text{M}\phi) = \text{SIR}(\text{M}\phi) * [\text{SS}(\text{M}\phi) +$
$+ \text{SS}(\text{NM})]/2,$ $\text{M}\phi = 1,\ldots,12,$
$\text{NM} = \text{M}\phi + 1,$
$\text{SS}(\text{M}\phi)\ldots\text{see (9-35)};$

$$\text{SSI}(13) = \sum_{\text{M}\phi=1}^{12} \text{SSI}(\text{M}\phi).$$

(8-13) $\text{SLI}(\text{M}\phi)$ *short-term loans' interest;*
in dollars per month;
$\text{SLI}(\text{M}\phi) = \text{SLR}(\text{M}\phi) * \text{SL}(\text{M}\phi),$
$\text{SL}(\text{M}\phi)\ldots\text{see (9-32)}.$
Obviously, this is a crude averaging
hypothesis which assumes that the size
of a loan at the beginning of a month
remains constant during this month (minimum duration of loan is assumed to be
one month);

$$\text{SLI}(13) = \sum_{\text{M}\phi=1}^{12} \text{SLI}(\text{M}\phi)$$

(8-14) $\boxed{\text{SLR}(\text{M}\phi)}$ *short-term loans' interest rate;*
(monthly or annual average).

Basic hypotheses and equations of the projected income statement:

(8-i) $\text{CT}(13) \begin{cases} = 0.3 * \text{PBT}(13), \\ \quad \text{if PBT}(31) \leq 25.000 \\ \text{or} \\ = 0.3 * 25.000 + 0.52 * [\text{PBT}(13) - 25.000], \\ \quad \text{if PBT}(13) > 25.000 \end{cases}$

$\text{PBT}(\text{M}\phi)\ldots\text{see (8-8)}$
(our model states $ figures in thousands,

otherwise it would be 25,000 instead of
25.000.)

(8–ii) $\emptyset LI(M\emptyset) = \emptyset IR(M\emptyset) * [TLL(M\emptyset) + TLL(NM)]/2$;
                                                    cf. (8–6).

(8–iii) $SSI(M\emptyset) = SIR(M\emptyset) * [SS(M\emptyset) + SS(NM)]/2$;
                                                    cf. (8–12).

(8–iv) $CGS(M\emptyset) = VMI(M\emptyset) + TPV(M\emptyset) - VMI(NM) +$
          $+ TLC(M\emptyset) + F\emptyset(M\emptyset) + TFI(M\emptyset) - TFI(NM)$;
                              $M\emptyset = 1, \ldots, 12$;
               see also (3–13), (3–11), (4–5), (5–7), and (9–4).
          $CGS(13) = VMI(1) + TPV(13) - VMI(13) + TLC(13) +$
          $+ F\emptyset(13) + TFI(1) - TFI(13)$.

(8–v) $GP(M\emptyset) = TSV(M\emptyset) - CGS(M\emptyset)$;
                      $M\emptyset = 1, \ldots, 13$; cf. (8–4).

(8–vi) $PAT(M\emptyset) = TSV(M\emptyset) - CGS(M\emptyset) - T\emptyset E(M\emptyset) -$
          $- FME(M\emptyset) - CT(M\emptyset)$,
                      $M\emptyset = 1, \ldots, 13$, cf. (8–7).

(8–vii) $SLI(M\emptyset) = SLR(M\emptyset) * SL(M\emptyset)$,
                      cf. (8–13), (8–14).

(9) Projected Balance Sheet (or Position) Statement:

(9–1) $AAR(M\emptyset)$ *allowance for accounts receivable:*

         $\boxed{AAR(1)}$ in dollars;

                                      $AAR(NM) = AAR(M\emptyset) + \emptyset E(M5,$
                                      $M\emptyset) - ARX(M\emptyset) = AAR(1) +$

                                      $+ \sum_{M\emptyset=1}^{MI} [\emptyset E(M5, M\emptyset) - ARX(M\emptyset)]$,

                                      $M\emptyset = 1, \ldots, MI, \ldots, 12$,
                                      $NM = M\emptyset + 1 = MI + 1$;
                                      hereby MI represents the *month indicated*
                                      by $M\emptyset$ in the variables $AAR(M\emptyset)$, etc.;

                                      when the $\sum$ notation is used in connec-
                                      tion with stock variables, a *second* symbol
                                      MI becomes necessary (otherwise it

                                      would read $\sum_{M\emptyset=1}^{M\emptyset} \ldots$ which is meaningless).

                                      The fourth operating expense item
                                      $[\emptyset E(M5, M\emptyset), M5 = 4$, see (6–2)] is
                                      assumed to refer to the "depreciation" of
                                      accounts receivables;
                                      $ARX(M\emptyset) \ldots$ see (9–10).

(9–2)   ABF(Mϕ)   *allowance for buildings and fixtures,*
         ABF(1)   *depreciation* in dollars;

$$ABF(NM) = ABF(M\phi) + F\phi C(12, M\phi) + $$
$$+ \phi E(M6, M\phi) - ABFX(M\phi)$$

$$= ABF(1) + \sum_{M\phi=1}^{MI} [F\phi C(12, M\phi) + $$

$$+ \phi E(M6, M\phi) - ABFX(M\phi)],$$

$$M\phi = 1,\ldots,MI,\ldots,12,$$

NM = Mϕ + I = MI + 1, (see also 9–1).
The twelfth factory overhead cost item
[FϕC(L, Mϕ), L = 12, see (5–9)] and
the *last* operating expense item [ϕE
(MM, Mϕ), MM = 5, see (6–2)] are in
our model assumed to represent building
and fixtures depreciation expenses.

(9–3)   ABFX(Mϕ)   *allowance for buildings and fixtures' special
                               changes,*
                               in dollars; this item reflects the increases or
                               decreases in allowances other than through
                               depreciation, e.g., sale of a fixture, re-
                               valuations of buildings' depreciation al-
                               lowance.

$$ABFX(13) = \sum_{M\phi=1}^{12} ABFX(M\phi).$$

(9–4)   AE(Mϕ)   *accrued expenses,*
         AE(1)   in dollars;

$$AE(NM) = AE(M\phi) + AEX(M\phi)$$

$$= AE(1) + \sum_{M\phi=1}^{MI} AEX(M\phi),$$

$$M\phi = 1,\ldots,MI,\ldots,12,$$
$$NM = M\phi + 1 = MI + 1.$$

(9–5)   AEM(Mϕ)   *allowance for equipment and machinery de-
                               preciation,*
         AEM(1)   in dollars;

$$AEM(NM) = AEM(M\phi) +$$

$$+ AEMX(M\phi) + \sum_{L=L4}^{L5} F\phi C(L, M\phi)$$

$$= AEM(1) + \sum_{M\phi=1}^{MI} [AEMX(M\phi) +$$

$$+ \sum_{L=L4}^{L5} F\phi C(L, M\phi)];$$

$$M\phi = 1, \ldots, 12,$$
$$NM = M\phi + 1 = MI + 1,$$
$$F\phi C(L, M\phi) \ldots \text{see } (5-9);$$

in our model the factory overhead cost items four and five [$F\phi C(L, M\phi)$; L = 4 and 5] are assumed to constitute equipment and machinery depreciation charges.

(9–6) $\boxed{AEX(M\phi)}$ *accrued expenses—changes,*
in dollars;

$$AEX(13) = \sum_{M\phi=1}^{12} AEX(M\phi).$$

(9–7) $\boxed{AEMX(M\phi)}$ *allowance for equipment and machinery—changes,*
in dollars;
increase or decrease in allowance through other than depreciation.

$$AEMX(13) = \sum_{M\phi=1}^{12} AEMX(M\phi).$$

(9–8) $AR(M\phi)$ *accounts receivables, etc.,*
in dollars;
$\boxed{AR(1)}$ $AR(NM) = AR(M\phi) + TSV(M\phi) -$
$- CS(M\phi) - ARC(M\phi) - ARX(M\phi).$
$$M\phi = 1, \ldots, 12,$$
$$NM = M\phi + 1;$$
$AR(13) = AR(1) + TSV(13) -$
$- CS(13) - ARC(13) - ARX(13),$
$$TSV(M\phi) \ldots \text{see } (1-9),$$
$$CS(M\phi) \ldots \text{see } (7-6),$$
$$ARC(M\phi) \ldots \text{see } (7-3),$$
$$ARX(M\phi) \ldots \text{see } (9-10).$$

(9–9) $ARN(M\phi)$ *accounts receivable net of allowances,*
in dollars;
$ARN(M\phi) = AR(M\phi) - AAR(M\phi);$
$$M\phi = 1, \ldots, 13,$$
$$AAR(M\phi) \ldots \text{see } (9-1).$$

(9–10) $\boxed{ARX(M\phi)}$ *accounts receivable's special changes,*
in dollars;
increase or decrease (through other than sales and collection) which are connected with $AAR(M\phi)$—see (9–1).

$$ARX(13) = \sum_{M\phi=1}^{12} PEX(M\phi).$$

(9–11)   BF(Mϕ)

$\boxed{\text{BF}(1)}$

buildings and fixtures;
in dollars;
BF(NM) = BF(Mϕ) + BFX(Mϕ) –
– ABFX(Mϕ),
$$M\phi = 1, \ldots, 12,$$
$$NM = M\phi + 1,$$
BF(13) = BF(1) + BFX(13) – ABFX(13),
ABFX(Mϕ) ... see (9–3).

(9–12)   BFN(Mϕ)

buildings and fixtures net of allowances for depreciation,
in dollars;
BFN(Mϕ) = BF(Mϕ) – ABF(Mϕ),
$$M\phi = 1, \ldots, 13$$

(9–13) $\boxed{\text{BFX}(M\phi)}$

buildings and fixtures' changes,
in dollars;

$$\text{BFX}(13) = \sum_{M\phi=1}^{12} \text{BFX}(M\phi).$$

(9–14)   DD(Mϕ)

$\boxed{\text{DD}(13)}$

dividends to be declared (flow variable),
in dollars;
DD(Mϕ) = DD(13)/12.

(9–15)   EM(Mϕ)

$\boxed{\text{EM}(1)}$

equipment and machinery,
in dollars;
EM(NM) = EM(Mϕ) + EMX(Mϕ) –
– AEMX(Mϕ) = EM(1) +

$$+ \sum_{M\phi=1}^{MI} [\text{EMX}(M\phi) - \text{AEMX}(M\phi)],$$

$$MN = M\phi + 1 = MI + 1.$$

(9–16)   EMN(Mϕ)

$\boxed{\text{EMN}(1)}$

equipment and machinery net of allowances for depreciation,
in dollars;
EMN(Mϕ) = EM(Mϕ) – AEM(Mϕ),
$$M\phi = 1, \ldots, 13,$$
AEM(Mϕ) ... see (9–5).

(9–17) $\boxed{\text{EMX}(M\phi)}$

equipment and machinery's changes,
in dollars;

$$\text{EMX}(13) = \sum_{M\phi=1}^{12} \text{EMX}(M\phi).$$

(9–18)   HL(Mϕ)

$\boxed{\text{HL}(1)}$

holdings of land,
in dollars;
HL(NM) = HL(Mϕ) + HLX(Mϕ)

$$= \text{HL}(1) + \sum_{M\phi=1}^{MI} \text{HLX}(M\phi),$$

$$M\phi = 1, \ldots, 12,$$
$$NM = M\phi + 1 = MI + 1.$$

(9–19) $\boxed{\text{HLX}(M\phi)}$ *holdings of land's changes;*
in dollars;

$$\text{HLX}(13) = \sum_{M\phi=1}^{12} \text{HLX}(M\phi).$$

(9–20) $\phi\text{EQ}(M\phi)$ *owners' equity;*
in dollars;
$$\phi\text{EQ}(M\phi) = \text{SC}(M\phi) + \text{PIS}(M\phi) +$$
$$+ \text{RE}(M\phi), \qquad\qquad M\phi = 1, \ldots, 13,$$
$$\text{SC}(M\phi)\ldots\text{see } (9\text{--}30),$$
$$\text{PIS}(M\phi)\ldots\text{see } (9\text{--}24),$$
$$\text{RE}(M\phi)\ldots\text{see } (9\text{--}28).$$

(9–21) $\boxed{\text{PER}(M\phi)}$ *prepaid expense reversal,*
in dollars; $M\phi = 1, \ldots, 13;$
interpreted as a credit to the prepaid
expense account and a debit *directly* to
profit and loss.

(9–22) $\boxed{\text{PEX}(M\phi)}$ *prepaid expenses' changes;*
in dollars;

$$\text{PEX}(13) = \sum_{M\phi=1}^{12} \text{PEX}(M\phi),$$

see also (9–27).

(9–23) $\text{PI}(M\phi)$ *participations and investments* in other enter-
$\boxed{\text{PI}(1)}$ prises (long-term securities), in dollars;
$$\text{PI}(NM) = \text{PI}(M\phi) + \text{PIX}(M\phi)$$

$$= \text{PI}(1) + \sum_{M\phi=1}^{MI} \text{PIX}(M\phi),$$

$$M\phi = 1, \ldots, 12,$$
$$NM = M\phi + 1 = MI + 1,$$
$$\text{PIX}(M\phi)\ldots\text{see } (9\text{--}25).$$

(9–24) $\text{PIS}(M\phi)$ *paid-in surplus,*
$\boxed{\text{PIS}(1)}$ in dollars;
$$\text{PIS}(NM) = \text{PIS}(M\phi) + \text{PISX}(M\phi)$$

$$= \text{PIS}(1) + \sum_{M\phi=1}^{MI} \text{PISX}(M\phi),$$

$$M\phi = 1, \ldots, 12,$$
$$NM = M\phi + 1 = MI + 1.$$

(9–25) $\boxed{\text{PISX}(M\phi)}$ *paid-in surplus' changes,*
in dollars;

$$PISX(13) = \sum_{M\emptyset=1}^{12} PISX(M\emptyset).$$

(9–26) $\boxed{PIX(M\emptyset)}$ *participations and investments—changes,*
in dollars;

$$PIX(13) = \sum_{M\emptyset=1}^{12} PIX(M\emptyset).$$

(9–27) PPE(M$\emptyset$) *prepaid expenses,*

$\boxed{PPE(1)}$ in dollars;

$PPE(NM) = PPE(M\emptyset) + PEX(M\emptyset) -$
$- PER(M\emptyset)$

$$= PPE(1) + \sum_{M\emptyset=1}^{MI} PEX(M\emptyset) - PER(M\emptyset).$$

$$M\emptyset = 1, \ldots, 12,$$
$$NM = M\emptyset + 1 = MI + 1,$$
$$PEX(M\emptyset) \ldots \text{see } (9\text{--}22).$$

(9–28) RE(M$\emptyset$) *retained earnings,*

$\boxed{RE(1)}$ in dollars;

$RE(NM) = RE(M\emptyset) + PAT(M\emptyset) -$
$- DD(M\emptyset)$

$$= RE(1) + \sum_{M\emptyset=1}^{MI} [PAT(M\emptyset) - DD(M\emptyset)]$$

$$M\emptyset = 1, \ldots, 12,$$
$$NM = M\emptyset + 1 = MI + 1,$$
$$PAT(M\emptyset) \ldots \text{see } (8\text{--}7),$$
$$DD(M\emptyset) \ldots \text{see } (9\text{--}14).$$

(9–29) REX(M$\emptyset$) *retained earnings' changes,*
in dollars;
increases and decreases through profits
(after taxes) minus dividends;
$REX(M\emptyset) = PAT(M\emptyset) - DD(M\emptyset),$
$$M\emptyset = 1, \ldots, 13,$$

$$REX(13) = \sum_{M\emptyset=1}^{12} REX(M\emptyset).$$

"Special" changes of retained earnings
that might eventually occur must be taken
care of separately.

(9–30) SC(M$\emptyset$) *stock capital,*

$\boxed{SC(1)}$ in dollars;

$SC(NM) = SC(M\emptyset) + SCX(M\emptyset)$

$$= SC(1) + \sum_{M\emptyset=1}^{MI} SCX(M\emptyset);$$

$$M\emptyset = 1, \ldots, 12,$$
$$NM = M\emptyset + 1 = MI + 1.$$

(9–31) $\boxed{SCX(M\emptyset)}$ *stock capital changes,*
in dollars;

$$SCX(13) = \sum_{M\emptyset=1}^{12} SCX(M\emptyset),$$

(9–32) $SL(M\emptyset)$ *short-term loans;*
in dollars;
     $\boxed{SL(1)}$ $SL(NM) = SL(M\emptyset) + SLX(M\emptyset)$

$$= SL(1) + \sum_{M\emptyset=1}^{MI} SLX(M\emptyset);$$

$$M\emptyset = 1, \ldots, 12,$$
$$NM = M\emptyset + 1 = MI + 1.$$

(9–33) $\boxed{SLX(M\emptyset)}$ *short-term loans' changes,*
in dollars;

$$SLX(13) = \sum_{M\emptyset=1}^{12} SLX(M\emptyset).$$

(9–34) $SS(M\emptyset)$ *short-term securities* (marketable securities to be held for a limited time) in dollars; the size or value of $SS(M\emptyset)$ depends on the accumulation or depletion of cash and in turn may influence and determine the cash balance $CHB(M\emptyset)$—see (7–4). If $CHB(M\emptyset)$ tends to go beyond the absolute cash maximum CASMAX (which cannot be surpassed—in our model CASMAX = 8.000, in thousand dollars) the excess amount $SSM(LM)$—see (7–16)—will increase $SS(M\emptyset)$; if $CHB(M\emptyset)$ tends to go below the relative or *conditional* cash minimum CASMIN (in our model CASMIN = 6.000, in thousand dollars) the shortage, a negative value of $SSM(LM)$ decreases $SS(M\emptyset)$ and increases $CHB(M\emptyset)$ until the cash minimum is reached or until $SS(M\emptyset)$ is depleted, which means reduced to zero. In the latter case $CHB(M\emptyset)$ may assume a value below the conditional cash minimum.

     $\boxed{SS(1)}$

$$SS(NM) = SS(M\phi) + SSM(M\phi) + \\ + SSX(M\phi) = SS(1) +$$

$$+ \sum_{M\phi=1}^{MI} [SSM(M\phi) + SSX(M\phi)],$$

$$M\phi = 1,\ldots,12,$$
$$NM = M\phi + 1 = MI + 1.$$

(9–35) $\boxed{SSX(M\phi)}$ *short-term securities' special changes,*
in dollars;
increases or decreases in the value of
$SS(M\phi)$ other than those incurred automatically by fluctuations of $CHB(M\phi)$—
see (7–4), (7–16), and (9–34),

$$SSX(13) = \sum_{M\phi=1}^{12} SSX(M\phi).$$

(9–36) $TA(M\phi)$ *total assets,*
in dollars;
$TA(M\phi) = TCA(M\phi) + TFA(M\phi),$
$TA(M\phi) = TE(M\phi),$
due to rounding off or up in the computer a minor discrepancy between
$TA(M\phi)$ and $TE(M\phi)$ may occur.

(9–37) $TCA(M\phi)$ *total current assets,*
in dollars;
$TCA(M\phi) = CHB(M\phi) + SS(M\phi) +$
$+ ARN(M\phi) + VMI(M\phi) +$
$+ TFI(M\phi) + PPE(M\phi).$
$M\phi = 1,\ldots,13,$
$CHB(M\phi)\ldots$ see (7–4),
$SS(M\phi)\ldots$ see (9–34),
$ARN(M\phi)\ldots$ see (9–9),
$VMI(M\phi)\ldots$ see (3–13).

(9–38) $TE(M\phi)$ *total equity,*
in dollars;
$TE(M\phi) = TSL(M\phi) + TLL(M\phi) +$
$+ \phi EQ(M\phi),$
$TE(M\phi) = TA(M\phi)$ see remark at
(9–36),
$M\phi = 1,\ldots,13,$
$TSL(M\phi)\ldots$ see (9–42),
$TLL(M\phi)\ldots$ see (9–41),
$\phi EQ(M\phi)\ldots$ see (9–20).

(9–39) $TFA(M\phi)$ *total fixed assets,*
in dollars;
$TFA(M\phi) = PI(M\phi) + EMN(M\phi) +$
$+ HL(M\phi) + BFN(M\phi),$
$M\phi = 1,\ldots,13,$

$$PI(M\phi)\dots \text{see } (9\text{--}23),$$
$$EMN(M\phi)\dots \text{see } (9\text{--}16),$$
$$HL(M\phi)\dots \text{see } (9\text{--}18),$$
$$BFN(M\phi)\dots \text{see } (9\text{--}12).$$

(9–40)   TFI(Mϕ)   *total finished (and partly finished) goods inventory value,*
in dollars;

$$TFI(1) \quad = \sum_{I=1}^{N} PUC\phi(I) * BI(I, 1),$$

$$PUC(I, M\phi)\dots \text{see } (2\text{--}8),$$
$$PUC\phi(I)\dots \text{see } (2\text{--}8),$$
$$BI(I, 1)\dots \text{see } (2\text{--}1);$$

$$TFI(M\phi) = \sum_{I=1}^{N} PUC(I, LM) * BI(I, M\phi),$$

$$M\phi = 2,\dots, 13.$$

(9–41)   TLL(Mϕ)

     $\boxed{TLL(1)}$

total long-term liabilities,
in dollars;
$$TLL(NM) = TLL(M\phi) + TLLX(M\phi) =$$

$$= TLL(1) + \sum_{M\phi=1}^{MI} TLLX(M\phi),$$

$$M\phi = 1,\dots, 12,$$
$$NM = M\phi + 1 = MI + 1.$$

(9–42) $\boxed{TLLX(M\phi)}$ *total long-term liabilities' changes;*
in dollars;

$$TLLX(13) = \sum_{M\phi=1}^{12} TLLX(M\phi).$$

(9–43)   TSL(Mϕ)   *total short-term liabilities;*
in dollars;
$$TSL(M\phi) = VP(M\phi) + SL(M\phi) +$$
$$+ AE(M\phi),$$
$$M\phi = 1,\dots, 13,$$
$$VP(M\phi)\dots \text{see } (9\text{--}43),$$
$$SL(M\phi)\dots \text{see } (9\text{--}32),$$
$$AE(M\phi)\dots \text{see } (9\text{--}4).$$

(9–44)   VP(Mϕ)

     $\boxed{VP(1)}$

vouchers payable,
in dollars;
$$VP(NM) = VP(M\phi) - VPE(M\phi) +$$

$$+ TPV(M\phi) + \sum_{L=L2}^{L3} F\phi C(L, M\phi) +$$

$$+ \ V\phi E(3, M\phi) + [F\phi E(3)/12]$$

$$= \ VP(1) + \sum_{M\phi=1}^{MI} [- \ VPE(M\phi) +$$

$$+ \ TPM(M\phi) + \sum_{L=L2}^{L3} F\phi C(L, M\phi) +$$

$$+ \ V\phi E(3, M\phi) + (F\phi E(3)/12)],$$

$$M\phi = 1, \ldots, 12,$$
$$NM = M\phi + 1 = MI + 1,$$
$$L2 = 4,$$
$$L3 = 9.$$

Basic hypotheses and equations of the projected balance sheet:

(9–i) $TFI(1) \quad = \sum_{I=1}^{N} PUC\phi(I)* BI(I, 1);$

$TFI(NM) = \sum_{I=1}^{N} PUC(I, M\phi) * BI(I, NM),$

$$M\phi = 1, \ldots, 12,$$
$$NM = M\phi + 1;$$

(9–ii) $DD(M\phi) = DD(13)/12;$
(9–iii) $TA(M\phi) = TE(M\phi);$
(9–iv) $TA(M\phi) = TCA(M\phi) + TFA(M\phi);$
(9–v) $TE(M\phi) = TSL(M\phi) + TLL(M\phi) +$
$\qquad\qquad + \ \phi EQ(M\phi);$
(9–vi) $TCA(M\phi) = CHB(M\phi) + SS(M\phi) +$
$\qquad\qquad + \ ARN(M\phi) + VMI(M\phi) +$
$\qquad\qquad + \ TFI(M\phi) + PPE(M\phi);$
(9–vii) $TFA(M\phi) = PI(M\phi) + EMN(M\phi) +$
$\qquad\qquad + \ HL(M\phi) + BFN(M\phi);$
(9–viii) $TSL(M\phi) = VP(M\phi) +$
$\qquad\qquad + \ SL(M\phi) + AE(M\phi);$
(9–ix) $\phi EQ(M\phi) = SC(M\phi) + PIS(M\phi) +$
$\qquad\qquad + \ RE(M\phi);$

$M\phi = 1, \ldots, 13.$

(9–x) $TLL(M\phi) = TLL(1) +$

$\qquad\qquad + \sum_{LM=1}^{M\phi-1} TLLX(LM);$

(9–xi) $RE(M\phi) = RE(1) +$

$M\phi = 2, \ldots, 13.$

$\qquad\qquad + \sum_{LM=1}^{M\phi-1} [PAT(LM) -$

$\qquad\qquad - \ DD(LM)];$

9.28   Summary and Conclusions

The budget approach presented herein demonstrates the way in which an accounting system may serve as a unifying frame for an *over-all model of the firm*, a model which does not merely describe the past but which projects into the future, a model which serves managerial planning through a *formalized procedure of satisficing* toward specified goals. But in spite of all the behavioral-analytic paraphernalia this budget remains at bottom an accounting system. We might illustrate this with the following set of twenty-eight accounts (beginning and ending balance sheets are excluded) that conform fully with our preceding discussion and which summarize concisely our budget model. An approach such as this could be addressed as *meta-accounting* since the individual entries are represented not by figures but by symbols of respectable generality.[22]   Many of these symbols have behavioral, technological, or institutional functions that combine the "sterile" accounting identities with working hypotheses resulting in a model of "predictive" or at least "projective" power. This and a further aspect may manifest some affinity of our approach with Leontief's interindustry model. The utilization of a great number of simple coefficients—e.g., (1–3), (2–4), (3–2), etc.—derived from past experience and based on relatively crude assumptions about the behavior of an economic entity (macro-economic in Leontief's case, micro-economic in ours) indicates another parallel.

The reason why our model is so sizable and has to cope with so considerable a number of variables lies in the very nature of accounting. This discipline, in contrast to economics and theoretical operations research, can be understood only under the impact of such details. As we have already hinted, model building in micro- and macro-accounting is something different from model building in mathematical economics; above all, this model must provide an unifying frame into which alternate sets of hypotheses can be "plugged-in." Such a framework calls for many variables, especially if it is general enough to serve as a prototype for practical applications and as a basis for a computer program. We have demonstrated elsewhere [see Mattessich, 1961a, pp. 392–93] that it is possible to present the main features of such a budget approach within a limited number of equations and variables and

---

[22]Such a "meta-accounting" has been used already in outlining the *analytical* budget model (Section 9.1).

even without the memnonic support of source languages. But in accounting so concise a model can merely serve the casting of ideas in broad strokes; to be operational, a more detailed model is called for. This "operationality" stands in the foreground of accounting and details cannot be relinquished. But the comprehensiveness of such an accounting model, in contrast to many a bulky economic model, is not necessarily a token of specificity; it need not diminish the general validity of the chief structure; rather it is a prerequisite for this generality. Therefore such a model fulfills a purpose embracing far more than a mere illustration; it articulates the individual variables and parameters, reveals the mathematical structure of accounting in general (not only that of budgeting) much more succinctly and with greater precision than traditional accounting ever could afford to do.

Besides, this huge model can always be presented in a "reduced" form through an accounting matrix (see Chapter 3 of companion volume) or the corresponding T-accounts as demonstrated in the comparatively small meta-accounting system that follows. There, the variables are aggregates that serve the closing at the end of the entire budget period (a similar approach could be used for the closing at the end of every month, if such details were required). For the components of these aggregates the reader is referred to the discussion of the variables in the individual subbudgets. To facilitate a check upon the double classification principle, the number in front of every entry conveys the account number of the counterentry (something that would not be necessary if a matrix approach were used). The Greek letters α and ω refer to the beginning and ending balances of *real accounts*. The residual of *any* account, on the other hand, is indicated by an asterisk, while a cross $(+)$ points at those variables which may assume negative values and then should be envisaged as belonging to the other side of the same account.

To facilitate the reconciling of the cash account with some of the equations of the model, we have indicated the main variables of which the individual entries are components. Reminding the reader of the basic identities

$$\text{CHB}(13) = \text{CHB}(1) + \text{TCR}(13) - \text{TC}\phi(13) \quad \text{cf. } (7\text{--}4);$$
$$\text{TCR}(13) = \text{CS}(13) + \text{ARC}(13) + \phi\text{CR}(13) \quad \text{cf. } (7\text{--}18);$$
$$\text{TC}\phi(13) = \text{VPE}(13) + \text{PE}(13) + \phi\text{C}\phi(13) \quad \text{cf. } (7\text{--}17);$$

(see furthermore 7–10, 7–11, 7–12, 7–14, and 7–15), this reconciliation should not be difficult. Yet it has to be borne in mind that several simplifications—some of which may be more pardon-able in a budget model than in an historic-descriptive model—are here implied (e.g., the counterentries to the reversal of pre-paid expenses and to the change in accrued expenses are found in account No. 27 bypassing, for convenience sake, the possibly numerous expense accounts [see PER(13) and AEX(13)].

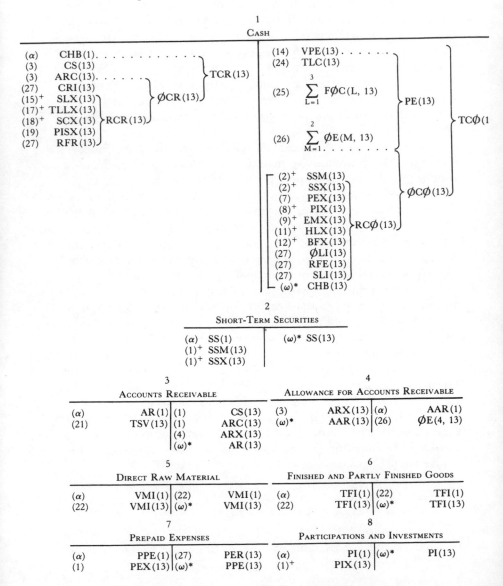

9
EQUIPMENT AND MACHINERY

(α)	EM(1)	(10)	AEMX(13)
$(1)^+$	EMX(13)	$(\omega)^*$	EM(13)

10
ALLOW. FOR EQUIP. AND MACH. DEPREC.

(9)	AEMX(13)	(α)	AEM(1)
$(\omega)^*$	AEM(13)	(25)	$\sum_{L=10}^{11} F\phi C(L,\ 13)$

11
HOLDINGS OF LAND

(α)	HL(1)	$(\omega)^*$	HL(13)
$(1)^+$	HLX(13)		

12
BUILDINGS AND FIXTURES

(α)	BF(1)	(13)	ABFX(13)
$(1)^+$	BFX(13)	$(\omega)^*$	BF(13)

13
ALLOW. FOR BLDG. AND FIXT. DEPREC.

(12)	ABFX(13)	(α)	ABF(1)
$(\omega)^*$	ABF(13)	(25)	$F\phi C(12,\ 13)$
		(26)	$\phi E(5,\ 13)$

14
VOUCHERS PAYABLE

(1)	VPE(13)	(α)	VP(1)
$(\omega)^*$	VP(13)	(23)	TPV(13)
		(25)	$\sum_{L=4}^{9} F\phi C(L,\ 13)$
		(26)	$\phi E(3,\ 13)$
		(28)	DD(13)
		(28)	CT(13)

15
SHORT-TERM LOANS

$(\omega)^*$	SL(13)	(α)	SL(1)
		$(1)^+$	SLX(13)

16
ACCRUED EXPENSES

$(\omega)^*$	AE(13)	(α)	AE(1)
		$(27)^+$	AEX(13)

17
LONG-TERM LIABILITIES

$(\omega)^*$	TLL(13)	(α)	TLL(1)
		$(1)^+$	TLLX(13)

18
STOCK CAPITAL

$(\omega)^*$	SC(13)	(α)	SC(1)
		$(1)^+$	SCX(13)

19
PAID-IN SURPLUS

$(\omega)^*$	PIS(13)	(α)	PIS(1)
		(1)	PISX(13)

20
RETAINED EARNINGS

$(\omega)^{*+}$	RE(13)	$(\alpha)^+$	RE(1)
		$(28)^+$	REX(13)

21
SALES REVENUES

$(28)^*$	TSV(13)	(3)	TSV(13)

22
COST OF GOODS SOLD

(5)	VMI(1)	(5)	VMI(13)
(6)	TFI(1)	(6)	TFI(13)
(23)	TPV(13)	$(28)^*$	CGS(13)
(24)	TLC(13)		
(25)	$F\phi(13)$		

23
DIRECT MATERIAL PURCHASES

(14)	TPV(13)	$(22)^*$	TPV(13)

24
DIRECT LABOR

(1)	TLC(13)	$(22)^*$	TLC(13)

25
FACTORY OVERHEAD COSTS

(1) $\sum_{L=1}^{3}$ FØC(L, 13) |(22)*   FØ(13)

(14) $\sum_{L=4}^{9}$ FØC(L, 13)

(10) $\sum_{L=10}^{11}$ FØC(L, 13)

(13) FØC (12, 13)

26
OPERATING EXPENSES

(1) $\sum_{M=1}^{2}$ ØE(M, 13) |(28)*   TØE(13)

(14) ØE(3, 13)
(4)   ØE(4, 13)
(13) ØE(5, 13)

27
FINANCIAL AND MISC. EXP. AND REV.

(1)	ØLI(13)	(1)	CRI(13)[23]
(1)	RFE(13)	(1)	RFR (13)
(1)	SLI(13)	(28)*+	FME (13)
(16)+	AEX(13)		
(7)	PER(13)		

28
PROFIT AND LOSS

(22)	CGS(13)	(21)	TSV(13)
(26)	TØE(13)		
(27)+	FME(13)		
(14)	DD(13)		
(14) }*	CT(13)		
(20) }+	REX(13)		

This presentation may be taken as evidence that the translation of accounting into mathematical terms is not a mere pasttime of idle scholars but has important clarificational if not epistemological functions and, above all, has a great practical potential. The application of matrix algebra in the economic sciences, the advent of electronic data processing, and the creation of memnonic source languages have provided the preconditions which were lacking until recently—an explanation of why previous attempts at formulating accounting in comprehensive algebraic terms were defeated, or disregarded, or remained limited to a few definitional equations. As a further consequence it ought to be considered whether *meta-accounting*—that is to say, *an accounting system whose entries are not mere numerals but behavioral functions and identities*—cannot also be employed beyond budgeting in the narrow sense of the word. Indeed, the spreading of this approach to other areas of accounting, to financial and cost accounting, to national income and flow of funds accounting, etc., is only a matter of time.

List of All Variables and Parameters in Alphabetic Order. Exogenous variables are in boxes, parameters are underlined. The first figure of the reference number refers to the subbudget (sales = 1, production = 2, material = 3, labor = 4, manufacturing cost = 5,

---

[23]Note that CRI(13) = SSI(13), but that CRI(MØ) ≠ SSI(MØ); for MØ = 1, . . . , 12; cf. (7–5).

operating expense = 6, cash = 7, projected income statement = 8, projected balance sheet = 9), the second refers to the place the variable assumes within the list of the pertinent subbudget.

Reference Number	Symbol	Name
(9–1)	AAR(M∅)	allowance for accounts receivable
	AAR(1)	
(9–2)	ABF(M∅)	allowance for buildings and fixtures
	ABF(1)	
(9–3)	ABFX(M∅)	allowance for buildings and fixtures' special changes
(7–1)	AC1	accounts receivable collection coefficient— for sales of last month
(7–2)	AC2	accounts receivable collection coefficient—for sales before last month
(9–4)	AE(M∅)	accrued expenses
	AE(1)	
(9–5)	AEM(M∅)	allowance for equipment and machinery depreciation
	AEM(1)	
(9–7)	AEMX(M∅)	allowance for equipment and machinery—changes
(9–6)	AEX(M∅)	accrued expenses—changes
(2–1)	APQ(I, M∅)	adjusted production quantity
(3–14)	APRM(J, M∅)	adjusted purchases of raw material
(9–8)	AR(M∅)	accounts receivables, etc.
	AR(1)	
(7–3)	ARC(M∅)	accounts receivable collection
(9–9)	ARN(M∅)	accounts receivable net of allowances
(9–10)	ARX(M∅)	accounts receivable's special changes
(9–11)	BF(M∅)	buildings and fixtures
	BF(1)	
(9–12)	BFN(M∅)	buildings and fixtures net of allowances for depreciation
(9–13)	BFX(M∅)	buildings and fixtures changes
(2–2)	BI(I, M∅)	beginning inventory, of finished and partly finished goods (in equivalent units)
	BI(I, 1)	
	BI(I, 13)	
(7–20)	CASMAX	cash maximum level allowed
(7–21)	CASMIN	cash minimum level desired
(8–1)	CGS(M∅)	cost of goods sold
(7–4)	CHB(M∅)	cash on hand and in bank at the beginning of month
	CHB(1)	
(3–1)	CMR(J, M∅)	cost of material requirement
(7–5)	CRI(M∅)	cash receipts of interest on short-term securities
(7–6)	CS(M∅)	cash sales
(7–7)	CSC	cash sales coefficient
(8–2)	CT(M∅)	corporation taxes (federal income taxes)
(9–14)	DD(M∅)	dividends to be declared
	DD(13)	
(5–1)	DFF(K, L)	departmental fixed factory overheads
(5–2)	DF∅(K)	departmental fixed overheads
(4–1)	DLC(I, K, M∅)	direct labor cost
(5–3)	DVF(K, L, M∅)	departmental variable factory overheads

(5-4)	$DV\emptyset(K, M\emptyset)$	departmental variable overheads
(2-3)	$EI(I, M\emptyset)$	ending inventory
(9-15)	$EM(M\emptyset)$	equipment and machinery
	$\boxed{EM(1)}$	
(9-16)	$EMN(M\emptyset)$	equipment and machinery net of allowances for
	$\boxed{EMN(1)}$	depreciation
(9-17)	$\boxed{EMX(M\emptyset)}$	equipment and machinery's changes
(5-5)	$FF\emptyset(M\emptyset)$	fixed factory overheads
(5-6)	$\boxed{FFR(K, L)}$	fixed factory overhead rate
(8-3)	$FME(M\emptyset)$	financial and miscellaneous expenses (net)
(5-7)	$F\emptyset(M\emptyset)$	factory overheads
(5-8)	$F\emptyset B(K, L, M\emptyset)$	factory overheads before proration
(5-9)	$F\emptyset C(L, M\emptyset)$	factory overhead cost for all departments
(7-24)	$F\emptyset CD(L)$	factory overhead costs of (past) December
(7-25)	$F\emptyset CN(L)$	factory overhead costs of (past) November
(6-1)	$\boxed{F\emptyset E(M)}$	fixed operating expenses
(7-8)	$F\emptyset F(I, K, M\emptyset)$	factory overheads of finished (and partly finished) goods (inventory)
(5-10)	$F\emptyset K(K, KI, M\emptyset)$	factory overhead coefficient
(5-11)	$F\emptyset P(K, M\emptyset)$	factory overheads prorated
(5-12)	$F\emptyset S(K, L, M\emptyset)$	factory overheads of service departments
(7-9)	$FPC(L, MS)$	factory overhead payments coefficient
(5-13)	$\boxed{FPF(L)}$	fixed part of factory overheads
(8-4)	$GP(M\emptyset)$	gross profit
(9-17)	$HL(M\emptyset)$	holdings of land
	$\boxed{HL(1)}$	
(9-18)	$\boxed{HLX(M\emptyset)}$	holdings of land's changes
(7-10)	$\emptyset C\emptyset(M\emptyset)$	other cash outlays
(7-11)	$\emptyset CR(M\emptyset)$	other cash receipts
(6-2)	$\emptyset E(M, M\emptyset)$	operating expenses
(6-3)	$\emptyset EK(I, M)$	operating-expense coefficient
(9-20)	$\boxed{\emptyset EQ(M\emptyset)}$	owners' equity
(8-5)	$\boxed{\emptyset IR(M\emptyset)}$	ordinary long-term liabilities' interest rate (monthly or annual average)
(8-6)	$\emptyset LI(M\emptyset)$	ordinary long-term liabilities' interest (expense)
(8-7)	$PAT(M\emptyset)$	profit after (federal income) taxes
(8-8)	$PBT(M\emptyset)$	profit before taxes
(2-4)	$PC(I, M\emptyset)$	production cost
(7-12)	$PE(M\emptyset)$	payroll expenditures
(9-21)	$\boxed{PER(M\emptyset)}$	prepaid expense reversal
(9-22)	$\boxed{PEX(M\emptyset)}$	prepaid expenses' changes
(7-13)	$PFK(K)$	product factory overhead coefficient
(9-23)	$PI(M\emptyset)$	participations and investments
	$\boxed{PI(1)}$	
(9-24)	$PIS(M\emptyset)$	paid-in surplus
	$\boxed{PIS(1)}$	
(9-25)	$\boxed{PISX(M\emptyset}$	paid-in surplus' changes
(9-26)	$\boxed{PIX(M\emptyset)}$	participations and investments—changes
(2-5)	$PK(I, M\emptyset)$	product coefficient

(2–6)	PKN(I, M∅)	new production coefficient
(3–2)	PMC(J, M∅)	purchases: monthly coefficient
(3–15)	PMCN(J, M∅)	purchases: new monthly coefficient
(2–13)	PMI(I)	product minimum inventory level
(3–3)	PMK(I, J)	purchases: material coefficient
(9–27)	PPE(M∅)	prepaid expenses
	PPE(1)	
(2–7)	PQ(I, M∅)	production quantity
(3–4)	PRM(J, M∅)	purchases of raw material
(3–4)	PRMD(J)	purchases of raw material of (past) December
(1–1)	PSQ(I)	previous sales quantity
(2–8)	PUC(I, M∅)	product unit cost
	PUC∅(I)	product unit cost at beg. of budget period
(7–14)	RC∅(M∅)	remaining cash outlays
(7–15)	RCR(M∅)	remaining cash receipts
(9–28)	RE(M∅)	retained earnings
	RE(1)	
(9–29)	REX(M∅)	retained earnings' (regular) changes
(8–9)	RFE(M∅)	remaining financial (and other) expenses
(8–10)	RFR(M∅)	remaining financial (and other) revenues
(3–5)	RMI(J, M∅)	raw material inventory
	RMI(J, 1)	
(3–16)	RMMI(J)	raw material minimum inventory level (units)
(3–6)	RMR(I, J, M∅)	raw material requirement
(9–30)	SC(M∅)	stock capital
	SC(1)	
(9–31)	SCX(M∅)	stock capital changes
(1–2)	SI(I)	sales index
(8–11)	SIR(M∅)	short-term securities' interest rate (monthly average if M∅ < 13)
(1–3)	SK(M∅)	sales coefficient
(9–32)	SL(M∅)	short-term loans
	SL(1)	
(4–2)	SLC(K)	standard labor cost
(4–3)	SLH(I, K, M∅)	standard labor hours
	SLH(I, K, 13)	
(8–13)	SLI(M∅)	short-term loans' interest
(8–14)	SLR(M∅)	short-term loans' interest rate (monthly average if M∅ < 13)
(9–33)	SLX(M∅)	short-term loans' changes
(1–4)	SP(I)	sales price
(1–5)	SQ(I, M∅)	sales quantity
(9–34)	SS(M∅)	short-term securities
	SS(1)	
(8–12)	SSI(M∅)	short-term security interest income
(7–16)	SSM(M∅)	short-term securities manipulation
(9–35)	SSX(M∅)	short-term securities' special changes
(1–6)	SV(I, M∅)	sales volume

(9–36)	TA(MØ)	total assets
(2–9)	TBI(MØ)	total beginning inventory (finished and partly finished goods in equiv. whole units)
(9–37)	TCA(MØ)	total current assets
(7–17)	TCØ(MØ)	total cash outlays
(3–7)	TCM(MØ)	total cost of material
(7–18)	TCR(MØ)	total cash receipts
(4–4)	TDLC(K, MØ)	total (direct) departmental labor cost
(9–38)	TE(MØ)	total equity
(2–10)	TEI(MØ)	total ending inventory
(9–39)	TFA(MØ)	total fixed assets
(5–16)	TFF	total fixed factory overheads
(9–40)	TFI(MØ)	total finished (and partly finished) goods inventory value ($)
(5–14)	TFØ(MØ)	total factory overheads
(5–17)	TFØA(K, MØ)	total factory overheads after proration
(5–15)	TFØB(K, MØ)	total factory overheads before proration
(6–4)	TFØE	total fixed operating expenses
(5–18)	TFØS(K, MØ) or TFØS(KI, MØ)	total factory overheads of service
(4–5)	TLC(MØ)	total labor cost
(4–6)	TLCP(I)	total labor cost per product
(9–41)	TLL(MØ) TLL(1)	total long-term liabilities
(9–42)	TLLX(MØ)	total long-term liabilities' changes
(3–8)	TMI(MØ)	total material inventory
(3–9)	TMR(J, MØ)	total material requirement
(6–5)	TØE(MØ)	total operating expenses
(2–11)	TPC(MØ)	total product cost
(3–10)	TPM(MØ)	total purchases of materials
(6–7)	TPØE(M)	total period operating expenses
(2–12)	TPQ(MØ)	total product quantity
(1–8)	TPSQ	total previous sales quantity
(3–11)	TPV(MØ)	total purchases of material—value
(9–43)	TSL(MØ)	total short-term liabilities
(1–7)	TSQ(MØ)	total sales quantity
(1–9)	TSV(MØ)	total sales volume
(7–22)	TSVD	total sales volume of (past) December
(7–23)	TSVN	total sales volume of (past) November
(5–19)	TTV	total of total variable factory overheads
(5–20)	TVF(L)	total variable factory overheads
(6–6)	TVØE(MØ)	total variable operating expenses
(5–21)	TVR(K)	total variable factory overhead rate
(3–12)	UCM(J, MØ)	unit cost of material
(3–12)	UCMØ(J)	unit cost of material of beginning inventory
(5–22)	VFØ(MØ)	variable factory overheads
(5–23)	VFR(K,L)	variable factory overhead rate
(3–13)	VMI(MØ)	value of (direct) material inventory
(6–8)	VØE(M, MØ)	variable operating expenses
(9–44)	VP(MØ) VP(1)	vouchers payable
(7–19)	VPE(MØ)	vouchers payable expenditures

Chapter 10

ACCOUNTING, A
MANAGEMENT SCIENCE

10.1 GENERAL REMARKS

MANAGEMENT SCIENCE—as the occasional application of the plural of this term betrays—is an interdisciplinary effort, an attempt to fuse branches of various social sciences with those of engineering, mathematics, and philosophy. Should accounting be considered as one of the management sciences? This book has demonstrated that some areas of management science are so closely related to the affairs of accounting that it is difficult to exclude our discipline from this new, interdisciplinary movement. Indeed, a glance into the pertinent literature confirms our concensus that accounting is part of this interdisciplinary effort. A small sample of quotations may serve to reinforce this statement.

In an article originally written for the *Encyclopaedia Britannica*, Churchman [1959b] says: "... especially in accounting, the management sciences have presented a challenge to a well-entrenched profession which some of its young Turks wish to meet." But several years before the above statement was made, Hermann and Magee [1953, p. 107] pointed at the close relationship between accounting and operations research: "It is true, however, that in the analysis and construction of measures of control, the functions of operations research and accounting do tend to overlap. Also, the men working in these functions have strong mutual interests. Accountants have served a useful purpose in bringing the importance of control measures to the attention of business management, while operations research has shown ability in building new methods for developing and implementing these concepts of control." Miller and Starr [1960, p. 7] referring to the long-standing tradition of accounting as *the* quantitative area of business practice, remark that the: "underlying accounting problems were problems of observation and measurement, systems analysis, model construction, and decision theory. Certainly, operations research is not an offshoot of accounting. But the forces that brought accounting practices to the fore were not unlike the forces that have introduced operations research to the business world." And Morse and Kimbal [1960, p. 104] make an even more radical assertion: "Replace operations research in the definition by cost accounting and it holds equally well."

Accountants, too, join in the chorus of voices that emphasize the connection between accounting and management science:

A substantial infusion of managerial analysis enriches financial reporting and gives it a more realistic, meaningful look. It is also true that much of the analysis now being carried on under the names of operations research, management sciences and management. services can use the sobering effect that the traditional accounting standards of audit and objectivity impose. The notion of managerial analysis and financial reporting as separated, fragmented, and even opposing activities should, and I am confident will, be soon supplanted by the view which emphasizes the basic unity of the accounting function. Accounting is an information system which provides significant, meaningful financial information about the firm—both for internal management use and for external financial reporting. What it needs is more management analysis! (Davidson [1963], p. 117.)

Also a cost expert asserts that the accountant "will become aware that cost accounting methodology has a vital interrelationship with other areas, such as engineering, statistics, mathematics, economics, organization theory, decision theory, and social psychology" (Horngren [1962], p. 766). This author then castigates the view of those colleagues who refuse to recognize this interrelationships as a concern of accounting with the following words: "This unrealistic view implies that accounting is an art that should be practiced for its own sake and that business operations are heavily compartmentalized with practically no interaction between functions. The point is that the cost accountant is most effective when he is highly conscious of these interrelationships" (Horngren [1962], p. 767). This statement is by no means in contradiction with the tight definition of accounting offered in Section 2.1. Obviously our concern is the accounting model, but the operation of this model, as was demonstrated in the Chapters 8 and 9, may well require knowledge and tools of management science. In addition to that, we showed in the Chapters 2, 3, and 6 that analytical concepts, introduced into business administration by other management sciences, may profitably be applied in clarifying concepts of the accounting model and the valuation model in general. This revelation confronts us with the question whether there exists a basic conflict between the operations analyst and the accountant. What are the roots of this conflict and how can it be resolved? The following section attempts to answer these questions.

10.2 OPERATIONS RESEARCH AND ACCOUNTING: COMPETITORS OR PARTNERS?[1]

For centuries accounting has dominated the area of practical quantitative problems in business administration. In actual practice the accounting department was the major source for quantitative financial information until the operations research team challenged this monopoly position. This challenge was badly needed; it may envigorate the organism of our discipline, and may awaken antibodies; but it may also have serious effects if this "organism" does not "react" in time. For not only do operations analysts pretend to have solutions for problems which accountants refuse to attack, the OR men even claim the ability to solve less forbidding tasks *better* and *more accurately* than accountants do. In consequence some of the radical members of this new discipline suggest that in time they will replace accountants altogether. With a strong, though implied, hint at accounting, Ackoff [1961b, p. 4] remarks: "I think it will become apparent that the expanding body of operations researchers does itself a disservice if it applies the standards of performance and concepts of methodology inherent in more traditional and less expanding areas of science." This controversy is by no means purely academic; it intimately concerns the welfare of a country's industry and warrants further introspection. But first, it seems opportune to review the genealogy of these two areas.

---

[1]This section is an expanded and revised version of a previous publication (see Mattessich [1962c] bearing the same title. However, Subsections 10.23 and 10.24 bear little resemblance to the original version.

10.21   The Case of Accounting

Trade, manufacturing, and governmental activities require internal and external control systems that traditionally have been provided for by accounting. There have been two decisive criteria of custodial control, (1) custodianship, i.e., control primarily directed toward checking the honesty and stewardship of the person subject to it, and (2) objective evidence, i.e., control based on documentation of a highly "objective" nature. But both criteria refer to *custodial control* which is only one control aspect, the other one, *efficiency control*, checks upon the ability manifested by a person or an organization. For a long time efficiency control was restricted to crude and global evaluative criteria such as sales and profit figures. Even then the accounting system could not and did not need to indicate what better sales volume or amount of profit could have been attained under a more efficient, or the most efficient management. In many cases the entrepreneur exercised the function of manager; furthermore, the industrial structure was simple enough to let experience and intuition control the aspects of efficiency. With increasing complexity of industry, the problem of efficiency control became more urgently felt. Obviously, it was the accountant's task to remedy the situation by extending and articulating the bookkeeping system. Thus control and cost figures for products, individual departments, distribution channels, etc., were generated on a large scale—data that proved useful, even if highly imprecise. Allocation assumptions are made more on grounds of thrift than of accuracy, a fact that limits the usefulness and validity of cost accounting data. Thus accounting has been confronted with a problem (which it shares with OR and any other "practical," quantitative discipline) that has not yet found a systematic solution: the question of the optimal relationship between the amount to be spent on measurement and the degree of accuracy to be desired. The difficulty in determining this point of equilibrium between these two "conflicting" variables lies not so much in the lack of analytical thought, as in finding a measure for the degree of accuracy of an accounting system, and above all in relating various accuracies to the benefits attained from them by the enterprise. In other words, the setting up of a reliable function between "degree of accuracy" and "yield" is the major hurdle.

As a result of this difficulty and the traditional methodology, accountants (even cost accountants) have restricted themselves to tasks of a quantitative descriptive nature.   Thus the activities of classification and allocation, as well as the definitional and evaluative problems connected with them, have constituted the main concern of the accountant.   This is comprehensible in the face of the bearing which accounting has upon many legal aspects, the taxation system, and the credit rating, as well as the security trading procedures.   Even cost accounting occasionally affects these areas more than the realm of managerial decision making.   The choice between the Fifo and Lifo inventory evaluation methods and the controversies connected with it amply illustrate this assertion.   Traditional cost accounting, however, does perform functions of direct use to the various echelons of management, and the emergence of "managerial accounting" (about fourteen years ago[2]) was no surprise.   This term is still not clearly defined—some identify it with cost accounting, some with accounting in general, and others with something in between these two concepts.[3]   It has, however, succeeded in deceiving many laymen and even some accountants about the capability and range of this discipline.

Thus accounting grew out of the immediate need of actual practice and was chiefly developed by practitioners who adjusted the accounting model (1) to the availability of documentary and documentable material, (2) to their relatively unsophisticated mathematical abilities, and occasionally (3) to the need of a particular purpose or department without regard to general or over-all managerial considerations.   Therefore, accounting and its effectiveness can be understood much better from a psychological than from a logical point of view.   It may be farfetched to compare its main function to that which Tolstoy assigned to General Kutuzov in his War and Peace, but a certain analogy undoubtedly exists.   There, an institution (the commanding general of the Russian Army) was painted as one whose importance lay in the representation of a stable (but perhaps purely fictitious) authority in the midst of chaos.   It would be too dangerous to carry this analogy further but it is notable that this commander, whose actions were not backed by any systematic strategy and whose actions usually defied logical

---

[2]See Vatter [1950].
[3]Cf. the definition of management accounting in R. I. Dickey (ed.), *Accountants' Cost Handbook* (2nd ed.; New York: Ronald, 1960), pp. 1–5.

analysis, ultimately carried the victory over the precisely logical and highly strategical war machinery of Napoleon.   Certainly, it was not Kutuzov but the Russian winter that won the
war.   The lesson of Tolstoy, however, consists in the implication that in spite of the winter Napoleon might have won, had it
not been for the *belief* of the Russian people in an undefeated
—though constantly retreating—army.   Likewise the effectiveness of traditional accounting lies not in the preciseness of
information to management for maximizing profit or any other
entrepreneurial goal, but in its authoritative character.   The
institution of control checks upon people and enables the de-
piction of the firm's financial structure in a simple and crude but
over-all model which constitutes a mighty bulwark against chaos.
This comparison is by no means intended as a defense of ir-
rationalism or unscientific methods; it has been presented
merely in the hope of facilitating the understanding of accounting by OR men and other people in whose logical system accounting seems to constitute a stumbling block.   There can be
no doubt that more scientific methods are better, absolutely
speaking.   There is merely the question about the threshold
where they become more profitable for a certain firm.

Thus accounting is being criticized for many reasons: that
it is based on irrelevant historical costs instead of opportunity
costs; that it provides only a description of the past, but no prediction of the future; that its models consist exclusively of identities but lack behavioral functions and do not lend themselves to
optimization procedures; that it ignores psychological factors
and uses "arbitrary" allocation procedures without consideration to the optimal organization structure; that the balance sheet
is not comprehensive enough because its inclusion-criterion of
"measurability" is too superficial; that the additivity assumption on which it operates is illusionary; that its measures are not
accompanied by error estimates, etc.   The preceding chapters
have discussed most of these problems at some detail; there it
was demonstrated that, at a closer look, some of the above-stated
complaints are unjustified, and others already prove to be invalid because of the present effort to overcome many shortcomings of our discipline.   The strongest counterargument to
most of the objections lies, to our mind, in the fact that, surprisingly enough, such criticism ignores the previously mentioned relationship between the costs of operating an account-

ing system and the yield from it. All these agruments seem to assume that the way of creating more accurate information by operations analysts costs no more, in relation to its marginal yield, than the way of creating less accurate information by accountants. We imply, of course, that both accounting and OR can attain only approximations to reality, approximations of lesser or greater accuracy, under lesser or greater costs, of a relative benefit that is not necessarily in proportion to these costs. It can well be argued that accounting is what it is, not because accountants reject analytical thinking but because under past circumstances every more sophisticated approach would have been financially unbearable to the enterprise.

10.22   The Case of Operations Research

Operations research emerged from the wartime need for solving decision-making problems of a military nature by way of mathematical-scientific methods. In many complex situations the intuition of the strategist was inferior to the solution which the mathematicians provided by means of their models. Thus it is understandable that OR methods came into vogue, not only with regard to military problems, but especially within the realm of business where the problem structure is similar, or at least amenable to the same methodology. The main feature of this approach is the construction of analytical models that permit the determination of maximum or minimum solutions. Some of these methods are nowadays well known under the names of linear, nonlinear, integer, and dynamic programing; solutions are occasionally attained in an iterative way only (e.g., the simplex method). This trend to substitute, in highly complex situations, purely analytical devices by iterative, heuristic, or even simulation approaches is another characteristic of modern OR and was strongly furthered by the advent of electronic data processing.

Out of all this grows an additional idiosyncrasy which OR shares with activity analysis[4] and which may be covered by the term "systems approach." This is the conceptualization of the problem under a viewpoint that considers the interdependence of all variables incorporated in the model. As previously pointed

---

[4]In the case of applying this new approach to macro-economics one usually speaks of activity analysis.

out, Charnes and Cooper [1957, p. 40–41] call such models *mutatis mutandis*, in contrast to the *ceteris paribus* models. The latter assume all but one variable constant whereas the former take all possible feedback reactions to other variables into consideration.

With respect to the mathematical tools Herbert Simon offers a "general recipe for using them in management decision-making."

1. Construct a *mathematical model* that satisfies the conditions of the tool to be used and which, at the same time, mirrors the important factors in the management situation to be analysed.
2. Define the *criterion function*, the measure that is to be used for comparing the relative merits of various possible courses of action.
3. Obtain *empirical estimates* of the numerical parameters in the model that specify the particular, concrete situation to which it is to be applied.
4. Carry through the mathematical process of finding the course of action which, for the specified parameter values, maximizes the criterion function. (Simon [1960], p. 16–17).

Operations research may, then, be regarded as a field of applied mathematics and statistics whose concern is the developing of sets of standard models—as well as their modification for practical application—in the micro-economy (e.g., inventory, queuing, allocation, replacement, game, transportation, learning and search theory, and so forth). These models control the efficiency of particular, limited areas within an organization.[5] The last part of this description will be stressed because it hints at one of the major shortcomings of OR: the inability (at least so far) to provide models for over-all optimization. This is partly conditioned by the technical limitations that a huge number of variables impose even on a computer, and partly by the unfortunate fact that the sum total of a series of suboptima does not necessarily yield the over-all optimum. A thorough analysis even reveals something more embarrassing, namely, that in order to optimize a part correctly, the whole ought to be optimized first. The ambition toward a global model of the firm is thus restricted to the area of simulation and to "satisficing" instead of optimizing. We have seen that attempts are under way

---

[5]There exist many attempts to define operations research. See for instance Part I of Shuchman [1963, pp. 12–60] or Ackoff [1961b] who offers a thorough inquiry into the essence of OR. Ackoff, however, does not make a distinction between operations research and management science and thus defines OR very broadly.

to construct comprehensive control models of the firm and the persons interested in this area expect great theoretical insight from the final results. With regard to the practical application of such complex models, however, skepticism is justified, for the huge number of unwieldy variables and the exceedingly high costs of such a project exclude any hope for establishing in the near future a control model of this sort for most of the industry.[6] It seems instead that a combination of OR models with the accountant's budgeting model as an over-all frame is, from the point of view of practicality of realization, a more promising solution.

A further characteristic of OR is the claim, made by leading operations analysts, that their *scientific* methods yield *superior advice* not only in technical respect but *also in matters of value judgement.* To put it bluntly, this science aims at assuming functions of morale and ethics. From this, an interesting circularity can be inferred. Originally religion fulfilled two functions: It imposed value judgements and tried to explain natural phenomena. In modern times the second function was absorbed by science which now seems to aspire to the first function as well. Yet, by imposing norms of "ethical" behavior, science infallibly returns to the womb of religion and enters into competition with politics—which since the nineteenth century has become the breeding ground for many a new creed. Although it might be preferable to be dominated by the scientists' value judgements, it is doubtful whether this new "religion" is more successful than its predecessors in overcoming the *hereditary* preferences so different in each individual. Connected with this problem, though going somewhat beyond hereditary traits, is the quest for profit maximization. The assertion that the entrepreneurs maximize profit is, in the face of overwhelming empirical contradictions, no longer tenable. But the "moral" inclinations of some management scientists makes them prone to transform this factual assertion into the normative proposition that "the entrepreneur *ought to* maximize over-all profit." Accountants, on the other hand plead that the manager tries to

---

[6]This is confirmed by a management scientist in the following sentences: "But primarily, management science has failed to assist top management because the philosophy and objectives of management science have often been irrelevant to the manager.... In many professional journal articles the attitude is that of an exercise in formal logic rather than that of a search for useful solutions to real problems." Reprinted from *Industrial Dynamics*, 1961, p. 3, by Jay W. Forrester, by permission of The M.I.T. Press. Copyright.

satisfy a plausible combination of enterprise goals which depend
on his own value judgement; they reject the thought to impose
upon him an obligation which is neither in conformity with his
intention nor attainable under the present technical limitations.

10.23   Decline and Revival

Wherever a new discipline infringes upon the territory of
another well-established one, a potential source of conflict arises.
In the case of operations research versus accounting, this conflict is, thus far, felt locally only—mainly in academic circles—,
but in general it has not yet demonstrated the strength of its
possible virulence. Whether a forceful conflict comes into being
or not depends on the power, or the equality of power, of the
opposing parties, as well as on their ability to reconcile and to
join in unison. In Subsection 4.22 we pointed out that accounting has lost much prestige during recent years; there we referred
the reader to the current chapter. This diminishing significance
of accounting as an academic field is most obviously manifested
in the enrollment figures at major universities of this country.
While the number of students electing accounting as a field of
emphasis is declining or remaining stagnant, the enrollment in
operations research has shot up and keeps on rising. Especially
serious is the fact that this shift is predominantly caused by
students of high intellectual acumen, who find OR problems
more challenging than the accounting exercises requested from
them.

The gravest problems, however, must be sought in the ignorance of many operations analysts and economists in matters
of accounting. While previously it was understood that an
economist has to be well trained in our discipline, nowadays
many students of economics are never exposed to the more profound problems of accounting; at best such students acquire familiarity with bookkeeping techniques. With regard to operations analysts the situation is even worse, the schooling of many
of them is in mathematics, engineering, behavioral science, philosophy, etc. Their accounting knowledge usually stems from
the superficial reading of an introductory text book, a learning
process that can neither enable a profound understanding of, nor
inspire enthusiasm for, our discipline. However, the apparently
simple basic mathematical structure of the accounting model
makes these scientists believe they have exhausted accounting,

and judge and criticize this discipline without having grasped its essence, often without having put a foot into an accounting department—not to speak of some practical experience with a CPA firm. The long-run danger for the industry from such an educational gap of our economists and operations analysts is obvious—one should suppose. The main hazard was illuminated from a theoretical viewpoint in Chapter 7. It lies in the eventuality of employing highly sophisticated hypotheses (as contained in most of the OR models) that are not warranted from the practical standpoint of economical operations—something closely connected with the failure to distinguish between scientific and pragmatic hypotheses.

It is surprising that operations analysts have not yet systematically explored the interrelationship between the following four properties of a model or system: (1) its degree of specification and sophistication, (2) its degree of reliability, (3) the cost of its development and operation, (4) the gross benefit derived from it. This neglect is characteristic for technocrats who are interested primarily in an elegant and impressive machinery without giving due consideration to its profitability. The area of control and planning is especially prone to such dangers, for here the benefits derived are difficult to measure. Thus it seems that *a cost accounting for systems* (similar to cost accounting for distribution, administration, research and development, etc.) seems to be called for in order to facilitate the appropriate choice between competing hypotheses, models, or systems.[7]

A further danger must be sought in the possible loss of benefits which only the accounting model affords. The wide acceptance of the duality approach in many areas of micro- and macro-accounting is sufficient evidence for such advantages. In Section 2.3 the belief was affirmed that if today business accounting were abandoned and substituted by a new information system of the firm, tomorrow the duality aspect would emerge in one form or the other and dominate this new system. Thus an unnecessary roundabout way might be avoided by paying more at-

---

[7]The "feasibility studies" carried out in actual practice rarely live up to the above quest. They neither afford a *continuous* control nor do they refer to choices between entirely different systems that compete with each other. Usually they concentrate on the choice between alternatives of similar systems. Thus far they are primarily used in substituting conventional, historical accounting systems by computerized, historical accounting systems; they are not used for choosing between budgetary planning systems and management control systems, etc.

tention to our discipline and to the advantages of the model which it offers.

Yet, the decline of accounting is not entirely due to the competition from operations research, or due to the one-sided orientation of economists and OR experts.   Accountants—as a profession, not necessarily as individuals—have failed, on one side to keep up with the mental progress of business administration, and on the other, to accept principles that enable the creation of financial statements meaningful for managerial and investment decisions.   To bring forth evidence we quote Leonard Spacek, one of the most eminent and most conscientious public accountants in this country:

Our responsibility to the public is exhibited in so many ways that it leads the public to believe we are rendering a service that we know in our own minds does not square with what the public expects of our profession....

Can we in good faith state that our work is for the protection of the public from "fraud and misrepresentation" until the standards of performance in our profession meet the requirements stated in the APB letter to the Executive Committee of the AICPA...to which I referred previously?   Bear in mind that gross negligence can be construed as fraud.   I ask you, has not the profession been guilty of such negligence in not straightening up its house? (p. 9)

What can be done to correct this situation?   The profession must show that it has the conscience of an independent professional having responsibility to all parties who rely on its opinions on financial statements—a conscience that compels it to act in defining and correcting major deficiencies in so-called generally accepted accounting principles, and then to defend the soundness of these principles before the regulatory commissions and the general public.

...The machinery is all in order; all that the profession and the Board have to do is to use it.   To do so will require initiative; and lack of initiative has thus far created our dilemma.   To develop *initiative*, we need only listen to our conscience.   This will inevitably lead us to assume our proper responsibility (pp. 13–14). [From a speech given by Leonard Spacek at the 1963 Convention of the American Accounting Association at Stanford University, reprinted by Arthur Andersen and Co. under the title "A Suggested Solution to the Principles Dilemma".]

Thus it is hardly surprising if the insufficient strive of the profession—technically and, as it seems from the preceding quotation, also ethically—has discouraged many a highly qualified student from specializing in accounting.   But, no doubt, there are many strong personalities left who believe in the mission of accounting.

10.24   The Mission of Accounting

What is this future mission?   Management scientists find the *raison d'être* of accounting in procuring data for operations research.   Indeed, the process of generating "raw material" for OR models is a great embarrassment to operations analysts. Many of the data needed are not regularly supplied; a fairly accurate measurement of most of these data is still, and will in future be, forbiddingly expensive.   Some cannot be measured at all, and accountants mock the OR men with the question of whether the crystal ball that might supply them with the required information has already been found.   The only way out of this dilemma obviously is to make a crude, and often very arbitrary, estimate of the magnitude of these variables; this, however, defeats the operations analyst's claim to supply more accurate information than the accountant does.   Therefore, even if cost accounting and OR were direct competitors, the problem would be more complex than it appears to the operations analyst who sees only the mathematical superiority of his own approach. The question must be posed in a different fashion, we have to ask instead: where in a particular enterprise does the golden middle lie between "the pitfalls of oversimplification and the morass of overcomplication" (Bellman [1957], p.x).   Since this middle road is differently situated in every firm, no pat answer is available.   It will take considerable time to find the critical size of enterprise for which the mathematical overcomplication and "technical" oversimplification of OR models are less disadvantageous than the mathematical oversimplification and "technical" overcomplication of the accounting model.   This in itself is an optimization problem; one that might be solved some day by OR's own methods, such as learning theory and so on.   Until then the superiority of OR methods will have to find its proof by trial and error, which means through the evidence of practical results on a large scale.   Thus the hope for abandoning accounting, or an immediate general acceptance of a "universal" information system of the firm, in accord with the suggestions of some operations analysts, is not great.

But does the future of accounting merely rest in providing the input data for OR models?   We should rather assume that accountants will not accept this assignment, that they are unwilling to fetch the chestnuts out of the fire, that they refuse to be blamed for the failure of a model for which they shall supply

unprocurable data.   To our mind the accountant's mission lies
in the function to control the validity of the models recommended by the operations analysts, to reject these models if
they prove to be unrealistic, to aid in making them acceptable if
they prove to be uneconomically expensive, to smooth the difficulties if these models prove unmanageable.   In other words to
co-operate closely with the OR men, to advise them with the
accountant's rich store of practical know-how, with his intuition
for the feasible, and his wisdom of the golden middle.   However,
the accountant can fulfill this task only if prepared for it, if
competent to judge the doing of the model builders, if familiar
with their tools and methods.

Once accountants and OR analysts learn to recognize their
own deficiencies and discover that their strong points are not
of a competitive but of a complementary nature, the "optimal
solution" might be found in a co-operative effort of both groups.
The advent of "management science" (a much broader area than
"operations research" in the conventional sense) may be interpreted as a start in this direction.   The founders of this interdisciplinary field have recognized that a close collaboration
between scholars from many disciplines is required to develop
tools which master the ever-increasing complexity of our economic environment.   They are becoming aware that a co-ordination between applied mathematics, behavioral economics, and
accounting contains the ingredients required to master the economic problems of the future.

Indeed, the more moderate advocates of management science
recognize that cost accounting provides an effective control
mechanism and supplies important (though not all) raw material to the operations researcher; they realize that imple-
ments as well entrenched as those of cost accounting cannot be
displaced overnight without a serious damage to the whole industry.   Another category of operations analysts, however, in-
sist on a complete break with the past, they reject any compromise or co-ordination with accounting and plead for an entirely
novel approach.   If we examine the camp of the accountants we
observe here, too, various reactions to the new movement of management science.   One group, and it appears to us that it still is
the dominating one, wants to disregard or deny the impact
which this new development makes upon accounting; they refuse
to acquire even the basic mathematical knowledge necessary to

understand operations research methods and behave in a manner which is erroneously attributed to the African ostrich. The second group, which seems to grow slowly but steadily in number, recognizes the importance of the achievements of operations research for the field of accounting, is willing to sacrifice enough time and energy to learn and understand the working methods of management's new science, and admits that major revisions are due in managerial accounting, but firmly believes that the main structure of accounting will survive in this process of reformation. Most of the members of this group do not favor sudden and radical adjustments, and some believe that a first step toward co-operation with operations research is to analyze and describe the mathematical-behavioral structure of accounting models. On one hand, they are aware that the future accounting system of the firm cannot do without many technical and often trivial-appearing details, but, on the other hand, they are skeptical of the idea that a central information system of the firm— in which are also stored and elaborated the innumerable, purely technological, personnel, psychological, and market data—can fulfill all the functions of traditional accounting. In our opinion such an information system may perform useful services to many departments, but can neither be identified with what is commonly understood as accounting, nor replace it overnight. Finally those few accountants must be mentioned who have lost all hope for the future of their discipline and hasten to abandon what they believe to be a sinking ship.

10.3 SUMMARY OF THE BOOK

It is difficult to reflect the spirit of a book in a synopsis, and it is impossible to recapitulate all the essential details and conclusions of our book. Yet, the unorthodox character of this work warrants the attempt to offer a concise and integrated view of major ideas contained in the individual chapters. Thereby our concern with the following three aspects of accounting will be illuminated: its essence, the purification of its concepts, and its future under the impact of analytical methods.

Chapter 1 ("Introduction") offers a survey of the various theoretical and practical needs to "overhaul" accounting. Recent developments in management science and electronic data processing make themselves felt already. Soon they will gather mo-

mentum and will surprise those accountants who are unwilling
to keep pace with the accelerated progress of science and technology. If the majority of our colleagues are reluctant to face
this problem, severe and painful repercussions to our profession are inevitable. It is not sufficient to breed an esoteric cast
of specialists—versed in accounting, mathematics, and computer systems—nor is it necessary that all accountants become
experts in operations research. The problem is to get hold of
the majority of accountants, to make them realize the fundamental
nature of this shift, to make them see its implications for their
own future, and to help them master this critical period of
transition.

This change entails a rethinking that must start at the very bottom of our discipline. There, the analytical approach begins by
staking the border of accounting, and by clarifying its basic assumptions. This task is attacked in *Chapter 2* ("Basic Assumptions
and Definitions")—a chapter that, together with Appendix A,
constitutes the most fundamental part of our book. It offers a
definition of accounting which is in conformity with clear boundaries. It suggests a flexible definition of income, and examines the
concepts of income and wealth. It explains the "duality principle"
as a reflection of a series of two-dimensional processes such as
giving and receiving, producing and consuming, selling and purchasing, possessing and owning, lending and borrowing, saving
and investing. The description of these processes enforces the
accounting model which offers a double classification and enables
the interrelating of these activities, connecting purchasing with
investing or consuming, receiving with purchasing or borrowing,
selling with paying or lending, etc. Thus *the accounting model
imposes legal and economic dualities upon a host of otherwise unstructured
commercial data.* Above all, this chapter contains a set of eighteen
basic assumptions which hold for all micro- *as well as* macro-accounting systems.

These assumptions—presented in great detail and supplemented by a set-theoretical formulation in Appendix A—are as
follows:

1. *Monetary Values:* There exists a set of additive values, expressed
   in a monetary unit; this set is isomorphic to the system of (positive and negative) integers plus the number zero.
2. *Time Intervals:* There exists a set of elementary (or minimal),
   additive time intervals (instances).

3. *Structure:* There exists a structured set of classes (a hierarchy of equivalence classes) reflecting significant categories of an entity.
4. *Duality:* For all accounting transactions, it is true that a value is assigned to a three-dimensional concept (vector or ordered triple) consisting of two accounts and a time instance.
5. *Aggregation:* Every balance assigns a (monetary) value—i.e., the arithmetic sum of all (positive and negative) values aggregated during a period in an account—to an ordered pair; the latter consists of the pertinent account and the above-stated period which starts with the accounting period.
6. *Economic Objects:* There exists a set of economic objects whose values and physical properties are subject to change.
7. *Inequity of Monetary Claims:* There exists a custom to enter debts with the understanding to redeem them in legal tender at face value—whether meanwhile price level changes vis-à-vis this legal tender have occurred or not.
8. *Economic Agents:* There exists a set of economic agents who set specific goals to an accounting system, command resources, and make plans and decisions with regard to economic actions.
9. *Entities:* There exists a set of entities setting the frame for economic actions.
10. *Economic Transactions:* There exists a set of empirical phenomena, called "economic transactions." Each of these transactions assigns, by means of empirical hypotheses, a value to an ordered pair of transactors (categories) and a time instance.
11. *Valuation:* There exists a set of hypotheses determining the value assigned to an accounting transaction.
12. *Realization:* There exists a set of hypotheses, specifying which of the following three mutually exclusive effects are exercised by a change (in quantity, value, legal status, etc.) of an entity's economic object(s). Such a change either:
    a) Affects the value assigned to the current income of the entity; or
    b) Does not affect the owner's equity of this entity (within the specified period); or
    c) Affects the owner's equity without affecting the current income of the entity.
13. *Classification:* There exists a set of hypotheses required to establish a chart of accounts.
14. *Data Input:* There exists a set of hypotheses required to determine the form of data input and the level of aggregation for which accounting transactions are to be formulated.
15. *Duration:* There exists a set of hypotheses about the expected life of the entity (or entities) under consideration, and the duration of individual accounting periods or subperiods.
16. *Extension:* There exists a set of hypotheses specifying the empirical conditions under which two or more accounting systems can be consolidated and extended to a more comprehensive system.

17. *Materiality:* There exists a set of hypotheses (criteria) determining if and when an economic transaction, or related event, is to be reflected by an accounting transaction.
18. *Allocation:* There exists a set of hypotheses determining the allocation of an entity's economic objects or flows of services to subentities and similar categories.

Some of these assumptions deal exclusively with logical concepts, others contain empirical notions as well. This set of eighteen assumptions—though amenable to further refinement—is, in contrast to preceding attempts, rigorous enough to form the key to *a general theory of accounting*: a meta-theory which provides a frame for alternative hypotheses tailor-made for individual objectives, a theory which accepts the objective of *profit maximization* as a possible *specific* hypothesis, but *not* as a basic assumption.

Since accounting is defined as the *quantitative description* and projection of income circulation and of wealth aggregates, the task of *Chapter 3* ("Modern Measurement Theory and Accounting") is to explore thoroughly the notion of quantitative description. Thus modern measurement theory—as advanced by Stevenson, Torgerson, Churchman, Coombs, Ackoff, and others—is discussed and serves to illuminate the essence of accountancy. This chapter emphasizes the predominant role of the "nominal scale" and utilizes the *basic charts of accounts*—extensively employed in Continental Europe—as a conspicuous illustration to support the view which regards classification as the root of measurement.   Classification in accounting has strong empirical overtones and the resulting identities are by no means "arbitrary definitions."   Furthermore, it is demonstrated that ordinal and interval scales are used to some extent in accounting, while the ratio scale dominates valuation.   But since *valuation* is merely *measurement by fiat* it is, in spite of the most rigorous scale, a more precarious activity than other commensurations (based on fundamental or derived measurement).   An additional difficulty arises out of the frequent failure to provide probabilistic realiability measures for accounting values, a problem of which some aspects are illuminated here, others are dealt with in Chapter 7.   Finally, this Chapter 3 illustrates the various modes in which accounting measures and the duality aspect can be expressed.   Thus the following forms are discussed: the net-work form, the double-entry form, the matrix form, the journal entry, and vector form. This comparison is enhanced by juxtaposing schemata of the four modes.

Chapter 4 ("Evolution of the Accounting Model") illuminates the basic assumptions from an historical viewpoint. It also presents opinions about accounting by prominent nonaccountants— something that is supplemented in other chapters. Although this collection of pronouncements is far from being exhaustive, it contains names like Boulding, Cayley, Churchman, Copeland, Fisher, Friedell, Gilbert, Goethe, Jaszy, Kuznets, V. and W. Lutz, Morgenstern, Schumpeter, Schwartz, Sombart, Spengler, Stone and others. This chapter also demonstrates Quesnay's *tableau économique* as a manifestation of the *duality* principle, one that got along without utilizing double-entry. In consequence, a detailed version of the tableau is presented in traditional accounting as well as in matrix form. From this presentation three conclusions are drawn: (1) that Quesnay could have made his analysis considerably more lucid by taking advantage of the traditional accounting frame; (2) that the *tableau économique* can easily be converted into a system which closely resembles our present-day national income and product accounting; and (3) that Quesnay's failure to produce a meaningful net product figure (regarding agriculture as the sole productive economic sector) is in close connection with *his neglect to distinguish properly between intermediate and final consumption.*

This chapter emphasizes the significance of Irving Fisher's endeavor to connect our discipline with economics by exploiting the accounting approach for the analysis of income and wealth in general. After some historical references to cost accounting, opportunity is taken to introduce the reader to various areas of macro-accounting, illuminating the validity of our basic assumptions in these areas. These first four chapters comprise Part I ("On the Essence and Foundations of Accounting").

Part II ("On Valuation and Hypotheses Formulation") embraces the chapters 5, 6, and 7. *Chapter 5* ("Towards a General View of Valuation—Economics and Accounting") first offers a recapitulation and a criticism of the economist's and the accountant's traditional approaches to valuation. On the one side, conventional marginal value theory is helpful as a theoretical prop, as an exercise in logical deduction, as a study in isolated economic phenomena; but it is dangerous to apply it to practical situations which do not meet the required preconditions. On the other side, it is difficult to accept the accountant's historical cost basis as a value measure for managerial decisions. We assert that different objectives call for different valuation methods and demonstrate that the historical cost basis is, contrary to common belief, by no means unbiased. The question whether acquisition costs *adjusted* for depreciation and price-level changes constitute a basis of measurement to be preferred to the "present value" method may be answered in three stages (1) determining the likelihood of the assumption that a present trend will continue, (2) determining the degree of uncertainty attributed to the estimation of future net receipts to be discounted and (3) comparing the likelihood of 1 with the degree of uncertainty of 2.

Beyond this, three important new developments toward a more realistic valuation procedure in actual practice (emphasizing *current cost basis* and the *need for price-level adjustments*) are examined and discussed in this chapter. The first advance is Edwards and Bell's [1961] *theory of measuring business income.* The discussion of this contribution is complemented by *a test* of Edwards and Bell's theory that was *carried out in actual practice* by our research assistant. This test reveals that, in spite of some difficulties it is possible to adjust, on working papers, the data of traditional accounting in an inexpensive way that provides financial statements relevant to managerial decisions and that is in accord with Edwards and Bell's suggestions. The second advance is the proposal for a realistic set of accounting principles made by Sprouse and Moonitz [1962] in the *AICPA-Accounting Research Study No. 3.* The eight principles (realization, profit separation, inclusion, asset valuation, valuation of cash-liabilities, valuation of noncash liabilities, classification of owners' equity, classification of profit components) are concisely summarized, while the principle of asset valuation is discussed and presented in full detail. The third advance is represented by the most recent recommendation on *Reporting the Effects of Price-Level Changes—AICPA-Accounting Research Study No. 6* [1963] which primarily is concerned with *general* price-level adjustments. Among other aspects, the possible future transition to *specific* price-level adjustments, and thus to a *promising* version of *current cost* evaluation, is discussed.

This analysis of valuation problems is continued in *Chapter 6* ("Toward a General View of Valuation—Management Science"). It begins with an examination of the criticism of accounting valuation put forth by one of the most eminent theoreticians of management science. Yet, Churchman's criticism is tenable only under the premise that the objective of management, and thus of accountancy, is profit maximization. But how can economists assert that entrepreneurs *do* maximize profits if no one knows how to go about it? Which manager can tell where in the end the maximum is to be found? How can management scientists pretend that entrepreneurs *would like to*, or ought to, maximize profit, as long as we cannot formulate a realistic profit concept that lends itself to over-all maximization. The major variables dominating microeconomic behavior are manifold and the constraints are highly complex; thus far no one has succeeded in presenting an image of the firm that comes close enough to reality and at the same time is amenable to an optimization procedure. Since empirical evidence does not confirm the profit maximization assumption—something admitted by many scholars—a good deal of Churchman's criticism can be refuted. His own outline of a "transaction theory" is also shortly discussed.

In due course, this chapter gives emphasis to those aspects of management science which are, in one way or the other, concerned with value, and which help to clarify the various aspects of valuation. In this connection the following areas are referred to: the phenomenon of the *dual* of linear programing and its value imputation (offering opportunity to acquaint the reader with the basic concepts of linear programing); the new investment theory which proposes a *simultaneous solution* of the problems how to invest *and* how to finance this investment (Massé [1959, 1962] and Albach [1960, 1962]); the measuring of the enterprise value by econometric means; and above all the decisive contribution of decision theory and Bayesian statistics to valuation. Out of these examinations grow *some propositions that might form the launching basis for a general and functional theory of valuation.* A theory that respects the context in which valuation occurs, and that recognizes the need for assigning to an asset a *set of values* instead of a single value only. Our proposal also contains an accounting solution to the dilemma of nonlinearity of value functions and the resulting nonadditivity.

Chapter 7 ("Empirical Hypotheses in Accounting") begins with examining empirical hypotheses in general; it discusses the originally hesitating and nowadays universal acceptance of statistical hypotheses. Predominantly, the chapter is concerned with the problem and the difficulties of hypotheses formulation in accounting and with the epistemological difference between hypotheses for decision making in everyday life and business practice (pragmatic hypotheses) on one hand and purely scientific hypotheses on the other (related to this distinction is the difference between *a priori* hypotheses and rigorous statistical hypotheses). The criterion suggested for distinguishing pragmatic from scientific hypotheses is the process of invalidation. A pragmatic hypothesis is invalidated (rejected) by demonstrating (or believing) that in the long-run, or on the average, the actions based on it, yield results that are less *satisfactory* than the results of actions based on another, available hypothesis; while a scientific hypothesis is refuted by instances (acceptable to the experts) which testify reliably to the falsity of this hypothesis. Since the term "satisfactory" refers to the *net* benefits derived from a pragmatic hypothesis (or set of hypotheses), the costs involved in generating and operating a specific hypothesis will be a decisive factor in deciding for or against its validity. Thus the empirical task of the normative scientist (accountant, operations analyst, econometrician, etc.) lies primarily in formulating and ranking competing pragmatic hypotheses, and not in a search for rigorous scientific hypotheses. This viewpoint must not be confused with that of Friedman, who neglects to make a distinction between these two kinds of hypotheses. Pragmatic hypotheses are closely related to the *persistency assumption* (the premise of continuation of a present trend in the absence of contrary evidence) and to the *trial and error principle* which justifies an hypothesis by the ultimate result arising from corrective interactions between a series of preliminary attempts and the observations of their outcome. Morgenstern's [1963] profound insight into the idiosyncrasies of accounting measures and his suggestions for improvement are also given some play by paying special attention to the problem of reliability of accounting data and accounting hypotheses. Thus the complementation of accounting statements by error estimates and judgment probabilities is considered.

Traditional accounting rarely employs the term "hypothesis" whereas the term "rule" belongs to its standard vocabulary. Thus the last section of this chapter examines the distinction between basic assumptions, rules, and empirical hypotheses. In many situations the accounting rules constitute constraints within which the actual hypotheses are being formulated. Since the concept "rule" and "hypothesis" are not identical, future accounting, inspired by management science, is expected to shift its emphasis from *rules* to *hypotheses*. Yet, one ought to be aware that the low level of generalization of most accounting hypotheses makes it difficult to evolve a comprehensive and generally valid deductive system—a trait that is characteristic for all disciplines that are in an early stage of scientific development. This chapter closes with a comprehensive survey of present-day accounting rules as recommended by The American Institute of Certified Public Accountants.

The last three chapters of the book form Part III ("On Projection and Planning for the Future"). *Chapter 8* ("Planning Models for the Micro- and Macro-Economy,") offers a concise introduction to interindustry accounting and analysis, to Tinbergen-type models, to macro-economic simulation models, and to management control models. It points out the relation of accounting to these approaches, and constitutes an important pedagogic means to acquaint business accountants with instruments for planning and projection that have some common ground with periodic budgeting.

In the area of input-output analysis special attention is paid to the explanation of the matrix presentation, and of such concepts as transaction matrix, input-coefficient matrix, technology matrix, inverse technology matrix, etc. Also discussed are the major assumptions underlying the Leontief-type models (closed and open models as well as dynamic models), the linear programing interpretation, and the meaning of the primal and dual of an input-output system.

Tinbergen-type models are discussed and illustrated by means of the Klein-Goldberger [1955] model for the United States. The twenty basic equations of this model are presented, and details are illuminated at the investment function. The connection between Tinbergen-type models and national income accounting, input-output analysis, and macro-simulation models are indicated.

A short introduction to system simulation in general is offered. Hereby the reader's attention is drawn to *macro-simulation* models by Adelman, Balderston and Hoggatt, Cohen, Fisher, Gillespie, Holland, Orcutt, and *micro-simulation* models by Bonini, Cyert and March, Forrester, Sprowls and Asimow, and the Systems Development Corporation.

Chapter 9 ("Budget Models of the Firm") recognizes that two extreme possibilities of constructing a model of the firm can be envisaged: the accountant's simple balance sheet model and the operations analyst's sophisticated management control model. A great variety of alternative models in between these extremes are imaginable, and the task of accounting as a management science will be to evolve a general construct that compromises between theoretical needs and practical means. Such a compromise would supply the basis for individual over-all models of the firm, useful in business practice. Since the author believes in an evolutionary rather than in a revolutionary solution, a simulation model is recommended which, at first, reflects an existing budget system but which is flexible enough to permit step-by-step refinements. Thus, from time to time additional constraints may be formalized, new adaptive controls may be incorporated, supplementary OR features may be connected, etc.—all this without abandoning the basic accounting frame. Before the initial form of such a model is presented, the possibility of constructing "analytical" budget models (which seem to have less prospect of practical application than simulation models) is explored. This offers opportunity to demonstrate some structural peculiarities of budget models which have not been articulated by traditional budgeting theory. A budget system is conceived as an accounting model for which (1) the transactions are highly aggregated, (2) a limited number of main accounts are used, (3) some global transactions (e.g., anticipated sales, investment, etc.) are exogenously given, and above all, (4) the remaining global transactions (endogenous variables like production input, receivable collection, etc.) can be expressed as functions of the given or predetermined transactions. This is achieved by means of a set of empirically determined parameters not unlike the input coefficients in Leontief models. The possibility of explicitly introducing side-constraints and an objective function in order to formulate the budget system as a (linear) programing model is shortly discussed and reference is made to related suggestions by Charnes, Cooper and Ijiri [1963] and Stedry [1960].

The second part of Chapter 9 provides a fairly *general formulation* of a periodic budget, designed for simulating the financial aspects of the firm. The master budget consists of nine subbudgets (sales, production, material, labor, factory overheads, operating expenses, cash flows, projected income statement, projected balance sheet), each of these subbudgets consists of a list of variables and parameters with detailed explanations. At the end of each sub-budget the hypotheses, similar to those encountered in actual practice, are stated. Traditional budgeting, as a crude way of simulating the firm is here being refined by translating an existing budget system into a formalized model. The corresponding computer program is contained in the companion volume *Simulation of the Firm through a Budget Computer Program* (Homewood: Irwin, 1964). The purpose is to provide a *proto-type* for actual practice and a means of demonstration for classroom use. This "budget simulation" is less ambitious than, and distinct from, the simulation through management control models. While the latter models are well suited to improve the organizational structure and the long-run decision pattern of a firm, *budget models* serve the *short-run planning*. The proposed budget model yields many benefits, above all, it enables computation of a large number of alternative (short-run) factor combinations, and greatly facilitates the frequent revisions of a firm's budget. (These revisions have been called the nightmare of the controller; frequently they require months, and provide data too obsolete for attaining optimal control.)

This Chapter 9 is not a mere "appendix" to the main ideas of this book; it is an organic part of it, since it demonstrates that the essence of the budget model does not lie in a set of empirical hypotheses (which can easily be exchanged against an alternative set) but lies in a general and permanent structure manifested in the *accounting* frame. Hereby the "entries" need be no longer individual figures but may be conceived as variables of respectable generality which may represent behavioral functions or definitional equations.

Chapter 10 ("Accounting as a Management Science"), including this summary, tries to convey the need for regarding accounting as part of an interdisciplinary effort which calls for a close co-operation between accountants and operations analysts. To achieve such a collaboration—it not only is necessary that accountants acquire some understanding of analytical tools and methods—the ignorance of many operations analysts and economists as to the essence of accounting must also be overcome. The basic conflict between operations research and accounting is rooted in their genealogies and may be related to the tension between idealism and realism. This chapter tries to make both groups, the accountants as well as the operations analysts, see their shortcomings, tries to demonstrate where they failed in the past, and tries to point out a way for a fruitful teamwork.

Thus a novel viewpoint of accountancy was introduced, not a complete theory, but a foundation and outline to such a theory. Undoubtedly, this book is plagued with all the shortcomings of a pioneering attempt, but it affords a bridge between accounting and operations research, though one that is still to be converted into a permanent structure. The need for such a construct is not of recent origin, but it becomes more urgent with the progress of time. Indeed, this need was foreshadowed, years ago, in Boulding's [1955, p. 270] portentous remark: "It may be that the time is almost ripe for a thorough overhauling of both accounting and statistical procedures."

Appendixes

APPENDIX A

SET-THEORY
AND THE AXIOMATIZATION
OF ACCOUNTING

THIS APPENDIX is designed to fulfill a twofold task. First, it explains some expressions of the logic of extension (set-theory),[1] encountered in the text and required for the understanding of the second part of this appendix. Second, it offers a set-theoretical interpretation of the foundations of accounting in order to overcome linguistic impurities of some accounting concepts. In conformity with this attempt is the reduction of accounting to a small number of basic notions from which the remaining concepts can be derived. Hereby the accountant is offered the opportunity to get acquainted with the elements of the algebra of sets through their application to his own discipline, an approach that ought to facilitate the comprehension of some facets of this much talked-about common territory of logic and mathematics. On the other hand, the management scientist, familiar with set-theory, will gain deeper insight into the essence of accounting by reading Section A.2. In order to understand the second part of this appendix no mathematical prerequisites beyond high-school algebra and the few concepts explained in Section A.1. are required. But in absorbing novel ideas and in handling new tools, patience and persistency can hardly be dispensed with. In the face of the immense success and vast spread which set-

---

[1] Elementary logic may be presented in form of the *logic of extension* or by means of the *logic of intension*. The former directs its attention to the *classes* of objects with specific properties (i.e., the logic of classes or algebra of sets of which the English mathematician George Boole [1854] may be regarded as the originator). The logic of intension, on the other hand, is a logic of predicates, it compares qualities and attributes of objects. In many cases the logic of intension can be translated into the more economical expressions of set theory; beyond this a combination of intensional and extensional logic is possible. Of special significance for the logic of intension are the *two quantifiers*. The distinction between *existential quantifier* ($\exists x$ "there exists *some* x such that") and *universal quantifier* ($\forall x$ "for *all* x it is true that") prevents much confusion encountered in classical logic and philosophy.

theory can score, the effort to attain some grasp of modern logic will not be in vain.[2]

A.1 EXPLANATION OF SOME CONCEPTS OF THE ALGEBRA OF SETS

This section is not designed to teach set-theory, its intent is *to explain a few notions* of the algebra of sets that have been utilized in this book. The strength of set-theory lies in its rigor and in its generality of application. The following presentation illustrates concepts and operations by graphical means, but it must be borne in mind that a graph constitutes only one out of many possible interpretations of a specific set-theoretical notion. For the sake of suggestive illustration we use the commonly applied Venn diagrams and similar devices which represent a set by a circular or rectangular frame; where this frame is drawn in strong lines, a particular set is emphasized; dots within this frame depict the elements of this specific set (the elements of the remaining sets are usually not shown explicitly). What here is demonstrated for two sets, holds analogously for three or more sets as well. The universe of discourse U is itself a set, of which the sets under discussion are subsets (independent of whether U is implied or stated explicitly).

I.   A *set* is a well-defined collection or class of objects; the objects are called elements or members. The content of a set may be conveyed either

    (1) by *listing* all elements, e.g.:
        the set $A = \{a_1, a_2, a_3, a_4\}$,
        in this connection the expression "$a_1 \epsilon A$" means "a_1 *is an element of* A";
        the set $N = \{1, 3, 5, 7, 9\}$;
        the set $E = \{\text{Napoleon I, Napoleon III}\}$; or
    (2) by generic *description* e.g.:
        the set $A = \{a_i : i = 1, \ldots, 4\}$;
        the set $N = \{n : 0 < n < 10 \text{ and } n \text{ is odd}\}$;
        the set $E = \{e : e \text{ was a reigning emperor of the French}\}$;
    the elements a_i, n, and e in the above sets are called generic elements and the colon stands for the expression "such that." Fundamentally, these two ways of constructing sets are equivalent, but in cases of infinite sets the generic description is mandatory, and in the case of large finite sets, it obviously is more convenient than the individual listing of all ele-

---

[2]The reader interested in an introduction to modern logic is referred to the works by Carnap [1958], Kershner and Wilcox [1950], Langer [1953], Lewis and Langford [1959]. Suppes [1957], Wilder [1952]. For a set-theoretic treatment of value theory see Debreu [1959], and for a set-theoretical presentation of some facets of biology see Woodger [1952], a book not only of value for biologists but for every scholar interested in the axiomatization of a natural or social science.

ments. The empty set contains *no* element and is designated by the symbol $\emptyset = \{\quad\}$; it is an important concept, the set-theoretical meaning of which corresponds to the *zero* in number theory.

II. The *union* of two or more sets is a set resulting from the "addition" operation of set-theory:

FIGURE A-1

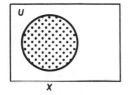 $\cup$ 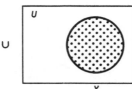 $=$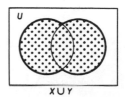

Hence $X \cup Y$ is the set of all elements which are contained either in X or in Y or in both: $X \cup Y = \{z: z \epsilon X$ or $z \epsilon Y$ or both$\}$.

III. The *intersection* of two or more sets is the result of one of the two "multiplication" operations of set-theory:

FIGURE A-2

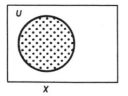 $\cap$ 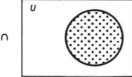 $=$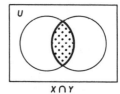

Hence $X \cap Y$ is the set of all elements which are contained simultaneously in X and Y; $X \cap Y = \{z: z \epsilon X$ and $z \epsilon Y\}$. The reader may verify (perhaps by means of graphs) that the operations of "union" and "intersection" obey the following laws:

1. The commutative law for unions: $X \cup Y = Y \cup X$
2. The associative law for unions: $(X \cup Y) \cup Z$
   $= X \cup (Y \cup Z)$
3. The commutative law for intersections: $X \cap Y = Y \cap X$
4. The associative law for intersections:
   $(X \cap Y) \cap Z = X \cap (Y \cap Z)$
5. The distributive law: $X \cap (Y \cup Z) = (X \cap Y) \cup (X \cap Z)$

IV. A *subset* Y of the set X is a set which contains no other elements than those contained in X. Hence Y may contain fewer elements than X but not more.

FIGURE A–3

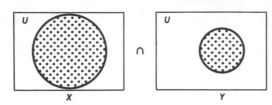 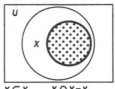

$$Y \subset X \qquad X \cap Y = Y$$

(frequently the symbol $\subseteq$ is used for designating the notion "is a subset of," while the symbol $\subset$ is used for the notion "is a *true* subset of." In this exposition we do not need the latter notion, hence we use the symbol $\subset$ to indicate all subsets including the case $X \subset X$. If $X \subset Y$ and $Y \subset X$ then $X = Y$. The reader may verify that $X \cap Y = Y$ and $X \cup Y = X$ if $Y \subset X$.

V.   The *difference* of two sets (X minus Y) is a set comprising all elements contained in X except those elements also contained in Y: $X - Y = \{z : z \epsilon X \text{ and } z \notin Y\}$; the symbol $\notin$ indicates "is *not* an element of."

FIGURE A–4

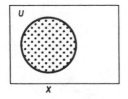 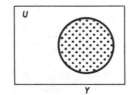 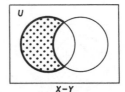

VI.   The *complement* of a set X is a set $\overline{X}$ which contains all elements of the universe except those contained in X, hence: $\overline{X} = \{z : z \epsilon U \text{ and } z \notin X \text{ and } X \subset U\}$

FIGURE A–5

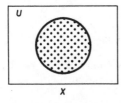 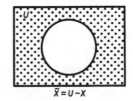

VII.   The second "multiplication" operation of set theory leads to the *Cartesian product* which is the *set of all ordered couples* or *n*-tuples that can be formed from two or n sets respectively.

Figure A–6 demonstrates the two sets X and Y and the set of all ordered couples $X \times Y$ (the Cartesian product X times Y) which can be formed out of them.   In an analogous way the Cartesian product of three, four, or n sets would result in a three, four, or n-dimensional system with ordered triples, quadruples, or n-tuples respectively.

In contrast to the operations of union and intersection, the Cartesian product is *not commutative*.   Hence $X \times Y \neq Y \times X$ (unless $X = Y$) (e.g., $(x_1, y_1) \neq (y_1, x_1)$) the *order* of the elements is decisive and a strict distinction between the two sets (X and Y) has to be made by calling the first set the *domain* and the second set the *counterdomain* (or range) of the Cartesian product

$$X \times Y = \{(x, y) : x \epsilon X \text{ and } y \epsilon Y\}$$

FIGURE A–6

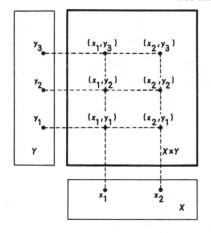 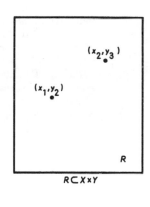

In a less naïve and more formal way the set $X \times Y$ and its subset R (see item VIII) are written as follows:
$$X \times Y = \{(x_1, y_1), (x_2, y_1), (x_1, y_2), (x_2, y_2), (x_1, y_3), (x_2, y_3)\},$$
$$R = \{(x_1, y_2), (x_2, y_3)\}, \text{ hence } R \subset X \times Y$$

VIII. A *relation* is a subset of a Cartesian product.   The elements of this subset are ordered n-tuples; (in the special case of ordered *couples* one speaks of a binary relation).   This is illustrated in Figure A–7 as well as in the following examples:

(a) $M = \{(x, y) : x \text{ is a mother, and } y \text{ is her child}\}$

expresses the motherhood relation ("is the mother of") which could also be written xMy or $M(x, y)$; hence $x_1 M y_1$ is a propositional function expressing that x_1 is the mother of y_1; if x_1 is Eva and y_1 is Abel than we obtain the proposition "Eva is the mother of Abel."

(b) $L = \{(x, y) : x \epsilon X$ and $y \epsilon Y$ and x is larger than $y\}$
expresses the relation "is larger than" (hence $L = >$);

(c) $F = \{(a_1, a_2, t, v) : a_1, a_2 \epsilon A, t \epsilon T, v \epsilon V\}$
expresses the relation "is an *accounting transaction*"—from a_1 (credit) to a_2 (debit) at time t with value v—if A is a set of accounts, t the set of time instances, and V the set of values. It can also be written in form of an operation $F(a_1, a_2, t) = v$ (since an operation is a special kind of function, and a function is a special kind of relation—see item VIII). This relationship is a subset of the following Cartesian product $A \times A \times T \times V$ and is no longer a binary but a quaternary relation. However, every "n-ary" relation can be reduced to a binary relation by treating the first two elements of each n-tuple as a single element.

Obviously, relations and sets in general are characterized by properties. Some of the generally significant properties (commutativity, associativity) were already encountered in item III, others (reflexivity, symmetry, transitivity) will be found in items XI and XII of this appendix. The relation of a "one-to-one correspondence" repeatedly encountered— but not yet properly explained—shall be discussed under item X. The distinction made in item VII between domain and counterdomain also holds for relations and functions (see item IX).

IX. A *function F* is a relation on the sets X and Y such that for every element of the domain X there exists exactly one element of the counterdomain Y.[3]

FIGURE A-7

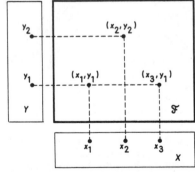

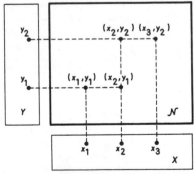

The set F is a function on X to Y since for every $x \epsilon X$ there is exactly one element of $y \epsilon Y$.

The set N is not a function since for $x_2 \epsilon X$ there exist *two* elements $y_1, y_2 \epsilon Y$.

Note that the converse[4] of a function (also called "singular function") need not be a function.

---

[3] Obviously the sets X and Y of item X are not identical with those of item IX.

[4] The *converse* of a function is attained by making the domain of the original function to the counterdomain and vice versa.

FIGURE A-8

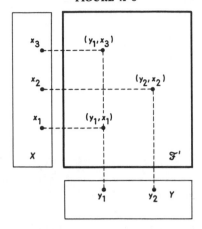

The set $F' = \{(y_1, x_1), (y_1, x_3), (y_2, x_2)\}$ is the converse of the set $F = \{(x_1, y_1), (x_2, y_2), (x_3, y_1)\}$. But while F is a function, F' is not a function since to an element of the (new) domain $y_1 \epsilon Y$ there correspond *two* elements of the (new) counterdomain $x_1, x_3 \epsilon X$.

X.   If A and B are sets and ϑ is a function on $A \times B$ then ϑ is a *one-to-one correspondence* between A and B, if
(*i*)   the domain of ϑ is A;
(*ii*) the counterdomain of ϑ is B;
(*iii*) the converse of ϑ is also a function.
Less rigorously this may be expressed as follows: two sets are in one-to-one correspondence when there is a *reversible* mapping that assigns to each element of one set, *one and only one* element of the other set.

FIGURE A-9

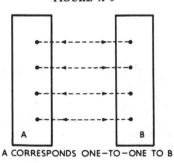

A CORRESPONDS ONE–TO–ONE TO B

Figure A-9 should not be confused with a one-to-one *mapping* which is a *one-directional* matching operation between two sets such that to each member of the set C one corresponding member of the set B is assigned (see Figure A–10).

FIGURE A–10

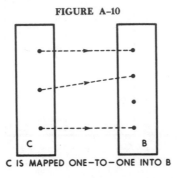

C IS MAPPED ONE–TO–ONE INTO B

If several members of C are mapped into one member of B we speak of a many-to-one mapping (Figure A–11).

FIGURE A–11

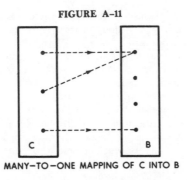

MANY–TO–ONE MAPPING OF C INTO B

A concept closely related to that of "one-to-one correspondence," as well as to that of "equivalence class" (see item XI), is that of *isomorphism* (= of equal structure). This notion is usually applied in the comparison of two structures that are ordered pairs or triples, each consisting of a set and one or two relations; the major conditions involve a one-to-one correspondence between the two structures.

XI.   A relation $\sim$ in a set X which has the following properties is called an *equivalence relation:*

    (*i*) it is reflexive: $x \sim x$;

    (*ii*) it is symmetric: If $x \sim y$ then $y \sim x$;

    (*iii*) it is transitive: If $x \sim y$ and $y \sim z$, then $z \sim x$;

          $x, y, z \epsilon X$.

The following relations constitute equivalence classes: "has the same parents as," "belongs to the same account as," "is congruent to," "was born in the same calendar year as," etc. Note that the relation "was born within one year of" is not an equivalence class (cf. Kershner and Wilcox [1950], p. 238).

A concept closely related to "equivalence" is that of *equivalence class*. It is a set or collection of nonempty subsets of X whose union is X; the equivalence class $[x]$ with respect to equivalence relation $\sim$ is the set of all those elements $y \epsilon X$ for which $x \sim y$. Formally expressed this yields $[x] = \{y : y \epsilon X, \ x \sim y\}$. Hence a set on which an equivalence relation is defined is *partitioned* into equivalence classes by the convention that two elements belong to the same class if and only if they are equivalent with regard to the specific equivalence relation (e.g., the set of objects belonging to an entity may be envisaged as being partitioned into equivalence classes, called "accounts").

XII. Another important category of relations, especially with regard to measurement, are *order relations*. The various order relations are distinct through the different properties listed in Table A–1.

TABLE A–1

Properties: / Order Relations:	Transitive	Reflexive	Antisymmetric	Asymmetric	Connected
Quasi-ordering	✓	✓			
Partial ordering	✓	✓	✓		
Simple ordering	✓	✓	✓		✓
Weak ordering	✓	✓			✓
Strictly partial ordering[5]	✓			✓	
Strictly simple ordering	✓			✓	✓

The properties of reflexivity, symmetry, and transitivity were pointed out in item XI. The remaining properties here mentioned are characterized as follows:

A relation R

(i) is antisymmetric if $R(x, \ y) \cap R(y, \ x)$ implies that $x = y$; e.g., the relation "is equal or larger than": $x \geq y$, because if $x \geq y$ and $y \geq x$ then $x = y$.

(ii) is asymmetric if $R(x, \ y) \supset \bar{R}(y, \ x)$, ($\bar{R}$ is the complement relation of R); e.g., the relation "is larger than": $x > y$, because $(x > y)$ implies that $(y < x)$.

(iii) is connected if $x \neq y$ implies that $R(x, \ y) \cup R(y, \ x)$. e.g., the relation "is larger than": $x > y$; because $x \neq y$ implies that either $x > y$ or $y > x$.

(Obviously connectedness would *not* hold for incompar-

---

[5]The terminology is not quite uniform, strict simple ordering (cf. Suppes [1957], p. 222) seems to come close to what Ackoff [1962, p. 188] calls "simple order." Occasionally the property of irreflexivity is stated explicitly.

able objects; *neither* is the relation "is a father of" a connected relation: if x is not identical to y it is not necessarily true that either x is a father of y or y is a father of x, because x may be in no family relation to y).

A.2   ATTEMPT OF A SET-THEORETICAL FORMULATION OF ACCOUNTING

The second part of this appendix does not merely restate the eighteen basic assumptions by means of the algebra of sets, it aims at further conceptual clarification by reducing the foundations of accounting to the notions of *ownership* and *debt claim*. Another purpose of this section is to illustrate how accounting theorems can be deduced by asserting and proving some conclusions which are of fundamental importance for our discipline. The significance of this illustration might be recognized by the fact that not all of the theorems presented are mere refinements of propositions found in a less rigorous form in current accounting texts. The *combination theorem* for example (see proposition 25 and comments) constitutes an insight of theoretical consequence that goes beyond the simple conventional notion of "combined entries." Indeed, this theorem enables us to express accounting entries in terms of ownership or debt claim in a way that essentially contributes to the disclosure of relations concealed by traditional theory.

A further refinement over the basic assumptions of Chapter 2 will be found in the clear distinction between primitive (undefined) notions and basic propositions. The numbering of the latter is—due to the difference in structure—independent of the numbering of the basic assumptions of Chapter 2. At the end of this appendix we juxtapose the numbers of basic assumptions (of Chapter 2) to corresponding numbers of the propositions of this appendix. This will help the reader in tracing the main ideas of this axiomatic presentation to the less formal treatment. The propositions[6] beyond the primitive notions are consecutively numbered; where a theorem is involved, it is explicitly expressed as such, but no distinction is made between axioms and definitions. The number of true axioms might ultimately prove to be small, yet most of the propositions presented are conditional definitions, that means definitions the conditions of which have axiomatic character.

As the title of this section betrays, our exposition is a mere *attempt* of a set-theoretical axiomatization of accounting, it is not exhaustive, neither with regard to comprehensiveness nor with regard to

---

[6]A proposition is taken as "any statement which makes an assertion which is either true or false, or which has been designated as true or false," from *Mathematics Dictionary* edited by Glenn James and Robert C. James (New York: Van Nostrand, 1959), p. 315. In the following these propositions are usually referred to as "items."

mathematical rigor.   Yet, the basic ideas of accounting—including important *empirical* notions such as ownership and debt claim—are all reflected in it; thus compared with previous attempts this treatment constitutes (together with Subsection 2.41 of this book) the most comprehensive formalistic presentation of accounting so far available.[7] It is not a finished structure, but a foundation hopefully stable enough to serve others as a basis for further ventures.

The following axiomatic presentation assumes as given the fundamental concepts and propositions of set-theory and economics.   Furthermore, propositions corresponding to the surrogate assumptions (basic assumptions 11 to 18) are not repeated; yet, for the sake of illustration a simple empirical hypothesis growing out of one of these surrogate assumptions (basic assumption 13—Extension) is developed in item 27.   Finally it should be stressed that in set-theory it is customary that variables are *bound-out* after every proposition, that means every variable has to be redefined in every new proposition.   This obviously economizes the number of symbols used, since one and the same symbol in two propositions may have entirely different meanings. In the following we have adhered to this practice with regard to *elements* of sets (though we attempt to use the same or a similar symbol for the same variable wherever possible); with regard to *major sets* however the symbols are *not bound out*.   An alphabetic list of these symbols with explanations and references is given at the very end of this appendix.

---

[7] A less comprehensive presentation was attempted seven years ago by the author (see Mattessich [1957], cf. the reproduction of parts of this article by Devine [1962a], vol. I, and by Williams and Griffin [1964]); independently of this, Dr. Marilynn G. Winborne [1962] presented in her dissertation a set-theoretical formulation of some accounting concepts.   Her original and meritorious contribution—which has not been exploited in this appendix primarily because of a different viewpoint assumed and because of our limited emphasis of the classificational task of formulating concepts such as costs, expenses, revenue, profit, etc.—to some extent complements our own effort.   Future attempts of a more complete or exhaustive axiomatization of our discipline hopefully will benefit from these various experiments.

On the other hand the study "Zur Axiomatik der Buchführungs und Bilanztheorie (Stuttgart, 1936—translated title: "The Axiomatization of Accounting and Balance-Sheet Theory") by Hans Holzer does *not* aim at a rigorous set-theoretical formulation of accounting.   The paper "Axioms and Structures of Conventional Accounting" by Ijiri [1964] is limited to the valuation aspect of historical costing and thus presents—from the viewpoint of our book—one out of several alternative sets of *hypotheses* for basic assumption 11 (Valuation).   Hence Ijiri's "axioms" (or in our terminology "hypotheses") are highly *specific* propositions valid for conventional accounting only, the formulation of these propositions is a valuable supplement to Subsection 5.33 of the present work.

The mathematical development of any science culminates in the axiomatic formulation of its contents. . . . The axiomatic method is simply a superb technique for summarizing our knowledge in a given field and for finding further knowledge deductively. This involves inevitably logico-mathematical operations, sometimes of great complexity. If the state of axiomatization of an empirical field has been reached, which is a state of some perfection, mathematics is indispensable . . . . Axiomatics does not burst upon the scene unprepared. There will have been a vast amount of preparatory exploration and thinking, much of it tentative and in parts. Some will have been in mathematical form, some not.

MORGENSTERN [1963b], pp. 23–24.

A.21 Set-Algebraic Formulation of the Foundations of Accounting

PRIMITIVE TERMS

The set of values V
The set of time instances (intervals)......................... T
The set of (economic) agents................................. G
The set of (economic) objects .... O
The set of positive[8] transactors .... π
The set of negative transactors .... ν

1. An element e belongs to the set of entities E if and only if
   (i) *the (state of the) entity at a time instance* τ *is* $e^\tau = e = \{x : x \epsilon G$ or $x \epsilon O\}$ such that $(e \cap G) \cup (e \cap O) \neq \emptyset$ whereby $G \cap O = \emptyset$;
   (ii) there exists a subset **E**, *the entity proper* (**E** $\subset E$), such that

   $$\mathbf{E} = \{e^\tau : \tau = 1, \ldots, \vartheta\}, \text{ and } \sum_{\tau=1}^{\vartheta} t^\tau \text{ is the duration of the}$$

   entity,[9] $t^\tau \epsilon T$.
   Remark: This asserts, first, that the entity e (or e_n or e_m, etc.), or more precisely the state of this entity at a specific time instance, consists of some agents or some objects or both (whereby no agent can be an object nor vice versa) and, second, that there exists a subset **E**, the entity proper, which contains all the states of the entity during its existence.
2. The relation ω $(e_i, \ o_j, \ t^\tau) = v_{ij}^\tau$ is an *ownership right* if and only if
   (i) $e_i \epsilon E$ or $e_i \subset E$ (the latter may hold in case of joint ownership);
   (ii) $o_j \epsilon O$ or $o_j \subset O$ (the latter holds in case the ownership refers to a collection of objects);

---

[8]The term "positive" and "negative" are mere mathematical conventions and do not imply a value judgment.
[9]The duration of an entity is given by empirical hypotheses (see Chapter 2, basic assumption 15).

(*iii*) $t^\tau \epsilon T$ a time instance at which the ownership right holds.

(*iv*) $v_{ij}^\tau > 0$, $v_{ij}^\tau \epsilon V$, the value attributed to the ownership right at time t^τ.

(*v*) the legal or economic conditions are fulfilled.[10]

3. The relation δ $(e_i,\ e_j,\ t^\tau)\ =\ v_{ij}^\tau$ is a *debt claim* if and only if

   (*i*) $e_i \epsilon E$ or $e_i \subset E$ (e_i is the party which owes)

   (*ii*) $e_j \epsilon E$ or $e_j \subset E$ (e_j is the claiming party);

   (*iii*) $e_i \neq e_j$;

   (*iv*) $t^\tau \epsilon T$ a time instance at which the debt claim exists;

   (*v*) $v_{ij}^\tau > 0$, $v_{ij}\epsilon V$, the value attributed to the debt claim at time t^τ;

   (*vi*) the legal or economic conditions of a debt claim are fulfilled.

4. A *transaction* (or flow) F is a relation between a negative and a positive transactor to both of which a time instance (or sequence index) is attached and a value is assigned by means of an empirical hypothesis.

Thus the relation

$$F\ (k_i,\ k_j,\ t^\tau)\ =\ v_{ij}^\tau$$

is a transaction, if and only if

   (*i*) the negative transactor (representing a specific equivalence class[11]) is $k_i \epsilon \nu$;

   (*ii*) the positive transactor[12] (also representing an equivalence class—perhaps the same as the negative transactor) is $k_j \epsilon \pi$;

   (*iii*) $k_i \subset e_m$, $k_j \subset e_n$;

   (*iv*) either $k_i \approx k_j$ and $e_m \neq e_n$, or $k_i \neq k_j$ and $e_m \equiv e_n$;

   (*v*) the time instance[13] is $t^\tau \epsilon T$;

---

[10]Ownership need not be interpreted in the narrow legalistic sense. In macro-accounting, for instance, an owning entity may not itself have the legal right to own but may consist of subentities holding this right. Similar holds for debt claims (see item 3).

[11]In contrast to the relations of ownership rights and debt equities, a transaction is here not defined as a relation between an entity and an object, or between entities or sets of entities, etc., but as a relation between equivalence classes. The notion of a transactor representing an equivalence class becomes more articulate in item 15. It is important to realize that these equivalence classes are independent of the entity to which a transaction refers. Therefore we shall use the symbol $\approx$ to signify that two transactors "*represent*" the same equivalence class" (but may belong to different entities). The symbol $\neq$ denotes "do not represent the same equivalence class."

All equivalence classes are to be specified by empirical hypotheses (see basic assumption 13).

[12]The following transactions *imply* that the *negative* transactor is represented by the *first* element of the ordered triple (of a transaction), the positive transactor by the second, and the time dimension by the third element.

[13]Here and in the following the symbol τ and other superscripts (λ, s, z, etc.) do not represent "powers," but dimensions; hence these superscripts are equivalent to subscripts. For the sake of better distinction, and for other technical reasons, superscripts are here used to express time instances (or sequences).

Accounting and Analytical Methods

(vi) the value assigned[14] is $v_{ij}^\tau > 0$, $v_{ij}^\tau \epsilon V$.

5. A transaction F_I $(k_i,\ k_j,\ t^\tau) = v_{ij}^\tau$ is an *intra*-entity *transaction* if and only if
    (i) $k_i \subset e_m$;
    (ii) $k_j \subset e_n$;
    (iii) $e_m \equiv e_n$, $e_n \epsilon E$;
    (iv) $k_i \neq k_j$.

6. A transaction F_E $(k_i,\ k_j,\ t^\tau) = v_{ij}^\tau$ is an *inter*-entity *transaction* if and only if
    (i) $k_i \subset e_m$;
    (ii) $k_j \subset e_n$;
    (iii) $e_m \neq e_n$, $e_m, e_n \epsilon E$
    (iv) $k_i \approx k_j$.

7. Two inter-entity transactions F_1 $(k_i,\ k_j,\ t^\tau) = v_{ij}^\tau$ and F_2 $(k_r, k_s, t^\lambda) = v_{rs}^\lambda$ are called *a pair of requited transactions* if and only if .
    (i) $k_i \subset e_m$, $k_j \subset e_n$, $k_r \subset e_p$, $k_s \subset e_q$ such that $e_m \equiv e_q$ and $e_n \equiv e_p$, $e_m \neq e_n$, $e_m, e_n \epsilon E$, $k_i \approx k_j$, $k_r \approx k_s$;
    (ii) $v_{ij}^\tau = v_{rs}^\lambda$, $v_{ij}^\tau, v_{rs}^\lambda \epsilon V$;
    (iii) $t^\tau \equiv t^\lambda$, $t^\tau \epsilon T$;
    (iv) there is empirical evidence that one transaction is the legal or economic consideration of the other.

8. The *converse of a transaction* is a transaction attained by interchanging the transactors (i.e., the transactor originally negative becomes positive and *vice versa*).
    Or more precisely: let the original transaction F be F $(k_i,\ k_j,\ t^\tau) = v_{ij}^\tau$, $k_i \epsilon \nu$, $k_j \epsilon \pi$, then the converse is

    $$F'\ (k_j,\ k_i,\ t^\lambda) = v_{ji}^\lambda,$$

    if and only if
    (i) $k_j \epsilon \nu$;
    (ii) $k_i \epsilon \pi$;
    (iii) $t^\lambda \gtrless t^\tau$, (i.e. t^λ may be larger, equal, or smaller than t^τ);
    (iv) v_{ij}^τ, $v_{ji}^\lambda \epsilon V$, $v_{ji}^\lambda = v_{ij}^\tau$, (the equality sign merely expresses that the *same value* is attributed to both transactions; with regard of origin, v_{ji}^λ is not identical to v_{ij}^τ).

9. A transaction P $(k_i,\ k_j,\ t^\tau) = v_{ij}^\tau$ is called a *transfer of ownership* (or property) from entity e_m to entity e_n if and only if
    (i) $\omega\ (e_m,\ o_j,\ t^{\tau-1}) = v_{mj}^{\tau-1} > 0$ and $\omega\ (e_m,\ o_j,\ t^\tau) = v_{mj}^\tau = 0$;
    (ii) $\omega\ (e_n,\ o_j,\ t^{\tau-1}) = v_{nj}^{\tau-1}$. $= 0$ and $\omega\ (e_n,\ o_j,\ t^\tau) = v_{nj}^\tau = v_{mj}^{\tau-1} > 0$;
    (iii) $e_m \neq e_n$; $e_m, e_n \epsilon E$,
    (iv) $k_i \subset e_m$; (e_m is the entity giving up ownership);
    (v) $k_j \subset e_n$; (e_n is the entity assuming ownership—cf. Table A-2);

---

[14] A frame for the empirical valuation hypotheses is provided by basic assumption 11 (see Chapter 2).

(vi) $k_i \approx k_j$, $k_i = [o_j]$ (i.e., k_i is the equivalence class categorizing object $o_j \epsilon O$).

(vii) $t^{\tau-1}$, $t^\tau \epsilon T$;

(viii) $v_{mj}^{\tau-1}$, v_{mj}^τ, $v_{nj}^{\tau-1}$, $v_{nj}^\tau \epsilon V$.

10. A transaction Q $(k_i, k_j, t^\tau) = v_{ij}^\tau$ is called the *creation of an owners' equity* if and only if

   (i) ω $(e_m, e_n, t^{\tau-1}) = v_{mn}^{\tau-1} = 0$ and ω $(e_m, e_n, t^\tau) = v_{mn}^\tau > 0$;

   (ii) $k_i \subset e_m$ (e_m is the entity being owned);

   (iii) $k_j \subset e_n$ (e_n is the owning entity);

   (iv) $k_i \approx k_j$ (both, an owner's equity and its corresponding claim belong to the same equivalence class;[15] the difference merely lies in the negativity or positivity of the transactors which belong to different entities);

   (v) $e_m \neq e_n$, e_m, $e_n \epsilon E$;

   (vi) $t^{\tau-1}$, $t^\tau \epsilon T$;

   (vii) $v_{mn}^\tau = v_{ij}^\tau$, $v^{\tau-1}$, v_{mn}^τ, $v_{ji}^\tau \epsilon V$.

Remark: Based on items 1(i) and 2(ii) a theorem may assert and be proved that in owning an entity only the objects contained in it but not the agents are being owned.

11. A transaction D $(k_i, k_j, t^\tau) = v_{ij}^\tau$ is called the *creation of a debt claim* from entity e_n to entity e_m if and only if

   (i) δ $(e_m, e_n, t^{\tau-1}) = v_{mn}^{\tau-1} = 0$ and δ $(e_m, e_n, t^\tau) = v_{mn}^\tau > 0$;

   (ii) $k_i \subset e_m$, (e_m is the owing entity);

   (iii) $k_j \subset e_n$, (e_n is the claiming entity—cf. Table A-2);

   (iv) $k_i \approx k_j$, (both, a debt equity and its corresponding debt claim belong to the same equivalence class;[16] the difference merely lies in the momentary positivity or negativity of the transactor and its pertaining to a specific entity).

   (v) $e_m \neq e_n$, e_m, $e_n \epsilon E$;

   (vi) $t^{\tau-1}$, $t^\tau \epsilon T$;

   (vii) $v_{mn}^\tau = v_{ij}^\tau$, $v_{mn}^{\tau-1}$, v_{mn}^τ, $v_{ij}^\tau \epsilon V$.

12. A transaction Q' $(k_i, k_j, t^\lambda) = v_{ji}^\lambda$ is called *cancellation of an owners' equity* (or part of it) if and only if

   (i) ω $(e_m, e_n, t^{\lambda-1}) = v_{mn}^{\lambda-1} > 0$ and ω $(e_m, e_n, t^\lambda) = v_{mn}^\lambda = 0$;

   (ii) $k_j \subset e_n$ (e_n is the entity previously owning e_m);

   (iii) $k_i \subset e_m$ (e_m is the entity previously being owned by e_n);

   (iv) $e_m \neq e_n$, e_m, $e_n \epsilon E$;

   (v) $t^{\lambda-1}$, $t^\lambda \epsilon T$;

---

[15] This seems to be unaccustomed to accountants since the two accounts involved may bear such different lables as "Stock Capital of X Co." on one side and "Investment in Stock Capital of X Co." on the other (see basic assumption 3, item (e) of Chapter 2).

[16] This may surprise no less than the remark in the preceding footnote since one equivalence class seems to represent "Accounts Payable," the other "Accounts Receivable." However, this is imprecise, in both cases the equivalence class is "Amount payable by Y to X." Thus traditional practice and customary labeling must not deceive us about the identity of these equivalence classes. This identity becomes obvious in case of consolidations of firms with intercompany debts.

(*vi*) $v_{ji}^{\lambda} = v_{mn}^{\lambda-1}$, $v_{ji}^{\lambda}, v_{mn}^{\lambda-1}, v_{mn}^{\lambda} \epsilon V$.

Remark: It can be proved that the cancellation of an owners' equity is the converse of the creation of this owners' equity.

13. A transaction D' $(k_j, \; k_i, \; t^{\lambda}) = v_{ij}^{\lambda}$ is called a *redemption of a debt claim* (or part of it), if and only if

    (*i*) $\delta \; (e_m, \; e_n, \; t^{\lambda-1}) = v_{mn}^{\lambda-1} > 0$ and $\delta \; (e_m, \; e_n, \; t^{\lambda}) = v_{ij}^{\lambda} = 0$;

    (*ii*) $k_j \subset e_n$,   (e_n is the entity to be redeemed);

    (*iii*) $k_i \subset e_m$,   (e_m is the redeeming entity);

    (*iv*) $e_m \neq e_n$, $e_m, e_n \epsilon E$;

    (*v*) $t^{\lambda-1}, t^{\lambda} \epsilon T$;

    (*vi*) $v_{ij}^{\lambda} = v_{mn}^{\lambda-1}$, $v_{mn}^{\lambda-1}, v_{ij}^{\lambda} \epsilon V$.

Remark: It can be proved that the redemption of a debt claim is the converse of the creation of this debt claim.

14. An *accounting period* p^z is the sum of an uninterrupted series of time intervals. Hence,

$$p^z = \sum_{\tau=1}^{z} t^{\tau} \quad \text{if} \quad t^{\tau} \epsilon T.$$

A *period* p^s is defined as a subperiod of p^z which has the same beginning as the accounting period p^z. Hence

$$p^s = \sum_{\tau=1}^{s} t^{\tau}$$

hereby $s \leq z$ and 1 is the beginning of p^z.

15. The set A_n is called *the chart of accounts* of entity e_n if[17]

    (*i*) $A_n = \{a_i : a_i \subset e_n, i = 1, \ldots, y\}$, $e_n \epsilon E$;

    (*ii*) The accounts a_i, $(i = 1, \ldots, y)$ are equivalence classes;

    (*iii*) some of the accounts (equivalence classes) are subsets of others:

      e.g.: $a_d = [o_d]$, $o_d \epsilon e_n$, $d = 1, \ldots, k$, $o_d \epsilon O$,

           $a_l = [o_l]$, $a_l \subset a_d$, $l = k+1, \ldots, m$,

           $\vdots$ $\vdots$

           $a_r = [o_r]$, $a_r \subset a_n$, $r = q + 1, \ldots, w$,

           $a_x = [o_x]$, $a_x \subset a_r$, $x = w + 1, \ldots, y$,

           $a_d, a_l, \ldots, a_r, a_x \epsilon A_n$;

    (*iv*) There exists an account a_i' such that $a_i \approx a_i'$, $(i = 1, \ldots, y)$, and $a_i \subset e_n$, $a_i' \subset e_m$, $e_m \neq e_n$;

Remark: The notion "account" as used in this appendix goes slightly beyond that of traditional bookkeeping. Accounts are here envisaged primarily as means for *structured (or hierarchical)*

---

[17] (*i*) to (*iv*) are *sufficient* conditions, while (*i*) and (*ii*) are *necessary* conditions as well.

categorization, and not so much as recording devices; thus a subtotal or subconcept of the balance sheet for instance, may well be regarded as an account, though a debit-credit mechanism might not be visible.

16. A topological space C_n, consisting of the set L_n and some subsets of L_n, is called the *chart of accounts* of entity e_n, if and only if

(*i*) L_n is the list (set) of accounts of *lowest order;*

(*ii*) the set C_n corresponds one-to-one (is isomorphic) to a set of transactors relevant for entity e_n;[18]

(*iii*) $L_n \epsilon C_n$ and $\emptyset \epsilon C_n$ ($\emptyset$ is the symbol for the empty set—see item I (2) of Section A.1).

(*iv*) the union of any number of specified subsets of L_n is an element of C_n;

(*v*) the intersection of any two elements (sets) of C_n also belongs to C_n.

Remarks: (*i*) and (*ii*) are accounting conditions and (*iii*) to (*v*) are the mathematical conditions of a topological space (which are redundant in as far as we presuppose all set-theoretical concepts in this presentation—if these items are listed, it is because the conditions for a topological space were not stated in the preceding set-algebraic introduction). In order to illustrate the chart of accounts as a topological space we choose the simple example depicted in Figure A–12. Each rectangle, except the largest represents an account (designated in the upper left hand corner).

FIGURE A–12

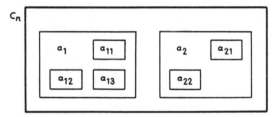

Then the list of ultimate accounts is $L_n = \{a_{11}, a_{12}, a_{13}, a_{21}, a_{22}\}$, and the subsets of L_n, also contained in C_n are:

$$a_1 = \{a_{11}, a_{12}, a_{13}\},$$
$$a_2 = \{a_{21}, a_{22}\},$$
$$\emptyset = \{\quad\};$$

hence

$$C_n = \{L_n, a_1, a_2, \emptyset\} = \{\{a_{11}, a_{12}, a_{13}, a_{21}, a_{22}\}, \{a_{11}, a_{12}\}, \{a_{21}, a_{22}\}, \emptyset\},$$

---

[18]The set of transactors (or categories) relevant for entity e_n has to be determined by empirical hypotheses (see basic assumption 13—Classification).

whereas the *set of accounts* is
$A_n = \{a_{11}, a_{12}, a_{13}, a_{21}, a_{22}, a_1, a_2\}$
which, in contrast to the set C_n, would not reveal a "structure" without the subscripts. The reader may verify that the three conditions of a topological space (*iii*) to (*v*) are fulfilled for the set L_n and the collection of sets C_n. Something similar holds for more complex structures possessing longer hierarchies of accounts.

17. A transaction $F(a_i, a_j, t^\tau) = v_{ij}^\tau$ in which the transactors are accounts, is called an *accounting transaction* of entity (or superentity) e_n if and only if
    (*i*) $a_i, a_j \in A_n$, $a_i \in \nu$, $a_j \in \pi$;
    (*ii*) $t^\tau \in T$;
    (*iii*) $v_{ij}^\tau \in V$.
Remarks: If A_n represents the set of accounts of entity e_n, the expression $a_i \in A_n$ implies $a_i \subset e_n$ (see item 15).

To illustrate the notions of inter- and *intra*-entity transactions, transfers of ownership, creation of owners' equity, and creation of debt claim by means of accounting transactions, we relate in Table A–2 our set-theoretical abstractions to an accounting matrix.

The following two events are depicted in Table A–2 for the superentity e_l to which the set of accounts
$A_l = \{a_1, a_2, a_3, a_4, a_5, a_6, a_7\}$
pertains. Superentity e_l consists of entities e_m and e_n:
(1) The purchase of shares of entity e_n by entity e_m in compensation for cash (the four flows involved in this pair of requited transactions are v_{13}^1, v_{15}^1, v_{75}^1 and v_{73}^1).
(2) The borrowing of cash by entity e_n from entity e_m (the four flows involved in this second pair of requited transactions are v_{21}^2, v_{26}^2, v_{56}^2, and v_{51}^2).
The northwest quadrant (upper left) of Table A–2 represents the accounting system of entity e_m and the southeast quadrant (lower right) represents the accounting system of entity e_n. These two quadrants exclusively contain *intra*-entity transactions (from the viewpoint of entity e_m or e_n respectively), while the northeast and southwest quadrants merely contain inter-entity transactions between the two entities.

(1) $F_1(a_1, a_5, t^1) = v_{15}^1$ *transfer of ownership* (of cash), since $a_1 \subset e_m$ and $a_5 \subset e_n$, and $a_1 \approx a_5$, etc.
$F_2(a_7, a_5, t^1) = v_{75}^1$ *intra*-entity transaction within e_n, since $a_7 \subset e_n$, $a_5 \subset e_n$ and $a_7 \neq a_5$.
$F_3(a_7, a_3, t^1) = v_{73}^1$ *creation of owners' equity* (e_n is the entity being owned), since $a_7 \subset e_n$ and $a_3 \subset e_m$ and $a_7 \approx a_3$, etc.
We ought to remind the reader that the accounts "Investment in e_n" and "Owners Equity of e_n" represent identical equivalence classes; so do the accounts "Re-

ACCOUNTING MATRIX OF INTRA- AND INTER-ENTITY TRANSACTIONS

		ENTITY e_m				ENTITY e_n		
		CASH a_1	PAYABLES a_2	INVESTMENT a_3	OWNERS' EQUITY a_4	CASH a_5	RECEIVABLE a_6	OWNERS' EQUITY a_7
e_m	CASH a_1			v^1_{13}		v^1_{15}		
	PAYABLES a_2	v^2_{21}					v^2_{26}	
	INVESTMENT a_3							
	OWNERS' EQUITY a_4							
e_n	CASH a_5	v^2_{51}					v^2_{56}	
	RECEIVABLE a_6							
	OWNERS' EQUITY a_7			v^1_{73}		v^1_{75}		

$v^1_{15}, v^1_{73}, v^2_{26}, v^2_{51}$ are (observable) inter-entity flows, whereas $v^1_{13}, v^1_{75}, v^2_{21}, v^2_{56}$ are (derived) intra-entity transactions.

ceivables" and "Payables" in this particular case.

$$F_4 (a_1, a_3, t^1) = v^1_{13}$$ *intra*-entity transaction within e_n, since $a_1 \subset e_m$ and $a_3 \subset e_m$ and $a_1 \neq a_3$.

(2) $$F_5 (a_2, a_6, t^2) = v^2_{26}$$ *creation of a debt claim* from e_n to e_m, since $a_2 \subset e_m$, $a_6 \subset e_n$ and $a_2 \approx a_6$, etc.

$$F_6 (a_5, a_6, t^2) = v^2_{56}$$ *intra*-entity transaction, since $a_5 \subset e_n$, $a_6 \subset e_n$ and $a_5 \neq a_6$.

$$F_7 (a_5, a_1, t^2) = v^2_{51}$$ *transfer of ownership* (of cash), since $a_5 \subset e_n$, $a_1 \subset e_m$, and $a_5 \approx a_1$, etc.

$$F_8 (a_2, a_1, t^2) = v^2_{21}$$ *intra*-entity transaction, since $a_2 \subset e_m$, $a_1 \subset e_m$, $a_2 \neq a_1$.

18. The relation $B(a_i, p^s) = v^s_i$ is called "the operation[19] *to balance*" and v^s_i is called "the balance of account a_i" $(i = 1, \ldots, y)$ at the end of period p^s if and only if

(i) $$v^s_i = \sum_{\tau=1}^{s} \sum_{j=1}^{y} (v^\tau_{ji} - v^\tau_{ij}), \qquad\qquad i = 1, \ldots, y;$$

(ii) $$a_i \epsilon A_n, \qquad\qquad i = 1, \ldots, y;$$

(iii) $$p^s = \sum_{\tau=1}^{s} t^\tau;$$

(iv) v^τ_{ij}, v^τ_{ji}, $v^s_i \epsilon V$, $i, j = 1, \ldots, y$, $\tau = 1, \ldots, s$; v^τ_{ij} and v^τ_{ji} are values assigned to accounting transactions in conformity with item 17.

(We remind the reader that the first subscript refers to the row of a matrix or credit side of an account, whereas the second subscript refers to the column or debit side).

19. The balance $$v^s_i = \sum_{\tau=1}^{s} \sum_{j=1}^{y} (v^\tau_{ji} - v^\tau_{ij}) \quad \text{is called}$$

a *debit balance* if $v^s_i > 0$,
a *credit balance* if $v^s_i < 0$, and
a *zero balance* if $v^s_i = 0$.

20. The set $\mathbf{B}^s$, a relation on the Cartesian product $A_n \times V$, is called a *trial balance* if and only if

$$\mathbf{B}^s = \{(a_i, v^s_i) : i = 1, \ldots, y\},$$

such that
(i) $a_i \epsilon A_n$, $i = 1, \ldots, y$;
(ii) $v^s_i = V$.

21. *Trial Balance Equality Theorem.*

In a trial balance the total of all debit balances (positive

---

[19] An *operation* (or more precisely *binary* operation) is a special case of a function.

balances) is equal to the *negative* total of all credit balances (negative balances).

Or formulated more precisely:

Assume the following debit balances $v_k^s > 0$ $(k = 1, \ldots, m)$, and the following credit balances $v_p^s < 0$ $(p = 1, \ldots, q)$, and the following zero balances $v_r^s = 0$ $(r = 1, \ldots, u)$, of a trial balance $\mathbf{B}^s$ with y accounts such that $m + q + u = y$ and

$$v_{Bd}^s = \sum_{k=1}^{m} v_k^s, \; v_{Bc} = \sum_{p=1}^{q} v_p^s, \; \text{and} \; v_k^s, v_p^s, \; v_{Bd}^s, v_{Bc}^s \in V \quad (k = 1, \ldots, m;$$

$p = 1, \ldots, q)$, then

$$v_{Bd}^s = - v_{Bc}^s.$$

Below we state an *attempt of a formal proof* of this theorem (which requires first the proof of a lemma):[20]

Lemma $\displaystyle\sum_{i=1}^{y} v_i^s = 0$:

according to item 17 (i): $\displaystyle v_i^s = \sum_{\tau=1}^{s} \sum_{j=1}^{y} (v_{ji}^\tau - v_{ij}^\tau)$,

hence $\displaystyle\sum_{i=1}^{y} v_i^s = \sum_{i=1}^{y} \sum_{j=1}^{y} \sum_{\tau=1}^{s} v_{ji}^\tau - \sum_{i=1}^{y} \sum_{j=1}^{y} \sum_{\tau=1}^{s} v_{ij}^\tau = 0;$

according to the

above assumption: $\displaystyle v_{Bd}^s = \sum_{k=1}^{m} v_k^\pi$ and $\displaystyle v_{Bc}^s = \sum_{p=1}^{q} v_r^\pi;$

since there exist in $\mathbf{B}^s$ (by definition) y balances: m positive ones, q negative ones, and u zero balances, and since $m + q + u = y$ it follows that:

$$\sum_{i=1}^{y} v_i^s = \sum_{k=1}^{m} v_k^s + \sum_{p=1}^{q} v_p^s + \sum_{r=1}^{u} v_r^s;$$

since $\displaystyle\sum_{r=1}^{u} v_r^s = 0$, and since according to our lemma $\displaystyle\sum_{i=1}^{y} v_i^s = 0$, it

follows that:

$$\sum_{k=1}^{m} v_k^s + \sum_{p=1}^{q} v_p^s = 0$$

---

[20]A lemma is an auxiliary theorem of no direct significance but necessary for proving another theorem.

$$\sum_{k=1}^{m} v_k^s = -\sum_{p=1}^{q} v_p^s$$

$$v_{Bc}^s = -v_{Bd}^s \qquad\qquad \text{Q.E.D.}$$

22. A set S^s is called an accounting statement if and only if
$S^s = \{\{(a_b, v_b^s) : b = 1, \ldots, d\}, \{(a_e, v_e^s) : e = 1, \ldots, h\}, (v_{Cb}^s, v_{Ce}^s, v_C^s)\}$
such that

   (i) $a_b, a_e \in A_n$, $A_n\{a_i : i = 1, \ldots, y\}$ $b = 1, \ldots, d$, $e = 1, \ldots, h$,

   (ii) $v_{Cb}^s = \sum_{b=1}^{d} v_b^s$, $v_{Ce}^s = \sum_{e=1}^{h} v_b^s$

   (iii) $v_C^s = v_{Cb}^s + v_{Ce}^s$ (is called the *balance* of the *accounting
   statement.*)

   (iv) $d + h \leq y$

   (v) $v_b^s, v_e^s, v_{Cb}^s, v_{Ce}^s, v_C^s \in V$.

23. *The Two-Statements Theorem.*

   If there are two accounting statements comprising together
all the accounts with nonzero balances contained in A_n (at the
end of a period p^s), then the balance of the first accounting
statement is equal to the negative of the balance of the second
accounting statement.

   Or formulated more precisely:
Let S_B^s and S_P^s be two accounting statements, then according to
item 22:

$$S_B^s = \{\{(a_b, v_b^s) : b = 1, \ldots, d\}, \{(a_e, v_e^s) : e = 1, \ldots, h\}, (v_{Bb}^s, v_{Be}^s, v_B^s)\},$$
$$S_P^s = \{\{(a_p, v_p^s) : p = 1, \ldots, l\}, \{(a_f, v_f^s) : f = 1, \ldots, g\}, (v_{Pb}^s, v_{Pc}^s, v_P^s)\},$$

such that
$a_b, a_e, a_f, a_p \in A_n = \{a_i : i = 1, \ldots, y\}$ and $d + h + l + g + u = y$
(u is the number of accounts with zero balances).

$$v_b^s, v_e^s, v_f^s, v_p^s, v_{Bb}^s, v_{Be}^s, v_B^s, v_{Pb}^s, v_{Pc}^s, v_P^s \in V$$

then it is true that:

$$v_B = -v_P \text{ or } v_{Bb}^s + v_{Be}^s = -(v_{Pb}^s + v_{Pc}^s)$$

Attempt of Proof:
By definition (see above) $d + h + l + g + u = y$, or

$$\sum_{b=1}^{d} v_b^s + \sum_{e=1}^{h} v_e^s + \sum_{p=1}^{l} v_p^s + \sum_{f=1}^{g} v_f^s + \sum_{x=1}^{u} 0 = \sum_{i=1}^{y} v_i^s;$$

according to items 22, 23, and the lemma of item 21 this yields:

$$v_{Bb}^s + v_{Be}^s + v_{Pb}^s + v_{Pc}^s = 0$$

hence

$$v_{Bb}^s + v_{Be}^s = -(v_{Pb}^s + v_{Pc}^s) \qquad\qquad \text{Q.E.D.}$$

Remark: In a similar fashion a more general theorem can be proved which asserts that the sum of the balances of *all* accounting statements is zero (there may be more than two accounting statements), provided *all* accounts of A_n with nonzero balances are represented in this collection of statements.

24. An operation o on two or more accounting transactions is permissible if these transactions occur at the same time and if the balances of all the accounts, affected by these transactions, remain the same in spite of the operation.

Or more precisely: the operation

$$o\ (F_1(a_i, a_j, t^\tau)\ =\ v_{ij}^\tau, \ldots, F_m(a_r, a_s, t^\lambda)\ =\ v_{rs}^\lambda)$$

is permissible if

(*i*) the balances $B(a_i,\ p^s)\ =\ v_i^s, \ldots, B(a_r,\ p^s)\ =\ v_r^s$
$$B(a_j,\ p^s)\ =\ v_j^s, \ldots, B(a_s,\ p^s)\ =\ v_s^s$$
are unaffected by the operation o;

(*ii*) $t^\tau\ =\ \ldots\ =\ t^\lambda,\ t^\tau \epsilon\, T,$

hereby $p^s\ =\ \displaystyle\sum_{\tau=1}^{s} t^\tau,$

$a_i, a_j, \ldots, a_r, a_s \epsilon A_n,$
$v_{ij}^\tau, \ldots, v_{rs}^\tau, \ldots, v_i^s, v_j^s, \ldots, v_r^s, v_s^s \epsilon\, V.$

25. *The Combination Theorem.*

Two accounting transactions F_1 and F_2 occurring simultaneously and belonging to the same entity can together be substituted by a third accounting transaction F_3, provided the credit account of one original transaction is identical with the debit account of the other original transaction.

Or more precisely: Assume two transactions

$$F_1(a_i, a_j,\ t^s)\ =\ v_{ij}^s$$
$$F_2(a_r, a_u,\ t^\lambda)\ =\ v_{ru}^\lambda$$

then there exists an operation that substitutes

$$F_3 \text{ for } (F_1 \text{ and } F_2);$$

if either   (*a*) $F_3(a_i, a_u, t^s)\ =\ v_{iu}^s,$ if $a_r \equiv a_j;$

or (*b*) $F_3(a_r, a_j, t^s)\ =\ v_{rj}^s,$ if $a_i \equiv a_u;$

provided

(*i*) $t^s\ =\ t^\lambda,\ t^s \epsilon\, T;$

(*ii*) $v_{ij}^s\ =\ v_{ru}^\lambda\ =\ v_{iu}^s\ =\ v_{rj}^s$ (equal as *values* only), $v_{ij}^s, v_{ru}^\lambda, v_{iu}^s, v_{rj}^s \epsilon\, V;$

(*iii*) $a_i, a_j, a_r, a_u \epsilon A_n.$

Attempt of Proof:

(Step 1) Assume the following balances after the occurrence of F_1 and F_2:

$B(a_i, p^s)\ =\ v_i^s,$ $B(a_r, p^\lambda)\ =\ v_r^\lambda,$
$B(a_j, p^s)\ =\ v_j^s,$ $B(a_u, p^\lambda)\ =\ v_u^\lambda;$

(recalling that according to item 25 (*i*) $t^s = t^\lambda$). According to item 18 we may write:

$$v_i^s = \sum_{\tau=1}^{s-1} \sum_{l=1}^{y} (v_{li}^\tau - v_{ul}^\tau) - v_{ij}^s \quad \text{and}$$

$$v_u^\lambda = \sum_{\tau=1}^{\lambda-1} \sum_{l=1}^{y} (v_{lu}^\tau - v_{ul}^\tau) + v_{ru}^\lambda.$$

If we assume in accord with item 25 (*a*) that $a_r \equiv a_j$, then (according to item 18):

$$v_r^\lambda \equiv v_j^s = \sum_{\tau=1}^{s-1} . \sum_{l=1}^{y} (v_{lj}^\tau - v_{jl}^\tau) + v_{ij}^s - v_{ru}^\lambda,$$

but by item 25 (*ii*) $v_{ij}^s = v_{ru}^\lambda$, hence

$$v_r^\lambda \equiv v_j^s = \sum_{\tau=1}^{s-1} \sum_{l=1}^{y} (v_{lj}^\tau - v_{jl}^\tau).$$

(Step 2) If transaction F_3 (instead of F_1 and F_2) occurs and if $a_r \equiv a_j$ then the accounts a_r and a_j remain unaffected and we can write

$$w_r^s \equiv w_j^s = w_j^{s-1} = \sum_{\tau=1}^{s-1} \sum_{l=1}^{y} (v_{lj}^\tau - v_{jl}^\tau) = v_r^\lambda \equiv v_j^s,$$

$$w_r^s, w_j^{s-1}, \ldots, v_r^\lambda \epsilon V.$$

The balances of the accounts a_i and a_u then become (according to item 18):

$$w_i^s = \sum_{\tau=1}^{s-1} \sum_{l=1}^{y} (v_{li}^\tau - v_{ul}^\tau) - v_{ij}^s, \quad w_i^s, \ldots, w_u^s \epsilon V,$$

$$w_u^s = \sum_{\tau=1}^{s-1} \sum_{l=1}^{y} (v_{lu}^\tau - v_{ul}^\tau) + v_{ru}^\lambda, \quad [v_{ij}^s = v_{ru}^\tau = v_{iu}^\lambda \text{ by item 25 } (ii)]$$

(Step 3)   Hence from comparison of the first two steps we conclude that:

$$w_i^s = v_i^s, \qquad w_j^s = v_j^s,$$
$$w_r^s = v_r^\lambda, \qquad w_u^s = v_u^\lambda;$$

we also remember that according to 25 (*i*) $t^s = t^\lambda$; thus both conditions of item 24 are fulfilled [if (*a*) $a_r \equiv a_j$ or if (*b*) $a_i \equiv a_u$ —the proof for variation (*b*) is analogous to that demonstrated for (*a*)], hence the operation of substituting the transaction F_3 for the two transactions (F_1 and F_2) is permissible. Q.E.D.

26. *The Substitution Theorem.*
A pair of requited (inter-entity) transactions can be substituted by two *intra*-entity transactions each of which belongs to one of the two entities involved.

Or more precisely: the operation of *substituting* the pair of requited transactions

$$F_{R1}(a_i, a_j, \dot{t}^\tau) = v_{ij}^\tau \text{ and } F_{R2}(a_r, a_u, t^\lambda) = v_{ru}^\lambda$$

by the two *intra*-entity transactions

$$F_{I1}(a_i, a_u, t^\tau) = v_{iu}^\tau \text{ and } F_{I2}(a_r, a_j, t^\tau) = v_{ru}^\tau,$$

is permissible provided $v_{iu}^\tau = v_{rj}^\tau = v_{ij}^\tau = v_{ru}^\tau.$

Attempt of Proof:

According to item 7 the following conditions hold for the above stated pair of requited transactions:

(*i*) $a_i \subset e_m$, $a_j \subset e_n$, $a_r \subset e_p$, $a_u \subset e_q$ such that $e_m \equiv e_q$, and $e_n \equiv e_p$, $e_m \neq e_n$, e_m, e_n, ϵE, $a_i \approx a_j$, $a_r \approx a_u$;

(*ii*) $v_{ij}^\tau = v_{ru}^\lambda$, v_{ij}^τ, $v_{ru}^\lambda \epsilon V$;

(*iii*) $t^\tau \equiv t^\lambda$, $t^\lambda \epsilon T$;

(*iv*) there is empirical evidence that one transaction is the legal or economic consideration of the other.

(Step 1) Assume the following balances before the occurrence of F_{R1} and F_{R2} (or before the occurrence of F_{I1} and F_{I2}):

$$B(a_i, p^{s-1}) = v_i^{s-1}, \qquad\qquad B(a_r, p^{s-1}) = v_r^{s-1},$$
$$B(a_j, p^{s-1}) = v_j^{s-1}, \qquad\qquad B(a_u, p^{s-1}) = v_u^{s-1};$$

then we have the following balances after the occurrence of F_{R1} and F_{R2}:

$$v_i^s = v_i^{s-1} - v_{ij}^\tau, \qquad\qquad v_r^s = v_r^{s-1} - v_{ru}^\lambda,$$
$$v_j^s = v_j^{s-1} + v_{ij}^\tau, \qquad\qquad v_u^s = v_u^{s-1} + v_{ru}^\lambda;$$

or the below-stated balances after the occurrence of F_{I1} and F_{I2}:

$$v_i^\sigma = v_i^{s-1} - v_{iu}^\tau, \qquad\qquad v_r^\sigma = v_r^{s-1} - v_{ru}^\tau,$$
$$v_j^\sigma = v_j^{s-1} + v_{iu}^\tau, \qquad\qquad v_u^\sigma = v_u^s + v_{ru}^\tau;$$

but since $v_{iu}^\tau = v_{rj}^\tau = v_{ij}^\tau$, and since $v_{ij}^\tau = v_{ru}^\lambda$, it is true that $v_i^s = v_i^\sigma$, $v_j^s = v_j^\sigma$, $v_r^s = v_r^\sigma$, $v_u^s = v_u^\sigma$. Thus the balances of the accounts a_i, a_j, a_r, a_u are unchanged by substituting F_{I1} and F_{I2} for F_{R1} and F_{R2} which fulfills condition (*i*) of item 24.

(Step 2) According to condition (*iii*) of item 8 it is true that $t^\tau = t^\lambda$ which fulfills condition (*ii*) of item 24. This proves that the operation of substituting the pair of requited transactions F_{R1} and F_{R2} by the *intra*-entity transactions F_{I1} and F_{I2} is permissible. Q.E.D.

A corollary may prove the reverse relationship, namely that F_{I1} and F_{I2} can be substituted by F_{R1} and F_{R2}.

Though accountants are intuitively aware of these relations, the above-stated theorem is never pronounced in traditional accounting theory. Yet it constitutes the main vehicle for converting basic inter-entity transactions (such as transfers of ownership and the creation or redemption of debt claims, etc.) into *intra*-entity accounting transactions. Thus, *through this theorem (and its corollary) can accounting be reduced to the basic ownership and debt relations; only in this way can one prove that purely intra-entity accounting transactions can reflect relations that transgress into other entities.*

The next and last two items are of particular interest. First, because proposition 27 actually pertains to a surrogate assumption (it is the simplest and most natural hypothesis for which basic assumption 16—Extension—may stand), and second, because the construction of consolidated statements is of extreme importance in micro- and especially in macro-accounting.

Item 27 does not look like a *specific* empirical hypothesis, because it seems to be a self-evident truth. The proof that it is not so, is given by business practice which, surprisingly enough, frequently rejects this hypothesis in favor of others that are artificial and more complex—as shall be explained in the "remarks" of item 27.

27. A trial balance $\mathbf{B}_n^s$ of an entity (of higher order) e_n is a *consolidation* of the trial balances of two or more distinct entities e_l, and e_m, if it is identical to a fictitious trial balance that would result from all transactions of e_l to e_m (during the period specified) applied directly to the superentity e_n.

Or in symbolic form:
Assume the following trial balances $\mathbf{B}_l^{s-1}, \ldots, \mathbf{B}_m^{s-1}, \mathbf{B}_n^{s-1}$ (at the beginning of period p^s and referring to entities $e_l, \ldots, e_m$ and e_n respectively) have only zero values assigned to their accounts. Also assume that the sum totals of all transactions (during period p^s) of each of these entities are designated with $\mathbf{S}_l, \ldots, \mathbf{S}_m$, and $\mathbf{S}_n$, respectively.[21] Finally assume the trial balances of these entities at the *end* of period p^s given as

$$\mathbf{B}_l^s = \mathbf{B}_l^{s-1} \cup \mathbf{S}_l$$
$$\vdots \quad \vdots \quad \vdots$$
$$\mathbf{B}_m^s = \mathbf{B}_m^{s-1} \cup \mathbf{S}_m$$
$$\mathbf{B}_n^s = \mathbf{B}_n^{s-1} \cup \mathbf{S}_n$$

then $\mathbf{B}_n^s$ is a *consolidated trial balance* of the entities e_l to e_m, if and only if

$$(\mathbf{S}_l \cup \ldots \cup \mathbf{S}_m = \mathbf{S}_n) \text{ implies } (\mathbf{B}_l^s \cup \ldots \cup \mathbf{B}_m^s = \mathbf{B}_n^s).$$

Remarks: This statement is by no means a matter of course. Indeed, the practice and theory of consolidated financial balance sheets of parent and subsidiary companies often introduces additional transactions that would not occur if the entity of higher order (e.g., entity e_n) were regarded from the very outset as the only entity under consideration. A typical case in point is the situation where the parent company does not hold all stocks of the subsidiaries; in consequence the embarrassing class of "minority

---

[21] The assumption that only zero balances are assigned to the beginning trial balances is permissible because nonzero balances eventually present can be regarded to be transactions belonging to $\mathbf{S}_l$, $\mathbf{S}_m$, and $\mathbf{S}_n$.

stockholders" enters the picture. However, if originally parent and subsidiaries would have been considered as a single entity the minority stockholders would have been considered as ordinary stockholders and no transaction separating them in the balance sheet would ever have occurred. This is not a critique of present practices but an illustration that the process of stripping accounting from its habituary cloak makes us aware of important but often concealed assumptions.

28. *The Consolidation Theorem.*

Two or more trial balances $\mathbf{B}_l^s, \ldots, \mathbf{B}_m^s$ of distinct entities $e_l, \ldots, e_m$ (at the end of period p^s) are being consolidated in a single trial balance $\mathbf{B}_n^s$ of an entity e_n by performing the following operations:

(i) *Identifying* whether
$a_i^l \approx a_j^m$ or $a_i^l \neq a_j^m$,
hereby $a_i^l \epsilon A_l$ (hence $a_i^l \subset e_l$)
and $a_j^m \epsilon A_m$ (hence $a_j^m \subset e_m$);

(ii) *Adding the values* assigned to accounts which represent identical equivalence classes:

if $(a_d^l, v_d^s) \epsilon \mathbf{B}_d^s$, $d = 1, \ldots, g$,
$(a_f^m, v_f^s) \epsilon \mathbf{B}_f^s$, $f = 1, \ldots, g$
and if $a_d^l \approx a_f^m$,
then $\mathbf{B}_l^s \cup \mathbf{B}_m^s = \mathbf{B}_n^s$, $(a_k^n, v_k^s) \epsilon \mathbf{B}_n^s$
implies $v_k^s = v_d^s + v_f^s$ if $a_k^n \approx a_d^l$.

(iii) *Incorporating the accounts* of (ii) with their accumulated values as well as the remaining accounts of all trial balances (to be consolidated) with their original values *into the consolidated trial balance:*
Assume
$\mathbf{B}_l^s = \{(a_i^l, v_i^s) : i = 1, \ldots, r\}$
$\mathbf{B}_m^s = \{(a_j^m, v_j^s) : j = 1, \ldots, q\}$
$\mathbf{B}_n^s = \{(a_k^n, v_k^s) : k = 1, \ldots, y\}$;

also assume the following auxiliary subsets of $\mathbf{B}_l^s$, $\mathbf{B}_m^s$ and $\mathbf{B}_n^s$:
$\beta_l^s = \{(a_i^l, v_i^s) : i = 1, \ldots, d\}$
$\gamma_l^s = \{(a_i^l, v_i^s) : i = d + 1, \ldots, r\}$, (hence $\mathbf{B}_l^s = \beta_l^s \cup \gamma_l^s$);
$\beta_m^s = \{(a_j^m, v_j^s) : j = 1, \ldots, d\}$,
$\gamma_m^s = \{(a_j^m, v_j^s) : j = d + 1, \ldots, q\}$, (hence $\mathbf{B}_m^s = \beta_m^s \cup \gamma_l^s$);
$\delta_n^s = \{(a_k^n, v_i^s + v_j^s) : i, j = 1, \ldots, d\}$ if
$a_i^l \approx a_j^m \approx a_k^n, i, j, k = 1, \ldots, d$, then
$\mathbf{B}_l^s \cup \mathbf{B}_m^s = \mathbf{B}_n^s$ implies that $\mathbf{B}_n^s = \delta_n^s \cup \gamma_l^s \cup \gamma_m^s$.

What was outlined above for two trial balances or entities to be consolidated, holds analogously for any finite number of trial balances or entities.

We suggest that the reader himself attempts to prove this last theorem and reflects upon the formulation of further propositions. By now it will be obvious that there is still much to accomplish in accounting theory, and that its problems are no less exciting than those of other mathematical and empirical sciences. Apart from the further development of the general basis, hypotheses fitting the major objectives or even specific purposes have to be formulated in a more systematic way than has been done thus far.

As regards the method employed, a superficial judgment may lead to the conclusion that the foundations of accounting can be cast better and in a simpler fashion by the unsophisticated notation of high school algebra. This deceptive belief can easily be disproved by a practical attempt; the result will be either a loss of generality and rigor, or a much more involved maze of variables which have to get along without sub- and superscripts, without the sigma notation, and without the highly efficient concepts of set-theory. These devices enable modern algebra to achieve a concise, rigorous and concomitantly most general presentation. Besides, this approach avoids the unacademic dogmatism of convincing the student about the truth of a conclusion by submitting an array of specific instances numerous enough to make the conclusion *plausible* without ever proving it rigorously. As long as accounting is taught in such a way, our discipline is rightly criticized by the academic community.

Basic Assumptions (from Chapter 2)	Propositions of Set-Theoretical Formulation (from Appendix A)
1. Monetary values	primitive term
2. Time intervals (instances)	primitive term
3. Structure	item 15
4. Duality	item 17
5. Aggregation	item 18
6. Economic objects	primitive term
7. Inequity of monetary claims	(identical, not listed)
8. Economic agents	primitive term
9. Entities	item 1
10. Economic transactions	item 4
11. Valuation	(identical, not listed)
12. Realization	(identical, not listed)
13. Classification	(identical, not listed)
14. Data input	(identical, not listed)
15. Duration	(identical, not listed)
16. Extension	(an example of the simplest extension-hypothesis offered in item 27)
17. Materiality	(identical, not listed)
18. Allocation	(identical, not listed)

Subitems of Basic Assumptions (from Chapter 2)	Propositions of Set-Theoretical Formulation (from Appendix A)
2 b, c	14
3 a	16
5 a	19
5 c	20
5 d	22
6 a–d	2, 3, (also related to 9, 10, 11, 12, 13)
10 c, d	7, 24
10 e	5, 6

ALPHABETIC LIST OF SYMBOLS OF MAJOR SETS

(Subscripts or superscripts may vary,
hence are here omitted.)

Symbol	Explanation	Reference to Item
A	set of accounts (of an entity)	15
B	balancing operation (on an account at the end of a period)	18
B	trial balance of an entity (at the end of a period)	20
C	chart of accounts	16
D	creation of debt claim relation	11
D'	redemption of debt claim relation	13
δ	debt claim relation	3
E	set of entities (precisely: set of all states of *all* entities)	1
E	set of all states of *one* entity (= entity proper)	1
F	transaction (or flow) relation	4
F'	a transaction which is the *converse* of another transaction F	8
L	set or list of accounts of lowest order (of an entity)	16
ν	set of negative transactors	primitive
O	set of (economic) objects	primitive
$\emptyset$	the empty set	II
P	transfer of ownership relation	9
π	set of positive transactors	primitive
Q	creation of owners' equity relation	10
Q'	cancellation of an owners' equity	12
S	accounting statement (of an entity as at the end of a period)	22
S	auxiliary symbol for sums of transactions	27
T	set of time instances (intervals)	primitive
V	set of values	primitive
ω	ownership relation	2

APPENDIX B

INTRODUCTION TO MATRIX ALGEBRA

Appendix B introduces the reader to the basic notions of matrix algebra; it is reproduced from Chapter 12 of *Mathematical Analysis for Business Decisions* by James E. Howell and Daniel Teichroew (Homewood: Richard D. Irwin, Inc., 1963); pp. 234 to 246.

1. MATRICES

A matrix is a rectangular array of numbers or elements and is represented by writing down the elements and enclosing them in brackets; for example,

$$\begin{bmatrix} 5 & 4 & 6 \\ 3 & 2 & 7 \end{bmatrix}$$

is a matrix. For convenience, matrices may be represented by a single symbol, which by convention is usually a capital letter. The matrix given above might be called the matrix A, and this definition would be written as

$$A = \begin{bmatrix} 5 & 4 & 6 \\ 3 & 2 & 7 \end{bmatrix}$$

The array of elements of a matrix must be rectangular; for example,

$$\begin{bmatrix} 5 & 4 & 6 \\ & 2 & 7 \end{bmatrix}$$

is not a matrix because one element is missing. Other examples of matrices are:

$$B = \begin{bmatrix} 25 & 50 & 75 \\ 15 & 25 & 35 \\ 0 & 1 & 1 \end{bmatrix}; \quad X = \begin{bmatrix} x_1 \\ x_2 \\ x_3 \end{bmatrix}; \quad Y = [y_1 \ y_2];$$

and

$$C = \begin{bmatrix} 1750 \\ 850 \\ 25 \end{bmatrix}$$

These examples illustrate the fact that matrices may have one or more rows of elements and one or more columns of elements; the matrix B has 3 rows and 3 columns; X has 3 rows and 1 column; Y has 1 row and 2 columns; and C has 3 rows and 1 column. A matrix which has the same number of rows as columns is a *square matrix*; B is a square matrix.

Addition and subtraction of matrices, defined as one might expect, are easily performed: two matrices, A and B, may be added (or subtracted) one to (from) the other provided only that they have the same number of rows and columns. The resulting sum (or difference) will be a matrix, call it C, with the same number of rows and columns as the given matrices. If

$$A = \begin{bmatrix} 1 & 3 \\ 0 & 4 \end{bmatrix} \quad \text{and} \quad B = \begin{bmatrix} 0 & 2 \\ 3 & 3 \end{bmatrix}$$

and if $C = A + B$, then, since the elements of C are simply the sums of the correspondingly positioned elements of A and B,

$$C = \begin{bmatrix} 1 + 0 & 3 + 2 \\ 0 + 3 & 4 + 3 \end{bmatrix}$$

$$= \begin{bmatrix} 1 & 5 \\ 3 & 7 \end{bmatrix} \tag{1}$$

Also

$$\text{if } A + B = C, \quad \text{then} \quad B + A = C \quad \text{and}$$
$$\text{if } C - B = A, \quad \text{then} \quad C - A = B$$

It should be emphasized that matrix addition (or subtraction) requires only that the matrices which are to be added (or subtracted) have the same numbers of rows and columns (although they need not be square).

Matrix multiplication is more complex, interesting, and important. First, a matrix A can be multiplied by a matrix B if and only if *B has the same number of rows as A has columns.* Suppose *A* has *q* rows and *p* columns whereas *B* has *s* rows and *r* columns. Then the product *AB* is defined if and only if $p = s$. Note that nothing is said about *q* and *r* in this case: they need not be equal.

Finding the elements of the product matrix, call it *C*, involves finding a number of sums of products. For example, suppose

$$A = \begin{bmatrix} a & b & c \\ d & e & f \end{bmatrix} \quad \text{and} \quad B = \begin{bmatrix} g & j \\ h & k \\ i & m \end{bmatrix}$$

Then if $C = AB$,

$$C = \begin{bmatrix} a & b & c \\ d & e & f \end{bmatrix} \begin{bmatrix} g & j \\ h & k \\ i & m \end{bmatrix} = \begin{bmatrix} (ag + bh + ci) & (aj + bk + cm) \\ (dg + eh + fi) & (dj + ek + fm) \end{bmatrix} \quad (2)$$
$$\text{(2 × 3)} \quad \text{(3 × 2)} \qquad \text{(2 × 2)}$$

$$= \begin{bmatrix} t & v \\ u & w \end{bmatrix}$$

where $t = (ag + bh + ci)$, $u = (dg + eh + fi)$, $v = (aj + bk + cm)$, and $w = (dj + ek + fm)$.

Notice that *A* is a "2 by 3" matrix, meaning only that it has 2 rows and 3 columns, whereas *B* is a 3 × 2. Thus, they meet the condition for multiplication. Note also that the product *C* is 2 × 2. In general, if a $p \times r$ matrix *B* is premultiplied ("pre-" referring to the order, whether *AB* or *BA*) by a $q \times p$ matrix *A*, the product *AB* is a $q \times r$ matrix. Of course, if *A* and *B* are square matrices of order $r (= q = p)$, then an $r \times r$ matrix is being multiplied by one which is $r \times r$ and the product matrix *C* will be $r \times r$.

The order of multiplication is important, for even if *AB* is defined, *BA* may not be. Thus, if *A* is 2 × 3 and *B* is 3 × 4, the 2 × 4 matrix *AB* exists but *BA* does not. If the matrices are square and of the same order, both *AB* and *BA* are defined but they are not, in general, equal; that is, in general,

$$AB \neq BA$$

Consider the matrices

$$A = \begin{bmatrix} 1 & 3 \\ 0 & 4 \end{bmatrix} \quad \text{and} \quad B = \begin{bmatrix} 0 & 2 \\ 3 & 3 \end{bmatrix}$$

Then,

$$AB = \begin{bmatrix} (1 \cdot 0 + 3 \cdot 3) & (1 \cdot 2 + 3 \cdot 3) \\ (0 \cdot 0 + 4 \cdot 3) & (0 \cdot 2 + 4 \cdot 3) \end{bmatrix} = \begin{bmatrix} 9 & 11 \\ 12 & 12 \end{bmatrix}$$

and

$$BA = \begin{bmatrix} (0 \cdot 1 + 2 \cdot 0) & (0 \cdot 3 + 2 \cdot 4) \\ (3 \cdot 1 + 3 \cdot 0) & (3 \cdot 3 + 3 \cdot 4) \end{bmatrix} = \begin{bmatrix} 0 & 8 \\ 3 & 21 \end{bmatrix}$$

Hence, the order of multiplication—whether A is premultiplied (BA) or postmultiplied (AB) by B—is of great importance.

2. MATRIX SOLUTIONS OF LINEAR SYSTEMS

Suppose a problem generates a system of three equations,

$$\begin{align} 25x + 50y + 75z &= 1750 \\ 15x + 25y + 35z &= 850 \\ y + z &= 25 \end{align} \tag{3}$$

which must be solved simultaneously for values of x, y, and z. This is, essentially, a simple problem: elementary methods will do.

Solution of (3) by Method of Elimination:

Given:

i) $25x + 50y + 75z - 1750 = 0$
ii) $15x + 25y + 35z - 850 = 0$
iii) $\qquad y + z - 25 = 0$

From (*iii*):

iv) $y = 25 - z$

Substitute (*iv*) into (*i*) and (*ii*):
$5x + 10(25 - z) + 15z - 350 = 0$
$5x + 5z - 100 = 0$ (divide by 5)

v) $x + z = 20$
$3x + 5(25 - z) + 7z - 170 = 0$

vi) $3x + 2z = 45$

From (*v*):

vii) $x = 20 - z$

Substitute (*vii*) into (*vi*):
$$3(20 - z) + 2z = 45$$
$$- z = 45 - 60$$
$$z = 15$$

viii)

Substitute into (*vii*) and (*iii*):

ix) $x = 20 - 15$
$x = 5$

x) $y + 15 - 25 = 0$
$y = 10$

Thus (3) has a solution, and it is unique: 5, 10, 15.

Consider now a solution using *matrices*. Just as algebraic symbols have been used, e.g., x and $f(x)$, to express relationships, so matrices can be used to represent systems of equations such as (3).

Let the coefficients of x, y, and z in (3) be rewritten but without the unknowns:

$$25 \quad 50 \quad 75$$

$$15 \quad 25 \quad 35$$

$$1 \quad 1$$

This is not quite a matrix, for a matrix must be a rectangular array of elements. Thus, it is necessary to recognize explicitly that the coefficient of x in the third equation of the system is 0. The resulting array can then be defined as the matrix A:

$$A = \begin{bmatrix} 25 & 50 & 75 \\ 15 & 25 & 35 \\ 0 & 1 & 1 \end{bmatrix}$$

Now let the variables, the unknowns, be relabeled x_1, x_2, and x_3, respectively, and be represented by the matrix X where

$$X = \begin{bmatrix} x_1 \\ x_2 \\ x_3 \end{bmatrix}$$

Finally, let the right-hand side of (3) be represented by the matrix C where

$$C = \begin{bmatrix} 1750 \\ 850 \\ 25 \end{bmatrix}$$

The system of (3)

$$25x_1 + 50x_2 + 75x_3 = 1750$$
$$15x_1 + 25x_2 + 35x_3 = 850$$
$$x_2 + x_3 = 25$$

may now be conveniently written in matrix notation as

$$AX = C \qquad (4)$$

where A, X, and C are as defined above since

$$\begin{bmatrix} 25 & 50 & 75 \\ 15 & 25 & 35 \\ 0 & 1 & 1 \end{bmatrix} \begin{bmatrix} x_1 \\ x_2 \\ x_3 \end{bmatrix} = \begin{bmatrix} 25x_1 + 50x_2 + 75x_3 \\ 15x_1 + 25x_2 + 35x_3 \\ x_2 + x_3 \end{bmatrix}$$

Clearly, in a two-equation system little is gained notationally; equally clearly, much is gained if the system becomes even moderately large, say six or seven variables and equations. It should be noted that nothing new has been brought into the original problem; it has simply been described in a more economical way.

But matrices are more than a very useful notational convention. They also are a part of a technique for solving equation systems such as (3). Furthermore they are particularly useful in the analysis of systems where the number of unknowns and variables are not equal—certainly the usual condition for business and economic problems. Before matrix solutions can be explored, however, it is necessary to define two special matrices.

First, define the *identity matrix* which has the special characteristics that (*i*) it is square, (*ii*) its diagonal elements (those going from the top left-hand corner to the bottom right-hand corner) are all 1, and (*iii*) its nondiagonal elements are all 0. In other words, the identity matrix, always designated *I* and playing a role which is analogous to that played by 1 in elementary algebra, is defined as

$$I = \begin{bmatrix} 1 & 0 & \cdots & 0 \\ 0 & 1 & \cdots & 0 \\ \cdot & \cdot & \cdots & \cdot \\ 0 & 0 & \cdots & 1 \end{bmatrix} \tag{5}$$

where the number of rows and number of columns are equal. It is easy to verify that $IA = AI = A$, where A is any matrix and I has the necessary rows and columns.

Next, define the *inverse matrix*. This matrix is analogous to the reciprocal of a number; that is, it is defined only in relation to something else. Thus, if A is a given *square* matrix, its inverse is designated A^{-1} and is defined as that matrix which will, when properly multiplied by A, result in a product which is the identity matrix, I. Thus A^{-1} is the inverse matrix of A if and only if

$$A^{-1}A = I = AA^{-1} \tag{6}$$

The inverse will also be square and have the same number of rows and columns as do A and I. The inverse does *not* always exist, even if A is square; but when it does, it can be of great value in solving equation systems.

Now return, thus equipped, to the problems of solving the equation system

$$AX = C$$

for the matrix of unknowns, X. Consider first the analogous problem, using the familiar algebraic rules. Given

$$ax = c \tag{7}$$

where x is the unknown to be determined, one procedure would be to multiply both sides by $1/a$, that is, by a^{-1}. Thus

$$a^{-1}ax = a^{-1}c$$

Recognizing that

$$a^{-1}a = 1$$
$$x = a^{-1}c \tag{8}$$

and it is possible to assert, correctly, that an analytical solution to the original problem ("solve $ax = c$") has been obtained.   Notice that the procedure depends on understanding what is meant by a^{-1} and by the product $a^{-1}a$.

The matrix solution to (4) depends on similar understandings. First, where A^{-1} is the inverse of A, premultiply both sides of the equation by A^{-1}:

$$A^{-1}AX = A^{-1}C$$

Next, recognize that

$$A^{-1}A = I$$

and that

$$IX = X$$

Thus,

$$IX = A^{-1}C$$
$$X = A^{-1}C \tag{9}$$

i.e., the product matrix $(A^{-1}C)$ is the desired solution just as $(a^{-1}c)$ was the solution in the elementary case.

For the system in (3)

$$A = \begin{bmatrix} 25 & 50 & 75 \\ 15 & 25 & 35 \\ 0 & 1 & 1 \end{bmatrix} \text{ and } C = \begin{bmatrix} 1750 \\ 850 \\ 25 \end{bmatrix}$$

Since A is a 3×3 matrix, A^{-1}, if it exists at all, will also be 3×3. And pre-multiplication of C, a 3×1 matrix, by a 3×3 matrix is possible, the product being a 3×1 matrix.   This state of affairs will always prevail with systems such as (3).   Thus, the only question is that of finding A^{-1}.

The first step is to return to the definition of an inverse as that matrix A^{-1} whose product with A is the identity matrix, I:

$$A^{-1}A = I$$

Substituting for A and I yields

$$A^{-1} \cdot \begin{bmatrix} 25 & 50 & 75 \\ 15 & 25 & 35 \\ 0 & 1 & 1 \end{bmatrix} = \begin{bmatrix} 1 & 0 & 0 \\ 0 & 1 & 0 \\ 0 & 0 & 1 \end{bmatrix}$$

Let the elements of A^{-1} be designated by the letters a, b, c, etc.

$$\begin{bmatrix} a & b & c \\ d & e & f \\ g & h & i \end{bmatrix}$$

Then, recalling the procedure for multiplication of matrices, the following can be written:

$$A^{-1}A = \begin{bmatrix} a25 + b15 + c0 & a50 + b25 + c1 & a75 + b35 + c1 \\ d25 + e15 + f0 & d50 + e25 + f1 & d75 + e35 + f1 \\ g25 + h15 + i0 & g50 + h25 + i1 & g75 + h35 + i1 \end{bmatrix}$$

Equating corresponding elements in $A^{-1}A$ and I gives

$$\left.\begin{aligned} (a25 + b15 + c0) &= 1 \\ (a50 + b25 + c1) &= 0 \\ (a75 + b35 + c1) &= 0 \end{aligned}\right\} \text{which can be solved for } a, b, c$$

$$\left.\begin{aligned} (d25 + e15 + f0) &= 0 \\ (d50 + e25 + f1) &= 1 \\ (d75 + e35 + f1) &= 0 \end{aligned}\right\} \text{which can be solved for } d, e, f \tag{10}$$

$$\left.\begin{aligned} (g25 + h15 + i0) &= 0 \\ (g50 + h25 + i1) &= 0 \\ (g75 + h35 + i1) &= 1 \end{aligned}\right\} \text{which can be solved for } g, h, i$$

Solving these nine equations in sets of three for the elements of A^{-1} gives

$$A^{-1} = \begin{bmatrix} -\frac{2}{25} & \frac{1}{5} & -1 \\ -\frac{3}{25} & \frac{1}{5} & 2 \\ \frac{3}{25} & -\frac{1}{5} & -1 \end{bmatrix}$$

Finally, pre-multiplication of C yields

$$X = A^{-1}C$$

$$= \begin{bmatrix} -\frac{2}{25} & \frac{1}{5} & -1 \\ -\frac{3}{25} & \frac{1}{5} & 2 \\ \frac{3}{25} & -\frac{1}{5} & -1 \end{bmatrix} \begin{bmatrix} 1750 \\ 850 \\ 25 \end{bmatrix}$$

$$= \begin{bmatrix} 5 \\ 10 \\ 15 \end{bmatrix}$$

as before.

At this point the reader deserves the assurance that no one ever uses matrix methods of solution for small systems since, clearly, aside from the notational convenience, it is at least as difficult to solve by elementary methods of elimination for the elements of the inverse matrix as it is to solve the original problem. This is not the whole picture, however, since there are many standard procedures for the inversion of matrices for large systems, procedures which rely on electronic computers rather than on tedious hand calculations. It is this development, the ability to invert large coefficient matrices, that has made linear analysis so important and powerful in the analysis of business and economic problems. It is also relevant to note that many problems involve finding the matrix X for various C matrices while the coefficient matrix A—and hence A^{-1}—stays fixed. Under such circumstances, the matrix method of solution becomes quite efficient.

3. SUBSCRIPT NOTATION

A matrix with m rows and n columns has mn elements and each one appears in some row and some column. It is often quite convenient to identify the elements by using the row and column in which they appear as subscripts. If A is a matrix with 2 rows and 3 columns, it can be written as

$$\begin{bmatrix} a_{11} & a_{12} & a_{13} \\ a_{21} & a_{22} & a_{23} \end{bmatrix} \tag{11}$$

Using this notation, the operations of addition, subtraction, and multiplication can be defined in general as follows, where the subscript indices i and j indicate, respectively, the row and column positions of the element:

if $C = A + B$, then $c_{ij} = a_{ij} + b_{ij}$
if $C = A - B$, then $c_{ij} = a_{ij} - b_{ij}$ $\qquad\qquad$ (12)

if $C = AB$, then $c_{ij} = \sum_{k=1}^{r} a_{ik} b_{kj}$ (where r is the number of rows of B and the number of columns of A)

if $C = A^{-1}$, then $CA = I$ or $\sum_{k=1}^{r} c_{ik} a_{kj} = 1 \quad$ if $i = j$
$\qquad\qquad\qquad\qquad\qquad\qquad = 0 \quad$ if $i \neq j$

4. EXISTENCE OF AN INVERSE

In the previous sections it has been stated that a system of equations may or may not have a unique solution and that a matrix may or may not have an inverse. It is desirable to obtain or develop a criterion to determine whether or not a system has a solution or whether a matrix has an inverse. The condition is most easily stated in terms of the *determinant*.

An intuitive feeling for the definition of the determinant can be

obtained by considering the general case of two equations in two unknowns:

$$a_{11}x_1 + a_{12}x_2 = b_1 \tag{13}$$
$$a_{21}x_1 + a_{22}x_2 = b_2 \tag{14}$$

in which neither a_{11} nor a_{22} is zero. Since a_{11} is not zero,

$$x_1 = \frac{b_1 - a_{12}x_2}{a_{11}} \text{ from (13)} \tag{15}$$

And similarly, since a_{22} is not zero,

$$x_2 = \frac{b_2 - a_{21}x_1}{a_{22}} \text{ from (14)} \tag{16}$$

Substituting (16) into (15) gives

$$x_1 = \frac{b_1}{a_{11}} - a_{12}\left[\frac{b_2 - a_{21}x_1}{a_{22}}\right]$$

or

$$a_{11}a_{22}x_1 - a_{12}a_{21}x_1 = a_{22}b_1 - a_{12}b_2$$

and

$$x_1 = \frac{a_{22}b_1 - a_{12}b_2}{a_{11}a_{22} - a_{21}a_{12}} \tag{17}$$

Substituting (15) into (16) gives

$$x_2 = \frac{a_{11}b_2 - a_{21}b_1}{a_{11}a_{22} - a_{21}a_{12}} \tag{18}$$

The symbol

$$\begin{vmatrix} a_{11} & a_{12} \\ a_{21} & a_{22} \end{vmatrix} \tag{19}$$

is called a *determinant* of the system of equations, and its value is defined to be

$$a_{11}a_{22} - a_{12}a_{21} \tag{20}$$

Using this definition, the solutions to the system of equations can be
written as the ratio of two determinants:

$$x_1 = \frac{\begin{vmatrix} b_1 & a_{12} \\ b_2 & a_{22} \end{vmatrix}}{\begin{vmatrix} a_{11} & a_{12} \\ a_{21} & a_{22} \end{vmatrix}} \tag{21}$$

$$x_2 = \frac{\begin{vmatrix} a_{11} & b_1 \\ a_{21} & b_2 \end{vmatrix}}{\begin{vmatrix} a_{11} & a_{12} \\ a_{21} & a_{22} \end{vmatrix}} \tag{22}$$

Expression (21) is merely another way of writing (17), and expression (22) is another way of writing (18). The solution to the set of equations

$$4x_1 + 2x_2 = 4800$$
$$2x_1 + 13x_2 = 4800$$

is

$$x_1 = \frac{\begin{vmatrix} 4800 & 2 \\ 4800 & 13 \end{vmatrix}}{\begin{vmatrix} 4 & 2 \\ 2 & 13 \end{vmatrix}} = \frac{13(4800) - 2(4800)}{13(4) - 2(2)} = \frac{11(4800)}{48} = 1100$$

$$x_2 = \frac{\begin{vmatrix} 4 & 4800 \\ 2 & 4800 \end{vmatrix}}{\begin{vmatrix} 4 & 2 \\ 2 & 13 \end{vmatrix}} = \frac{4(4800) - 2(4800)}{48} = 200$$

The expression of the solution to a system of n linear equations as a ratio of two determinants is known as Cramer's Rule. Equations (21) and (22) are the application of this rule to the case where $n = 2$.

It has been shown above that the inverse of the matrix

$$\begin{bmatrix} a_{11} & a_{12} \\ a_{21} & a_{22} \end{bmatrix}, \text{ namely } \begin{bmatrix} c_{11} & c_{12} \\ c_{21} & c_{22} \end{bmatrix} \tag{23}$$

can be obtained by solving two sets of simultaneous linear equations:

$$a_{11}c_{11} + a_{12}c_{21} = 1$$
$$a_{21}c_{11} + a_{22}c_{21} = 0$$

$$a_{11}c_{12} + a_{12}c_{22} = 0$$
$$a_{21}c_{12} + a_{22}c_{22} = 1$$

Using (21) and (22), the inverse of A can be written as

$$\begin{bmatrix} c_{11} & c_{12} \\ c_{21} & c_{22} \end{bmatrix} \tag{24}$$

where

$$c_{11} = \frac{\begin{vmatrix} 1 & a_{12} \\ 0 & a_{22} \end{vmatrix}}{\begin{vmatrix} a_{11} & a_{12} \\ a_{21} & a_{22} \end{vmatrix}} \qquad c_{21} = \frac{\begin{vmatrix} a_{11} & 1 \\ a_{21} & 0 \end{vmatrix}}{\begin{vmatrix} a_{11} & a_{12} \\ a_{21} & a_{22} \end{vmatrix}} \tag{25}$$

$$c_{12} = \frac{\begin{vmatrix} 0 & a_{12} \\ 1 & a_{22} \end{vmatrix}}{\begin{vmatrix} a_{11} & a_{12} \\ a_{21} & a_{22} \end{vmatrix}} \qquad c_{22} = \frac{\begin{vmatrix} a_{11} & 0 \\ a_{21} & 1 \end{vmatrix}}{\begin{vmatrix} a_{11} & a_{12} \\ a_{21} & a_{22} \end{vmatrix}} \tag{26}$$

For example, if

$$A = \begin{bmatrix} 4 & 2 \\ 2 & 13 \end{bmatrix}$$

then

$$C = \begin{bmatrix} +\frac{13}{48} & -\frac{2}{48} \\ -\frac{12}{48} & \frac{4}{48} \end{bmatrix}$$

From these solutions it is clear that if the determinant $\begin{bmatrix} a_{11} & a_{12} \\ a_{21} & a_{22} \end{bmatrix}$ is zero, the inverse matrix will not exist since division by zero is not defined. On the other hand, if the determinant is not zero, the inverse matrix will exist and satisfy the necessary equations.

The same reasoning can be extended to cases of more variables; for example, consider the system of three equations in three unknowns:

$$\begin{aligned} a_{11}x_1 + a_{12}x_2 + a_{13}x_3 &= b_1 \\ a_{21}x_1 + a_{22}x_2 + a_{23}x_3 &= b_2 \\ a_{31}x_1 + a_{32}x_2 + a_{33}x_3 &= b_3 \end{aligned} \qquad (27)$$

The solution to this set of equations may be written formally as:

$$x_1 = \frac{\begin{vmatrix} b_1 & a_{12} & a_{13} \\ b_2 & a_{22} & a_{23} \\ b_3 & a_{32} & a_{33} \end{vmatrix}}{\begin{vmatrix} a_{11} & a_{12} & a_{13} \\ a_{21} & a_{22} & a_{23} \\ a_{31} & a_{32} & a_{33} \end{vmatrix}}$$

$$x_2 = \frac{\begin{vmatrix} a_{11} & b_1 & a_{13} \\ a_{21} & b_2 & a_{23} \\ a_{31} & b_3 & a_{33} \end{vmatrix}}{\begin{vmatrix} a_{11} & a_{12} & a_{13} \\ a_{21} & a_{22} & a_{23} \\ a_{31} & a_{32} & a_{33} \end{vmatrix}} \qquad (28)$$

$$x_2 = \frac{\begin{vmatrix} a_{11} & a_{12} & b_1 \\ a_{21} & a_{22} & b_2 \\ a_{31} & a_{32} & b_3 \end{vmatrix}}{\begin{vmatrix} a_{11} & a_{12} & a_{13} \\ a_{21} & a_{22} & a_{23} \\ a_{31} & a_{32} & a_{33} \end{vmatrix}}$$

where the determinant in the denominator is the determinant of the system, and the determinant in the numerator is obtained by replacing the elements in the ith column of the system matrix by the right-hand side of (27) while leaving the remaining elements unchanged.

The value of a third-order determinant may be found by using the following rule:

a) Write the determinant and then repeat the first two columns:

$$
\begin{array}{ccccc}
a_{11} & a_{12} & a_{13} & a_{11} & a_{12} \\
a_{21} & a_{22} & a_{23} & a_{21} & a_{22} \\
a_{31} & a_{32} & a_{33} & a_{31} & a_{32}
\end{array}
$$

b) Sum the three products of the three terms linked by solid lines, and subtract the sum of the three products of the three terms linked by broken lines; i.e., the value of the determinant, D, shown above is:

$$
D = (a_{11}a_{22}a_{33} + a_{12}a_{23}a_{31} + a_{13}a_{21}a_{32}) -
$$
$$
- (a_{13}a_{22}a_{31} + a_{11}a_{23}a_{32} + a_{12}a_{21}a_{33}) \qquad (29)
$$

Reasoning as before, the system matrix will have a unique inverse if and only if its determinant is different from zero.

This same reasoning can be extended to cases of four, five, and a higher number of variables, although the computation of the determinant becomes more difficult and other rules are used to compute determinants with more coefficients. This generalization, which shall be shown without proof, is as follows:

a) The system of equations

$$
AX = C
$$

has a solution if and only if the determinant of A, written as $|A|$, is different from zero.

b) The matrix A has an inverse if and only if the determinant of A is different from zero.

c) From this it follows that the solution to the system of equations exists if and only if the matrix A has an inverse.

APPENDIX C

INTRODUCTION
TO LINEAR PROGRAMMING

Appendix C introduces the reader to the basic notions of linear programming; it is reproduced mainly from Chapter 13 of *Mathematical Analysis for Business Decisions* by James E. Howell and Daniel Teichroew (Homewood: Richard D. Irwin, Inc., 1963) pp. 257 to 272. The treatment of the "Dual" is taken from Chapter 15 of *Quantitative Analysis for Business Decisions* by Harold Bierman, Lawrence E. Fouraker, and Robert K. Jaedicke (Homewood: Richard D. Irwin, Inc., 1961), pp. 218–23. For further mathematical details and references the reader is referred to both of these books.

Linear programming is a mathematical technique for determining the most desirable or most profitable course of action for a situation where a number of variables are involved, where many possible courses of action are available, and where the problem can be expressed in linear terms. Thus, linear programming is another optimizing technique, a technique, however, which is applicable to many types of decision problems for which the methods of Chapters 4 and 7 do not work.

1. THE LINEAR PROGRAMMING MODEL

It would not be necessary to resort to linear programming if the conditions of the decision situation could be expressed as, for example,

$$x + 2y = 100$$
$$3x + y = 100 \tag{1}$$

There is only one solution ($x = 20$, $y = 40$), and this (necessarily optimal) solution can be determined easily by elementary methods. See Figure 13-1.

Suppose, however, that *many* acceptable, or feasible, solutions exist; e.g., suppose the system is

$$x + 2y \leq 100$$
$$3x + y \leq 100 \qquad (2)$$
$$x \geq 0$$
$$y \geq 0$$

There are now many possible solutions which would satisfy the inequalities of (2). The graph of these inequalities, Figure 13–2, shows that any point (x, y) within the shaded area will satisfy the restrictions set forth in the problem. Linear programming provides a method for deciding which of the possible points is optimal.

First, consider a specific industrial problem which might lead to a situation such as (2). Suppose that the Proteus Company makes two products—X and Y. Each of these musf be processed on a milling machine and on a turret lathe. The total amount of machine time available weekly on each machine is 100 hours, approximately a two-shift operation, six days a week.

Now suppose that product X requires *one* hour of machine time on the milling machine and *three* hours on the turret lathe; whereas product Y requires *two* hours on the milling machine and *one* hour

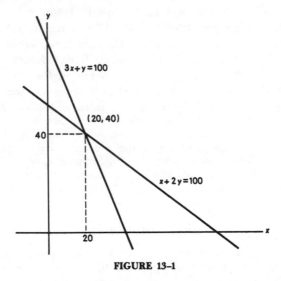

FIGURE 13–1

on the turret lathe. To describe the quantities of X and Y which may be produced in a week, where x is the quantity of product X and y is the quantity of product Y, it is necessary and sufficient that

$$x + 2y \leq 100$$
$$3x + y \leq 100$$
$$x \geq 0 \qquad (3)$$
$$y \geq 0$$

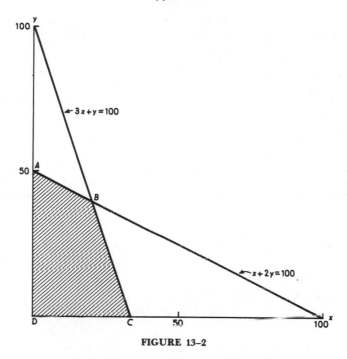

FIGURE 13-2

It can be seen that $x = 33\frac{1}{3}$ if only X is produced, or that $y = 50$ if only Y is produced. Both of these possibilities, however, would result in considerable idle machine time: $y = 0$, $x = 33\frac{1}{3}$ gives $66\frac{2}{3}$ hours of idle time on the milling machine; while $x = 0$, $y = 50$ gives 50 hours idle time on the turret lathe; and seldom would either be considered a practical alternative. A third alternative is to produce nothing at all; the machines would be idle all the time. Each of these three possibilities is *feasible* since the conditions of (3) would be satisfied. Negative values of x and y, on the other hand, are excluded from consideration by (3).

Is it possible to identify the optimal values for x and y? Clearly, not, since no decision criterion has been stated. Suppose therefore that the company wishes to maximize its net revenues (earnings) from the production and sale of these two products. It is still impossible to set a production program, i.e., choose x^* and y^*, the optimum values. It is necessary to introduce economic information—as opposed to the engineering information embodied in (3)—in order to specify the company's objective in terms of x and y.

This can be accomplished by introducing the information that the company's earnings are $4.00 per unit on X and $3.00 per unit on Y. Letting $E(x, y)$ represent earnings, the earnings function is thus

$$E(x, y) = 4x + 3y \tag{4}$$

The firm's management wants to maximize (4), subject to the restrictions on output which are imposed by machine time limitations as represented by the inequalities in (3). E is a function of x and y, and its graph is shown in Figure 13–3 along with the two equations implicit in the system of (3). For instance, if E is \$900, then $4x + 3y = 900$; if $x = 210$, y must equal 20; if $x = 180$, y must equal 60, etc. Construction of the graph is facilitated by rewriting the earnings function $E = 4x + 3y$ explicitly in terms of y, as

$$y = \frac{E}{3} - \frac{4x}{3}$$

so that by choosing any value for E and x the corresponding value y can be determined. For any given value of E there exists a line having the y-intercept $E/3$ and a slope of $-4/3$. Several such lines are shown in Figure 13–3.

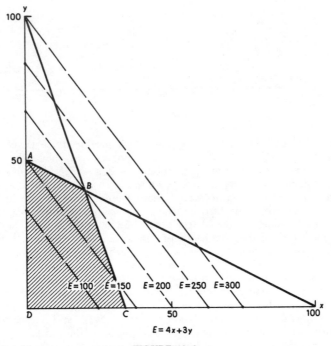

FIGURE 13–3

The decision problem is to find the highest value of E obtainable within the machine time restrictions stated in (3). This means that the line expressing E must contain at least one point which will satisfy the inequalities, $x + 2y \leq 100$, $3x + y \leq 100$, $x \geq 0$, and $y \geq 0$.

Clearly, the highest value of E, say E^*, is represented by the line which is tangent to the shaded area on the graph at the point ($x = 20$, $y = 40$). At this point, B, the equation $E = 4x + 3y$ has the value 200 and maximum earnings are \$200. The graph of the equation $E = 4x + 3y$ for all values of $E \geq 200$ is entirely outside the shaded area.

By finding that E^* requires a production plan such that $x = 20$ and $y = 40$, a simple linear programming problem has been solved— one in which the solution was intuitively clear as soon as the profit function and the constraints were shown on the same graph (Figure 13–3). This simple problem, however, has illustrated certain aspects of the linear programming method which will be helpful in considering more complicated problems later on. These features are:

a) The set of all *feasible solutions* to the problem is represented graphically by a polygon—*ABCD*—the shaded area in Figure 13–2.

b) The *optimum solution* appears at a vertex, or corner, of the polygon. It does not matter what the coefficients are as long as the earnings function and the constraints are linear; the solution will always be at one of the corner points of the polygon. For instance, suppose there were no earnings at all on product Y, and the earnings function was $E = 4x$; the optimum solution would have been at vertex C. Or if the earnings function had been $E = 2x + 10y$, the vertex A would have been the optimum solution. Clearly the optimum vertex position depends only on the ratio of the two coefficients in (4).

c) A linear programming problem may not have any feasible solution. If the lines were such that no point in the positive quadrant (when $x, y > 0$) satisfied both inequalities, there would be no feasible solution.

d) If a linear programming problem has a feasible solution, then there also exists an optimum solution.

The graphical method for solving linear programming models is useful only for small problems, in fact, only for problems with two variables. For problems with more than two variables, more powerful techniques are necessary. One such technique is that of enumerating all the alternatives, computing E for each one, choosing the optimum, E^*, by inspection. This technique is useful for explanatory purposes. However, it quickly becomes less useful in practice as the problem grows in size and complexity.

The *enumeration technique* is applicable because of properties (a) and (b), for if a linear programming problem has any feasible solutions, the optimum solution is at one of the vertices and the number of vertices is limited. The technique consists of enumerating all the vertices, computing the earnings at each one and selecting as the optimum the vertex giving the highest earnings. For example for (3) and (4) the following table can be developed:

Vertex	x	y	E
A	0	50	150
B	20*	40*	200*
C	33⅓	0	133⅓
D	0	0	0

Simply by inspection of the last column, and remembering that the objective is to maximize E, it is seen that E^* implies $x^* = 20$ and $y^* = 40$, the same solution as before.

2. A THREE-PRODUCT PROBLEM

Now suppose that the Proteus Company has added a third product, Z, to its line. The earnings on each unit of Z are $5.00. Product Z requires two hours of machine time on the milling machine and three hours on the turret lathe.

The company's earnings function is now $E = 4x + 3y + 5z$, and the problem is to find x^*, y^*, and z^* which will result in E^*. In other words, how much of each of the three products should the company produce each week? The machine time restrictions governing the output of X, Y, and Z are expressed by

$$x + 2y + 2z \le 100$$
$$3x + y + 3z \le 100 \tag{5}$$

and also

$$x \ge 0$$
$$y \ge 0$$
$$z \ge 0$$

The equations implicit in (5) now represent planes instead of simply straight lines. It is necessary to imagine a three-dimensional graph of these planes. Considering the axes of this graph as perpendicular (technically, orthogonal) planes instead of as lines, the two additional planes described by the equations ($x + 2y + 2z = 100$ and $3x + y + 3z = 100$) will form a polyhedron whose sides are planes. (If this is difficult to visualize, take a look at a cardboard box. Seen from the top, it is a rectangle whose edges are four straight lines. Seen from any other angle, the sides are observed as planes.)

This polyhedron has corner points, or vertices, just as did the two-dimensional polygon. The previous result that the optimum solution of the problem will be found at one of these vertices applies here, and even though it is not easy to construct the graph, the values at each vertex can be computed. Then the vertex having the highest value in terms of earnings can be selected as the optimum point.

To evaluate the vertices by a process of enumeration, it is necessary first to identify the several planes which intersect to form the several vertices. The equations

$$x + 2y + 2z = 100 \tag{6}$$
$$3x + y + 3z = 100$$

make up two sides of the polyhedron. The other three sides of the polyhedron are the yz-plane, the xz-plane, and the xy-plane. These planes are represented by the equations

$$x = 0$$
$$y = 0 \tag{7}$$
$$z = 0$$

When any two of the five planes intersect, a straight line, rather than a point, is formed. When three planes intersect, i.e., when there is a common solution to any three of the five equations, the intersection may be a straight line or a single point. If it is a point, it may form a vertex of the feasible polyhedron. (Cf. the example of the cardboard box; when three sides of the box come together simultaneously, a corner of the box—a "point"—is formed.)

Given the set of five equations, x, y, and z must be evaluated at each vertex. That is, each combination of three equations is solved for the three unknowns as follows:

The Equations (Planes)

$$a)\ x + 2y + 2z = 100$$
$$b)\ 3x +\ y + 3z = 100$$
$$c)\ x = 0$$
$$d)\ y = 0$$
$$e)\ z = 0$$

Vertex	x	y	z	$E =$ $4x + 3y + 5z$
a, b, c	0	25	25	200
a, b, d	−33⅓	0	66⅔	. .
a, b, e	20	40	0	200
b, c, d	0	0	33⅓	166⅔
b, c, e	0	100	0	. .
c, d, e	0	0	0	0
b, d, e	33⅓	0	0	133⅓
a, c, d	0	0	50	. .
a, c, e	0	50	0	150
a, d, e	100	0	0	. .

There are ten vertices. Only six of them, however, are within the set of feasible solutions, i.e., are vertices of the polyhedron of feasible solutions. Examine the vertex formed by the intersecting planes of equations a, b, and c. The values of x, y, and z are, respectively, 0, 25, and 25. Each of these is an allowable value; hence, the resulting value of $E = 200$ is feasible. Consider the next intersection, the one formed by equations a, b, and d. The respective values of x, y, and z are—33⅓, 0, and 66⅔. Clearly, x cannot be −33⅓; hence, this intersection is outside the set of feasible solutions and the E-value implied by (−33⅓, 0, 66⅔) is irrelevant since it is not feasible.

Similarly, three other vertices must be excluded as being unobtainable; (b, c, e) because y cannot be greater than 100/2 by equation (a); (a, c, d) because z cannot be greater than 100/3 by equation (b); and (a, d, e) because x cannot be greater than 100/3 by equation (b).

Now that six potential optima have been isolated, it is a simple task to glance at the E-value implied by each in order to find the optimal course of action. The largest possible profit is $E^* = 200$, and it is obtainable with either of two production plans: (0, 25, 25) or (20, 40, 0). The fact that there are two optima is not particularly significant. It is significant, however, that each optimum involved produces only two of the three products. This point will be considered below.

The reader should not be concerned if the spatial aspects of the foregoing example are difficult to grasp. The use of analytic geometry in linear programming is limited, and visual or spatial concepts are of no use when more than three dimensions are involved anyway. It is only important to know that the vertices or edges of the geometric figures formed will always be the only points (or lines) which are potentially optimal points. In the particular example, the earnings plane happened to be parallel to an edge of the polyhedron rather than intersecting the polyhedron at a single point so that there was more than one optimum.

To summarize the argument to this point:

1. The first step was to realize that the feasible solutions were contained within or on a polyhedron created by the intersection of the planes implied in the several inequalities.
2. Next, the values of the vertices of this polyhedron were identified by solving each set of three equations in three unknowns; the values of x, y, and z thus obtained were substituted into the profit function to find the value of each vertex—i.e., the value of the profit function at that vertex.
3. Those vertices which lay outside the feasible polyhedron were discarded. The feasible region does not include the solutions which have values of x, y, or z which are too high or too low in view of the machine-time restrictions or of the restriction that x, y, z are all nonnegative.
4. The vertex at which profit was highest was determined by inspection. In this case, there were two, indicating that the profit plane touched an edge rather than a corner of the polyhedron. (Strictly speaking, there were more than two optimal production schedules, although there were only two identified by the enumeration procedure. Why?)

The results suggest that the Proteus Company gained nothing by adding product Z. It can make no more profit now than it did with products X and Y only. On the other hand, it would be just as well off to drop product X and to produce only Y and Z.

In order to illustrate a case where the optimum is unique, suppose the company has found ways of improving the profitability of product Z so that the earnings function is now

$$E = 4x + 3y + 7z \qquad (8)$$

The results are somewhat different, as the enumeration procedure reveals:

Vertex	x	y	z	E
a, b, c	0	25	25	250
a, b, d	$-33\frac{1}{3}$	0	$66\frac{2}{3}$	. .
a, b, e	20	40	0	200
b, c, d	0	0	$33\frac{1}{3}$	$233\frac{1}{3}$
b, c, e	0	100	0	. .
c, d, e	0	0	0	0
b, d, e	$33\frac{1}{3}$	0	0	$133\frac{1}{3}$
a, c, d	0	0	50	. .
a, c, e	0	50	0	150
a, d, e	100	0	0	. .

The feasible region has not changed; the same four vertices must still be excluded. But now there is a unique optimum at the vertex defined by (a, b, c). Under these circumstances, it is clear that the company should now drop product X and manufacture 25 units per week of product Y and 25 units of product Z.

It may seem strange that the company can obtain more profit by producing two products than it can by producing all three, a result which is generally true. A careful statement of this important result is as follows:

> Suppose there is limited time available on each of m machines which can produce n different products each of which requires time on each machine $(n \geq m)$. Suppose further that earnings is a linear function of the number of units of each product produced. Then the optimum earnings can be obtained by producing only k products where $k \leq m \leq n$.

To show intuitively why this is true, consider the last example described. In mathematical terms the problem is:

$$\text{Maximize: } E = 4x + 3y + 7z \tag{9}$$
$$\text{Subject to: } x + 2y + 2z \leq 100 \tag{10}$$
$$3x + y + 3z \leq 100 \tag{11}$$

x, y, and z nonnegative. The answer is, as already seen, $x = 0$, $y = 25$, $z = 25$, which gives

$$E^* = 250$$

Now write the inequalities as equations in the form

$$2y + 2z = c_1 \tag{12}$$
$$y + 3z = c_2 \tag{13}$$

where $c_1 = 100 - x$ and $c_2 = 100 - 3x$. Then solve for y and z. Subtracting 2 times (13) from 3 times (12) and dividing by 4 gives

$$1 \cdot y + 0 \cdot z = \frac{3c_1 - 2c_2}{4}$$
$$= \tfrac{1}{4}[300 - 3x - 200 + 6x]$$
$$= 25 + \tfrac{3}{4}x$$

Similarly, subtracting (12) from 2 times (13) and dividing by 4 gives

$$0y + 1z = \frac{2c_2 - c_1}{4}$$
$$= \tfrac{1}{4}[200 - 6x - 100 + x]$$
$$= 25 - \tfrac{5}{4}x$$

or

$$y = 25 + \tfrac{3}{4}x \tag{14}$$
$$z = 25 - \tfrac{5}{4}x \tag{15}$$

This solution says that if there is to be no idle time, i.e., the euqality sign holds in (10) and (11), then

a) $y = 25$ and $z = 25$ if $x = 0$,
b) $y = 28$ and $z = 20$ if x has some positive value, say $x = 4$.

These results can, of course, be obtained from (10) and (11), but it is much easier to get them from (14) and (15). Furthermore, the set (14) and (15) can be substituted in (9) to give

$$E = 4x + 3[25 + \tfrac{3}{4}x] + 7[25 - \tfrac{5}{4}x]$$
$$= 250 - \tfrac{10}{4}x \qquad (16)$$

This form of the earnings function says that $x = 0$ is the optimum production level for if $x > 0$, then $E < 250$, i.e., as x increases from 0, E declines: product X should not be produced.

The reason why only two products should be produced is now clear. From (14) and (15) it follows that since all the machine time is already being used to produce Y and Z, some X can be produced only by reducing the amount of time for Y and Z. In particular (14) and (15) say that if $x = 1$, i.e., one unit of X is produced, and the rest of the machine time is used for Y and Z, then $y = 25\tfrac{3}{4}$ and $z = 23\tfrac{3}{4}$. The net increase in earnings will be the earnings from one unit of x *less* the earnings that would have been received if the machine time was used to produce $\tfrac{3}{4}$ of a unit less of Y and $\tfrac{5}{4}$ units more of Z, namely.

$$4(1) - [3(-\tfrac{3}{4}) + 7(+\tfrac{5}{4})] = 4 + \tfrac{9}{4} - \tfrac{35}{4}$$
$$= -\tfrac{10}{4}$$

which is the coefficient that appears in (16). The same conclusion can be read directly from (16):

$$E = 250 - \tfrac{10}{4}x$$

Considering this as a function of one variable, the other two having been eliminated by the substitution of (14) and (15), it is clear by inspection that E^* implies $x = 0$.

The "new" form of the earnings function can be computed for each vertex of the polyhedron. The results for the example at hand are shown in the following table. It should be noted that there is at least one

Products	Equations from		Earnings Function
X	$x = \dfrac{100}{3} - \dfrac{y}{3} - z$	(11)	$E = 4x + 3y + 7z$ $E = \tfrac{400}{3} + 1\tfrac{2}{3}y + 3z$
Y	$y = 50 - \dfrac{x}{2} - z$	(10)	$E = 150 + 2\tfrac{1}{2}x + 4z$
Z	$z = \dfrac{100}{3} - x - \dfrac{y}{3}$	(11)	$E = \tfrac{700}{3} - 3x + \tfrac{2}{3}y$
X and Y	$x = 20 - \tfrac{1}{3}z$ $y = 40 - \tfrac{2}{3}z$	(10) (11)	$E = 200 + 2z$
X and Z	$x = -\tfrac{100}{3} + \tfrac{1}{3}y$ $z = \tfrac{200}{3} - \tfrac{2}{3}y$	(10) (11)	(not feasible since x cannot be negative)
Y and Z	$y = 25 + \tfrac{3}{4}x$ $z = 25 - \tfrac{5}{4}x$		$E = 250 - \tfrac{5}{2}x$

positive coefficient in each case. In the case where only one product is produced, one of the inequalities, (10) or (11), is redundant. The controlling inequality is shown in the table. The equations for X and Z only show that the solution must be $x = -100/3$, $y = 200/3$ if there is to be no idle time. This solution, of course, is not feasible.

3. ADDITIONAL INFORMATION FROM LP SOLUTIONS

It has been shown in the preceding section that if there are two restricting inequalities, only two products are produced even though there were three possible products. The optimal number of products would have been the same even if there had been four, five, or a hundred possible products. The number of products which will be produced in a linear programming solution can never be larger than the number of constraints, regardless of how many products are technologically possible.

This fact can be used to elicit additional information from the linear programming model. First, define two fictitious products: U and W, and let u and w denote the quantities produced of each. Suppose each unit of U requires one hour of milling machine time and no time on the lathe, while each unit of W requires one hour of lathe time but no milling machine time. In fact, u and w are nothing more than the quantity of *idle* time on the milling machine and turret lathe, respectively. Since the time required to produce products *plus* the idle time on each machine must *equal* the total time available, the restricting inequalities of (5) become the equations of (17).

$$x + 2y + 2z + 1u + 0w = 100$$
$$3x + y + 3z + 0u + 1w = 100 \qquad (17)$$
$$x \geq 0, y \geq 0, z \geq 0, u \geq 0, w \geq 0$$

This is a set of two linear equations in five unknowns. From Chapter 12 it is known that two equations in two unknowns can have a unique solution, but that if the number of unknowns is greater than the number of equations, there can be an infinite number of solutions.

It is known that the optimum solution in the linear programming model of the preceding section calls for the production of at most two products, the other products not being produced. In terms of the equation this means that at most two of the variables will have non-zero values while the others will be zero. From the previous section, the optimum solution requires production of y and z so that the solution is known to require that $x = 0$, $u = 0$, $w = 0$. The optimum values of y and z can then be found by solving (18) which is derived directly from (17):

$$2y + 2z = 100$$
$$y + 3z = 100 \qquad (18)$$

Of course, $y^* = 25$, and $z^* = 25$, as before.

The earnings function of (9) becomes

$$E = 4x + 3y + 7z + 0u + 0w \qquad (19)$$

since U and W do not contribute to earnings. In this case $E^* = 3(25) +$

$7(25) = 250$. The solution indicates what should be produced and what the earnings will be.

Frequently the management also wants to know whether it should acquire more machine time or what the decrease in earnings will be if some X must be produced. These questions can be answered relatively easily by the method given above if x, u, and w are not set to zero but are carried along as variables.

The equations of (17) become

$$2y + 2z = 100 - x - 1u - 0w \qquad (20a)$$
$$y + 3z = 100 - 3x - 0u - 1w \qquad (20b)$$

and the solutions can be obtained as follows:

Subtracting 2 times (20b) from 3 times (20a) and dividing by 4

$$1 \cdot y + 0 \cdot z = 25 + \tfrac{3}{4}x - \tfrac{3}{4}u + \tfrac{1}{2}w \qquad (21)$$

Subtracting (20a) from 2 times (20b) and dividing by 4 gives

$$0 \cdot y + 1 \cdot z = 25 - \tfrac{5}{4}x + \tfrac{1}{4}u - \tfrac{1}{2}w \qquad (22)$$

The system of (21) and (22) has the same solutions as (18). Because (21) does not contain z and (22) does not contain y, the solutions obtained when $x = u = w = 0$ can be read off directly as $y = 25$ from (21) and $z = 25$ from (22). Furthermore, if, for example, $x = 4$, $u = 8$, and $w = 2$, the solution can also be obtained easily as

$$y = 25 + 3 - 6 + 1 = 23$$
$$z = 25 - 5 + 2 - 1 = 21 \qquad (23)$$

It should be noted that to obtain this solution from (17) would require the solution of a system of two equations in two unknowns.

Equations (21) and (22) can be substituted in (19) to give

$$E = 4x + 3[25 + \tfrac{3}{4}x - \tfrac{3}{4}u + \tfrac{1}{2}w] + 7[25 - \tfrac{5}{4}x + \tfrac{1}{4}u$$
$$- \tfrac{1}{2}w] + 0u + 0w = 250 - 2\tfrac{1}{2}x - \tfrac{1}{2}u - 2w \qquad (24)$$

This formula for earnings reveals the following:

1. Since the coefficients of x, u, and w are negative, and since x, u, and w themselves must, by definition, be nonnegative it follows that the solution $x = u = w = 0$, $y = 25$, $z = 25$, which results in earnings of 250, is optimum.
2. The coefficient of x in (24), namely $-2\tfrac{1}{2}$, says that earnings will be reduced by $2\tfrac{1}{2}$ dollars if one unit of X is produced. This can easily be verified as follows: to produce one unit of X requires one hour of milling machine time and three hours of lathe time. Therefore the quantities of Y and Z that can be produced are given by the solution of the equation

$$2y + 2z = 99$$
$$y + 3z = 97$$

which is

$$y = 25\tfrac{3}{4}, \qquad z = 23\tfrac{3}{4} \qquad (25)$$

and

$$E = 4 + 3(25\tfrac{3}{4}) + 7(23\tfrac{3}{4}) = 247\tfrac{1}{2}$$

3. If an additional hour of milling machine time is available the earnings will be increased by \$.50 and if an additional hour of lathe time is available, earnings will be increased by \$2.00.

To show the third conclusion, suppose the new problem is written in the form,

$$\text{Maximize } E = 4x + 3y + 7z$$
$$\text{Subject to} \quad x + 2y + 2z \leq 100 + F_1$$
$$3x + \ y + 3z \leq 100 + F_2 \tag{26}$$
$$x \geq 0, y \geq 0, z \geq 0$$

where F_1 is the change in the amount of milling machine time and F_2 the change in the amount of lathe time (the changes may be $+$ or $-$). Adding the "slack variables" (i.e., the fictitious variables u and w) gives:

$$x + 2y + 2z + u = 100 + F_1$$
$$3x + \ y + 3z + w = 100 + F_2 \tag{27}$$

Solving for y and z yields

$$y = 25 + \frac{3F_1}{4} - \frac{1F_2}{2} + \tfrac{3}{4}x - \tfrac{3}{4}u + \tfrac{1}{2}w$$

$$= 25 + \tfrac{3}{4}x - \tfrac{3}{4}(u - F_1) + \tfrac{1}{2}(w - F_2)$$

$$z = 25 + \frac{F_2}{2_2} - \frac{F_1}{4} - \tfrac{5}{4}x + \tfrac{1}{4}u - \tfrac{1}{6}w \tag{28}$$

$$= 25 - \tfrac{5}{4}x + \tfrac{1}{4}(u - F_1) - \tfrac{1}{2}(w - F_2)$$

These values are substituted into the earnings function:

$$E = 250 - 2\tfrac{1}{2}x - \tfrac{1}{2}(u - F_1) - 2(w - F_2) \tag{29}$$

In the case where an additional hour of milling machine time is available, i.e., $F_1 = 1, F_2 = 0$, the optimum solution, if $x = u = w = 0$, is

$$y = 25 + \tfrac{3}{4}$$
$$= 25\tfrac{3}{4}$$
$$z = 25 - \tfrac{1}{4} \tag{30}$$
$$= 24\tfrac{3}{4}$$

This solution is certainly feasible since

$$0 + 2(25\tfrac{3}{4}) + 2(24\tfrac{3}{4}) = 101 \leq 100 + 1$$
$$0 + \ (25\tfrac{3}{4}) + 3(24\tfrac{3}{4}) = 100 \leq 100$$

Then, by substituting into (29)

$$E = 250 + \tfrac{1}{2}$$
$$= 250\tfrac{1}{2} \tag{31}$$

It is possible, of course, that the products produced in the optimal program if 100 hours of milling machine time are available will not be produced by the optimal program if 101 hours of milling machine time are available. It is therefore essential to check that the solution obtained by this method is in fact feasible.

This technique of examining the change in earnings under unit changes of machine time is an important aspect of the application of linear programming. From a theoretical point of view it shows the relationship between linear programming and marginal analysis.

The technique also makes it possible to compute the solution of a slightly changed linear programming problem with much less effort than was required for solving the original problem.

An outline summary of the linear programming model follows.

SUMMARY OF THE LINEAR PROGRAMMING MODEL

A. *Description*

A problem can be placed in the linear programming format if it satisfies the following conditions:
1. There are n variables which must be nonnegative.
2. There are m linear inequalities restricting these variables.
3. The earnings function is a linear function of the n variables.

B. *Major Results*

The major results are:
1. There may or may not be any feasible solution. A feasible solution is one which satisfies the m linear inequalities and in which all the variables are nonnegative.
2. If there is a feasible solution, then there is also an optimum solution; an optimum solution is one which results in at least as high a value of the profit function as does any other feasible solution.
3. In the optimum solution no more than m of the variables will be different from zero and at least $n - m$ of the variables will be equal to zero.

C. *Computation*

The solution to a linear programming problem can be determined numerically by selecting a set of m variables out of the $n + m$, taking the other n, placing them on the right-hand side of the equation and then solving the m equations in m unknowns. The solutions are substituted into the earnings function, and the coefficients of the n variables computed. If all of these coefficients are negative, an optimum solution has been obtained. If one or more of the coefficients is positive, then the solution is not optimum.

If n and m are relatively small, the solution can be obtained by trial-and-error enumeration of all sets of m variables until all coefficients are negative. If the number of variables is large, a more systematic procedure known as the Simplex Method is used. The Simplex Method may be applied "by hand" or on a computer.

D. *Other Information*

The information obtained in the solution of the linear programming model is as follows:
1. The solution is the set of values of the m variables which jointly maximize the earnings function.
2. The earnings which can be obtained by choosing alternative, non-optimal solutions can be computed using the coefficients in the earnings function.
3. The value of additional resources can be computed using the coefficients in the earnings function.

LINEAR PROGRAMMING—THE DUAL PROBLEM

Every linear programming problem that we have solved has been of the type designated as "primal"; the primal being the first problem

to which our attention is generally directed.   Each primal problem
has a companion problem which is called the "dual."   The dual has the
same optimum solution as the primal, but it is derived by an alternative
procedure and the analysis of this procedure may be instructive for
several types of decision problems.

Example—The Primal

Assume that two products X_1 and X_2 are manufactured on two
machines, 1 and 2.

Product X_1 requires three hours on machine 1 and one-half hour on
machine 2.

Product X_2 requires two hours on machine 1 and one hour on
machine 2.

There are six hours of excess capacity on machine 1 and four hours
on machine 2.

Each unit of X_1 produces a net increase in profit of \$12, and each
unit of X_2 an incremental profit of \$4.00.

The objective function (or profit function) to be maximized is $P =
12X_1 + 4X_2$, or after including the slack variables, $P = 12X_1 + 4X_2 +
0X_3 + 0X_4$.

The restraints are:

$3X_1 + 2X_2 \leq 6$. There are six hours available on machine 1.   Each unit
of X_1 requires three hours; X_2 requires two hours.

$\frac{1}{2}X_1 + X_2 \leq 4$. There are four hours available on machine 2.   Each unit
of X_1 requires one-half hour; X_2 requires one hour.

$X_1 \geq 0, X_2 \geq 0$.   The X's cannot be negative. (We cannot produce a negative
amount of product.)

After slack variables are introduced to convert the inequalities into
equalities, we have:

$$3X_1 + 2X_2 + X_3 + 0X_4 = 6,$$
$$\tfrac{1}{2}X_1 + X_2 + 0X_3 + X_4 = 4.$$

Continuing the example, we shall examing the dual problem.   The
following characterizes the dual:

1. If the objective function is *maximized* in the primal, the objective
function of the dual is *minimized*. In this example, the objective function
is a cost equation.

2. The coefficients of the variables of the cost equation (the dual
objective function) are the constants of the primal restraints.   In this
example, they are six and four and represent the hours of each machine
available. The variables U_1 and U_2 of the cost equation of the dual are
the respective costs per hour of using machine 1 and machine 2.[1]   The
cost equation (or objective function) is:

$$C = 6U_1 + 4U_2 + 0U_3 + 0U_4 + MU_5 + MU_6.$$

---

[1] The U_1 and U_2 are opportunity cost measures and are not related to conventional
accounting costs.

3. The restraints are formed by transposing the coefficients used in the primal. In the primal the equations and coefficients were:

Equation	Coefficients	
$3X_1 + 2X_2 \leq 6$	3	2
$\frac{1}{2}X_1 + X_2 \leq 4$	$\frac{1}{2}$	1

The transposition is as follows (A^T indicates that A has been transposed):

$$A = \begin{pmatrix} 3 & 2 \\ \frac{1}{2} & 1 \end{pmatrix}, \qquad\qquad A^T = \begin{pmatrix} 3 & \frac{1}{2} \\ 2 & 1 \end{pmatrix}.$$

The first column of A is regarded as the first row of A^T, and the second column of A is regarded as the second row of A^T.

The constants for the primal restraints are obtained from the profit function (the objective function) of the primal. Thus, the constants will be 12 and 4.

4. If we are maximizing a primal objective function, and if the restraints of the primal are "less than or equal to," the restraints of the dual will be "greater than or equal to." Thus, the restraints are:

$$3U_1 + \tfrac{1}{2}U_2 \geq 12,$$
$$2U_1 + U_2 \geq 4.$$

The interpretation of these restraints should illuminate the relationship between the primal and dual problems. The first inequality states that the time to produce product X_1 on machine 1 (three hours) times the cost per hour of using machine 1 (U_1) plus the time to produce product X_1 on machine 2 (one half hour) times the cost per hour of using machine 2 (U_2) is greater than or equal to $12. The $12 is the net profit of a unit of X_1 (see the profit function of the primal). Thus, the cost of producing X_1 is either going to be equal to the net profit (in which case X_1 will be produced) or greater than the net profit (in which case no units of X_1 will be produced).

The interpretation of the second restraint is similar. The total cost per unit of producing product X_2 is $2U_1$ (cost of using machine 1) plus U_2 (cost of using machine 2). The total cost per unit is equal to or greater than $4.00, where $4.00 is the net increase in profit per unit of product X_2. Thus, the cost of producing X_2 is either going to be equal to the net profit per unit of X_2 (in which case X_2 will be produced) or greater than the net profit (in which case no units of X_2 will be produced).

It should be noted that the form of solution does not allow for the costs of producing either product to be less than the incremental profit of the product. This is reasonable since the value of the machine hours is measured by the profit they can produce. To have the total costs less than the profit would imply that more units of the product should be produced; but if the product is produced to the limit of productive capacity, the costs of the last unit will be equal to the profit. The only time the costs will be greater than the incremental profit will be when it is not desirable to produce any units of the product. Remember that these are opportunity, not accounting, costs.

This type of analysis has important applications. For example, a foreman could be told of the current alternative cost of each machine. Jobs must have an incremental profit of $4.00 per hour or more to be placed on machine 1. Jobs which have an incremental profit of less than $4.00 per hour (theoretically anything in excess of zero) can be assigned to machine 2. This procedure could be used to evaluate common costs, i.e., the value of production factors which are used in producing two or more products. The cost information evolved, using the dual of the linear programming primal problem, is sometimes referred to as a "shadow price" or an "accounting" price.

Limitations of the Example

The above example is typical of a large classification of economic problems, but it is important to note the limitations of the procedures described.

The significant characteristics of the problem from the viewpoint of the present discussion were:

1. The objective function of the primal was being maximized.
2. The sense of the primal restraints was equal-to or less-than.

With these characteristics we proceeded to make the sense of the dual restraints opposite to those of the primal. Unfortunately different combinations of the above characteristics require different procedures in the dual. Two possibilities are as follows:

If Primal Has—		Then Set up Dual—	
Objective Function	Sense of Restraint Equation	Objective Function	Sense of Restraint Equation
Maximize	$\leq$	Minimize	$\geq$ (opposite sense)
Minimize	$\geq$	Maximize	$\leq$ (opposite sense)

We may have a primal with an objective function which we are directed to maximize, but the sense of the restraint equations is "equal to or greater than." We can use the above directions by multiplying the objective function by minus one and changing it from a maximizing to a minimizing problem. For example, maximize $f = 2X_1 - 3X_2$ is equivalent to minimize $g = -2X_1 + 3X_2$, but the change would enable us to construct the dual from the primal.

The analyst may prefer to bypass solving the dual as a by-produ :t of the primal. He may initially solve the problem which might be thought of as the dual. The facts of the situation should indicate how the restraints are to be set up.

APPENDIX D

LIST OF ERRATA
IN FIRST EDITION

The first figure refers to the page; the second figure refers to the paragraph, item or footnote (n); the third figure refers to the line. The correct expression is then stated in quotation marks.

4/n2/1: "Joel Dean (1951a)"
24/1/1: "Fisher chooses the first, Hicks the second"
34/c/3: "same date"
52/1/1: "(see Section 2.1)"
53/2/10: "non-restrictive"
58/n6/5: "Section 3.4"
60/n8/2: "Reaumur"
69/n3 of Table 3-2/2: "by the order relation shall be"
69/n3 of Table 3-2/5: "if both $a \leq b$ and $b \leq a$ then $a = b$"
70/Table 3-3/5: "$1 > a/b \geq 0.5$"
85/3/11: "Section 2.2"
87/2/8: "Section 9.1"
94/2/3: "consists of a date"
95/1/11: "(4) that the right-hand side"
95/n27/4: "*fourth* dimension"
96/3-11/middle section of the first part of equation:
  "+ $(t_{12} + t_{22} + t_{32})$ +"
104/3/8: "our assumption 3"
108/I/12: "(see our basic assumption 12)"
110/1/2: "'000,000 £"
110/2/6: "Food—farmers"
112/6/2: "'000,000£"
113/Table 4-1/3rd line of title: "(in '000,000£)"

113/Table 4-1/I-Row 1:   "$^{(1)}$2,000" should be in third column instead of second

113/Table 4-1/III-Row 1:   "$^{(6)}$1,000" should be in first column

117/first account, credit side/7:   "$(i'' + b'')$"

117/second account, debit side/3:   "$(b' + b'' + i')$"

117/second account, credit side: "(c) Rent 2,000

(d) Agri. Profits . . . . 1,200"

118/n13/11:   "18th century"

124/Subsection 4.53/3:   "eighteenth century"

128/Account II, 2.3:   "Transfers to r.o.w."

129/Account IV, 4.7:   "Transfers from pers. sector"

130/2/24:   "assumption 16"

134/second presentation: "71.6

$\underline{22.2}$

$\underline{\underline{93.8}}$"

160/1/3:   "our views"

161/1/4:   "hence often undifferentiable"

164/2/26:   "in Chapter 2"

166/2/10:   "often supply"

176/E/2:   "payments where the yield rate"

176/E/3:   "practices. This was"

195/Objective Function: "$R = c_1 x_1 + \ldots$"

202:   The right side of lambdas (including indices) not in bold letters:

"$\leq - \lambda_1$

$\leq - \lambda_2$

$\ldots$

$\ldots$

$\leq - \lambda_t$"

205/1/3:   "$\mathbf{c}^1, \ldots, \mathbf{c}^k \ldots$"

218/Figure 6-2:   The arrow upwards should point downwards.

223/10a/4:   "footnote 19"

225/Column C of illustration/2:   "5.00" instead of "4.00"

232/1/2:   "or less well tested"

240/2/4:   "Russell"

300/Table 8-2/right-most bottom corner of Quadrant I: "x_{nn}"

301/1/11:   delete "$= X_j$"

304/Algebraic notation/1:   "$\ldots - a_{1n} X_n = Y_1$"

304/Sigma notation/1:   "$-\sum_{j=1}^{n} a_{ij} X_j =$"

309/2:   add a new item "d) There is constant return to scale."

335/Figure 9-1/Material:

$$\text{``} \underline{\quad\quad\quad I \quad\quad\quad} \text{''}$$

BM | - - - - - →'
      | t_{MW}
- - - - - → | ME

336/Table 9-1/Payables, Column L: cancel "t_{PL}"

337/1/19:   "t_{WF}"

337/equation (16):   "+ t_{SR}"

337/equation (17):   "− t_{CA}"

337/equation (18):   "+ t_{CA}"

337/equation (20):   "− t_{NB}"

339/equation (16):   "− t_{SR}"

339/equation (17):   "+ t_{CA}"

339/equation (18):   "− t_{CA}"

339/equation (20):   "− t_{NB}"

355/1/1:   "causal"

363/1-ii/1:   "SQ (I, MØ) ="

363/2-2/5:   "MØ = 2, . . . , 12"

366/1/2:   "(I, 13) +"

368/3-5/16:   "RMMI(J)"

370/3-13/5:   "VMI(1) ="

371/3-iv/1:   "VMI(NM) = VMI(MØ) + TPV(MØ) − TCM(MØ),
    MØ = 1, . . . , 12"

402/Cash Account: the right-most symbol "TCØ(1" should be "TCØ(1,13)"

444/XI(iii)/1:   "then $x \sim z$"

445/XII(ii)/1:   "$R(x, y)$ implies $\bar{R}(y, x)$"

452/13(i)/1:   "= $v_{mn}^{\lambda} = 0$;"

453/16/27:   "$\{a_{11}, a_{12}, a_{13}\}$" instead of "$\{a_{11}, a_{12}\}$"

456/1/3:   "within e_m"

456/20(ii)/1:   "$v_i^s \in V$"

457/2/6:   "$v_{Bc}^{\ s} =$" instead of "$v_{Bc}^{\ s}$"

457/3/4:   "according to item 18(i)"

457/3/7:   "$\displaystyle\sum_{k=1}^{m} v_k^s$ and $v_{Bc}^s = \displaystyle\sum_{p=1}^{q} v_p^s$"

458/22(ii)/1:   "$v_{Ce}^s = \displaystyle\sum_{e=1}^{h} v_p^s$"

458/23/17:   "$v_B^s = - v_p^s$ or $v_{Bb}^s + v_{Be}^s = - (v_{Pb}^s + v_{Pc}^s)$"

461/1/5:   "= v_{rj}^{τ}"

461/1/6:   "= v_{ru}^{λ}"

461/Step 1/2:   "F_{I2}):"

461/Step 2/1:   "(iii) of item 7"

463/28(iii)/13:   "$\beta_m^s \cup \gamma_m^s$"

$475/1/10:$ "$x_1 = \dfrac{b_1}{a_{11}} - \dfrac{a_{12}}{a_{11}} \Big[$ "

477/equation 28, last equation: "$x_3 =$"

501/Bierman, Fouraker . . ./2:   "*Business Decisions*"

502/Braithwaite/1:   "*Scientific Explanation*"

503/Churchman, Ratoosh: "*Measurement:*"

513/Mattessich, item before last/3:   "(1964c)"

513/Mattessich, last item/2:   "1964b."

517/Samuelson 3/1:   "*American Economic Review*"

519/Sombart/2:   add "(quotations refer to 2nd ed. 1917)"

528/after line 17 insert: "Cotruglio, Raugeo Benedetto, 101n"

528/D/2:   delete "Dantzig, George, 247"

530/R: delete line 4

531/W/25:   "19n, 522"

542/L/2:   "Lagrange"

545/N/27:   "178, 179, 257"

Bibliography

BIBLIOGRAPHY

The following bibliography contains mainly literature cited in the preceding text. Occasionally publications relevant to the topics of this work have been added for the purpose of reference.

ACKOFF, RUSSELL I. (ed). *Progress in Operations Research*. Vol. 1. New York: John Wiley & Sons, Inc, 1961a.

————. "The Meaning, Scope and Methods of Operations Research," *Progress in Operations Research*. Vol. I. New York: John Wiley & Sons, Inc., 1961b.

————. *Scientific Method*. New York: John Wiley & Sons, Inc., 1962.

ADAM, A. *Messen und Regeln in der Betriebswirtschaft*. Würzburg: Physica, 1959.

ADELMAN, IRMA, AND ADELMAN, FRANK. "The Dynamic Properties of the Klein-Goldberger Model," *Econometrica*, Vol. 27, No. 4 (October, 1959), pp. 596–625.

ALBACH, HORST. "Lineare Programmierung als Hilfsmittel betrieblicher Investitionsplanung," *Zeitschrift für handelswissenschaftliche Forschung*, Vol. 12, No. 9 (September, 1960), pp. 526–549.

————. *Investition und Liquidität—Die Planung des optimalen Investitionsbudgets*. Wiesbaden: Gabler, 1962.

ALDERSON, WROE. "Review of Churchman's *Prediction and Optimal Decision*," *Management Science*, Vol. 8, No. 3 (April, 1962), pp. 375–380.

ALEXANDER, SIDNEY S. "Income Measurement in a Dynamic Economy," *Five Monographs on Business Income*. New York: Study Group on Business Income of the American Institute of Accountants, July 1, 1950.

ALLAIS, M. *Les fondements comptables de la macro-économique*. Paris: Presses Universitaires de France, 1954.

ALLEN, R. G. D. *Mathematical Economics*. London: Macmillan & Co., Ltd., 1956.

ANTHONY, ROBERT N. *Management Accounting: Text and Cases*. Rev. ed. Homewood: Richard D. Irwin, Inc., 1960.

503

ANTON, HECTOR R. *Accounting for the Flow of Funds.* New York: Houghton Mifflin, 1962; a revision of "A Critical Evaluation of Techniques of Analysis of the Flow of Business Funds" (unpublished Ph.D. thesis, University of Minnesota, 1953).

————. "Some Aspects of Measurement Theory and Accounting," *Journal of Accounting Research*, Vol. 2, No. 1 (Spring, 1964), pp. 1–9.

ANTON, HECTOR R., and BOUTELL, WAYNE S. *FORTRAN and Business Data Processing.* To be published. New York: McGraw-Hill Book Co., Inc., 1965.

ARROW, K. J. *Social Choice and Individual Values.* New York: John Wiley & Sons, Inc., 1951.

ARTLE, ROLAND. *Studies in the Structure of the Stockholm Economy.* Stockholm: Bus. Res. Inst., 1959.

ASHBY, W. ROSS. *An Introduction to Cybernetics.* New York: John Wiley & Sons, Inc., 1956.

AUKRUST, ODD. *Nasjonalregnskap-Teoretiske Prinsipper.* Oslo: Statistisk Sentralbyrå, 1955; contains English Summary.

AYER, ALFRED JULES. *Language, Truth and Logic.* New York: Dover-Edition, 1946.

————. *The Problem of Knowledge.* Harmondsworth: Penguin Books Ltd., 1956.

BACKER, MORTON (ed.). *Handbook of Modern Accounting Theory.* New York: Prentice-Hall, Inc., 1955.

BAIRD, D. C. *Experimentation: An Introduction to Measurement and Experiment Design.* Englewood Cliffs, N. J.: Prentice-Hall, Inc., 1962.

BALDERSTON, FREDERICK E., and HOGGATT, AUSTIN C. *Simulation of Market Processes.* Berkeley: Institute of Business and Economic Research, 1962.

BANBURY, J., and MAITLAND, J. (eds.). *Proceedings of the Second International Conference on Operational Research.* London: English Univ. Press, 1961.

BARGER, HAROLD, and KLEIN, L. R. "A Quarterly Model for the U.S. Economy," *Journal of the American Statistical Association*, Vol. 49 (September, 1954), pp. 413–37.

BARONE, ENRICO. *Principi di Economia Politica.* Rome: Athenaeum, 1920.

BARRETT, WILLIAM, and AIKEN, HENRY D. (eds.). *Philosophy in the Twentieth Century*, Vols. 1, 2, 3, 4. New York: Random House, 1962.

BAUER, STEPHAN. "Quesnay's 'Tableau économique,'" *Economic Journal*, Vol. 5, No. 2 (March, 1895), pp. 1–21.

BAUMOL, WILLIAM J. *Business Behavior, Value and Growth.* New York: Macmillan Co., 1959.

————. *Economic Theory and Operations Analysis.* Englewood Cliffs, N.J.: Prentice-Hall, Inc., 1961.

BAXTER, W. T., and DAVIDSON, SIDNEY (eds.). *Studies in Accounting Theory.* Homewood: Richard D. Irwin, Inc., 1962.

BAYES, THOMAS. "An Essay towards Solving a Problem in the Doctrine of Chances," *Philosophical Transactions of the Royal Society of London*, Vol. 53, No. 1763, pp. 370–418. See *Facsimile of Two Papers by Bayes*, Washington: Graduate School of the Department of Agriculture, 1940.

BEACH, E. F. *Economic Models—An Exposition.* New York: John Wiley & Sons, Inc., 1957.

BEDFORD, NORTON M. "Behavioral Science and Accounting Research," *Proceedings: International Conference on Accounting Education,* pp. 93–99. Urbana: Center for Internat. Educ. and Res. in Acctg., 1962.

BEER, STAFFORD. *Cybernetics and Management.* New York: John Wiley & Sons, Inc., 1959.

BELLMAN, RICHARD. *Dynamic Programming.* Princeton: Princeton Univ. Press, 1957.

BIERMAN, HAROLD. *Managerial Economics.* New York: Macmillan Co., 1959.

————. "Probability, Statistical Decision Theory, and Accounting," *Accounting Review,* Vol. 37, No. 3 (July, 1962), pp. 400–405.

————. "Measurement and Accounting," *Accounting Review,* Vol. 38, No. 3, (July, 1963) pp. 501–7.

————. *Topics in Cost Accounting and Decisions.* New York: McGraw-Hill Book Co., Inc., 1963.

BIERMAN, HAROLD, and SMIDT, SEMOUR. *The Capital Budgeting Decision.* New York: Macmillan Co., 1960.

BIERMAN, H., FOURAKER, L. E. and JAEDICKE, R. K. *Quantitative Analysis for Business Decision.* Homewood: Richard D. Irwin, Inc., 1961a.

————. "Use of Probability and Statistics in Performance Evaluation," *Accounting Review,* Vol. 36 (July, 1961b), pp. 409–417.

BLACK, HOMER A., and CHAMPION, JOHN E. *Accounting in Business Decisions: Theory, Method and Use.* Englewood Cliffs, N. J.: Prentice-Hall, Inc., 1961.

BLOCKER, JOHN G., and WELTMER, W. KEITH. *Cost Accounting.* 3rd ed. New York: McGraw-Hill Book Co., Inc., 1954.

BÖHM-BAWERK, EUGEN V. *Kapital und Kapitalzins.* 1st ed. Vienna: 1889.

BONINI, CHARLES P. "A Simulation of a Business Firm," *Proceedings of the Spring Joint Computer Conference,* AFIPC, May, 1962.

————. *Simulation of Information and Decision Systems in the Firm.* Englewood Cliffs, N. J.: Prentice-Hall, Inc., 1963. Ford Foundation Doctoral Dissertation Series.

BOOLE, GEORGE. *An Investigation of the Laws of Thought on which are Founded the Mathematical Theories of Logic and Probabilities.* London: 1854.

BOTT, KARL (ed.). *Lexikon des kaufmännischen Rechnungswesens,* Vols. I to IV. 2nd ed. Stuttgart: Mut'sche Verlagsbuchhandlung, 1955.

BOULDING, KENNETH E. *A Reconstruction of Economics.* New York: John Wiley & Sons, Inc., 1950.

————. *Economic Analysis.* 3rd ed. New York: Harper & Bros., Inc., 1955.

————. "The Present Position of the Theory of the Firm," *Linear Programming and the Theory of the Firm,* pp. 1–17. New York: Macmillan Co., 1960.

————. "Economics and Accounting: the Uncongenial Twins," *Studies in Accounting Theory,* pp. 44–55. W. T. BAXTER, and S. DAVIDSON (eds.). Homewood: Richard D. Irwin, Inc., 1962.

BOULDING, K. E., and SPIVEY, W. A. *Linear Programming and the Theory of the Firm*. New York: Macmillan Co., 1960.

BOUTELL, WAYNE S. "The Impact of Electronic Data Processing on Professional Auditing Procedures" (Doctoral dissertation). To be published. Berkeley: University of California Press, 1964.

BRAITHWAITE, R. B. *Scientific Explanations*. Cambridge: Cambridge Univ. Press, 1953.

BROWN, GENE R., and JOHNSTON, KENNETH S. *Paciolo on Accounting*. New York: McGraw-Hill Book Co., Inc., 1963.

BURDETT, D. K. "Social Accounting in Relation to Economic Theory," *Economic Journal*, Vol. 64 (1954), pp. 679–97.

CAMPBELL, N. R. *Physics: The Elements*. Cambridge: University Press, 1920.

————. *An Account of the Principles of Measurement and Calculation*. London: Longmans Green, 1928.

————. "Measurement and its Importance for Philosophy," *Symposium of the Aristotelian Society for the Systematic Study of Philosophy*, pp. 121–42. London: Harrison & Sons, Ltd., 1938.

CANNING, JOHN B. *The Economics of Accountancy*. New York: Ronald Press, 1929.

CARNAP, RUDOLF. *Introduction to Symbolic Logic and its Applications* (trans., WILLIAM H. MEYER and JOHN WILKINSON). New York: Dover, 1958.

CAYLEY, ARTHUR. *The Principles of Book-keeping by Double Entry*. Cambridge: Univ. Press, 1894.

CHAMBERS, R. J. *Towards a General Theory of Accounting*, a reprint of the Annual Endowed Lecture of the Australian Society of Accountants held at the University of Adelaide, 1961.

————. "Measurement in Accounting" (mimeographed), p. 48, University of Sydney, January, 1963.

CHARNES, A., and COOPER, W. W. "Management Models and Industrial Applications of Linear Programming", *Management Science*, Vol. 4, No. 1 (October, 1957), pp. 38–91.

————. *Management Models and Industrial Applications of Linear Programming*, I, II. New York: John Wiley & Sons, Inc., 1961.

————. "On Some Works of Kantorovich, Koopmans and Others." *Management Science*, Vol. 8, No. 3 (April, 1962), pp. 246–63.

CHARNES, A., COOPER, W. W., and IJIRI, Y. "Breakeven Budgeting and Programming to Goals," *Journal of Accounting Research*, Vol. 1, No. 1 (Spring, 1963), pp. 16–43.

CHARNES, A., COOPER, W. W., and MILLER, N. H. "Application of Linear Programming to Financial Budgeting and the Costing of Funds," an O.N.R. research report presented in 1957. Reprinted by EZRA SOLOMON [1959], pp. 229–55.

CHENERY, HOLLIS B., and CLARK, PAUL G. *Interindustry Economics*. New York: John Wiley & Sons, Inc., 1959.

CHERNOFF, HERMAN, and MOSES, LINCOLN E. *Elementary Decision Theory*. New York: John Wiley & Sons, Inc., 1959.

CHRIST, CARL F. "An Econometric Model of the United States, 1921–1947," *Conference on Research in Business Cycles*, pp. 35–107. New York: National Bureau of Economic Research, 1951.

————. "On Econometric Models of the U.S. Economy," International Association of Income and Wealth, *Income and Wealth Series*, No. 6. London: Bowes & Bowes, 1957.

CHURCHILL, NEIL. "Linear Algebra and Cost Allocations: Some Examples," (to be published in *Accounting Review*, 1964).

CHURCHMAN, C. WEST. *Elements of Logic and Formal Science.* Philadelphia: Lippincott, 1940.

————. *Theory of Experimental Inference.* New York: Macmillan Co., 1948.

————. "A Materialists Theory of Measurement," *Philosophy for the Future* (eds., R. W. SELLARS, V. J. McGILL, and M. FARBER). New York: Macmillan Co., 1949.

————. "Why Measure?" *Measurement: Definitions and Theories* (eds., C. W. CHURCHMAN and P. RATOOSH), pp. 83–94. New York: John Wiley & Sons, Inc., 1959.

————. "The Management Sciences," *Working Paper No. 1* of the Management Science Nucleus of the University of California. Berkeley, 1959b (mimeographed).

————. *Prediction and Optimal Decision: Philosophical Issues of a Science of Values.* Englewood Cliffs, N.J.: Prentice-Hall, Inc., 1961.

CHURCHMAN, C. W., and ACKOFF, R. L. *Methods of Inquiry—An Introduction to Philosophy and Scientific Method.* Saint Louis: Educational Publ., 1950.

————. "Operational Accounting and Operations Research," *Journal of Accountancy*, Vol. 99 (1955), pp. 33–39.

CHURCHMAN, C. W., ACKOFF, R. L., and ARNOFF, E. L. *Introduction to Operations Research.* New York: John Wiley & Sons, Inc., 1957.

CHURCHMAN, C. W., and RATOOSH, P. (eds.). *Management: Definitions and Theories.* New York: John Wiley & Sons, Inc., 1959.

CHURCHMAN, C. W., and VERHULST, M. (eds.). *Management Sciences: Models and Techniques*, Vols. I and II. New York: Pergamon, 1960.

CLARK, COLIN. "A System of Equations Explaining the United States Trade Cycle 1921 to 1941," *Econometrica*, Vol. 17, No. 2 (April, 1949), pp. 93–124.

CLARKSON, G. P. E. *Portfolio Selection: A Simulation of Trust Investment.* Englewood Cliffs, N. J.: Prentice-Hall, Inc., 1962.

COHEN, KALMAN J. *Computer Models of the Shoe, Leather, Hide Sequence*, 1959 Award Winner of the Ford Foundation Doctoral Dissertation Series. Englewood Cliffs, N. J.: Prentice-Hall, Inc., 1960.

COOMBS, C. H. "Theory and Methods of Social Measurement," *Research Methods in the Behavioral Sciences* (eds., L. FESTINGER, and D. KATZ). New York: Dryden Press, 1953.

COOMBS, C. H., RAIFFA, H., and THRALL, R. M. "Some Views on Mathematical Models and Measurement Theory," *Decision Processes*, (eds., THRALL, COOMBS, and DAVIS). New York: John Wiley & Sons, Inc., 1954.

COPELAND, MORRIS A. *A Study of Moneyflows in the United States.* New York: National Bureau of Economic Research, 1952.

COURNOT, A. *Recherches sur les principes mathématiques de la théorie des richesses.* Paris: Hachette, 1838.

CYERT, R. M., and TRUEBLOOD, R. M. *Sampling Techniques in Accounting.* New York: Prentice-Hall, Inc., 1957.

CYERT, RICHARD M., and DAVIDSON, H. JUSTIN. *Statistical Sampling for Accounting Information.* Englewood Cliffs, N. J.: Prentice-Hall, Inc., 1962.

CYERT, R. M., DAVIDSON, H. J., and THOMPSON, G. L. "Estimation of the Allowance for Doubtful Accounts by Markov Chains," *Management Science*, Vol. 8, No. 3 (April, 1962), pp. 287–303.

CYERT, R. M., and MARCH, JAMES G. *A Behavioral Theory of the Firm.* Englewood Cliffs, N. J.: Prentice-Hall, Inc., 1963.

DAVIDSON, D., SIEGEL, S., and SUPPES, P. "Some Experiments and Related Theory on the Measurement of Utility and Subjective Probability," *Technical Report no. 1 of Applied Mathematics and Statistics Laboratory.* Stanford: Stanford University Press, 1955.

DAVIDSON, D., SUPPES, PATRICK, and SIEGEL, SIDNEY. *Decision Making: An Experimental Approach.* Stanford: Stanford Univ. Press, 1957.

DAVIDSON, SIDNEY. "The Day of Reckoning—Managerial Analysis and Accounting Theory," *Journal of Accounting Research*, Vol. 1, No. 2 (Autumn, 1963), pp. 117–231.

DEAN, JOEL. *Managerial Economics.* New York: Prentice-Hall, Inc., 1951.

————. *Capital Budgeting.* New York: Columbia Univ. Press, 1951.

DEBREU, G. *Theory of Value: An Axiomatic Analysis of Economic Equilibrium,* Cowles Foundation Monograph No. 17. New York: John Wiley & Sons, Inc., 1959.

DENIZET, J. "Les problèmes techniques posés par l'établissement de comptes d'opérations financières," *Studies in Social and Financial Accounts* —Income and Wealth Series, Vol. 9 (ed., P. DEAN). London: Bowes & Bowes, 1961.

DE STE. CROIX (see STE. CROIX, G.E.M. DE).

DEVINE, C. T. *Cost Accounting and Analysis.* New York: Macmillan Co.,1950.

————. "Integration of Accounting and Economics in the Elementary Accounting Course," *Accounting Review*, Vol. 27, No. 3 (July, 1952), pp. 329–33.

————. (ed.) *Readings in Accounting Theory*, Vols. I and II (mimeographed). Djakarta, 1962a.

————. "Accounting—A Behavioral Approach" *Readings in Accounting Theory*, Vol. I (ed., C. DEVINE), 1962b, pp. 12–20.

————. *Essays in Accounting Theory*, Vols. I and II (mimeographed). Djakarta, 1962c.

DICKERSON, PETER J. "A Case Study in the Implementation of the Theory and Measurement of Business Income," M.B.A.—thesis (mimeogr.) Berkeley: Univ. of California.

DICKEY, R. I. (ed.). *Accountants Cost Handbook.* 2nd ed. New York: Ronald Press, 1960.

DICKIE, H. F., and THRONDSEN, E. C. "Manufacturing Systems Simulation," *Factory*, Vol. 118 (October, 1960), pp. 114–17.

DORFMAN, ROBERT. "Operations Research," *American Economic Review*, Vol. 50, No. 4 (September, 1960), pp. 575–623.

DORFMAN, ROBERT, SAMUELSON, PAUL A., and SOLOW, ROBERT M. *Linear Programming and Economic Analysis*. New York: McGraw-Hill Book Co., Inc., 1958.

DORRANCE, GRAEME S. "The Present Status of Financial Accounts: A Review of Recent Developments," *Studies in Social and Financial Accounts* —Income and Wealth Service, Vol. 9 (ed., P. DEAN). London: Bowes & Bowes, 1961.

DUESENBERRY, J. S. *Business Cycles and Economic Growth*. New York: McGraw-Hill Book Co., Inc., 1958.

DURAND, DAVID. "The Cost of Capital, Corporation Finance and the Theory of Investment: Comment," *American Economic Review*, Vol. 49, No. 4 (September, 1959), pp. 639–55. Reprinted and slightly revised under the title "The Cost of Capital in an Imperfect Market: A Reply to Modigliani and Miller" in EZRA SOLOMON [1959], pp. 182–97.

DURANT, WILL. *The Renaissance*, Vol. V of *The Story of Civilization*. New York: Simon and Schuster, 1953.

EDEY, HAROLD, and PEACOCK, ALAN T. *National Income and Social Accounting*. London: Hutchinson, 1954.

EDWARDS, EDGAR O., and BELL, PHILIP W. *The Theory and Measurement of Business Income*. Berkeley: Univ. of California Press, 1961.

ENGELS, WULFRAM. *Betriebswirtschaftliche Bewertungslehre im Licht der Entscheidungstheorie*. Opladen: Westdeutscher Verlag, 1962.

ENRICK, NORBERT L. *Cases in Management Statistics*. New York: Holt, Rinehart & Winston, 1963.

EVANS, W. D., and HOFFENBERG, M. "The Interindustry Relations Study for 1947," *Review of Economics and Statistics*, Vol. 34, No. 2 (May, 1952), pp. 97–142.

FEIGL, HERBERT, and BRODBECK, MAY. *Readings in Philosophical Analysis*. New York: Appleton, 1949.

FELDMAN, JULIAN, and FEIGENBAUM, EDWARD A. (eds.). *Artificial Intelligence*. New York: McGraw-Hill Book Co., Inc., 1963.

FELLNER, WILLIAM *Emergence and Content of Modern Economic Analysis*. New York: McGraw-Hill Book Co., Inc., 1960.

FIRMIN, PETER. "Measurement Theory and Accounting Measurements," a paper presented at the 1963 American International Meeting of the Institute of Management Sciences. New York, September 12–13, 1963 (mimeographed).

FISHER, IRVING. *The Nature of Capital and Income*. London: Macmillan & Co., Ltd., 1906.

————. "Income," *Encyclopedia of the Social Sciences*, Vol. 7, pp. 622–25. New York: Macmillan Co., 1932.

————. *The Theory of Interest*. New York: Macmillan Co., 1930; reprinted by Kelly, New York, 1961.

FLANDERS, DWIGHT P. "Accountancy, Systematized Learning and Economics," *Accounting Review*, Vol. 36, No. 4 (October, 1961), pp. 564–76.

——————. "Accounting and Economics: A Note with Special Reference to 'The Teaching of Social Accounts,'" *Accounting Review*, Vol. 34, No. 1 (January, 1959), pp. 68–73.

FORD, L. R., and FULKERSON, D. R. *Flows in Networks*. Princeton: Princeton Univ. Press, 1962.

FORRESTER, JAY W. *Industrial Dynamics*. New York: John Wiley & Sons, Inc. and Cambridge, Mass.: M.I.T. Press, 1961.

FRANK, J. D. "Individual Differences in Certain Aspects of the Level of Aspiration," *American Journal of Psychology*, Vol. 47, No. 1 (January, 1935), pp. 119–28.

FRIEDELL, EGON. *A Cultural History of the Modern Age*, 3 vols. New York: Alfred A. Knopf, Inc., 1930, 1950—a translation of *Kulturgeschichte der Neuzeit*. Munich: C. H. Beck'sche Verlag, 1927.

FRIEDMAN, MILTON. "The Methodology of Positive Economics," *Essays in Positive Economics*, pp. 3–43. Chicago: Univ. of Chicago Press, 1953.

FRIEND, IRWIN. "Financial Statements for the Economy," *Accounting Review*, Vol. 24, No. 3 (July, 1949), pp. 230–47.

FRISCH, RAGNAR. Økosirk-systemet. Oslo, 1942 (mimeographed).

——————. "Axiomatic Remarks on some National Income Concepts," October 16, 1949, a mimeographed paper from Oslow University cited by Ohlsson 1953.

——————. "Attempt at Clarification of Certain National Income Concepts," October 8, 1949, a mimeographed paper from Oslo University cited by Ohlsson 1953.

FUÀ, GIORGIO. *Reddito nazionale e politica economica*. Torino: Edizioni Scientifiche Enaudi, 1957.

GALBRAITH, JOHN KENNETH. *American Capitalism*. 2nd ed. Cambridge, Mass.: Riverside Press, 1956.

GALE, DAVID, *The Theory of Linear Economic Models*. New York: McGraw-Hill Book Co., Inc., 1960.

GALE, D. H., KUHN, H. W., and TUCKER, A. W. "Linear Programming and the Theory of Games," *Activity Analysis of Production and Allocation* (ed. T. C. KOOPMANS). New York: John Wiley & Sons, Inc., 1951.

GAYNOR, E. W. "Use of Control Charts in Cost Control," *N.A.C.A. Bulletin*, Vol. 35 (June, 1954), pp. 1300–1309. (Now, *National Association of Accountants Bulletin*.)

GEISLER, MURRAY A. "Appraisal of Laboratory Simulation Experiences," *Management Science*, Vol. 8, No. 3 (April, 1962), pp. 239–45.

GILBERT, M., JASZI, G., DENISON, E. F., and SCHWARTZ, C. F. "Objectives of National Income Measurement: A Reply to Professor Kuznets," *Review of Economics and Statistics*, Vol. 30, No. 3 (August, 1948), pp. 179–95.

GILLESPIE, R. W. "Simulation of Economic Growth with Alternative Balance of Payments Policies," Ph.D. Dissertation, M.I.T., 1961 (cited from Holland [1962]).

GILMAN, STEPHEN. *Accounting Concepts of Profits*. New York: Ronald Press, 1939.

GOETZ, BILLY E., and KLEIN, FREDERICK R. *Accounting in Action—Its Meaning for Management*. Boston: Houghton Mifflin, 1960.

GOLDBERG, LOUIS. *An Outline of Accounting.* Sydney: Law Book Co., 1957.

GOLDBERG, SAMUEL. *Introduction to Difference Equations.* New York: John Wiley & Sons, Inc., 1958.

GOLDSMITH, RAYMOND W. *A Study of Savings in the United States,* 3 vols. Princeton: Princeton Univ. Press, 1956.

————. *The National Wealth of the United States in the Postwar Period* (NBER). Princeton: Princeton Univ. Press, 1962.

GOLDSMITH, RAYMOND W., and SAUNDERS, CHRISTOPHER (eds.). *The Measurement of National Wealth*—Income and Wealth Series, Vol. 8. London: Bowes & Bowes, 1959.

GOMBERG, LÉON. *Eine geometrische Darstellung der Buchhaltungsmethoden.* Berlin: Weiss, 1927.

GOODMAN, LEO A. "Statistical Methods for the Preliminary Analysis of Transaction Flows," *Econometrica,* Vol. 31, No. 1-2 (January–April, 1963), pp. 197–208.

GORDON, MYRON J. "Dividends Earnings and Stock Prices," *Review of Economics and Statistics,* Vol. 41, No. 2 (May, 1959), pp. 99–105.

————. "Scope and Method of Theory and Research in the Measurement of Income and Wealth," *Accounting Review,* Vol. 35, No. 4 (October, 1960), pp. 603–618.

————. *The Investment, Financing, and Valuation of the Corporation.* Homewood, Ill · Richard D. Irwin, Inc., 1962.

GORDON, ROBERT A. "Short Period Price Determination in Theory and Practice," *American Economic Review,* Vol. 38, No. 3 (June, 1948), pp. 265–88.

GORDON, ROBERT AARON, and HOWELL, JAMES EDWIN. *Higher Education for Business.* New York: Columbia Univ. Press, 1959.

GOSSEN, HERMANN H. *Entwicklung der Gesetze des menschlichen Verkehrs und der daraus fliessenden Regeln für menschliches Handeln.* Berlin: 1854; new edition, Berlin: Prager, 1889.

GRAHAM, B., and DODD, D. L. *Security Analysis: Principles and Technique.* New York: McGraw-Hill Book Co., Inc., 1951.

GRAY, ALEXANDER. *The Development of Economic Doctrine.* London: Longmans, Green & Co., 1931.

GREGORY, ROBERT H., and VAN HORN, RICHARD L. *Automatic Data-Processing Systems*—*Principles and Procedures.* 2nd ed. Belmont: Wadsworth, 1963.

GUTENBERG, ERICH. *Grundlagen der Betriebswirtschaftslehre,* Vols. I and II. Berlin: Springer, 1951 and 1955 respectively.

HADLEY, G. *Linear Programming.* Reading: Addison-Wesley, 1962.

HANSEN, PALLE. *The Accounting Concept of Profit*—An Analysis and Evaluation in the Light of the Economic Theory of Income and Capital. Kopenhagen: Einar Harcks, 1962.

HANSON, N. R. *Patterns of Discovery.* Cambridge: Cambridge Univ. Press, 1958.

HECKERT, J. BROOKS, and WILSON, JAMES D. *Business Budgeting and Control.* 2nd ed. New York: Ronald Press, 1955.

HELMHOLZ, H. VON. "Zählen und Messen erkenntnistheoretisch betrachtet," *Wissenschaftliche Abhandlungen.* Leipzig: Barth, 1895.

HENDERSON, JAMES MITCHELL, and QUANDT, RICHARD E. *Microeconomic Theory: a Mathematical Approach.* New York: McGraw-Hill Book Co., Inc., 1958.

HERRMANN, CYRIL C., and MAGEE, JOHN F. "'Operations Research' for Management," *Harvard Business Review*, Vol. 31, No. 4 (July–August, 1953), pp. 100–112.

HEYNE, J. B. "Planning for Research in Management Control Systems," *Technical Memorandum* (TM–546). Santa Monica: *System Development Corporation*, 1960a.

————. "MARK I Operational Specifications," *Technical Memorandum* (TM–536). Santa Monica: System Development Corporation, 1960b.

HICKS, J. R. "The Valuation of the Social Income," *Economica*, Vol. 7 (new series), No. 25 (February, 1940), pp. 105–24.

————. *Value and Capital.* 2nd ed. Oxford: Clarendon Press, 1946.

————. "The Valuation of the Social Income—A Comment on Professor Kuznets' Reflections," *Economica*, Vol. 15, No. 59 (August, 1948), pp. 163–72.

HIRSCHLEIFER, J. "On the Theory of Optimal Investment Decision," *Journal of Political Economy*, Vol. 46, No. 4 (August, 1958), pp. 329–52.

HOGGATT, AUSTIN C., and BALDERSTON, FREDERICK E. (eds.). *Symposium on Simulation Models: Methodology and Applications to the Behavioral Sciences.* Cincinnati: South-Western, 1963.

HOLLAND, EDWARD P. "Simulation of an Economy with Development and Trade Problems," *American Economic Review*, Vol. 52, No. 3 (June, 1962), pp. 408–30.

HOLLAND, E. P., TENCER, BENJAMIN, and GILLESPIE, R. W. "A Model for Simulating Dynamic Problems of Economic Development," Report no. C160–10 of the Center for International Studies, Massachusetts Institute of Technology, 1960.

HOLT, C. C., MODIGLIANI, FRANCO, MUTH, J. F., and SIMON, H. A. *Planning Production, Inventories and Work Force.* Englewood Cliffs, N. J.: Prentice-Hall, Inc., 1960.

HOMBURGER, RICHARD H. "Measurement in Accounting," *Accounting Review*, Vol. 36, No. 1 (January, 1961), pp. 94–99.

HONKO, JAAKKO. *Yrityksen Vuositulos*, English Summary: "The Annual Income of an Enterprise and its Determination—A Study from the Standpoint of Accounting and Economics." Helsinki: 1959.

HOOD, U. C., and KOOPMANS, T. C. *Studies in Econometric Method.* New York: John Wiley & Sons, Inc., 1953.

HORNGREN, CHARLES T. *Cost Accounting—A Managerial Emphasis.* Englewood Cliffs, N. J.: Prentice-Hall, Inc., 1962.

HOWELL, JAMES E., and TEICHROEW, DANIEL. *Mathematical Analysis for Business Decisions.* Homewood, Ill.: Richard D. Irwin, Inc., 1963.

IJIRI, YUJI. "An Application of Input-Output Analysis to some Problems in Cost Accounting," unpublished term paper. Minneapolis: Univ. of Minnesota, 1960.

————. "Axioms and Structures of Conventional Accounting Measurement," Technical Report No. 128, Institute for Mathematical Studies in the Social Sciences, Stanford University, 1964 (to be published in *Accounting Review*).

—————. *Goal Oriented Models for Accounting and Control* (Doctoral dissertation, Carnegie Institute of Technology, Pittsburgh, 1963). To be published, Amsterdam: North-Holland Publishing Co., 1965.

IJIRI, Y., LEVY, F. K., and LYON, R. C. "A Linear Programming Model for Budgeting and Financial Planning," *Journal of Accounting Research*, Vol. 1, No. 2 (Autumn, 1963), pp. 198–212.

JAEDICKE, ROBERT K. "Improving Break-Even Analysis by Linear Programming Techniques," *NAA Bulletin*, Sec. 1, March, 1961, pp. 5–12.

JOHNSTON, J. *Statistical Cost Analysis*. New York: McGraw-Hill Book Co., Inc., 1960.

JOURDAIN, PHILIP E. B. *The Nature of Mathematics,* (1910), reprinted in Newman [1956] Vol. 1, pp. 4–71.

KAGDIS, J., and LACKNER, M. R. *Introduction to Management Control Systems Research*, TM-708/100/00. Santa Monica: System Development Corporation, 1962.

KALDOR, NICOLAS. *An Expenditure Tax*. London: Allen & Unwin, 1955.

KANTOROVICH, L. V. *Mathematical Methods of Organizing and Planning Production*. Leningrad Univ., 1939. An English translation from Russian prepared by R. W. CAMPBELL and W. H. MARLOW, *Management Science*, Vol. 6, No. 4 (July, 1960), pp. 366–422.

————— "On the Translocation of Masses," *Comptes Rendus* (Doklady) de l'Academie des Sciences de l'URSS, Vol. 37 (1942), pp. 199–201, republished in *Management Science*, Vol. 5, No. 1 (October, 1958).

—————. "On Methods of Analysis of Some External Problems in Planning Production," *Doklady Akademii Nauk SSSR*, Vol. 115 (1957), pp. 441–44. English translation by R. D. BURKE, Rand Corporation T-86, April 15, 1958.

KAYSEN, CARL. "A Dynamic Aspect of the Monopoly Problem," *Review of Economics and Statistics*, Vol. 31, No. 2 (May, 1949), pp. 109–13.

KEMENY, JOHN G., SCHLEIFER, ARTHUR, SNELL, J. LAURIE, and THOMPSON, GERALD L. *Finite Mathematics with Business Applications*. Englewood Cliffs, N.J.: Prentice-Hall, Inc., 1962.

KENNEDY, MILES. "The Values of Accounting and of Corporations: A Review Article," *Journal of Accounting Research*, Vol. 1, No. 1 (Spring, 1963), pp. 108–15.

KERSHNER, R. B., and WILCOX, L. R. *The Anatomy of Mathematics*. New York: Ronald Press, 1950.

KEYNES, JOHN MAYNARD. *The General Theory of Employment Interest and Money*. London: Macmillan & Co., Ltd., 1936.

KLEIN, LAWRENCE R. *Economic Fluctuations in the United States 1921–1941*. New York: John Wiley & Sons, Inc., 1950.

—————. *A Textbook of Econometrics*. Evanston: Row, Peterson & Co., 1953.

—————. "The Dartmouth Conference on an Econometric Model of the United States," *Social Research Council ITEMS*, Vol. 15, No. 3 (September, 1961).

————. *An Introduction to Econometrics.* New York: Prentice-Hall, Inc., 1962.

KLEIN, L. R., and GOLDBERGER, A. S. *An Econometric Model of the United States 1929–1952.* Amsterdam: North Holland Publishing Co., 1955.

KLEIN, L. R., BALL, R. J., HAZELWOOD, A., and VANDOME, P. *An Econometric Model of the United Kingdom.* Oxford: Blackwell, 1961.

KOCH, EDWARD G. "Managerial Strategy through Classification and Coding," *California Management Review,* Vol. 1, No. 4 (1959), pp. 56–66.

KOHLER, ERIC L. "Accounting Concepts and National Income," *Accounting Review,* Vol. 27, No. 1 (January, 1952), pp. 52–56.

————. *A Dictionary for Accountants.* Englewood Cliffs, N.J.: Prentice-Hall, Inc., 1952, 1957.

KOLMOGOROV, A. "Über die analytischen Methoden in der Wahrscheinlichkeitrechnung," *Mathematische Annalen,* Vol. 104 (1931), pp. 415–58.

————. "Grundbegriffe der Wahrscheinlichkeitrechnung," *Ergebnisse der Mathematik.,* Vol. 2, No. 3 (1933).

KOOPMANS, TJALLING C. (ed.). *Statistical Inference in Dynamic Economic Models.* New York: John Wiley & Sons, Inc., 1950.

———— (ed.). *Activity Analysis of Production and Allocation,* Cowles Commission for Research in Economics, Monograph No. 13. New York: John Wiley & Sons, Inc., 1951.

————. "A Note about Kantorovich's Paper 'Mathematical Methods of Organizing and Planning Production,'" *Management Science,* Vol. 6, No. 4 (July, 1960), pp. 363–65.

————. "On the Evaluation of Kantorovich's Work of 1939," *Management Science,* Vol. 8, No. 3 (April, 1962), pp. 264–65.

KOPLIN, H. T. "The Profit Maximization Assumption," *Oxford Economic Papers,* Vol. 15, No. 2 (July, 1963), pp. 130–39.

KOSIOL, ERICH. "Pagatorische Bilanz," *Lexikon des kaufmännischen Rechnungswesens* (ed. Karl Bott), pp. 2085–120. 2nd ed. Stuttgart: Muth, 1955.

————. "Modellanalyse als Grundlage unternehmerischer Entscheidungen," *Zeitschrift für handelswissenschaftliche Forschung,* Vol. 13, No. 7 (July, 1961), pp. 318–34.

KRELLE, WILHELM. *Volkswirtschaftliche Gesamtrechnung.* Berlin: Duncker & Humblot, 1959.

————. *Volkswirtschaftliche Gesamtrechnung—Einzelberechnungen.* Berlin: Duncker & Humblot, 1960.

KUH, EDWIN. "Capital Theory and Capital Budgeting," *Metroeconomica,* Vol. 12, No. 2/3 (August–December, 1960), pp. 64–80.

KUZNETS, SIMON. *National Income and Its Composition,* 1919–1938. New York: National Bureau of Economic Research, 1941.

————. "Discussion of the New Department of Commerce Income Series—National Income: A New Version," *Review of Economics and Statistics,* Vol. 30, No. 3 (August, 1948), pp. 179–95.

————. "On the Valuation of Social Income—Reflection on Professor Hicks' Article," Part I, *Economica,* Vol. 15, No. 57 (1948), pp. 1–16; Part II, *Economica,* Vol. 15, No. 58 (1948), pp. 116–31.

LANGER, SUSANNE K. *An Introduction to Symbolic Logic.* 2nd ed. New York: Dover, 1953.

LANZILLOTTI, ROBERT F. "Pricing Objectives in Large Companies," *American Economic Review*, Vol. 48, No. 5 (December, 1958), pp. 921–40.

LAZARSFELD, P. F., and BARTON, A. H. "Qualitative Measurement in the Social Sciences: Classification, Typologies, and Indices," *The Policy Sciences*, (eds. DANIEL LERNER and H. D. LASSWELL) Stanford: Stanford Univ. Press, 1951.

LEE, M. W., et al. *Views on Business Education.* Chapel Hill: Univ. of North Carolina, 1960.

LEONTIEF, WASSILY W. *The Structure of American Economy 1919–1939.* 2nd ed. New York: Oxford University Press, 1951. Note: compare improvements over the first edition, 1941.

————, et al. *Studies in the Structure of the American Economy.* New York: Oxford Univ. Press, 1953.

LESOURNE, J. *Technique économique et gestion industrielle.* Paris: Dunod, 1960.

LESTER, RICHARD A. "Shortcomings of Marginal Analysis for Wage-Employment Problems," *American Economic Review*, Vol. 36, No. 1 (March, 1946), pp. 63–82.

LEWIN, K., DEMBO, TEMARA, FESTINGER, L., and SEARS, PAULINE S. "Level of Aspiration," *Personality and the Behavior Disorders*, 2 vols (ed. J. M. Hunt), pp. 356–77, New York: Ronald Press, 1954.

LEWIS, CLARENCE IRVING, and LANGFORD, COOPER HAROLD. *Symbolic Logic.* 2nd ed. New York: Dover, 1959.

LEWIS, CLEONA. *The International Accounts.* New York: Macmillan Co., 1927.

LIPS, J., and SCHOUTEN, D. B. "The Reliability of the Policy Model Used by the Central Planning Bureau of the Netherlands," *Income and Wealth Series VI*, International Association for Income and Wealth, (eds. M. GILBERT, and R. STONE), pp. 24–51. London: Bowes & Bowes, 1957.

LITTLE, I. M. D. "The Valuation of the Social Income," *Economica*, Vol. 16, No. 61 (Feb., 1949), pp. 11–26.

————. *A Critique of Welfare Economics.* Oxford: Clarendon Press, 1950.

LITTLETON, A. C. *Accounting Evolution to 1900.* New York: American Institute Publ. Co., 1933.

————. *Structure of Accounting Theory.* Menasha: American Accounting Association, 1953.

LITTLETON, A. C., and YAMEY, B. S. (eds.). *Studies in the History of Accounting.* Homewood, Ill.: Richard D. Irwin, Inc., 1956.

LITTLETON, A. C., and ZIMMERMAN, V. K. *Accounting Theory: Continuity and Change.* Englewood Cliffs, N.J.: Prentice-Hall, Inc., 1962.

LUTZ, FRIEDRICH, and LUTZ, VERA. *The Theory of Investment of the Firm.* Princeton: Princeton Univ. Press, 1951.

MACK, RUTH N. *Consumption and Business Fluctuations: A Case Study of the Shoe, Leather, Hide Sequence.* New York: National Bureau of Economic Research, 1956.

MAILLET, PIERRE. "État actuel des travaux d'input-output dans le mond," *Revue d'Economie Politique*, Vol. 73, No. 1 (Jan.–Feb., 1963), pp. 39–61.

MALCOLM, DONALD G. "Foreword" to *Report of System Simulation Symposium*. New York: American Institute of Industrial Engineers, 1957.

————. "Bibliography on the Use of Simulation in Management Analysis," *Operations Research*, Vol. 8, No. 2 (March–April, 1960), pp. 169–77.

MALCOLM, DONALD G., and ROWE, A. J. (eds.). *Management Control Systems: The Proceedings of a Symposium*. New York: John Wiley & Sons, Inc., 1960.

MARCH, JAMES G., and SIMON, HERBERT A. *Organizations*. New York: John Wiley & Sons, Inc., 1958.

MARGOLIS, JULIAN. "National Economic Accounting: Reorientation Needed," *Review of Economics and Statistics*, Vol. 34, No. 4 (November, 1952), pp. 291–304.

————. "The Analysis of the Firm: Rationalism, Conventionalism, and Behaviorism." *Journal of Business*, University of Chicago, Vol. 31, No. 3 (July, 1958), pp. 187–99.

MARKOWITZ, HARRY M. *Portfolio Selection*. New York: John Wiley & Sons, Inc., 1959.

MARKOWITZ, HARRY M., HAUSER, BERNARD, and KARR, HERBERT W. *SIMSCRIPT—A Simulation Programming Language*. Englewood Cliffs, N.J.: Prentice-Hall, Inc., 1963; copyright 1963 by the Rand Corporation.

MARSCHAK, J., and RADNER, R. "Economic Theory of Teams," 2nd and 3rd chapters mimeographed. *Cowles Foundation Discussion Paper* No. 59. New Haven, 1958.

MARSHALL, ALFRED. *Principles of Economics*. London: Macmillan & Co., Ltd., 1920.

MASON, PERRY. *Price-Level Changes and Financial Statements*. New York: American Accounting Association, 1956.

————. *Cash Flow Analysis and the Funds Statement*. Accounting Research Study, No. 2. New York: American Institute of Certified Public Accountants, 1961.

MASSÉ, PIERRE. *Le choix des investissments—critères et méthodes*. Paris: Dunod, 1959. English translation by Scripta Technica, Inc., *Optimal Investment Decisions, Rules for Action and Criteria for Choice*. Englewood Cliffs, N.J.: Prentice-Hall, Inc., 1962. References in the present book refer to the English translation.

MATTESSICH, RICHARD. "The Constellation of Accountancy and Economics," *Accounting Review*, Vol. 31, No. 4 (October, 1956), pp. 551–64.

————. "Towards a General and Axiomatic Foundation of Accountancy—With an Introduction to the Matrix Formulation of Accounting Systems," *Accounting Research*, Vol. 8, No. 4 (London; October, 1957), pp. 328–55. Reprinted in *Readings in Accounting Theory*, Vol. I (ed. Carl Devine), pp. 123–45 (proofs omitted).

————. "Mathematical Models in Business Accounting," *Accounting Review*, Vol. 33, No. 3 (July, 1958a), pp. 472–81.

————. "Prolegomena zu einer universalen Rechnungswissenschaft," *Zeitschrift für Betriebswirtschaft*, Vol. 28, No. 10 (October, 1958b), pp. 601–13.

————. "Messung, Vorausberechnung und Buchhaltungsmodelle," *Zeitschrift für handelswissenschaftliche Forschung*, Vol. 11, No. 4 (April, 1959a), pp. 179–94.

————. "Accounting Reconsidered," *California Management Review*, Vol. 2, No. 1 (October, 1959b), pp. 85–91.

————. "Budgeting Models and System Simulation," *Accounting Review*, Vol. 36, No. 3 (July, 1961a), pp. 384–97.

————. "Unternehmungsforschung," *Zeitschrift für handelswissenschaftliche Forschung*, Vol. 13, No. 819 (Aug.–Sept., 1961b), pp. 411–23.

————. "To the Problem of Measurement and Statistical Estimation of Errors in Accounting," *Management International*, Vol. 2, No. 2 (April, 1962a), pp. 37–58.

————. "Philosophie der Unternehmungsforschung," *Zeitschrift für handelswissenschaftliche Forschung*, Vol. 14, No. 5 (May, 1962b), pp. 249–58.

————. "Operations Research and Accounting: Competitors or Partners?" *Quarterly Review of Economics and Business*, Vol. 2, No. 2 (August, 1962c), pp. 7–14.

————. "Opportunities for Research in Accounting—Mathematical Applications," *Proceedings: International Conference on Accounting Education*, pp. 100–106. Urbana: Center for Internat. Educ. and Res. in Acctg., 1962.

————. "Wertrealismus und Addierbarkeit von Entscheidungswerten im betrieblichen Rechnungswesen," *Zeitschrift für Betriebswirtschaft*, Vol. 34, No. 2 (1964), pp. 65–75.

————. *Simulation of the Firm through a Budget Computer Program.* Homewood: Richard D. Irwin, Inc., 1964.

McCLOSKEY, J. F., and TREFETHEN, F. N. (eds.). *Operations Research for Management*, Vols. I and II. Baltimore: Johns Hopkins Press, 1954.

MEADE, J. E. *The Balance of Payments*, The Theory of International Economic Policy, Vol. I. London: Oxford University Press, 1951.

MELLEROWICZ, KONRAD. *Wert und Wertung im Betrieb.* Essen: W. Girardet, 1952a.

————. *Der Wert der Unternehmung als Ganzes.* Essen: W. Girardet, 1952b.

MENGER, KARL (1840–1921). *Grundsätze der Volkswirtschaftslehre*, published in Vienna, 1871; in English translation in *Principles of Economics.* Glencoe: Free Press, 1950.

MENGER, KARL (1902–). "Mensuration, a Mathematical Connection of Observable Material" in Churchman and Ratoosh [1959], pp. 97–128.

MEYER, H. A. (ed.). *Symposium on Monte Carlo Methods.* New York: John Wiley & Sons, Inc., 1956.

MEYER, JEAN. *Comptabilité d'entreprise et comptabilité nationale.* Paris: Dunod, 1962.

MILLER, DAVID W., and STARR, MARTIN K. *Executive Decisions and Operations Research.* Englewood Cliffs, N.J.: Prentice-Hall, Inc., 1960.

MILLER, ROBERT W. *Schedule, Cost and Profit Control with Pert.* New York: McGraw-Hill Book Co., Inc., 1963.

MINAS, J. SAYER. "Science and Operations Research," in Banbury and Maitland [1961], pp. 26–33.

MITCHEL, WESLEY C. "The Flow of Payments, a Preliminary Survey of Concepts and Data" (an unpublished memorandum), June, 1944.

MODIGLIANI, FRANCO, and MILLER, MERTON H. "The Cost of Capital, Corporation Finance and the Theory of Investment," presented at the annual meeting of the Econometric Society, 1956. Reprinted as a revised version by Solomon [1959], pp. 150–81.

MOONITZ, MAURICE. *The Basic Postulates of Accounting,* Accounting Research Study No. 1 of the American Institute of Certified Public Accountants. New York: AICPA, 1961.

————. "The Nature of Research in Accounting," *Proceedings: International Conference on Accounting Education,* pp. 83–86. Urbana: Center for Internat. Educ. and Res. in Acctg., 1962.

MOONITZ, MAURICE, and STAEHLING, CHARLES C. *Accounting: An Analysis of its Problems,* Vols. I and II. Brooklyn: Foundation Press, 1950 and 1952.

MOONITZ, MAURICE, and JORDAN, LOUIS H. *Accounting: An Analysis of its Problems,* Vol. I. Rev. ed. Holt, Rinehart & Winston, Inc., 1963.

MORGENSTERN, OSKAR (ed.). *Economic Activity Analysis.* New York: John Wiley & Sons, Inc., 1954.

————. *On the Accuracy of Economic Observations.* 1st and 2nd ed. Princeton: Princeton Univ. Press, 1950 and 1963.

————. "Limits to the Uses of Mathematics in Economics," *Mathematics and the Social Sciences* (ed. J. C. CHARLESWORTH), pp. 12–29. Philadelphia: American Academy of Political and Social Sciences, 1963b.

MORSE, PHILIP M., and KIMBALL, GEORGE E. *Methods of Operations Research.* New York: John Wiley & Sons, Inc., 1951.

————. *Executive Decisions and Operations Research.* Englewood Cliffs, N.J.: Prentice-Hall Inc., 1960.

MOSTELLER, FREDERICK, ROURKE, ROBERT E. K., and THOMAS, GEORGE B. *Probability with Statistical Applications.* Reading: Addison-Wesley, 1961.

MUHS, KARL. "Die 'wertlose' Nationalökonomie—Eine Auseinandersetzung mit Fr. v. Gottl-Ottlilienfeld," *Jahrbücher für Nationalökonomie und Statistik,* Vol. 129, No. 6 (December, 1928), pp. 801–28.

MURPHY, MARY E. "The Teaching of Social Accounting: A Research Planning Paper," *Accounting Review,* Vol. 32, No. 4 (October, 1957), pp. 630–45.

MYERS, JOHN H. *Reporting of Leases in Financial Statements,* Accounting Research Study No. 4. New York: American Institute of Certified Public Accountants, 1963.

MYRDAL, GUNNAR. *The Political Element in the Development of Economic Theory.* Cambridge: Harvard University Press, 1955. Original version: *Vetenskap och politik i nationalekonomien.*

NAGEL, ERNEST. "Assumptions in Economic Theory," *American Economic Review*, Vol. 53, No. 2 (May, 1963), pp. 211–19.

NEUMANN, JOHN VON. *The Computer and the Brain.* New Haven: Yale University Press, 1958.

NEUMANN, JOHN VON, and MORGENSTERN, OSKAR. *Theory of Games and Economic Behavior.* Princeton: Princeton Univ. Press, 1944 (1st ed.), 1947 (2nd ed.).

NEWMAN, JAMES R. (ed.). *The World of Mathematics*, Vols. I to IV. New York: Simon & Schuster, 1956.

NIELSEN, OSWALD. New Challenges in Accounting," *Accounting Review*, Vol. 35, No. 4 (October, 1960), pp. 583–89.

NOBLE, C. E. "Calculating control limits for cost control data," *N.A.C.A.-Bulletin*, Vol. 35 (June, 1954), pp. 1309–17 (Now, National Association of Accountants).

OHLSSON, INGVAR. *On National Accounting.* Stockholm: Konjunkturinstitutet, 1953.

ONCKEN, AUGUST (ed.). *Oeuvres Économiques et Philosophiques de F. Quesnay.* Francfort: Baer, 1888.

ORCUTT, GUY H. "Simulation of Economic Systems," *American Economic Review*, Vol. 50, No. 5 (December, 1960), pp. 893–907.

ORCUTT, GUY H., GREENBERGER, M., KORBEL, J. and RIVLIN, A. *Microanalysis of Socioeconomic Systems: A Simulation Study.* New York: Harper & Bros., Inc., 1961.

ORGANICK, ELLIOT I. *A FORTRAN primer.* Reading: Addison-Wesley, 1963.

PACIOLI, LUCA B. *Summa de arithmetica, geometria, proportioni et proportionalita.* Venice, 1494.

PAPANDREOU, ANDREAS G. "Some Basic Problems in the Theory of the Firm," *A Survey of Contemporary Economics*, 2, (ed. BERNARD F. HALEY). Homewood, Ill.: Richard D. Irwin, Inc., 1952.

—————. *Economics as a Science.* Chicago: Lippincott, 1958.

—————. "Explanation and Prediction in Economics," *Science*, Vol. 129, No. 3356 (April, 1959), pp. 1096–1100.

—————. "Theory Construction and Empirical Meaning in Economics," *American Economic Review*, Vol. 53, No. 2 (May, 1963), pp. 205–10.

PAPANDREOU, ANDREAS G., and WHEELER, JOHN T. *Competition and its Regulation.* Englewood Cliffs, N.J.: Prentice-Hall, Inc., 1955.

PATINKIN, DON. *Money, Interest and Prices—An Integration of Monetary and Value Theory.* Evanston, Ill.: Row, Peterson & Co., 1956.

PATON, WILLIAM A. "Cost and Value in Accounting," *Journal of Accountancy*, Vol. 81, No. 3 (March, 1946), pp. 192–99.

—————. "Accounting Procedures and Private Enterprise," *Journal of Accountancy*, Vol. 85, No. 4 (April, 1948), pp. 278–91.

PATON, WILLIAM A., and LITTLETON, A. C. *Introduction to Corporate Accounting Standards.* Iowa City: American Accounting Association, 1940.

PERAGALLO, EDWARD. *Origin and Evolution of Double Entry Bookkeeping.* New York: American Institute Publishing Co., 1938.

PERRY, KENNETH W. "Statistical Relationship of Accounting and Economics," *Accounting Review*, Vol. 30, No. 3 (July, 1955), pp. 500–506.
PFANZAGL, J. *Die axiomatischen Grundlagen einer allgemeinen Theorie des Messens*. Würzburg: Physica Verlag, 1962.
PHILLIPS, A. W. "Mechanical Models of Economic Dynamics," *Economica*, Vol. 17, No. 67 (August, 1950), pp. 283–305.
————. "Stabilization Policy and the Time-Form of Lagged Responses," *Economic Journal*, Vol. 67 (June, 1957), pp. 265–77.
PHILLIPS, ALMARIN. "The Tableau Économique as a Simple Leontief Model," *Quarterly Journal of Economics*, Vol. 69, No. 1 (February, 1955), pp. 137–44.
PICHLER, O. "Anwendung der Matrizenrechnung auf betriebswirtschaftliche Aufgaben," *Ingenieur Archiv*, Vol. 21, No. 3 (1953), pp. 119–40.
PIERSON, FRANK, et al. *The Education of American Businessmen*. New York: McGraw-Hill Book Co., Inc., 1959.
POPPER, KARL R. *Conjectures and Refutations*. New York: Basic Books, Inc., 1962.
————. *The Logic of Scientific Discovery*. New York: Basic Books Inc., 1959. Original version: *Logik der Forschung*, Vienna, 1935.
POWELSON, JOHN P. *Economic Accounting*. New York: McGraw-Hill Book Co., Inc., 1955a.
————. "Social Accounting," *Accounting Review*, Vol. 30, No. 4 (October, 1955b), pp. 651–59.
PRINCE, THOMAS R. *Extension of the Boundaries of Accounting Theory*. Cincinnati: South-Western, 1963.
QUESNAY, FRANÇOIS. *Oeuvres économiques et philosophiques*, publieé avec une introduction et des notes par Auguste Oncken. Francfort: Baer, 1888.
RAIFFA, HOWARD, and SCHLAIFER, ROBERT. *Applied Statistical Decision Theory*. Boston: Harvard University, 1961.
REICHENBACH, HANS. "Kausalität der Wahrscheinlichkeit," *Erkenntnis*, Vol. 1, No. 158 (1930).
————. "The Logical Foundations of the Concept of Probability," (in translation by FEIGL and BRODBECK [1949]). Originally published in German: "Die Logischen Grundlagen des Wahrscheinlichkeitskonzepts," *Erkenntnis*, Vol. 3, No. 4 (Leipzig, 1932), pp. 401–25.
————. *The Theory of Probability*. Berkeley: University of California Press, 1949.
RICHARDS, ALLEN B. "Input-Output Accounting for Business," *Accounting Review*, Vol. 35, No. 3 (July, 1960), pp. 429–36.
RILEY, VERA, and ALLEN, R. L. *Interindustry Economic Studies*. Baltimore: J. Hopkins Press, 1955.
ROLPH, EARL R. "The Concept of Transfers in National Income Estimates," *Quarterly Journal of Economics*, Vol. 62, No. 3 (1948), pp. 327–61.
ROOVER, RAYMOND DE. "The Development of Accounting Prior to Luca Pacioli According to The Account-books of Medieval Merchants," *Studies in the History of Accounting*, pp. 114–74, by A. C. LITTLETON and B. S. YAMEY (eds.). Homewood, Ill.: Richard D. Irwin, Inc., 1956.

ROSENBLATT, DAVID. "On Linear Models and the Graphs of Minkowski-Leontief Matrices," *Econometrica*, Vol. 25, No. 2 (April, 1957), pp. 325-38.

ROTHSCHILD, K. W. "Price Theory and Oligopoly," *Economic Journal*, Vol. 57 (1947), pp. 299-320; reprinted in *Readings in Price Theory*, pp. 440-64, (eds., GEORGE J. STIGLER and KENNETH E. BOULDING). Homewood, Ill.: Richard D. Irwin, Inc., 1952.

ROWE, A. J. "Computer Simulation Applied to Job Shop Scheduling," *Report on Simulation Symposium*, American Institute of Industrial Engineers, 1958.

RUSSELL, BERTRAND. *A History of Western Philosophy*. New York: Simon & Schuster, Inc., 1945.

SAMUELSON, PAUL A. *Foundations of Economic Analysis*. Cambridge: Harvard Univ. Press, 1947.

————. "Evaluation of Real National Income," *Oxford Economic Papers*, Vol. 2, No. 1 (1950), pp. 1-29.

————. "Problems of Methodology—Discussion," *American Accounting Review*, Vol. 53, No. 2 (May, 1963), pp. 231-36.

SASIENI, MAURICE, YASPAN, ARTHUR, and FRIEDMAN, LAWRENCE. *Operations Research—Methods and Problems*. New York: John Wiley & Sons, Inc., 1959.

SAVAGE, I. RICHARD, and DEUTSCH, KARL. "A Statistical Model of the Gross Analysis of Transaction Flows," *Econometrica*, Vol. 28 (July, 1960), pp. 551-72.

SAVAGE, LEONARD J. *The Foundations of Statistics*. New York: John Wiley & Sons, Inc., 1954.

SCHERPF, PETER. *Der Kontenrahmen*. Munich: Hueber, 1955.

SCHLAIFER, ROBERT. *Probability and Statistics for Business Decisions*. New York: McGraw-Hill Book Co., Inc., 1959.

————. *Introduction to Statistics for Business Decisions*. New York: McGraw-Hill Book Co., Inc., 1961.

SCHMALENBACH, EUGEN. *Der Kontenrahmen*. Leipzig, 1927.

————. *Dynamische Bilanz*. 6th ed. Leipzig: Gloeckner, 1933; English translation: *Dynamic Accounting*. London: Gee & Co., 1959.

SCHNEIDER, ERICH. *Industrielles Rechnungswesen*. 2nd ed. Tübingen: J. C. B. Mohr, 1954.

SCHUMPETER, JOSEPH ALOIS. *History of Economic Analysis*. New York: Oxford Univ. Press, 1954.

SCITOVSKY, TIBOR. "A Note on Profit Maximization and its Implications," *Review of Economic Studies*, Vol. 11 (1943), pp. 57-60; reprinted in *Readings in Price Theory*, pp. 352-58 (eds., GEORGE J. STIGLER and KENNETH E. BOULDING). Homewood, Ill.: Richard D. Irwin, Inc., 1952.

SHANNON, C. E., and WEAVER, W. *The Mathematical Theory of Communication*. Urbana: University of Illinois Press, 1949.

SHUBIK, MARTIN. "Bibliography on Simulation, Gaming, Artificial Intelligence and Allied Topics," *Journal of the American Statistical Association*, Vol. 55, No. 4 (December, 1960), pp. 736-51.

SHUCHMAN, ABE (ed.). *Scientific Decision Making in Business.* New York: Holt, Rinehart & Winston, 1963.

SIGEL, STANLEY J. "An Approach to the Integration of Income and Product and Flow-of-Funds National Accounting Systems: A Progress Report," *The Flow-of-Funds Approach to Social Accounting;* Vol. 26 of Studies in Income and Wealth of the National Bureau of Economic Research, Princeton: 1962.

SILK, L. S. *The Education of Businessmen.* New York: Committee for Economic Development, 1960.

SIMON, HERBERT A. *Administrative Behavior.* New York: Macmillan Co., 1948.

————. "A Behavioral Model of Rational Choice," *Quarterly Journal of Economics,* Vol. 69, (1952), pp. 99–118.

————. *Models of Man.* New York: John Wiley & Sons, Inc., 1957.

————. "Theories of Decision-Making in Economics and Behavioral Science," *American Economic Review,* Vol. 49, No. 3 (June, 1959), pp. 253–83.

————. *The New Science of Management Decision.* New York: Harper & Brothers, 1960.

————. "New Developments in the Theory of the Firm," *American Economic Review,* Papers and Proceedings), Vol. 52, No. 2, May 1962.

————. "Problems of Methodology—Discussion," *American Accounting Review,* Vol. 53, No. 2 (May, 1963), pp. 229–231.

SINGER, E. A. (ed. C. W. CHURCHMAN). *Experience and Reflexion.* Philadelphia: Univ. of Pennsylvania Press, 1959.

SMITH, ADAM. *The Wealth of Nations.* New York: Random House, Inc., Edition, 1937. (*An Inquiry into the Nature and Causes of the Wealth of Nations.* London: 1776).

SMITH, CALEB A. "How Can Accounting be Integrated with Economics?" *Accounting Review,* Vol. 3, No. 1 (January, 1952), pp. 100–123.

SMITH, NICOLAS M. "Stochastic Processes and the Theory of Value." First Natl. Meeting, Oper. Res. Soc. Amer., November 17, 1952.

————. "Value and the Decision Process." Third Annual Fall Meeting, Oper. Res. Soc. Amer., November 19, 1954.

————. "A Calculus for Ethics: A Theory of the Structure of Value—Part I." *Behavioral Science,* Vol. 1, No. 2 (April, 1956), pp. 111–42.

SMITH, NICOLAS M., WALTERS, STANLEY S., BROOKS, FRANKLIN C., and BLACKWELL, DAVID H. "The Theory of Value and the Science of Decision—A Summary," *Operations Research,* Vol. 1, No. 3 (May, 1953), pp. 103–13.

SMYTH, J. E. "A Cast for National Income Accounting in the Accounting Curriculum," *Accounting Review,* Vol. 34, No. 3 (1959), pp. 376–80.

————. "Opportunities for Research in National Income Accounting," *Proceedings: International Conference on Accounting Education,* pp. 100–106. Urbana: Center for Internat. Educ. and Res. in Acctg., 1962.

SOLOMON, EZRA (ed.). *The Management of Corporate Capital.* New York: Glenco, 1959.

SOLOMONS, DAVID. "Economic and Accounting Concepts of Income," *Accounting Review*, Vol. 3, No. 36 (July, 1961), pp. 374–84.

————. "The Integration of Accounting and Economic Studies," *Accounting Research*, Vol. 6, (1955), pp. 106–11.

SOMBART, WERNER. *Der moderne Kapitalismus*. Leipzig: Duncker & Humblot, 1902.

SPACEK, LEONARD. "Suggested Solution to the Principles Dilemma," a speech given at the 1963 Convention of the American Accounting Association at Stanford University. Reprinted by Arthur Andersen and Co.

SPENGLER, OSWALD. *The Decline of the West*. Vol. 2: English translation, New York: Alfred A. Knopf, Inc., 1928; original version, *Der Untergang des Abendlandes—Welthistorische Perspektiven*. Munich: Beck'sche Verlag, 1918.

SPROUSE, ROBERT T., and MOONITZ, MAURICE. *A Tentative Set of Broad Accounting Principles for Business Enterprises*. Accounting Research Study no. 3 of the American Institute of Certified Public Accountants. New York, 1962.

SPROWLS, CLAY R. "A Model of Customer Behavior for the Task Manufacturing Corporation," *Management Science*, Vol. 8, No. 3 (April, 1962), pp. 311–24.

————. "A Role of Computer Simulation in Accounting Education," *Accounting Review*, Vol. 37, No. 3 (July, 1962), pp. 515–20.

SPROWLS, CLAY R., and ASIMOW, M. "A Computer Simulated Business Firm," *Management Control Systems*, pp. 321–32, D. G. MALCOLM, A. J. ROWE, and L. F. McCONNELL (eds.). New York: John Wiley & Sons, Inc., 1960.

STAUBUS, GEORGE J. *A Theory of Accounting to Investors*. Berkeley: University of California Press, 1961.

STE. CROIX, G. E. M. DE. "Greek and Roman Accounting," *Studies in the History of Accounting*, pp. 14–74 (eds. A. C. LITTLETON and B. S. YAMEY). Homewood, Ill.: Richard D. Irwin, Inc., 1956.

STEDRY, ANDREW C. *Budget Control and Cost Behavior*, 1959 Award Winner of the Ford Foundation Doctoral Dissertation Series. Englewood Cliffs, N. J.: Prentice-Hall, Inc., 1960.

STERN, MARK E. *Mathematics for Management*. Englewood Cliffs, N.J.: Prentice-Hall, Inc., 1963.

STEVENS, S. S. "On the Theory of Scales of Measurement," *Science*, Vol. 103 (Jan.–June, 1946), pp. 677–80.

————. "Mathematics, Measurement and Psychophysics," *Handbook of Experimental Psychology* (ed. S. S. STEVENS). New York: John Wiley & Sons, Inc., 1951.

————. "Measurement and Man," *Science*, Vol. 127, No. 21 (February, 1958), pp. 383–409.

————. "Measurement, Psychophysics, and Utility," *Measurement* (eds. WEST C. CHURCHMAN and PHILBURN RATOOSH). New York: John Wiley & Sons, Inc., 1959.

STIBITZ, G. R., and LARRIVEE, J. A. *Mathematics and Computers*. New York: McGraw-Hill Book Co., Inc., 1957.

STIGLER, GEORGE J. *Production and Distribution Theories—The Formative Period*. New York: Macmillan Co., 1941.

STONE, RICHARD. "Definition and Measurement of the National Income and Related Totals," Appendix of *Measurement of National Income and The Construction of Social Accounts*. Geneva: United Nations—Studies and Reports on Statistical Methods, No. 7, 1947.

————. "Functions and Criteria of a System of Social Accounting," *Income and Wealth* (ed. ERIC LUNDBERG), Series I, pp. 1–74. Cambridge: Bowes & Bowes Publishers Ltd., 1951.

————. "Simple Transaction Models, Information and Computing," *Review of Economic Studies*, Vol. 19, No. 49 (1951/52), pp. 67–84.

————. "Transaction Models with an Example Based on the British National Accounts," *Accounting Research*, Vol. 6, No. 3 (July, 1955) (England), pp. 202–26.

STUDENSKI, PAUL. *The Income of Nations*. New York: New York University Press, 1958.

SUPPES, PATRICK. *Introduction to Logic*. Princeton, N. J.: Van Nostrand, 1957.

SZYPERSKI, NORBERT. *Zur Problematik der quantitativen Terminologie in der Betriebswirtschaftslehre*. Berlin: Duncker & Humblot, 1962.

TEIL, H. *Linear Aggregation of Economic Relations*. Amsterdam: North Holland Publ. Co., 1954.

THRALL, R. M., COOMBS, C. H., and DAVIS, R. L. (eds.). *Decision Processes*. New York: John Wiley & Sons, Inc., 1954.

TINBERGEN, JAN. *Statistical Testing of Business Cycle Theories, II, Business Cycles in the United States of America 1919–1932*. Geneva: League of Nations Economic Intelligence Service, 1939.

————. *Econometrics*. New York: Blakiston, 1951. (Traduction anglaise de *Econometrics*, Groninghen, 1941).

TINBERGEN, JAN, and POLAK, J. J. *Dynamics of Business Cycles*. Chicago: University of Chicago Press, 1950.

TINTNER, GERHARD. *Econometrics*. New York: John Wiley & Sons, Inc., 1952.

TRUEBLOOD, ROBERT M., and CYERT, RICHARD M. *Sampling Techniques in Accounting*. Englewood Cliffs, N.J.: Prentice-Hall, Inc., 1957.

TORGERSON, WARREN, S. *Theory and Methods of Scaling*. New York: John Wiley & Sons, Inc., 1958.

ULRICH, HERBERT. "Zur Berechnung von Input-Output Koeffizienten aus Kostenrechnungsunterlagen in der Eisen- und Stahlindustrie," *Zeitschrift für die Gesamte Staatswissenschaft*, Vol. 120, No. 1 (January, 1964), pp. 106–25.

VAJDA, S. *The Theory of Games and Linear Programming*. New York: John Wiley & Sons, Inc., 1956.

VALVANIS-VAIL, STEFAN. "An Econometric Model of Growth, U.S.A., 1869–1953," *American Economic Review*, Vol. 45, No . 2 (May, 1955), pp. 208–21.

VANCE, LAWRENCE L., and NETER, JOHN. *Statistical Sampling for Auditors and Accountants.* New York: John Wiley & Sons, Inc., 1956.

VAN CLEEFF, E. "Nationale boekhounding: proeve van cen jaaroverzicht Nederland 1938," *De Economist* (Netherlands) July, 1941, pp. 415–24.

VATTER, WILLIAM J. *The Fund Theory of Accounting and its Implications for Financial Reporting.* Chicago: Univ. of Chicago Press, 1947.

—————. *Managerial Accounting.* Englewood Cliffs, N. J.: Prentice-Hall, Inc., 1950.

—————. "Another Look at the 1957 Statement," *Accounting Review*, Vol. 37, No. 4 (October, 1962), pp. 660–69.

VAZSONYI, ANDREW. *Scientific Programming in Business and Industry.* New York: John Wiley & Sons, Inc., 1958.

VON NEUMANN (see NEUMANN, JOHN VON).

WAGNER, HARVEY M. "Practical Slants on Operations Research," *Harvard Business Review*, Vol. 41, No. 3 (May–June, 1963), pp. 61–71.

—————. "Review of Forrester's *Industrial Dynamics,*" *Management Science*, Vol. 10, No. 1 (October, 1963), pp. 184–86.

WALD, ABRAHAM. *Statistical Decision Functions.* New York: John Wiley & Sons, Inc., 1950.

WALRAS. LÉON M. J. *Éléments d'économie politique pure.* Lausanne: Corbaz, 1874. English translation, *Elements of Pure Economics.* London: Unwin, 1954.

WASSERMAN, PAUL, and SILANDER, FRED S. *Decision-Making, an Annotated Bibliography.* Ithaca: Graduate School of Business and Public Administration, Cornell University, 1958.

WEISS, LIONEL. *Statistical Decision Theory.* New York: McGraw-Hill Book Co., Inc., 1961.

WENKE, KLAUS. "Kostenanalyse mit Matrizen," *Zeitschrift für Betriebswirtschaftslehre*, Vol. 26, No. 10 (October, 1956), pp. 558–76.

—————. "On the Analysis of Structural Properties of large scale microeconomic input-output models," *Reprints of the International Meeting of the Institute of Management Sciences.* London: Pergamon, 1959.

WEYL, HERMANN. *Philosophie der Naturwissenschaften.* Munich, 1927.

WHEELER, JOHN T. "Economics and Accounting," *Handbook of Modern Accounting Theory*, pp. 41–76. (ed. MORTON BACKER.) New York: Prentice-Hall, Inc., 1955.

WHITIN, T. M. *The Theory of Inventory Management.* Princeton: Princeton Univ. Press, 1953.

WICKSTEED, PHILIP H. "The Scope and Method of Political Economy in the Light of the 'Marginal' Theory of Value and of Distribution," *Economic Journal*, Vol. 24, No. 93 (March, 1914).

WIENER, N. *Cybernetics.* New York: John Wiley & Sons, Inc., 1948.

—————. *The Human Use of Human Beings: Cybernetics and Society.* Boston, 1950.

WILDER, RAYMOND L. *The Foundations of Mathematics.* New York: John Wiley & Sons, Inc., 1952.

WILLIAMS, J. D. *The Compleat Strategyst.* New York: McGraw-Hill Book Co., 1954.

WILLIAMS, THOMAS H., and GRIFFIN, CHARLES H. *The Mathematical Dimension of Accountancy.* Cincinnati: South-Western Publ. Co., 1964a.

———. "Matrix Theory and Cost Allocation," *Accounting Review,* Vol. 39, No. 3 (July, 1964b), pp. 671–78.

WINBORNE, MARILYNN G. "Application of Sets and Symbolic Logic to Selected Accounting Principles and Practices" (Doctoral Dissertation, unpublished). Austin, 1962.

WITTGENSTEIN, L. V. *Philosophical Investigations.* Translated by G. E. M. AUSCOMBE, Oxford: Blackwell, 1953. Originally published in German as *Philosophische Untersuchungen,* 1945.

WITTMANN, WALDEMAR, *Der Wertbegriff in der Betriebswirtschaftslehre.* Köln: Westdeutscher Verlag, 1956.

WOODGER, J. H. *Biology and Language.* Cambridge: Cambridge Univ. Press, 1952.

WYATT, ARTHUR R. *A Critical Study of Accounting for Business Combinations,* Accounting Research Study No. 5, New York: American Institute of Certified Public Accountants, 1963.

ZANNETOS, ZENON S. "Statistical Attributes of Group Depreciation," *Accounting Review,* Vol. 37, No. 4 (October, 1962), pp. 713–20.

AMERICAN ACCOUNTING ASSOCIATION. *A Survey of Economic Accounting,* 1957.

AMERICAN INSTITUTE OF CERTIFIED PUBLIC ACCOUNTANTS (previously American Institute of Accountants). *Accounting Research and Terminology Bulletins* — Final Edition (containing the 1953 revisions and restatements of earlier bulletins with all subsequent bulletins issued). New York: AICPA, 1961.

AMERICAN INSTITUTE OF CERTIFIED PUBLIC ACCOUNTANTS (Staff of the Accounting Research Division). *Reporting the Financial Effects of Price-Level Changes.* New York: AICPA, 1963.

ARTHUR ANDERSEN & CO. *Accounting and Reporting Problems of the Accounting Profession.* 2nd ed., AC 2040, Item 3, October, 1962.

CENTRAL STATISTICAL OFFICE (of the United Kingdom). *National Income Statistics—Sources and Methods.* London: Her Majesty's Stationary Office, 1956.

FEDERAL RESERVE SYSTEM (Board of Governors). "A Flow-of-Funds System of National Accounts, Annual Estimates, 1939–54," *Bulletin,* Vol. 41, No. 10 (October 1955), pp. 1085–1124.

———. "Summary Flow-of-Funds Accounts 1950–55," *Bulletin,* Vol. 43, No. 4 (April, 1957a), pp. 372–91.

———. "Summary of Flow-of-Funds Accounts for 1954," *Bulletin,* Vol. 43, No. 10 (October, 1957b), pp. 1190–94.

———. "A Quarterly Presentation of Flow-of-Funds, Saving, and Investment," *Bulletin,* Vol. 45, No. 8 (August, 1959), pp. 828–1062.

———. "The Balance Sheet of Agriculture, 1961," *Bulletin,* Vol. 47, No. 8 (November, 1961), pp. 908–16.

———. "Flow of Funds Seasonally Adjusted," *Bulletin,* Vol. 48, No. 11 (Nov. 1962), pp. 1393–407.

Index of Economic Journals, Vols. I (1886–1924), II (1925–39), III (1940–49), IV (1950–54), V (1954–59) prepared under the auspices of the American Economic Association. Homewood, Ill.: Richard D. Irwin, Inc., 1961–62.

INTERNATIONAL MONETARY FUND. *Balance of Payments Manual.* Washington, 1950.

NATIONAL ASSOCIATION OF ACCOUNTANTS (previously: National Assoc. of Cost Accts.). Some important *Research Reports:*
The Analysis of Cost-Volume-Profit Relations, Combined Research Series 16, 17, and 18. New York: NACA, 1950.
Direct Costing, Research Series No. 23. New York: NACA, 1953.
Accounting for Intra-Company Transfers, Research Series No. 30. New York: NAA, 1956.
Costing Joint Products, Research Series No. 31. New York: NAA, 1957a.
Accounting for Labor Costs and Labor-Related Costs, Research Series No. 32. New York: NAA, 1957b.
Current Practice in Accounting for Depreciation, Research Report No. 33. New York: NAA, 1958.
Classification and Coding Techniques to Facilitate Accounting Operations, Research Report No. 34. New York: NAA, 1959.

NATIONAL BUREAU OF ECONOMIC RESEARCH. *Input-Output Analysis: An Appraisal*—Studies in Income and Wealth, Vol. 18. Princeton: Princeton Univ Press, 1955.

————. *Problems in the International Comparison of Economic Accounting*—Studies in Income and Wealth, Vol. 20. Princeton: Princeton Univ. Press, 1957.

————. *A Critique of the United States National Income and Product Accounts*—Studies in Income and Wealth, Vol. 22. Princeton: Princeton Univ. Press, 1958.

————. *The Flow-of-Funds Approach to Social Accounting*—Studies in Income and Wealth, Vol. 26. Princeton: Princeton Univ. Press, 1962.

ORGANIZATION FOR EUROPEAN ECONOMIC COOPERATION. *A Standardized System of National Accounts.* Paris, 1952a.

————. *Cost Accounting and Productivity—The Use and Practice of Cost Accounting in the U.S.A.* Paris. OEEC, 1952b.

Report of (first) System Simulation Symposium. New York: American Institute of Industrial Engineers, 1957.

Report of the Second System Simulation Symposium. New York: American Institute of Industrial Engineers, 1960.

STUDY GROUP ON BUSINESS INCOME. *Changing Concepts of Business Income*, New York: Macmillan Co., 1952.

UNITED NATIONS. *A System of National Accounts and Supporting Tables*—Studies in Methods, No. 2. New York, 1953.

U.S. CONGRESS. *The National Economic Accounts of the United States*, Joint Economic Committee, 85th Congress of the United States. Washington, 1957.

U.S. DEPARTMENT OF COMMERCE, Office of Business Economics. *National Income*, A Supplement to the Survey of Current Business (1954 edition).

U.S. DEPARTMENT OF COMMERCE. *U.S. Income and Output*, A Supplement to the Survey of Current Business (1958 edition).

U.S. GENERAL ACCOUNTING OFFICE—Office of Staff Management. *Outline of AICPA Accounting Research and Terminology Bulletins—Prepared for Advanced Accounting and Auditing Study Program.* Washington, D.C.: U.S. Government Printing Office, 1962

Indexes

INDEX OF AUTHORS

INDEX OF SUBJECTS

Groups (mathematical)—*Cont.*
structure of scales, 69
transformation, 59n

H

Hedonism, 155–56, 160
Historical costing, 25, 161–64; *see also* Acquisition (or historic) cost
adjustments of, 171
basis of, 224, 428
History, 54, 185
and learning process, 238
Homo oeconomicus, 147
Homogeneity assumption in interindustry analysis, 308
Household threshold; *see* Domestic threshold as income criterion
Hurwicz' criterion of optimisim (maximax), 208n
Hypotheses: *see also* Empirical hypotheses
alternative, 426
a priori (or primary), 234, 239
in budgeting, 337–40, 358–60, 363, 367, 371, 372, 377, 378, 386–87, 399, 400
cost of operating, 236
falsity of, 235
formulation, 241, 326n, 429, 464
pragmatic (or action), 232–39, 430
pragmatic vs. scientific, 235–36, 419, 429–30
vs. rules, 251–52, 291, 430–31
scientific, 232–36, 430
selection of, 330
statistical, 232–36
universal, 233n

I

IBSYS monitor system, 352n
Identities; *see also* Accounting identities *and* Definitions
corporate savings, 316
of gross national product, 316
of net investment, 316
wage rate and labor, 316
Idle capacity, 339–40; *see also* Slack variables
Imported
opportunity costs, 136
prices, 196, 199
Income
AICPA definition of, 289
the author's general definition, 21
disposable, 86–89, 130
earned, 22
and earned surplus, 262–63
essence of, 20–26
farm, equation, 315
Fisher's definitions, 21–25
Hick's definition, 23
and investment, 152
Keynes' definition, 24
Marshall's definition, 24

measurement, 22–23, 43
money, 22
national, 86–89
personal, 129
psychic, 22
real (realized), 22
value of, 25
Income distribution in macro-accounting, 86–89
Income statement; *see also* Profit and loss statement
AICPA definition of, 286
combined with earned surplus, 254–55
for economic analysis, 121–22
heterogenity of, 44
projected, 387–90
Index
Gross National Product Implicit Price Deflator, 183
for price-level fluctuations, 181–83
Index of Economic Journals, 523
Indifference curve(s)
in Boulding's theory, 157
in interindustry analysis, 309
and valuation, 150
Induction, 232–33
principle (Hume's rejection), 232 33n
Industrial dynamics, 323–25
Inequalities in linear programing (general), 480–83, 487f.
Inequity of monetary claims, basic assumption, 19, 36, 48, 100, 425
Inflation; *see* Price level changes
Information
accuracy vs. cost of, 415
through financial statements, 212, 244
imprecise, 237
loss, 213
multipurpose, system, 251
net work, 232
procurement of, 237
system (of firm), 29, 166, 421
value, 248
Input coefficients, 303–5, 308, 431
Input-output analysis (or system), 28, 29, 295–311, 431; *see also* Interindustry analysis
Installment(s)
on deferred items, 255
of long-term payments, 256
Intangible(s)
assets, 258–59
evaluation of, 172, 175, 179
Integers, 32
Interdependence; *see also* *Mutatis-mutandis* phenomenon
of economic variables, 298
in simulation model, 328
Interest
and cash flow, 205

Value—*Cont.*
  concept, 159–61
  of consumption goods, 149–50
  conventions, 213
  cost, 216; *see also* Cost
  current (or market); *see* Current value
  deduction of, 214
  of enterprise, 200–201, 210–11, 226–31
  equation, 207
  ethical aspects, 206
  expected, 245–46
  extrapolation of, 25
  functional vs. subjective, 143–48
  functions, 161, 201, 211, 226–31, 429
  of goods of higher order, 151
  in linear programing, 193–99, 306
  liquidation, 224, 225
  military aspects, 206
  monetary, 200
  multidimensional, 225–26, 250
  of object vs. state, 206–9, 222–23
  of output, 136
  present, 25, 216, 428
  replacement; *see* Replacement value
  scale, 221
  subjective, 144, 168–69
  of system state, 206–9, 220–23
  of ultimate state, 221
  utility vs. monetary, 210–11, 226–31
  vector, 224–26, 250
Value added, 43
Value judgement(s); *see also* Normative
  in accounting, 12, 176
  and acquisition cost, 162
  and decision criteria, 208
  in measuring relative frequency, 240
  in operations research, 417
  and valuation, 145
  in value theory, 214
Value system(s), 206–10
  basic state of, 224
  conflict resolutions in, 209
  preliminary state of, 222, 224
  subdividing, 209
  ultimate state of, 222, 224
Value theories
  constituents of, 163
  of management science, 184–231

Value—*Cont.*
  for production, 150
  relation to valuation, 144
  search for functional, 160–61
  some postulates of, 208
  subjective, 153–57
Variables
  accounting, 311
  alphabetic list of, budget model, 404–8
  of budget model, 335–39
  control of, 318
  endogenous, 313n, 345
  exogenous, 313n, 345, 353–56, 360
  flow, 353, 361
  index, 351, 360–61
  predetermined, 313n
  slack, 339–40, 491
  stochastic (random), 313–18
  stock, 353, 361
Vector(s); *see also* Ordering
  in matrix algebra, 470
  presentation in accounting, 94–97, 426
  value, 224–26, 250
Venn diagrams, 438–40

W

Wage adjustment equation, 315
Wald's criterion of pessimism (maximin),
    208n
Waiting line models; *see* Queuing
Wealth
  aspects of, 20–26
  as capital goods, 25
  as capital value, 25
  relation to income, 24–25
Working capital, 255
Working papers (of accounting), 174–75

Y

Yield; *see* Return on capital, *and* Rate of
    return

Z

Zero point (class); *see also* Set, empty
  absolute, 59
  in measurement, 59

This book has been set by Photon in 11 point Baskerville, leaded 2 points and 10 point Baskerville, leaded 1 point. Chapter numbers are in 18 point Techno Medium italics and chapter titles in 18 point Baskerville caps. The size of the type page is 27 by 46½ picas.